Botticelli Past and Pre

Botticelli Past and Present

Edited by Ana Debenedetti and Caroline Elam

UCLPRESS

First published in 2019 by
UCL Press in association with the Victoria and Albert Museum
University College London
Gower Street
London WC1E 6BT

Available to download free: www.ucl.ac.uk/ucl-press

A CIP catalogue record for this book is available from The British Library.

ISBN: 978-1-78735-461-6 (Hbk.)
ISBN: 978-1-78735-460-9 (Pbk.)
ISBN: 978-1-78735-459-3 (PDF)
ISBN: 978-1-78735-462-3 (epub)
ISBN: 978-1-78735-463-0 (mobi)
ISBN: 978-1-78735-464-7 (html)
DOI: https://doi.org/10.14324/111.9781787354593

The publication of this book was made possible in part thanks to the generosity of the Kress Foundation.

The publishers would like to thank the Italian Cultural Institute in London for their generous support for the publication of this book.

ISTITUTO italiano DI CULTURA LONDRA

Contents

List of illustrations vii
List of contributors xix

Introduction
Ana Debenedetti, Victoria and Albert Museum 1

Part 1: Botticelli in his own time

Introduction
Michelle O'Malley, Warburg Institute 7

1. *Sandro Botticelli and the birth of modern portraiture*
Patrizia Zambrano, Università degli Studi del Piemonte Orientale 10

2. *Botticelli's* Portrait of a Lady known as Smeralda Bandinelli*: a technical study*
Nicola Costaras, Victoria and Albert Museum and Clare Richardson, Courtauld Institute 36

3. *Classicism and invention: Botticelli's mythologies in our time and their time*
Paul Holberton, independent scholar 53

4. *Jacopo del Sellaio's adaptation of the* Primavera
Jerzy Miziołek, Museum of the University of Warsaw 73

Part 2: The Botticelli effect

Introduction
Julius Bryant, Victoria and Albert Museum 91

5. *Whigs and primitives: Dante and Botticelli in England from Jonathan Richardson to John Flaxman*
Mark Evans, Victoria and Albert Museum 94

6. *Befriending Botticelli: psychology and connoisseurship at the fin de siècle*
Francesco Ventrella, University of Sussex 116

7. *A woman's touch, Michael Field, Botticelli and queer desire*
Anna Gruetzner Robins, University of Reading 148

Part 3: Botticelli between art history and connoisseurship

Introduction
Caroline Elam, Warburg Institute 161

8. *Crowe and Cavalcaselle on Botticelli: new results*
Donata Levi, University of Udine 166

9. *Why Botticelli? Aby Warburg's search for a new approach to Quattrocento Italian art*
Claudia Wedepohl, Warburg Institute 183

10. *'A Japanese Critic on Botticelli': fragmentation and universality in Yashiro's 1925 monograph*
Jonathan K. Nelson, Syracuse University, Florence 203

11. *Jacques Mesnil's Botticelli*
Michel Hochmann, Ecole Pratique des Hautes Etudes, Paris (EPHE, PSL) 218

Part 4: Botticelli now

Introduction
Stefan Weppelmann, Gemäldegalerie, Kunsthistorisches Museum Wien 233

12. Ninfa fluida *(a post-scriptum)*
Georges Didi-Huberman, Ecole des Hautes Etudes en Sciences Sociales, Paris 237

13. *Into the abyss. On Salvador Dalì's* Dream of Venus
Riccardo Venturi, Académie de France, Villa Medici, Rome 266

14. *Giving an edge to the beautiful line: Botticelli referenced in the works of contemporary artists to address issues of gender and global politics*
Gabriel Montua, Neue Nationalgalerie, Staatliche Museen zu Berlin 290

Index 307

List of illustrations

Fig 1.0 Sandro Botticelli, *The Birth of Venus*, *c*.1480, tempera on canvas, 172.5 × 278.5 cm, Galleria degli Uffizi, Florence, Inv.1890 no.878. © 2018 Photo Scala – courtesy of the Ministero Beni e Att. Culturali e del Turismo. 9

Fig.1.1 Sandro Botticelli, *Portrait of a Young Man with a Mazzocchio*, *c*.1470, tempera on wood, 51.2 × 35.2 cm, Galleria Palatina, Florence, Inv.1912 no.372. © 2018 Photo Scala – courtesy of the Ministero Beni e Att. Culturali e del Turismo. 12

Fig.1.2 Attributed to Piero del Pollaiuolo, *Male Portrait*, *c*.1465, tempera on wood, 55.5 × 41.2 cm, The National Gallery of Art, Washington, Inv.1937.I.17. © Courtesy National Gallery of Art, Washington. 13

Fig.1.3 Piero del Pollaiuolo (1443–96), *Portrait of Galeazzo Maria Sforza*, *c*.1471, tempera on wood, 65 × 42 cm,Uffizi Gallery, Florence, Inv.1890 no.1492. © 2018 Photo Scala, Florence – courtesy of the Ministero Beni e Att. Culturali e del Turismo. 14

Fig.1.4 Sandro Botticelli, *Portrait of a Man*, *c*.1475, tempera on wood, 51 × 37 cm, formerly Museo Filangieri, Naples, destroyed in 1943. © Bologna, Fototeca Federico Zeri inv.1259. 16

Fig.1.5 Sandro Botticelli, *Portrait of a Lady known as Smeralda Bandinelli*, *c*.1470, tempera on wood, 65.7 × 41 cm, Victoria and Albert Museum, London, inv.CAI.100 © Victoria and Albert Museum, London. 17

Fig.1.6 Sandro Botticelli, *Sant'Ambrogio altarpiece*, detail of St Catherine, *c*.1470, tempera on wood, 167 × 195 cm, Uffizi Gallery, Florence, Inv.1890 no.8657. © Wikimedia Commons. 18

Fig.1.7 Sandro Botticelli, *Portrait of a Young Man with the Medal of Cosimo de' Medici*, c.1475, tempera on wood, 57.5 × 44 cm, Uffizi Gallery, Florence, Inv.1890 no.1488. © Wikimedia / source DirectMedia / public domain. 19

Fig.1.8 Sandro Botticelli, *Adoration of the Magi*, detail, c.1475–6, tempera on wood, 111 × 134 cm, Uffizi Gallery, Florence, Inv.1890 no.882. © 2018 Photo Scala – courtesy of the Ministero Beni e Att. Culturali e del Turismo. 20

Fig.1.9 Sandro Botticelli, *Portrait of Giuliano de' Medici*, after 1478, tempera on wood, 56.8 × 38.5 cm, Accademia Carrara, Bergamo, 58MR0006. © Courtesy of the Accademia Carrara, Bergamo. 22

Fig.1.10 Sandro Botticelli, *Portrait of Giuliano de' Medici*, after 1478, tempera on wood, 56.8 × 38.5 cm, Gemäldegalerie, Staatliche Museen zu Berlin, Berlin, no.106 B. © Staatliche Museen zu Berlin – Gemäldegalerie. Photo: Christoph Schmidt. 23

Fig.1.11 Bertoldo di Giovanni (1420–91), *Bronze Medal of Lorenzo and Giuliano de' Medici*, 1478, bronze, diam. 6.35 cm, Victoria and Albert Museum, London, Inv.7139-1860. © Victoria and Albert Museum, London. 24

Fig.1.12 Florentine sculptor (Michele Marini da Fiesole?), *Marble Bust of Giuliano de' Medici*, detail, 1480-90, height 64 cm, Museo Nazionale del Bargello, Florence, inv.Sculture 360. © 2018 DeAgostini Picture Library/Scala, Florence. 25

Fig.1.13 Sandro Botticelli, *Portrait of Giuliano de' Medici*, after 1478, tempera on wood, 75.6 × 52.6 cm, National Gallery of Art, Washington, inv.1952.5.56. © Courtesy National Gallery of Art, Washington. 27

Fig.1.14 Sandro Botticelli, *Portrait of a Young Man*, c.1485, tempera and oil on panel, 37.5 × 28.3 cm, The National Gallery, London, NG 626. © 2018 The National Gallery, London/ Scala, Florence. 29

Fig.1.15 Sandro Botticelli, *Portrait of a Lady known as Smeralda Bandinelli*, *c.* 1475, before treatment, tempera on wood, 66.8 × 42.5 cm, Victoria and Albert Museum, London, inv. CAI.100. © Victoria and Albert Museum, London. 37

Fig.1.16 Sandro Botticelli, *Portrait of a Lady known as Smeralda Bandinelli*, X-ray image, Victoria and Albert Museum, London, inv.CAI.100. © Victoria and Albert Museum, London. 39

Fig.1.17 Sandro Botticelli, *Portrait of a Lady known as Smeralda Bandinelli*, infrared reflectography. © Victoria and Albert Museum and the National Gallery, London. IRR carried out by Rachel Billinge, The National Gallery, London, using an OSIRIS camera. 41

Fig.1.18 Sandro Botticelli, *Portrait of a Lady known as Smeralda Bandinelli*, X-ray detail showing incised lines. © Victoria and Albert Museum, London. 42

Fig.1.19 Sandro Botticelli, *Portrait of a Lady known as Smeralda Bandinelli*, detail after cleaning showing scoring upper right. © Victoria and Albert Museum, London. 46

Fig.1.20 Sandro Botticelli, *Portrait of a Lady known as Smeralda Bandinelli*, virtual reconstruction by Nicola Costaras. © Victoria and Albert Museum, London. 47

Fig.1.21 D. G. Rossetti (1828–82), *La Donna della Finestra*, 1870, coloured chalks on paper, 84.8 × 72.1 cm, Bradford Art Gallery (104.26). © Bradford Art Galleries and Museums, West Yorkshire, UK / Bridgeman Images. 49

Fig.1.22 Filippino Lippi (*c.* 1457–1504), *The Muse Erato*, c. 1500, tempera on wood, 61 × 51 cm, Gemäldegalerie, Staatliche Museen zu Berlin, Berlin, Inv.no.78A. © Staatliche Museen zu Berlin – Gemäldegalerie. Photo: Christoph Schmidt. 56

Fig.1.23 Sandro Botticelli, *Camilla and the Centaur*, early 1480s, tempera on canvas, 207 × 148 cm, Uffizi, Florence, Inv.1911 no.OdA 752. © 2018 Photo Scala, Florence – courtesy of the Ministero Beni e Att. Culturali e del Turismo. 57

Fig.1.24 Sandro Botticelli, *The Calumny of Apelles*, 1490s, tempera on panel, 62 × 91 cm, Uffizi, Florence Inv.1890, no.1496. © 2018 Photo Scala – courtesy of the Ministero Beni e Att. Culturali e del Turismo. 58

Fig.1.25 Sandro Botticelli, *The Calumny of Apelles*, detail, Uffizi, Florence Inv. 1890 no. 1496. © 2018 Photo Scala – courtesy of the Ministero Beni e Att. Culturali e del Turismo. 59

Fig.1.26 Sandro Botticelli, *The Calumny of Apelles*, detail, Uffizi, Florence Inv. 1890, no. 1496. © 2018 Photo Scala – courtesy of the Ministero Beni e Att. Culturali e del Turismo. 61

Fig.1.27 Sandro Botticelli, *Mars and Venus*, *c.*1485, tempera and oil on wood, 69.2 × 173.4 cm, National Gallery, London (Inv.NG915). © 2018 The National Gallery, London/Scala, Florence. 62

Fig.1.28 Florentine, *Mirror frame with two lovers*, 1470–80, painted stucco, diam. 50.8 cm, Victoria and Albert Museum, London, Inv.no.5887-1859. © Victoria and Albert Museum, London. 63

Fig.1.29 Anonymous, '*Qui regna amor*', early fifteenth century, fresco detached and re-inserted in a wall, figure life-size, Cini collection, Castello, Monselice (PD). © Photograph by the author. 64

Fig.1.30 Sandro Botticelli, *Primavera*, *c.*1475, tempera on wood, 203 × 314 cm, Uffizi, Florence, Inv.1890 no.878. © Photo Scala – courtesy of the Ministero Beni e Att. Culturali e del Turismo. 65

Fig.1.31 Jacopo del Sellaio (1441–93), *Story of Cupid and Psyche*, detail of *cassone* front panel, *c.*1490, tempera and oil on wood, 43.5 × 152.8 cm, Riggisberg, Abegg-Stiftung. © Riggisberg, Abegg-Stiftung. 74

Fig.1.32 Master of the Argonauts, *Story of Psyche*, part 1, *cassone* front, *c.*1470, tempera on wood, 40 × 130 cm, Berlin, Gemäldegalerie. © Staatliche Museen zu Berlin – Gemäldegalerie. Photo: Christoph Schmidt. 76

Fig.1.33 Master of the Argonauts, *Story of Psyche*, part 2, *cassone* front, *c.*1470, tempera on wood, 40 × 130 cm, Berlin, Gemäldegalerie. © Staatliche Museen zu Berlin – Gemäldegalerie. Photo: Christoph Schmidt. 76

Fig.1.34 Master of the Argonauts, *Story of Psyche*, *cassone* side panel, *c.*1470, tempera on wood, 43.5 × 51 cm, Kraków, Royal Castle (no.7966). © Kraków, Royal Castle. 77

Fig.1.35 Virtual reconstruction of the second *cassone* with the *Story of Psyche*. © Maciej Tarkowski, following the author's instructions. 78

Fig.1.36 Jacopo del Sellaio, *Story of Cupid and Psyche*, part 1, *spalliera*, tempera and oil on panel, *c.*1480, 58.4 × 178.8 cm, Cambridge, Fitzwilliam Museum. © Fitzwilliam Museum, Cambridge. 78

Fig.1.37 Jacopo del Sellaio, *Story of Cupid and Psyche*, part 2, *spalliera*, tempera and oil on panel, *c.*1480, 59 × 179 cm, private collection. © Courtesy Moretti Gallery. 78

Fig.1.38 Jacopo del Sellaio, *Story of Cupid and Psyche*, part 1, *cassone* front, tempera and oil on panel, *c.*1490, 43 × 152.8 cm, Boston, Museum of Fine Arts (12.1049). Photograph © 2018 Museum of Fine Arts, Boston. 79

Fig.1.39 Jacopo del Sellaio, *Story of Cupid and Psyche*, *cassone* front, part 2, tempera and oil on panel, *c.*1490, 42 × 158.5 cm, Riggisberg, Abegg-Stiftung. © Riggisberg, Abegg-Stiftung. 79

Fig.1.40 Jacopo del Sellaio, *Story of Cupid and Psyche*, detail of fig.1.31. © Riggisberg, Abegg-Stiftung. 80

Fig.1.41 Master of the Argonauts, *Marriage of Cupid and Psyche*, detail of fig.1.33. © Staatliche Museen zu Berlin -- Gemäldegalerie. Photo: Christoph Schmidt. 81

Fig.1.42 *The Seven Planets and Seven Heavenly Spheres*, miniature, Dijon, Bibliothèque Municipale, Ms.448, fol.63v. © Bibliotheque Municipale, Dijon (Ms. 448, fol. 63v). 83

Fig.2.1 Joseph Strutt (1749–1802), after Baccio Baldini and Botticelli, *The monster Fraud, with the guide seated upon his back, desiring the author to follow his example[...]from the rare edition of the works of Dante, published at Florence, A.D. 1481 (1785)*, engraving from Joseph Strutt, *A Biographical Dictionary; containing an historical account of all the Engravers from the earliest period of the art of engraving to the present times (1785/6)*, vol.1, plate VII facing p.25 © Victoria and Albert Museum, London. 97

Fig.2.2 Sandro Botticelli, *The Mystic Nativity*, 1500, oil on canvas, 108.6 × 74.9 cm, The National Gallery, London, NG 1034. © 2018: The National Gallery, London/Scala, Florence. 99

Fig.2.3 Henry Fuseli (1741–1825), *Dante and Virgil on the ice of Cocythus*; 'Inferno', canto XXXII, inscribed Roma Aug. 74 (1774), ink, sepia and watercolour, 43.7 × 31.2 cm, inv.1916/13, Kunsthaus, Zurich. © Kunsthaus Zürich. 102

Fig.2.4 Sandro Botticelli, *Dante and Virgil on the ice of Cocythus*; 'Inferno', canto XXXII, 1490s, metalpoint and ink on vellum, cod.Hamilton 201, Kupferstichkabinett, Berlin (detail). © bpk / Kupferstichkabinett, SMB / Philipp Allard. 103

Fig.2.5 John Flaxman (1755–1826), *The Punishment of the Sodomites*; 'Inferno', canto XVI, 1807, ink on paper, 13.7 × 19.6 cm, Houghton Library, Harvard University, PF MS TYP 26.4, fol.19r. © Houghton Library, Harvard University. 105

Fig.2.6 Sandro Botticelli, *The Punishment of the Sodomites*; 'Inferno', canto XVI, 1490s, metalpoint and ink on vellum, Biblioteca Apostolica Vaticana, cod.Reg. lat.1896, fol.98v (detail). © Vatican Library. 105

Fig.2.7 John Flaxman, *Lucifer*; 'Inferno', canto XXXIV, 1807, ink on paper, 13.9 × 19.5 cm, Houghton Library, Harvard University, PF MS TYP 26.4, fol.39r. © Houghton Library, Harvard University. 107

Fig.2.8 Sandro Botticelli, *Lucifer*; 'Inferno', canto XXXIV, 1490s, metalpoint and ink on vellum, cod.Hamilton 201, Kupferstichkabinett, Berlin (detail). © bpk / Kupferstichkabinett, SMB / Philipp Allard. 107

Fig.2.9 John Flaxman, *Penance of the proud*; 'Purgatorio', canto XI, 1807, ink on paper, 14 × 19.3 cm, Houghton Library, Harvard University, PF MS TYP 26.4, fol.55r. © Houghton Library, Harvard University. 109

Fig.2.10 Sandro Botticelli, *Penance of the proud*; 'Purgatorio', canto XI, 1490s, metalpoint and ink on vellum, cod. Hamilton 201, Kupferstichkabinett, Berlin (detail). © bpk / Kupferstichkabinett, SMB / Philipp Allard. 109

Fig.2.11 Bac, 'Leurs Almanachs', illustration by Rougeron Vignerot, detail, *La Vie Parisienne*, 32 (January 1894): 20, The British Library, London. © British Library Board. 116

Fig. 2.12 Page from Bernard Berenson's '*Amico di Sandro*', *Gazette des Beaux-Arts*, 22 (July 1899): 33. Warburg Institute Library, London. © Warburg Institute. 118

Fig.2.13 Bernard Berenson's study at Villa Kraus in Michael Field, *Works and Days*, f.43 (1895), Add. Ms.46783, The British Library, London. © British Library Board. 123

Fig.2.14 Sandro Botticelli, *Madonna of the Pomegranate*, *c*.1487, tempera on wood, 143.5 cm diameter, Uffizi Galleries, Florence, inv.1890 no.1609. © Wikimedia Commons. 125

Fig.2.15 Bernard Berenson's manuscript notes on 'Botticelli' [*c*.1894?], Bernard and Mary Berenson Papers, Biblioteca Berenson, Villa I Tatti. The Harvard University Center for Italian Renaissance Studies © President and Fellows of Harvard College. 134

Fig.2.16 Guido Landra (1913–80), '*Concetti del razzismo italiano*', *La Difesa della razza* 1: 2 (1938): 9, The Museum of English Rural Life. © The University of Reading. 138

Fig.2.17 Michael Field (Katherine Bradley 1848–1914 and Edith Cooper 1862–1913), photograph, silver gelatin carte-de-visite (likely a copy of a platinotype), 1884–1889 by Bromhead, Clifton, Collection Mark Samuels Lasner, Special Collections, University of Delaware. © Wikimedia Commons. 148

Fig.2.18 Settle designed by Arthur H. Mackmurdo and Herbert P. Horne (The Century Guild), made by E. Goodall & Co., 1886, satinwood, with panels of marquetry and brass; upholstery of printed cotton, Victoria and Albert Museum, London (W.16:1 to 4-1967). © Victoria and Albert Museum, London. 151

Fig.2.19 Photograph of the 'Botticelli room' at Durdans, Bodleian Library – Ms Eng Misc 304, 22 & 23. © The Bodleian Libraries, The University of Oxford (MS. Eng. Misc. c. 304, fol. 22r) 156

Fig.3.1 G. B. Cavalcaselle (1819–97), from S. Botticelli, *Saint Sebastian* (Berlin, Gemäldegalerie), Venice, Biblioteca Nazionale Marciana, cod.It. IV 2037 (=12278), notebook 15, c.80v. © Biblioteca Nazionale Marciana, Venice. 169

Fig.3.2 G. B. Cavalcaselle, from F. Botticini, *Tobit and three Archangels* (Florence, Uffizi), Venice, Biblioteca Nazionale Marciana, cod.It. IV 2030 (=12271), 16, c.334. © Biblioteca Nazionale Marciana, Venice. 171

Fig.3.3 G. B. Cavalcaselle, from F. Botticini, *The Assumption of the Virgin* (London, National Gallery), Venice, Biblioteca Nazionale Marciana, cod.It. IV 2033 (=12274), XXII, cc.186v–187r. © Biblioteca Nazionale Marciana, Venice. 177

Fig.3.4 J. A. Crowe (1825–96), from F. Botticini, *Tabernacle of St Sebastian* (Empoli, Museo della Collegiata), London, National Art Library, 86.ZZ.33, box 1. © Victoria and Albert Museum, London. 178

Fig.3.5 J. A. Crowe, from F. Botticini, *Tabernacle of the Sacrament* and *Annunciation* (Empoli, Museo della Collegiata), London, National Art Library, 86.ZZ.33, box 1. © Victoria and Albert Museum, London. 179

Fig.3.6 Title page of Aby Warburg's personal copy of his Sandro Botticelli's *'Geburt der Venus' und 'Frühling'. Eine Untersuchung über die Vorstellungen von der Antike in der italienischen Frührenaissance,* Hamburg und Leipzig, Leopold Voss 1893, Warburg Institute Archive, III.38.1.1.1. © The Warburg Institute. 186

Fig.3.7 Aby Warburg (1866–1929), List of recipients of his Sandro Botticelli's *'Geburt der Venus' und 'Frühling'* (1893) and their responses, first of three folios, Warburg Institute Archive, III.38.1.5.1, fol.1. © The Warburg Institute. 187

Fig.3.8 Aby Warburg, *Collation of the Homeric Hymn to Aphrodite, Poliziano's Stanze per la Giostra (I, 99–103) and Botticelli's Birth of Venus,* Warburg Institute Archive, III.39.4.2, fol. 7. © The Warburg Institute. 189

Fig.3.9 Agostino di Duccio (1418–81), *The Journey of St Sigismund,* detail of an angel appearing to the saint, *c.*1450, bas-relief (originally in the St Sigismund-Chapel, Tempio Malatestiano), Museo d'Arte Antica, Castello Sforzesco, Milan. © Photograph by the author. 190

Fig.3.10 Aby Warburg, *Lecture Notes of August Schmarsow's 'Von Nicolo Pisano bis Michelangelo', Winter Semester 1888–89,* Kunsthistorisches Institut, Florence, Warburg Institute Archive, III.33.2.8, p.104: 'extremely sheer, fluttering garments en masse'. © The Warburg Institute. 194

Fig.3.11 Aby Warburg, Diary entry of 3 May 1890: 'citation in Poliziano for the Spring found', WIA, III.9.6, p.64. © The Warburg Institute. 195

Fig.3.12 Yukio Yashiro (1890–1975), *Botticelli,* 1925, vol.II, 95: detail of *Primavera.* © Photograph by the author. 206

Fig.3.13 Yashiro, *Botticelli*, 1925, vol.II, 47: detail of *Saint Sebastian* (Berlin, Gemäldegalerie). © Photograph by the author. 209

Fig.3.14 Yashiro, *Botticelli*, 1925, vol.II, 50: detail of *Saint Sebastian.* © Photograph by the author. 210

Fig.3.15 Jacques Mesnil (1872-1940), altered photograph (date unknown; 1905?). © Wikimedia Commons. 219

Fig.4.1 Ferdinand de Saussure (1857–1913), *Les 'royaumes flottants'*, 1906–11, in *Cours de linguistique générale* (1906–1911), ed. Charles Bally and Albert Sechehaye (1915), revised by Tullio de Mauro (Paris: Payot, 1972), pp.155–6. 246

Fig.4.2 Illustration from Hungarian journal *Fidibusz*, 1900, repr. in Sigmund Freud, *The Interpretation of Dreams* (1899), trans. James Strachey (London: Allen & Unwin 1954), p.368. 247

Fig.4.3 Gustav Klimt (1862–1918), *Reclining Female in Underwear with Spread Legs and Head Bent Backwards, Masturbating*, 1916/17, pencil, white chalk on Japanese paper, 37.4 × 57 cm, Leopold Museum, Vienna, Inv.1355. © Leopold Museum, Vienna. 248

Fig.4.4 Jean Arp (1886–1966), *L'air est une racine*, 1933. Poems and drawings published in *Le Surréalisme au service de la révolution,* no.6 (1933): 33. 250

Fig.4.5 Albert von Schrenk-Notzing (1862–1929), *Le Medium Stanislawa P. avec un voile ectoplasmique*, 1913, photograph, Fribourg-en-Brisgau, Institut für Grenzgebiete der Psychologie und Psychohygiene. © Institut für Grenzgebiete der Psychologie & Psychohygiene e. V. (IGPP), Fribourg-en-Brisgau. 251

Fig.4.6 Pierre Jahan (1909–2003), *Jaillissement d'écume*, l'estacade, Le Havre, 1935. © Pierre Jahan/Roger-Viollet. 252

Fig.4.7 Rogi André (Rosza Klein) (1900–70), *Jacqueline Breton: la nymphe*, Recueil.EP-825-BOITE FOL. © Paris, Bibliothèque nationale de France (BnF). Photo © BnF, Dist. RMN-Grand Palais / image BnF. 253

Fig.4.8 Man Ray (1890–1976), *Le Retour à la raison*, 1923. Segment of the film roll, Paris, Centre Georges Pompidou. 254

Fig.4.9 Jean Painlevé (1902–89), *Ouverture de la poche incubatrice du mâle hippocampe*, 1931. Silverprint. © Paris, Les documents cinématographiques. 255

Fig.4.10 Jean Vigo (1905–34), *L'Atalante*, 1934; photographic still from the film. 257

Fig.4.11 Ana Mendieta (1948–85), *Flower Person, Flower Body*, 1975, Super-8mm film transferred to high-definition media, colour, silent; running time: 6:20 minutes, edition of 6 + 3 Aps (GP1218). © The Estate of Ana Mendieta Collection, LLC. Courtesy Galerie Lelong & Co. 260

Fig.4.12 Facade of Salvador Dalí's *Dream of Venus* pavilion, 1939, The Dalí Museum in St. Petersburg, Fla. Dalí Museum/Fundacio Gala-Salvador Dalí via Agency Press. © Salvador Dalí, Fundació Gala-Salvador Dalí, DACS 2018. 267

Fig.4.13 Salvador Dalí (1904–89), cover image of his solo show at Julien Levy Gallery, New York 1939. © Salvador Dali, Fundació Gala-Salvador Dalí, DACS 2018. 269

Fig.4.14 *Dream of Venus* invitation card, 1939, reproduced in Lewis Kachur, *Displaying the Marvelous. Marcel Duchamp, Salvador Dalí, and Surrealist Exhibition Installations*, Cambridge, Mass.: The MIT Press, 2001. © Salvador Dalí, Fundació Gala-Salvador Dalí, DACS 2018. 270

Fig.4.15 'Dalí's Surrealist Dream House at the World's Fair', in *Vogue*, June 1939. © Salvador Dalí, Fundació Gala-Salvador Dalí, DACS 2018. 271

Fig.4.16 Salvador Dalí, sketch for *Dream of Venus*, 1939, tempera, charcoal, pencil and collage on illustration board, reproduced in Ingrid Schaffner, *Salvador Dalí's Dream of Venus. The Surrealist Funhouse from the 1939 World's Fair*, New York: Princeton Architectural Press, 2002. © Salvador Dalí, Fundació Gala-Salvador Dalí, DACS 2018. 272

Fig.4.17 Salvador Dalí, *Declaration of the Independence of the Imagination and the Rights of Man to His Own Madness*, 1939, ink on paper, 40.3 × 24.35 cm, National Art Library. © Salvador Dalí, Fundació Gala-Salvador Dalí, DACS 2018. 274

Fig.4.18 Photograph of female models for *The Dream of Venus* watertank show directed by Salvador Dalí, with a reproduction of Botticelli's *Venus*, 1939. Photographer unknown. 283

Fig.4.19 Carl Van Vechten (1880–1964), Dalí's *Dream of Venus*, side view of exterior, 11 August 1939, Museum of the City of New York, Print Archives. 286

Fig.4.20 Eglė Otto (b. 1976), *Botticelli, Giotto, Grünewald, da Vinci, Dürer, Mantegna, Rossetti, Ensor, Parmigianino, Lippi, Raffael, van der Weyden, Ingres, Ernst*, 2012, oil on canvas, 130 × 107 cm. © Courtesy of the Artist. 292

Fig.4.21 Sylvia Sleigh (1916–2010), *Venus and Mars: Maureen Conner and Paul Rosano*, 1974, oil on canvas, 69.2 × 173.7 cm, Milwaukee Art Museum, Gift of the Artist and Dr and Mrs James Stadler (M1990.137). © Courtesy of the Estate of Sylvia Sleigh and Andrew Hottle. 293

Fig.4.22 Gülsün Karamustafa (b. 1946), *Gold Venus with Mirror*, 1985, found object, wood, plastics, mirror, 65 × 88 cm, courtesy the Artist and Rampa Gallery, Istanbul. Photo © Thomas Bruns, Staatliche Museen zu Berlin, Nationalgalerie. 294

Fig.4.23 Faraḥ Osūlī (b. 1953), *Botticelli and I*, 2014, gouache on cardboard, 75 × 100 cm. © Courtesy of the Artist. 296

Fig.4.24 Left: Sandro Botticelli, *Portrait of a Man with a Medal of Cosimo the Elder*, c.1475, tempera and gilded stucco on wood, 57.5 × 44 cm, Galleria degli Uffizi, Florence; Right: Aydin Aghdashlou (b. 1940), *Portrait by Sandro Botticelli* (*Taṣvīrī az Sāndro Bottečellī*), 1975, gouache on paper, 71 × 50 cm, Tehran Museum of Contemporary Art, Tehran. © Courtesy of the Artist. 299

Fig.4.25 Juan O'Gorman (1905–82), *Proyecto de Monumento al Nacimiento de Venus*, 1976, tempera on wood, 122 × 82 cm, Pérez Simón Collection, México. © Pérez Simón Collection, México. 301

Fig.4.26 Sokari Douglas Camp (b. 1958), partial view of the work ensemble *Primavera* (presented at October Gallery between 7 April–14 May 2016), 2015–16 steel, gold and copper leaf, acrylic paint, various dimensions. © Courtesy of the Artist and October Gallery, London. 302

List of contributors

Ana Debenedetti is an art historian specialising in Florentine art, artistic literature and workshop practice in the Renaissance. She is Curator of Paintings at the Victoria and Albert Museum, responsible for the collections of paintings, drawings, watercolours and miniatures. She has written and published on Renaissance art, philosophy and poetry, and holds a PhD in History of Art focusing on the artistic and cultural milieu of Quattrocento Florence, especially the interaction between philosophy and artistic literature through the work of Marsilio Ficino (1433–99). She co-curated the exhibition *Constable: The Making of a Master* (V&A, 2014–15) and *Botticelli Reimagined* (V&A, 2016), and was co-author of the accompanying catalogue. Current projects include a display and a catalogue of French Master drawings in the V&A, and a book on Botticelli (Reaktion books).

Caroline Elam is an art historian who has published widely on architecture, art and patronage in the Italian Renaissance. She has held academic positions at the University of Glasgow, King's College, Cambridge and Westfield College, University of London. From 1987 to 2002 she was Editor of *The Burlington Magazine*. From 2002 to 2004 she was Andrew W. Mellon Professor for the History of Art at the Center for Advanced Studies for the Visual Arts in the National Gallery of Art, Washington DC. She has held a fellowship and visiting professorships at the Harvard Center for Italian Renaissance Studies at Villa I Tatti, Florence, and was awarded the I Tatti Mongan Prize in 2003. She is an honorary fellow of King's College, Cambridge. Her book *Roger Fry and Italian Art* is scheduled for publication in 2019.

Michelle O'Malley is Deputy Director and Professor of the History of Art at the Warburg Institute. She is particularly interested in issues of commissioning, pricing, production and quality in Italian Renaissance art. She has published numerous articles and is author of *The Business of Art: Contracts and the Commissioning Process in Renaissance Italy* (Yale 2005) and *Painting under Pressure: Fame, Reputation and Demand in Renaissance Florence* (Yale 2013). She is the co-editor of *The Material*

Renaissance (2007) and *Re-thinking the Renaissance Object* (2009). Her most recent research considers the work of Alessandro Botticelli and his assistants, specifically in terms of economics, ownership and production practices in the workshop.

Patrizia Zambrano is Professor of Modern Art History at Università del Piemonte Orientale, Italy. She is co-author of the 2004 monograph on Filippino Lippi, and author of many articles, reviews and contributions to exhibition catalogues, several of them devoted to Botticelli. In 2005 she wrote a book on Bernard Berenson and the creation of 'Amico di Sandro', between Filippino Lippi and Sandro Botticelli. She was on the board of advisors for the exhibition *Filippino Lippi e Sandro Botticelli nella Firenze del '400* (Rome, Scuderie del Quirinale, 2011) and contributed to the catalogue. Over the last five years she has given several lectures on Botticelli rediscoveries, on connoisseurship, and on the birth and developments of Italian Renaissance individual portrait in the fifteenth century. She is preparing a book on Botticelli's portraiture, after having contributed to the 2010 exhibition on the artist at the Poldi Pezzoli Museum in Milan, writing about the Giuliano de' Medici portraits. She has always also maintained an interest in antique frames and in the story of conservation in nineteenth-century Italy, and has published extensively on these subjects.

Nicola Costaras is Head Paintings Conservator at the Victoria and Albert Museum. She trained at Gateshead Technical College (now the University of Northumbria) and joined the V&A in 1996. Prior to that position, she worked at the Mauritshuis, in The Hague for six years. She graduated with an MA in Medieval Cultures from Birkbeck College, University of London in 2008. The major projects she has worked on at the V&A include the British Galleries (2001), Paintings Galleries (2003), Medieval & Renaissance Galleries (2009), Europe Galleries (2015), and, most recently, the exhibition *Botticelli Reimagined*.

Clare Richardson is a specialist in infrared imaging. As a partner in Tager Stonor Richardson, she has undertaken infrared imaging for public and private collections since 2002. She trained at the Courtauld Institute of Art and has also worked at the Institute as a lecturer and research fellow. Her research interests include the early works of Rubens and nineteenth-century painting. Clare was Senior Manager, Painting, Frame and Paper conservation at Royal Museums Greenwich from 2015 to 2017. Prior to this she was at the V&A for five years, working on projects including a large touring exhibition of Constable Sketches, the Europe Galleries and *Botticelli Reimagined* at the V&A.

Paul Holberton completed his PhD at the Warburg Institute in 1989, after obtaining degrees in Classics (Cambridge) and Art History (London). His first publication was on Botticelli's *Primavera* in the *JWCI* (*Journal of the Warburg and Courtauld Institutes*) in 1982. His last article was published in 2004, since when he has been writing a book on 'A History of Arcadia in Art and Literature: Idyll and Idleness', spinning off into occasional papers, two of which are in press. He is a partner in Paul Holberton Publishing Ltd, which specialises in art books.

Jerzy Miziołek is Professor of the Classical Tradition in the Visual Arts at the Institute of Archaeology at the University of Warsaw, and Director of the University's Museum. His academic interests focus on themes related to the symbolism of light, the secular art of the Italian Renaissance (*cassoni* and *spalliere*), the reception of antiquity in Italian and Polish art, and the ways in which archaeological research influenced the art of the Enlightenment. Currently, the main subject of his research is the artistic culture of Rome in the neoclassical era, in particular Polish artists, architects and archaeologists who were active there (A. F. Moszyński, S. K. Potocki, F. Smuglewicz). In parallel with his research work, he is involved in didactic activities.

Julius Bryant is Keeper of Word and Image at the Victoria and Albert Museum, where the collections in his care include drawings, designs, architecture, photography, posters, watercolours, paintings, the art of the book and the National Art Library. He was previously Chief Curator and Director of Museums and Collections at English Heritage (1990–2005). Among the major exhibitions he has co-curated are *James 'Athenian' Stuart, 1713–1788: The Rediscovery of Antiquity* (V&A and Bard Graduate Center, New York, 2007); *Art and Design for All: The Victoria and Albert Museum* (Bonn and Budapest, 2011), *William Kent: Designing Georgian Britain* (BGC and V&A, 2013) and *John Lockwood Kipling* (V&A and BGC, 2017). His publications include *Kenwood: Paintings in the Iveagh Bequest* (Yale, 2005) and *Caro: Close Up* (Yale, 2012).

Mark Evans, FSA is Senior Curator of Paintings at the Victoria and Albert Museum, with responsibility for oil paintings, drawings, miniatures and watercolours. He was formerly a lecturer at the University of St Andrews, Assistant Keeper of Foreign Art at the Walker Art Gallery in Liverpool (from 1979–1984) and Curator of Fine Art at the National Museum of Wales in Cardiff from 1984–99. He has held his present post at the V&A since 2000. He is the author of numerous books, exhibition catalogues and scholarly articles, and was editor of *Art Collecting and Lineage in the*

Elizabethan Age: The Lumley Inventory and Pedigree (Roxburghe Club, 2010) and *Dutch and Flemish Drawings at the Victoria and Albert Museum* by Jane Turner and Christopher White (V&A Publishing, 2014). Mark Evans has curated several major V&A exhibitions including *Raphael: Cartoons and Tapestries for the Sistine Chapel* (2010), the touring show *John Constable: Oil Sketches from the Victoria and Albert Museum* (2010–12), *John Constable: The Making of a Master* (2014–15) and *Botticelli Reimagined* (2016).

Claudia Wedepohl has studied Art History and Italian Literature at the Universities of Göttingen and Hamburg. She finished her studies with a doctoral thesis on the Cappella del Perdono and Tempietto delle Muse in the Ducal Palace of Urbino (published in 2009). She joined the staff of the Warburg Institute in 2000 after two years spent at the institute as Aby-Warburg-Scholar. Since 2006 she has been the Archivist of the Warburg Institute. Her academic work focuses on fifteenth-century Italian art and architecture, and art historiography around 1900. She has published widely on the genesis of Aby Warburg's ideas and key terms, with a special interest in his concept of myth and mythology. Her main current project relates to the genesis of Warburg's *Bilderatlas*. Claudia Wedepohl is also engaged in transcribing Warburg's autographs and editing his works. She is co-editor of the *Gesammelte Schriften* series (De Gruyter, Berlin) and of the volume *Aby Warburg: 'Kleine Schriften und Vorträge'*.

Francesco Ventrella is Lecturer in Art History at the University of Sussex. He is co-editor, with Meaghan Clarke, of a special issue of Visual Resources on 'Women and the Culture of Connoisseurship' (forthcoming), and has written on the relationship between art historiography and modern body cultures. Francesco is completing his first monograph titled *Connoisseurial Intimacies: Sexuality, Physiological Aesthetics and the Making of Modern Artwriting*, which is funded by a Leverhulme Early Career Fellowship. He is the former editor of *Parallax*.

Anna Gruetzner Robins is Emerita Professor, University of Reading. She has written widely on cross-culture exchange between Britain and France. Her publications include *Modern Art in Britain 1910–1914* (1997), *Walter Sickert: The Complete Writings on Art* (2000), *Degas, Sickert, Toulouse-Lautrec, Paris and London 1870–1910*, (with Richard Thomson, 2005), and *A Fragile Modernism Whistler and his Impressionist Followers* (2007). She is currently completing a book on the 1890s.

Jonathan K. Nelson is Associate Professor of Art History at Syracuse University, Florence. In 2004 he co-authored a major monograph on Filippino Lippi, the subject of his PhD dissertation at the Institute of Fine Arts; the same year he co-curated an exhibition devoted to Botticelli and Filippino at the Palazzo Strozzi, Florence. He has also co-curated two exhibitions at the Galleria dell'Accademia in Florence: *Venus and Cupid. Michelangelo and the New Ideal of Beauty* (2002) and *Robert Mapplethorpe: Perfection in Form* (2009). Other books include *Leonardo e la reinvenzione della figura femminile: Leda, Lisa e Maria* (2007) and, with Richard J. Zeckhauser, *The Patron's Payoff: Economic Frameworks for Conspicuous Commissions in Renaissance Italy* (2008). On the I Tatti website he curated two online exhibitions: *Berensons and Harvard: Bernard and Mary as Students* (2012),and *Yashiro and Berenson: Art History between Japan and Italy* (2015). Current book projects include a monograph on Filippino (Reaktion Books) and a volume on *Representing Infirmity in Early Modern Italy* (Routledge, as contributor and co-editor).

Michel Hochmann is Professor at the Ecole Pratique des Hautes Etudes in Paris, where he has taught the history of Italian painting (sixteenth–seventeenth centuries) since 2000. He specialised in Italian (especially Venetian) art of the Renaissance. His doctoral dissertation was dedicated to the relationship between painters and patrons in Venice during the sixteenth century (*Peintres et Commanditaires à Venise. 1540–1628*, Rome: 1992). He was Head of the Department of Art History at the French Academy in Rome.

Stefan Weppelmann is Director of the Picture Gallery in the Kunsthistorisches Museum in Vienna. He was formerly Curator of early Renaissance Italian and Spanish Painting at the Gemäldegalerie of Staatlichen Museen in Berlin (2003–15). Among his exhibitions are *Fantasy and Craftmanship* (2008), *Rothko/Giotto* (2009) and *The Renaissance Portrait from Donatello to Bellini* (2011). His current research focuses on European Renaissance and Baroque Painting; he is equally interested in forms of contemporary receptions of Old Masters.

Georges Didi-Huberman is a French philosopher and art historian whose research spans the visual arts, the historiography of art, psychoanalysis, the human sciences and philosophy. He is a lecturer at the Ecole des Hautes Etudes en Sciences Sociales (EHESS) in Paris since 1990, and has been guest lecturer and visiting professor in numerous universities. In 1997 Didi-Huberman curated *L'Empreinte* at the Centre Georges Pompidou in Paris (with Didier Semin), and in 2001 *Fables du* *lieu* at the Studio national des arts contemporains in Tourcoing. Georges Didi-Huberman is Membre du Conseil artistique du Centre G. Pompidou, Membre du Conseil scientifique de la Mission de préfiguration du musée de l'Homme, des Arts et des Civilisations (Paris), Fellow of the Courtauld Institute of Art (London), Honorary Member at the Center for Literature and Cultural Studies in Berlin and on the editorial board of various magazines and journals, such as *L'Inactuel*, *Études photographiques*, *Les Cahiers du musée national d'art moderne* and *Journal of Visual Culture*. He received the Adorno Prize in 2015 and was elected a Corresponding Fellow of the British Academy (FBA) in 2017.

Riccardo Venturi is Pensionnaire in history and theory of the arts at Académie de France, Villa Medici, Rome (2018–19) and was post-doctoral scholar at Institut national d'histoire de l'art (INHA) in Paris (2012–16). He has published *Mark Rothko. Lo Spazio e la sua disciplina* (Electa, Milan 2007), *Black paintings. Eclissi sul modernismo* (Electa, Milan 2008) and *Passione dell'indifferenza. Francesco Lo Savio* (Humboldt Books, Milan 2018). He recently co-curated the retrospective 'Francesco Lo Savio' at the MART in Rovereto. He contributes regularly to 'Artforum', 'Alias – Il Manifesto' (with the rubric entitled *Cristalli Liquidi*) and to www.doppiozero.com (Screen Tests blog).

Gabriel Montua is Curator of the Collection at Museum Berggruen, Nationalgalerie, Staatliche Museen zu Berlin (National Museums in Berlin), which he joined in 2013. He was part of the Gemäldegalerie's curatorial team for the exhibition *Botticelli Reimagined* in Berlin and London before joining the State Museum's Nationalgalerie for the exhibitions *The Tehran Collection. The Tehran Museum of Contemporary Art in Berlin* (scheduled for 2016–17, but eventually cancelled) and *Wanderlust. From Caspar David Friedrich to Auguste Renoir* (2018). He was Visiting Fellow at Harvard University in 2009 and received a PhD from Humboldt Universität zu Berlin in 2013 with a thesis on arts and politics in the twentieth century, in which he analysed the communication of artists, notably Salvador Dalí, through their works, texts, newspaper features and television appearances. He teaches contemporary art at the Université Paris Nanterre. His research focuses on Western and global art from the nineteenth century to the present.

Botticelli Past and Present

Introduction

Ana Debenedetti

I

This book brings together the proceedings of a two-day international conference held at the Victoria and Albert Museum (13–14 May 2016) to coincide with the exhibition *Botticelli Reimagined* in London.

The recent exhibitions dedicated to Botticelli around the world show, more than ever, the actuality of the debate about this old master.[1] This new 'Botticelli craze', no longer particularly English, but now with a global reach, led the curators of the exhibition *Botticelli Reimagined*, staged in 2015–16 at the Gemäldegalerie in Berlin and the V&A in London, to question the use and re-use of Botticelli's types and formulae, the migration of his images across time and their adaptation in new contexts.

This new methodological approach has been explored in subsequent shows such as *Reflections: Van Eyck and the Pre-Raphaelites* at the National Gallery in London, as well as *Truth and Beauty: The Pre-Raphaelites and the Old Masters* at the Legion of Honour Museum in San Francisco; both are based on similar principles.[2] Elizabeth Prettejohn, who contributed to the *Botticelli Reimagined* exhibition catalogue, has returned to this central question of artistic legacy in her recent book, *Modern Painters, Old Masters*. In this work she analyses the response of Victorian painters to the artists of the past, with Botticelli prominent among them.[3]

The process of redefining Botticelli's art is part of a wider modern phenomenon which extracts works of art from historically grounded settings and inserts them into new, 'contemporary' narratives. Today the presentation of old master works in art fairs, such as London Frieze Masters and the Paris FIAC, is a good example of this trend. Displayed alongside modern and contemporary works of art, historic objects are further isolated from their primary function and locus. Yet through such display these works gain new audiences and meanings, simultaneously casting new light on the contemporary pieces presented alongside them.

This is only the latest episode of a long history of de-contextualisation. Since the late eighteenth century, early Italian paintings have been removed from their original settings, often dismembered and anachronistically reframed, then transferred to private collections and museums. In this process their function as objects of devotion for the pious, or of intellectual enjoyment for a cultural elite, was forgotten. However, their rediscovery as objects of interest to artists, of moral and then aesthetic enjoyment to art writers and collectors and of monetary value to the art trade led in turn to new critical approaches, new artistic vocabularies and, finally, to the rise of connoisseurship. The paintings of Botticelli have a central role in this story.[4]

Reacting against the aestheticism of Swinburne and Pater, and the purely visual judgements of Morelli and Berenson, art historians such as Gaetano Milanesi, John Crowe, Giovanni Battista Cavalcaselle and Herbert Horne took to the archives to rediscover the original authorship and settings of the works, as well as the ways in which old masters had been appraised in the period. Meanwhile there has been a burgeoning interest in the historiography of the taste for early Italian painting and its study, in which writing on Botticelli plays a pivotal part.

This rediscovery is still an ongoing process today, fuelled by the art-historical turn to social history and the study of material culture. Among the positive results of de-contextualisation is the increasing importance of the scientific and diagnostic examination of paintings in museum conservation departments, where we continue to learn about the original techniques of paintings and their physical histories over time.

The exhibition *Botticelli Reimagined* focused on a visual reassessment of the master and his influence over time. However, it inevitably engaged with a rather abbreviated selection of works, displayed in an enclosed, limited space. The need for a coherent narrative and the decision to draw the visitors backwards in time through the artistic reappraisal of Botticelli did not permit the curators to explore fully other types of reception, by critics and historians. The main question was, of course, what was left to cover in the wake of the show and its accompanying catalogue. We hope to have made some inroads into this monumental task in the present volume. In that daunting gap between Medicean Florence and our day lie both the impossibility of a return and the chance for a new start.

We have asked questions about Botticelli's workshop practices and iconographic innovations, as well as meanings of pictures we have failed to decipher since their rediscovery. What may be perceived as a desperate attempt to reactivate the past is somewhat redeemed when its art is translated into a new mode of artistic expression. Modern literature and poetry had remained the least developed topic, introducing a new category of actors in Botticelli-mania with a new set of psychological motivations. Women as poets and connoisseurs in their own right, even if hidden behind a masculine pen-name, were able to challenge the white Western male viewpoint, which has dominated art criticism and all its ramifications over centuries.

Questions of gender and canon recur in the pre- and post-First World War era, while figures such as the anarchist Jacques Mesnil attempted to challenge the 'bourgeois' interpretation of the art of the past. Mesnil made a point of living like a Florentine '*contadino*' to experience a life as close as possible to that of the painter whose work he was studying. He tried to understand Botticelli's habits and customs, as well as the emotive response elicited by his art. Another modern route, or rather an ironic take on the serious and respectable interpretation of the past, can be found in Dalì's reinvention of what had become the quintessential representation of love and beauty: Botticelli's figure of Venus. Dalì and the surrealists paved the way to contemporary means of expression such as video art, installations and performances as well as the cinema – a topic only touched on in the exhibition.

Even today Botticelli's ethereal pictures are transformed and adapted into these new media, whose power of universal reach and immediate reception seem to challenge new forms of religious and political expression. Yet this field seems too close to us to be acknowledged fully and understood as a true societal phenomenon. We are still struggling to understand what contemporary interpretations of the Botticellian nymph say about our times. As Aby Warburg foresaw, the fluid quality of Botticelli's art lies in the embryonic phase of ever-morphing forms, always expandable but never fully resolved.

II

The book comprises four thematic parts, spanning four centuries of Botticelli's artistic fame and reception from the fifteenth century to the present day. Organised chronologically, each part is preceded by a short introduction that contextualises and positions the essays that follow within the wider scholarly literature.

The first part focuses on Botticelli's working practice and his role as the head of an important workshop. Patrizia Zambrano shows the artist's pivotal role in the rise of modern portraiture during the second half of the Quattrocento by exploring the influence of contemporary sculpture as well as the literary tradition that presented portraits as living and speaking memories (*imagines spirantes*). Using both contemporary written sources and recent technical investigation, Nicola Costaras and Clare Richardson investigate Dante Gabriel Rossetti's alleged restoration of Botticelli's *Portrait of a Lady known as Smeralda Bandinelli* (Victoria and Albert Museum). The analysis reveals earlier alterations, providing an important insight into the master's working practice. Paul Holberton offers a survey of the interpretations of Botticelli's 'mythologies' since Aby Warburg's seminal work in identifying a passage from Ovid's *Fasti* at the origins of the *Primavera*'s iconography. Jerzy Miziołek presents an early adaptation of Botticelli's *Primavera* by his contemporary fellow artist Jacopo del Sellaio for a *spalliera* painting depicting the story of Cupid and Psyche.

The second part deals with the progressive rediscovery of Botticelli from the late eighteenth century to the turn of the twentieth. Mark Evans provides a richly illustrated account of Flaxman's recourse to Botticelli's Dante drawings. Francesco Ventrella looks at *fin-de-siècle* connoisseurship and aesthetic theories in the unpublished notes and letters of Mary and Bernard Berenson as well as Vernon Lee (aka Violet Paget) to reveal the psychological motivations behind their understanding of Botticelli as a 'modern' artist. Anna Gruetzner Robins shows how the lovers and collaborators Katherine Bradley and Edith Cooper, known as 'Michael Field', challenged male interpretations of Botticelli's art and offered – in their poetry and journal – a unique, subjective response, tempered by their sexuality and gender, to what they regarded as highly desirable paintings.

The third part is dedicated to the reception of Botticelli's art by scholars and critics from the late nineteenth century to the 1930s. Donata Levi presents new results emerging from Cavalcaselle's and Crowe's approach to Sandro Botticelli, drawing from their unpublished archives. Levi outlines the position of the two art historians in regard to the new evaluations of Botticelli's work within the art criticism of the period, driven by the critics Ruskin and Pater, as well as the connoisseur Giovanni Morelli (1864–94). Claudia Wedepohl goes back to Aby Warburg's doctoral dissertation on Botticelli's mythological paintings to demonstrate how Warburg had first shaped his ideas regarding emotions, physiognomy and body language while studying Filippino Lippi's figures and Masaccio's types in the Brancacci Chapel before deciding to apply them to Botticelli. Jonathan Nelson investigates how 'Japanese' Yukio Yashiro's perception of Botticelli really was, and to what extent he appealed to universal values that grew out of debates in Japan in the early twentieth century. This approach remained understudied by Botticelli scholars, while it provided the foundation for Yashiro's highly influential work on Asian art. Michel Hochmann presents the introspective approach of Jacques Mesnil to Botticelli in his book on the artist published in 1938.

A political activist and an anarchist, Mesnil identified himself with the poorer classes of Florence, challenging the 'bourgeois' interpretations of fellow art historians such as Bernard Berenson and Herbert Horne.

The last part takes the reader into the present day and considers contemporary manifestations of Botticelli's art. Georges Didi-Huberman reconsiders Aby Warburg's key concept of 'imaginary breeze' as a characteristic aspect of Botticelli's painting to propose a new interpretation of the 'fluid' quality of his art which the author extends to film and the new media used in contemporary art. Riccardo Venturi revives Salvador Dalí's provocative use of Botticelli's *Venus* in his pavilion '*Dream of Venus*' for the 1939 New York World's Fair. Finally Gabriel Montua explores contemporary artists' use of Botticelli in specific political contexts, chiefly the status of women in the Middle East, allowing for a reappraisal of the migration of Botticelli's motives through cultures and time.

The editors would like to thank the contributors who enthusiastically agreed to provide a written version of their lecture, which made this book possible. We are grateful to the Kress Foundation who sponsored the organisation of the conference and generously contributed to this publication. Special thanks are due to Marco Delogu, Director of the Italian Cultural Institute in London, for lending his ongoing support to the organisation of the conference and the publication of its proceedings. I am personally grateful to my co-editor Caroline Elam, whose knowledge and kindness were instrumental in bringing the project to completion, and to Tom Windross, Head of Content, Digital Media and Publishing at the V&A, for believing in this editorial adventure, which may initiate a new partnership with UCL Press. A personal thanks to Kira d'Alburquerque and finally many thanks to Lara Speicher and Jaimee Biggins at UCL Press for their enthusiasm for the project, and for their help and patience in preparing this book for publication.

Notes

1 From Japan to the US: see, for example, *Money and Beauty: Botticelli and the Renaissance in Florence*, Bunkamura Museum of Art, Tokyo (21 March–28 June 2016); *Botticelli and His Time*, Tokyo Metropolitan Art Museum (16 January–3 April 2016); jointly organised *The Botticelli Renaisssance*, Gemäldegalerie, Berlin (24 September 2015–24 January 2016) and *Botticelli Reimagined*, The Victoria and Albert Museum, London (5 March–3 July 2016); *Botticelli and the Search for the Divine*, The Museum of Fine Arts, Boston (15 April–9 July 2017).

2 *Reflections: Van Eyck and the Pre-Raphaelites*, The National Gallery, London (2 October 2017–2 April 2018); *Truth and Beauty: The Pre-Raphaelites and the Old Masters*, Legion of Honour Museum, San Francisco (30 June–30 September 2018).

3 Elizabeth Prettejohn, *Modern Painters, Old Masters. The Art of Imitation from the Pre-Raphaelites to the First World War* (London: Yale University Press, 2017).

4 See Jeremy Melius, *Art History and the Invention of Botticelli*, PhD thesis, University of California, Berkeley, 2010, https://escholarship.org/uc/item/98rtqomq.

Part 1
Botticelli in his own time

Introduction

Michelle O'Malley

The essays in part 1 largely discuss Alessandro Botticelli's work from the 1470s, the early years of his career. It is notable that from his earliest recorded commission in 1470, Botticelli was hired by patrons with connections to the Medici family or to Lorenzo's government. For example, the commission for the *Fortitude* panel, made to hang in the Audience Hall of the palace of the Merchants' Tribunal on Piazza della Signoria in Florence, was driven by Tommaso Soderini, the uncle and advisor of the young Lorenzo de' Medici. It must have been around this time that Botticelli was hired by the bankers' guild, the prestigious Arte del Cambio to which the Medici belonged, to paint the *Virgin and Child surrounded by Cherubim,* now in the Uffizi, and by the Pucci family, great supporters of the Medici, to paint an image of the *Adoration of the Magi* for their palazzo. Botticelli designed the standard that Giuliano de' Medici, Lorenzo's brother, carried in the joust of 1475, while around 1476 Gaspare di Zanobi del Lama hired him to produce an altarpiece of the *Adoration of the Magi.* This work presented three generations of the Medici family as the kings and members of their courts (see p.20, fig.1.8).

In about 1477 Botticelli was commissioned, probably by Lorenzo or his wards, to paint the *Primavera*. The following year he was selected by the Florentine government to depict the hanged collaborators of the Pazzi conspiracy, in which Lorenzo's brother Giuliano had been assassinated; either Lorenzo himself or members of his circle asked the painter to produce images of the murdered Giuliano. In 1480 the Vespucci family, of which father and son served as notaries in key government positions, commissioned Botticelli to paint half of the choir screen of their church, the Ognissanti. By this time, when he attracted the attention of the agents of Pope Sixtus IV, who were seeking artists to paint the Sistine Chapel in Rome, Botticelli was probably regarded as one of the Medici family's painters of choice. This undoubtedly enhanced his reputation.

While high-level patrons do not necessarily mean that a painter's work was particularly visible, Botticelli's pictures could often be found in prominent public locations. This means that many people could have been familiar with his work. For example, the *Fortitude* panel hung in the court that dealt with issues of Florentine commerce, commonly visited by merchants. Gaspare di Zanobi del Lama's *Adoration of the Magi* altarpiece stood just to the side of the central door of Santa Maria Novella. Another of Botticelli's images of this subject was on the stair of the Palazzo della Signoria that led to the Sala dei Gigli, in which government committee meetings were held. The image of St Augustine on the choir screen of the Ognissanti faced the main portal, while Botticelli's huge fresco of the *Annunciation* graced the wall under the loggia that formed the entrance to the hospital of San Martino. The *pitture infamanti* of the Pazzi conspirators, painted quickly in 1478 on the walls of the Customs House alongside the Palazzo della Signoria, remained in this prominent spot for 17 years.

The visibility of Botticelli's work contributed to the image Florentines had of their city; it may also have influenced their sense of the visuality both of recognisable individuals and of holy figures. That, along with the reputation Botticelli gained from the excellence of his art and the status of his patrons, must have contributed to the high level of demand for his work – not only from those who commissioned paintings directly from him, but also from those who bought the many pictures he and his assistants produced speculatively for sale in the *bottega*.

It is evident that Botticelli was a careful image maker, often adjusting and readjusting the design of a work after he had transferred his preparatory drawings to a panel or canvas. His manner of working is clear in Nicola Costaras and Clare Richardson's discussion of the *Portrait of a Lady known as Smeralda Bandinelli* in the collection of the Victoria and Albert Museum (see p.17, fig. 1.5). Their analysis provides a detailed example of the complex approach to picture making that Botticelli practised throughout his career. It demonstrates the many changes the painter made to the design at both the drawing and the painting stages, as he re-thought the figure and its relationship to the window in which 'Smeralda' is framed. This kind of close attention was undoubtedly behind Botticelli's pivotal role in the development of portraiture during the second half of the Quattrocento, explored here by Patrizia Zambrano. She argues that Botticelli was among the pioneers of the modern painted portrait, creating innovative compositions of the figure within the picture space and experimenting with the expressive power of the face. Some of this is likely to have been worked out on the panel itself.

Botticelli brought to the depiction of mythological subjects the same close attention to detail found in the portraits, and the same intelligence directed to conveying of meaning. The mythological pictures were based on written sources and, as there is no evidence that Botticelli read Latin, the subject matter was presumably conveyed to the painter in the course of the commissioning process. Only after designing *The Birth of Venus* (fig.1.0), for example, did he fully comprehend the visual import of the winds always included in this classical subject, altering during the painting stage the way in which Venus's hair streams out and her garment, held by one of her attendants, flutters. Paul Holberton argues that *The Birth of Venus* was, like the *Primavera*, conceived as a marriage picture. He focuses on Ovid's *Fasti* as the origin of the complex *Primavera* iconography.

Jerzy Miziołek's contribution underlines the fact that Botticelli's pictures not only influenced future patrons, but also inspired other artists – even when they were destined for private settings. He discusses an early adaptation of the *Primavera* by Botticelli's fellow painter, Jacopo del Sellaio, who reproduced the characters of the picture in a *cassone* panel depicting the story of Cupid and Psyche (see p.74, fig.1.31). He argues that Sellaio's presentation of the figures in this subject supports a case for Apuleius's *Metamorphoses* or *Golden Ass* as a source for the *Primavera*, an idea originally put forward by Ernst Gombrich. In the course of this, Miziołek demonstrates that the material that informed the original conception of Botticelli's *Primavera* was accessible to artists decades after its creation. The Sellaio *cassone* appears to be the only example yet found of a direct quotation from the figures in the *Primavera*, but it suggests that Botticelli's work provided exempla to painters and to patrons in fifteenth-century Florence.

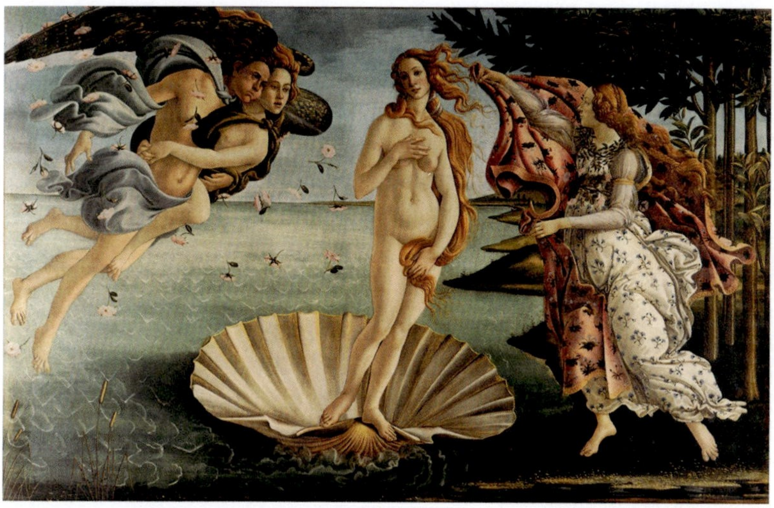

Fig.1.0 Sandro Botticelli, *The Birth of Venus*, c.1480, tempera on canvas, 172.5 × 278.5 cm, Galleria degli Uffizi, Florence, Inv.1890 no.878. © 2018 Photo Scala – courtesy of the Ministero Beni e Att. Culturali e del Turismo.

1. Sandro Botticelli and the birth of modern portraiture

Patrizia Zambrano

Botticelli's fame certainly does not rest on his relatively few portraits – a dozen according to Ronald Lightbown, a few more according to other scholars – though all are of enormous importance.[1] Instead, he is known and appreciated for his mythological works, for his Madonnas and, to a lesser extent, for his magnificent altarpieces. In the course of his career Botticelli painted both group portraits in narrative scenes and autonomous likenesses. None of the latter is signed, dated or securely documented. In 1966 John Pope Hennessy wrote that Sandro emerges, in the Quattrocento context, 'as a giant among portraitists. He can animate the human face, he can apprehend its contours and its planes, he can invest it with a sentient response to the scene when it occurs'.[2] Of course one should add that Botticelli is a giant among other giants – Antonello da Messina, Andrea Mantegna, Giovanni Bellini, Leonardo da Vinci. For this very reason it is important to understand the particular position Sandro occupies in the history of modern autonomous portraiture, and to analyse the works through which he arrived at it.

Group portraits of private citizens within a sacred scene are commonly found in Italy from the 1420s. They appear in a well-known linear development that runs from Masaccio's *Sagra* in the Carmine in Florence to the feats of portraiture in the Sistine Chapel in 1482 to the Vatican Stanze, reaching a climax in the sixteenth century. This trajectory has much to do with the social and political history of Florence, Rome and Venice.[3] By contrast, the autonomous portrait has a much less linear history, still partly obscure. It seems that while private citizens had little hesitation in having themselves depicted in social contexts, they were somewhat more resistant to seeing their individual image fixed in painting.[4] It is also true that, at least in the second half of the Quattrocento, Florentine patrons with the requisite economic and social means favoured the option of a sculpted portrait, as witnessed by the portrait busts in terracotta and marble executed between 1450 and 1500. These seem in many respects to be a more conspicuous phenomenon than painted likenesses.[5] A decisive element in this preference was the influence of the antique, especially Pliny the Elder's account of ancient busts in his *Natural History*. Portrait busts also offered the possibility of using life and death masks, ensuring greater verisimilitude and producing the quality of 'breathing images' (*imagines spirantes*) – lacking only a voice to seem alive – so highly valued by humanists since the time of Petrarch.[6]

Rather than being the mirror and visual expression of a social group, like the collective and 'civic' portrait, the autonomous likeness at this period often (if not always) has to do with private history and identity; it commemorates a single individual and has a personal, introspective and speculative character. For that reason it requires a profound and explicit psychological characterisation.[7] However, up to and beyond the middle of the fifteenth century the autonomous portrait in Italy remains prisoner to the profile pose-derived either from earlier conventions of donor portraiture or from ancient coins – allowing only limited psychological characterisation and physiognomic accuracy. This restriction hampered the development of the portrait, which in Flanders had already changed in direction from the 1420s following the experiments of Jan van Eyck. Only at the end of the 1460s did the situation in Italy and Florence change, with subjects now 'turning around' into three-quarter poses – partly, but not solely, under the influence of Flemish examples.

Botticelli is among the protagonists in this shift. In Florence, it is he who took the portrait on from the first experiments, in the late 1460s, to the fully modern form the genre assumed in the 1480s. This is why his works of the 1470s, a period when he was working on some of his most radically innovative portraits, are so important. For a decade, in fact, Botticelli continues to experiment in two registers in particular: with different compositional structures of the figure within the picture space, and with the expressive capacities of figure and face. Naturally, for Sandro, the point of departure is the work of his master Filippo Lippi and of Antonio and Piero Pollaiuolo, the artists in whose orbit he was formed, but it is of course possible that he also knew portraits by Flemish artists and others from outside Florentine culture. At the beginning of this period Botticelli (born in 1445) was about 25 years old, and the very first portrait securely attributable to him shows that he could paint a figure in three-quarters view and rotated in space. A comparison between the *Portrait of a Young Man with a Mazzocchio* in the Galleria Palatina, Florence (fig.1.1), which can be dated around 1470,[8] but is unfortunately in poor condition,[9] and the *Male Portrait* now in the National Gallery of Art, Washington (fig.1.2)[10] reveals how carefully the young Sandro looked at a work such as the latter.

The attribution of the Washington picture to Andrea del Castagno has been questioned by Miklòs Boskovits in favour of Piero del Pollaiuolo, with a date around the middle of the 1460s – shortly before the altarpiece

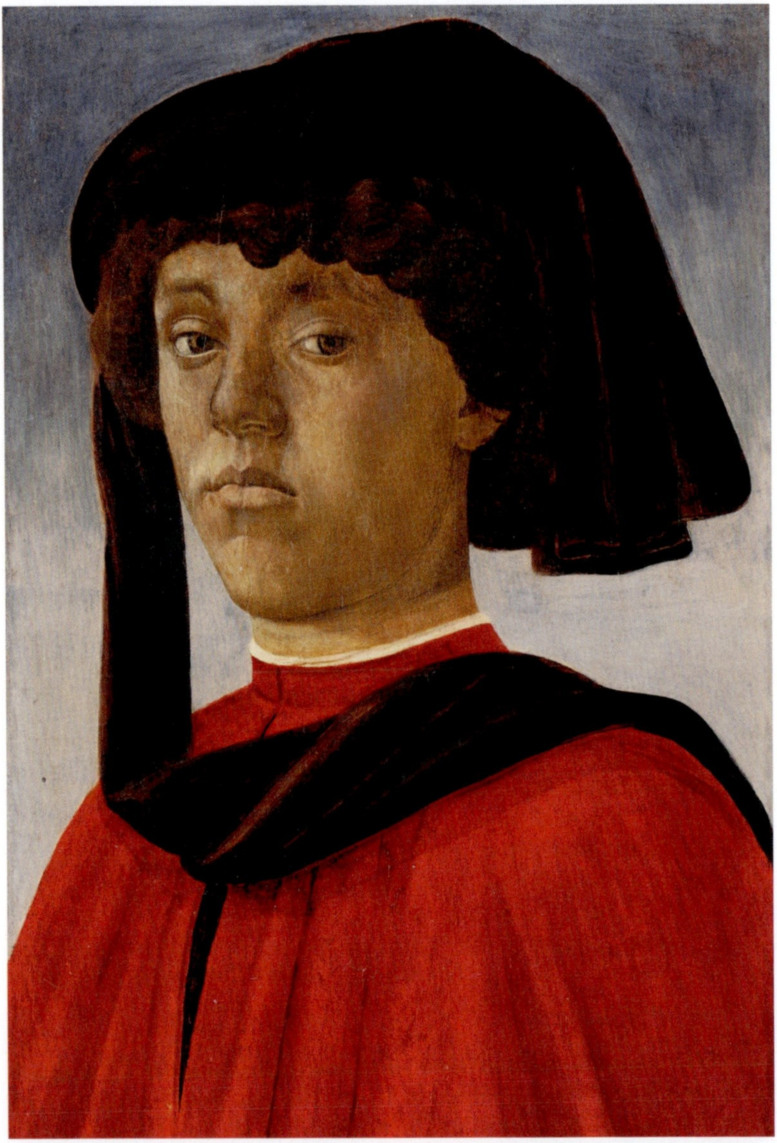

Fig.1.1 Sandro Botticelli, *Portrait of a Young Man with a Mazzocchio*, *c.*1470, tempera on wood, 51.2 × 35.2 cm, Galleria Palatina, Florence, Inv.1912 no.372. © 2018 Photo Scala – courtesy of the Ministero Beni e Att. Culturali e del Turismo.

with *Saint James between Saint Vincent and Saint Eustace* from the Chapel of the Cardinal of Portugal in San Miniato al Monte in Florence, now in the Uffizi.[11] According to Boskovits (with whom I agree), 'the innovative

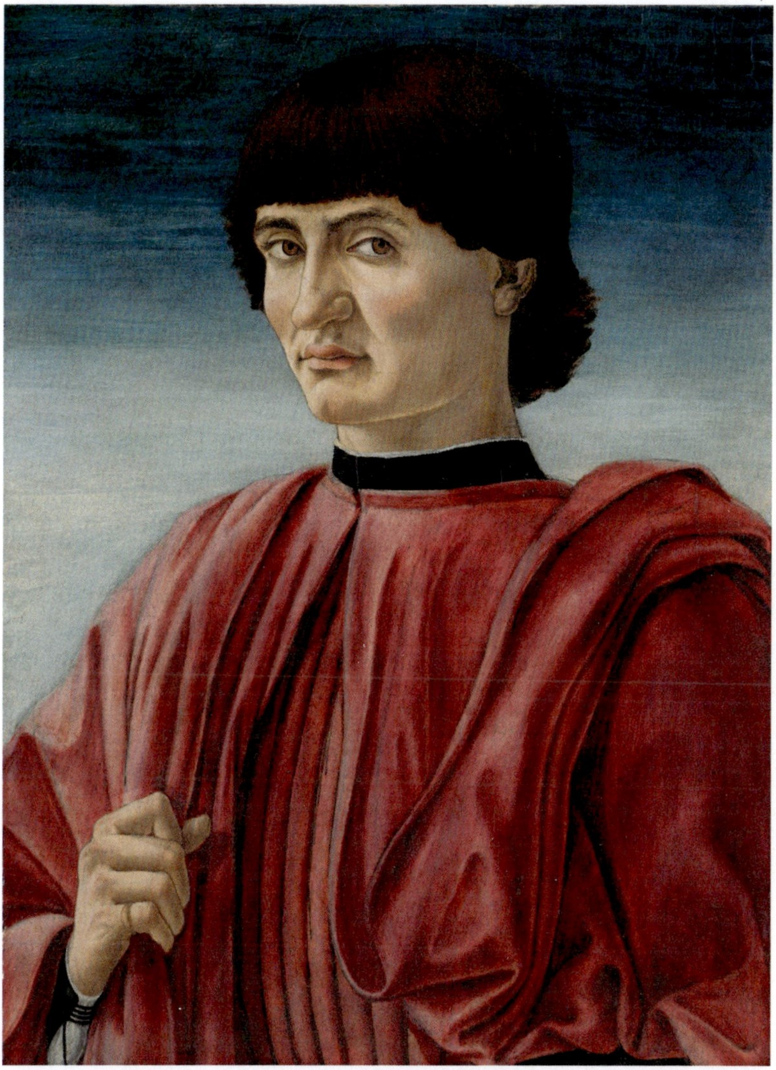

Fig.1.2 Attributed to Piero del Pollaiuolo, *Male Portrait*, *c*.1465, tempera on wood, 55.5 × 41.2 cm, The National Gallery of Art, Washington, Inv.1937.I.17. © Courtesy National Gallery of Art, Washington.

composition suggests that the panel postdates Andrea's death' in 1457.[12] The panel would therefore be later than Mantegna's *Portrait of Cardinal Ludovico Trevisan* of 1459 (now in Berlin), in which the sitter's hands are not included in the image, as they are by contrast in Piero del Pollaiuolo's *Portrait of Galeazzo Maria Sforza* in the Uffizi (fig.1.3).

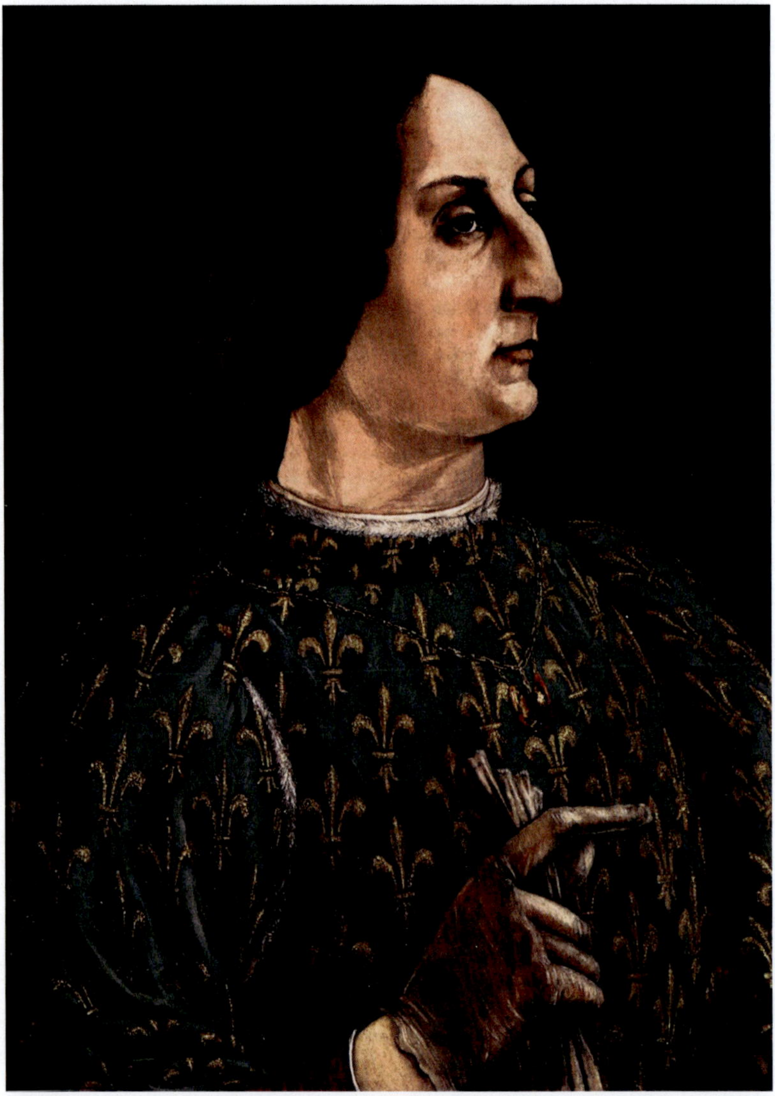

Fig.1.3 Piero del Pollaiuolo (1443–96), *Portrait of Galeazzo Maria Sforza*, *c.*1471, tempera on wood, Uffizi Gallery, Florence, Inv.1890 no.1492. © 2018 Photo Scala, Florence – courtesy of the Ministero Beni e Att. Culturali e del Turismo.

This latter painting, which was in Lorenzo the Magnificent's ground-floor *camera* (‘*Camera grande terrena*’) at the time of his death in 1492, was probably executed from life during the Duke of Milan's visit to Florence in March 1471; it shows Galeazzo half-length and in profile, but in a pose slightly rotated to the left.[13] The two figures (Washington and Palatina) have the same chromatic range of blue, red, black and white and the same rotation of the body in space, against a background of sky. The head is slightly rotated in relation to the bust, and turned to look directly out. The eyes follow the spectator wherever he or she moves, holding the gaze and demanding attention. This point may seem banal, but it is not: in his search for a direct *rapport* with the viewer, Botticelli not only eliminates the foreground hand that distances the figure in the Washington picture, but also reduces the space between the figure and the frame, bringing it closer to us. This abolition of distance through a gaze turned directly towards the spectator is the quality that will characterise all of Sandro's portraits. The same immediacy and the same engagement of the spectator is found in the *Portrait of a Man*, formerly in the Museo Filangieri in Naples (fig.1.4), destroyed in 1943 and known to us only from old reproductions.[14] In this painting, which should probably be dated to the mid-1470s, the figure has an identical pose to that of the boy in the Palatina (fig.1.1). Botticelli places him within an architectural setting, but brings him close to us, making the hand in the foreground seem to enter our space.

In the course of the 1470s, Sandro painted three other portraits in which the figure is seen through an opening and is placed within an architectural setting: the so-called *Smeralda Bandinelli* (fig.1.5) and two of the versions of the *Portrait of Giuliano de' Medici*. This type of composition would have been familiar to Sandro because it had been developed to a complex and refined degree by his first master, Filippo Lippi – as we see in the double portrait now in New York and in the single likeness in Berlin.[15] The *Smeralda Bandinelli* represents a turning point in the history of the modern portrait. It is in fact the first known female likeness to be presented to us not in profile but in a three-quarters pose, seen through a window and framed within an architectural space; the setting is more highly articulated than in the Naples painting.[16] In line with his other portraits, Botticelli takes care to establish a strong contact between figure and spectator, by means of the direct gaze. A comparison with the head of St Catherine in the *Sant'Ambrogio altarpiece* in the Uffizi (fig.1.6), datable around 1470, is instructive. St Catherine too turns her head towards the spectator and looks out, but her gaze avoids direct contact and slips away, eluding the viewer. So she remains in her own sacred space, distant, remote and unapproachable.

Scholars date the problematic *Portrait of a Young Man with the Medal of Cosimo de' Medici* (fig.1.7) in the Uffizi to the middle of the 1470s.[17] In reality this is a double portrait, and it is distinct in several respects from the other likenesses that Sandro produced in these years;

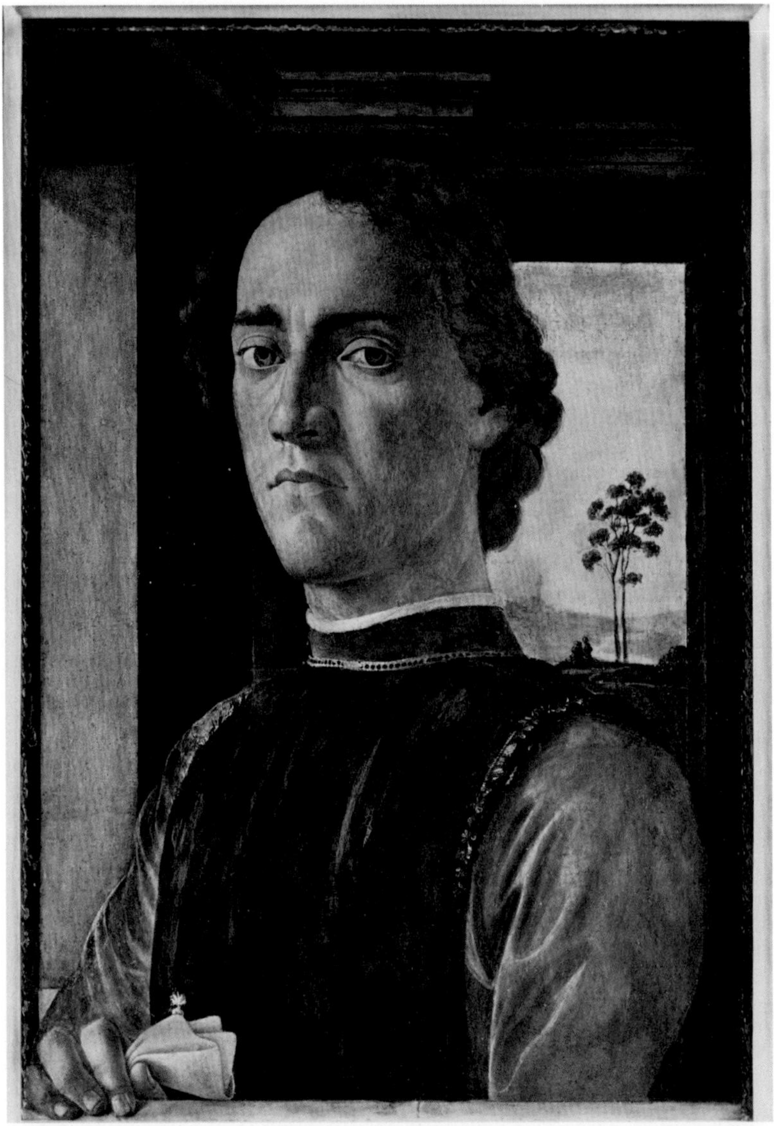

Fig.1.4 Sandro Botticelli, *Portrait of a Man*, *c*.1475, tempera on wood, 51 × 37 cm, formerly Museo Filangieri, Naples, destroyed in 1943. © Bologna, Fototeca Federico Zeri inv.1259.

Lightbown aptly defines it as essentially an 'ambitious essay in a manner ultimately Flemish'[18] – a description that would not apply to other paintings of this period, which do not exhibit northern characteristics, either in the landscape or in the treatment of the figure. The portrait is

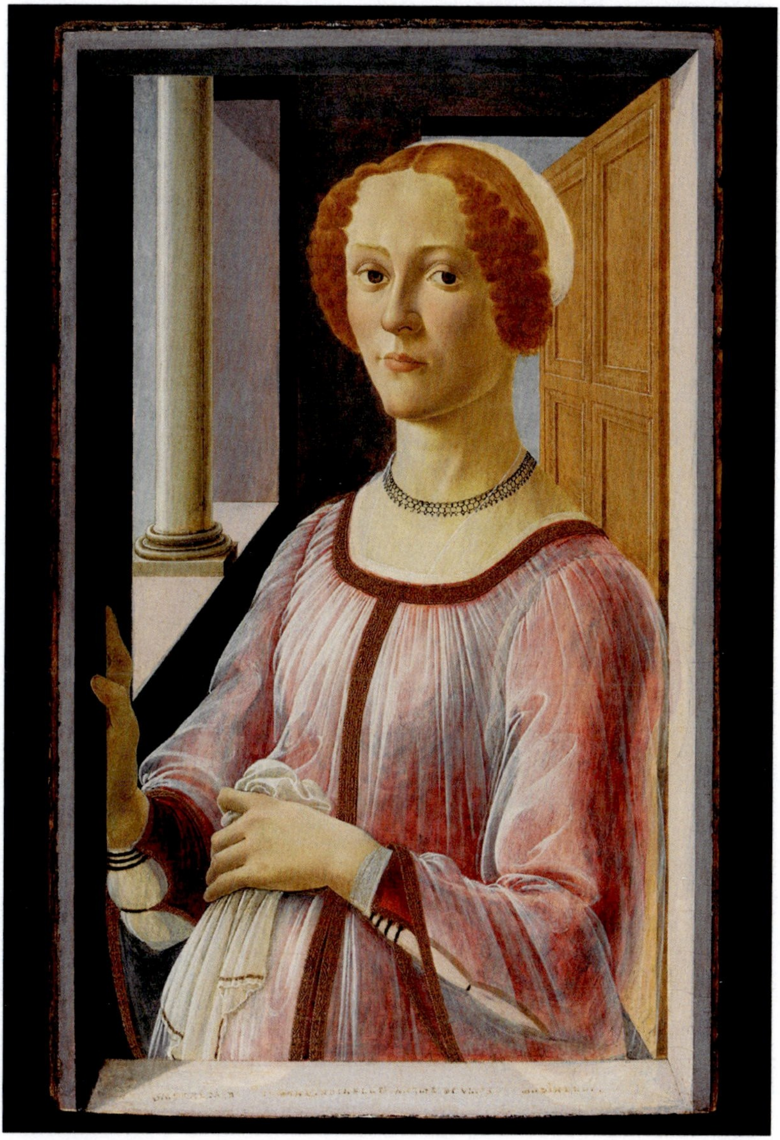

Fig.1.5 Sandro Botticelli, *Portrait of a Lady known as Smeralda Bandinelli*, *c.*1470, tempera on wood, 65.7 × 41 cm, Victoria and Albert Museum, London, inv. CAI.100 © Victoria and Albert Museum, London.

problematic, primarily because the sitter has not been identified, despite displaying the medal with the profile of Cosimo il Vecchio. For both author and patron, this was probably intended to permit an immediate identification.[19] The medal's presence has led to suggestions that the

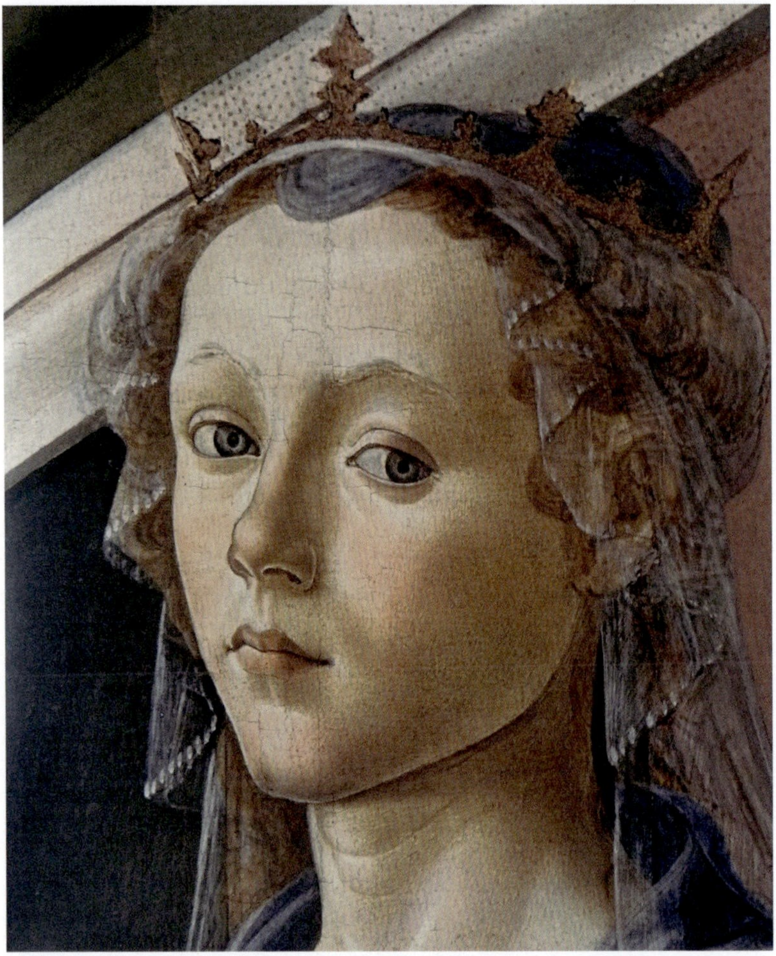

Fig.1.6 Sandro Botticelli, *Sant'Ambrogio altarpiece*, detail of St Catherine, *c.*1470, tempera on wood, 167 × 195 cm, Uffizi Gallery, Florence, Inv.1890 no.8657. © Wikimedia Commons.

young man could be a member of the Medici family, or a goldsmith or a medallist (perhaps the author of this very medal, which was made after 1465 and before 1469) – or perhaps Sandro's brother, Antonio, or even a self-portrait. However, none of these hypotheses is fully convincing.[20] Moreover, unlike Leonardo, Ghirlandaio, Lorenzo di Credi or Luca Signorelli, Botticelli was never again, so far as we know, to paint portraits with landscape backgrounds, nor with the sitter holding objects.

In the two decades following the experiments of the 1470s his portraits have undifferentiated backgrounds, as one sees in the two

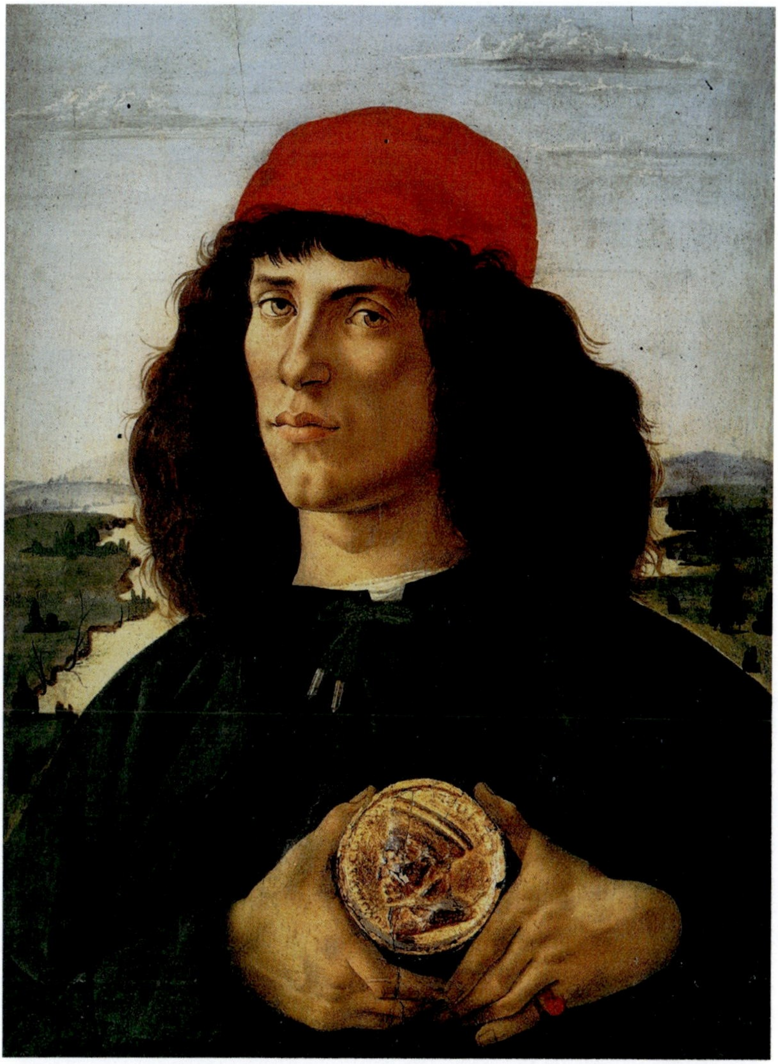

Fig.1.7 Sandro Botticelli, *Portrait of a Young Man with the Medal of Cosimo de' Medici*, c.1475, tempera on wood, 57.5 × 44 cm, Uffizi Gallery, Florence, Inv.1890 no.1488. © Wikimedia / source DirectMedia / public domain.

young men in London (see p.29, fig.1.14) and Washington, in the portraits of the humanist *Michele Marullo Tarchaniota* in Barcelona[21] and of *Lorenzo de' Lorenzi* in Philadelphia.[22] A comparison between the background of the Uffizi *Portrait* and the *St Sebastian* in Berlin, executed in January 1474 for the church of Santa Maria Maggiore in Florence, shows two different visual worlds: in the latter case a typically Florentine landscape, to be placed alongside those of the Pollaiuolo brothers (very familiar to Sandro); in the former a landscape with a blueish tonality of Flemish character, which finds no analogies with other works of these years, beginning with the Uffizi *Adoration of the Magi*, which can be dated around 1475–6 (fig.1.8).

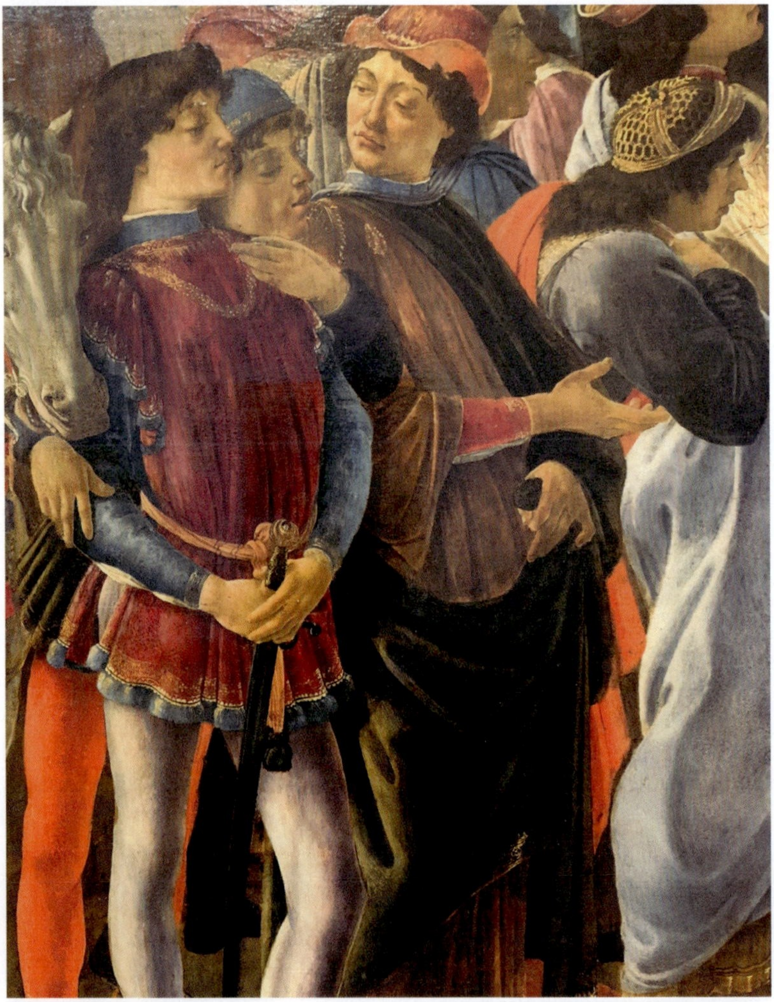

Fig.1.8 Sandro Botticelli, *Adoration of the Magi*, detail, *c.*1475–6, tempera on wood, 111 × 134 cm, Uffizi Gallery, Florence, Inv.1890 no.882. © 2018 Photo Scala – courtesy of the Ministero Beni e Att. Culturali e del Turismo.

To understand the impact this latter work must have had on Botticelli's contemporaries, even Giorgio Vasari's words are insufficient. In his *Lives,* Vasari testifies to the amazement of mid-sixteenth-century viewers: 'every artist today still marvels at it',[23] describing it in detail and dwelling on the heads – *'le teste'* – which 'are turned in various attitudes – some full-face, some in profile, some three-quarter [*'mezo occhio'*], and some looking down [...] – with a great diversity of expressions on the faces of young and old alike'.[24] If the impression left on Vasari many years later was so vivid, in the mid-1470s Botticelli's portraits must have had an effect similar to that of Antonello's on a Venetian clientele in the same years. In Peter Humfrey's words, they would have conveyed a 'powerful physical and personal presence that must have been mesmerizing for viewers'.[25]

The *Adoration of the Magi* was painted for Guasparre di Zanobi del Lama. It includes portraits of members of the Medici family and many others, among them Sandro himself and probably the patron.[26] The altarpiece was originally on the interior facade of the church of Santa Maria Novella, where Sandro's formidable powers as a portraitist must have been visible to the largest possible public. Among the likenesses present are those of Giuliano de' Medici and of his friend Angelo Poliziano who, in 1475, had dedicated the *Stanze per la giostra* to him. A few months after Giuliano's assassination, Poliziano recounted in his *Commentary on the Pazzi Conspiracy* the drama in Florence cathedral on 26 April 1478: the death of Giuliano, the flight of Lorenzo, the hunting down of the conspirators, the vendetta against the Pazzi and their accomplices.[27] At least three portraits of *Giuliano de' Medici* by Botticelli (now in Bergamo, Washington and Berlin) are tied to these events and were painted shortly afterwards.[28] The first of these to be realised must have been the one today in the Accademia Carrara, Bergamo (fig.1.9).[29] In this panel Giuliano appears in a three-quarters view, turned to his left, his head slightly inclined and his gaze lowered. His head stands out against a background of sky seen through an open box in a rudimentary architectural setting, barely sketched out. The painting was conserved in 2011 by Carlotta Beccaria and Roberto Buda, after the exhibition at the Poldi Pezzoli Museum in Milan, but discontinuities in the execution had been visible even before the restoration. Both the background and the red hatching on the garment seemed to be unfinished. By contrast, technical analysis has confirmed that the head is highly finished, painted in oil, with an ivory-like surface and an extraordinary mastery and subtlety of execution that reveals the hand of Botticelli himself.[30] The analyses carried out during the conservation campaign have shown that the background was completely

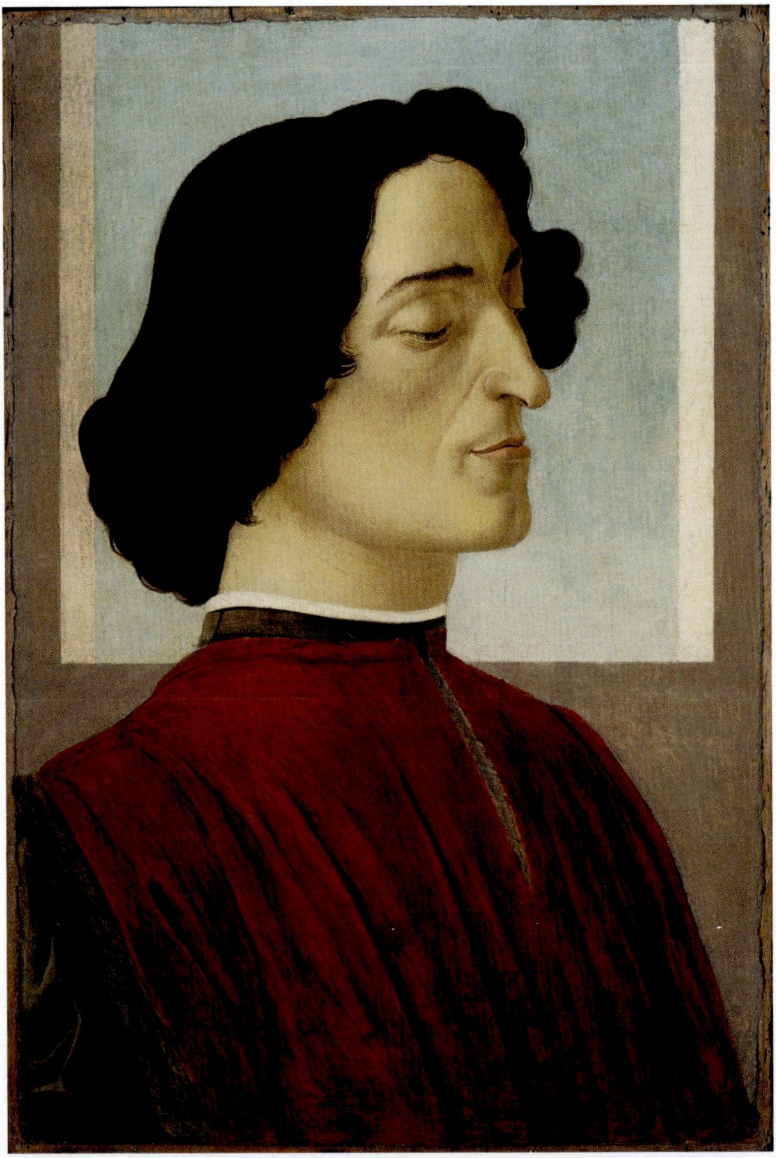

Fig.1.9 Sandro Botticelli, *Portrait of Giuliano de' Medici*, after 1478, tempera on wood, 56.8 × 38.5 cm, Accademia Carrara, Bergamo, 58MR0006. © Courtesy of the Accademia Carrara, Bergamo.

repainted, some time after the original was made, with a uniform blue colour. This was removed before Morelli acquired the picture in 1883, making it similar to the version in Berlin (fig.1.10).[31]

While in the case of the portraits discussed above the identity of the subjects is unknown, and we are not even sure if they were alive or dead – one of the most important questions for the study of portraiture – the case of Giuliano's portrait is very different. In this work Botticelli had to

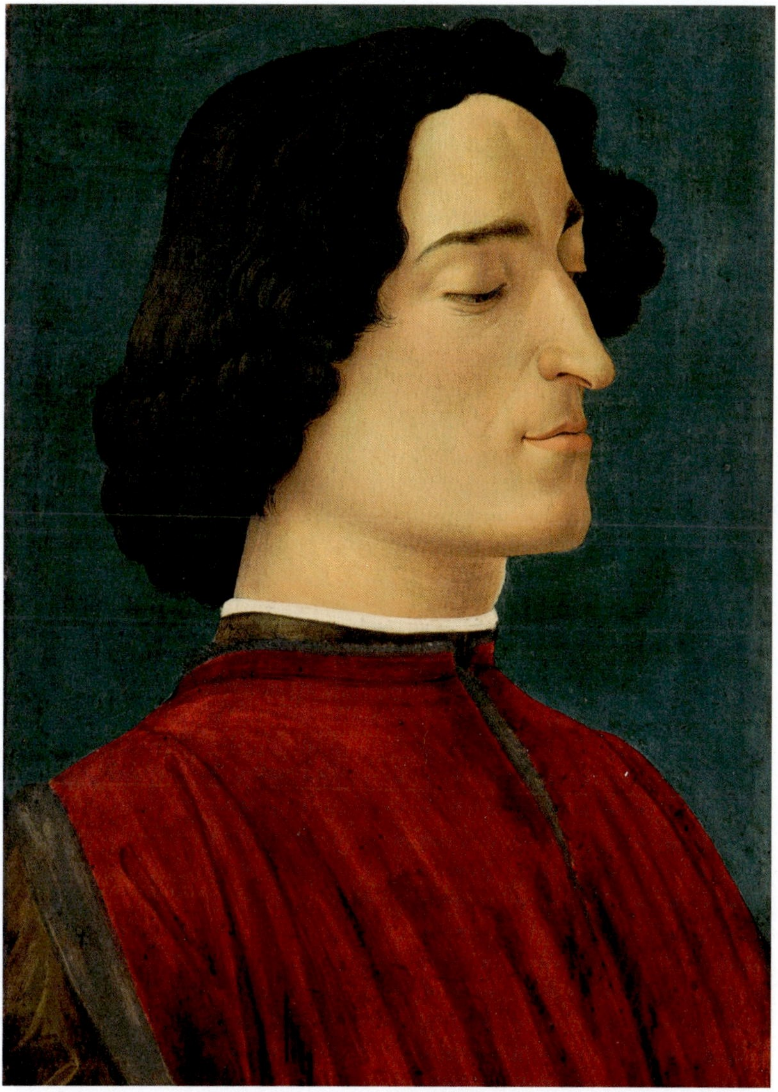

Fig.1.10 Sandro Botticelli, *Portrait of Giuliano de' Medici*, after 1478, tempera on wood, 56.8 × 38.5 cm, Gemäldegalerie, Staatliche Museen zu Berlin, Berlin, no.106 B. © Staatliche Museen zu Berlin – Gemäldegalerie. Photo: Christoph Schmidt.

grapple with the image of a public figure only recently deceased, still very much present in the Florentine collective imagination – a man whom very many contemporaries had seen or indeed known. It is more than likely that in order to execute the portrait Botticelli may have had to hand the medal (fig.1.11) that Lorenzo de' Medici commissioned from Bertoldo di Giovanni as a *memento* of the conspiracy, with his brother's portrait and his own.[32] It is also probable that the artist used a death mask of Giuliano (something analogous to the extant death mask of Lorenzo, taken in 1492).[33] Karla Langedijk claims that no such mask was made of Giuliano, on the grounds that his head was too disfigured to permit a cast, but the sources give contradictory information on the location of the wounds.[34] Francesco Caglioti has proposed that both Bertoldo and Botticelli used such a mask, which allowed them 'the less exploited option of a three-

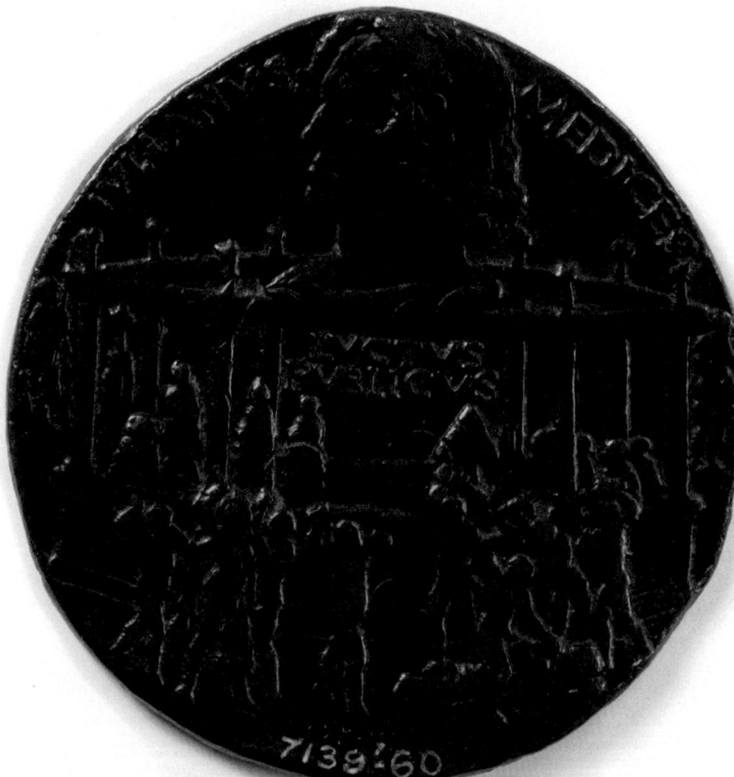

Fig.1.11 Bertoldo di Giovanni (1420–91), *Bronze Medal of Lorenzo and Giuliano de' Medici*, 1478, bronze, diam. 6.35 cm, Victoria and Albert Museum, London, Inv. 7139-1860. © Victoria and Albert Museum, London.

quarters view, as though the three-dimensional object took the place of a model in flesh and blood'.[35] Confirmation of the existence of such a relic comes from the marble *Bust of Giuliano* in the Bargello which Caglioti attributes to a Florentine sculptor working in the 1480s–90s, perhaps Michele Marini da Fiesole (fig.1.12). Here the features reveal the use of a death mask – for example, the lifeless, half-closed eyes and the hollow cheeks, the same traits evident in the Bergamo portrait.[36]

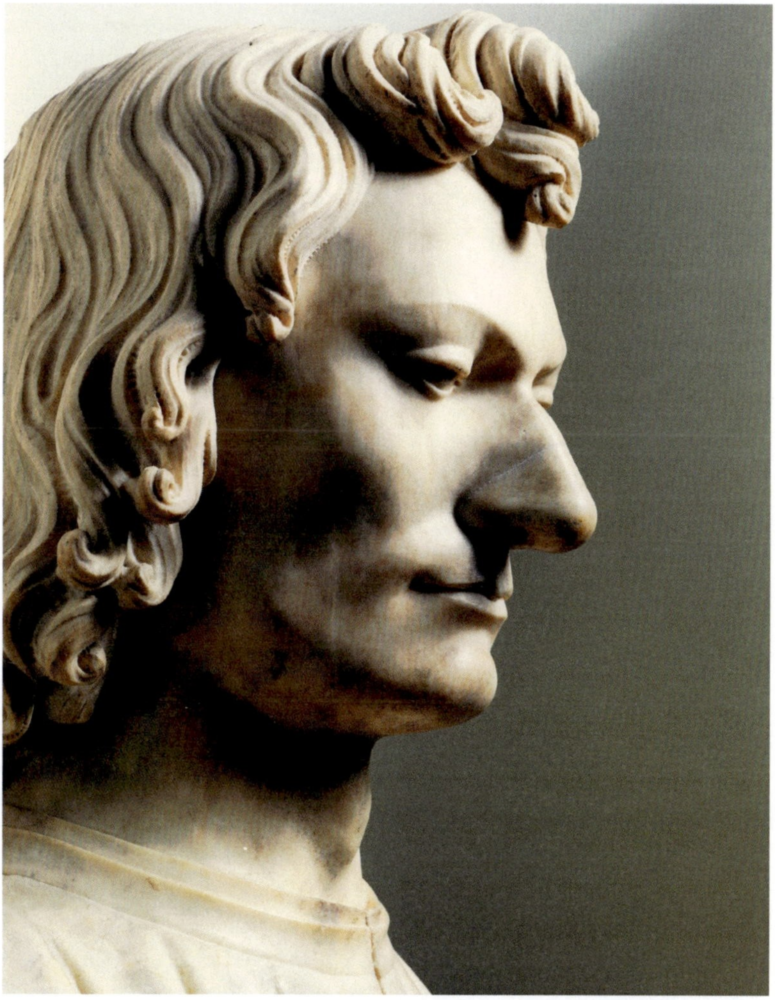

Fig.1.12 Florentine sculptor (Michele Marini da Fiesole?), *Marble Bust of Giuliano de' Medici*, detail, 1480–90, height 64 cm, Museo Nazionale del Bargello, Florence, inv.Sculture 360. © 2018 DeAgostini Picture Library/Scala, Florence.

That Botticelli was entrusted, after April 1478, with the task of making an effigy of Giuliano shows that his experience as a portraitist must have been sufficient to justify a commission at the highest level. We can imagine that to research and recompose the image of Lorenzo's young brother, he proceeded on the basis of his own memory. He knew Giuliano, having designed the standard for his Giostra of 1475 showing Pallas Athena dressed in gold and white, and had already portrayed him in the Del Lama *Adoration*. In addition, he would have had access to important visual testimony such as Verrocchio's terracotta bust, now in Washington DC, and probably, as already mentioned, Bertoldo's medal.[37] However, the mask was in my view probably the point of departure and the decisive model – just as it is equally decisive to contrast the face in the Bergamo portrait with that of the version in the National Gallery of Art, Washington (fig.1.13), from which Botticelli tried to erase the traces of death, in an operation akin to plastic surgery.[38]

The Bergamo head should be considered as a first study, 'photographing' and adapting to the painted panel what was visible in the death mask. In the second version Botticelli eliminated the deep hollow of the eyebrows, the black marks under the eyes and the bridge of the nose, the long furrows across the lower part of the face around the mouth, which was made to project more prominently. He gave more volume to the cheeks, sunken by the inevitable collapse of tissues in death. He also turned the head slightly, changing the inclination, lifting it from the chest and raising the chin, so that the jaw line fell less heavily. In so doing the artist sought to make Giuliano more of a living, 'breathing' likeness in a painting which, this time, had to be a finished work, bound up with memory, commemoration, celebration of the young Medici butchered in the cathedral. In the Washington panel, in fact, Giuliano de' Medici (fig.1.13) is shown in a more elaborate composition, framed between two openings. In front of him are a turtle dove (which may be a symbol of eternal love, conjugal fidelity or affliction) and a dry, broken twig – a sombre reference to a life cut short. Behind the young man is a window with one shutter open and one closed, to signify the transition from life to death or the hope for immortality – which Botticelli's image had certainly given him.[39] It is probable that the third version of the portrait (Gemäldegalerie, Berlin; fig.1.10),[40] in which Giuliano is presented in the same pose but against a uniform blue background, is the culmination of the process of elaboration Botticelli went through to retrieve Giuliano's lost image. This seems to be indicated by the freer treatment of the clothing, the softer modelling in the face and the vibrant handling of the thick, full hair. In addition, the figure is liberated from any architectural background, as was to be the case in all Botticelli's subsequent portraits.

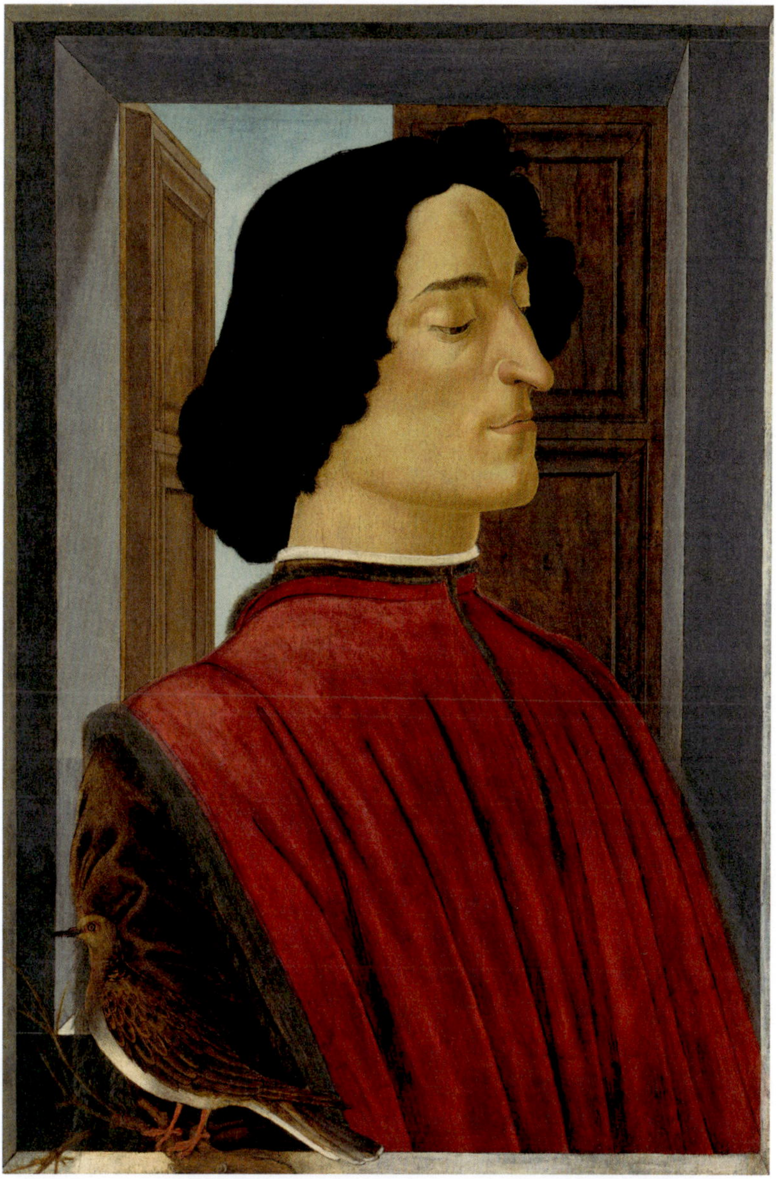

Fig.1.13 Sandro Botticelli, *Portrait of Giuliano de' Medici*, after 1478, tempera on wood, 75.6 × 52.6 cm, The National Gallery of Art, Washington, inv.1952.5.56. © Courtesy National Gallery of Art, Washington.

If we look at these paintings as a series, not as individual pieces, and try to grasp the relationships between them, it seems clear that the three (or perhaps more)[41] versions of the subject testify to the various phases in the elaboration of the image, starting from what Botticelli knew and what he was able to see. They make visible to us the difficult passage from the three-dimensional values of mask and sculpture to the two-dimensional ones of painted portraiture – or, in a different sense, the difficulty of translating sculpture into painting. Furthermore, the reciprocal ties between these paintings show us something about the birth of this genre, and throw light on the development of Botticelli's portraiture at the end of the 1470s – a time when, as should not be forgotten, he was still taking, as the basis for his portrait of Giuliano, the model of Piero Pollaiuolo's *Portrait of Galeazzo Maria Sforza* (fig.1.3). Even if it has not yet been possible to identify who commissioned the portrait of Giuliano de' Medici, in its various versions, I believe it to be a complex image requiring multiple readings linked to the history and culture of Florence, at the end of the 1470s. Nonetheless I see it, above all, as the expression of a humanistic idea – the ability of the image to preserve the memory of the dead. The portrait of Giuliano has to do with the political life of Florence, with the Medici family, with Lorenzo the Magnificent, with the public and private dimension of mourning, with power, with sorrow, with remembrance.[42]

It is hard to establish with certainty or to delineate with precision what provoked the transformation so apparent in Botticelli's portraiture between the end of the 1470s and the early years of the next decade. The two male portraits, the one in London (fig.1.14),[43] datable to the mid-1480s, and the one in Washington[44] from some years later, demonstrate a decisive and evident change from the previous work. The narrative dimension that had been supplied by setting, architecture, background and atmospheric movement has been abandoned in favour of a dark background against which only the figure stands out, fully frontal. The panels are smaller, around 40 by 30 cm and the light comes from the left; space is compressed around the subject, who is thereby brought closer to and looks at the viewer. This is a compositional and expressive choice that marks a new phase in Botticelli's portraiture. It is accompanied by a drastic reduction in chromatic range in favour of a greater concentration on the expressive and plastic characterisation of the painted subject, which, by this means, attains greater relief. These are works which make one suspect that Sandro had in some way come into contact with a portrait by Antonello da Messina, not just with northern European importations.[45] The frontal pose, specific and peculiar to these two works, the use of light to modulate the tones of the few colours employed, the use of a dark but not opaque background and the choice of a close-cropped format all indicate a new direction apparently without correspondence or parallel in Florence in the 1480s.

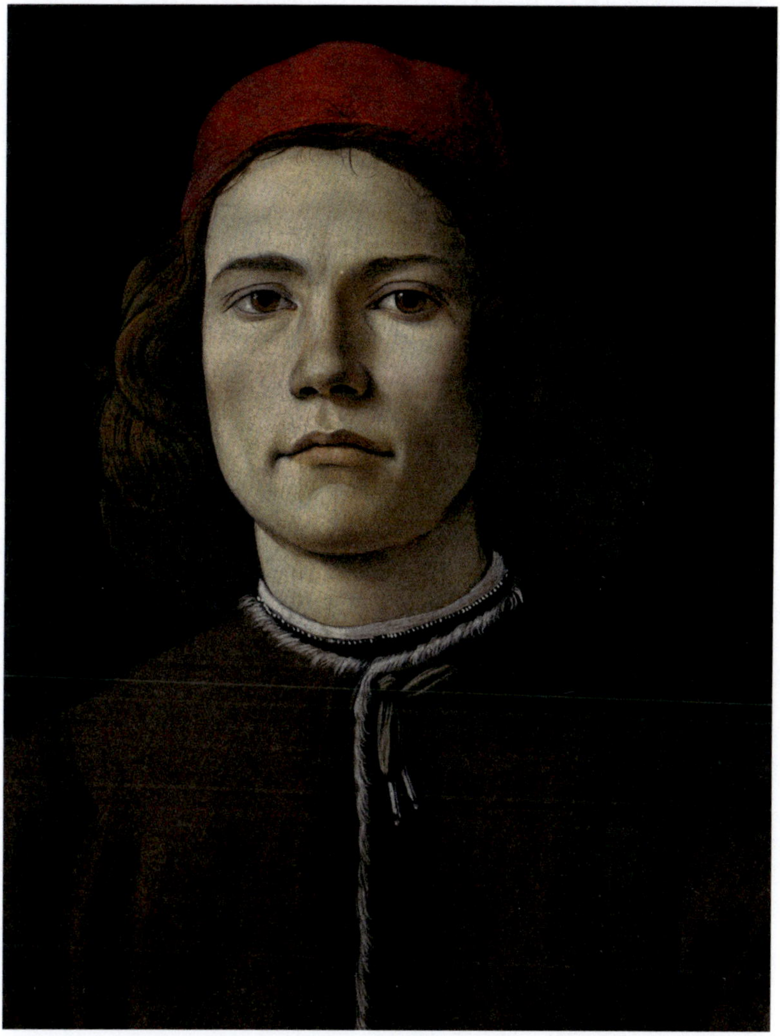

Fig.1.14 Sandro Botticelli, *Portrait of a Young Man*, *c.*1485, tempera and oil on panel, 37.5 × 28.3 cm, The National Gallery, London, NG 626. © 2018 The National Gallery, London/Scala, Florence.

A useful key to understanding the direction on which Botticelli was embarking in this phase of his portraiture is provided by a passage in *Della pittura* in which Leon Battista Alberti discusses lighting, the treatment of light and shade, the use of white and black, 'because light and shade make things appear in relief'. He continues: 'I shall praise those faces which seem to come out of the picture as though sculpted and I shall criticise those faces in which no other skill is visible than perhaps that of drawing'.[46] Without referring directly to portraiture, Alberti gives painters a very important direction, not towards an imitative *paragone* with sculpture, but towards 'relief' in painting. This is what Botticelli achieves in these portraits, responding to Alberti's powerful exhortation.

Acknowledgements

My thanks to Ana Debenedetti for giving me the chance to share some reflections on *Sandro Botticelli and the birth of modern portraiture*, a theme at the centre of my current research and the subject of a book in preparation. I am grateful to Carlotta Beccaria, Carmen Belmonte, Andrea di Lorenzo, Jonathan K. Nelson, Paolo Plebani, Maria Cristina Rodeschini and Giovanni Valagussa for exchanges of ideas, and to Clare Richardson and the conservation staff of the V&A for their kind collaboration. To Caroline Elam, Mary Crettier and Nicholas Penny, my deepest gratitude. Translation of the Italian text is by Caroline Elam.

References for Botticelli's works are to Ronald Lightbown, *Sandro Botticelli. Life and Work. Complete Catalogue*, 2 vols (London: Paul Elek, 1978); Caterina Caneva, *Botticelli. Catalogo completo* (Florence: Cantini, 1990); *The Renaissance Portrait from Donatello to Bellini*, exh. cat. (Berlin 2011–New York 2012), ed. Keith Christiansen and Stefan Weppelmann (New Haven & London: Yale University Press, 2011).

Notes

1 Ronald Lightbown, *Sandro Botticelli. Life and Work. Complete Catalogue*, 2 vols (London: Paul Elek, 1978), 137–8, 'eight or so portraits by him survive', five of them 'early works'. In Caterina Caneva, *Botticelli. Catalogo completo* (Florence: Cantini, 1990) 11 portraits are catalogued (including the one formerly in Naples, destroyed in the Second World War, p.150). More optimistically, Frank Zöllner assigns to Botticelli *'presque deux douzaines de portraits'*; Frank Zöllner, *'Botticelli Portraitiste. Réflexion sur l'histoire du portrait en tant que genre artistique'*, in *Le Portrait individuel. Réflexions autour d'une forme de représentation, XIIIe–XVe siècles*, ed. Dominic Olariu (Bern: Peter Lang, 2009), 249.

2 John Pope-Hennessy, *The Portrait in the Renaissance* (London and New York: Bollingen Foundation, 1966, repr.1989), 23.

3 Pope-Hennessy, *The Portrait*, 11–23. The ample bibliography on group portraits need not be listed here.

4 On the birth of the autonomous portrait and its connections with medieval conventions, see the crucial study by Marco Collareta, 'Modi di presentarsi: taglio e visuale nella ritrattistica autonoma', in *Visuelle Topoi*, ed. Ulrich Pfisterer and Max Seidel (München: Deutscher Kunstverlag, 2003), 131–45. In contrast with Jacob Burckhardt's theory that the affirmation of the portrait corresponded with the affirmation of the individual in the fifteenth century, Andrew Butterfield has written: 'in 15th-century Florence, portraits regularly celebrated individuals as the exemplary representatives of groups, most especially of the patrician family'; Andrew Butterfield, 'The rebirth of sculpted portrait in 15th-century Florence', in *The Springtime of the Renaissance: sculpture and the arts in Florence 1400–1460*, ed. Beatrice Paolozzi Strozzi and Marc Bormand (Florence: Mandragora, 2013), 212–21, esp. 214. On the theme of the 'individualisation' of sculpted figures in the first two decades of the Quattrocento, a phenomenon, which anticipates painted portraiture, see Aldo Galli, 'Almost like living people, and no longer figures of stone', in *The Springtime*, 88–95. Opportunities for studying autonomous portraiture were provided by two exhibitions: *Renaissance Faces. Van Eyck to Titian* (London, The National Gallery, 2008–9), ed. Lorne Campbell, Miguel Falomir, Jennifer Fletcher and Luke Syson (London: National Gallery Publishing, 2008) and *The Renaissance Portrait: from Donatello to Bellini* (Berlin, Bode Museum and New York, The Metropolitan Museum of Art, 2011–12), ed. Keith Christiansen and Stefan Weppelmann (New Haven and London: Yale University Press: 2011) – see in particular the essay by Patricia Rubin, 'Understanding Renaissance Portraiture', 2–25. Among the many contributions of the last 25 years see Alison Wright, 'The Memory of Faces: Representational Choices in Fifteenth-Century Florentine Portraiture', in *Art, memory, and family in Renaissance Florence*, ed. Giovanni Ciappelli and Patricia Lee Rubin (Cambridge: Cambridge University Press, 2000), 86–113; Janette Kohl, 'Casting Renaissance Florence: the bust of Giovanni de' Medici and indexical portraiture' in *Carvings, Casts & Collectors. The Art of Renaissance Sculpture*, ed. Peta Motture, Emma Jones and Dimitri Zikos (London: V&A Publishing, 2013), 58–71. On functions and meanings, the fundamental text is John Shearman, 'Portraits and Poets', in *Only connect [...] Art and the spectator in the Italian Renaissance* (Princeton: Princeton University Press, 1992), 108–48.

5 Irving Lavin, 'On the Sources and Meaning of the Renaissance Portrait Bust', *The Art Quarterly* XXXIII (1970): 207–26, reprinted in *Looking at Italian Renaissance Sculpture*, ed. Sarah Blake McHam (Cambridge: Cambridge University Press, 1998), 60–78; Anthony Radcliffe, 'Portrait-busts in Renaissance Florence: Patterns and Meanings', in *Pollaiolo e Verrocchio? Due ritratti fiorentini del Quattrocento*, exh. cat. (Florence, Museo Nazionale del Bargello, 2001), ed. Maria Grazia Vaccari (Florence: S.P.E.S., 2001), 15–34; Butterfield, 'The rebirth', 212–21, 221). Interesting reflections on the 'feeling' of Florentine portrait busts compared with Venetian examples are in Alison Luchs, 'Grounds for an absence', in *Tullio Lombardo and Ideal Portrait Sculpture in Renaissance Venice, 1490–1530* (Cambridge: Cambridge University Press, 1995), 17–20.

6 A brief listing of the information on the theme of the portrait provided by Pliny may be found in Massimo Bernabò, 'Ritratti di autori: dall'antichità ai classicisti, a Bisanzio', in *Immaginare l'autore. Il ritratto del letterato nella cultura umanistica*, ed. Giovanna Lazzi and Paolo Viti (Florence: Edizioni Polistampa, 2000), 17. On the reception of Pliny in Florentine art-historical writings see Eliana Carrara, 'Plinio e l'arte degli antichi e dei moderni. Ricezione e fortuna dei libri XXXIV–XXXVI della Naturalis Historia nella Firenze del XVI secolo (dall'Anonimo Magliabechiano a Vasari)', *Archives Internationales d'Histoire des Sciences*

61, 166–7 (2011): 367–81. On Petrarch and portraiture see Maurizio Bettini, 'Tra Plinio e sant'Agostino: Francesco Petrarca sulle arti figurative', in *Memoria dell'antico nell'arte italiana (l'uso dei classici)*, ed. Salvatore Settis, 3 vols (Turin: Einaudi, 1984), vol.1, 219–67 (enlarged and revised ed., Livorno: Sillabe, 2002); Nicholas Mann, 'Petrarch and Portraits', in *The Image of the Individual. Portraits in the Renaissance*, ed. Nicholas Mann and Luke Syson (London: British Museum Press, 1998), 15–21; Patrizia Castelli, 'Imagines spirantes', in Lazzi and Viti ed., *Immaginare l'autore*, 35–62.

7 Regarding Venetian portraiture of the Quattrocento, however, Peter Humfrey has noted that its development 'was often constrained by a political and social ethos that placed a higher value on the collective interest of the Venetian state than on individual self-expression. Before about 1500, autonomous Venetian portraits – including those of the greatest exponent, Giovanni Bellini – tended to be simple in pose, objective in treatment, and impassive in mood'. Peter Humfrey, 'The Portrait in Fifteenth-Century Venice', in *The Renaissance Portrait*, 63.

8 Sandro Botticelli, *Portrait of a Young Man*, Florence, Galleria Palatina, Inv.1912, n.372, panel, 51.2 × 35.2 cm; Lightbown, *Sandro Botticelli*, 1, 38; 2, 26, B12, (with date: 'c.1475'); Caneva, *Botticelli*, 38, cat. no.17; Nicoletta Baldini, entry on 'Sandro Botticelli 33 *Ritratto di giovane uomo*', in *I dipinti della Galleria Palatina e degli Appartamenti Reali. Le scuole dell'Italia Centrale 1450–1530, I cataloghi di Palazzo Pitti. 3*, ed. Serena Padovani (Florence: Giunti, 2014), 153–6 (with bibliography and notes on conservation).

9 On the state of conservation and restoration of the work see Ciro Castelli, Marco Ciatti, Carlo Lalli and Alessandra Ramat, 'Il Restauro del Ritratto di *Giovane con mazzocchio* di Sandro Botticelli', *ODP Restauro* 23 (2011): 141–54.

10 *Male Portrait*, Washington, The National Gallery of Art, Andrew W. Mellon Collection, 1937.I.17, tempera on wood, 55.5 × 41.2 cm.

11 Miklós Boskovits, '*Studi sul ritratto fiorentino quattrocentesco – II*', *Arte Cristiana*, 85, 782 (1997): 336–9, 341–2; Miklós Boskovits, entry 'Attributed to Piero del Pollaiolo *Portrait of a Man*', in Miklòs Boskovits and David Alan Brown, *National Gallery of Art. Italian Paintings of the Fifteenth Century* (The Collections of The National Gallery of Art Systematic Catalogue) (Washington DC: The National Gallery of Art, 2003), 588–95. The panel is attributed to Andrea del Castagno by Keith Christiansen, entry 'Andrea del Castagno, 21. *Portrait of a Man*', in *The Renaissance Portrait*, 123–5, cat. no.21. Alison Wright, *The Pollaiuolo Brothers. The Arts of Florence and Rome* (New Haven and London: Yale University Press, 2005), 133, writes that the painting 'has been unconvincingly attributed to one or other of the Pollaiuolo brothers at various moments', 454, note 94.

12 Boskovits in Boskovits and Brown, *National Gallery of Art. Italian Paintings of the Fifteenth Century*, 589.

13 Piero del Pollaiuolo, *Galeazzo Maria Sforza*, 1471, tempera on wood, 65 × 42 cm, Florence, Galleria degli Uffizi, Inv.1890 no.1492; Wright, *The Pollaiuolo Brothers*, 131–6, 521, cat. no.50; Andrea Bayer, entry 'Piero del Pollaiolo. 48. *Galeazzo Maria Sforza*', in *The Renaissance Portrait*, 169–71, cat. no.48; Aldo Galli, *La sorte dei Pollaiolo*, in *Antonio e Piero del Pollaiolo. 'Nell'argento e nell'oro, in pittura e nel bronzo [...]'*, exh. cat. (Milan, Museo Poldi Pezzoli, 2014–15), ed. Andrea Di Lorenzo and Aldo Galli (Milan: Skira editore, 2014), 68–9.

14 Sandro Botticelli, *Portrait of a Man*, 1470s, panel, 51 × 37 cm, formerly Naples, Museo Gaetano Filangeri (destroyed in 1943, during the Second World War); Lightbown, *Sandro Botticelli*, 1, 38; 2, 37, no.B24, with a date 'c.1478'; Caneva, *Botticelli*, 150.

15 Filippo Lippi, *Portrait of a Woman and a Man at a Casement*, c.1440, tempera on wood, 64.1 × 41.9 cm, New York, The Metropolitan Museum of Art, Marquand Collection, 89.15.19 and *Portrait of a Lady*, c.1440, tempera on poplar, 49.5 × 32.9 cm, Berlin, Gemäldegalerie, Staatliche Museen, 1700.

16 Sandro Botticelli, *Portrait of a Lady known as Smeralda Bandinelli*, tempera on panel, 65.7 × 41 cm, London, Victoria and Albert Museum, CAI.100. Lightbown, *Sandro Botticelli*, 1, 38–9; 2, 28–9, n.B15; Caneva, *Botticelli*, 43, cat. no.20; entry online: http://collections.vam.ac.uk/item/O17317/portrait-of-a-lady-known-painting-botticelli-sandro/, with up-to-date bibliography. For the proposal to identify the subject as Simonetta Vespucci and a connection between Smeralda Bandinelli with the *Lady with a Bunch of Flowers* in the Museo Nazionale del Bargello, Florence (Inv. Sculture no.115), see: Alison Luchs, 'Verrocchio and the Bust of Albiera degli Albizzi: Portraits, Poetry and Commemoration', *Artibus et Historiae*, 33, 66 (2012): 87–90, 91. See also in this volume Nicola Costaras and Clare Richardson, 'Botticelli's *Portrait of a Lady known as Smeralda Bandinelli*: a technical study'.

17 Sandro Botticelli, *Portrait of a Young Man with the Medal of Cosimo de' Medici*, c.1475, tempera on wood, 57.5 × 44 cm, Florence, Galleria degli Uffizi, Inv.1890 n.1488. Lightbown, *Sandro Botticelli*, 1, 38; 2, 33–5, n.B22; Caneva, *Botticelli*, 51, cat. n.25.

18 Lightbown, *Sandro Botticelli*, 1, 38.

19 The inscription on the medal of Cosimo de' Medici (1389–1464) reads: 'Magnus Cosmus Medices PPP'. The title of 'Primus Pater Patriae' was assigned to Cosimo in 1465 and a representation of the medal already appears in a manuscript of 1469 in the Biblioteca Laurenziana. See Francesco Caglioti, entry 46, '*Cosimo de' Medici*', in *The Renaissance Portrait*, 164–6, cat. no.46.

20 For the principal attempts to identify the sitter see Ilaria Ciseri, entry 18, '*Ritratto di giovane con la medaglia di Cosimo il Vecchio*', in *Gli Uffizi. Studi e ricerche. 10. Itinerario laurenziano* (Florence: Centro Di, 1992), 46–7; Nicoletta Pons, entry 34, 'Sandro Botticelli, *Ritratto d'uomo con medaglia di Cosimo il Vecchio*', in *Botticelli e Filippino Lippi. L'inquietudine e la grazia nella pittura fiorentina del Quattrocento*, exh. cat. (Paris, Musée du Luxembourg–Florence, Palazzo Strozzi, 2004), ed. Daniel Arasse, Pierluigi De Vecchi and Jonathan K. Nelson (Milan: Skira, 2004), 220–3.

21 Sandro Botticelli, *Michele Marullo Tarchaniota*, tempera on panel, transferred from wood to canvas, 49 × 35 cm, The Guardans Cambò Family, Barcelona; Lightbown, *Sandro Botticelli*, 1, 141; 2, 81–2, no.B72; Caneva, *Botticelli*, 111, cat. no.55; Stefan Weppelmann, 'Sandro Botticelli, *Michele Marullo Tarchaniota*'. in *The Renaissance Portrait*, 150–1, cat. no.38.

22 Sandro Botticelli, *Portrait of Lorenzo de' Lorenzi*, oil on panel, 50.8 × 36.5 cm, Philadelphia, John G. Johnson Collection, 1917, cat.48; Lightbown, *Sandro Botticelli*, 1, 141; 2, 96–7, no.B86; Caneva, *Botticelli*, 125, cat. no.66.

23 'Ogni artefice ne resta oggi maravigliato'; Giorgio Vasari, *Le Vite de' più eccellenti pittori, scultori e architettori nelle redazioni del 1550 e 1568*, 'Vita di Sandro Botticello', vol.3, ed. Rosanna Bettarini and Paola Barrocchi, 1971 (Florence: Sansoni Editore, 1966–87), 516.

24 'Le quali con diverse attitudini son girate, quale in faccia, quale in proffilo, quale in mez[z]o occhio e qual chinata, et in più altre maniere, e diversità d'arie di giovani, di vecchi'; Vasari, *Le Vite*, 3, 515.

25 Peter Humfrey, 'The Portrait in Fifteenth-Century Venice', in *The Renaissance Portrait*, 51.

26 Sandro Botticelli, *Adoration of the Magi*, tempera on panel, 111 × 134 cm, Florence, Galleria degli Uffizi, Inv.1890 no.882. For the identification of the portraits in the picture see Rab Hatfield, *Botticelli's Uffizi Adoration: a Study in Pictorial Content* (Princeton: Princeton University Press, 1976), 66; Nicoletta Pons, *Botticelli* (Milan: Rizzoli, 1989), 61; Ciseri in *Itinerario laurenziano*, 44.

27 Angelo Poliziano, *Della Congiura dei Pazzi (Coniurationis Commentarium)*, ed. Alessandro Perosa (Padova: Editrice Antenore, 1958).

28 Patrizia Zambrano, entry 1, 'Sandro Botticelli, *Ritratto di Giuliano de' Medici*', in *Sandro Botticelli nelle collezioni lombarde*, exh. cat. (Milan, Museo Poldi Pezzoli, 2010–11), ed. Andrea Di Lorenzo (Milan: Silvana editoriale, 2010), 54–7, where the other known versions of the portrait of Giuliano are also examined. The three portraits were exhibited and catalogued by Stefan Weppelmann in *The Renaissance Portrait*, nos.50 (Bergamo), 51 (Washington), 52 (Berlin), 174–7. For the Bergamo portrait see also Andrea Di Lorenzo, '*Ritratto di Giuliano de' Medici*', in *Sandro Botticelli 'Persona sofistica'. I dipinti dell'Accademia Carrarra*, exh. cat. (Bergamo, Palazzo della Ragione, 2012), ed. Maria Cristina Rodeschini (Bergamo: Lubrina, 2012), 20–5, Andrea Di Lorenzo, entry I.1, 'Sandro Filipepi detto Botticelli, *Ritratto di Giuliano de' Medici*', in *Le storie di Botticelli. Tra Boston e Bergamo*, exh. Cat. (Bergamo, Accademia Carrara, 2018-19), ed. M. Cristina Rodeschini and Patrizia Zambrano (Milan: Officina Libraria, 2018), 72-75, and publications cited in the following notes. The present author discussed the problems of the three portraits in a lecture entitled *Il ritratto di Giuliano de' Medici di Sandro Botticelli. Tra storia, filologia e connoisseurship*, Bergamo, Accademia Carrara, *Letture morelliane*, 23 September 2016.

29 Sandro Botticelli, *Giuliano de' Medici*, tempera and oil on panel, 59.5 × 39.5 cm, Bergamo, Accademia Carrara, inv. no.58 MR 00006.

30 The restoration was carried out in 2011 by Carlotta Beccaria and Roberto Buda (for the wooden support); see Roberto Buda and Carlotta Beccaria, 'Sandro Botticelli, *Ritratto di Giuliano de' Medici*', in *Sandro Botticelli 'Persona sofistica'*, 59–73 and also Maria Cristina Rodeschini, '*I Botticelli dell'Accademia Carrara di Bergamo: i risultati dei recenti restauri e nuovi esisti di studio*', in *Sandro Botticelli (1445–1510). Artist and Entrepreneur in Renaissance Florence*, ed. Gert Jan der Sman and Irene Mariani (Florence: Centro Di, 2015), 63–73.

31 Carlotta Beccaria, 'Sandro Botticelli, *Ritratto di Giuliano de' Medici*', 2012, 'Ipotesi sulla stesura del fondo', 66–8. According to the restorer, the composition would have been originally as we see it today, but in a subsequent moment, difficult to date, the original paint layers were '*ricoperte da uno strato bianco steso su tutte le parti cromatiche del fondo. Questo strato potrebbe avere avuto funzione di imprimitura al fine di uniformare l'intera area di fondo e rendere possibile la successiva stesura di colore azzurro, evitando l'interferenza cromatica delle stesure originali sottostanti. La coloritura soprastante era costituita di azzurrite[...] Altrettanto difficile è immaginare per quanto tempo il dipinto abbia mantenuto questa ridipintura del fondo. Sicuramente, in un momento precedente o concomitante all'acquisto dell'opera da parte di Giovanni Morelli, la ridipintura è stata rimossa, altrimenti se ne avrebbe notizia nelle carte d'archivio conservate in Accademia*'.

32 Some scholars have proposed that it was the Botticelli portrait that furnished the model for Bertoldo's representation. See James David Draper, *Bertoldo di Giovanni. Sculptor of the Medici Household. Critical Reappraisal and Catalogue Raisonné* (Columbia, MO and London: University of Missouri Press, 1992), 86–95, cat. no.3 (with earlier bibliography).

33 Lorenzo il Magnifico's funeral mask is in the Museo degli Argenti, Florence.

34 Karla Langedijk, *The Portraits of the Medici. 15th to 18th Century*, 3 vols (Florence: S.P.E.S., 1981–7), I, 1981, 33.

35 Francesco Caglioti, entry 26, 'Maestro degli Apostoli sistini' (Matteo del Pollaiuolo?), *Busto di Giuliano di Piero de' Medici*', in *Eredità del Magnifico 1492–1992*, exh. cat. (Florence, Museo Nazionale del Bargello, 1992), ed. Giovanna Gaeta Bertelà, Beatrice Paolozzi Strozzi and Marco Spallanzani (Florence: S.P.E.S., 1992), 58.

36 Florentine sculptor working in the 1480s–90s, Michele Marini da Fiesole?, *Busto di Giuliano di Piero de' Medici*, ht. *c*.63, cm Florence, Museo Nazionale del Bargello, Inv. Sculture 360,; Caglioti, 'entry 26', 56–9; Francesco Caglioti, 'Da una costola di Desiderio: due marmi giovanili del Verrocchio', in *Desiderio da Settignano*, atti del convegno internazionale di studi (Florence, Kunsthistorisches Institut – Settignano, Villa I Tatti, The Harvard University Center for Italian Renaissance Studies, 9–12 May 2007), ed. Beatrice Paolozzi Strozzi, Joseph Connors, Alessandro Nova and Gerhard Wolf (Venice: Marsilio, 2011), 123–150; Francesco Caglioti, entry I.3, 'Scultore fiorentino (Michele Marini da Fiesole?), *Giuliano de' Medici*', in *Le storie di Botticelli. Tra Boston e Bergamo*, exh. cat. (Bergamo, Accademia Carrara, 2018–19), ed. M. Cristina Rodeschini and Patrizia Zambrano (Milan: Officina Libraria, 2018), 78–83.

37 Andrea del Verrocchio, *Giuliano de' Medici*, terracotta, ht. 61 cm, National Gallery of Art, Andrew W. Mellon Collection, 1937.1.127. A list of the numerous existing and lost images of Giuliano de' Medici can be found in Langedijk, *The Portraits*, 2, 1983, 1062–76 and in Lightbown, *Sandro Botticelli*, 2, 31.

38 Sandro Botticelli, *Giuliano de' Medici*, 75.6 × 52.6 cm, Washington DC, National Gallery of Art, Samuel H. Kress Foundation, 1952.2.56. Miklòs Boskovits, 'Sandro Botticelli, *Giuliano de' Medici*', in Boskovits and Brown, *National Gallery of Art*, 170–5 (with earlier bibliography).

39 Patricia Lee Rubin, entry 1, 'Sandro Botticelli, *Portrait of Giuliano de' Medici*', in *Renaissance Florence, The Art of the 1470s*, exh. cat. (London, The National Gallery, 1999), ed. Patricia Lee Rubin and Alison Wright (London: National Gallery Publications, 1999), 126–7.

40 Sandro Botticelli, *Giuliano de' Medici*, tempera on wood, 56.8 × 38.5 cm, Berlin, Gemäldegalerie, Staatliche Museen zu Berlin, 106 B.

41 A fourth portrait of Giuliano, with a darkish white background, transferred from panel to canvas, was once in the Otto H. Kahn collection, New York, then in the Thyssen-Bornemisza collection, Lugano, then with Mario Crespi, Milan. Roger Fry ('Note on a Portrait of Giuliano de' Medici by Sandro Botticelli', *The Burlington Magazine* 25 (1914): 2–3), indicated this panel as the prime example in the series. Luisa Vertova ('*Botticelli tra falsificazioni e reinvenzioni*', *Antichità Viva* 30, 6 (1991): 24–9) concluded that this version was a fake, followed by Hans Körner, *Botticelli* (Köln: DuMont, 2006), 93. See also Miklós Boskovits, entry in Boskovits and Brown, *The National Gallery of Art*, 175, note 17, who observes that Giuliano seems younger in this version; he considers it to be a work independent of the three in Washington, Bergamo and Berlin, to be connected instead with the Washington bust of Giuliano (1937.1.127), 'in which Giuliano appears as a young man of about twenty years'. Caneva, *Botticelli*, 56, no.28, believes this to be the only portrait made while Giuliano de' Medici was still alive (whereas the others were done after his death).

42 On the presence of Giuliano de' Medici in the panel with the *Story of Nastagio degli Onesti*'s *Wedding Feast* (private collection), see Patricia Lee Rubin, *Images and Identity in Fifteenth-Century Florence* (New Haven and London: Yale University Press, 2007), 262–5.

43 Sandro Botticelli, *Portrait of a Young Man*, tempera and oil on panel, 37.5 × 28.3 cm, London, The National Gallery, NG 626. Lightbown, *Sandro Botticelli*, 1, 114; 2, 65, no. B47; Caneva, *Botticelli*, 94, cat. no.44. For an analysis of the construction of this image see Lorne Campbell, *Renaissance Portraits. European Portrait-Painting in the 14th, 15th and 16th Centuries* (New Haven and London: Yale University Press, 1990), 12; for the poem that Herbert P. Horne dedicated to it, see Antonella Francini, 'Herbert Horne and an English "Fable"', in *Sandro Botticelli and Herbert Horne: New Research*, ed. Rab Hatfield (Florence: Syracuse University Press, 2009), 227–50.

44 Sandro Botticelli, *Portrait of a Youth*, tempera on poplar, 41.7 × 30.9 cm, Washington DC, The National Gallery of Art, Andrew Mellon Collection, 1937.I.19. Lightbown, *Sandro Botticelli*, 1, 114; 2, 78–9, no.B67; Caneva, *Botticelli*, 105, cat. no.50; Miklòs Boskovits, 'Sandro Botticelli, *Portrait of a Youth*', in Boskovits and Brown, *The National Gallery of Art*, 176–80.

45 Simona di Nepi, entry 14, 'Sandro Botticelli, *Portrait of a Young Man*', in *Renaissance faces. Van Eyck to Titian*, 106–7, holds that some of the distinctive characteristics of the painting are due – as in Antonello da Messina's portrait in the National Gallery, London (NG1141) – to the influence of 'Netherlandish models'. She points in particular to the unified dark backgrounds in portraits such as those of Tommaso and Maria Portinari (New York, The Metropolitan Museum, Bequest of Benjamin Altman, 1913, 14.40.6267).

46 '*Però che il lume e l'ombra fanno parere le cose rilevate, così il bianco e 'l nero fa le cose dipinte parere rilevate[...]*'; Leon Battista Alberti, *De Pictura*, in Leon Battista Alberti, *Opere Volgari*, ed. Cecil Grayson (1960–73), vol.3, *De Pictura*; reprint *De Pictura*, ed. Cecil Grayson (Roma-Bari: Laterza, 1975), vol.2, 46, 1–2, 82; '*Io, coi dotti e non dotti, loderò quelli visi quali come scolpiti parranno uscire fuori della tavola, e biasimerò quelli visi in quali vegga arte niuna altra che solo forse nel disegno*'; Alberti, *De Pictura*, vol.2, 46, 7–10, 82.

2. Botticelli's *Portrait of a Lady known as Smeralda Bandinelli*: a technical study

Nicola Costaras and Clare Richardson

Botticelli's portrait known as *Smeralda Bandinelli* was treated in the paintings conservation studio of the Victoria and Albert Museum in 2013–14 with the support of the Friends of the V&A. The painting had been identified for treatment in preparation for the recent *Botticelli Reimagined* exhibition (fig.1.15). While removal of the highly discoloured natural resin varnish was recommended to re-establish the cooler tonality of Botticelli's original composition, the history of the painting and its ownership by Dante Gabriel Rossetti (1828–82), a founding member of the Pre-Raphaelite Brotherhood, complicated matters. Technical examination was undertaken to understand fully the condition of the painting and the interventions that had taken place to restore it in the past, shedding new light on Botticelli's creation of the work as well as on its subsequent history. Ultimately we were able to go ahead with the cleaning and conservation treatment of the work, which revealed it to be a particularly beautiful example of Botticelli's portrait oeuvre (fig.1.5).

Rossetti and Ionides

Rossetti's inscriptions on labels on the reverse of the painting are still visible, giving his name and address as owner and suggesting that the model for this portrait is the same as that of the Venus in the *Primavera* now in the Uffizi (see p.65, fig.1.30). Rossetti acquired the picture at a Christie's sale for £20 on 23 March 1867, after it had been in the Pourtalès collection until 1865.[1] Just 13 years after acquiring the painting, Rossetti sold it to the businessman and collector Constantine Alexander Ionides, who later bequeathed it to the Victoria and Albert Museum.[2] A letter from Rossetti to Ionides negotiating the sale is in the archives of the museum. In it Rossetti sets out his price for the picture and describes it as being in 'an exceptionally pure state'.[3]

However, we know from other correspondence that this description may be a little misleading. Research by Gail Weinberg established that Rossetti had the painting restored by Henry Merritt, as well as adding to it himself.[4] It is clear from Rossetti's correspondence with Merritt

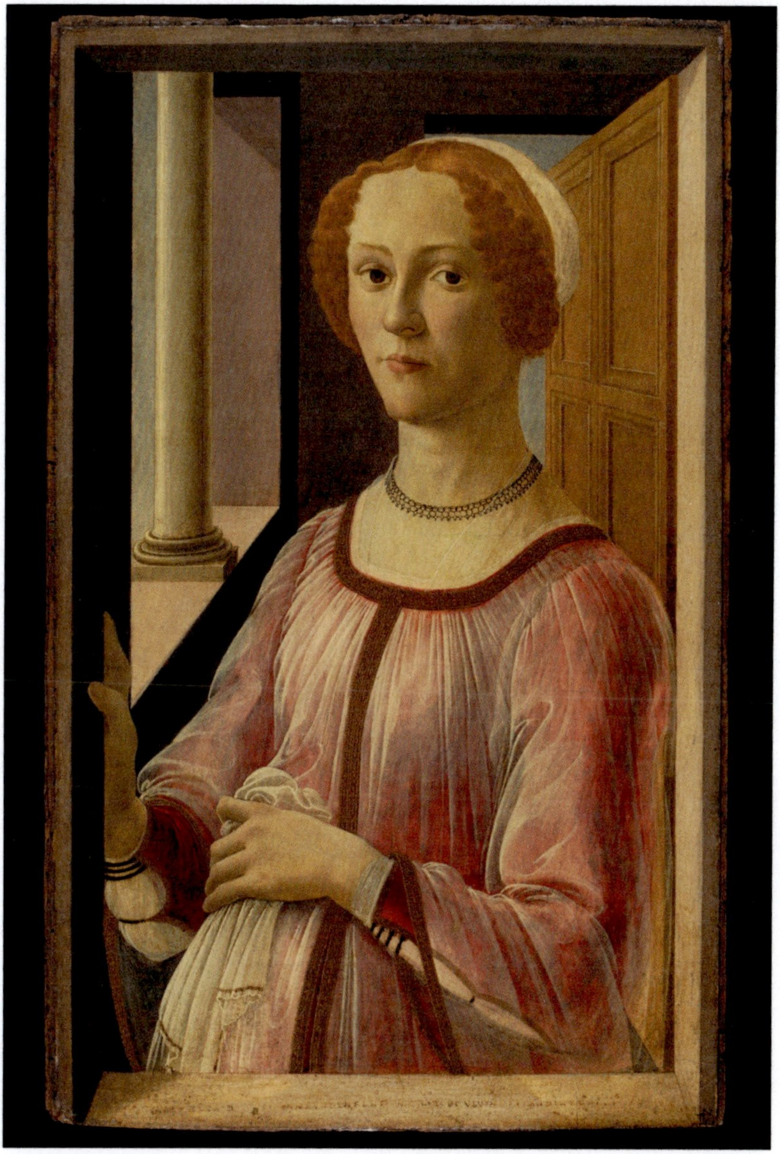

Fig.1.15 Sandro Botticelli, *Portrait of a Lady known as Smeralda Bandinelli*, c. 1475, before treatment, tempera on wood, 66.8 × 42.5 cm, Victoria and Albert Museum, London, inv.CAI.100. © Victoria and Albert Museum, London.

that he had the painting cleaned, and during the cleaning the restorer established that the inscription identifying the sitter as Smeralda Bandinelli was a later addition.[5] Rossetti bought the picture on the last day of the Christie's sale and received it three days later. It seems that the cleaning of the picture took place in the interim. Two subsequent references are made to Rossetti himself restoring the picture: on 29 March Rossetti's brother describes him as painting on 'the back of the head of his Botticelli', which has been 'injured by previous cleaning'.[6] A few days later, Rossetti himself writes to his secretary that he has been 'restoring the head-dress, but don't mean to tell'.[7]

Examining the painting through the obscuring and discoloured varnish, it was difficult to distinguish how far Rossetti's repainting of the 'head-dress' and 'back of the head' extended to the sitter's hair. There were retouchings on both the white cap and her hair, as well as in the background top centre where it covered damage caused by scoring into the paint surface. The striking red-blonde hair of 'Smeralda' obviously brought to mind Rossetti's fondness for models such as Elizabeth Siddal, with their auburn curls. One of our principal concerns when approaching the cleaning of this painting was to determine how much Rossetti's intervention had altered the painting's aesthetic. A number of artists of the eighteenth and nineteenth centuries worked as restorers, with varying approaches. Joshua Reynolds is known for his often substantial interventions – for example, his repainting of large sections of Rembrandt's *Susanna and the Elders* now in the Gemäldegalerie, Berlin.[8] Perhaps rather than simply restoring it, Rossetti had reimagined the portrait through his Pre-Raphaelite lens. In the latter case, we would be faced with an ethical dilemma. Should we attempt to remove all later additions in order to return to the earliest, Botticellian paint? Or should we value the restorations in the light of the later artist's engagement with the Renaissance prototype, and present the object's metamorphosis over the ages?

Botticelli's painting technique

To establish the condition of the original paint and to determine the extent of later additions, we undertook a technical study using X-radiography, infrared reflectography (IRR), cross-section analysis, medium analysis and close examination under the microscope.[9]

X-radiography revealed much about the original panel construction (fig.1.16).The panel is a single poplar board, which was repaired prior to any painting taking place. There are several white vertical lines on the right of the X-radiograph of the panel, suggesting the presence of an X-ray opaque fill material such as gesso or lead white. This would represent repairs to the panel, undertaken before the gesso layer was applied. In two places a wider band is associated with this filler, appearing

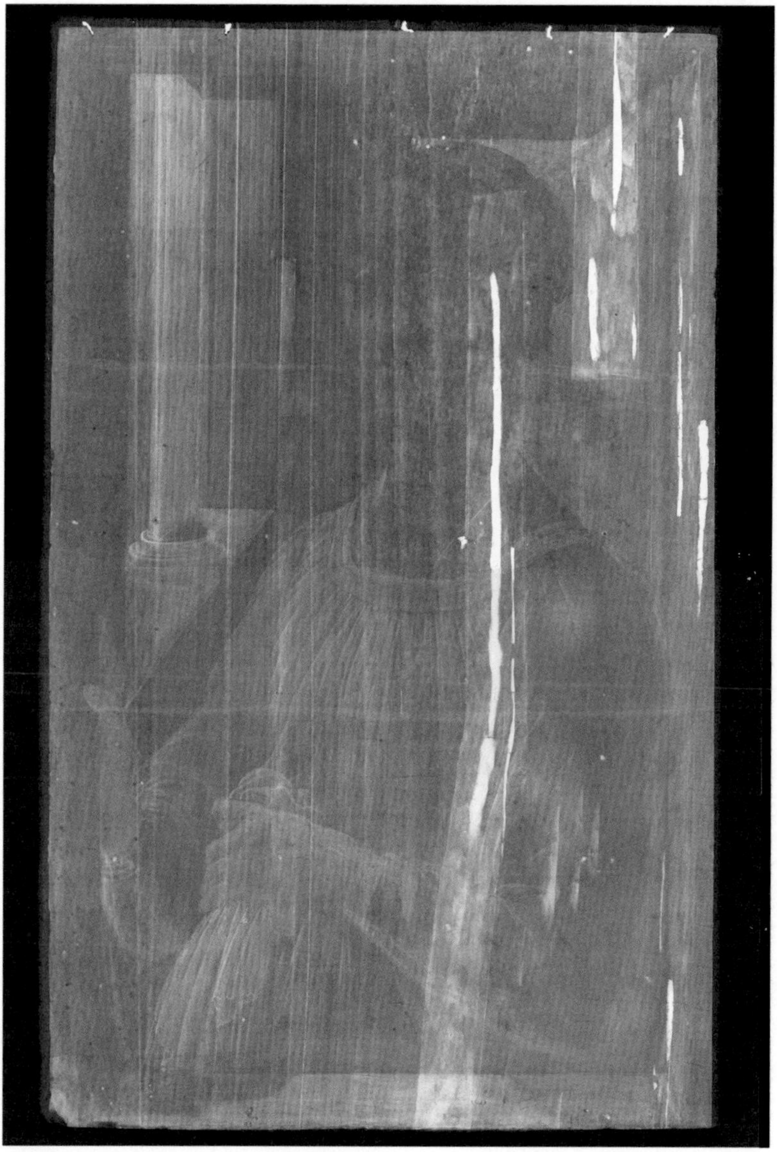

Fig.1.16 Sandro Botticelli, *Portrait of a Lady known as Smeralda Bandinelli*, X-ray image, Victoria and Albert Museum, London, inv. CAI.100. © Victoria and Albert Museum, London.

to be part of this repair – perhaps a recessed area in the wood where the filler is present but thinner. The use of damaged boards for Italian panel painting of this period is not unusual, and is usually related to prior insect attack.[10] Further, unrepaired insect channels can be seen at the right of the X-radiograph as a mottled pattern of dark lines, where the overall thickness of the wood has been reduced.

After the panel had been repaired, the entire surface was covered with a fabric layer, in three horizontal strips. The weave of the fabric is visible in the X-radiograph image; narrow gaps between the strips are visible as pale horizontal lines where the ground is thicker. Although this type of panel preparation is mentioned in Cennino Cennini's *Libro dell'Arte* in the late fourteenth century, by this date an almost complete fabric layer was unusual.[11] Instead, fabric is often found only over knot holes or local defects. Perhaps in this case it was applied to overcome the significant damage to the right side of the panel. If so it was successful, since no hint of these problems is visible on the surface of the painting.

The nails that show up as white along the upper edge of the X-radiograph are evidence for an original engaged frame – as are the borders of unpainted wood and the step at the edge of the gesso and paint layers visible at the front.[12] The cropping of the window frame on the lower edge and the fact that the painting continues to the edge are evidence that the panel has been cut down from its original size.

Infrared reflectography (IRR) revealed several stages of the drawing and planning process. IRR detects the presence of infrared-absorbing materials in all parts of the painting's structure. The red draperies and flesh tones have become completely transparent in infrared, while the grey paints of the background, which contain carbon black, hide any drawing beneath (fig.1.17).

Around the sitter's white cap we can see the initial setting out of the figure, using a simple line that appears quite uniform in thickness. This first setting out of the composition may be following a transfer or cartoon – there appear to be spots from pouncing around the nose in the IR image.[13] This was followed by the incision of architectural features. This has been found on other works by Botticelli, and comes after the setting out of the figures.[14] Importantly, these incised lines do not encroach into the figure areas (fig.1.18).

Incision is confined to the straight lines of the architecture, suggesting the use of ruler and stylus. Although the incising appears at first to be related to mathematical perspective, there is no single vanishing point. The receding lines of the architecture from left and right do not converge in the same place, suggesting there was little desire for perspectival precision.

Infrared examination reveals a large-scale compositional change to the arrangement of the sitter's arms, hands and sleeves. Using microscope examination of the painting during cleaning, there was evidence that

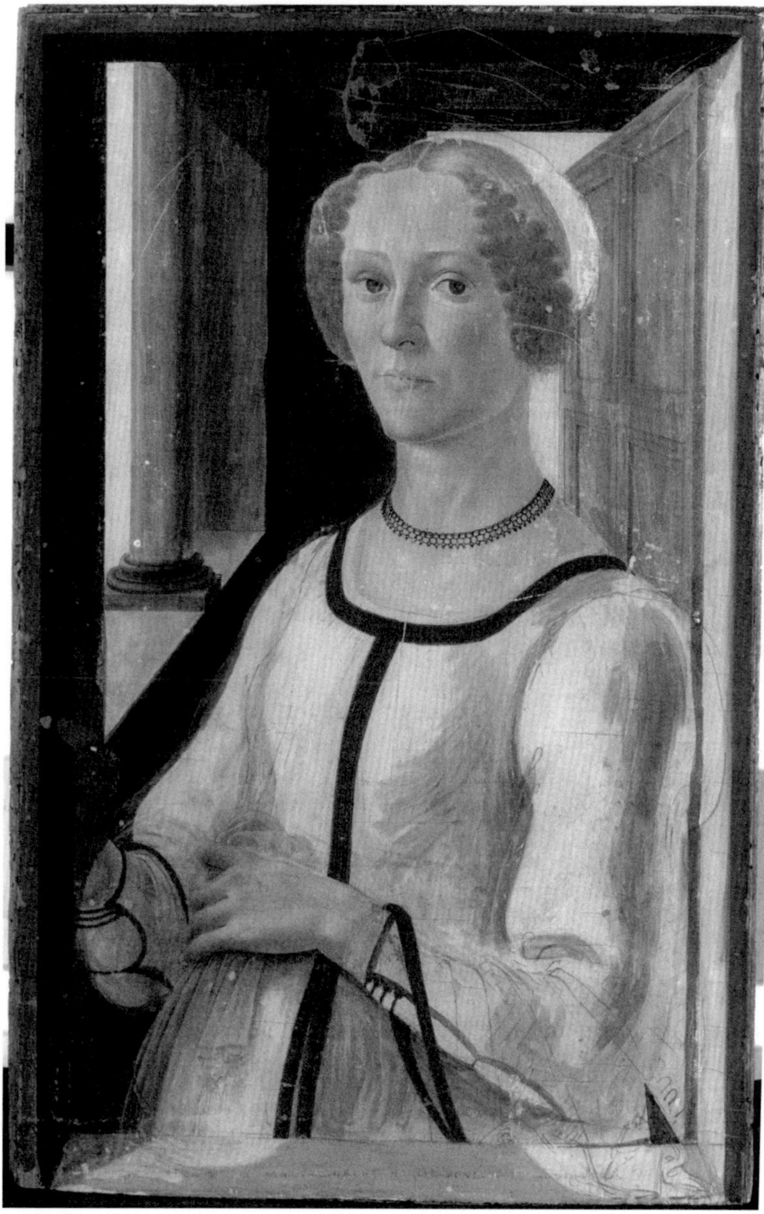

Fig.1.17 Sandro Botticelli, *Portrait of a Lady known as Smeralda Bandinelli*, infrared reflectography. © Victoria and Albert Museum and the National Gallery, London. IRR carried out by Rachel Billinge, The National Gallery, London, using an OSIRIS camera.

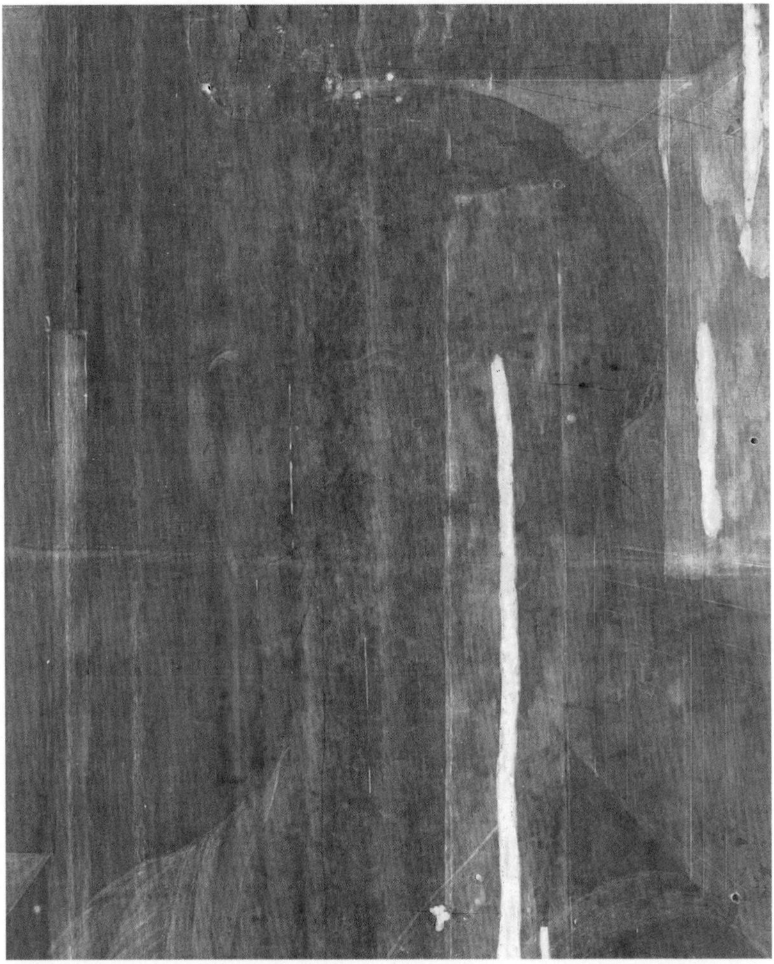

Fig.1.18 Sandro Botticelli, *Portrait of a Lady known as Smeralda Bandinelli*, X-ray detail showing incised lines. © Victoria and Albert Museum, London.

these changes were made as the painted composition was evolving. The red paint of the larger sleeve design is visible to the naked eye beneath the final paint of the window embrasure at the right-hand side. However, this red paint was then painted out as the design for the sleeve narrowed, and the brown paint of the shutter behind the sitter was inserted at the edge of her shoulder. The new design of the sleeve is not drawn, but shaded with black washes, which can be seen to have been applied with a broad brush.[15] Similarly, the dark wash is used either to narrow the bosom or to change the pose to a more frontal position. This black wash can be seen through the upper paint layers, and it seems that it may lie higher up in the painting structure than other underdrawn lines. Certainly, it must lie above some of the preparatory red paint layers, which the artist had begun before the sleeve was narrowed.

It is clear in infrared that the position of the sitter's left arm has been moved up from drawing to painting. The X-radiography reveals a slightly greater thickness of lead-white paint in the new position, indicating that it was painted on top of the first design for the drapery. The presence of the completed dress, both the red paint and the white layer of the *guarnello* (a loose, informal gown of linen or cotton) visible in a loss to the sitter's left hand, show that its position was moved at an advanced stage in the painting process.

The drawn position of the sleeve also featured draperies spilling out onto the windowsill in the right-hand corner, and this drawing is now partially visible through the white paint. It seems to indicate the *guarnello* resting higher up on the arm, closer to the elbow, and falling out onto the sill, suggesting a more projecting position for the elbow. We also see a design for drapery on the left-hand side of the sill. This seems at first to be an extension of the draperies held in the sitter's left hand; however, neither hand is indicated in the underdrawing, so the function of this drapery is open to interpretation.

It is possible that this drapery could also have been a draping cuff of the *guarnello* garment. The original position of the sitter's right arm is unclear, but the oval reserved area visible in infrared at the elbow suggests that the arm was intended to come forward, in foreshortening, towards the other hand. Perhaps the original plan was for both hands to be clasped together.

The position of the sitter's right hand is a last-minute change. The hand appears much darker in colour, having been painted over the underlying grey paint of the background. The thumb was painted over the window frame and the incision for the edge. Elsewhere the incising does not encroach into any of the figure areas, as these had been set out in the very first stage of the underdrawing. The right arm also shows alterations to the red sleeve of the costume.

The palette of the painting includes a well-preserved red lake with an intensely saturated colour. Because of the difference in refractive index between tempera and oil, red lake can appear differently in the two media. In oil the pigment is transparent and can be layered to create rich, deep red colours. It has been reported that Botticelli added oil to his tempera paints to get a more sophisticated range of effects.[16] Medium analysis of the V&A panel confirmed the use of egg tempera in all of the sampled areas, including the hair, architecture and red draperies.[17]

Red lake is present throughout the composition, in mixtures with lead white and black to compose both the delicate lilac hues and the dark purple of the background architecture. Red lake is among the more expensive pigments available to artists of this period, and this represents a quite lavish use of it.[18] The red lake also stands for an expensively dyed fabric in the sitter's dress, which would have used the same dyestuff as found in the pigment. In both the sitter's dress and the inherent materials used to depict it, the painting reveals the wealthy status of the sitter and of the unknown patron of the work.

The dress is characteristic of a well-to-do person of the time, rich but not aristocratic.[19] The edging of the *guarnello* appears to be a woven metal braid, another indicator of the expense of her costume. The paint application here is simple but very effective: a dark ochre layer, a brighter yellow ochre and highlights of lead-tin yellow. The red dress is visible under the first ochre layer. Lead soap aggregates, formed through the reaction of lead pigments with oily fats present in the binding medium, and visible as transparent inclusions, identify the presence of lead-tin yellow.[20]

The flesh painting uses a modelled yellow-brown underlayer of a semi-translucent earth pigment, in a manner similar to the traditional *verdaccio*.[21] The upper pink layers are applied in thin strokes over this warm under layer; this gives them a cool, pearlescent tone, manipulating the effect of the turbid medium. In an X-radiograph the face and neck are dark; only a few highlights on the cheek and eyelid revealing a thicker application of lead-white-containing paint. Botticelli employed the luminosity of the white gesso for the lights of the flesh tones. Using remarkably little paint, the artist conjures up extraordinarily lifelike and three-dimensional effects.

Later restoration and conservation treatment

One of our initial concerns was that the red hair of 'Smeralda' might have been applied or at least tinted by Rossetti. Cross-section samples from the red hair were essential to answer this question. They were taken from the edge areas of damage and restoration to capture the full layer structure of the paint and varnish. In one section retouching by Rossetti or a later restorer can be seen at the right-hand edge, but this is not a uniform layer. The retouching is associated with the upper varnish layers and may be in a varnish medium. A second cross-section showed particles of vermilion in the upper paint layers of the original hair – indicating that it was always red-blonde.

If Merritt treated the painting at the instruction of Rossetti's secretary Charles Augustus Howell immediately after it was acquired, he had it for only three days before William Rossetti records that his brother received it. Merritt was one of the foremost nineteenth-century restorers, and the author of a book on ethical approaches to the cleaning and restoration of paintings, *Dirt and pictures separated, in the works of the Old Masters*, published in 1854. Given the time frame, it seems likely that Merritt only cleaned the picture and returned it to Rossetti to restore, at which point Rossetti wrote to him:

> 16 Cheyne Walk
>
> Wednesday
>
> Dear Sir
> I am greatly obliged to you for what you have done to my picture, the tone of which is now exquisite and everything apparently as it first left the painter's hand. One cannot help regretting to find the lady a good deal aged; but if so she was, so be she. I was surprised to hear from Howell firstly, that you thought the picture probably not a Botticelli but a Lippo Lippi; & secondly, that your impression was that the inscription at the bottom is not original. Do you still retain these opinions? One cannot help feeling a weakness for the inscription it is evidently old, & if not by the painter, may still possibly be a true record of the person painted.
> The letter which your messenger brought does not tell me what I am owing you for your successful treatment of my picture. Will you kindly let me know.
>
> DG Rossetti[22]

We have the account of William Michael Rossetti that Rossetti had 'painted on the back of the head of his Botticelli, and improved it very sensibly – the previous condition of this part of the picture being obviously wrong, and I understand injured by previous cleaning'.[23] While Rossetti himself writes to Howell, 'I forgot to ask Kate to tell you not to shriek when you see the Botticelli if others are here – I have been restoring the head-dress, but don't mean to tell'.[24] The only area that we found to be substantially repainted was the much damaged white cap, and we believe that this was the area referred to both by D. G. Rossetti in his letter and by W. M. Rossetti in his diary (fig.1.19).

We were satisfied that Rossetti had not made a significant compositional alteration to the painting with his retouching, and that while this was a little generous by today's standards, it was in the main

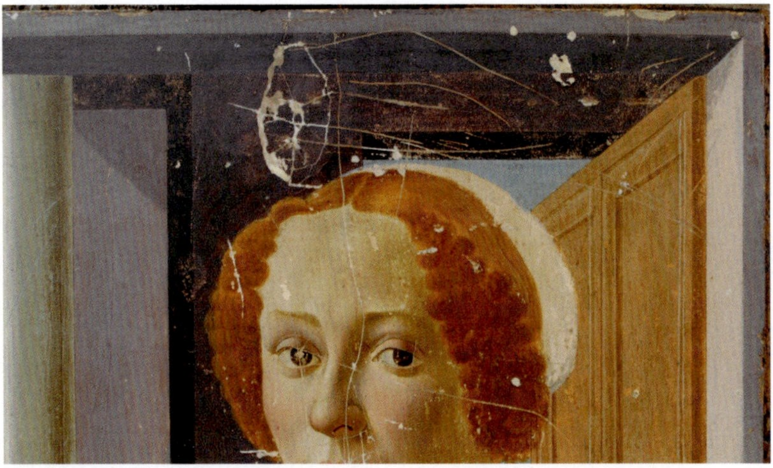

Fig.1.19 Sandro Botticelli, *Portrait of a Lady known as Smeralda Bandinelli*, detail after cleaning showing scoring upper right. © Victoria and Albert Museum, London.

confined to losses. It seems he did not entirely follow Merritt's precepts that retouching should not 'be on the work of the master, but over cavities'.[25] We removed the retouching with the varnish.

The inscription is not original to the painting, but is thought to have been added in the seventeenth century.[26] As we have seen, Merritt doubted its authenticity. The inscription was thin and somewhat abraded, but the consensus was to retain it as it was part of the painting's history. The inscription has a distorting effect on the spatial illusion since it gives the viewer the impression that it is painted on a vertical surface, whereas the windowsill should be read as a receding horizontal.[27] This has a profound effect on the assessment of the quality of the perspective design and the composition as a whole. To give an idea of how the painting might have looked originally, we manipulated a digital image to remove the inscription and replace the lower edge of the window frame (fig.1.20).

After our removal of the varnish and retouching, the original paint was revealed as it was last seen in 1867. The paint layers are in a variable condition across the surface. The face and neck are abraded, particularly in the darks, revealing the yellow-brown underpaint, and have suffered additionally from numerous scratches from what appears to have been a mixture of vandalism and carelessness. Scoring through the sitter's mouth and right eye suggests the former, while several deep horizontal grooves above her head, a long scratch virtually from top to bottom and other scratches in the background look less deliberate. The scores above

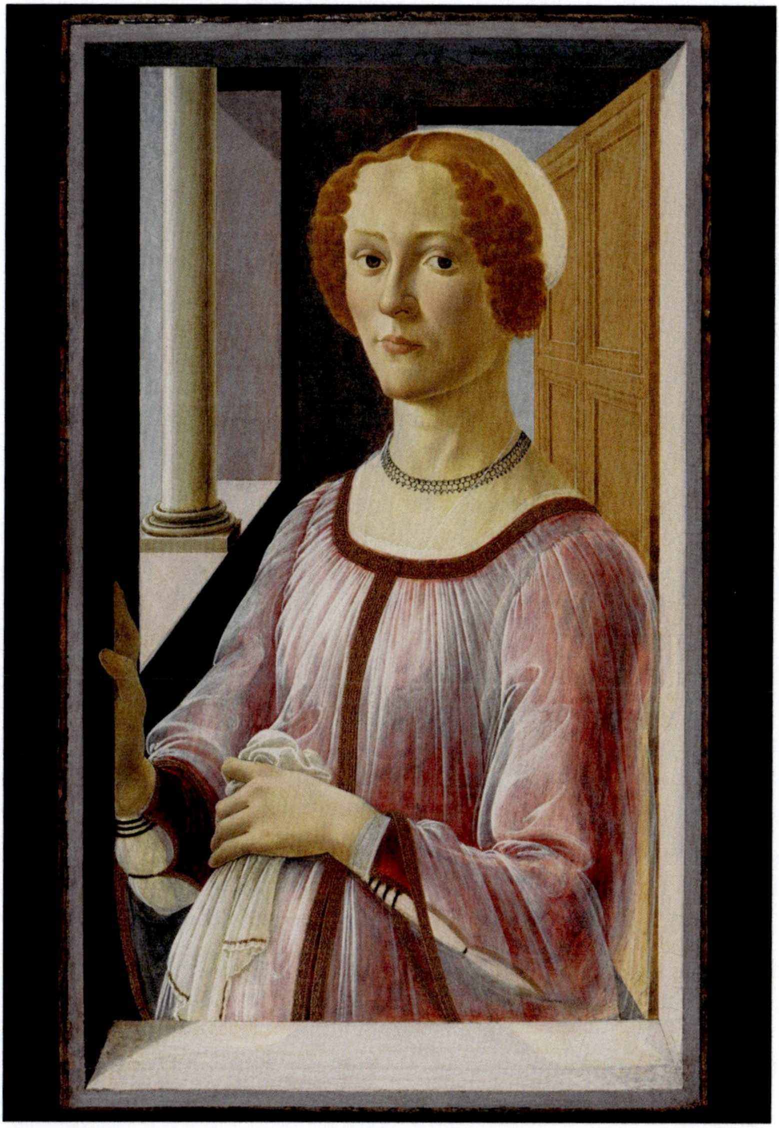

Fig. 1.20 Sandro Botticelli, *Portrait of a Lady known as Smeralda Bandinelli*, virtual reconstruction by Nicola Costaras. © Victoria and Albert Museum, London.

the sitter's head end in a concavity where pressure caused the collapse of the insect-damaged wood. The draperies are in excellent condition, with very well-preserved passages of red lake.

After removal of the overpaint, the spot to the left of the sitter's head and in the architecture above it had a pitted look, as if damaged by something caustic in a previous cleaning treatment; this seems likely to be the area referred to by William Michael Rossetti.[28] The paint surface had been eroded, revealing minute spots of the white ground. Apart from the obvious mechanical damage and the areas mentioned, the rest of the painting has a lovely gloss where the paint surface is intact. In our restoration of the painting, we retouched the areas of loss and abrasion to recapture Botticelli's subtle layered effects. We did not fill indented paint to restore a smooth surface as this would have obscured the original paint. The scoring is evident only in raking light.

Conclusion

The 2016 exhibition *Botticelli Reimagined* traced the painter's critical fortunes throughout the ages. In our treatment of the painting, slowly uncovering the original paint, but also the various damages, we traced the portrait's physical fortunes. The removal of the yellowed, slightly opaque varnish revealed exquisite brushwork typical of egg tempera and showed the greys of the architecture to be a range of optical purples. The composition regained a three-dimensional quality that had been flattened by the degraded varnish. The generous use of red lake, not only to depict the rich red velvet of the sitter's dress but also her surroundings, gives the portrait the satisfying chromatic unity of a limited palette.

Following in the footsteps of Dante Gabriel Rossetti in our restoration of the picture, we pondered what the artist might have taken away from his similarly close study of the painting. Perhaps he too observed the traces of Botticelli's earlier design for the folds of drapery spilling out over the windowsill. Whilst Botticelli abandoned this projection of the sitter into the viewer's space, perhaps for reasons of contemporary decorum, Rossetti embraced it in the pose of his *La Donna della Finestra* of 1870 (Bradford Art Gallery, 104.26) (fig.1.21). *La Donna della Finestra* also features an inscription, an area of our portrait for which Rossetti confessed to having a weakness.

Glossary

X-radiography: An X-radiograph image reveals the presence of heavy metal elements throughout the entire structure of the painting. These can be found in paint layers, for example lead and mercury in lead white and vermilion respectively, or as metal incorporated into the panel

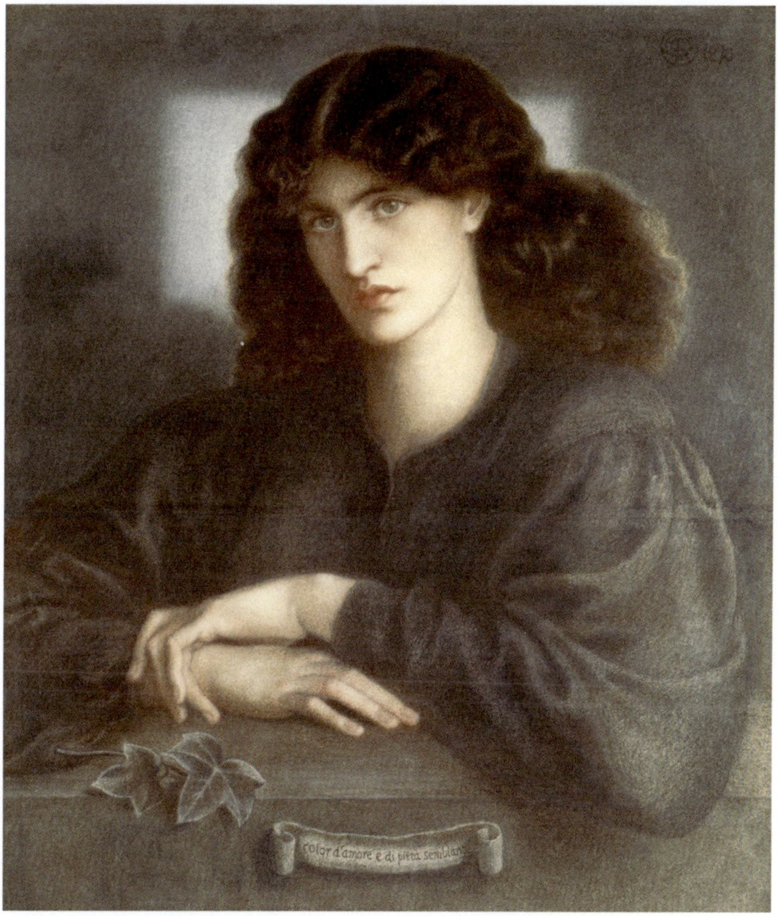

Fig.1.21 D. G. Rossetti (1828–82), *La Donna della Finestra*, 1870, coloured chalks on paper, 84.8 × 72.1 cm, Bradford Art Gallery (104.26).

structure such as nails or screws. Organic materials register more weakly in an X-ray image, but can be seen, particularly if a thick structure such as a panel or stretcher.

Infrared Reflectography (IRR): infrared reflectography uses a camera sensitive to wavelengths in the near infrared region. It is often used to detect underdrawing by exploiting the difference in infrared (heat) absorption by different colours, particularly carbon black and white.

Cross-section analysis: A cross-section through the paint layers is prepared by embedding a tiny paint sample in resin and polishing one side.

Engaged or integral frame: The frame members were fixed to the panel before the ground layer was applied. In the absence of the frame, indicators are an absence of ground or paint at the edges of the panel, and a slight ridge to the ground bordering these edges.
ATR-FTIR: Attenuated total reflectance-Fourier transform infrared spectroscopy can be used to identify organic materials.
Red lake: A pigment created from precipitating an organic red dye such as cochineal or madder onto a colourless substrate.
Egg tempera: A paint that uses egg yolk as the binding medium.

Acknowledgements

The painting was treated with financial support from the Friends of the Victoria and Albert Museum. We are grateful to Rachel Billinge, Kate Stonor and David Peggie of the National Gallery, London, for undertaking technical study of the picture, and to Gail Weinberg for discussing her work with us. Thanks too to all our colleagues at the V&A who have contributed to this project and helped us to prepare this paper – in particular Ana Debenedetti, Mark Evans, Susan North and Paul Robins.

Notes

1 Gail S. Weinberg, 'D.G. Rossetti's ownership of Botticelli's "Smeralda Brandini"', *The Burlington Magazine* CXLVI (January 2004): 24. For detailed provenance see Mark Evans, 'The Portrait of a Lady known as *Smeralda Bandinelli*' and cat. no.162, in Mark Evans and Stefan Weppelmann, ed., *Botticelli Reimagined* (London: V&A Publishing, 2016): 36–4, and cat.162.

2 V&A inventory number: CAI.100.

3 National Art Library: MS.L. 2601.3 – 1979.

4 Weinberg, 'D. G. Rossetti's ownership', 24.

5 William E Fredeman, ed., *The Correspondence of Dante Gabriel Rossetti, vol.3: The Chelsea Years, 1863–1872: Prelude to Crisis I. 1863–1867* (London: Boydell & Brewer Ltd, 2003), 523, no.67.51, dated by Fredeman to *c*.10 April 1867. We are grateful to Gail Weinberg for drawing our attention to this correspondence and to W. M. Rossetti's diary entry.

6 William Michael Rossetti, *Rossetti Papers 1862–1870, A Compilation* (London: Sands & Co, 1903), 228.

7 Fredeman, *Correspondence,* 520–1, no.67.46.

8 Gabriela Walde, '*Wie ein englischer Malerfürst Rembrandt verbessern wollte*', *Berliner Morgenpost*, 4 March 2015, accessed May 2017, https://www.morgenpost.de/kultur/berlin-kultur/article138061006/Wie-ein-englischer-Malerfuerst-Rembrandt-verbessern-wollte.html.

9 See glossary at the end of this article.

10 Luca Uzielli, 'Historical overview of panel-making techniques in Central Italy', in *The Structural Conservation of Panel Paintings,* ed. Kathleen Dardes and Andrea Rothe (Los Angeles: Getty Conservation Institute, 1998), 116.

11 Cennino Cennini, *Il Libro dell'Arte,* trans. Lara Broecke (London: Archetype Publications, 2015), 149.

12 Nails securing moulding to the edges of a panel can be seen in an X-ray image of Giotto's *Crucifix* in Santa Maria Novella. Uzielli, 'Historical Overview', 121.

13 For the use of cartoons and other transfer methods see David Bomford, ed., *Underdrawing in Renaissance Paintings* (London: National Gallery, 2002): 61–71, particularly 66.

14 Jill Dunkerton et al., ed., *Giotto to Dürer: Early Renaissance Painting in the National Gallery* (New Haven and London: Yale University Press, 1991), 312.

15 A similar technique seems to have been employed for the *Portrait of a Young Man with a Mazzocchio* (Galleria Palatina, Pitti Palace, Florence: fig.1.1). See Ciro Castelli, Marco Ciatti, Carlo Lalli, Alessandra Ramat, 'Il restauro del *Ritratto di giovane con mazzocchio* di Sandro Botticelli', *Note di Restauro, Opificio delle Pietre Dure* (Florence: Centro Di, 2012), 141–54, esp. 146. Examples of this type of wash lay-in by Botticelli can be found in the work of Andrea del Sarto, used to obliterate large-scale changes from an initial drawn design; see Gabriele Finaldi and Carmen Garrido ed., *El Trazo Oculto, dibujos subyacentes en pinturas de los siglos XV y XVI* (Madrid: Museo Nacional del Prado, 2006), 158–73.

16 Catherine Higgitt and Raymond White, 'Analyses of Paint Media: New Studies of Italian Paintings of the Fifteenth and Sixteenth Centuries', *National Gallery Technical Bulletin*, vol.26 (2005): 88–97, 89.

17 Medium analysis was carried out by David Peggie at the National Gallery using ATR-FTIR.

18 On the relative expense of red lake compared to other pigments see Susie Nash, '"*Pour couleurs et autres choses prises de lui*[...]": The supply, acquisition, cost and employment of painters' materials at the Burgundian Court, *c*.1375–1419', in Jo Kirby, Susie Nash and Joanna Cannon ed., *Trade in Artists' Materials: Markets and Commerce in Europe to 1700* (London: Archetype Publications, 2010), 141–8.

19 Susan North, personal communication to Nicola Costaras, 1 April 2016.

20 David Peggie, personal communication to Clare Richardson, 2014.

21 Cennini, *Il Libro dell'Arte,* ch.CXLVII, 'How to paint faces'. See also Glossary.

22 Fredeman, *Correspondence,* 2003, 523, no.67.51, dated by Fredeman to *c*.10 April 1867.

23 Rossetti, *Rossetti Papers,* 228.

24 Fredeman, *Correspondence,* 520–1, No.67.46.

25 Henry Merritt, *Dirt and pictures separated, in the works of the old masters* (London: Holyoake and Co., 1854), 19. 'Yet these holes may be filled and tinted by the fine point of a sable pencil, so as to mingle the specks with the neighbouring colours, thus restoring the painting to its

original completeness. It will be borne in mind that the whole of the processes described and recommended are performed, not on the work of the master, but over cavities.'

26 Evans, in *Botticelli Reimagined*, 38, footnote 12.

27 The window frame is still complete in the *Portrait of a Lady with the attributes of St Catherine*, Lindenau Museum, Altenburg (inv.100).

28 For historic cleaning methods see Christine Sitwell and Sarah Staniforth, ed., *Studies in the History of Painting Restoration* (London: Archetype Publications, 1998), for example 155, which describes mixtures containing vitriol. See also Hero Boothroyd Brooks, *Practical Developments in English easel-painting conservation, c. 1824–1968, from written sources*, PhD thesis, Courtauld Institute of Art, 1999; see 196 describing the use of warm beer and alkalis made from wood ashes. The authors are grateful to Katharine Waldron for her notes from this thesis.

3. Classicism and invention: Botticelli's mythologies in our time and their time

Paul Holberton

For Liz and Charles

In an age of discovery – across a broad range of knowledge – there were also 'inventions', not only mechanical but also cultural. In the visual arts, in more or less a single generation, we find Botticelli, Mantegna, Jheronimus Bosch and, slightly younger, Giorgione: all 'inventive' artists in the sense that they devised novel pictorial representations. Botticelli is perhaps the odd man out among these, in that generally he was probably not responsible for the invention proper – for the *ennoia* as opposed to the *methodos* (the content/intent as opposed to the technique), to use the terms of the last great Greek writer on rhetoric, the second-century AD Hermogenes of Tarsus. Botticelli illustrated *The Divine Comedy* after Dante, while Bosch himself almost certainly composed his cosmic '*Garden of Delights*'.[1] But style must be suited to content, and myths, according to Hermogenes, or fiction in general, are 'sweet' matter, requiring a sweet style of delivery, which Botticelli surely offered.[2]

I introduce rhetoric because I believe Botticelli's so-called mythologies, a small but unique group of paintings featuring classical subject matter,[3] can better be understood by studying how they might have been composed and read as examples of *inventio*. Such a process is more familiar to the viewers of the artist's time than of ours.[4] It means that, relying of course on intervening contributions, I can give a better answer to the question in the concluding third part of Aby Warburg's 1898 Botticelli dissertation, 'How Botticelli's mythologies came to be made' – an answer that Warburg himself did not satisfactorily provide, for all the strengths of his dissertation's first two parts.[5]

Warburg investigated the motivations of the 'renewal', *Erneuerung*, of classical antiquity in Renaissance Florence, but provided only a partial and rather distorted account, epitomised in his famous 'ninfa'. Championing Warburg for our own age, Charles Dempsey has claimed that this 'nymph', which he regards as Botticelli's greatest creation, was both 'classical, even Greek' and at the same time firmly contemporary and Florentine.[6] But today we must regard the 'ninfa' as part of a wider and longer Italian Renaissance phenomenon of the cult of the *bella donna*, which as such has recently been the object of a fair amount of scholarly study;[7] and more seriously ask what, though they may employ classicistic form or format, there was that is truly Greek, or Roman, about the *ninfa* or any of Botticelli's creations – or could possibly have been.

Some notion of rhetoric can help us understand how a desire for a new or expanded range of expression induced certain Florentines to look for material in the classical past – much as an orator would seek material directly in history or mythology, or indirectly in one of the thousands and thousands of handbooks eventually provided for the purpose, under such headings as '*inventio*' or, more specifically, '*amplificatio*' or '*copia*'.[8] In his *De pictura,* which fulfilled the same role for a painter, Alberti takes over the term '*inventio*', stating: 'For their own enjoyment, artists should associate with poets and orators. These could be very useful in beautifully composing the story whose greatest praise consists in the invention'. 'A beautiful invention has such force,' continues Alberti, 'that even without painting it is pleasing in itself alone.'[9] This phrasing anticipates the idea we find later in the poem by Giovanni Battista Augurelli on the standard of Pallas/Minerva that Botticelli painted for Giuliano de' Medici's *giostra*: it seems to claim that the invention is superior to the painting.[10] Erasmus in one of his *Colloquies* will make play with feeding the belly (with food), the eyes (with a painting) and the mind (with a suitable subject).[11] The *Giostra* invention itself is derived almost whole from Petrarch's *Trionfi*, substituting Minerva for Chastity, a classicising revision which a 'poet' might have advised.

In signis quare Medici sit, Bembe, requiris
Post tergum vinctis pictus amor manibus
Sub pedibusque tenens arcus fractamque pharetram
Pendeat ex humeris nullaque penna suis;
Atque solo teneat fixos immotus ocellos,
Immeritam veluti sentiet ille crucem.
Horrida cui tereti Pallas supereminet hasta
Et galea et saeva gorgone terribilis.
Multi multa ferunt, eadem sententia nulla est:
Pulchrius est pictis istud imaginibus.

You ask, Bembo, why love is painted in Medici emblems with his hands tied behind his back and holding his bow and broken quiver beneath his feet and why no wings hang from his shoulders, and he keeps his eyes fixed on the ground as if he were enduring undeserved punishment; and over him there towers Pallas with her smooth-shafted spear and helmet and shield terrible with the fierce Gorgon. Well, many people

> *say many things, no opinion is the same; and that is prettier than any painted images.*[12]

The *inventio* Alberti himself mentions is the *Calumny of Apelles* (after Lucian), concluding: 'If this story pleased as it was being told, think how much pleasure and delight there must have been in seeing it painted by the hand of Apelles'. This emphasis contrasts with the view, not uncommon among early humanists, that as long as we have the inventions we do not need images displaying them. Alberti goes on to suggest a second *inventio*, this time taken from Seneca.

> I should like to see those three sisters to whom Hesiod gave the names of Aglaia, Euphrosyne and Thalia, who were painted laughing and taking each other by the hand. [...] How much praise similar inventions give to the artist should be clear [...] the painter will surely acquire much praise and renown in his painting.

Seneca is brief and waspish about this invention he had seen in a painting in which Mercury, accompanied by the Three Graces, was supposed to represent reason or oratory – but in fact was there, according to Seneca, only at the caprice of the painter.[13] Maybe it suited Alberti to cite this example because, representing Liberality, it made a good alternative or companion to Calumny – a virtue of a ruler as opposed to a vice. Was there something about its being the whim of the painter – which Alberti does not mention – that also appealed? Alberti gives only these two examples, then concludes with a non-story: Phidias painting (*sic*) Zeus (a distortion of the classical facts to make his point). Alberti apparently anticipated the creation of a secular painting such as the *Primavera* (see p.65, fig.1.30) and his text might have served as a guide to a patron who, wanting to have a splendid painting made, was pointed towards the passage in Seneca – much as he might dip into a rhetorical handbook if he were making a speech.

So the 'poets' the patron and painter of the *Primavera* should have consulted came up with something, but how and what? In his article on Botticelli's mythologies of 1945, Ernst Gombrich spoke of 'vast tracts of this [humanist] literature still remain[ing] unexplored' and of an 'assumption which may any day be overthrown by an important find'.[14] He meant probably a textual find, such as the account of a wedding pageant Warburg found featuring an iconography much like Filippino Lippi's *Erato*[15] (fig.1.22) – otherwise baffling, though we might have guessed the belt stood for chastity. However, today those tracts are less vast, and there is less expectation of 'the' text popping up; there has surely been only one

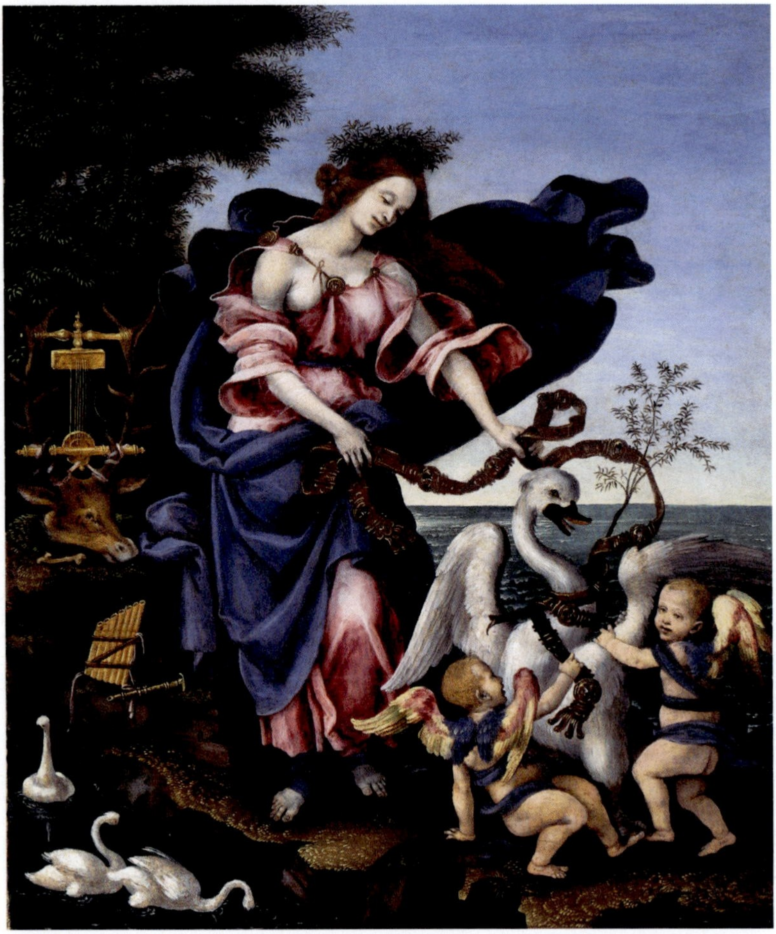

Fig.1.22 Filippino Lippi (c. 1457–1504), *The Muse Erato*, c. 1500, tempera on wood, 61 × 51 cm, Gemäldegalerie, Staatliche Museen zu Berlin, Berlin, Inv.no.78A. © Staatliche Museen zu Berlin – Gemäldegalerie. Photo: Christoph Schmidt.

important find since he or Warburg wrote, the Medici Palace inventory of 1498. Published in 1975,[16] this unpaired *The Birth of Venus* from the *Primavera* and gave a new title for the *Camilla and the Centaur (Satyr)* (fig.1.23). Indeed it has been asserted that we know as much as we need to know about the *Primavera* – patron, location, textual sources, function and typology: 'it belongs to the genre of paintings intended for *spalliere* [...] in the tradition of decorative frescos for secular rooms'.[17] Meanwhile an article by Barbara Deimling, though as recent as 2009,[18] definitively settles the iconography of Camilla and the satyr/centaur – equivalent to

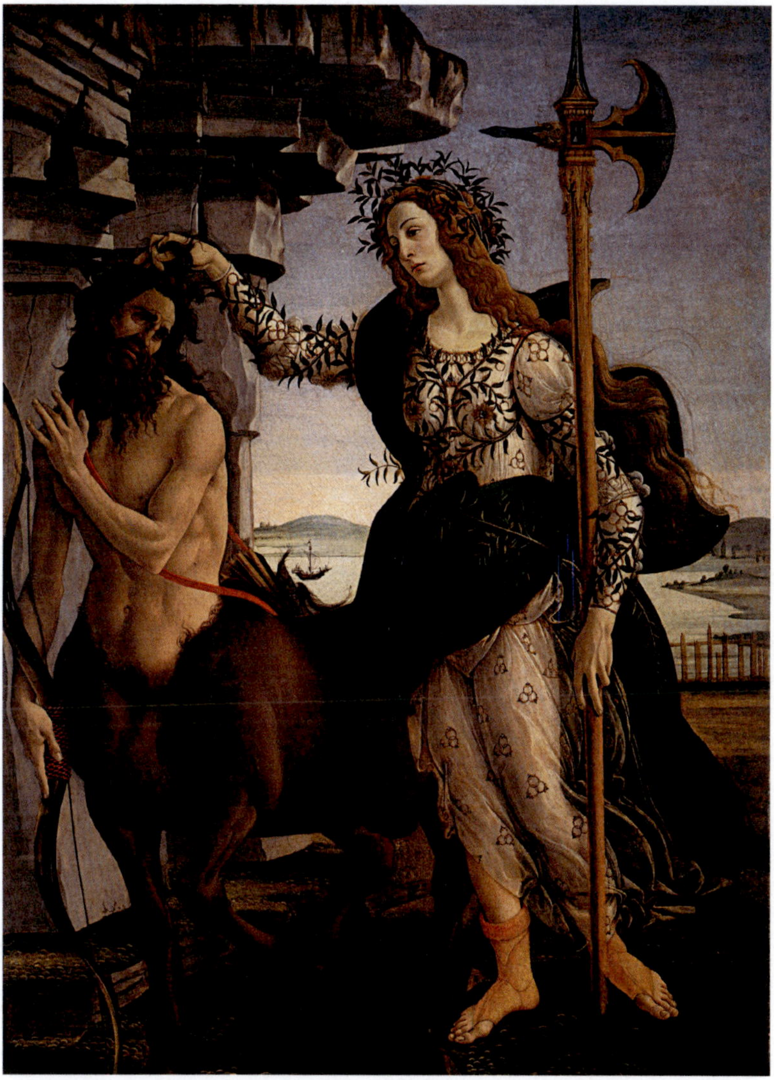

Fig.1.23 Sandro Botticelli, *Camilla and the Centaur*, early 1480s, tempera on canvas, 207 × 148 cm, Uffizi, Florence, Inv.1911 no.OdA 752.

a satyr in Botticelli's eyes, at least, since he shows a centauress having given birth to satyrs in his re-creation of *The Calumny of Apelles* (see p.58, fig 1.24).[19] His figure is certainly Camilla, even if in 1516 she was already being called Minerva. One more argument to add to Deimling's is that 'Camilla' represents the *lectio difficilior* – the principle that the more

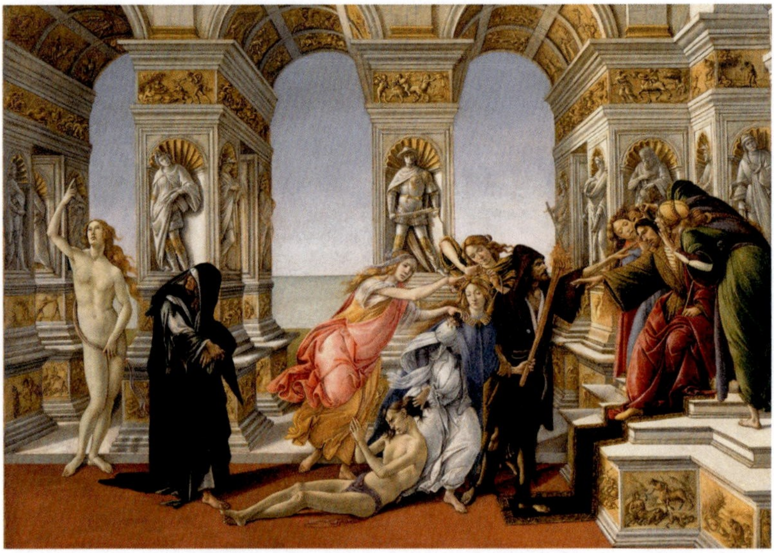

Fig.1.24 Sandro Botticelli, *The Calumny of Apelles*, 1490s, tempera on panel, 62 × 91 cm, Uffizi, Florence Inv.1890 no.1496. © 2018 Photo Scala – courtesy of the Ministero Beni e Att. Culturali e del Turismo.

awkward or unexpected reading in a manuscript tradition is more likely to be closer to the right one.

We are again like Augurelli's viewers before Minerva, however. The action and identity of the figures are clear: the halberd she holds is the weapon of the infantry man against the horseman – or horse-man: she will deal with him with it; and the source for Camilla is Virgil's *Aeneid* VII, 803ff. and XI, 498ff. – '*o decus Italiae virgo*'. She is a maid, Tuscan and a warrior (specifically against horsemen, XI, 504: '*solaque Tyrrhenos equites ire obvia contra*'; [she promises] to go alone out into their way against the Trojan horsemen). We know who Camilla is,[20] what halberds do, what centaurs are like in Renaissance terms. We can see she holds a straight pole and he a crooked bow; he seems to writhe and grimace beneath her spell while she is serene. Within this, we can generate our own *sententia*. Centaurs can stand for all sorts of beastly passions, but also, according to a passage in Boccaccio's *Genealogie deorum gentilium*, book IX, for tyranny; she, by the device on her dress, is Medicean (also adamantine). That the painting is about love or lust, however, seems proven by Botticelli's return to the theme in a fictive relief in his *Calumny*. In this Cupid breaks his bow; lust is conquered; Cupid rides the centaur; he is driven by love; a woman leads him by the bridle, and finally tames him (fig.1.25). Camilla, a warrior maid, has surely been picked as a

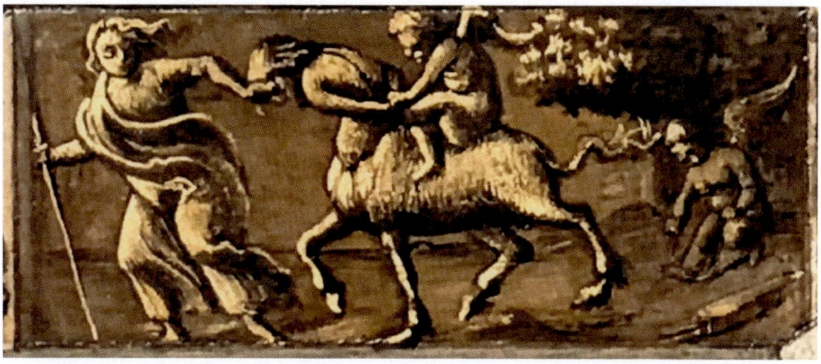

Fig.1.25 Sandro Botticelli, *The Calumny of Apelles*, detail, Uffizi, Florence Inv. 1890 no. 1496.

specifically Tuscan – and still classical – Minerva, to provide a classicising periphrasis or invention for the rule of Chastity.

A poem comparable to Augurelli's was published in his collection of neo-Latin poetry in 1496 by Battista Guarini (son of Guarino da Verona). It commemorates a lost work by Pirgotele (Giovanni Giorgio Lascaris), who is now perhaps best known for his *Madonna* above the portal of Santa Maria dei Miracoli in Venice:

Signum Veneris Cupidinem verberantis

Quid sibi suspenso vult Cypria diva flagello?
Tristia cur meruit verbera nudus amor?
An punit quod sit laqueis deprensa mariti?
An quod sit blando lentus in officio?
An pueri curas plagis docet illa domari?
An solitos ficto contegit ore dolos?
Quicquid id est timeo divae Sybaritidos iram
Et quamvis caesus me tamen urit amor.
Pyrgotelis Veneti signum: neque Cous Apelles
Nec vincet clari dextera Praxitelis
Egrediens pelago celebres dea reddidit illos:
Iste flagellanti notus erit Venere.
A statue of Venus delivering a beating to Cupid

What does Venus mean by holding aloft a whip?
Why has naked love incurred her painful blows? Does she punish him because she was caught [thanks to him] in the net of her husband? Or

because he is tardy in his sweet duty? Or does she demonstrate how his pains may be overcome with her blows? Or has he disguised his usual tricks under a feigned countenance? Whatever the answer I fear the anger of the Sybarite goddess, and love still burns me even though he suffers these cuts.

This is a statue of the Venetian Pirgotele, superior both to Coan Apelles and to the craft of famous Praxiteles: the goddess emerging from the sea made them famous; Pirgotele will be known for his Venus flagellant.[21]

Again there is no classical source, but possibly this is a development, a further invention, stimulated by Moschus's 100-line poem (*Eros drapetes*) on Aphrodite searching for her runaway son Eros, vengefully at one point. This poem was published in a Latin verse translation by Battista in this same collection: this might be what Venus will do when she catches the little devil. The iconography encourages *sententiae* about love while identity and action are clear.

Following these examples, one might oneself compose something like this for the *Camilla*:

En formosa caput centauri nympha ferocis
Captat, et ille manu ducitur invalidus.
Quale nefas, quidnam male sanum corde revolvit?
Virgine quoque dolo iam dominabitur?
Frustra: pendet inops arcus flaccetque lacertus:
Vi propria monstrum casta puella premit.
Scutum ornata adamantinis sua vestis anellis
mensque armis duris fortior alma deae.
Cuspide nempe terit Volsca de gente Camilla
et Tuscis medicina Italiaeque decus.
Fecit Alexander florentis opus civitatis:
cunctis ingenio complacet iste novo.

See the beautiful nymph grasping the head of a ferocious centaur, and he is led strengthless by her hand. What crime, what unhealthy evil does he contemplate in his heart? What trick will he now use to overcome the virgin? In vain – his bow hangs useless and his arm is flabby: the chaste girl controls the monster with some power of her own. Her shield is her dress adorned with diamond rings and the gentle mind of this goddess is stronger than hard weapons. For Camilla of the Volscan race crushes him with her spear – Camilla, both balm for

Tuscany and the glory of Italy. Sandro of the flowering city made the work; by the novel power of his devising he greatly pleases everyone.[22]

Are Botticelli's other 'mythologies' like the *Camilla*? Clearly the *Camilla* is an allegory, drawing on classical material but not reproducing a classical story, and least of all a classical meaning. By contrast Botticelli's *Calumny* is a re-creation of a classical *ekphrasis* – a notable Renaissance procedure and the basis of the programme of Alfonso d'Este's Camerino, for instance. Botticelli nevertheless added much more into his *Calumny*, namely a series of other *inventiones* in fictive reliefs, some old – such as Zeuxis' *Family of Centaurs*, praised by Lucian as an 'audacity', when the painter was fed up with doing routine work (fig.1.26), others new, and all concerned with love. The 'new' include more than one version of a scene resembling Boccaccio's story of Cimon and, on the far left, a reprise of Botticelli's workshop production of the story of Nastagio degli Onesti, both from the *Decameron*.[23] Yet chief of these contemporary inventions, right in the centre, is that of Cupid on a lion (fig.1.26). This one will run and run: we find it in Titian's painting, now in Oxford, and in Anton Francesco Doni's notice in *I Marmi*, '*discorremo molto della bella inventione*' of a bronze lion ridden by a Cupid.[24] In Erasmus's colloquy referred to above the interlocutors frequently say that this or that motif 'speaks' ('*loquitur*'): that is, they moralise out of it.

A picture such as Botticelli's so-called *Mars and Venus* (fig.1.27) does not seem to be of the same kind. Given the position of the two reclining figures, one must suppose it to be a marriage picture, resembling several surviving vernacular objects or images of the kind. Among them are Otto prints, paintings in *cassoni*, a mirror frame in the Victoria and

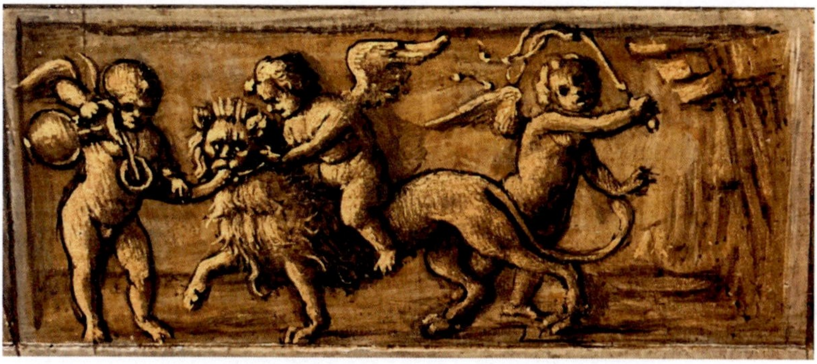

Fig.1.26 Sandro Botticelli, *The Calumny of Apelles*, detail, Uffizi, Florence Inv. 1890 no. 1496. © 2018 Photo Scala – courtesy of the Ministero Beni e Att. Culturali e del Turismo.

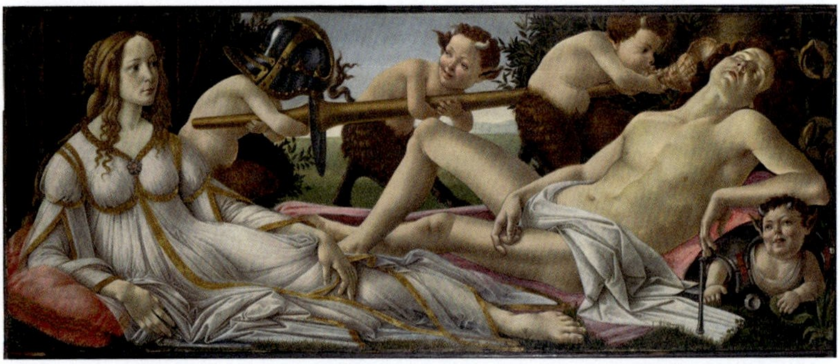

Fig.1.27 Sandro Botticelli, *Mars and Venus*, *c.*1485, tempera and oil on wood, 69.2 × 173.4 cm, National Gallery, London (Inv.NG915). © 2018 The National Gallery, London/Scala, Florence.

Albert Museum (fig.1.28), *spalliere* paintings like more than one in the Museo Horne, and so on.[25] Also surely epithalamial are two detached frescoes of perhaps 1425–50, re-inserted into a room in the Castello at Monselice. One of them is a *Judgement of Paris*, the other (fig.1.29) a reclining female nude on whom a Cupid pours flowers, following the '*qui regna Amore*' passage in Petrarch's *canzone* 127 – used again by Lotto in the picture now in Washington, DC, often called '*The Dream of the Maiden*'.[26]

The pose of the nude resembles not so much the '*Mars and Venus*' as a second painting in the National Gallery, not necessarily derived from it but suggesting a larger tradition.[27] Into this kind of imagery there has been imported, thanks to a friendly poet, parts of a text by Lucian; this describes Aetion's picture representing the wedding night of Alexander and Roxana. The little satyrs play some of the games that Lucian describes the putti playing in that work. It is surely clear that this element serves as an '*amplificatio*' of the invention Botticelli had already devised – an invention that included *satirelli* representing lasciviousness; we find them again in the *Cimon* scene (in which a man stares at a nude woman) in the right-hand bottom corner of the *Calumny* (fig.1.24).

By contrast to Peruzzi's fresco in the Villa Farnesina, which is properly a recreation of Lucian's *ekphrasis*, Botticelli's picture is a vernacular one with a classical flourish. We today look for a classical subject and take them to be Mars and Venus (in which case why do they have attributes belonging to Alexander and Roxana?). If we were familiar with marriage imagery of all kinds, however, nor had ever seen a Mars and Venus picture (I think none is attested in fifteenth-century Florence)

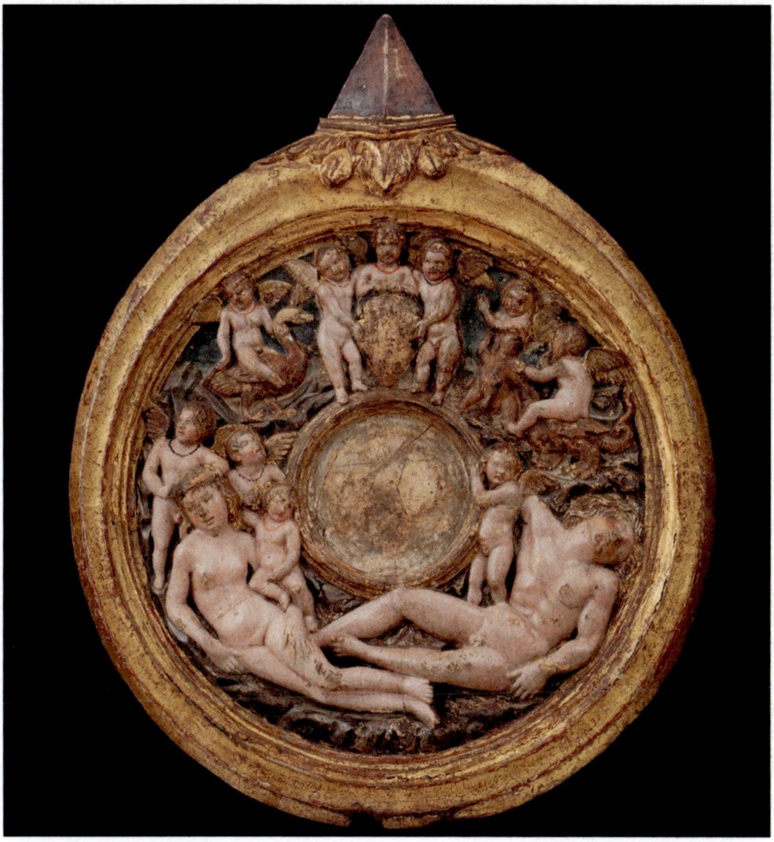

Fig.1.28 Florentine, *Mirror frame with two lovers*, 1470–80, painted stucco, diam. 50.8 cm, Victoria and Albert Museum, London, Inv. no.5887-1859. © Victoria and Albert Museum, London.

– let alone a Mars and Venus who lack their basic attributes, such as the sun, a net, a bed, Vulcan, Cupid and so on – would we call this couple Mars and Venus? Putting on period spectacles,[28] we should read it instead as a marriage gift of two lovers, to which the appropriate *amplificatio* 'games from the marriage of Alexander and Roxana, as reported by Lucian to have been painted by Aetion' has been added. We should call the two figures simply people, or, if pressed, 'portraits' but unidentified.[29]

Quite separately from this flourish (and from any notion of Mars and Venus), there is emphasis on the condition of the young man, or on his state of mind – that is, his enamourment or *innamoramento*. Precedent for this might be found in Dante's dream of enamourment in the *Vita Nuova*: the *chiasso* or din of the (venereal) conch blown in his ear

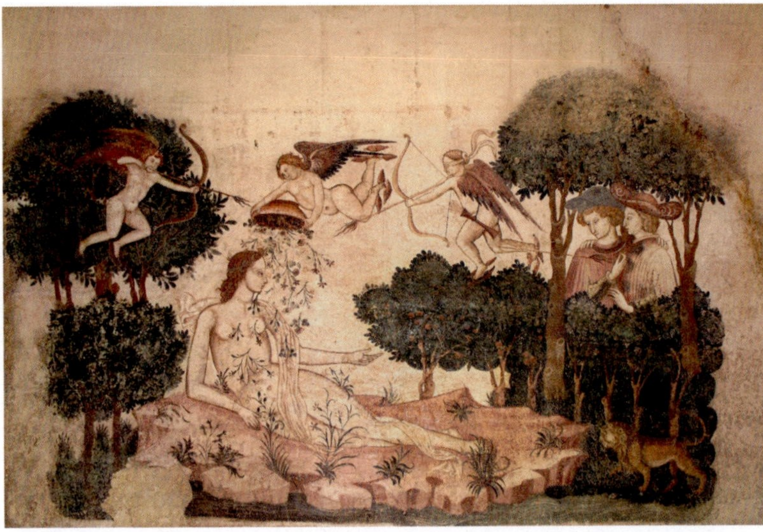

Fig.1.29 Anonymous, *'Qui regna amor'*, early fifteenth century, fresco detached and re-inserted in a wall, figure life-size, Cini collection, Castello, Monselice (PD). © Photograph by the author.

and the buzzing of the wasps must represent, together with the armour in disarray, that confused state of mind.[30] Petrarch's sonnet 227 refers to *'amorose vespe'* that buzz the poet. Gombrich suggested that these wasps or bees were explained by a Vespucci marriage, but to this there are two objections, apart from no suitable marriage being known. The first is that there is no second term or lemma, i.e. what they mean besides this (compare the bees and hornets in Piero di Cosimo's two paintings of Bacchus for the Vespucci, which have a place in the story, too).[31] The second is that for a marriage there would be two coats of arms: what or where is thc other one? So it would appear that this is a marriage picture on generic lines, nothing to do with Mars and Venus,[32] in which both classicising and vernacular imagery – the *satirelli*, their games like those of Aetion, the lasciviously wagging tongue of one of them,[33] the strident bees, the booming conch – bespeaks the amorous state of the young man.

There seems now to be a wide consensus that the *Primavera* too (fig.1.30) was a marriage painting.[34] We have physical context and here a probable occasion, the marriage of Lorenzo di Pierfrancesco de' Medici to Semiramide Appiani, even if we have no proof. The problem is the lack of parallel, by contrast to the *'Mars and Venus'*. Paul Watson brought his pioneering book *The Garden of Love in Tuscan Art* to an end or climax with Botticelli's *Primavera*, but the *Primavera* lacks a fountain, music and a

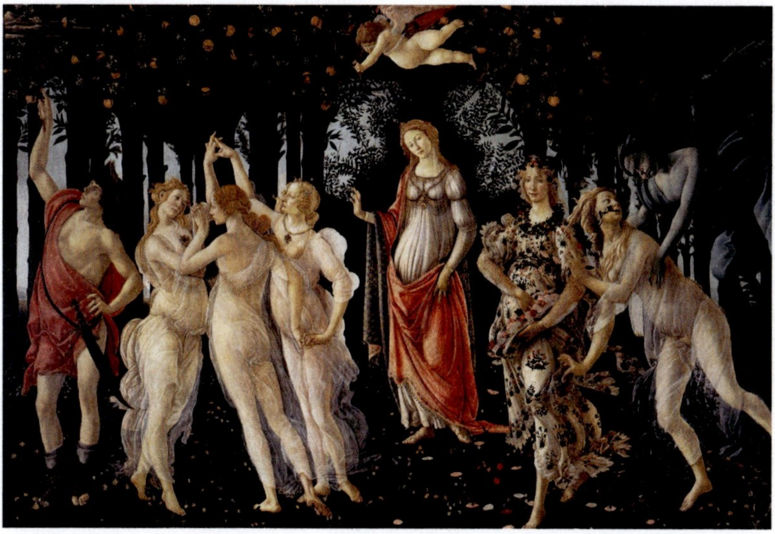

Fig.1.30 Sandro Botticelli, *Primavera*, *c.*1475, tempera on wood, 203 × 314 cm, Uffizi, Florence, Inv.1890 no.878. © 2018 Photo Scala – courtesy of the Ministero Beni e Att. Culturali e del Turismo.

wall: it is a grove, not a garden. Nor is it a Court of Love. This is perplexing, but we have to take into account the fact that there have been tremendous losses: the whole class of early Renaissance secular room decoration has been more than decimated, rather millesimated, over 500 years. I believe we have to presume that the *Primavera* is a classicisation of a pre-existent topic – a beautiful woman presented in a delightful grove – which has been rendered into a splendid and delightful picture in Albertian terms, particularly by its classicising figuration.

The only alternative to this hypothesis is that the *Primavera* is a re-created classical subject or classical description (*ekphrasis*). This is the position taken notably by Charles Dempsey in his book on the painting,[35] but unsustainable in so far as this re-creation re-creates three utterly disparate sources, as if the advising poet had gone crazy. What Dempsey (and others less explicitly but analogously) infers is that the central figure is the Venus invoked by Lucretius in *De rerum natura* (or some other source), with whom is yoked a passage from Ovid's *Fasti* on one side and an aside by Seneca on the other. If we ask the question how this picture came to be made, however, the only possible answer is that it was a representation in classical guise of a current subject – along the lines of the '*Mars and Venus*', but with two classical quotations instead of one. All the figures are declared by their attributes to be classical, except the central woman. If she were Venus she would be nude, and accompanied by doves, or the apple she won, or other attributes: all the more pressingly should she look like Venus – if she were Venus – because the others in the painting do have their full identifying properties. Instead, they are figures, and she is a person.[36]

The one significant action of the woman is that she greets.[37] Therefore the beholder has just met her – presumably she is looking at the beholder. When you meet a beautiful woman, you fall in love. This is what happens in Politian's *Stanze*, also in Girolamo Benivieni's *Amore* for Niccolò da Correggio, and of course elsewhere but in these two texts the (actual) woman met is surrounded by allegorical personages. Therefore this is an *innamoramento* picture. Indeed for all its crudity the Monselice fresco, in which an arrow enters the breast of one of the gazing figures, is clear precedent for the '*innamoramento* picture'.

We may surmise that this is why the passage of the *Fasti* represented conspicuously on the right was chosen: outstandingly in classical literature, it epitomises an enamourment, Zephyr's for Flora, encapsulated by Ovid in a virtuoso summary of the 'progress' of love, including its resolution in marriage (Zephyr was smitten with Chloris, and took her; he then married her, and she became Flora). By virtue of Flora's power, the ground in Botticelli's picture is spread with flowers. This quotation therefore classicises the lyric conceit that flowers spring up where the beloved walks (in the Monselice painting they fall). By analogy with other imagery (several erotic paintings by Titian, for example), the presence of Cupid does not serve as attribute, but rather as a non-attached mark that enamourment is taking place. The Three Graces will refer not only to her beauty, but also to interior qualities, such as her 'liberality'; Mercury appears because in the source that Alberti used the god was also present and, as the educator of Love, he can represent her reason and fair speech. The better to understand her 'liberality', consider the story of Nastagio degli Onesti, painted in a series by Botticelli's workshop. This involves an overt reversal of the Diana and Actaeon story: the manner of punishment is the same, but the crime is unyielding chastity in the woman instead of sexual desire in the man. We can plausibly read the 'liberality' of the *Primavera*'s central figure in this sense; her resistance would be a lack of liberality and reasonableness. The greeting lady comes with obliging, even wifely manners.

This moment of meeting, the *coup de foudre* in modern terms, is important because it happens once only, in an entrance through the eyes. It is then remembered in the heart, and it is to the image in his heart that the Petrarchan lover directs his thoughts and addresses his poetry.

The fact that it is construed as a memory may be why the *Primavera* appears to be sequenced from right to left, rather than left to right. The painting represents not a moment that is happening now, but a moment recalled, after the impulse of desire – felt first over on the right – has been institutionalised and accepted thanks to the qualities on the left. These indicate an acquiescence consonant with Flora's attitude, and are obviously beautiful and lovable in themselves.

The citation of the *Fasti* may still appear an oddity, despite its encapsulation of the transition from enamourment to marriage. However, this passage in Ovid also begins with an explanation as to why Flora's feast is celebrated in May and not in April, and we know Pierfrancesco de' Medici's marriage was scheduled for May; Mercury was also associated with this month, not least through his mother Maia.[38] These happy coincidences may have smoothed the way for the combining of the two passages. I am emboldened to reiterate in these new terms my proposal, first put forward in 1982, that this picture would represent the poetic experience of an *innamoramento*, even though no other scholar appears able to accept its essential premise: that the woman in the centre is not Venus (through whose power – allegorically – but not with whom the beholder becomes enamoured).[39] The others are figures; she, set against myrtle (inferring certain qualities in common with Venus) in the manner we find in surviving portraits from Verrocchio's circle, is a person.[40]

Since my 1982 paper does not seem to have changed many people's views,[41] it is perhaps redundant to take this opportunity to modify it; but my conclusion then that the picture epitomised 'sublimation' – which was certainly a feature of contemporary love discussion, and a term taken up by Gombrich himself in his subsequent discussion of the picture[42] – was too much swayed by Gombrich's idea of the work as an education for Lorenzo di Pierfrancesco. Nowadays, with the consensus, I would stress the picture's marriage topicality. In terms of decorum, this classicising commemoration of a regulated and accepted *innamoramento*, located in the month of May, was a splendid package for a marriage gift.

By contrast, Botticelli's *Birth of Venus* (fig.1.0) appears, like the *Calumny*, to be the realisation of an *ekphrasis*, though the precise text it illustrates is missing or adapted. These two pictures might be seen, as the latest in date of Botticelli's 'mythologies', to show a new phase. They represent a move from classicising embellishment of contemporary vernacular material to re-creation of classical material for contemporary purposes – even if the re-creation is (classicistically) imperfect. The cloak of flowers was an interpolation (though not without some classical justification), for Venus was not really the goddess of spring – even if, in Renaissance terms, spring was the season of love. It seems most likely the *Birth* was a marriage picture, or part of a nuptial event, though we lack any lead. This re-creation in *The Birth of Venus* perhaps also included the use of visual classical imagery, if the entwined Winds derive from the twin fluttering figures in the Tazza Farnese (which belonged to Lorenzo de' Medici at the time).[43] The Venus herself does not seem intended to cite any particular classical model.[44] At any rate with *The Birth of Venus* (and also his allegories from the Villa Lemmi, now in the Louvre), Botticelli joins the mainstream of the Renaissance use of classical figures as narrative or allegory (his '*Mars and Venus*' and *Primavera* by contrast are in these terms ungrammatical).[45] However, there is less to 'discuss' regarding this picture. In particular its elegant workshop derivations,[46] lacking attributes, recall Lorenzo Costa's very similar upright *Nude* in Budapest given, or like the one given, to François I. That philanderer king was looking for, and was delighted to receive, 'some nude figure or some Venus' – so not really an invention at all, however fine a painting (in fact the king seems to have regarded even this as the portrait of a person, desiring to know whose body it was).[47] In rhetorical terms, its *enargeia* (naturalism) was more important than its *inventio*.[48]

Acknowledgements

I offer this paper in homage to Professors Elizabeth McGrath and Charles Hope, from whose 'Iconography' classes at the Warburg Institute my 1982 article on the *Primavera* emerged ('Botticelli's "*Primavera*": *che volea s'intendesse*', *Journal of the Warburg and Courtauld Institutes* xlv (1982): 202–10); I am grateful to Ana Debenedetti and Caroline Elam for the opportunity to revisit that article.

Notes

1 For a summary of current views on Bosch, see Pilar Silva Maroto, ed., *Bosch: the 5th centenary exhibition*, exh, cat., Museo Nacional del Prado, Madrid (London: Thames & Hudson, 2016), and especially the work there cited of Reindert Falkenburg and Paul Vandenbroeck. Mantegna was credited by contemporaries specifically for his *inventio* (Paul Kristeller, *Andrea Mantegna* [Berlin and Leipzig, 1902] doc.71, Lorenzo da Pavia to Isabella d'Este, 16 July 1504: '*de invencione nesun non po arivare a M. andrea Mantegna*'); Bosch, judging by the inscription on the drawing in Berlin (KdZ 549), *The woods have ears, the fields have eyes – Miserrimi quippe est ingenii semper uti inventis et numquam inveniendis* – knew himself to be an inventor (see Vandenbroeck in Silva Maroto, *Bosch*, 91 and fig.III.2).

2 *Hermogenis opera (Rhetores Graeci VI)*, ed. Hugo Rabe (Leipzig: B. G. Teubner, 1913); *Hermogenes On Types of Style*, trans. Cecil W. Wooten (Chapel Hill and London: The University of North Carolina Press, 1987) and a rather better French one: Hermogène, *L'art rhétorique: exercices préparatoires, états de cause, invention, catégories stylistiques, méthode de l'habileté*, trans. Michel Patillon (Lausanne: L'Age d' homme, 1997).

3 This is not the place to provide a complete bibliography of Botticelli's 'mythologies'; I give citations only for specifics.

4 Frank Zöllner, '*Zu den Quellen und zur Ikonographie von Sandro Botticellis Primavera*', *Wiener Jahrbuch für Kunstgeschichte* 50 (1997): 131–58, 357–66, takes the view that Botticelli 'self-consciously countered the theoretical primacy of *inventio*' – a highly contrived position.

5 Aby Warburg, *Sandro Botticellis 'Geburt der Venus' und 'Frühling': eine Untersuchung über die Vorstellung von der Antike in der italienischen Frührenaissance* (Hamburg: Leopold Voss, 1893); Aby Warburg, *The renewal of pagan antiquity: contributions to the cultural history of the European Renaissance*, transl. David Britt (Los Angeles: Getty Research Institute for the History of Art and the Humanities, 1999).

6 Charles Dempsey, 'Love and the Figure of the Nymph in Botticelli's Art', in Daniel Arasse ed., *Botticelli: From Lorenzo the Magnificent to Savonarola*, exh. cat., Musée du Luxembourg, Paris, and Palazzo Strozzi, Florence, (Milan: Skira, 2003), 35. I shall also be referring to Charles Dempsey, *The Portrayal of Love: Botticelli's Primavera and Humanist Culture at the Time of Lorenzo the Magnificent* (Princeton: Princeton University Press, 1992) and his earlier articles.

7 See, for example, Andrea Bayer et al., ed., *Art and Love in Renaissance Italy*, exh. cat., The Metropolitan Museum of Art, New York (New Haven & London: Yale University Press, 2008), notably Luke Syson, '*Belle*: Picturing Beautiful Women', 246–54; Luke Syson and Dora Thornton, *Objects of Virtue: art in Renaissance Italy* (Los Angeles: J. Paul Getty Museum, 2001) ch.2, 37–77; David Alan Brown ed., *Virtue and Beauty: Leonardo's Ginevra de' Benci and Renaissance Portraits of Women*, exh. cat., National Gallery of Art, Washington (Princeton: Princeton University Press, 2003).

8 See Peter Mack, *A History of Renaissance Rhetoric 1380–1620* (Oxford: Oxford University Press, 2011).

9 I have used Leon Battista Alberti, *On Painting*, trans. John R. Spencer (London: Routledge & Paul, 1956 / New Haven & London: Yale University Press, 1966).

10 Salvatore Settis, '*Citarea "su una impresa di bronconi"*', *Journal of the Warburg and Courtauld Institutes* 34 (1971): 135–77, the details of the transmission of Augurelli's poem in his note 16 (1). Settis discusses Augurelli's verses only fleetingly in his long article, but his conclusion is drawn from Augurelli. Settis writes: '*ché, se questo significato non fosse risultato comprehensibile a tutti, 'pulchrius est pictis istud imaginibus*'. However, Augurelli does not say there was a deep meaning comprehensible only to a few (even though modern scholars tend to translate with similar prejudice); he says that the *inventio* encouraged discussion.

11 *Convivium religiosum*: *Opera omnia Desiderii Erasmi Roterodami: recognita et adnotatione critica instructa notisque illustrata*, Amsterdam (or later Leiden) 1965–, Ordo I, vol.iii, 231–66; *Collected Works of Erasmus: Colloquies*, trans. and ed. Craig R. Thomson (Toronto & London: University of Toronto Press, 1997), 171–243. This colloquy does not seem generally to be known to art historians: neither Reindert Falkenburg, 'Érasme de Rotterdam et la peinture de paysage aux Pays-Bas', in *De la puissance de l'image: les artistes du nord face à la Réforme; cycle de conférences organisé par le Musée du Louvre du 6 février au 27 mars 1997*, ed. Roland Recht (Paris: Documentation française: Musée du Louvre, 2002) 135–65, nor Erwin Panofsky, 'Erasmus and the Visual Arts', *Journal of the Warburg and Courtauld Institutes* 32 (1969): 200–27, refer to it.

12 Published by A. Della Torre, *'La prima ambasceria di Bernardo Bembo a Firenze'*, *Giornale Storico della Letteratura Italiana* XXXV (1900), 264–8, at 267: in modern citations (following one another) one may find *'pictus'* erroneously for *'pictis'* in the last line.

13 Seneca, *De beneficiis*, I, iii.

14 Ernst Gombrich, 'Botticelli's mythologies: A study in the neoplatonic symbolism of his circle', *Journal of the Warburg and Courtauld Institutes* 8 (1945): 7–60, at 7–8.

15 See Claudio Paolini, Daniela Parenti and Ludovica Sebregondi, *Virtù d'amore: pittura nuziale nel Quattrocento fiorentino*, exh. cat., Gallerie dell'Accademia and Museo Horne (Florence: Giunti, 2010), no.21 (Jonathan K. Nelson).

16 John Shearman, 'The Collections of the Younger Branch of the Medici, *The Burlington Magazine* cxvii, no.862 (January 1975): 12, 14–27; Webster Smith, 'On the Original Location of the "Primavera"', *The Art Bulletin* (March 1975): 31–9.

17 Frank Zöllner, *Sandro Botticelli* (Munich: Prestel, 2005), 66–7; he relies on the important article by Michael Rohlmann, *'Botticelli's "Primavera": zu Anlaß, Adressat und Funktion von mythologischen Gemälden im Florentiner Quattrocento'*, *Artibus et historiae* 33, no.17 (1996): 97–132.

18 Barbara Deimling, 'Who Tames the Centaur? The Identification of Botticelli's Heroine', in Rab Hatfield ed., *Sandro Botticelli and Herbert Horne: New Research* (Florence: S.E.I. – Syracuse: Syracuse University Press, 2009), 63–79; *Botticelli Reimagined*, exh. cat., London, Victoria and Albert Museum (London: V&A Publishing, 2016), cat.164. (entry by Ana Debenedetti).

19 Some close-up photographs in Zöllner, *Sandro Botticelli,* 165–6 and no.67.

20 Or Botticelli's circle may well have done: Politian addressed the Renaissance humanist Cassandra Fedele quoting Virgil's *'o decus Italiae virgo'*: see Lisa Jardine,'"O Decus Italiae Virgo", or The Myth of the Learned Lady in the Renaissance', *The Historical Journal* 28, no.4 (December 1985): 799–819.

21 B. G. [Battista Guarini], *poema divo Herculi Ferrariensium duci dicatum*, Modena: A. D. Rocociolo, 1496. For two small bronzes with this iconography see Herbert Beck, Dieter Blume and Sybille Ebert-Schifferer ed., *Natur und Antik in der Renaissance,* exh. cat. (Frankfurt am Main: Liebieghaus Museum alter Plastik, 1985) nos. 121, 122 (the latter a plaquette attributed to Riccio in the National Gallery of Art, Washington DC).

22 The words *'cuspide'* and *'Volsca de gente Camilla'* echo Virgil, *Aeneid* VII. The topic of *'medicina'* for love occurs in Virgil's *Eclogues* and in Propertius.

23 Giovanni Boccaccio, *Decameron*, V, 8; V, 1. See the four *spalliere* panels depicting the story of Nastagio degli Onesti made for the wedding of Gianozzo Pucci and Lucrezia Bini in 1483 and now dispersed between the Prado (Madrid: Inv.2838 to 2840) and a private collection.

24 Catherine Whistler, 'Uncovering beauty: Titian's *Triumph of Love* in the Vendramin collection', *Renaissance Studies* 26, no.2 (2011): 218–42, citing numerous examples, and Antonfrancesco Doni, *I marmi*, Venice, Francesco Marcolini, 1552, Parte III, fols. 40–1, in note 22. See also Beck et al., *Natur und Antik*, no.123.

25 Examples are Otto prints, Arthur M. Hind, *Early Italian Engraving* (London: [publ. unknown], 1948) A. IV (Otto prints), nos. 13, 20, etc.; Paul Schubring, *Cassoni: Truhen und Truhenbilder der italienischen Frührenaissance* (Leipzig: K. W. Hiersemann, 1915), nos. 156, 157; 289, 290; 184, 185; see also Bayer et al., *Art and Love*, no.58b; Caroline Campbell, ed., *Love and Marriage in Renaissance Florence*, exh. cat., Courtauld Gallery, London (London: Courtauld Gallery in association with Paul Holberton, 2009) fig.1 (example in the Statens Museum for Kunst, Copenhagen) and several more examples in Paolini et al., *Virtù d'amore*; for a *spalliera* painting attributed to Girolamo di Benvenuto see *Il Museo Horne a Firenze*, Filippo Rossi, ed. (Milan: Electa, 1967) no.59. The V&A relief is inv. no.5887-1859.

26 See Bernhard Hinz, '*"Amorosa Visione". Inkunabeln der profanen Malerei in Florenz*', *Städel-Jahrbuch*, n.f. xi (1987): 127–46. The frescoes were acquired by Count Vittorio Cini for his collection in Florence in 1938. Enrico Dal Pozzolo of the University of Verona has told me that Federico Zeri thought them fakes, but the unusual iconography makes this unlikely, in the lack of other evidence. The conception of Cupid recalls that of the descriptions of Cupid, and representations of him in illuminated manuscripts of his work, in Francesco da Barberino's *Documenti d'Amore* (notably Vatican, Barb. Lat.4076). For the Lotto see Giovanni Carlo Federico Villa, ed., *Lorenzo Lotto nelle Marche*, exh. cat., Scuderie del Quirinale, Rome (Milan: Silvana, 2011), no.50.

27 For this and another similar work in the Louvre see the website: https://www.nationalgallery.org.uk/paintings/research/being-botticelli (entry by Scott Nethersole); the second National Gallery picture is not necessarily derived from the Botticelli.

28 See also Paul Hills writing on the concept of the 'period eye' in Michael Baxandall's *Painting and Experience in Fifteenth-century Italy* (Oxford: Oxford University Press, 1972), in Richard Shone and John-Paul Stonard, eds, *The Books That Shaped Art History: From Gombrich and Greenberg to Alpers and Krauss* (London: Thames & Hudson, 2013), 150–63, at 157ff.

29 Here I retreat from my earlier suggestion (P. Holberton, 'Botticellli's *Hypnerotomachia* in the National Gallery, London: A Problem of the Use of Classical Sources in Renaissance Art', *Illinois Classical Studies* ix, no.2 [Fall 1984]: 149–82) that the woman is a 'venereal personification'. If classification is necessary she is an unidentifiable portrait (this is discussed further below).

30 For a detailed rejection of the idea that the conch, following an obscure classical source, was to induce panic in the young man see Holberton, 'Botticellli's *Hypnerotomachia*'. The central thesis in this article of a reference to a passage in Persius is untenable and it contains a number of errors – but not on this point.

31 Gombrich, 'Botticelli's Mythologies' and subsequent editions; for Piero di Cosimo's Vespucci series see Dennis Geronimus, *Piero di Cosimo: Visions Beautiful and Strange* (New Haven & London: Yale University Press, 2006), 100–5.

32 It is doubly absurd that the mirror frame in the V&A, with no armour at all, is nowadays labelled 'Mars and Venus' on the basis of the misidentification of the National Gallery Botticelli.

33 Beside the thigh of Annibale Carracci's nude *Venus* in the Uffizi a putto makes a similar gesture with his tongue, unmistakably *sensu obsceno*.

34 See Rohlmann, 'Botticelli's "Primavera"', 97–132; Cristina Acidini, 'For a Prosperous Florence: Botticelli's Mythological Allegories, in *Botticelli: Likeness, Myth, Devotion*, exh. cat., Städel Museum, Frankfurt-am-Main (Ostfildern: Hatje/Cantz, 2009) 73–97, at 74–9.

35 Dempsey, *Portrayal*, 27: he concludes the picture is a *fabula* or a *poesia*, even though he states it is not a myth: he does not resolve this question.

36 In a *cassone* panel representing the story of Cupid and Psyche by Jacopo del Sellaio in the Abegg-Stiftung in Riggisberg (see, for example, Jerzy Miziołek, 'Botticelli's masterpieces reflected: Jacopo del Sellaio's domestic panels with the fable of Cupid and Psyche', in *Center 22* (CASVA), *Record of Activities and Research Reports*, (June 2001–May 2002): 128–32; Paolini et al. ed., *Virtù d'amore* (Florence: Giunti, 2010), 74; and again his paper in this volume) there is an interpolation into the Psyche story of the *Primavera*'s figures, now of uncertain or, surely, decayed meaning. This panel cannot contribute conclusively to the elucidation of these figures' source – beyond perhaps the common association with a marriage – nor aid the identification of its central figure as Venus.

37 I have seen this doubted, but the meaning of her gesture was adequately demonstrated in Gombrich, 'Botticelli's Mythologies' (reference to a Baldovinetti *Annunciation*); it can be underscored by the gesture of the greeting innkeeper in a woodcut reproduced in Baxandall, *Painting and Experience*, 67–70.

38 On Mercury as May see Dempsey, *Portrayal* and his earlier articles there cited.

39 Holberton, 'Botticelli's "*Primavera*", see note 1.

40 The backing myrtle recalls such works as Leonardo's *Ginevra de' Benci* (National Gallery of Art, Washington DC) or Lorenzo di Credi's *Portrait of an Unknown Woman* (Metropolitan Museum of Art, New York). The woman is in effect an unidentified and unidentifiable portrait: compare the case of François I and Lorenzo Costa's nude cited further below. The name *Paris* inscribed on the traditional generic figure on a *cassone* lid in the Museo Horne (Paolini et al., *Virtù d'amore*, no.iii) and in other examples shows that the wish to identify these generic figures could be felt. But there is nothing visibly intended in Botticelli's picture to represent or refer to Simonetta Vespucci (see further Hans Körner, 'Simonetta Vespucci: The Construction, Deconstruction and Reconstruction of a Myth', in Schumacher, *Botticelli: Likeness*, 57–96, and literature cited in note 7: she is not 'the' exemplary *bella donna*, but a good example of one).

41 One who failed to engage with it – though aware of it – was Dempsey, *Portrayal*, and elsewhere.

42 See Elizabeth McGrath, 'Gombrich and "Warburgian" Iconography', in *Meditations on a Heritage: Papers on the Work and Legacy of Sir Ernst Gombrich*, ed. Paul Taylor (London: Paul Holberton Publishing, in association with the Warburg Institute, 2014), 36–57, at 49.

43 Toby E. S. Yuen, 'The Tazza Farnese as a source for Botticelli's *Birth of Venus* and Piero di Cosimo's *Myth of Prometheus*', *Gazette des Beaux-Arts* 74 (1969): 175–8.

44 Botticelli's Venus has long been connected with the Medici *Venus*, but I remain unconvinced. The basic composition recalls a Baptism of Christ and Eve covers her pudenda too. I would castigate the mistranslations by Dempsey and others of Politian's ekphrasis of an image of Venus in the *Stanze* in order to read in a classical reference: Dempsey (in Frankfurt 2003–4, p.25)

reads the word *pomo*, apple, as referring to the area between her legs that her hand covers, so he can claim that correspondingly Botticelli's *Venus* was deliberately related to the Medici *Venus* statue type. Apparently similarly influenced, David Quint in the *I Tatti* texts series renders the word with the coy phrase 'mound [sc. mount?] of flesh', traducing what translation is meant to do. In Renaissance poetry apples are women's breasts, and it is their breasts that are apples.

45 Again Piero di Cosimo's *Mars and Venus* in Berlin, though similar to and in the tradition of Botticelli's National Gallery work, is more plausibly actually a mythology. The putti do not echo Lucian's description directly. See further Geronimus, *Piero di Cosimo*, 89–95.

46 Evans et al., *Botticelli Reimagined*, nos. 169, 170. (entry by Ruben Rebmann).

47 The letters were published by C. M. Brown, 'Lorenzo Costa in Mantua – Five Autograph Letters', *L'Arte* xi–xii (1970): 120ff; the king sought '*qualche figura nuda hover una qualche Venere*' and was regarded as a '*bono judice di bellezze di corpi – maximamente di donne*'; when he received Costa's picture he enquired if the sitter was one of Francesco II Gonzaga's court ladies.

48 See, with reference to Erasmus's colloquy cited above, Terence Cave: 'Enargeia: Erasmus and the Rhetoric of Presence in the 16th Century', *L'Esprit créateur* 16, no.4 (1976): 5–19. It is worth remarking that Renaissance references to the lust aroused by pictures is also an expression or praise of their naturalism – in Leonardo's discussion of the *paragone*, in correspondence about Titian's erotic pictures, in several letters by Aretino. I would hazard that in the sixteenth century *inventio* widened its meaning to include the pictorial, rather than the strictly motival.

4. Jacopo del Sellaio's adaptation of the *Primavera*

Jerzy Miziołek

In his book *Renaissance and Renascences in Western Art* Erwin Panofsky argued for a link between Botticelli's two famous paintings, the *Primavera* (fig.1.30) and *The Birth of Venus* (fig.1.0). He interpreted the first of them as *amor humanus* (Natural Venus) and the second as *amor divinus* (Celestial Venus).[1] At the same time Panofsky severely criticised Ernst Gombrich's interpretation of the *Primavera*, advanced in 1945 and subsequently modified somewhat.[2] Gombrich suggested, *inter alia*, that along with other texts of both ancient and Renaissance authors such as Ovid, Lucretius and Poliziano – already indicated as written sources for the painting by Aby Warburg in his famous doctoral thesis of 1893 – one should also consider a passage from Book X of Apuleius's *Metamorphoses* or *Golden Ass*.[3] In opposition to Warburg, who was of the opinion that the painting was intended to commemorate the death of Giuliano de' Medici and Simonetta Vespucci, Gombrich argued, following Herbert Horne, that it was produced for Lorenzo di Pierfrancesco de'Medici, thus opening up the possibility of seeing the *Primavera* as a marriage picture.[4] In this paper I would like to put forward some evidence that Gombrich's reading of the panel may be correct, in particular his citation of Apuleius as a source.

While carrying out research on an end panel of a *cassone* depicting a scene showing Psyche, which once belonged to the Lanckoroński collection in Vienna and is now housed at the Royal Castle in Cracow, I came across a *cassone* front depicting the story of Cupid and Psyche, produced by Jacopo del Sellaio (*c*.1441–93) in the last decade of the fifteenth century (fig.1.31). The panel is kept in the Abegg-Stiftung in Riggisberg, near Bern, and contains a very interesting adaptation of the *Primavera* which has gone unnoticed by scholars.[5] The relevant figures are inserted between the scenes of the *Flagellation of Psyche by the Servants of Venus* and the *Marriage of Psyche with Cupid*. Next to the kneeling Psyche, who is shown being whipped, are the three Graces, Venus, Flora (or the personification of Spring) scattering flowers, and Zephyr pursuing Chloris. Zephyr and Chloris are shown not running to the left (as in the *Primavera*), but going in the opposite direction, towards the wedding of Cupid and Psyche. Curiously enough the nude goddess of love, as depicted in Botticelli's *Birth of Venus*, also appears in the scene;

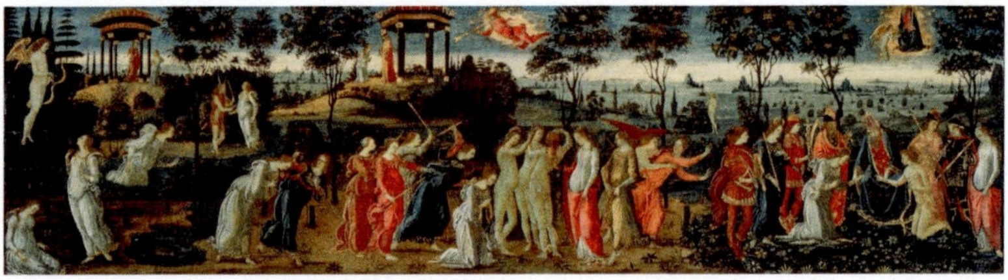

Fig.1.31 Jacopo del Sellaio (1441–93), *Story of Cupid and Psyche*, detail of *cassone* front panel, *c.*1490, tempera and oil on wood, 43.5 × 152.8 cm, Riggisberg, Abegg-Stiftung. © Riggisberg, Abegg-Stiftung.

she is represented in the background just above Chloris, while Mercury flies in the air over the Three Graces.

Thus a point of departure for my reconsideration of the *Primavera* is not a text but a painting. Needless to say, the present paper cannot pretend to exhaust the questions raised by this unusual adaptation of Botticelli's masterpiece due to lack of space.[6] Before considering the adaptation itself, it may be helpful to recall briefly the fable of Cupid and Psyche, and the surviving *cassone* and *spalliera* panels illustrating it. It should be remembered that the *Primavera* once adorned a *lettuccio* or day bed, and thus also belongs to the category of domestic painting. The 1498 inventory of the town house of the younger Medici line on the via Larga (now via Cavour) in Florence reads: '*Uno quadro dj lignamo apicato sopra elletucio nel q[ua]le e dipinto nove figure di don[n] e a hominj*'.[7]

The Cupid and Psyche tale and its depictions by the Master of the Argonauts

The myth of Cupid and Psyche (the Soul), which occupies the central section of Apuleius's masterpiece (IV, 28–VI, 24), unfolds in two parts. In the first, Cupid falls in love with Psyche. With the help of Zephyr, he takes her secretly to a palace where they live happily. However, she is not allowed to discover his identity, so the lovers meet only in the hours of darkness. One night, by the light of an oil lamp, she is able to see him; when burnt by a drop of burning oil, he immediately wakes up and flees, despite Psyche's tears. In the second part of the tale Psyche wanders over meadows and through the woods; she encounters some divinities, and at some point reaches the palace of Venus, who first subjects her to a flogging, administered by her servants, then sets her a series of tasks to fulfil. The most difficult tasks are to bring water from the Styx, and to descend into Hades for 'a little of Proserpine's beauty'. With the help of Cupid, who watches over her despite his wound, Psyche accomplishes all the tasks. The god reveals himself in person to save her when, on her return from the underworld, she opens the vial she has received there and falls into a deep sleep. Finally Jupiter heeds Cupid's plea and agrees to Cupid's marriage to Psyche. Mercury leads her to Olympus, where she receives a cup of nectar, after which she becomes immortal. All the inhabitants of Olympus take part in the celestial nuptials.

With the passing of time the myth took on an important symbolic meaning and lost its inherently pagan character. According to Martianus Capella, Psyche is no longer one of the daughters of a royal couple but the child of Endelechia (ripeness of time) and Apollo; after many adventures and much suffering, she embodies the Soul and hence becomes immortal.[8] In Fulgentius's interpretation Psyche is punished, like Adam and Eve, because of her disobedience.[9] Apuleius's tale and all its allegorical interpretations were synthesised in Boccaccio's *Genealogie deorum gentilium*.[10] The first printed edition of the *Metamorphoses*, prefaced by an introduction by the Bishop of Aleria Giovan Antonio Bussi, based on Fulgentius's interpretation, was published in Rome in 1469 and reprinted at least four times before 1500.[11] The first Italian version of the story, by Matteo Maria Boiardo, was produced in the 1470s. Thus in the last decades of the fifteenth century the story of Psyche and Cupid was known throughout Italy as an *exemplum* or a moralising tale of a more or less Christian character. A similar view of the story also appears in the commentary to Boiardo's *Capitoli del giuoco dei tarocchi*, written by Pier Antonio Viti.[12]

In addition to the aforementioned small Lanckoroński panel, which depicts *Psyche's journey down into Hades*, six long panels survive with the story of Cupid and Psyche (one of them being the Riggisberg painting), constituting three pairs. All were painted in Florence in the last 30 years of the fifteenth century. The earliest, dated *c.*1470, are two *cassone* fronts now in the Bode Museum, Berlin (figs 1.32 and 1.33).[13] Their painter, the so-called Master of the Argonauts, starts with Psyche's conception: a golden sun (Apollo) rises above the head of a naked maiden. Thus the artist took the inspiration from Boccaccio, who follows Martianus Capella in identifying Psyche's parents as Apollo and Endelichia.[14] Next, in the loggia, on the upper floor of the same building, Psyche appears as a grown woman before a group of young men standing below and admiring her beauty. The narrative ends with Cupid's flight. The painter also showed the visit of Psyche's sisters, who encouraged her to disobey her lover's order not to see him.

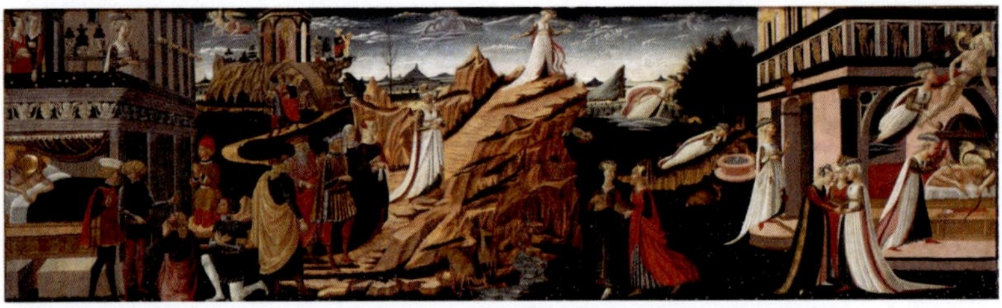

Fig.1.32 Master of the Argonauts, *Story of Psyche*, part 1, *cassone* front, *c*.1470, tempera on wood, 40 × 130 cm, Berlin, Gemäldegalerie. © Staatliche Museen zu Berlin – Gemäldegalerie. Photo: Christoph Schmidt.

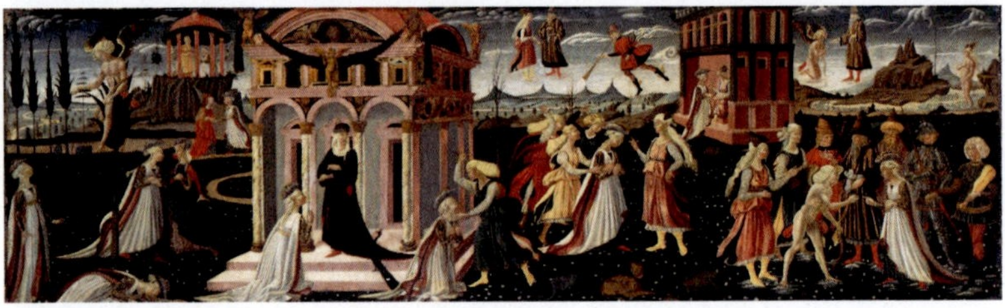

Fig.1.33 Master of the Argonauts, *Story of Psyche*, part 2, *cassone* front, *c*.1470, tempera on wood, 40 × 130 cm, Berlin, Gemäldegalerie. © Staatliche Museen zu Berlin – Gemäldegalerie. Photo: Christoph Schmidt.

The story unfolds in the second painting, which begins with a scene of Cupid admonishing Psyche from a tall cypress and ends happily with their marriage. The long gap between the parting of the lovers and their happy reconciliation is filled by nine scenes representing, *inter alia*, Psyche's meetings with Ceres and Juno (Ceres talks to the maiden in her *tempietto*, while Juno stands beside a splendid peacock on the steps of the magnificent portico of her Palace), and the capture and flogging of Psyche by the servants of Venus, whom we finally see inside her palace, most probably giving the girl the four seemingly impossible tasks.

The tasks themselves, by virtue of which Psyche becomes Cupid's wife and a deity, are not depicted in the Berlin paintings. Once they adorned the end panels, of which only one survives, in the Royal Castle in Cracow (fig.1.34). It depicts Psyche's journey into Hades for 'a little of Proserpine's beauty', the fourth task ordered by Venus, as related in Book VI of the *Metamorphoses*. First Psyche is shown on the top of a high tower, from which she hears a voice instructing her on how to descend into the realms of Hades and bring back the box from Proserpine. Subsequent scenes depict her prevailing upon the ferryman Charon to take her across the Styx; giving the fearsome dog Cerberus one of the sops, while keeping

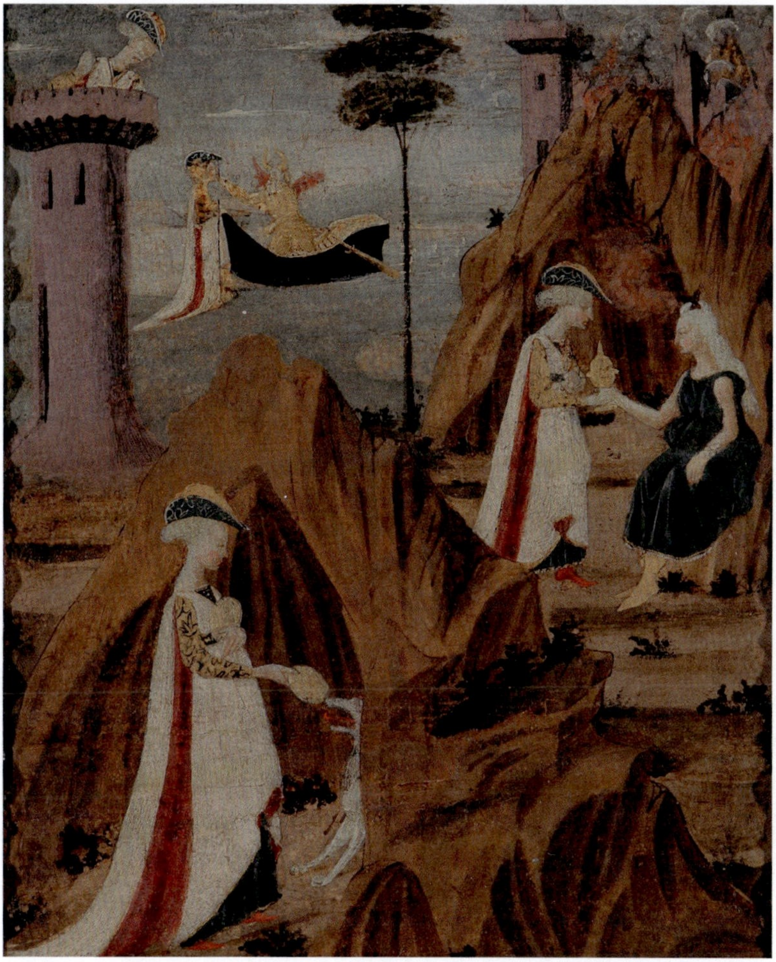

Fig. 1.34 Master of the Argonauts, *Story of Psyche*, *cassone* side panel, *c.*1470, tempera on wood, 43.5 × 51 cm, Kraków, Royal Castle (no.7966). © Kraków, Royal Castle.

the other for the return journey so that she can pass by him safely; and finally receiving the box from Proserpine, who is seated on a rock. Thus the Lanckoroński painting can be seen as a continuation of the narrative in the second Berlin panel (fig. 1.35).

Jacopo del Sellaio's *spalliere* and *cassoni*

The second pair of panels, which will not be considered in detail here, are *spalliere*: one is in the Fitzwilliam Museum in Cambridge, the other formerly in the collection of Mrs Hester Diamond in New York (figs 1.36 and 1.37).[15] Both were produced by Jacopo del Sellaio *c.*1480. According to Vasari, Sellaio studied painting in Fra Filippo Lippi's workshop,

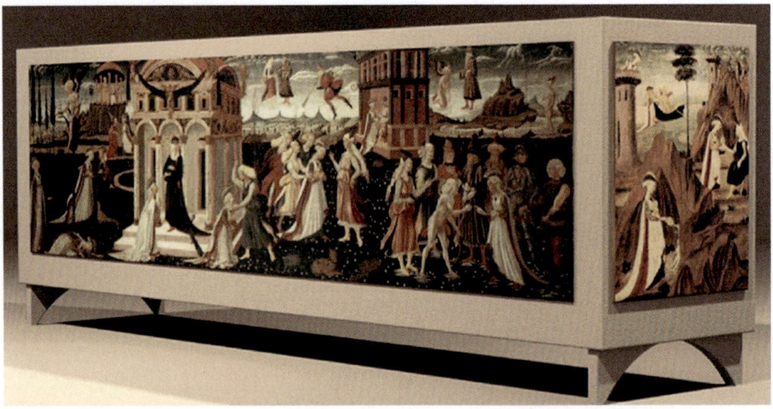

Fig.1.35 Virtual reconstruction of the second *cassone* with the *Story of Psyche*. © Maciej Tarkowski, following the author's instructions.

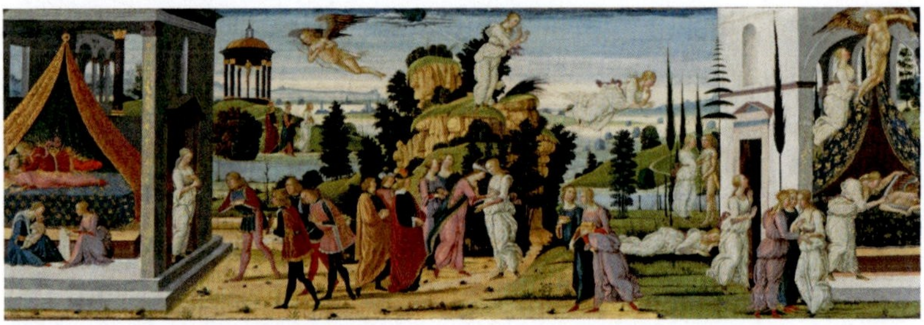

Fig.1.36 Jacopo del Sellaio, *Story of Cupid and Psyche*, part 1, *spalliera*, tempera and oil on panel, *c.*1480, 58.4 × 178.8 cm, Cambridge, Fitzwilliam Museum. © Fitzwilliam Museum, Cambridge.

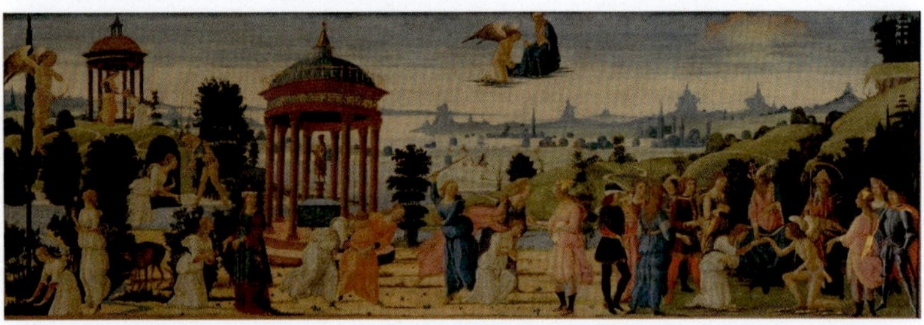

Fig.1.37 Jacopo del Sellaio, *Story of Cupid and Psyche*, part 2, *spalliera*, tempera and oil on panel, *c.*1480, 59 × 179 cm, private collection. © Courtesy Moretti Gallery.

alongside Sandro Botticelli, and many of his works are *cassoni* fronts and *spalliere*. Sellaio was a talented eclectic who often based his paintings on those of his more creative colleagues, such as Botticelli and Domenico Ghirlandaio. When producing his panels with Cupid and Psyche he followed the compositions created by the Master of the Argonauts to a significant degree, while also introducing some *novità* into his elaborate narrative scenes, set in beautiful Arcadian landscapes. The similarities between the two artists' depictions of the story are easy to explain. As Margaret Haines has demonstrated, Jacopo del Sellaio is documented as sharing a workshop and a dwelling with Biagio d'Antonio, an artist with whom the Master of the Argonauts also cooperated, and with whom he was often confused in the past.[16] It is only natural that compositional ideas should have circulated among these artists.

In the case of the third pair of panels, produced *c.*1490 and now divided between the Museum of Fine Arts, Boston and the Abegg-Stiftung in Riggisberg (figs 1.38 and 1.39), Jacopo del Sellaio used as models both the scenes shown on the Master of the Argonauts panels in Berlin and his own *spalliere*, currently in Cambridge and New York. However, the impact of Botticelli is clearly discernible, not only in the Riggisberg panel, but

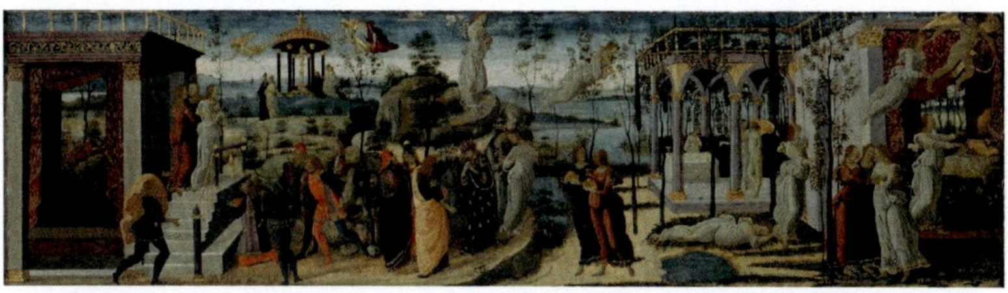

Fig.1.38 Jacopo del Sellaio, *Story of Cupid and Psyche*, part 1, *cassone* front, tempera and oil on panel, *c.*1490, 43 × 152.8 cm, Boston, Museum of Fine Arts (12.1049). Photograph © 2018 Museum of Fine Arts, Boston.

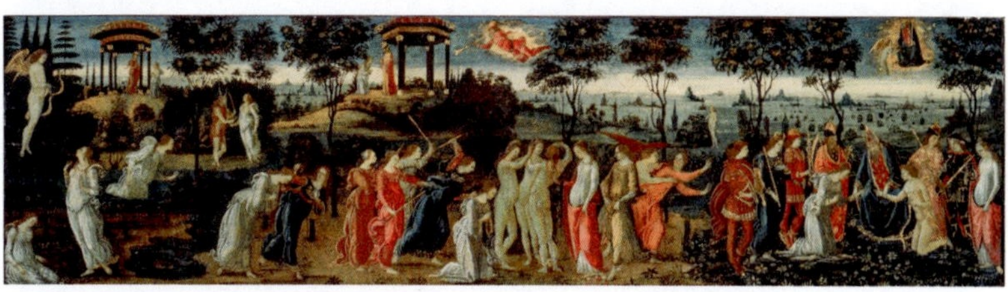

Fig.1.39 Jacopo del Sellaio, *Story of Cupid and Psyche*, *cassone* front, part 2, tempera and oil on panel, *c.*1490, 42 × 158.5 cm, Riggisberg, Abegg-Stiftung. © Riggisberg, Abegg-Stiftung.

also in the one in Boston. For example, the portrayal of Venus and Cupid shown in space is very reminiscent of the personification of the wind gods in Botticelli's *Birth of Venus*, which in turn was modelled on a portrayal of the wind in the famous *Tazza Farnese* (the famous engraved gem from the Hellenistic period, then in the collections of Lorenzo il Magnifico).[17] In addition the figure of Apollo in the *Marriage of Psyche* group (in both of Sellaio's depictions of this scene) appears to be borrowed from the left-hand figure in Botticelli's *Adoration of the Magi*, painted in 1475 for Gaspare di Zanobi del Lama's chapel at Santa Maria Novella in Florence and now in the Uffizi.[18] Moreover, it has recently been shown that the grouping of figures in the left foreground derives from Botticelli's fresco of *Moses and the Daughters of Jethro* of 1481–2 in the Sistine Chapel.[19]

A desire to depart from the previous compositions is evident in the Riggisberg *cassone*, although the marriage scene that ends the narration (fig.1.40) is modelled on the second panel in Berlin (fig.1.41) and the *spalliera* in New York. As we have seen, the most interesting departure is in the central section of the painting. It comprises three scenes of which only the first – the flogging of Psyche – is described in the *Metamorphoses.* Close to the kneeling Psyche the viewer sees the three Graces, then Venus, who is followed by Flora, or Spring, scattering flowers, and by Zephyr and Chloris.[20] It should be noticed that Sellaio's Flora is not wearing a dress decorated with flowers, as in Botticelli's panel. As in the *Primavera*, Zephyr is a winged youth with chubby cheeks, but his green wings have been replaced by red ones. Nor does he swoop down on his prey from a

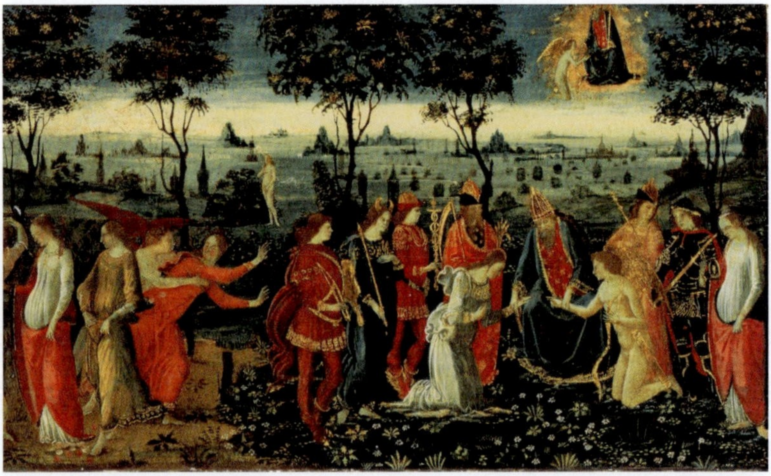

Fig.1.40 Jacopo del Sellaio, *Story of Cupid and Psyche*, detail of fig.1.31. © Riggisberg, Abegg-Stiftung.

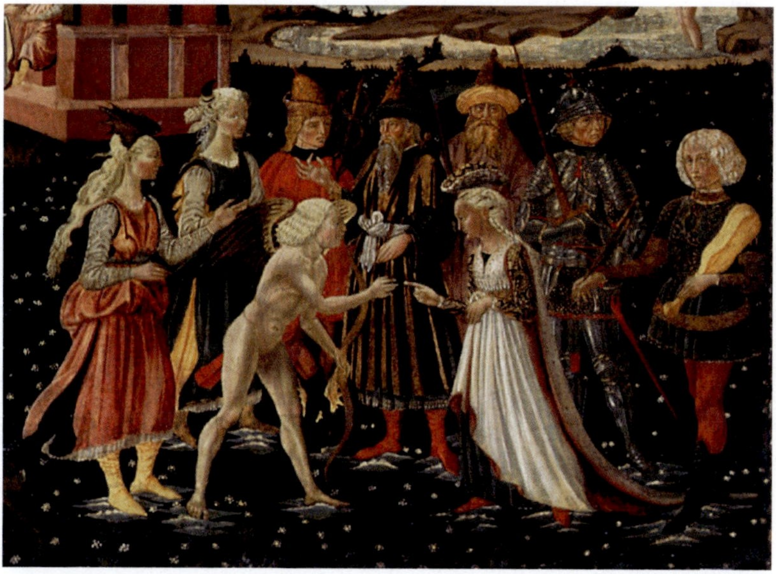

Fig.1.41 Master of the Argonauts, *Marriage of Cupid and Psyche*, detail of fig.1.33. © Staatliche Museen zu Berlin -- Gemäldegalerie. Photo: Christoph Schmidt.

tree, but instead runs along the ground grasping Chloris, who is dressed in a red rather than a white dress. She stretches her arms out, almost touching the garments of Apollo, who is one of the witnesses to the marriage depicted on the right of the panel. In the foreground, just above Chloris's hands, we see a small figure of *Venus pudica* – a reflection of the goddess as depicted in Botticelli's *Birth of Venus.*

Sellaio's adaptation of the *Primavera* is indeed an ingenious one. The changes made by the artist to the colours (wings and dresses) and actions of Botticelli's figures might suggest that the finer points of Botticelli's iconography have escaped him. Both Cupid and Mercury appear to be missing from the central group, yet Cupid is one of the two most important participants in the fable (and is depicted in several of the *cassone*'s other scenes). However, Mercury is in fact present. As the messenger of Jupiter and, this time, also of Venus, he is flying in the skies, just above the Three Graces. Three further points are worth noting. The first is that in the *Primavera* the narrative should be read from right to left, while in the case of the Abegg panel the opposite is the case. Secondly, in the Abegg painting Venus is not, as in the *Primavera*, somewhat elevated in comparison to other figures depicted in the scene. Instead she is shown on the same level as her retinue, and seems to be gesturing at Psyche.

The third observation is that the meadow with flowers, which plays so important a role in the *Primavera* on the Riggisberg panel, is moved into the final scene depicting the *Marriage of Cupid and Psyche*. There are two sources of inspiration for this part of the composition: contemporary Florentine marriage rituals and a cosmological scene.

Wedding rituals in Renaissance Florence consisted of three main stages: the *giuramento*, when the two families entered into a contract; the *anellamento*, in which the exchange of rings by the *sposi nuovi* took place in the presence of a notary, which was the most important part of the ceremony; and finally the *domumductio*, or wedding procession.[21] It is the scene of the *anellamento* that is depicted in all three pairs of panels under discussion. The Master of the Argonauts, and after him Sellaio, gave the myth a more contemporary feel, choosing as a conclusion to the narrative scenes not the wedding banquet, which Apuleius describes in great detail, but the wedding itself, which the author dismisses in a few words. However, the depictions of this scene vary. In the Berlin *cassone* the young couple are shown standing in the middle of a circle of witnesses.[22] The paintings in New York and Riggisberg, however, depict Cupid and Psyche kneeling face to face. As well as altering the poses, the artists also modified the number of deities present at the ceremony. In the Berlin painting seven gods attend: Venus, Proserpine,[23] Mercury, Saturn, Mars and Apollo/the Sun form a semi-circle around Jupiter, who stands in the centre and fulfils the function of celebrant. Thus Jupiter takes the place of the notary, who was present during the nuptials would later draw up the marriage contract. It would seem that because the Master of the Argonauts (and later Jacopo del Sellaio) did not have appropriate models for depicting a celestial wedding ceremony, they used a cosmological depiction of the seven planets.[24] Several examples of this kind of depiction executed in the fourteenth and fifteenth centuries have survived to date. One need only mention the miniature in the Bibliothèque Municipale in Dijon (ms.448, fol.63*v*), which portrays seven planets above seven celestial zones with Saturn in the centre, identifiable not by virtue of an attribute, but by an inscription (fig.1.42).[25] By contrast, in all the paintings under discussion he appears with his attribute, a scythe, as he also does in the engravings by the Florentine artist Baccio Baldini, executed in the 1470s.[26] Indeed the other divinities depicted by Baldini resemble the gods depicted in the *cassoni* and *spalliere* by the Master of the Argonauts and Sellaio.[27] The fact that Saturn, who does not appear in Apuleius's text, is present at the nuptials of Cupid and Psyche is proof that the artists of these paintings made use of cosmological depictions as ready-made iconographic models.

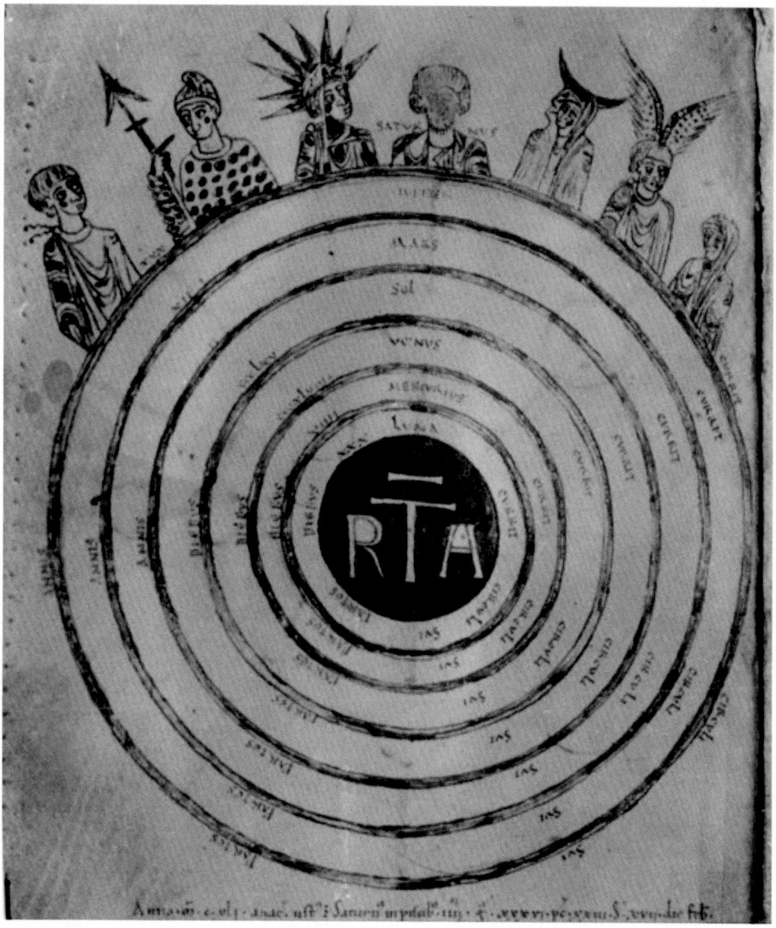

Fig.1.42 *The Seven Planets and Seven Heavenly Spheres*, miniature, Dijon, Bibliothèque Municipale, Ms.448, fol.63v. © Bibliotheque Municipale, Dijon (Ms. 448, fol. 63v).

Gombrich's reading of the *Primavera*

Now let us return to Ernst Gombrich's interpretation of the *Primavera,* often severely criticised by scholars.[28] As we have seen, Gombrich suggested that the text mainly consulted for the depiction of Venus and her train was a passage in Book X of Apuleius's *Metamorphoses* or *Golden Ass*, which describes a dumb show of the *Judgement of Paris*. It reads as follows:

> Then a radiantly beautiful boy appeared, naked except for an ephebic cape covering his left shoulder. He attracted all eyes with

> his blond curls, and from his hair projected little golden wings symmetrically attached; a caduceus and wand identified him as Mercury[...]. And now Venus, amidst loud applause from the audience, delightfully took her position at the very centre of the stage, smiling sweetly and surrounded by a whole mob of happy little boys. You would have said that those soft, round, milky-skinned babies where real Cupids who had just flown in from the sky or the sea. With their little wings and tiny arrows and all the rest of the costume they fitted the part splendidly, and they lit the way for their mistress with twinkling torches as if she were on her way to her wedding feast. Then in streamed handsome groups of unwed girls, on one side the graceful Graces, on the other the lovely Hours, worshipping their goddess by throwing garlands and loose flowers; they formed a most elegant dance-pattern as they beguiled the Queen of pleasures with the tresses of Spring.[29]

In this text then, in addition to Venus 'standing in the centre', several other *dramatis personae* depicted in the *Primavera* are present, i.e. the Graces on one side, the Horae (in the painting replaced by Flora), scattering the petals of Spring on the other, and even Mercury. It is to be noted that the Horae and the Graces are also mentioned in the story of Cupid and Psyche. They appear during the wedding feast where 'the Hours were colouring everything with roses and all the other flowers, the Graces were sprinkling balsam' (*Metamorphoses* VI, 24). To be sure, several other texts, pointed to by numerous students of Botticelli's art, were used to devise the *Primavera.*[30] Sellaio's adaptation of this masterpiece in the context of the Cupid and Psyche story suggests, however, that Book X of Apuleius's novel may well have been a point of departure for the author of the programme of the *Primavera*.

We may cite here a passage from Gombrich's 'Postscript' of 1970 to his article on 'Botticelli's Mythologies':

> In my paper I suggest that the text which was mainly consulted for this purpose [the painting of the *Primavera*] was a description of Venus and her train which occurs in the *Golden Ass* by Apuleius in the context of a dumb show of the Judgment of Paris. This hypothesis has fared very badly with my critics[...] I still think that the scholar eager to provide the painter with an authentic description of Venus as she was seen in antiquity may have remembered this passage[...] I would not want to exclude Apuleius from the list of authors remembered by Botticelli's instructor[...].

Gombrich returned to the interpretation of the *Primavera* once more. He did so in a film about this masterpiece made by Agnieszka Piotrowska for Channel 4 in 1996. He expressed his admiration for the painting, observing 'It is about the realm of Venus [...] the kingdom of Venus is a realm in which love and grace predominate, and which is important to human beings as a sublimation of their animal instincts[...]Finished'.[31] Thus he clearly refers once again to the Neoplatonic interpretation he proposed for the first time in 1945 and repeated 25 years later.

Conclusion

Now let us consider the question: what was the reason for an adaptation of the *Primavera* group on the Riggisberg *cassone* front? The idea may have been to show that through the flogging (a punishment for disobedience and excessive curiosity), which can be interpreted as a kind of *catharsis*, Psyche at last goes to heaven as a result of marrying her beloved Cupid. Originating from the same literary work as the rest of the painting, Apuleius's *Metamorphoses*, the insertion is presented in place of Psyche's tasks, absent in these portrayals. Instead of the *Descent into Hades* (as on the end panel in the former Lanckoroński collection) and the other seemingly impossible tasks achieved through divine intervention, there is a different, rather enigmatic 'bridge' between earthly reality and heaven: Venus surrounded by the Graces, Flora/ Hora and finally Venus Urania and the group of Chloris and Zephyr (the same wind that transported Psyche to Cupid's palace) running in the direction of the wedding ceremony. Here it is worth mentioning one of the Botticelli frescoes that once decorated the Villa Lemmi in Careggi (currently in the Louvre), which was painted for the wedding of Lorenzo Tornabuoni and his second wife Ginevra Gianfigliazzi (previously identified as Lorenzo's first wife, Giovanna degli Albizzi) *c.*1489–90.[32] In this fresco the bride is being presented to Venus by the Three Graces. In Florence in the times of Lorenzo il Magnifico, Venus and the three Graces also had matrimonial connotations. There is a superb medal bearing a portrait of Giovanna degli Albizzi on one side and the Three Graces on the obverse, which was probably struck to commemorate Lorenzo's first marriage in 1484.

Thus, while depicting the fable of Cupid and Psyche, which is an 'interpolation' within Apuleius's novel about the metamorphosis of Lucius being turned into an ass, Sellaio, most probably instructed by a learned advisor, produced this unique adaptation of what by now must have been a very famous *exemplum* executed by Botticelli, producing a kind of instruction for a newly-wed how to become a good wife and how to attain immortality. In his version of the fable of Cupid and his beloved, Boiardo presents Psyche as an *exemplum*:

> *Pazienza Psiche ebbe ne i casi soi,*
> *E però fu soccorsa ne li affani*
> *E facta Dea nel fin, ch'è exempio ad noi.*[33]

Acknowledgements

For Elizabeth McGrath and Jill Kraye for inspiring discussions on some interpretations of the *Primavera* and for Caroline Elam and Ana Debenedetti for emendations to my English and bibliographical references.

Notes

1 Erwin Panofsky, *Renaissance and Renascences in Western Art* (Stockholm: Almqvist and Wiksell, 1960), 191–200. Several attempts to solve the centuries-old puzzle of the *Primavera* have been published in the past 25 years. See, for example, Claudia Villa, '*Per una lettura della* Primavera. *Mercurio 'retrogrado' e la Retorica nella bottega di Botticelli*', *Strumenti critici* 86.1 (1998): 1–28, who interpreted 'Venus' as Philology, Flora as 'Rhetoric', 'Chloris' as Flora and 'Zephyr' as '*Genio ispiratore*'; Claudia La Malfa, '*Firenze e l'allegoria dell'eloquenza: una nuova interpretazione della* Primavera *di Botticelli*', *Storia dell'arte,* 97 (1999): 249–93 who saw in 'Venus' a 'celestial symbol of Philosophy-theology', in 'Flora' the Muse of Florence and in 'Zephyr' Atanasia, the goddess of immortality; Nicole Lévis-Godechot, '*La* Primavera *et la* Naissance de Vénus *de Botticelli ou le cheminement de l'âme selon Platon*', *Gazette des Beaux-Arts* 12, 1 (1993): 137–48, who discovered the story of Psyche in the painting (*sic*); Edith Balas, 'Botticelli's *Primavera* and the Story of Helen', *Gazette des Beaux-Arts* 137–8 (2001): 137–48, who saw in the painting 'the Abduction of Helen of Troy'; see also in this volume Paul Holberton, 'Botticelli's "Mythologies": Classicism and Invention'.

2 Ernst H. Gombrich, 'Botticelli's mythologies. A study in the neoplatonic symbolism of his circle', *Journal of the Warburg and Courtauld Institutes* 8 (1945): 7–60, repr. in *Symbolic Images. Studies in the Art of the Renaissance II* (Oxford: Phaidon, 1972), 31–81.

3 Aby Warburg, *The Renewal of Pagan Antiquity*, trans. David Britt (Los Angeles: Getty Research Institute for the History of Art and the Humanities, 1999), 89–156.

4 For *Primavera* as a painting for the bedchamber of the bride, see Ronald Lightbown, *Sandro Botticelli, vol.I, Life and Work* (London: Paul Elek, 1978), 73; Lilian Zirpolo, 'Botticelli's *Primavera*. A lesson for the bride', in *The Expanding Discourse: Feminism and Art History*, ed. Norma Broude et al. (New York: Icon Ed., 1992) 101–9.

5 Preliminary observations on this discovery are to be found in Jerzy Miziołek, 'Botticelli's masterpieces reflected: Jacopo del Sellaio's domestic panels with the fable of Cupid and Psyche', *Center 22. (CASVA) Record of Activities and Research Reports: June 2001–May 2002*: 128–32. See also Jerzy Miziołek, '*Alcune osservazioni sulla storia di Amore e Psiche nella pittura italiana del '300 e '400*', *Fontes* 5–6 (2000): 133–54; Jerzy Miziołek, 'I decori e le storie dipinte sui cassoni', in *Virtù d'amore. Pittura nuziale nel Quattrocento fiorentino*, ed. Claudio Paolini, Daniela Parenti and Ludovica Sebregondi (Florence: Giunti, 2010): 74–6. Regarding this *cassone* see Gaudenz Freuler, '*Manifestatori delle cose miracolose*', *Arte italiana del '300 e '400 da collezioni in Svizzera e nel Liechtenstein* (Einsiedeln: Eidolon, 1991): 290–1; Laurence B. Kanter, *Italian Paintings in the Museum of Fine Arts. Boston, vol.1: Thirteenth- Fifteenth Century* (Boston: Museum of Fine Arts, 1994), no.50: 172–3. Strangely enough neither Freuler (who first published the Abegg panel) nor Kanter, who reproduced and briefly discussed it, noticed this adaptation. See also Ellen Callmann, 'Subjects from Boccaccio in Italian painting 1375–1525', *Studi sul Boccaccio* 23 (1995): 58, who writes: 'In the centre two sets of figures have been inserted that do not appear in the story: a youth reaching for a fleeing maiden, and a group of three nymphs, the latter referring to the ancient statue of the Three Graces that had been found in Siena'.

6 Most of the previous interpretations of the *Primavera* are discussed by Giovanni Reale, *Botticelli. La Primavera o le Nozze di Filologia e Mercurio?: rilettura di carattere filosofico ed ermeneutico del capolavoro di Botticelli con la prima presentazione analitica dei personaggi e dei particolari simbolici* (Rimini: Idea Libri, 2001) 181–237. See also Mirella Levi d'Ancona, *Due quadri del Botticelli eseguiti per nascite in casa Medici* (Florence: Olschki, 1992) 7–15; Charles Dempsey, *The Portrayal of Love. Botticelli's Primavera and Humanist Culture at the Time of Lorenzo the Magnificent* (Princeton: Princeton University Press, 1992), 3–19; Frank Zöllner, *Sandro Botticelli* (Munich-London-New York: Prestel, 2015), 210–13. See also Holberton's essay in this volume.

7 See Webster Smith, 'On the original location of the Primavera', *Art Bulletin* 57 (1975): 34; John Shearman, 'The Collections of the Younger Branch of the Medici', *The Burlington Magazine* 117, no.862 (1975): 12–27, and Jerzy Miziołek, *Renaissance Weddings and the Antique. Italian Domestic Paintings from the Lanckoroński Collection* (Rome: L'"Erma" di Bretschneider, 2018), 189–221.

8 *Martianus Capella and the Seven Liberal Arts*, vol.2: *The Marriage of Philosophy and Mercury*, trans. William Harris Stahl et al. (New York: Columbia University Press, 1977), 6–8.

9 *Fulgentius the mythographer*, trans. Leslie George Whitbread Athens (Ohio: Ohio State University Press, 1971), 88–90.

10 *Della genealogia de gli Dei di M. Giovanni Boccaccio libri quindeci*, trans. Giuseppe Betussi (In Venetia): Spineda [Dr], 1606) k. 91–2; Giovanni Boccaccio, *Genealogie deorum gentilium libri, V*, ed. Vincenzo Romano (Bari: Laterza, 1951), ch.V, 22.

11 Edoardo Fumagalli, *Matteo Maria Boiardo volgarizzatore dell Asino d'oro. Contributo allo studio della fortuna di Apuleio nell'umanesimo* (Padua: Antenore, 1988).

12 Viti in Matteo Maria Boiardo, *Tutte le opere*, ed. Angelandrea Zottoli (Milan: Mondadori, 1936–7), 714. See also Jan de Jong, 'Renaissance representations of Cupid and Psyche: Apuleius versus Fulgentius', *Groningen colloquia on the novel* 2 (1989): 76–7.

13 Paul Schubring, *'Zwei Cassonetafeln mit Apuleius' Märchen von Amor und Psiche'*, *Zeitschrift für Bildende Kunst* 27 (1916): 315–20; Wilhelm Bode, *'Zwei Cassone-Tafeln aus dem Besitz des Piero de'Medici in der Sammlung Eduard Simon zu Berlin'*, *Mitteilungen des Kunsthistorischen Institutes in Florenz*, 2.1912/17 (1917), 5/6: 149–51; Paul Schubring, *Cassoni. Truhen und Truhenbilder der italienischen Frührenaissance* (Leipzig: Karl W. Hiersemann, 1923), nos. 911–12; Hans Werner Grohn, *'Zwei cassoni mit Darstellungen aus der Erzählung von Amor und Psiche. Frühwerke des Meisters der Argonauten-Tafeln'*, *Forschungen und Berichte-Staatliche Museen zu Berlin* 1 (1957): 90–100, 90–3, figs 1–2; Luisa Vertova, 'Cupid and Psyche in Renaissance painting before Raphael', *Journal of the Warburg and Courtauld Institutes* 42 (1979): 107–13, pl.30; Everett Fahy, 'The Argonaut Master', *Gazette des Beaux-Arts*, 6th ser. 114 (1989): 287–90, figs 5–6, with a date of 1475 for the Berlin panels; Callmann, 'Subjects from Boccaccio', no.91, 57–8; Colin Eisler, *Masterworks in Berlin. A City's Paintings Reunited. Paintings in the Western World, 1300–1914* (Boston: Little, Brown, and Co., 1996) 192–3; Graham Hughes, *Renaissance Cassoni. Masterpieces of Early Italian Art: Painted Marriage Chests 1400–1550* (London: Art Books International, 1997), 134–5.

14 Julia Haig Gaisser, *The fortunes of Apuleius and the Golden Ass: a study in transmission and reception* (Princeton and Oxford: Princeton University Press, 2008), 113.

15 See Deborah Krohn in Andrea Bayer, ed., *Art and Love in Renaissance Italy*, exh. cat., The Metropolitan Museum of Art, New York (New Haven & London: Yale University Press, 2008), 293–5.

16 Luciano Bellosi and Margaret Haines, *Lo Scheggia* (Florence: Maschietto & Musolino, 1999), 60–1; Roberta Bartoli, *Biagio d'Antonio* (Milan: Motta, 1999), 151; Patricia Lee Rubin and Alison Wright, *Renaissance Florence. The Art of the 1470s* (London: National Gallery Publications Limited, 1999), nos. 78–9, 316–19.

17 See Nicole Dacos, Antonio Giuliano, Ulrico Pannuti, *Il tesoro di Lorenzo il Magnifico: Le Gemme* (Florence: Sansoni, 1973), 69–72, no.43, figs 39–43.

18 For this panel, see Lightbown, *Sandro Botticelli*, 44–6. I would like to express my gratitude to Ana Debenedetti and Caroline Elam who drew my attention to this borrowing in Sellaio's panel.

19 Kanter, *Italian Paintings*, 172–3.

20 Nicolai Rubinstein, 'Youth and Spring in Botticelli's Primavera', *Journal of the Warburg and Courtauld Institutes* 60 (1997): 248–51.

21 For the wedding rituals and *cassoni* see Christiane Klapisch-Zuber, *'Zaccaria, o il padre spodestato. I riti nuziali in Toscana tra Giotto e il Concilio di Trento'* in *La famiglia e le donne nel Rinascimento a Firenze* (Bari-Roma: Laterza, 1988), 109–51; Christiane Klapisch-Zuber, *'Les femmes dans les rituels de l'alliance et de la naissance à Florence'* in *Riti e rituali nelle società medievali*, ed. Jacques Chiffoleau (Spoleto: Centro Italiano di Studi Sull'Alto Medioevo, 1994), 3–32; Christiane Klapisch-Zuber, 'Les coffres de mariage et les plateaux d'accouchée', in *A travers l'image. Lecture iconographiques et sens de l'œuvre*, ed. Sylvie Deswarte-Rosa (Paris: Éditions Klincksieck, 1994), 309–23.

22 Jerzy Miziołek, *Soggetti classici sui cassoni fiorentini alla vigilia del Rinascimento* (Warsaw: Instytut Sztuki Polskiej Akademii Nauk, 1996), 17 and plate 1. See also Max Seidel, *'Hochzeitsikonographie im Trecento'*, *Mitteilungen des Kunsthistorischen Institutes in Florenz*, 38.1 (1994): 1–40, with several illustrations showing marriage scenes.

23 For Diana/Luna produced by Baccio Baldini see Patrizia Castelli, *'Motivi astrologici ed ermetici nel governo Laurenziano'*, in *Per bellezza, per studio, per piacere. Lorenzo il Magnifico e gli spazi dell'arte*, ed. Franco Borsi (Florence: Giunti, 1991), 55–78, fig.16. For the iconography of Proserpine see Vertova, 'Cupid and Psyche', 111.

24 For the seven Planets: Bruno Archibald Fuchs, *Die Ikonographie der 7 Planeten in der*

Kunst Italiens bis zum Ausgang des Mittelalters (Munich: [s.n.], 1909); Anton Hauber, *Planetenkinderbilder und Sternbilder zur Geschichte des Menschlichen Glaubens und Irrens* (Strasbourg: Heitz, 1916); Dieter Blume, '*Planetengötter und ein christlicher Friedensbinger als Legitimation eines Machtwechsels. Die Ausmalung der Rocca di Angera*' in *Europäische Kunst um 1300, Akten des XXV. Internationalen Kongresses für Kunstgeschichte, Wien 1983*, ed. Gerhard. Schmidt (Vienna: H. Böhlau, 1986), 175–87. See also Sven Eriksson, *Wochentagsgötter, Mond und Tierkreis. Laienastrologie in der römischen Kaiserzeit* (Stockholm: Almqvist & Wiksell, 1956), fig.1 and *passim*. For the iconography of the pagan gods in the art of the Middle Ages see Nikolaus Himmelmann, *Antike Götter im Mittelalter* (Mainz am Rhein: von Zabern, 1986).

25 Jean Seznec, *The Survival of the Pagan Gods. The Mythological Tradition and Its Place in Renaissance Humanism and Art*, trans. Barbara F. Sessions (New York: Harper, 1961), 70, fig.20. See also Erwin Panofsky, Fritz Saxl, 'Classical mythology in medieval art', *Metropolitan Museum Studies*, 4.2 (1932–3): 240–5.

26 For Saturn and its attribute see Panofsky, Saxl, 'Classical mythology'; Arthur Mayger Hind, *Early Italian Engraving, Part I: Florentine Engraving and Anonymous Prints of other Schools* (London: Published for M. Knoedler, New York, by Bernard Quaritch, 1938), II, plates 114–15; *The Illustrated Bartsch. Early Italian Masters*, ed. Mark Zucker (New York: Abaris Books, 1980), 299–305 (192–8); Castelli, 'Motivi astrologici', 62–72, figs 7–24. See also Castelli for the carnival procession organised in Florence by Lorenzo il Magnifico in 1490, which featured a christianised 'Triumph of the Planets' ('*un trionfo cristianizzato dei pianeti*'). In his *Canzone dei sette pianeti* Lorenzo il Magnifico puts the following words: '*Sette Pianeti siam, che alta sede / Lasciam per far del Cielo in terra fede*', Castelli (as above), 70.

27 Note that Venus with winged cap is to be found both in Baldini's etchings and on the Berlin *cassoni*.

28 Thanks to Elizabeth McGrath's recent investigation, it is now known that Fritz Saxl was not convinced with Gombrich's interpretation. She published and commented on his letter of 4 April 1946 (preserved in the Archives of E. H. Gombrich at the Warburg Institute), which reads: 'I have read the *Primavera* with enthusiasm. Astute, subtle, full of invention & I would very much like to believe that Apuleius is the text. But you say that early Renaissance images are mostly illustrations and cite a splendid array from Bott[icelli] to Titian. The *Primavera* certainly does not fit into that array. You do not think that the traditional title is false, but it remains unexplained. Nor is the Judgement of Paris illustrated. On the one hand you try to save the link with Apuleius (emendations for Zephyr and Flora, Mercury's senseless gesture, senseless, since he is not delivering Jupiter's request to Paris, which however one would expect to see from the text of Apuleius), on the other hand Bott[icelli]'s overall theme has nothing to do with Apuleius. I fear Apuleius is not the text which served as the unique source. The source must have as its upshot the idea of Primavera and the grove of delight. Since apparently we do not yet know the source, we probably have to fall back on the old method of a *combinatio* of sources & then Apuleius will have his place, without our having to force the interpretation. [...] I wouldn't know what else to do, than to rephrase and say – that [*i.e.* Apuleius's text] was probably known in Florence, and influenced the unknown author of the programme'. See: Elizabeth McGrath, 'Gombrich and 'Warburgian' Iconography', in Paul Taylor, ed., *Meditations on a Heritage. Papers on the Work and Legacy of Sir Ernst Gombrich* (London: Paul Holberton Publishing, 2014), 49–50.

29 Apuleius, *The Golden Ass, being the Metamorphoses of Lucius Apuleius*, trans. William Adlington, Rev. Stephen Gaselee (London: William Heinemann, 1935): 275–7.

30 Dempsey, *The Portrayal of Love*; Edgar Wind, *Pagan Mysteries in the Renaissance* (London: Faber and Faber, 1958), 100–10.

31 McGrath, *Gombrich and 'Warburgian' Iconography*, 49.The present author possesses a copy of this film, *Botticelli: Primavera. Myths of fingerprints?*

32 Aby Warburg, '*La* Nascita di Venere *e la* Primavera *di Sandro Botticelli. Ricerche sull'immagine dell'Antichità nel primo Rinascimento italiano*', in *La rinascita del paganesimo antico* (Florence: La Nuova Italia, 1966), 29; Lightbown, *Sandro Botticelli*, 93–7; Horst Bredekamp, *Botticelli. La Primavera*, trans. S. Castri (Modena: Panini, 1996), ill. 9. See also Veronica Mertens, *Die Drei Grazien. Studien zu einem Bildmotiv in der Kunst der Neuzeit* (Wiesbaden: Harrassowitz, 1994) 190–4, fig.84. In Helen Ettlinger's opinion ('The Portraits in Botticelli's Villa Lemmi frescoes', *Mitteilungen des Kunsthistorischen Institutes in Florenz* 20 (1976): 404–7), these frescos were produced on the occasion of the wedding of Matteo d'Andrea Albizzi and Nanna di Niccolò Tornabuoni in 1484. But see also Patricia Simons, 'Giovanna and Ginevra: Portraits for the

Tornabuoni Family by Ghirlandaio and Botticelli', *I Tatti Studies in the Italian Renaissance*, vols 14/15 (2011–12): 103–35, 117; who conclusively demonstrated that the bride of Lorenzo Tornabuoni depicted at the Villa Lemmi is not Giovanna degli Albizzi, but Ginevra Gianfigliazzi, Lorenzo's second wife.

33 Boiardo, *Tutte le opere*, 711. Similar words are to be found in Pier Antonio Viti's commentary to Boiardo's *Capitoli del giuoco di tarrochi*: '*Questa è l'anima nostra, che cum grandissime fatiche da le brutture del mondo nostro levandose, piglia l'ale, da Jove per grazia concesseli, pogiando col divino adiuto insino al Cielo, dove, per merito de le sue fatighe, la felice vita prendendo, diventa Dea*'.

Part 2
The Botticelli Effect

Introduction

Julius Bryant

This second part takes a chronological approach to exploring the rediscovery of Botticelli, from the late eighteenth to the early twentieth centuries. From Rome and Florence to Harvard, South Kensington and Richmond, research takes us from the Vatican Library, where the neoclassical sculptor John Flaxman studied Botticelli's illustrations to Dante in 1792, to the cosy sofa in the 'Little Botticelli room' in Richmond of the lesbian couple Katherine Bradley and her niece Edith Cooper, better known by their shared pen name Michael Field. Bridging these research worlds, of the academic artist and Aesthete poets, are the connoisseur historians Hermann Ulmann and Bernard and Mary Berenson. Given their common interests as pioneers of Botticelli studies, these colourful characters could not be more varied in their priorities, nor in what they sought, found and used from studying the artist.

While the exhibition *Botticelli Reimagined* revealed the influence of a *Portrait of a Lady known as Smeralda Bandinelli* (fig.1.5) that Rossetti had bought in 1867, this section of the conference drew attention to the contribution to the artist's rediscovery made by a literary tradition, from Dante to William Roscoe, Rossetti and to Walter Pater. Another theme to emerge from the perspectives of these three papers is the role played by reproductions of Botticelli's actual paintings. From an edition of Dante's *Divine Comedy* with engravings after Botticelli (published in 1481) to chromolithographs published by the Arundel Society and on to photographic prints, the pioneers' understanding of the artist was formed more through small-scale reproductions than by any dramatic rediscovery and rehanging of large oil paintings in British galleries. The role of photographs as a tool of Berenson's connoisseurship has long been known, but we may ask how far reproductions on paper became a way of seeing Botticelli in the wider sense. In this way, the visual material culture of Botticelli favoured the intimate study of linear and tonal values over full-scale compositions and the subtleties of his actual palette.

The idea of ownership and portability of Botticelli in reproduction facilitated not only close scrutiny by connoisseurs, beyond the limited public space and opening times of public galleries, but also encouraged a more relaxed frame of mind – a freedom to dream, to meander through subjective readings of creative reinterpretation. Rossetti wrote a sonnet to the *Primavera* after seeing it in reproduction, but never visited Italy. As Anna Gruetzner Robins observes, when Walter Pater described *The Birth of Venus* (fig.1.0) as a weary prostitute with 'grey flesh and wan flowers', he may have only known the painting from the chromolithograph published by the Arundel Society in 1870.

Mark Evans traces the rediscovery of Botticelli in England from the portrait painter Jonathan Richardson, drawing on both a travel guide to Italy and France that Richardson and his son published in 1722 and from his collection of drawings, sold after his death in 1745. Despite English translations of Dante, and paintings and sketches by artists such as Fuseli, Flaxman and William Blake, when Fuseli's friend William Young Ottley tried to sell the only signed painting by Botticelli, *The Mystic Nativity* (National Gallery, London; see p.99, fig.2.2), acquired by Ottley from the Villa Aldobrandini in Rome, at auction in 1811, it found no buyer. In an edition of Fuseli's writings published in 1831, Botticelli's frescoes in the Sistine Chapel were described as by 'Sandro, the least qualified of the group, whose barbarous taste and dry minuteness palsied [...] his associates'.

Francesco Ventrella's study of Bernard Berenson and Botticelli focuses on the connoisseur's pursuit of a specific 'artistic personality'. In 1884, while a student at Harvard, he heard a lecture by Edmund Gosse that prompted him to rush not to a public gallery, but rather to a shop to purchase a reproduction of Botticelli's *Primavera* (fig.1.30). Berenson's first publication on art, in 1890, was an article about photographs of old master paintings. He decorated his study with photographs and used visual aids in the series of lectures on the Italian masters that he gave in 1893, not in a public art gallery but at 93 Onslow Square, South Kensington. When the first comprehensive monograph on Botticelli, by Hermann Ulmann, appeared in 1893, Berenson prepared for writing a review by asking his future wife, Mary Costelloe, to check for any gaps in his collection of photographs. This way of studying Botticelli through reproductions must have influenced Berenson's conclusion to the article (written with Mary Costelloe): 'Ulmann did not understand Botticelli's quality, which is the fact that he is a linealist'. Berenson saw Botticelli's use of line as the key to his character as an artist and to the 'tonic effects' of his art. Ventrella invites us to equate Berenson's attempt at psychological analysis of the artist with his own struggle to reconcile his anti-Semitism with his Jewish identity.

Anna Gruetzner Robins presents the writers known as Michael Field first in Paris in 1890, meeting Berenson on their way to Florence; they had been inspired by Walter Pater's essay on Botticelli (published in book form in 1873) and by Dante Gabriel Rossetti's sonnet 'For Primavera by Sandro Botticelli'. Bradley and Cooper knew Botticelli's *Mystic Nativity* in London's National Gallery, and they looked long and hard in the Uffizi and Accademia in Florence. Back home their 'little Botticelli room' was hung with framed photographs – until their neighbour Charles Ricketts persuaded them to prefer Burne-Jones; in 1900 they noted 'Photographs of Botticelli have recently been unhung'. As well as these graphic and literary drivers behind the rediscovery of Botticelli in Britain, the psychology of writers is shown to have been a key factor in his reception, as the Renaissance artist's paintings of androgynous figures appealed to such aesthetes of flexible sexuality.

The rediscovery of Botticelli can no longer be credited entirely to Pre-Raphaelite painters and to a literary cult in late nineteenth-century England. But while most of his paintings remained in Tuscan churches, houses and galleries, the appreciation of his art spread beyond eloquent texts and artistic emulations – for Botticelli travelled, and was savoured, in reproductions that had their own influence and appeal.

5. Whigs and primitives: Dante and Botticelli in England from Jonathan Richardson to John Flaxman

Mark Evans

The upsurge of interest in Dante towards the end of the Regency disconcerted 'the Honourable Mr Listless', a character in Thomas Love Peacock's satirical Gothic novella *Nightmare Abbey* (1818):

> I don't know how it is, but Dante never came my way till lately [...] and if I had had him, I should not have read him. But I find he is growing fashionable, and I am afraid I must read him some wet morning.[1]

Mr Listless was probably alluding to the blank verse translation of *The Divine Comedy* by Henry Cary (1772–1844) (first edition 1814), which had recently been favourably reviewed by the Italian poet Ugo Foscolo (1778–1827), Samuel Rogers (1763–1855) and Samuel Taylor Coleridge.[2] While Dante's writings seemed crude and obscure by the classicising standards of the seventeenth and eighteenth centuries, in 1818 William Hazlitt hailed him as 'the father of modern poetry [...] self-will personified' and Coleridge praised his 'endless subtle beauties', excusing his apparent faults as 'excellencies carried to an excess'.[3] The Tuscan poet's influence on British literature and art was soon manifest, for example, in Lord Byron's *The Prophecy of Dante* (1819) and William Blake's late watercolours of *The Divine Comedy* (1824–7).[4]

Like most fifteenth-century painters, Botticelli had been forgotten since Vasari. He was not mentioned in such travel guides as *Letters from Italy between the years 1792 and 1798* (first edition 1800) by Mariana Starke (1762–1838), and in 1787 even John Flaxman, an artist well-disposed to the so-called 'primitives', misattributed his *Madonna del Magnificat* to Taddeo Gaddi.[5] The starting point for Botticelli's rehabilitation in Britain is generally dated three-quarters of a century later, at the time of Dante Gabriel Rossetti's purchase in 1867 of his *Portrait of a Lady known as Smeralda Bandinelli* (fig.1.5) and the publication of Walter Pater's 'Fragment on Sandro Botticelli' in 1870.[6] However, as we shall see, the English rediscovery of Botticelli was closely linked to that of Dante, and both were inaugurated by a coterie of mostly nonconformist artists and men of letters, and by Whig grandee collectors.

At the dawn of the Georgian age, Dante was principally remembered for the criticism of the papacy which had caused his *Monarchia* to be put on the index of prohibited books.[7] Such a viewpoint would have been consistent with the political affiliations of Thomas Coke, earl of Leicester (1697–1759), a wealthy kinsman of Sir Robert Walpole. He made the grand tour in 1712–18 and assembled at his Palladian mansion, Holkham Hall in Norfolk, a library rich in Italian texts, with a superb group of early Dante manuscripts.[8] Coke and his family sat to Jonathan Richardson (1667–1745), a portrait painter of Low Church persuasion and the most perceptive art theorist of his generation; he was the first English commentator to express an interest in Dante and Botticelli.[9] Richardson and his son, also called Jonathan, wrote an account of works of art the latter had seen in Italy in 1720, which mentions Domenico di Michelino's fresco of *Dante and the Divine Comedy* in Florence Cathedral as well as an *Adoration of the Magi* (fig.1.8) attributed to Botticelli at the Uffizi.[10] The elder Richardson's remarkable collection of master drawings, sold after his death, included 100 early sheets, several ascribed to Botticelli.[11]

In his *Discourse on the Science of a Connoisseur* (1719), Richardson likened painting to poetry, citing 'Examples [...] very Curious, and very little Known', including that of the Ghibelline Count Ugolino, incarcerated with his sons and left to starve in a tower at Pisa, which had been reported in the *Florentine History* of Giovanni Villani.[12] Richardson provided a verse translation of Dante's account of this gruesome tale (*Inferno*, XXXIII) to show how 'The Poet carries this story farther than the Historian'. Arguing that sculpture had yet greater power over the imagination, he described a relief of this subject attributed to Michelangelo – whom he described as 'a *Dante* in his way' – and concluded that 'the same Story painted' with 'all the Advantages of [...] Colours' by 'a Genius Equal to that of Michelangelo' would be even more effective.[13]

Edward Gibbon considered fifteenth-century Florence to exemplify the values of civic humanism which imbued Georgian political thought, as well as the artistic theories of Sir Joshua Reynolds – a devotee of Richardson and a strong adherent of the Whigs.[14] Reynolds's extensive collection included a drawing of *Virgil, Dante and Ugolino*, now attributed to Luca Signorelli, and he responded in 1773 to Richardson's challenge with his own composition of *Count Hugolino and his Children in the Dungeon*.[15] Enormously influential, Reynolds's full-face image established the iconography of the despairing count for a century, as is apparent from later representations of the subject by Blake (1793), Henry Fuseli (1806) and Jean-Baptiste Carpeaux (1862).

Richardson also influenced the Swiss scholar Johann Jakob Bodmer (1698–1783), one of the first German-speaking authors to appreciate Dante. His tragedy on Ugolino, entitled *Der Hungerthurm in Pisa*, was published in 1769.[16] Bodmer's students at Zurich included Henry Fuseli, who acquired an extensive command of Greek and Latin and was ordained as a Zwinglian minister before moving in 1764 to London. Encouraged by Reynolds to become a painter, Fuseli spent the years 1770–8 in Rome, where he became enthralled by Michelangelo and made several drawings and paintings of subjects from *The Divine Comedy*.[17]

A blank verse translation of the *Inferno* was published in 1782 by Reynolds's friend, the connoisseur Charles Rogers (1711–84).[18] His 'Extensive Cabinet of Capital Drawings' included a double-sided sheet of *Pallas* and *A Head of a Lady*, attributed to Botticelli.[19] After Rogers's sale in 1799, this was acquired by the Keeper of Manuscripts at the British Museum, Francis Douce (1757–1834). Douce's collection was bequeathed in 1834 to the University of Oxford, and it has recently been rehabilitated as an autograph work.[20]

Rogers's friend, the painter George Romney, was an intimate of William Hayley (1745–1820), a fashionable liberal poet who declined the poet laureateship. In 1782 Hayley published his own rhyming translation of the first three cantos of the *Inferno*, to ascertain if the poem was sufficiently in tune with 'the sentiments of the public' to justify its complete translation.[21] This was followed in 1785 by a translation of the *Inferno* by Henry Boyd (1748/9–1832), dedicated to Frederick Augustus Hervey, Earl of Bristol and Bishop of Derry (1730–1803).[22] A political ally of Charles James Fox, this wealthy prelate lived for years in Italy and assembled a large art collection, mostly dispersed at auction at Rome in 1804. The Earl Bishop aspired to illustrate the entire 'Progress of Painting' as he put it in 1792: 'from *Cimabue* thro' Raphael [...] to Pompeo Battoni [...] & in Germany from Albert Durer's Master down to Angelica [Kauffmann]'.[23] Hayley ordered seven copies of Boyd's translation for friends, and perhaps gave Blake the copy which the latter angrily annotated: 'Every Principle in Dante is[...] proved Foolish by his Translator'.[24]

The bibliophile Whig MP Roger Wilbraham (1743–1829) had made the grand tour in 1770–3. He acquired 'all that is rare and curious in the classes of early poetry', including Cristoforo Landino's edition of *The Divine Comedy*, with engravings by Baccio Baldini after Botticelli's designs, published in 1481.[25] The printer left space for 96 engravings, but only 19 were made, and few copies include all of them. Wilbraham lent his choice volume, with all 19 illustrations, to his fellow antiquarian Joseph Strutt (1749–1802), who published two facsimiles of them in his *Biographical Dictionary of Engravers* (1785/6), accompanied by a lengthy account of Botticelli (fig.2.1).[26] Remarking that 'Boticelli [*sic*] is spoken of as a man of genius, in the history of the painters' and was also 'a man of letters', Strutt concluded that 'It was evidently from the works of Boticelli, or of his scholars, that Marc Antonio formed his first style of engraving'.[27]

Strutt's *Biographical Dictionary* was prefaced by an account of 'the use and excellency of the art of engraving [...] drawn up by a gentleman of great taste', which he modestly hoped would be 'still more acceptable to the public' than 'the remarks of an engraver', such as himself.[28] This disinterested 'man of science' and 'lover of the arts' was the Liverpool attorney William Roscoe (1753–1831), a self-taught polymath who also lent Strutt engravings by Mantegna for reproduction in his book.[29] Roscoe was friendly with Fuseli by 1782 and became a principal patron. He purchased from him a 'subject from Dante' in 1792, and also a large painting of *The Death of Lorenzo de' Medici* for his dining room at Allerton Hall.[30]

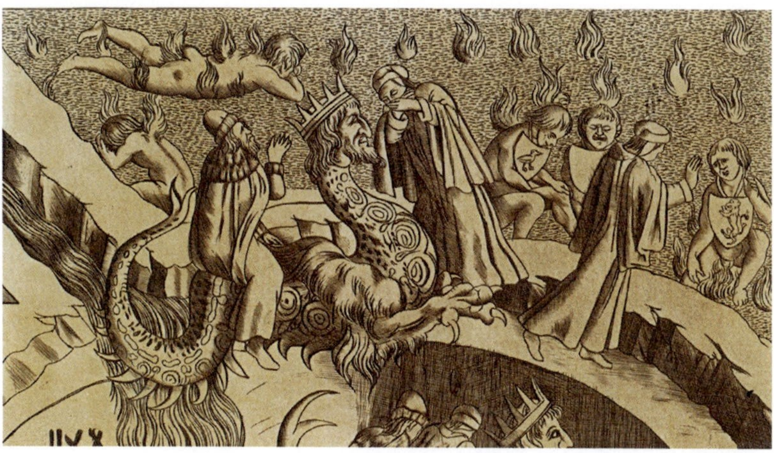

Fig.2.1 Joseph Strutt (1749–1802), after Baccio Baldini and Botticelli, *The monster Fraud, with the guide seated upon his back, desiring the author to follow his example[...]from the rare edition of the works of Dante, published at Florence, A.D. 1481 (1785)*, engraving from Joseph Strutt, *A Biographical Dictionary; containing an historical account of all the Engravers from the earliest period of the art of engraving to the present times (1785/6)*, vol.1, plate VII facing p.25 © Victoria and Albert Museum, London.

A Unitarian and a champion of toleration, who in 1806 was elected Whig MP for Liverpool and played a major role in the abolition of slavery, Roscoe considered Medicean Florence an auspicious model for his commercial city; he worked tirelessly to improve its cultural and intellectual life. When his life of Lorenzo the Magnificent was published in 1796 by the affluent antiquarian bookseller James Edwards (1756–1816), Roscoe acquired an international reputation as an authority on the Italian Renaissance, despite never going to Italy.[31] This biography proved immensely popular. Horace Walpole thought Roscoe 'the best of our historians, both for beauty and style, and for deep reflections', while the Earl Bishop of Bristol and Derry praised his 'superior talents and such indefatigable industry', offered the use of his apartments at Rome and Naples, and remarked that 'If, during my abode at Rome, I can in any way serve you by my connection with the Vatican Librarian, you may command me'.[32] These Whig noblemen encouraged Roscoe to write a longer sequel on Leo X (1805). This was less successful, but was also translated into French, Italian and German, and ran through numerous editions.

It may have been the historical range of the Earl Bishop's picture collection that inspired Roscoe also to acquire 'primitive' paintings. These included works by such painters as Simone Martini and Ercole de' Roberti (although these attributions were not yet established) 'for the purpose of illustrating [...] the rise and progress of the arts'.[33] In this he was assisted by another 'intimate friend of Fuseli', William Young Ottley (1771–1836). An established writer on art, collector and gentleman dealer, Ottley had acquired numerous works in Italy during the 1790s, including Botticelli's only signed painting, *The Mystic Nativity*, from the Villa Aldobrandini in Rome (fig.2.2).[34] He advised Roscoe on acquisitions and supplied him, directly or indirectly, with several pictures. However, he failed to sell *The Mystic Nativity* at auction in 1811, and was obliged to buy it in at 40 guineas.[35]

Roscoe's library boasted an impressive section on Dante, including the 1481 Landino's commentary to the *Divine Comedy*, prefixed with an 'original Folio Drawing by Botticelli of the Inferno, Purgatorio, and Paradiso' and 'ornamented with two of the prints designed by Sandro Botticelli [...] and with Drawings in Indian ink at the head of many of the cantos'.[36] He also owned two further sheets attributed to the artist: a 'very fine' *Man's Head* in metal point, formerly owned by Richardson, and a *Figure of a Man in Profile*, reputedly owned by Vasari.[37] When bankruptcy forced Roscoe to sell his collection in 1816 the illustrated *Divine Comedy* made a creditable 15 guineas, while the loose drawings realised £1 and 15/-.

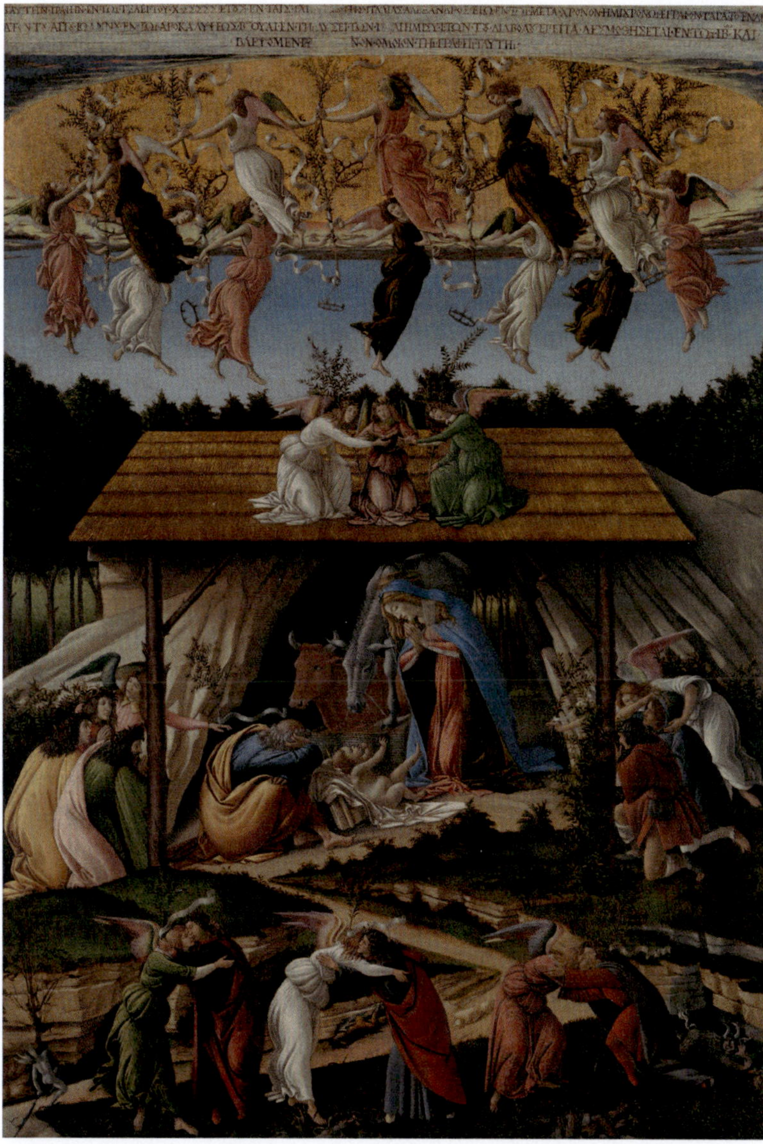

Fig.2.2 Sandro Botticelli, *The Mystic Nativity*, 1500, oil on canvas, 108.6 × 74.9 cm, The National Gallery, London, NG 1034. © 2018: The National Gallery, London/Scala, Florence.

In 1814 Roscoe accepted the invitation to visit the magnificent library inherited by Thomas William Coke, earl of Leicester (1754–1842) at Holkham Hall. Here he was 'delighted to find many volumes of extreme rarity and value [...] works of Italian history and poetry (amongst which were several copies of Dante) [...] the rarity of which was often equalled by their beauty'.[38] With characteristic generosity, Roscoe undertook to reorganise the library. He began a catalogue of its manuscripts and helped Coke to acquire two major fourteenth-century illuminated books, one English and the other Neapolitan: the *Holkham Bible Picture Book* and the *Bible of Clement VII*.[39]

Another of Roscoe's aristocratic admirers was the Marquess of Douglas, later the 10th Duke of Hamilton (1767–1852), who had spent the years 1792–1801 in Italy, collecting 'valuable manuscripts and printed books [...] estimable for their great antiquity, rarity and fine condition'; he went on to serve as Whig MP for Lancaster in 1802–6.[40] Just after returning home, and while still awaiting delivery of his books from Livorno, he wrote 'with particular pleasure' to this 'highly commended' author, 'whose extensive information and literary abilities have assured him the esteem of the public'.[41] In 1802 Roscoe outlined to Douglas his planned biography of Leo X, soliciting his aid 'in case anything should occur to you in your correspondence with your friends in Italy that may throw light on any of these subjects'.[42]

In the spring of 1803, towards the end of the Peace of Amiens, Roscoe's publisher, the bookseller James Edwards, made a visit to Paris. He wrote to inform Douglas of books he had seen at the premises of the *imprimeur-libraire* Giovanni Claudio Molini (1724–1812) and sold the marquess a fourteenth-century Dante and other manuscripts for £60.[43] By 27 April of that year the volume now known as the Hamilton Dante was in the possession of Molini, who ascribed its 88 full-page drawings to 'the hand of Botticelli or another draughtsman of that excellent period'.[44] The attribution was probably informed by Strutt's illustrated account of the artist's Dante engravings.

What would be later called the Hamilton Dante was reputedly made for one of Botticelli's principal patrons, Lorenzo di Pierfrancesco de' Medici – the younger cousin and ward of Lorenzo the Magnificent, who owned the *Primavera* (fig.1.30) and perhaps also *The Birth of Venus* (fig.1.0). It eschews the customary upright format of most manuscripts in favour of a horizontal layout, providing more space for multiple scenes expressive of the sequential, journey-like narrative of *The Divine Comedy*. The text was written in four columns, in humanist script, by the scribe Niccolò Mangona (active 1481–1503); one of the closing illustrations (*Paradiso*, XXVIII) is signed in tiny writing with Botticelli's proper name, 'Sandro di Mariano'. The manuscript remained uncompleted, and only a few of Botticelli's ethereal ink drawings were over-painted in colours. Seven illustrated leaves detached from the manuscript at an early date have since 1691 been at the Vatican Library, where they were catalogued in 1739 by the Benedictine scholar Bernard de Montfaucon (1655–1741).[45]

Although the whereabouts of the manuscript are undocumented prior to 1803, citations from it in works by Fuseli suggest it was also in Rome during the 1770s.[46] From 1797 the Napoleonic expropriation of works of art created a buyer's market in the papal capital, exploited by Ottley and many other dealers. During the Peace of Amiens in 1802–3 the arrival of numerous affluent British visitors in Paris offered propitious business opportunities for booksellers such as Molini, who co-operated with his brothers in Florence and London, as well as with other Italians. He probably sold the manuscript before 18 May 1803, when the resumption of hostilities between France and England severely reduced commerce until 1814, two years after his death. Sometime before July 1816 the manuscript was acquired by Douglas, perhaps through the agency of his dealer James Edwards or his future father in law, the opulent collector William Beckford (1760–1844), who had lived in Paris during the Peace.[47] He eventually owned no less than seven manuscripts of *The Divine Comedy*, plus a copy of the illustrated printed edition of 1481.[48]

Fuseli seems to have encountered this manuscript in Rome by August 1774, the date on his watercolour of *Dante and Virgil on the ice of Cocythus* (fig.2.3). In this work the protagonists are dwarfed by the immense truncated feet of giants, like those in the background of Botticelli's version of the subject (*Inferno*, XXXII, 17–18) (fig.2.4).[49] Another drawing by the Swiss artist, inscribed 'Roma 1777' and representing *Richard III Dreaming of the Ghosts of his Victims*, includes cowled, monk-like figures resembling the leaden-robed Hypocrites in Botticelli's *The Punishment of Hypocrites* and *The Punishment of Thieves* (*Inferno*, XXIII, XXIV).[50] After his return to London, during the 1780s, Fuseli painted a large picture of *A Midsummer Night's Dream* (Act IV, scene 1), now in the Tate Gallery. This combines a seductive figure of Titania based on the copy of Leonardo's lost *Leda and the Swan* in the Galleria Borghese, with tiny figures of elves diving into the calyx of a flower. The latter motif copies Botticelli's poetic interpretation of Dante's 'flowers and sparks changed before me' which make manifest 'the courts of heaven' (*Paradiso*, XXX, 94–6).[51]

It is unlikely that Fuseli recognised that the manuscript had been decorated by Botticelli, whose 'culinary abominations' he later disparaged in his account of the fifteenth-century frescoes on the side walls of the Sistine Chapel:

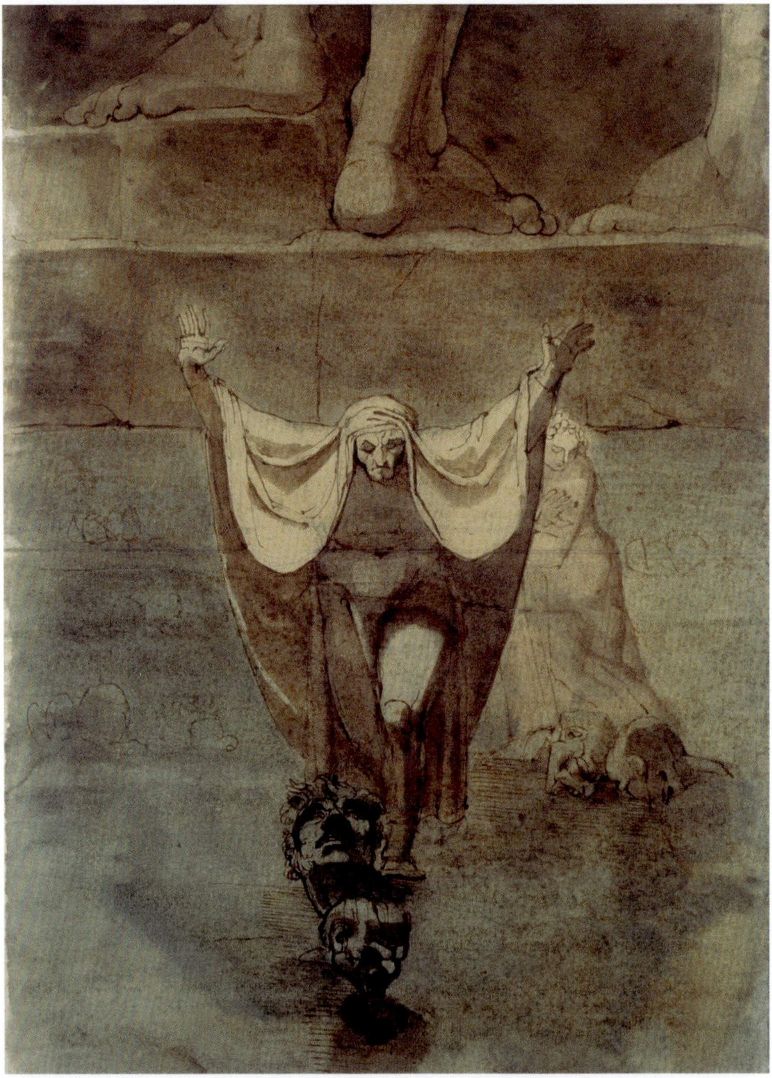

Fig.2.3 Henry Fuseli (1741–1825), *Dante and Virgil on the ice of Cocythus*; 'Inferno', canto XXXII, inscribed Roma Aug. 74 (1774), ink, sepia and watercolour, 43.7 × 31.2 cm, inv.1916/13, Kunsthaus, Zurich. © Kunsthaus Zürich.

> The superintendence [...] the Pope, with the usual vanity and ignorance of princes, gave to Sandro, the least qualified of the group, whose barbarous taste and dry minuteness palsied [...] his associates, and rendered the whole a monument of puerile ostentation, and conceits unworthy of its place.[52]

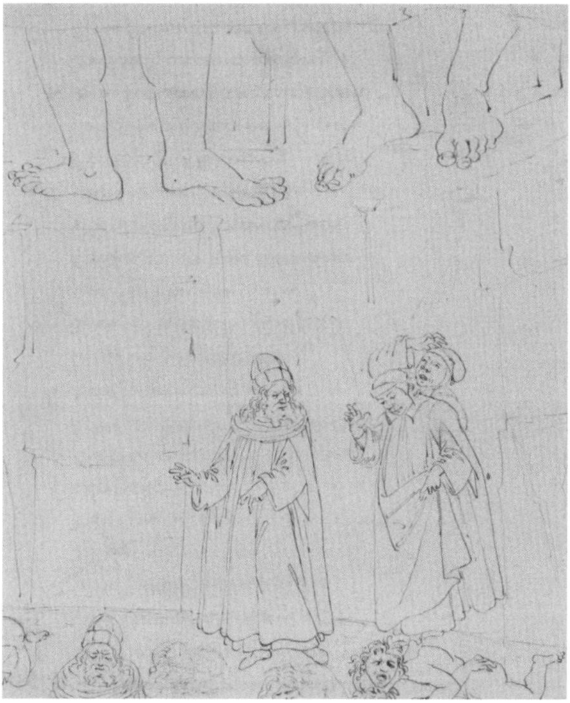

Fig.2.4 Sandro Botticelli, *Dante and Virgil on the ice of Cocythus*; 'Inferno', canto XXXII, 1490s, metalpoint and ink on vellum, cod. Hamilton 201, Kupferstichkabinett, Berlin (detail). © bpk / Kupferstichkabinett, SMB / Philipp Allard.

Fuseli's energetic compositions had a strong influence on the sculptor John Flaxman – a Swedenborgian whose fascination with mediaeval art rivalled that of his friend William Blake. Flaxman's mentors included William Hayley and George Romney, whose chaste classical style resembled his own. They encouraged him and his wife Ann to visit Rome, where the Flaxmans lived from 1787 to 1794. Sketches Flaxman made in Italy show that his interests extended to 'primitive' artists, such as Lorenzo Ghiberti and Luca Signorelli.[53] He went on sketching expeditions with William Ottley, whose drawings 'after the paintings and sculptures of the early Florentine school' were eventually published in 1826 as a volume of engravings dedicated to Flaxman.[54]

In Rome, Flaxman received commissions for statuary from the Earl Bishop of Bristol and Derry, and from the Anglo-Dutch banker, writer and collector Thomas Hope (1769–1831). Hope also paid him one guinea each for 109 outline drawings of the *Divine Comedy*, to be engraved by

Tomasso Piroli (1750–1824).[55] On 31 March 1792 Ann Flaxman wrote delightedly to Hayley announcing this 'Compleat set of drawings' of '*Your own dear Dante*, that old fashion crazy fellow with his [...] greasy Nightcap' who 'is all in fashion with the gay & Simple, & much beloved indeed by the discerning few'.[56]

Flaxman's contemporaries were alert to his characteristic method of assimilating figures and compositional devices from a wide range of sources, which caused the painter John Hoppner (1758–1810) to remark sourly in 1797 that his 'thoughts are all borrowed and purloined from a variety of things which he has seen. He has nothing original about him'.[57] In preparation for his commission to illustrate Dante, Flaxman acquired his own copy of *The Divine Comedy*, published by Antonio Zatta at Venice in 1784 and now in the British Institute at Florence.[58] However, its late Baroque vignettes by Cristoforo Dall'Acqua (1734–87) are utterly at odds with his neoclassical style, and had little influence on his designs, save for one of a demon 'burdened with the two legs of a sinner' (*Inferno*, XXI, 29–36).[59] Instead, his *Divine Comedy* illustrations incorporate appropriately archaic figures derived from Italian frescoes: Signorelli's *Last Judgement* in Orvieto Cathedral and a thirteenth-century depiction of *The Judgement of Count Henry* in the Roman Basilica of St Lawrence outside the Walls (San Lorenzo fuori le mura).[60]

Early in 1792 Flaxman and his wife visited the libraries of the Palazzo Barberini and the Vatican, where they found the librarian to be 'a civil and serviceable being'.[61] Six years later a highlight of their friend Mariana Starke's Vatican tour was the Duke of Urbino's copy of *The Divine Comedy*, 'adorned with exquisite paintings'.[62] Flaxman's Dante commission and his keen interest in early Italian art provided considerable incentive to study manuscripts of *The Divine Comedy* in the Vatican Library, where the leaves detached from the manuscript were readily identifiable as 'Dantis Aligherii Fragmentum cum figures' thanks to Montfaucon's catalogue.[63] That Flaxman perused these sheets is suggested by the spare and linear aesthetic of his Dante illustrations, and specifically by the balletic profile poses of the damned in his design of *The Punishment of the Sodomites* (fig.2.5), which closely resemble those in Botticelli corresponding scene (*Inferno*, XVI) (fig.2.6).[64]

At this time it is likely that Flaxman, like Fuseli two decades earlier, also viewed the manuscript itself later known as 'the Hamilton Dante'. Striking correspondences between his interpretations of Dante's text and Botticelli's may be listed:

1. Botticelli and Flaxman depict 'that foul image of Fraud' Geryon (*Inferno*, XVII, 1–27) as a Triton-like creature, lacking the

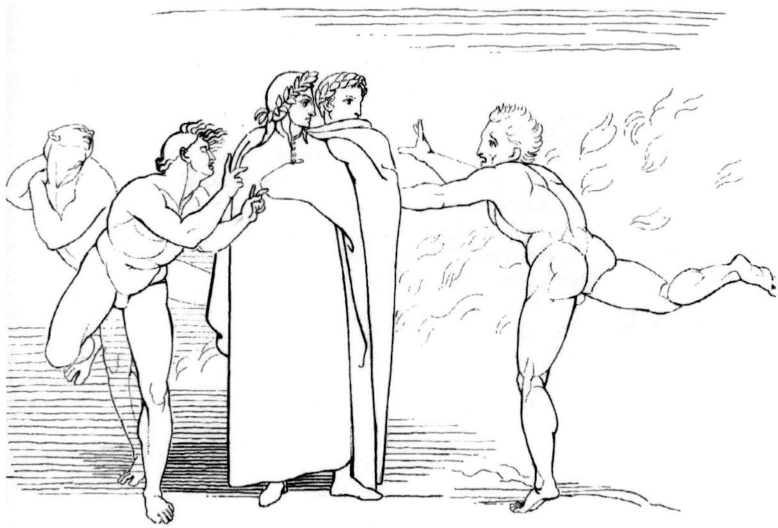

Fig.2.5 John Flaxman (1755-1826), *The Punishment of the Sodomites*; 'Inferno', canto XVI, 1807, ink on paper, 13.7 × 19.6 cm, Houghton Library, Harvard University, PF MS TYP 26.4, fol.19r. © Houghton Library, Harvard University.

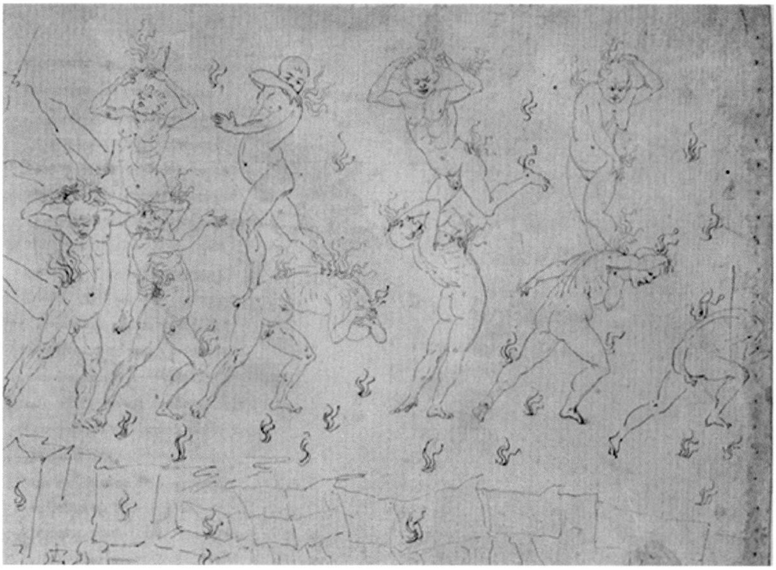

Fig.2.6 Sandro Botticelli, *The Punishment of the Sodomites*; 'Inferno', canto XVI, 1490s, metalpoint and ink on vellum, Biblioteca Apostolica Vaticana, cod.Reg. lat.1896, fol.98v (detail). © Vatican Library.

serpentine neck and bat's wings found in Dall'Acqua's vignette. Following Dante, both portray this hybrid creature with the face of a 'just man', nobly bearded and with flowing locks, but armed with leonine claws and a twisted tail with a 'venomous fork' and an 'armed point in the manner of a scorpion'.[65]

2. Flaxman's depiction of the torture of the corrupt servant Ciampolo by the demon Graffiacane (*Inferno*, XXII, 16–34) is based on a fresco in San Lorenzo fuori le mura.[66] Dante relates that the assailant 'grappled' his victim 'by his pitch-covered hair / And pulled him out' of the boiling pitch. Botticelli and Flaxman interpreted the remark that Ciampolo 'seemed to me like an otter' to mean that Grafficane hoisted his victim on an otter spear – a traditional hunting ritual depicted, for example, in the *Devonshire Hunting Tapestries* of 1425–50 and in a painting by Edwin Landseer of 1844.[67] Moreover, the agonised mask of Flaxman's Ciampolo closely resembles the screaming faces bobbing above the pitch in Botticelli's drawing.

3. Botticelli's and Flaxman's monk-like Hypocrites crush beneath their feet the high priest Caiaphas, condemned to lie 'crucified on the ground [...] naked' and 'obliged to feel the weight of everyone that has to pass' (*Inferno*, XXIII, 58–125). Unlike the published engraving, Flaxman's initial sketch of this subject also corresponded to Botticelli's drawing in depicting Caiaphas head-first, in extreme foreshortening.[68]

4. Dante describes the bridge over the final ditch of Malebolge (*Inferno*, XXIX, 25–72) as a *ponticello*, suggesting a modest structure resembling that in Dall'Acqua's vignette. Botticelli and Flaxman both depicted instead a massive span of Roman masonry, from which Dante and Virgil view the Falsifiers piled 'in [...] stacks', like ricks of hay.[69]

5. Dante describes the 'horrible giants', emerging waist-high from the well leading to the deepest point of Hell (*Inferno*, XXXI, 31–132), but Botticelli and Flaxman emphasise the nobility of these figures rather than their ferocity.[70] In 1504 Botticelli served on the Cathedral committee which advised on the location of Michelangelo's marble *David*, called 'The Giant' because of its huge size – a work that may have inspired both artists' depictions of this subject.

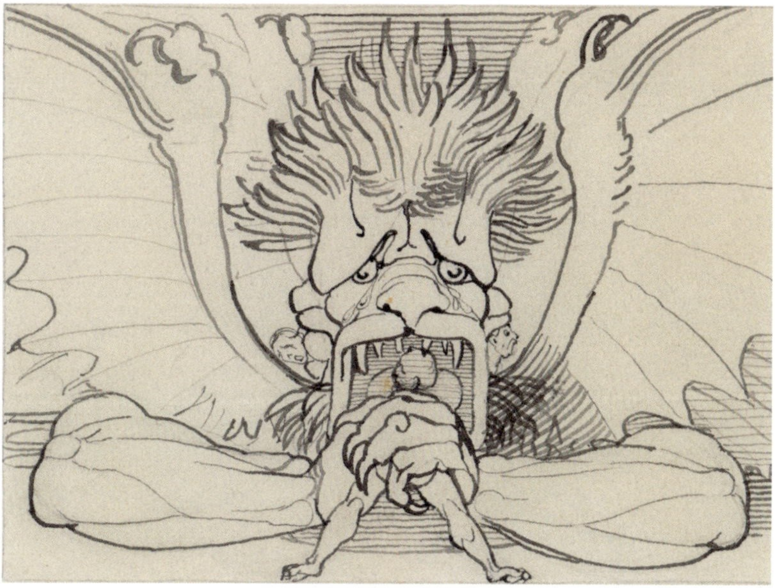

Fig.2.7 John Flaxman, *Lucifer*; 'Inferno', canto XXXIV, 1807, ink on paper, 13.9 × 19.5 cm, Houghton Library, Harvard University, PF MS TYP 26.4, fol.39r. © Houghton Library, Harvard University.

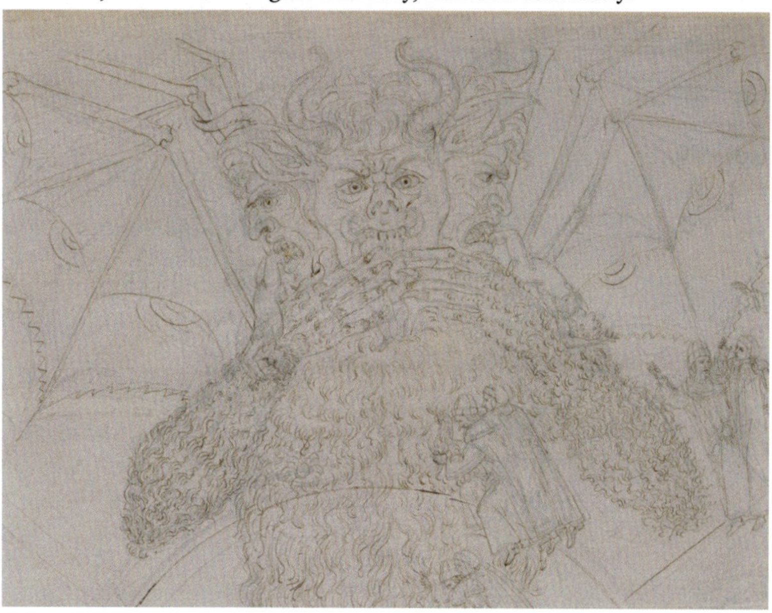

Fig.2.8 Sandro Botticelli, *Lucifer*; 'Inferno', canto XXXIV, 1490s, metalpoint and ink on vellum, cod.Hamilton 201, Kupferstichkabinett, Berlin (detail). © bpk / Kupferstichkabinett, SMB / Philipp Allard.

6. Dante describes Lucifer with 'half his chest sticking out of the ice' and emphasises his huge arms, 'three faces on his head' and 'great wings [...] like a bat's' (*Inferno*, XXXIV, 28–70). Flaxman's design (fig.2.7) has been likened to a fourteenth-century fresco at the Camposanto in Pisa, but his bust-length Lucifer, with forearms at right angles and elbows outwards, and clawed hands, more closely resembles Botticelli's drawing (fig.2.8).[71]

7. Dante describes how the Proud are condemned to bear a heavy rock on their necks, so they can only look down (*Purgatorio*, X, 112–39). Dall'Acqua shows them staggering past Dante and Virgil, who scrutinise an exemplary image of humility, 'The Justice of Trajan' (*Purgatorio*, X, 70–93). However, Flaxman's design (fig.2.9) and Botticelli's second illustration of this subject (fig.2.10) follow Dante's later passage, which likens the penitent souls to a figure with its 'knees [...] pressed up against his chest' supporting 'a floor or a roof' (*Purgatorio*, X, 130–2), like the anthropomorphic corbels found in medieval buildings.[72]

8. Flaxman and Botticelli portray the Lustful on the Seventh terrace of Purgatory with serpentine curlicues of flame embracing 'every shade [...] kissing one another' (*Purgatorio*, XXVI, 31–3).[73]

9. Dall' Acqua depicts Matilda showing Dante and Virgil the 'people dressed in white' singing "Hosanna" (*Purgatorio*, XXIX, 13–66). Botticelli and Flaxman represent instead the streamer-like illumination of the candles borne by the 24 elders: 'the flames [...] had the appearance of extended streamers [...] So that there remained seven bands Clearly marked [...] stretched [...] to the rear' (*Purgatorio*, XXIX, 73–9). Both depict the candlesticks with prominent drip-pans and embellish Dante's text by providing the elders with their books of the Old Testament, portrayed by Botticelli as codices and by Flaxman as classicising scrolls.[74]

The absence of similar citations from Flaxman's first ten designs 'in the beautiful Gothic taste' described by his wife on 31 March 1792 suggests that he viewed the manuscript between that date and 22 June 1793, when engraving of his designs was complete.[75] Access to the manuscript

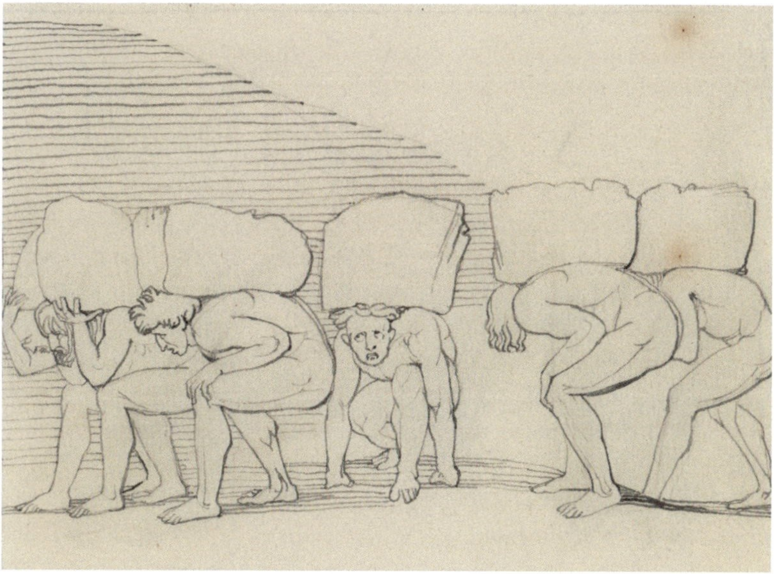

Fig.2.9 John Flaxman, *Penance of the proud*; 'Purgatorio', canto XI, 1807, ink on paper, 14 × 19.3 cm, Houghton Library, Harvard University, PF MS TYP 26.4, fol.55r. © Houghton Library, Harvard University.

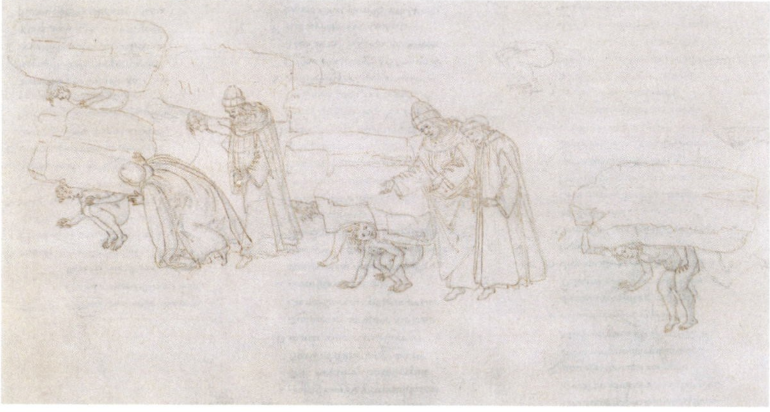

Fig.2.10 Sandro Botticelli, *Penance of the proud*; 'Purgatorio', canto XI, 1490s, metalpoint and ink on vellum, cod.Hamilton 201, Kupferstichkabinett, Berlin (detail). © bpk / Kupferstichkabinett, SMB / Philipp Allard.

could have been facilitated by his sketching partner William Ottley. Also a close friend of Fuseli, Ottley expressed his pleasure at following in the Swiss artist's footsteps by appending his own signature to the one Fuseli had left years earlier in a passage of graffiti on a fresco in Bologna.[76] Ottley's knowledge of the major Roman collections is evident in his acquisition of such paintings as Botticelli's *The Mystic Nativity*, Raphael's *Vision of a Knight,* Titian's *Holy Family with a Shepherd* and Garofalo's *Vision of St Augustine* from the Aldobrandini, Borghese and Corsini families; all are now in the National Gallery.[77] After returning to England he resumed socialising with Fuseli, and in 1803 accompanied him to see 'a few of *the* finest Pictures of the Italian School that ever came into the kingdom'.[78] Flaxman and Ottley were equally convivial, copying each other's sketches of primitives seen during their Italian travels.[79] A sense of this common endeavour between a 'discerning few', as Ann Flaxman put it, can be gained from the generous remark attributed to Fuseli after seeing the illustrations of *The Divine Comedy*: 'Now I confess that I hitherto thought myself the first composer, but I yield to F[laxman] as the greater man'.[80]

Before their popular rediscovery during the late Regency and in the mid-Victorian era, the linked fortunes of Dante and Botticelli were associated with a sequence of Whig cultural projects to do with Italian history. This was initiated by Gibbon's *Decline and Fall of the Roman Empire* (1776–89), consolidated with Roscoe's Medici biographies (1796, 1805) and concluded by the 5th Baron Vernon's lavish publications on Dante (1841–65).[81] Botticelli attracted notice as the illustrator of *The Divine Comedy*, but remained of marginal significance until Flaxman's encounter with the Florentine master's Dante drawings helped the sculptor to fashion a 'primitive' style appropriate to the archaic character of the medieval poem. His outline illustrations attained international celebrity, and were widely imitated. No less an authority than Goethe acknowledged Flaxman's 'gift of adopting the innocence of the older Italian school' while A. W. von Schlegel praised the imaginative freedom of his 'hieroglyphic-like' designs. [82] With such a pedigree, it was entirely fitting that by 1808–19 the outline style was being used by such Nazarene artists as Franz and Johannes Riepenhausen and Julius Schnorr von Carolsfeld to copy paintings by Botticelli.[83]

Acknowledgements

I was able to introduce the subject of this essay briefly in the exhibition catalogue; Mark Evans and Stefan Weppelmann ed., *Botticelli Reimagined* (London: V&A Publishing, 2016), 61, 244. Julius Bryant has since told me that he and David Bindman pondered this subject long ago, without pursuing it. I am grateful to Ana Debenedetti for the opportunity to do this here, and would also like to thank Adalbert Roth, Godfrey Evans and Mary McMahon for valuable assistance.

Notes

1 Cited in Michael Caesar, ed., *Dante. The Critical Heritage 1314(?)–1870* (London and New York: Routledge, 1989), 464–6.
2 David Bindman, Stephen Hebron and Michael O'Neill, *Dante Rediscovered. From Blake to Rodin*, exh. cat. (Grasmere: Wordsworth Trust, Dove Cottage, 2007), 4–8, 18–21, nos. 33–5; Nick Havely, *Dante's British Public. Readers and Texts, from the Fourteenth Century to the Present* (Oxford: Oxford University Press 2014), 135–7.
3 Cited in Caesar, *Dante*, 435–47.
4 Bindman, Hebron and O'Neill, *Dante Rediscovered*, 31–8, 57–8, 97, 206–7.
5 For Mariana Starke see Francis Haskell, *Rediscoveries in Art: some aspects of taste, fashion, and collecting in England and France* (Oxford: Phaidon Press, 1976), 107–8. For Flaxman's encounter with the *Madonna del Magnificat* see Hugh Brigstocke, 'Refocusing the Grand Tour: John Flaxman and the Reappraisal of Early Italian Painting and Sculpture' and 'Flaxman: The Fitzwilliam Journal', in *The Seventy-second Volume of the Walpole Society* (Leeds: Produced for Walpole Society by the Charlesworth Group 2010), 3, 89, 98, 106, 115.
6 See *Botticelli Reimagined*, 47–91, 186–245.
7 Havely, *Dante's British Public,* 50–3, 69–72.
8 Havely, *Dante*, 105–14.
9 Carol Gibson-Wood, *Jonathan Richardson. Art theorist of the English Enlightenment* (New Haven and London: Published for the Paul Mellon Centre for Studies in British Art by Yale University Press, 2000) 38–43. Richardson's portrait of Coke and his double portrait of his wife and son Edward are in the North State Bedroom at Holkham Hall.
10 Michael Levey, 'Botticelli and Nineteenth-Century England', *Journal of the Warburg and Courtauld Institutes* 23, nos. 3/4 (1960): 293; Jonathan Richardson, the senior and younger, *An Account of Statues, Bas-reliefs, Drawings and Pictures in Italy, France, &c. with remarks* (London: Printed for D. Browne, without Temple-Bar; J. Whiston and B. White, at Boyle's Head, and L. Davis, at Lord Bacon's Head, both in Fleet-street, 1754 [1st ed. 1722]), 49.
11 Levey, 'Botticelli', 293; Gibson-Wood, *Jonathan Richardson*, 96–7; Three drawings from Richardson's collection, formerly ascribed to Botticelli and now to Lorenzo di Credi and the circle of Filippino Lippi, are in the British Museum (1.24; 1895,0915.460; 1895,0915.462); A. E. Popham and Philip Pouncey, *Italian Drawings in the Department of Prints and Drawings in the British Museum. The Fourteenth and Fifteenth Centuries* (London: Trustees of the British Museum, 1950), 29–30, 86.
12 Jonathan Richardson, *Two Discourses, II, A Discourse on the Dignity, Certainty, Pleasure and Advantage, of the Science of a Connoisseur* (London, 1719) 26–35; Frances Yates, 'Transformations of Dante's Ugolino', *Journal of the Warburg and Courtauld Institutes,* vol.14 (1951): 92–117; Gibson-Wood, *Jonathan Richardson*, 200–1; Bindman, Hebron and O'Neill, *Dante Rediscovered*, 24–6.
13 This relief of Ugolino, thought to be by Michelangelo, was in fact by Pierino da Vinci, known in several versions.
14 John Hale, *England and the Italian Renaissance* (London: Fontana, 1996 [1954]), 36–45, 82–90; John Barrell, *The Political Theory of Painting from Reynolds to Hazlitt* (New Haven & London: Yale University Press, 1986), 1–13, 15, 32–3, 36–7, 69–76, 182–3.
15 British Museum (1885,0509.41); Popham and Pouncey, *Italian Drawings,* 149–50; Yates, 'Transformations', 106–7; Bindman, Hebron and O'Neill, *Dante Rediscovered,* 86–7, 90–1, nos. 11, 14.
16 Caesar, *Dante*, 385–7.
17 Gert Schiff, *Johann Heinrich Füssli 1741–1825* (Zurich and Munich: Prestel, 1973), 99–104, 437, 446–8, 490, 528, 530, 562, 589, 608, 639, 641, 653, nos. 361, 418–31, 720, 946, 959, 1200, 1398, 1537, 1799a, 1800, 1808, 76*.
18 Caesar, *Dante,* 53; Bindman, Hebron and O'Neill, *Dante Rediscovered,* 93, no.15.
19 *Catalogue of the Extensive Cabinet of Capital Drawings[...].collected with superior judgement by Charles Rogers Esq[...]*, Thomas Philipe, London, 15–24 April 1799 [Lugt 5901], lot 86: 'BOTTICELLI (Sandro, or Alessandro), 'A female holding an helmet and an olive branch – Indian ink, heightened with white – on the back is a lady's head – white and pencil, on a brown ground'.

20 Ashmolean Museum, Oxford (WA1863.613); Andreas Schumacher, ed., *Botticelli. Likeness, Myth, Devotion*, exh. cat., Städel Museum, Frankfurt am Main (Ostfildern: Hatje Cantz, 2009), 64, 67, 103–6.

21 Victor Chan, *Leader of my Angels. William Hayley and His Circle*, exh. cat. (Edmonton, Alberta: Edmonton Art Gallery, 1982), 9, 42; Bindman, Hebron and O'Neill, *Dante Rediscovered,* 3, 115, no.29.

22 Bindman, Hebron and O'Neill, *Dante Rediscovered,* 4, 111, 115–16, nos. 30–1; Gerard O'Brien, Hervey, Frederick Augustus (1730–1803), *Oxford Dictionary of National Biography*, Oxford University Press 2004–16; online edition, May 2009; http://www.oxforddnb.com/view/article/13111; accessed 28 April 2016.

23 Nicola F. Figgis, 'The Roman Property of Frederick Augustus Hervey, 4th Earl of Bristol and Bishop of Derry (1730–1803)', in *The Fifty-Fifth Volume of the Walpole Society 1989/90* (Leeds: Printed for the Walpole Society by W. S. Maney 1993), 77–103.

24 Bindman, Hebron and O'Neill, *Dante Rediscovered,* 115, no.30.

25 John Ingamells, *A Dictionary of British and Irish Travellers in Italy 1701–1800, compiled from the Brinsley Ford Archive* (New Haven and London: published for the Paul Mellon Centre for Studies in British Art by Yale University Press, 1997), 999–1000; John Rylands Library, Manchester, Spencer No.17280; Havely, *Dante*, 129, n.4.

26 Joseph Strutt, *Biographical Dictionary of Engravers*, London: 1785/6, vol.1, 14–15, 22–4, 55, 131–2 and pl.VII; vol.2, 16–17 and pl.III.

27 Strutt, 1785/6, vol.1, 23, 131; vol.2, 8–9.

28 Strutt, 1785/6, vol.1, 1–3.

29 Henry Roscoe, *The Life of William Roscoe* (London: Cadell, 1833), vol.1, 68–9; Emanuele Pellegrini, 'Between History and Art History: Roscoe's Medici Lives' and Xanthe Brooke, 'Roscoe's Italian Paintings in the Walker Art Gallery, Liverpool', in Stella Fletcher, ed., *Roscoe and Italy: the reception of Italian Renaissance history and culture in the eighteenth and nineteenth centuries* (Farnham: Ashgate, 2012), 32–3, 66; Donald A. MacNaughton, 'Roscoe, William (1753–1831)', *Oxford Dictionary of National Biography*, online edition, 2004–14; http://www.oxforddnb.com/view/article/24084 (accessed 16 October 2014).

30 Hugh Macandrew, 'Henry Fuseli and William Roscoe', *The Liverpool Bulletin*, vol.8 (1959–60): 5–52; Dongho Chun, '"Democratic Principles and Aristocratic Tastes": William Roscoe's Patronage and Art Collecting', *Transactions of the Historic Society of Lancashire and Cheshire,* vol.162 (2013), 107–35.

31 Pellegrini, 'Between History', 23–42; Francis Haskell, *History and its Images* (New Haven and London: Yale University Press, 1993), 209–14.

32 Cited in Roscoe, *The Life,* 162–4.

33 In the 'advertisement' to Roscoe's sale catalogue of 1816, cited in Michael Compton, 'William Roscoe and Early Collectors of Italian Primitives', *The Liverpool Bulletin*, vol.9 (1960–1): 29–33; Chun, 'Democratic Principles', 127–31.

34 John Knowles, *The Life and Writings of Henry Fuseli* (London: Henry Colburn and Richard Bentley, 1831), vol.1, 395; Nicholas Turner, 'Ottley, William Young (1771–1836)', *Oxford Dictionary of National Biography*, Oxford University Press 2004–16; online edition; http://www.oxforddnb.com/view/article/20941 (accessed 6 May 2016); E. K. Waterhouse, 'Some notes on William Young Ottley's Collection of Italian Primitives', in C. P. Brand, K. Foster & U. Limentani, eds., *Italian Studies presented to E.R. Vincent* (Cambridge: Heffer & Sons, 1962), 272–80; *The Mystic Nativity* is now in the National Gallery (inv.NG1034). Ottley also owned three fragments in tempera on linen of an *Adoration of the Magi*, formerly attributed to Filippino Lippi, but now to Botticelli (Fitzwilliam Museum, Cambridge, inv.910, 2888 and the Morgan Library, New York, inv.I, 5). He published an engraving of the bottom half of *The Mystic Nativity* in *A series of plates, engraved after the paintings and sculptures of the most eminent masters of the early Florentine School* (London, 1826), pl.L and an aquatint of one of the fragments in *The Italian School of Design* (London, 1823), pl. facing 14. See Hugh Brigstocke, 'A Series of Plates Engraved after the Paintings and Sculptures of the Most Eminent Masters of the Florentine School[...]by William Young Ottley, 1826', in *The Seventy-second Volume of the Walpole Society* (Leeds: Produced for Walpole Society by the Charlesworth Group 2010) 520, 571; *Botticelli Reimagined*, 59, 61, 248–9, 252–3, nos. 101, 104, 105.

35 Compton, 'William Roscoe', 42; Edward Morris and Martin Hopkinson, *Walker Art Gallery Liverpool. Foreign Catalogue: paintings, drawings, watercolour, tapestry, sculpture, silver, ceramics, prints, photographs*, Walker Art Gallery (Liverpool: Merseyside County Council,

1977), 100–1, 124–7, 205–6, 212–3, 251–2, 275–6; Brooke, 'Roscoe's Italian Paintings', 75–8, 90. See *Botticelli Reimagined*, 59, 61, 248–9, no.101.

36 *Catalogue of the very select and valuable library of William Roscoe Esq*, Mr. Winstanley, Marble Street, Liverpool, 19 August–3 September 1816, lot 999 [copy with prices in the Walker Art Gallery, Liverpool]; Corinna Salvadori Lonergan, 'Roscoe's Lorenzo: "Restorer of Italian Literature"', in Fletcher, *Roscoe and Italy*, 47.

37 *Catalogue of the genuine and entire collection of drawings and pictures, the property of William Roscoe Esq*, Mr. Winstanley, Marble Street, Liverpool, 23–8 September 1816 [Lugt 8970; copy with prices in the Rijksbureau voor Kunsthistorische Documentaties, The Hague], lots 39 and 40.

38 Roscoe, *The Life*, vol.2, 85–6; cited in Andrea M. Galdy, 'William Roscoe and Thomas Coke of Holkham', in Fletcher, *Roscoe and Italy*, 207.

39 Galdy in Fletcher, *Roscoe and Italy*, 208–10; A. N. L. Munby, *Connoisseurs and Medieval Miniatures 1750–1850* (Oxford: Clarendon Press, 1972), 68–71. Roscoe sold on *The Holkham Bible Picture Book* to Coke at its purchase price of £30. When he was obliged to sell *The Bible of Clement VII* for £178 at his auction in 1816, he induced its purchasers to sell it to Coke at a modest markup of 200 guineas. Both works are now in the British Library, as Add. MS. 47682 and 47672.

40 William Clarke, *Repertorium Bibliographicum; or some account of the most celebrated British Libraries*, London 1819, pp.257–64; Godfrey Evans, 'The Hamilton Collection and the 10th Duke of Hamilton', *Journal of the Scottish Society for Art History*, vol.8 (2003), 53–72.

41 Cited in Roscoe, *The Life*, 188–9.

42 Cited in D. S. Chambers, 'William Roscoe's *Life of Leo* X and Correspondence with Angelo Fabroni', in Fletcher, *Roscoe and Italy*, 138.

43 This is mentioned in correspondence between Edwards and Douglas, now in the Hamilton archive, for which information I am most grateful to Dr Godfrey Evans; personal communication, dated 9 June 2016. Originally from Florence, Molini had been based in Paris since 1763; Luigi Greco, 'Un libraire italien à Paris à la veille de la Révolution', in *Mélanges de l'Ecole française de Rome. Italie et Méditerranée*, vol.102, no.2 (1990), 261–80.

44 This is shown by Molini's signed and dated label inside the binding of the manuscript now known by Douglas's later title as 10th Duke of Hamilton; Hein-Thu. Schulze Altcappenberg, ed., *Sandro Botticelli. The Drawings for Dante's Divine Comedy*, exh. cat. (London: Royal Academy, 2000), 20–2; Dagmar Korbacher, ed., *Botticelli and Treasures from the Hamilton Collection*, exh. cat., Courtauld Gallery, London (London: Paul Holberton Publishing, 2016), 15–17.

45 Part of a miscellany once owned by Queen Christina of Sweden, these leaves were catalogued by Montfaucon as 'Dantis Aligherii Fragmentum cum figures' in his *Bibliotheca Bibliothecarum manuscriptorum nova*, published at Paris in 1739; *Les manuscrits de la reine de Suède au Vatican. Réédition du catalogue de Montfaucon et cotes actuelles* (Biblioteca Apostolica Vaticana, 1964), 15, no.183 (Reg. lat. 1896).

46 Schiff, *Johann Heinrich Füssli*, 99, 102, 447, 493–5; Victor Chan, 'Blake, Goya, Flaxman, Romney and Fuseli: Transcriptions and Transformations of a Dantesque Image', *Arts Magazine*, vol.55, (1981): 82.

47 William Clarke visited Douglas and compiled a list of his manuscripts in July 1816, in preparation for his published account of the library, which mentions the Hamilton Dante, which appeared in 1819; Clarke, *Repertorium Bibliographicum*, 257–64.

48 Havely, *Dante*, 243–5.

49 A version inscribed 'Roma Aug. 74' in the Kunsthaus, Zurich, inv. no.1916/13, and another in the British Museum, 1885,0314.267; Schiff, *Füssli* (note 17), p.447. nos. 425, 426; Bindman, Hebron and O'Neill, *Dante Rediscovered*, 148–9, no.50; Schulze Altcappenberg, *Sandro Botticelli*, 122–3; *Botticelli Reimagined*, 58–9.

50 British Museum (1885,0314.270); Chan, 'Blake, Goya', 82; Schulze Altcappenberg, *Sandro Botticelli*,100–3.

51 Tate Gallery, NO 1228; Schiff, *Johann Heinrich Füssli*, 495. no.753; Schulze Altcappenberg, *Sandro Botticelli*, 282–3.

52 John Knowles, ed., *The Life and Writings of Henry Fuseli* (London: Henry Colburn and Richard Bentley, 1831), vol.3, 183; cited in *Botticelli Reimagined*, 58.

53 David Irwin, *John Flaxman 1755–1826* (London: Studio Vista, 1979), 31–42; Brigstocke, 'Refocusing the Grand Tour', 3–24.

54 Brigstocke, 'William Young Ottley in Italy' and 'A Catalogue of Drawings after Early Florentine Paintings and Sculpture made by William Young Ottley in Italy', in *Walpole Society*, 341–69.
55 Irwin, *John Flaxman*, 53–8, 94. Francesca Salvadori et al., ed., *John Flaxman. The Illustrations for Dante's Divine Comedy* (London: Royal Academy of Arts, 2005).
56 Cited in G. E. Bentley Jr. 'Flaxman in Italy: A Letter Reflecting the Anni Mirabiles, 1792–3', *The Art Bulletin* 63, no.4 (Dec.1981), 660.
57 A remark recorded in Joseph Farington's diary entry of 11 January 1797, cited by Sarah Symmons, 'The Spirit of Despair: Patronage, Primitivism and the Art of John Flaxman', *The Burlington Magazine* 117, no.871 (Oct. 1975), 648.
58 Charlotte Miller, 'John Flaxman's working copy of Dante's *Divina Commedia*', *Italian Studies*, vol.58, 75–87, published online: 29 November 2013.
59 Salvadori, *John Flaxman*, 19–21.
60 Eckart Marchand, 'Flaxman: V&A Sketchbook 2790', in *Walpole Society*, 308, 332, fig.44; Salvadori, *John Flaxman*, 28–9, 164–5; Symmons, 'The Spirit of Despair', 648 (where the fresco in San Lorenzo is misidentified as *The Last Judgement*).
61 Mentioned in Ann Flaxman's latter of 31 March 1792, cited by Bentley, 'Flaxman in Italy', 659.
62 Mariana Starke, *Travels in Italy between the years 1792 and 1798* (London: Printed for R. Phillips, St. Paul's Church Yard; by T. Gillet, Salisbury-Square, 1802), vol. 2, 6. She describes the Urbino Dante (Biblioteca Apostolica Vaticana, Urb. Lat. 365) as 'begun by the Florentine School, and finished by Giulio Claudio' (i.e. Clovio). It was actually begun in the 1470s by the Ferrarese Matteo Contugi and completed by an anonymous seventeenth-century artist; Schulze Altcappenberg, *Sandro Botticelli*, 314–5.
63 For Montfaucon's catalogue see note 45 above.
64 Schulze Altcappenberg *Sandro Botticelli*, 78–9; Salvadori, *John Flaxman*, 84–5.
65 Schulze Altcappenberg *Sandro Botticelli*, 82–3; Salvadori, *John Flaxman*, 86–7.
66 See note 60 above.
67 Schulze Altcappenberg, *Sandro Botticelli*, 96–7; Salvadori, *John Flaxman*, 98–9. French or Flemish, *c.*1425–50, *The Otter and the Swan Hunt*, Victoria and Albert Museum, T.203-1957; Linda Wooley, *Medieval Life and Leisure in the Devonshire Hunting Tapestries* (London: V&A Publications, 2002), 30; Edwin Landseer, *The Otter Speared, portrait of the Earl of Aberdeen's Otterhounds*, Laing Art Gallery, Newcastle upon Tyne, TWCMS: B8130; Richard Ormond, *Sir Edwin Landseer*, exh. cat., Philadelphia Museum of Art and Tate Gallery (London: Thames and Hudson, 1981), 184–7.
68 Schulze Altcappenberg, *Sandro Botticelli*,100–1; Salvadori, *John Flaxman*, 100–1.
69 Schulze Altcappenberg, *Sandro Botticelli*, 116–17; Salvadori, *John Flaxman*, 112–13.
70 Schulze Altcappenberg, *Sandro Botticelli*, 120–1; Salvadori, *John Flaxman*, 116–17.
71 Irwin, *John Flaxman*, 96–7; Schulze Altcappenberg, *Sandro Botticelli*, 128–9; Salvadori, *John Flaxman*, 126–7.
72 Schulze Altcappenberg *Sandro Botticelli*, 156–61; Salvadori, *John Flaxman*,162–3.
73 Schulze Altcappenberg, *Sandro Botticelli*, 192–3; Salvadori, *John Flaxman*, 192–3.
74 Schulze Altcappenberg, *Sandro Botticelli*, 200–1; Salvadori, *John Flaxman*, 198–9.
75 *Botticelli Reimagined*, 61, n.36; cited in Bentley, 'Flaxman in Italy', 661.
76 Ottley's artistic style was based on that of Fuseli and he contributed an appreciative essay to the latter's posthumous biography; Brigstocke, 'William Young Ottley', 342, 357; Knowles, *The Life and Writings*, 422–7.
77 Turner, 'Ottley, William Young'; Brigstocke, 'William Young Ottley', 352; National Gallery inv. nos. 1034, 213, 4, 81.
78 Brigstocke, 'William Young Ottley', 342, 358, n.1.
79 Brigstocke, 'Ottley', 342.
80 Letter of Henry Crabb-Robinson, 17 January 1811, cited by Sarah Symmons, *Flaxman and Europe. The Outline Illustrations and their Influence* (London: Garland Publishing, 1984), 46.
81 Hale, *England*, 82–3; H. R. Tedder, 'Warren, George John, fifth Baron Vernon (1803–66)', rev. Alison Millbank, *Oxford Dictionary of National Biography*, online edition, 2004–14; http://www.oxforddnb.com/view/article/28242 (accessed 16 January 2017).
82 Irwin, *John Flaxman*, 95, Symmons, *Flaxman and Europe*, 204, 231.
83 See *Botticelli Reimagined*, 61, 240–1.

6. Befriending Botticelli: psychology and connoisseurship at the fin de siècle

Francesco Ventrella

> 'Perhaps no painter of the Renaissance has so peculiar a fascination for modern minds.'
>
> Julia Cartwright[1]

'An Anglo-Saxon fad'

In a lecture addressed to the Sorbonne in 1897, art critic Léon Rosenthal declared that the Botticelli infatuation had happened so fast that it would not be surprising if '*le krach des Botticellis*' were to be announced in a few days.[2] 'No article in the *Vie Parisienne* is complete without a reference to Botticelli, actresses do their hair à la Botticelli, so we have little *Botticellistes*' (fig.2.11).[3] The social critic Max Nordau had picked up on the vogue for women to cut their hair 'after the fashion of the fifteenth century, as may be seen in the young knights and pages of Gentile

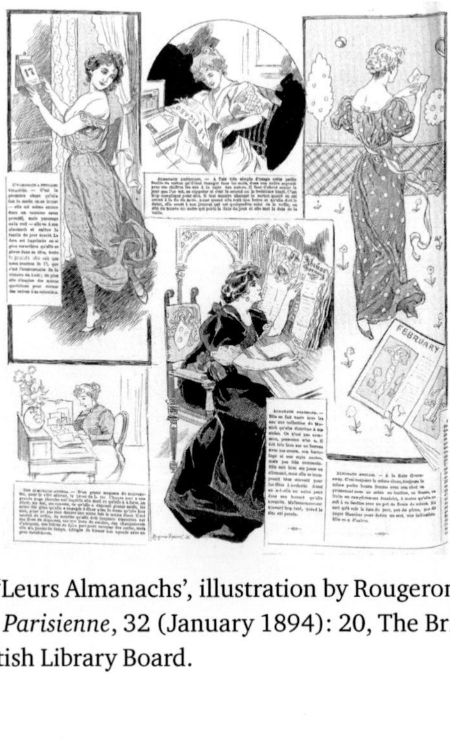

Fig.2.11 Bac, 'Leurs Almanachs', illustration by Rougeron Vignerot, (detail), *La Vie Parisienne*, 32 (January 1894): 20, The British Library, London. © British Library Board.

Bellini, Botticelli and Mantegna'.[4] For him, these trends represented the 'symptoms' of degeneration in fin-de-siècle European culture. The name of Botticelli could not only conjure up modern definitions of self and identity, but also point to signs of decadence.

The Botticelli consumed by popular culture was not separate from the Botticelli who art historians and connoisseurs were trying to identify, purify and separate from copyists, workshop and followers. Indeed Botticelli seems unique among old masters in his capacity to generate new ideas for different kinds of scholarship. He became a foil for testing the most diverse methodological approaches: imaginary criticism, philology, iconology and, above all, connoisseurship.[5] According to Constance Jocelyn Ffoulkes, her mentor Giovanni Morelli, the father of the 'new criticism', had arrived at his modern method of attribution by comparing the hands and ears of Botticelli with those of his disciple Filippino Lippi.[6] Following on from Morelli, in 1899 Bernard Berenson coined the artistic personality 'Amico di Sandro', an anonymous painter whose work occupied the space between Botticelli and Filippino (fig.2.12). Amico was the product of an experimental moment in art historiography, which witnessed the creation of many other *noms de commodité*.[7] Berenson announced that he had been able to reconstruct Amico's artistic personality by looking solely at the works and not at documents.[8]

> Considering our Anonimo's close following upon Sandro, in default a well-established historical name for him, we shall do well to call him AMICO DI SANDRO, for whatever were his relations in real life to Botticelli – an imitator is not always a friend! – in art, he was Sandro's companion.[9]

Berenson does not define Amico as a Botticellian type, but literally christens a singular and independent personality. In reconstructing Amico's *corpus*, he gives the artist's body and personal relations to Botticelli presence by furnishing him with specific psychological traits: 'He reveals a gayer, more easy-going temperament than Sandro's. He does not take his art at all so earnestly, is something of an improviser[...]'[10] These passages endorse Jeremy Melius's convincing suggestion that Berenson's scientific approach to the study of Amico di Sandro betrayed a 'reflex' that had bodily foundations, chiefly expressed in the continual recourse to psychological ideas in his writings.[11] But what were the cultural symptoms that informed the psychologising of art history at this time? In this essay I suggest that for Berenson Botticelli displayed some specific psychological qualities which spoke directly to his identity.

pino ; mais il est courant chez Amico. Ici, les draperies paraissent quelquefois comme mouillées et rappellent les panneaux d'Esther

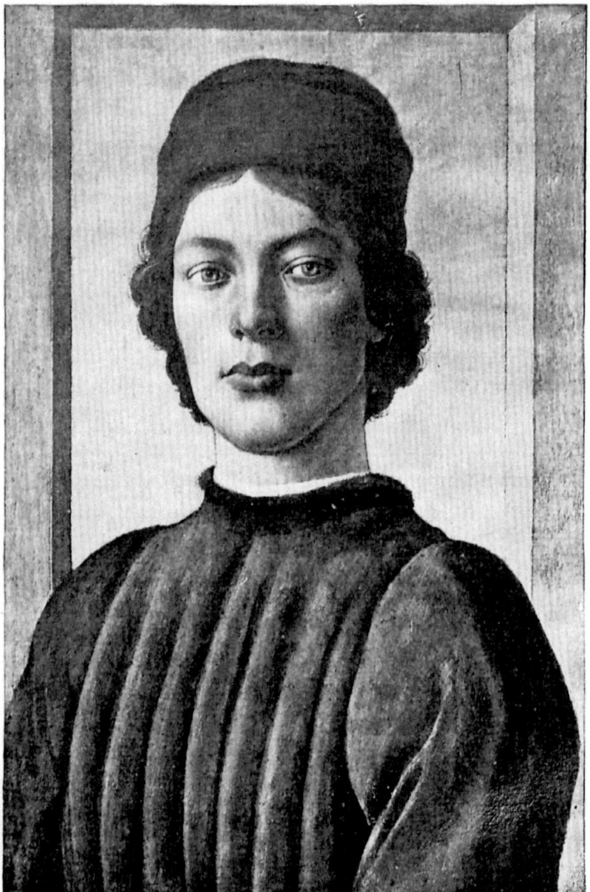

PORTRAIT DE JEUNE HOMME

(Galerie Liechtenstein, Vienne.)

par Amico. Même les mains (celles des anges, à gauche) offrent une singulière ressemblance avec celles de la Madone d'Amico à Berlin.

Ce sont là autant de témoignages des obligations de Filippino au peintre plus âgé que lui. Mais les autres anges, l'Enfant et la disposition générale des draperies, tout en n'étant pas exactement semblables

XXII. — 3e PÉRIODE. 5

Fig.2.12 Page from Bernard Berenson's '*Amico di Sandro*', *Gazette des Beaux-Arts*, 22 (July 1899): 33. Warburg Institute Library, London. © Warburg Institute.

As is well known, Berenson explained the way in which artists influence each other by looking at the psychology of habit and the platonic aesthetics of personality that he drew respectively from his tutor at Harvard, William James,[12] and from the texts of Walter Pater.[13] His early definition of an artistic personality as a plastic subjectivity that could be modelled and remodelled represents the major innovation of his connoisseurship in its intertwining of modern psychology and Paterian aesthetics. Patrizia Zambrano has aptly summarised this by stating that Berenson's essay on Amico di Sandro 'appears to our eyes as one of the most significant examples of psychological art history à la Pater to which, mixed with the Morellian method that he also embraced, Berenson remained loyal for his entire life'.[14] Pater imagined the task of the modern critic to be about distinguishing the specific 'sensations' he experienced in front of a picture, a landscape or a 'personality in life or in a book', in a manner akin to how 'a chemist notes some natural element'.[15] Within his rich aesthetic prose, Pater was displaying an early commitment to questions of consciousness and the psychological reality of sensations that William James had started to try out in his classroom, and that Berenson would later elaborate in his theory of tactile values.[16]

In this essay I will look at the years preceding the publication of the essay 'Amico di Sandro' in order to propose that Berenson's emphasis on the 'artistic personality' of Botticelli and his specific appreciation of the 'quality' of Botticelli's line (which paves the way for the theorisation of the 'tactile values') must be investigated in the context of the popularisation of the Botticellian type (disseminated since the Pre-Raphaelites). Drawing on a number of unpublished manuscripts and letters from the Mary and Bernard Berenson Archive, I demonstrate that the Anglo-Saxon infatuation with Botticelli's types represented a vexing methodological problem for Berenson, reflected in a middle-class consumer culture equally preoccupied with style and identity, physiognomy and psychology. Berenson's own engagement with psychological thinking cannot be disentangled from the social implications his ideas may have had in the context of decadence and degeneration. For Mary Costelloe, Berenson's future wife, the old scholarship on Botticelli was the symptom of an 'Anglo-Saxon fad' which required the renewal offered by scientific criticism.[17] Thus I suggest that Berenson's persistent critique of the typological method in connoisseurship directed him towards psychology, by which he constructed an argument about Botticelli's personality, but was also provided with the tools to deconstruct the way in which he may have been perceived as 'other' – both as a social outsider and as a Jew.

In the first part of the essay I consider how Berenson came to know Botticelli through readings of the aesthetics of Walter Pater and Vernon Lee. In the second part I show how competition with another Botticelli scholar, Hermann Ulmann, informed the novelty of Berenson's argument about Botticelli's personality. Finally I examine how Berenson's engagement with Botticelli's identity was developed in a dialogue with himself. Ernest Samuels, Berenson's biographer, has noted that his fashioning for himself of a new identity – 'the garment of Christianity' which he put on as a convert and as a scholar of Renaissance art – would not protect him from the anti-Semitism of the culture around him.[18] For the art historian Meyer Schapiro, Berenson's quest for the identity of artists and creative personalities was a transposition of the 'troubling' question about his own identity.[19] Building on these important remarks, this essay interrogates the identity of Botticelli for Berenson by taking into account the cultural anxieties of his time.

Befriending Botticelli: personality and influence

When Berenson arrived in Florence in spring 1889, he found a city crowded with middle-class tourists enthused by the writings of Walter Pater, John Ruskin and Vernon Lee. Growing up in Boston in a Jewish family that had moved from Lithuania when he was 10, Berenson had a gift and passion for languages; later, as a student at Harvard, he read Sanskrit, Hebrew and Aramaic. During this period he was introduced to 'the sacred word Botticelli' in a lecture given by Edmund Gosse in 1884, after which he 'went at once and bought himself a reproduction of Botticelli's "Primavera"'.[20] It was at university too that he discovered and became infatuated with Pater's *Studies in the History of the Renaissance*, a predilection to which his tutors William James and Charles Eliot Norton objected at the time.[21] Pater made a lasting impression. Writing to Mary Costelloe in 1890, Berenson tells her he was reading *The Renaissance* again in order to solve the riddle of how to translate aesthetic sensations into words:

> I still question whether it is at all possible to communicate a feeling for art to people except by personal contact[...] the real feeling with which a picture inspires me. The feeling is so wonderful, so delicate, so subtle, that I scarcely can define it to myself, not in language, but in other, more usual states of feeling.[22]

In his influential 'Fragment on Botticelli' (1870) Pater argued that the artist's work had a faculty to 'convey to us a peculiar quality of pleasure which we cannot get elsewhere'.[23] Our contact with an old master is mediated by the artwork which becomes the external manifestation or 'expression' of the artist's personality – thus Pater famously interpreted Buffon's aphorism *'le style c'est l'homme même'*.[24] It was according to this principle that Pater explained the interchangeability between artwork and personality, both and at once receptacle and transmitter.[25] This ability of the artwork to trigger physical sensations that equip life, both morally and – more importantly for him – physically, is an idea that shaped Berenson's theoretical imagination deeply.[26] Yet it was an idea he would not elaborate until 20 years later, when Pater's 'wistful' angels and 'peevish-looking Madonnas' had already entered the sphere of degeneration described by Nordau, and art historians such as Hermann Ulmann and Aby Warburg had committed themselves to a philological approach to purge Botticelli from the effeminate residues of aestheticism.

When Berenson arrived in Oxford, via Paris, at the beginning of a European grand tour sponsored by Isabella Stewart Gardner and a syndicate of wealthy Bostonians, he immediately mingled with the aesthetic crowd, including Lionel Johnson and fellow Bostonian Ned Warren, who were attending Pater's classics lectures.[27] At this time Berenson considered himself, and was seen by others, as a linguist: 'Berenson charmed Oxford for a term and vanished, leaving behind a memory of exotic epigrams,' wrote Johnson in a letter to their common friend George Santayana.[28] Johnson seems to register the difference of Berenson's interests by exoticising the student of ancient oriental languages.

Berenson was not admitted to the charmed circle. Pater explained that his lectures were not open to the public, and the course was in any case drawing to an end.[29] However, the European art galleries and the encounter with the Oxford classicists had a massive impact on the young graduate. Writing from Oxford to his sister Senda, he explained that his interests were moving away from literature:

> I am going through a stage of almost ferocious hatred towards all things literary. I can not [*sic*] bear to read and I have nothing to say worth reading. Yesterday I received a pile of Jewish books, and merely to look them over made me sick to fainting. I made up my mind, then and there, to toy no more with things Jewish and Oriental. I have wasted enough of my life and energy upon them already. Would I had put it all into Latin and Greek. If I had a boy to educate, he should never hear of Sanskrit, Hebrew, Assyrian, or any of those barbarous jargons. He should know his classics and his English by heart, and I should take care that until a certain age he should know nothing else.[30]

The disowning of Jewish heritage is a complicated issue in Berenson's training as a connoisseur. This passage seems to signal an opportunity to change his identity, reflecting the aesthetic opposition between Greeks and Jews which, as Éric Michaud suggests, was essential to the construction of modern cultural anti-Semitism.[31] The close study of the Italian Renaissance mediated for Berenson a sort of aesthetic assimilation. By the time he visited Oxford, Berenson had already become a convert to both Protestantism and aestheticism. Both were functional to his objective to live artistically. Like other Americans who embraced the Renaissance as a way of life (Isabella Stewart Gardner, Edith Wharton and Henry Adams, for instance), Berenson found and founded in the pleasures of Italian art a humanist retreat from the clatter of industrialised modernity. However, as Rachel Cohen aptly points out with reference to his Jewish identity, unlike his friends, 'Bernard Berenson was in physical, irremediable exile from his personal history'.[32]

Once the decision was taken to dedicate himself to Italian art, Berenson decided to settle in Florence to be close to his objects of study.[33] His second address there, Villa Kraus, had nothing of the grandeur, let alone the art collection, of the future Villa I Tatti. It may have looked like any other aesthetic interior decorated by the young generation of the Yellow Nineties. When the poet duo Michael Field (Katherine Bradley and Edith Cooper) house-sat for Berenson in April 1895, they sketched a plan of his study to document his gallery of prints and photographic reproductions after Melozzo, Leonardo, Giorgione, Bellini and Timoteo Viti, at the time he was working on the *Florentine Painters* (fig.2.13).[34] Right above a walnut photographic cabinet, hung on a wall covered in 'stretched brown sacking' next to Signorelli's *Pan*, was a print of Botticelli's *Primavera* – probably the one that Berenson had purchased in Boston 10 years earlier.[35]

Villa Kraus was part of the *podere* of Villa Rosa, where Mary Costelloe resided when in Florence. The working collaboration with Costelloe is instrumental to understanding the evolution of Berenson's scholarship in these early years; their relationship developed alongside their interest in Botticelli.[36] In her unpublished biography of Berenson, Costelloe tells us that he started to approach Botticelli at the end of 1890. Botticelli was 'an everlasting rebuke to people that want to submit art to newspaperology,' he intimated, adding 'There is nothing to be said about the Primavera.' Wrestling with the problem of aesthetic expression, Berenson claimed that the 'Primavera seems to me the greatest proof of what to me is so clear, that painting is a distinct manner of expression, and untranslatable', though he allowed that music could achieve this task: 'a

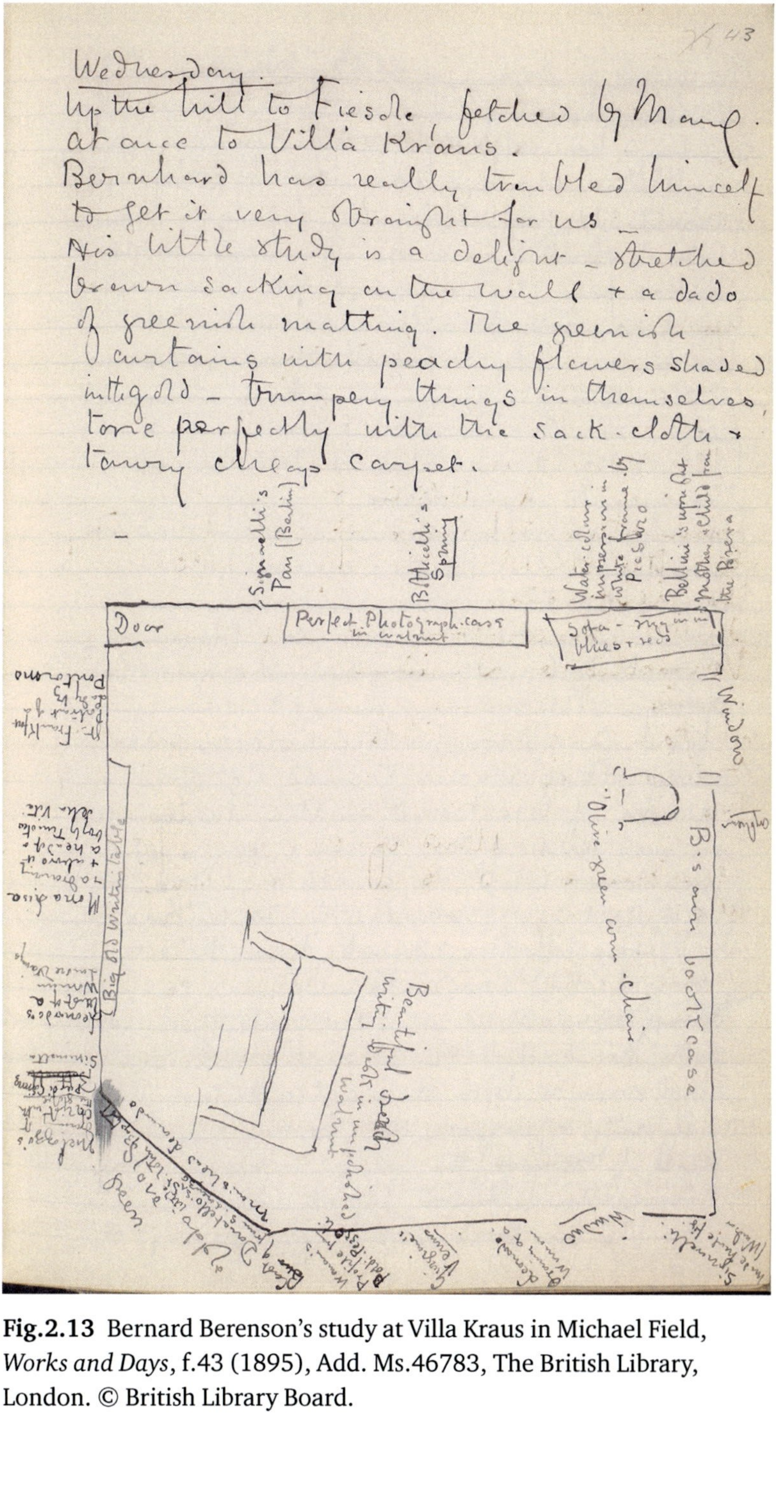
Wednesday.
Up the hill to Fiesole fetched by Mary. at once to Villa Kraus. Bernhard has really troubled himself to get it very straight for us – His little study is a delight – stretched brown sacking on the wall + a dado of greenish matting. The greenish curtains with peachy flowers shaded into gold – trumpery things in themselves tone perfectly with the sack-cloth + tawny cheap carpet.

Fig.2.13 Bernard Berenson's study at Villa Kraus in Michael Field, *Works and Days*, f.43 (1895), Add. Ms.46783, The British Library, London. © British Library Board.

symphony of Beethoven's let us say, but very different of course. I almost feel as if I could set it to music!'[37] Berenson perceived the modernity of Botticelli, although he was not yet able to express it fully. His turning of painting into music echoes Pater's famous idea that 'all art constantly aspires towards the condition of music', which was also an invitation to focus on the abstract qualities in a work of figurative art.[38] These problems would reveal to him the right path towards a novel interpretation of Botticelli's line as the single characteristic that the connoisseurs must apprehend as the test for a correct attribution.

Berenson initially struggled with Botticelli, and Costelloe's biography details the moody uncertainties he expressed in his letters at the time: 'Don't think I am going back on him, but at the same time I feel sure that about nine-tenths of the admiration he gets now is on false grounds. I would rather his admirers were fewer but truer.'[39] Although Pater had tried to describe Botticelli's personality as temperament, Berenson was also interested in ascertaining his identity.[40] The detective task of distinguishing between genuine and non-genuine works in fact informed his other conversion to Morellian connoisseurship.[41] Tackling Botticelli's iconic status intimidated the young art critic, but this was perhaps the very reason why Costelloe insisted he should pursue a serious study of the artist. In March 1893 Berenson and Costelloe re-read Pater's 'Botticelli' together.[42] That year, with her assistance, he finally started methodically to collect materials for a piece of writing on the artist, and in July he gave a lecture on his work in London – one of a series of 10 on Italian masters that provided much-needed income.[43]

In these early years in Florence, Berenson found in Vernon Lee (Violet Paget) the closest intellectual who had absorbed Pater's influence. A member of the aesthetic circles in London during the 1880s, Lee is still considered one of Pater's most successful disciples.[44] In the introduction to her Botticelli monograph of 1904, Julia Cartwright rightly listed Vernon Lee alongside Walter Pater and John Addington Symonds, in the first influential generation of writers on the master.[45] Our understanding of the intellectual friendship between Berenson and Lee has been clouded by the infamous accusation of plagiarism that Berenson levelled against her in 1897 concerning the sharing of their research on psychological aesthetics.[46] However, it is undeniable that in his early years in Florence he benefitted enormously from the dialogue with Lee and her network.[47] In spite of some unflattering descriptions of her presence and personality, Berenson typically respected Lee's authority.[48]

An undated note by Costelloe, possibly written after 1900, gives a colourful snapshot of their intellectual involvements 10 years earlier:

> Vernon was one of the most enthralling talkers I ever met – as well as at times one of the most irritating. I remember in particular one afternoon when she came to have tea in Bernard's room on the Lungarno and began to talk to us about Botticelli. Now we had laughed a good deal about her printed remarks on Botticelli, – his 'half-ravished angels' and the rest of her absurdities – but when she spoke of him that day, she spoke with the voice of an angel, neither holy nor 'half-ravished'. My husband sat at her feet like a little boy, drinking in her words.[49]

The 'half-ravished angels' derive from a description by Lee of the *Madonna of the Pomegranate* in the Uffizi (fig.2.14); it features in one of her most successful pieces of writing on Botticelli, 'Botticelli at the Villa Lemmi'

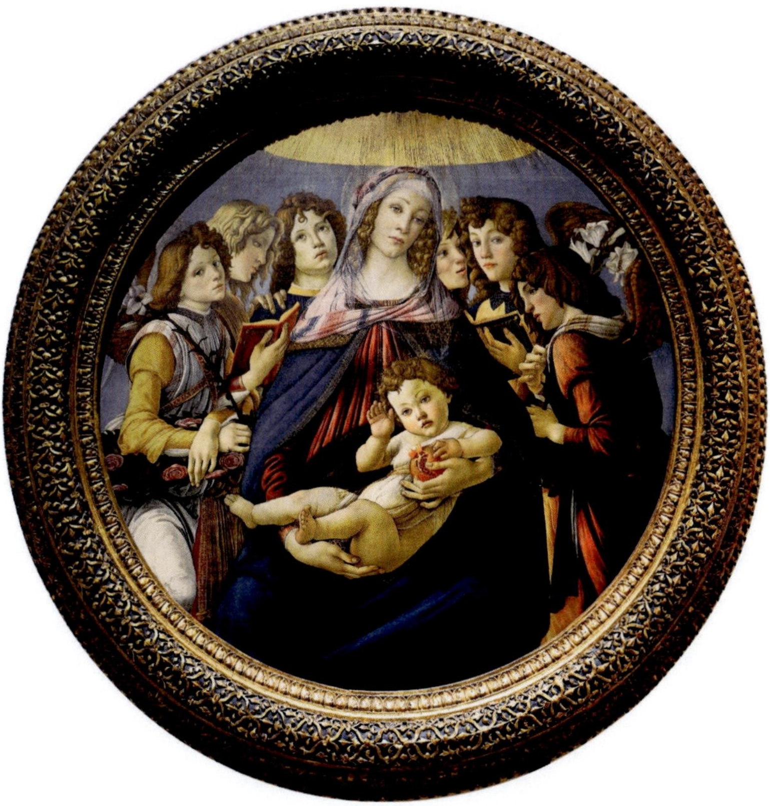

Fig.2.14 Sandro Botticelli, *Madonna of the Pomegranate*, c.1487, tempera on wood, 143.5 cm diameter, Uffizi Galleries, Florence, inv.1890 no.1609. © Wikimedia Commons.

(1882). The impact of this essay on the young Berenson has remained unacknowledged by scholars. Lee opens her essay with a painstaking description of the *strappo* technique used to remove the frescoes from the walls of the villa near Florence before they entered the Louvre that year. While Charles Ephrussi was celebrating their acquisition in the *Gazette des Beaux-Arts* as a success for French study of original Renaissance frescoes, Vernon Lee in the *Cornhill Magazine* instead lamented their removal, which she perceived as a 'loss' to Florence,[50] comparing the *strappo*'s loss to the 'departure of a friend'.[51] But what kind of friend was Botticelli for Vernon Lee?

> I know him well, familiarly; but he is as one of those persons whom you are forever meeting without ever especially seeking, familiar from sheer habit, perhaps justly appreciated for what they are.[52]

Lee's essay seems to follow the path inaugurated by Pater's psychological portraits. Anchoring her discussion in the materiality of communication between artistic personality and artistic output, Lee argues that Botticelli's temperament can be apprehended through the mood of the viewer: 'This is how the matter stands between me and Botticelli[…] […] I am made capricious by his capriciousness.' Like Pater, Lee was interested, not in reconstructing Botticelli's *corpus* for the advancement of connoisseurship, but in measuring rhythmic changes upon her body: 'I am never in tune, always too high and too low for him.'[53] Such ideas seem to point to Pater's 1873 'Preface' in *The Renaissance*, in which he notoriously wondered about the 'effects' that a song, an artwork or a personality 'produce on me'.[54]

Interestingly, Berenson also employed the metaphor of friendship in *The Central Italian Painters* (1897) to provide an explanation of the conversion of tactile values from the body of the painted figure to the body of the beholder:

> Tactile values and movement, then, are the essential qualities in the figure arts, and no figure-painting is real, — has a value of its own apart from the story it has to tell, the ideal it has to represent, — unless it conveys ideated sensations of touch and movement. If I may be pardoned a very childish parable, it is like someone who comes to us with a message. He tells us something we are very eager to know[…] But let him be a man of character and a gentleman, let him be sympathetic, and his message will have been but the happy accident that has initiated a life-long friendship. And so with

> a picture; long after, years after we have exhausted its message, if it has tactile values and movement, we are more in love with it than ever, because these qualities, as the attractions in a friend, have the power of directly enhancing life.[55]

This is a passage indebted as much to Pater's theory of personality and influence as it is to Lee's psychological writings on the master. Both Berenson and Lee were trying, in contiguous but different ways, to modernise the psychological implications of Pater's aestheticism.

Later on in Lee's essay, the metaphor of the loss of a friend leads the author to explore the aesthetic connectedness of consciousness and memory. There is an artistic possession which is more important than the physical artwork, she declares, and that has to do with the power 'of assimilating art into life'.

> Such assimilation means not only the enjoyment at the actual moment of seeing picture or statue, of hearing poem or symphony; but also (what is of more importance) the wealth of garnered-up impression which remains to us when the picture or statue has been long out of sight, the words of a poem have long been forgotten, the chords of the symphony have for ears ceased to vibrate.[56]

Lee proceeds to explain that, in order for artistic impressions to be assimilated into our life, 'there must already exist in our life a habit of impression akin to those given wholesale by art'. By insisting on the continuous structure of art and life, between culture and nature, Lee was opening up a way to test Pater's aesthetics in the nascent field of psychological and physiological aesthetics, which Berenson undoubtedly absorbed at a time when he too was thinking about Botticelli psychologically. However, while identifying similarities and continuities in the way in which Berenson and Lee remodelled *their* Pater, I also want to stress some fundamental differences.

Berenson's interest in psychological aesthetics was less scholarly and scientific than Lee's, as can be seen from the different ways in which they treated sensory responses to Botticelli. For Lee, Botticelli is not conducive to positive sensory effects; his 'wearisomely elaborated' world becomes the conduit for an unsatisfied longing, reminiscent of Pater.[57] Later in the 1890s, when Lee's aesthetic positions were informed by the experimental studies of psychologists such as Théodule Ribot and Karl Groos, she argued that the aim of beauty in art is to *maintain* a physiological equilibrium.[58] For Berenson, instead, art had a capacity to *elevate* our sensory experiences. His whole theory of aesthetics was predicated on the desire to explain how tactile values can have a 'direct tonic effect' upon us, which can be 'life-confirming and life-enhancing'.[59]

It was through an elaboration on Botticelli's line that Berenson was able to explore the capacity of art to augment life. In a passage from the *Florentine Painters* (1896), he first notes that Botticelli's lack of naturalism allows his line to stand out. Then he elaborates on this point:

> [T]ake these lines alone with all their power of stimulating our imagination of movement, and what do we have? Pure values of movement abstracted, unconnected with any representation whatsoever. This kind of line, then, being the quintessence of movement, has like the essential elements in all the arts, a power of stimulating our imagination and of directly communicating life. Well! Imagine an art made up entirely of these quintessences of movement-values, and you will have something that holds the same relation that music holds to speech.[60]

Berenson did not give up on the comparison with music, because it allowed him to illustrate an argument about abstraction that was instrumental to appreciate the tactile values of a work. Berenson's Botticelli is 'haunted by the idea of communicating the *unembodied* values of touch and movement'.[61] Devoted to 'the rhythm of the line', Botticelli's use of colour shows a 'contempt for its representative function' and is 'entirely subordinated to his lineal scheme'.[62] Berenson's interest in Botticelli's abstraction obviously finds a precedent in Pater's conception of 'impersonality', which was reflected in how he looked at the artist's line and colour as 'the medium of abstract painting'.[63] However, Pater's text alone does not explain the precision with which Berenson arrived in *The Florentine Painters* at a psychological definition of Botticelli's lack of naturalism. Indeed, his ideas about Botticelli's 'linealism' originated three years earlier, and developed in reaction to Hermann Ulmann's book on Botticelli. A close reading of how Berenson encountered this competing work during his study of Botticelli helps to explain how he came to psychologise this old master.

Ulmann, Berenson and the Botticelli formula

In December 1893 Costelloe received a letter from an alarmed Berenson about the publication of a new monograph on Botticelli:

> A huge book by a German on Botticelli has appeared. I have ordered it and will give you my notes on it which you must concoct into a review to pay for it. I doubt whether it will prove so good that we shall be tempted to give up our scheme.[64]

The book in question represented the first systematic study ever published of Botticelli's work. Its author, Hermann Ulmann, had been a fellow student with Aby Warburg, and one of eight students from various universities who attended August Schmarsow's seminar in Florence in 1889.[65] Berenson was not part of the academic networks through which German art historians had started to organise themselves in Florence.[66] The fact that he was so shocked about another's publication on a topic he had been researching for a while reveals his isolation as a scholar.

When the book eventually arrived, it made Berenson so angry 'that sticking it into the fire would scarcely alloy my rage'. His fury was especially levelled at the style of German scholarship, described as 'doting drivel' and 'nauseous as doze'. Initially Berenson changed his mind about reviewing the book: 'Writing about it is out of the question. You would have to write volumes and then it would not hit him or his kind, the worst in existence, the people who have not a spark of a feeling for what is specifically artistic, and yet make art their subject.'[67] Yet, as he continued reading, he became aware that, although the book might not be interesting or well written – Erwin Panofsky described Ulmann's art history as 'without accent' – it was still the first comprehensive monograph on Botticelli. 'It is a book many will praise but few read,' Berenson wrote across the paper on which he began to make his notes.[68] Eventually he overcome his aversion, and started to tackle Ulmann's monograph seriously, with a view to writing about it. His copy of the book in the I Tatti library and his handwritten notes in the archive document his attempts at demolishing Ulmann's attributions. At the same time they register his finding of a 'formula' to understand Botticelli, which he could claim as his own.

The first step was to look first hand at as many pictures as possible. Living in Florence, he could never have never accomplished this task without Costelloe's help from London.[69] Their letters also highlight the practicalities and moods of their collaboration:

> Look in the full catalogue of the New Gallery please, & see whether there is a portrait ascribed to Botticelli belonging to a Mr Ionides. If there is make a point of seeing it again, & noting it carefully. That Botticelli book is driving me distracted. You should note all the pictures in the New ascribed to Botticelli, & try to classify them.

> See if some of them are not Raffaellino. Look at my photos and see if I lack any of the B[otticelli]'s in the N[ational] G[allery]. If I have not one of the Magi in entrance hall, get a photo[...] You realise how important this is, so don't fail to attend [to] it.[70]

This letter is especially important because it shows that as early as 1893 Costelloe had already developed her own eye, which Berenson could trust to study the works on his behalf.[71] Eventually Ionides's *Portrait of a Lady known as Smeralda Bandinelli* (fig.1.5) was in 1899 to enter the list of works by 'Amico di Sandro': 'Ascribed to Botticelli, this is nevertheless a highly characteristic work by our Anonimo, dating from those years when he was most dependent on Sandro.'[72] So dependent was he, indeed, that scholars now believe the portrait to be Botticelli himself.[73]

Two months after receiving the book, Berenson again suggested that Costelloe write a review based on his annotations. Since the notes were 'far too copious and mixed up to send', he suggested they work on it together, the next time she came to Florence.[74] The manuscript notes, partly disarranged in the 'Botticelli' folder at I Tatti, eventually converged in the publication of two reviews, which have hitherto received little attention. The first, signed by Costelloe, appeared in *The Studio* in 1894.[75] The second, written by Berenson but signed 'Z.', appeared in *Revue Critique* a few months later.[76] Both were intended to deliver a critique of Ulmann's connoisseurship based on his inability to recognise the 'personality' of Botticelli. Both are thus important to understanding how Berenson, with Costelloe's collaboration, proposed a psychological approach to connoisseurship.

Costelloe was often the first person to register the progress of Berenson's thinking. In a letter sent to her in November 1894 he writes:

> I am still working on the review of that Botticelli. I have scrawled over what seems an endless number of sheets and the result is excessively modest. But it has cleared up my ideas on the subject, & I have at least found a formula for Botticelli which hits him 'every time', while furnishing an absolute test for authenticity, & method for tracing his evolution.[77]

'Tracing' could be seen as literal, for the formula was based on the idea that Botticelli was a 'linealist'. That he was a master of the outline was no novelty in the art criticism of the time, but Berenson was the first to endow Botticelli's line with a quality which could be claimed as a test for attribution. In his manuscript notes Berenson insists that Ulmann, 'Thus far never considers QUALITY of line, but merely TYPE, & interpretation' or 'type and composition'.[78] Berenson insisted that resemblances among types could not be relied on for correct connoisseurship. The connoisseur should be guided by the quality and value of the line alone, ignoring both type and iconography. Such ideas, developed in 1893 in reaction to Ulmann's monograph, were to inform the core of Berenson's theory of connoisseurship as he finally developed it in his 1902 methodological essay 'Rudiments of Connoisseurship', which appeared in the same sequence of volumes as the English translation of 'Amico di Sandro').[79] Here too Berenson distanced his method from the focus on type and iconographies and illuminated the path through which a connoisseur can identify the personality of an artist.

Some ideas from the manuscript first found their way into Costelloe's review, which the letters suggest they prepared together in Florence.[80] Here two passages from Berenson's unpublished notes were incorporated. In the first one, we read:

> Mr Ulmann never so much as hints at the existence of this quality of line, and, as it is the only adequate test, it is no wonder that his conclusions with regard to the genuineness of pictures ascribed to Botticelli are without great value.[81]

This review ultimately concluded that 'Ulmann did not understand Botticelli's quality, which is the fact that he is a linealist'[82] and suggested that without this knowledge it would be impossible to reconstruct Botticelli's 'artistic personality'. The review in *The Studio* was later corroborated by Berenson's anonymous intervention in the *Revue Critique*, in which he sums up his method:[83]

> The identity of details proves nothing about the paternity of a work: it is the identity of quality *alone* that can establish a presumption in this regard. But such an idea of quality is foreign to Mr Ulmann's mind. Like the majority of German critics, he imagines that one can arrive at qualitative proof by the accumulation of quantitative evidence. There is no worse mistake in art criticism.[84]

It is not surprising that Berenson chose not to sign this review. It was a vitriolic attack on the German connoisseurs which might have reminded the readers of the never-ending diatribe between Morelli and Wilhelm von Bode; and it was also the first time that Berenson was testing his theories in a publication.[85] He was still very young: he had to be cautious.

Ulmann's connoisseurship of Botticelli builds on the very uncertain corpus of Fra Diamante who, he claims, might have assisted Filippo Lippi in Prato and Spoleto. However, as Berenson makes a point of noting, Ulmann identifies no certain work by Fra Diamante, and therefore was missing any parameter of reference. Moreover, anything that is not good enough to be by Filippo Lippi he ascribes to Botticelli, thus ignoring the possibility that Filippo Lippi might have had imitators, apart from Botticelli, such as Pesellino, Giusto d'Andrea or Jacopo del Sellaio.[86] 'Very feeble proof', Berenson notes in the margin of one of Ulmann's pages.[87] Berenson compares Ulmann with the 'poor baronet' in Walter Scott's *The Antiquary* (1816), 'who hoped to reconstruct the Pictish language out of one remaining word, that a compound of which was Latin'.[88] For Berenson, Ulmann was a 'lexicographer'; he exemplified the problem that 'art-criticism is still where Comparative Philology was a century ago'.[89] Solidly grounded in a literary approach, this old-style critic must have reminded Berenson of himself before his conversion to Pater and Morellian connoisseurship. A new critic, instead, 'must be able to feel the artist, his character, his world, his soul in the only way they ever can be known thro' his touch'.[90] Such ideas inform the conclusion of Costelloe's review, which stresses that a monograph on Botticelli can only be written by someone who can add the connoisseurship of Morelli to the 'exact and subtle interpretation of Walter Pater':[91] such a connoisseur was, obviously, Berenson himself. The importance of Pater's aesthetics lay in his introduction of 'a certain tone, a style' as a more significant achievement for an artist than the illustration of an idea.[92] Berenson used this principle to organise his method of connoisseurship.

The quality of Botticelli's line is therefore situated in the cleavage between the economic value demanded by the art market – the quality of the line is the tool by which a connoisseur can separate a genuine Botticelli from the Botticellians – and aesthetic value, the gratification of the senses which allows for the enjoyment of the work of art. As Roberto Longhi put it in a sarcastic letter he sent to Berenson some years later: 'By starting from a positivist basis you inevitably arrive at a hedonistic criticism'.[93] However, in these years Berenson was trying to found his 'hedonistic criticism' on a different basis, and I believe that we need to make sense of his method not so much as an Epicurean revival, but rather as a response to his own times. Pater's aspiration towards an art for art's sake was based on the principle that the artist puts nothing of himself in the work: an art 'impersonal in its beauty, the perfection of nobody's style'. As Angela Leighton has pointed out, the saying that style is the man was 'never given as a proof of personality, but rather as an escape from personality'.[94] Pater's notion of personality represented a safe space of mimicry, but also an identity in exile which must have resonated with Berenson's own position.

Against the Botticellian type

An accidental encounter with Ulmann in Berlin in the summer of 1895 gave rise to a harsh anti-Semitic observation made by Berenson in a letter to his sister Senda: 'In the gallery I saw a nasty looking young Semite taking about another, and talking the most fabulous nonsense. I followed him about because it was so funny. It was Ulmann, Gronau told me.'[95] The following day he was introduced to Ulmann by Tschudi, 'but quite by the way. I did not wish to continue his acquaintance'.[96] Four months later, Berenson again bumped into Ulmann, this time in Florence: 'I joined the Buttles and Miss C[ruttwell] in the Academy after three. Ulmann was there, holding forth [to] about a score of Kommerzienräthe and –rathinnen [*sic*] about Botticelli's "Three Archangels"'.[97] These are not the only letters in which Berenson records his obsession with physiognomy, which was undoubtedly the symptom of a cultural (and personal) anxiety. They are instances of Berenson's ambiguous anti-Semitism which calls for a contextual interpretation.[98]

In Berenson's phraseology, type featured not only as a visual signifier of ethnicity, but also as a faulty methodology for connoisseurship. His reference to Ulmann's proximity to *Kommerzienrat* (business magnate) only exacerbates the anti-Semitism of his remark on Ulmann's appearance, reproducing the stereotype of the 'merchant Jew'. Funnily enough, this was the same basis on which another Jewish art historian, Meyer Schapiro, levelled his fierce criticism of Berenson's 'values'. Schapiro famously exposed Berenson's aesthetic paradigms as deeply implicated with his involvement in the picture trade; he opposed Berenson's commercial values to the 'more seriously philosophic' system of values expressed in the Jewish love for textual scholarship that Berenson firmly repudiated (at least on the surface of his methodology).[99] Schapiro's essay is vital in prompting speculation on how Berenson's conflicted relationship with Judaism must have influenced his life and work – and ultimately, as Catherine Soussloff suggests, in situating 'the function of Jewish identity in the epistemology of the discipline'.[100]

A manuscript on Botticelli by Berenson, drafted at the same time he was wading through Ulmann's hated book, opens with a scheme that may be useful in crafting an answer about these issues. The scheme is divided into four sections (fig.2.15):

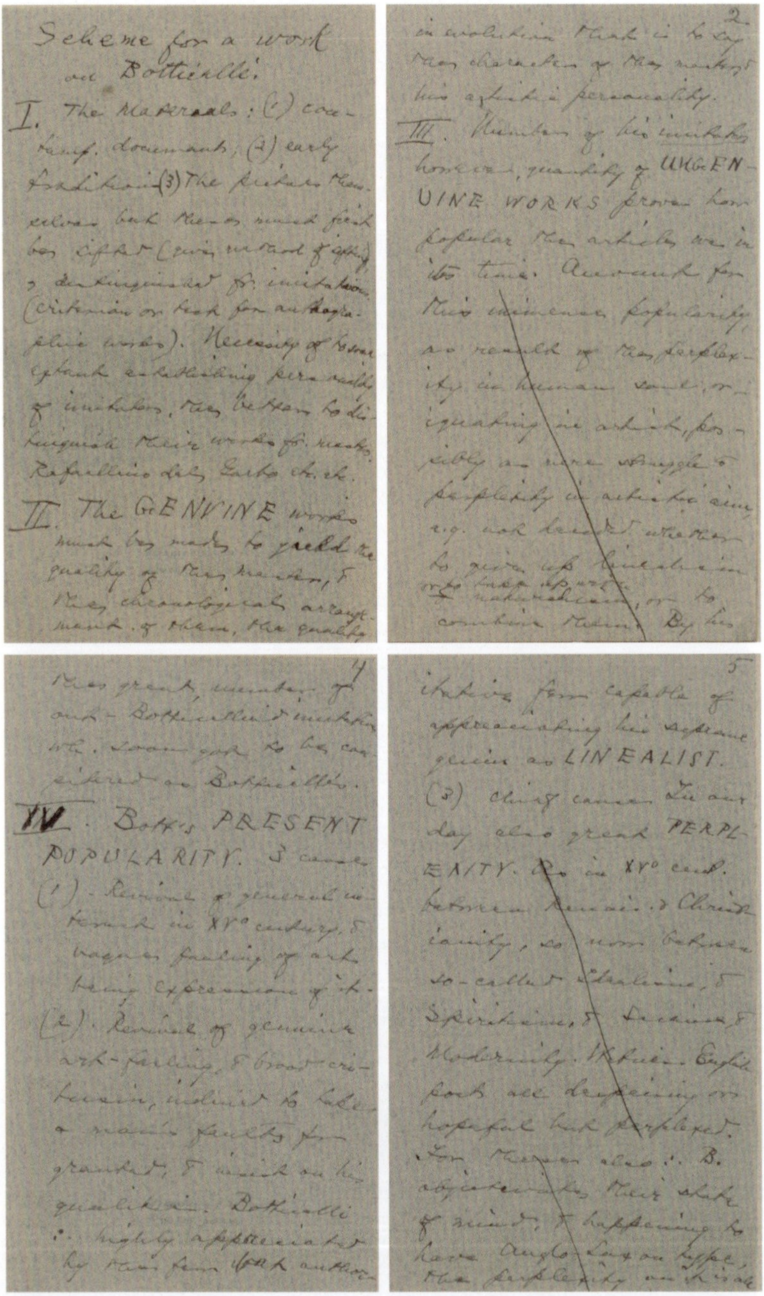

Fig.2.15 Bernard Berenson's manuscript notes on 'Botticelli' [*c.*1894?], Bernard and Mary Berenson Papers, Biblioteca Berenson, Villa I Tatti, The Harvard University Center for Italian Renaissance Studies © President and Fellows of Harvard College.

Scheme for a work in Botticelli.

I. The materials: (1) contemp. documents; (2) early traditions (3) The pictures themselves but these must first be sifted (give method of sifting) and distinguished fr. imitations (criterion on best for autographic works. Necessity of to some extent establishing personality of imitators, the better to distinguish their works fr. master's. Rafaellino del Garbo, etc. etc.

II. The GENUINE works must be made to yield the quality of the master, & the chronological arrangement of them, the quality [I.2] in evolution that is to say the character of the master, & his artistic personality.

III. Number of his imitators however, quantity of UNGENUINE WORKS prove how popular the article was in its time. Account for this immense popularity as result of the perplexity in human soul, originating in artist, possibly as mere struggle to perplexity in artistic aim, e.g. not decided whether to give up linealism or to take up more naturalism, or to combine them[…] the great numbers of out-Botticellian & imitations wh. soon got to be considered as Botticelli's.

IV. Bott's PRESENT POPULARITY. 3 causes.

(1) Revival of general interest in XV century, & vogue feeling of art being expression of it.

(2) Revival of genuine art-feeling, & broad criticism, inclined to take a man's faults for granted, & insist on his qualities. Botticelli is highly appreciated by the few but authoritative few capable of appreciating his supreme genius as LINEALIST.

(3) Chief causes. In our day also great PERPLEXITY. As in XV cent. between Renais. & Christianity, so now between so-called Idealism, & Spiritualism, & Science, & Modernity. Witness English poets all despairing or hopeful but perplexed. For these also: B[otticelli] objectivates their state of mind, & happening to have Anglo-Saxon type, the perplexity on it is all.[101]

Section I represents, in embryonic form, the very method Berenson was to explain in 'Rudiments of Connoisseurship', as I have already mentioned. Section II deals with his emphasis on the quality of Botticelli's line, which he presented as the major point of difference from Ulmann's approach. Both of these are extensively treated in the manuscript and developed further in the pages on Botticelli in *Florentine Painters*. Section III, instead, seems to echo Pater's opinion about Botticelli's 'sympathy for humanity in its uncertain condition'.[102] This is an aspect that preoccupied

Berenson, but one which he did not develop further in his scholarship – except obliquely, as I will indicate in my conclusion.[103] Section IV is subdivided into three paragraphs, each one of which deserves special discussion. However, here I want to concentrate on the last one, which points to the problem of the modernity of Botticelli in the Renaissance and in Berenson's own time.

The opposition between science and modernity mirrors the opposition between idealism and spiritualism. But as evidence to explain this dualism, Berenson does not draw on an iconology of the Renaissance exploration of Christian values enacted by the Renaissance mind (as Warburg did). Instead, he turns to the contemporary popularisation of Botticelli among the English poets, who allegedly recognise in the 'perplexity' embodied by the old master a resemblance with themselves and with the moods ('all despairing or hopeful but perplexed') of the 'Anglo-Saxon type'. These 'English poets' were specifically the Pre-Raphaelites. They had already been the subject of intense scrutiny in some pages in an unpublished notebook, written between 1892 and 1893, and later annotated by Costelloe under the title 'The Critic and Art: Pre-Raphaelites'.[104]

Trying to grapple with the popularisation of the primitives, Berenson lamented that the pre-Raphaelite movement had been driven by a mostly illustrative approach to early Renaissance literary themes. This did not encourage the painters to be 'pre-Raphaelite in means as well', just as it did not encourage the writers to use Chaucer's English in writing.[105] For the Pre-Raphaelite school, Berenson concluded, 'it did not matter whether painters tried to express anything of their own or not', and so they remained confined to illustrative means: 'On the whole your only chance of becoming somebody is by working hard to acquire knowledge, skill, and polish, and the power of thinking and of expressing yourself.'[106] What the Pre-Raphaelites failed to achieve, therefore, was wholly to embody the art of the Renaissance primitives without impersonating it.

This represented a pivotal problem for the young art critic, whose vocabulary had started to revolve around keywords such as authenticity, expression and personality. These issues would inform the modernity of Berenson's aesthetic doctrine of connoisseurship, mostly preoccupied with the formal qualities rather than the iconographic elements of a work of visual art. When Berenson was writing these notes Botticelli, already an established cipher in Pre-Raphaelite representations of female beauty, was becoming reproducible by art nouveau designers infatuated with the spiralling hair and interlaced flower branches. As Elizabeth Prettejohn explains, 'the Botticelli revival involves[...] an entire visual style, one in which the special character of Botticelli and that of the Pre-Raphaelites blend so persuasively that the sight of one seems to conjure up the other, without the viewer's conscious volition'.[107]

The recourse to the type in connoisseurship, therefore, remains faulty for Berenson because it gives access to Botticelli only according to the taste of a specific period, rather than allowing for an apprehension of the master's true character. Berenson chastises Ulmann on precisely this point, citing his passage on the identity of the portrait of Smeralda Bandinelli:

> The sitter even resembles the Venus there [i.e. in the *Primavera*]. Dante Gabriele Rossetti, from whose ownership the portrait originates (it was earlier in the Pourtales collection), considered both to be the same person. But I do not want to go that far. What a great stimulus the founder of the Pre-Raphaelite school, with his spiritual kinship to our master, must have derived from the old Italian's work for his female heads![108]

For Berenson, this passage represents an 'excellent instance' of Ulmann's method, and in a superscript annotation to his own text he adds 'His INTERPRETATION judged by fact that he finds Rossetti the kinsman in spirit of B.[otticelli]'.[109] But while the dismantling of Ulmann seems to provide Berenson with the bricks to build a new approach to Botticelli which exposes the shortcoming of the type as a methodological touchstone, it also illuminates the problematic of the type as a signifier of ethnicity. Although the passage may not appear immediately transparent, it nevertheless gives away some 'positions'. Berenson's fascination with how 'B.[otticelli] objectivates their state of mind', with what Botticelli is to *them* and how *they* see themselves reflected in Botticelli's Anglo-Saxon type, ultimately betrays his own anxiety about how others must see him. Although Berenson had previously insisted that the identification of types is not a reliable measure to substantiate an attribution, in matters of taste the type is employed as a touchstone to understand his own epoch. Yet Berenson's approach to Botticelli also represents one of the first attempts in art historiography to undermine the longstanding problematic of the type which, with major nationalistic implications, is drawn from Winckelmann. And although this may seem an unconscious process at this stage, Berenson had a reason to position himself against the type, for he would be able to witness the ideological uses of the Botticellian type to justify the scientific racism of the fascist regime in Italy.[110]

In an article published in *La Difesa della razza* in 1938, the anthropologist Guido Landra elaborated on the scientific and cultural bases for Italian racism by showing a reproduction of the *Allegorical Portrait of Simonetta Vespucci* (private collection; attributed to his workshop, 1480–90) to explain that the 'ideal type' of the Italian is not an abstraction, but corresponds to racial, physical and psychological characteristics that can be found in all men from the past and the present (fig.2.16):

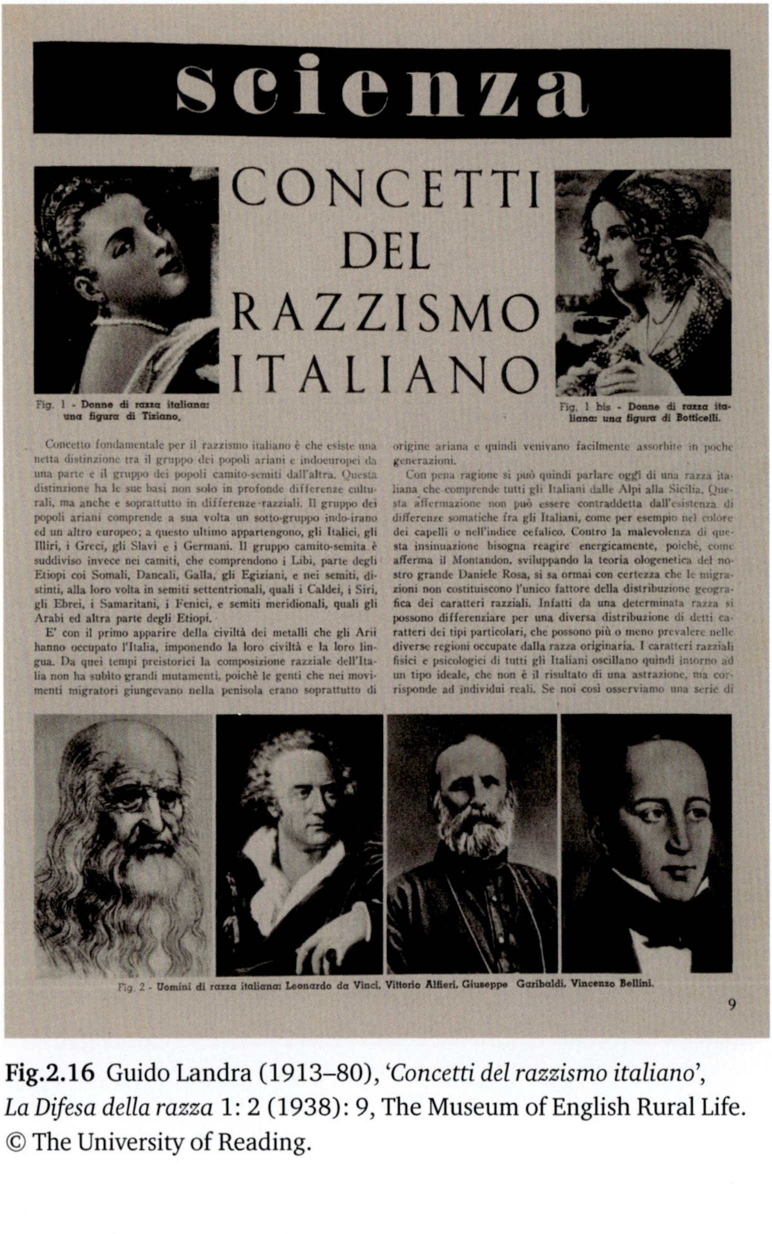

scienza

CONCETTI DEL RAZZISMO ITALIANO

Fig. 1 - **Donne di razza italiana: una figura di Tiziano.**

Fig. 1 bis - **Donne di razza italiana: una figura di Botticelli.**

Concetto fondamentale per il razzismo italiano è che esiste una netta distinzione tra il gruppo dei popoli ariani e indoeuropei da una parte e il gruppo dei popoli camito-semiti dall'altra. Questa distinzione ha le sue basi non solo in profonde differenze culturali, ma anche e soprattutto in differenze razziali. Il gruppo dei popoli ariani comprende a sua volta un sotto-gruppo indo-irano ed un altro europeo; a questo ultimo appartengono, gli Italici, gli Illiri, i Greci, gli Slavi e i Germani. Il gruppo camito-semita è suddiviso invece nei camiti, che comprendono i Libi, parte degli Etiopi coi Somali, Dancali, Galla, gli Egiziani, e nei semiti, distinti, alla loro volta in semiti settentrionali, quali i Caldei, i Siri, gli Ebrei, i Samaritani, i Fenici, e semiti meridionali, quali gli Arabi ed altra parte degli Etiopi.

E' con il primo apparire della civiltà dei metalli che gli Arii hanno occupato l'Italia, imponendo la loro civiltà e la loro lingua. Da quei tempi preistorici la composizione razziale dell'Italia non ha subìto grandi mutamenti, poichè le genti che nei movimenti migratori giungevano nella penisola erano soprattutto di origine ariana e quindi venivano facilmente assorbite in poche generazioni.

Con pena ragione si può quindi parlare oggi di una razza italiana che comprende tutti gli Italiani dalle Alpi alla Sicilia. Questa affermazione non può essere contraddetta dall'esistenza di differenze somatiche fra gli Italiani, come per esempio nel colore dei capelli o nell'indice cefalico. Contro la malevolenza di questa insinuazione bisogna reagire energicamente, poichè, come afferma il Montandon, sviluppando la teoria ologenetica del nostro grande Daniele Rosa, si sa ormai con certezza che le migrazioni non costituiscono l'unico fattore della distribuzione geografica dei caratteri razziali. Infatti da una determinata razza si possono differenziare per una diversa distribuzione di detti caratteri dei tipi particolari, che possono più o meno prevalere nelle diverse regioni occupate dalla razza originaria. I caratteri razziali fisici e psicologici di tutti gli Italiani oscillano quindi intorno ad un tipo ideale, che non è il risultato di una astrazione, ma corrisponde ad individui reali. Se noi così osserviamo una serie di

Fig. 2 - **Uomini di razza italiana: Leonardo da Vinci, Vittorio Alfieri, Giuseppe Garibaldi, Vincenzo Bellini.**

9

Fig.2.16 Guido Landra (1913–80), '*Concetti del razzismo italiano*', *La Difesa della razza* 1: 2 (1938): 9, The Museum of English Rural Life. © The University of Reading.

> We arrive at the same result when we observe a series of female beauties immortalised by our very own artists (fig. 1 and 1bis). One would try in vain to identify any of these figures with a regional type. They are above every regional type, because they represent the real image of the Italian race.[111]

The visual and verbal imbrication of Lambra's article demonstrates the central role art history played in the construction of imperialist discourses about race.[112] Above all, it shows that the type lends itself to a visual system of comparison which becomes self-explanatory, and therefore operates according to a pre-emptive epistemology: it looks like science, but it is only a flawed representation of objectivity.[113] In attacking typological connoisseurship, Berenson was ultimately rejecting the visual epistemology of the type that could have been used to define his otherness as well. At a time in which scientific racism was producing the methods and theories that explained the Jewish type, Berenson's disavowal of the type in connoisseurship becomes an act of resistance against public misconceptions and myths about the Jew's body.[114]

It has been central to my reading that Berenson challenged typological connoisseurship with a psychological argument about the quality of Botticelli's line as the true embodiment of the artist's character. He also proposed a physiological kind of apprehension of that quality which, as I have discussed above, pointed clearly at the 'tonic effects' that Botticelli's line has on the body of the beholder. Berenson's championing of such regenerative qualities in Botticelli's painting cannot be separated from the discourse of degeneration and decadence that informed the re-framing of the popularisation of Botticelli (and Paterian aesthetics) at the end of the nineteenth century. In his analysis of Schapiro's attack to Berenson, Donald Kuspit proposed to consider the effects of the 'Jewish position in society' for that generation of art historians: 'Berenson's Jewish identity gave him the strength of character and cunning to survive and flourish in alien circumstances'.[115] Consequently, it could be argued that his own explorations of the life-enhancing effects of Botticelli's line, which he developed fully in the *Florentine Painters*, must be taken as one individual's attempt to remove his body from the pathological system of – representation that entrapped the modern Jew.

The way in which Botticelli's 'values' operated upon Berenson's own body reveal the construction of a complicated intellectual armour in an environment that was becoming increasingly threatening, as he himself was to witness. For Schapiro, the authentically creative artist is also a survivor, 'that is a person who can establish an identity and sense of self and individuality against great odds'.[116] I agree with Kuspit that Schapiro must be considered as 'the last idealistic art historian-theorist-critic' of the twentieth century, but this is also what positions him closer to Berenson than he might have wished – at least in principle.[117] Indeed, Berenson's Botticelli too seems to have occupied a 'Jewish position in society' when Berenson was trying to establish him against the odds of the connoisseurs and art historians who continually disassembled and reassembled his body of work. But, in Berenson's opaque words, the fact that Botticelli reflected the tension 'in XV cent. between Renaissance [i.e. humanist values] & Christianity' meant that he occupied a marginal position also in his own society, which was expressed by the 'perplexity in human soul, originating in artist, possibly as mere struggle to perplexity in artistic aim'.[118] These ruminations take us back once again to Pater. Indeed, Pater had discussed Botticelli's character amidst apparently irreconcilable positions in his society. He made a visual commentary on Dante's Christian *Comedia* while also creating stunning interpretations of ancient pagan myths, but was in addition a follower of Savonarola's revolution. True or false, Pater writes in his 'Botticelli':

> […] the story interprets much of the peculiar sentiment with which he infuses his profane and sacred persons, comely, and in a certain sense like angels, but with a sense of displacement or loss about them – the wistfulness of exiles, conscious of a passion and energy greater than any known issue of them explains, which runs through all his varied work with a sentiment of ineffable melancholy.[119]

Perhaps it was this first encounter with such 'wistfulness of the exiles' which prompted Berenson to create – or preserve? – a Jewish position for Botticelli, in spite of his 'Anglo-Saxon type', while he was attempting to find one for himself as well. As his letters and manuscripts from the febrile and intense early years of the 1890s show, befriending Botticelli became a conduit for assimilation. The personality of Botticelli functioned for Berenson like a symptomatic transposition of the central question about his own identity.

Acknowledgements

This research was funded by a Leverhulme Early Career Research Fellowship at the University of Sussex (2013–16). Many thanks to Ilaria della Monica, Biblioteca Berenson Archive, Villa I Tatti, for her caring support to my research in the archive. Many thanks also to Jeremy Melius and Michelle O'Malley for productive discussions about this project. Jonathan Nelson has been particularly supportive and generous in showing me his papers in progress. My special gratitude to Michael Gorman for comparing transcriptions and, above all, for sharing his enthusiasm for handwritten traces.

Notes

1 Julia Cartwright, *The Painters of Florence* (London: John Murray, 1910), 197.

2 Léon Rosenthal, *Sandro Botticelli et sa réputation à l'heure présente* (Dijon: Librairie Générale Félix Rey, 1897), 6.

3 Rosenthal, *Sandro Botticelli*, 5–6: '*Un article de la Vie Parisienne n'est complet s'il n'y est parlé de Botticelli, nos actrices se coiffent à la Botticelli, nous avons des petits Botticellistes. L'Italie partage notre enthousiasme, et Botticelli, prophète en son pays, inspire le dessin des affiches qui annoncent l'Exposition de la Toscane. L'engouement a été si rapide que ceux-là mêmes qui s'imaginent en avoir été les premiers auteurs sont effrayés.*' [My translation]

4 Max Nordau, *Degeneration* [1892] (Lincoln: University of Nebraska Press, 1968), 7. Nordau here is especially concerned with a critique of consumerism and consuming the past through taste and fashionable commodities.

5 For a discussion of the Botticelli revival in nineteenth-century art writing see Michael Levey, 'Botticelli and Nineteenth-Century England', *Journal of the Warburg and Courtauld Institutes* 23, Nos. 3/4 (July–December 1960): 291–306; and Jeremy Melius, *Art History and the Invention of Botticelli*, unpublished PhD Thesis (Berkeley, 2010).

6 Constance Jocelyn Ffoulkes, 'Morelli, Giovanni', in *The Encyclopedia Britannica* 28 (London, 1911), 830.

7 Bernard Berenson, 'Amico di Sandro', *Gazette des Beaux-Arts* 41 (June 1899): 459–71; and 42 (July 1899), 21–36. Republished in English by Berenson, 'Amico di Sandro', in *The Study and Criticism of Italian Art* (London: George Bell, 1901), 46–69. For a study of the function of *notnamen*, *noms de convention* or *noms de commodité* in art historiography see Nicole Reynaud, 'Les Maîtres à nom de convention', *Revue de l'Art* 42 (1978): 41–52; and Enrico Castelnuovo, 'Attribution', in *Encyclopedia Universalis* II (1968), 1098–9.

8 It is interesting, however, that in proposing the identification of Amico with Berto Linaiuolo, Berenson makes reference to a passage in Vasari indicated to him by Herbert Horne. Berenson, 'Amico di Sandro', 67–9.

9 Berenson, 'Amico di Sandro', 64.

10 Berenson, 'Amico di Sandro', 49.

11 Jeremy Melius, 'Connoisseurship, Painting, and Personhood', *Art History*, 34: 2 (2011): 290.

12 In 1886 Berenson took the course 'Logic and Psychology', in which James taught the materials that he would develop into *Principles of Psychology* in 1890. See Rachel Cohen, *Bernard Berenson. A Life in the Picture Trade* (New Haven and London: Yale University Press, 2013), 38. For a discussion of Berenson's interest in psychological aesthetics see Alison Brown, 'Bernard Berenson and "Tactile Values" in Florence', in *Bernard Berenson. Formation and Heritage*, ed. Joseph Connors and Louis A. Waldman (Florence: Villa I Tatti, the Harvard University Center for Italian Renaissance Studies, 2014), 101–20; and Jeremy Melius, 'Connoisseurship, Painting and Personhood', *Art History* 34.2 (April 2011): 288–309, reprinted in *Creative Writing and Art History*, ed. Patricia Rubin and Catherine Grant (Oxford: Wiley-Blackwell, 2012), 66–87. According to Patricia Rubin, these theories also shaped Berenson's lifestyle. See Patricia Rubin, 'Bernard Berenson, Villa I Tatti, and the Visualization of the Italian Renaissance', in *Gli Anglo-Americani a Firenze: Idee e costruzione del Rinascimento*, ed. Marcello Fantoni (Rome: Bulzoni, 2000), 207–9.

13 Paul Barolsky, 'Walter Pater and Bernard Berenson', in *Walter Pater's Renaissance* (University Park and London: The Pennsylvania State University Press, 1987), 139–53; Jonah Siegel, 'Schooling Leonardo: Collaboration, Desire, and the Challenge of Attribution in Pater', in *Walter Pater: Transparencies of Desire*, ed. Laurel Brake, Lesley Higgins and Carolyn Williams (University of North Carolina: ELT Press, 2002), 139.

14 Patrizia Zambrano, 'Bernard Berenson e l'Amico di Sandro' in Bernard Berenson, *Amico di Sandro* (Milan: Electa, 2006), 22.

15 Walter Pater, 'Introduction', in *The Renaissance* (Oxford: Oxford University Press, 1998), xxx.

16 Matthew Beaumont, 'Pater as a Psychagogue: Psychology, Aesthetics, Rhetoric', *19: Interdisciplinary Studies in the Long Nineteenth Century*, 12 (2011): 1.

17 Mary Whitall Costelloe, 'The New and the Old Art Criticism', *The Nineteenth Century*, 35, n.207 (May 1894), 830.

18 Once in Boston, the Berensons changed their original surname from Valvrojensky. Berenson's birthplace was recorded as Vilnius, but he was actually born in the *shtetl* of Butremanz, or Butrimonys, in southern Lithuania. Ernest Samuels, *Bernard Berenson: The Making of*

a Connoisseur (Cambridge, Mass.: Belknap Press, 1981), 40. The Jewish population of Butrimonys was completely massacred by the *Einsatzgruppen* and Lithuanian collaborators on 9 September 1941. Nathan Cohen, 'The Destruction of the Jews from Butrimonys as Described in a Farewell Letter from a Local Jew', *Holocaust and Genocide Studies* 4: 3 (1989): 357–75.

19 Meyer Schapiro, 'Mr. Berenson's Values' [1961], in *Theory and Philosophy of Art: Style, Artist, and Society*, vol.4 of *Selected Papers* (New York: George Braziller, 1994), 225.

20 Logan Pearsall Smith, *Unforgotten Years* (Boston, 1939), 123. Quoted in Sanam Nader-Esfahani, 'Paths Intertwined: The 1884 Lowell Lecture and "The Sacred Word 'Botticelli'", in *Berenson and Harvard: Bernard and Mary as Students*, ed. by Jonathan K. Nelson. Available online: https://berenson.itatti.harvard.edu/berenson/items/show/3027#note [accessed 10/10/2017]. See Cohen, *Bernard Berenson*, 57–8.

21 The episode is detailed by Samuels, *Bernard Berenson*, 37.

22 B. Berenson to M. Costelloe, 7 November 1890, in *The Bernard Berenson Treasury*, ed. Hannah Kiel (Northampton: John Dickens & Co Ltd., 1964), 46.

23 Pater, *The Renaissance*, 40.

24 Stephen Cheeke, 'Pateresque: The Person, the Prose Style', *The Cambridge Quarterly* 43: 3 (2017): 254. Cheeke points out that 'the relation of style to body, and of body to identity, is an ancient philosophical question; the relation of style to thought – to *content* – equally so', 255. In this sense I agree with Beaumont that 'Pater's conception of psychology is a kind of late nineteenth-century pneumatology'. Beaumont, 'Pater as Psychagogue', 11.

25 Jonah Siegel, 'Schooling Leonardo: Collaboration, desire, and the challenge of attribution in Pater', in Laurel Brake, Lesley Higgins, Carolyn Williams, ed., *Transparencies of Desire* (Greensboro, NC: ELT Press, 2002), 144; quoted in Melius, 'Connoisseurship, Painting, and Personhood', 302. Melius coins the useful expression 'erotics of discipleship' (which echoes Siegel's 'erotics of instruction', p.150) to explain how the habits of one master inform the artistic outputs of the disciple.

26 Paul Barolsky, 'Walter Pater and Bernard Berenson', in *Walter Pater's Renaissance* (Philadelphia, Pennsylvania State University Press, 1987), 139–53.

27 Only a few years older, Ned Warren made it possible for Berenson to transfer from Boston University to Harvard by paying for the fees.

28 Samuels, *The Making of a Connoisseur*, 61.

29 Samuels, *The Making of a Connoisseur*, 61–2.

30 B. Berenson to S. Berenson, 10 February 1888. Box 23, folder 13. Bernard and Mary Berenson Papers, Biblioteca Berenson, Villa I Tatti, Harvard University Center for Italian Renaissance Studies, Florence (BMBP). See Samuels, *Bernard Berenson*, 69.

31 Éric Michaud, *Les invasions barbares. Une généalogie de l'histoire de l'art* (Paris: Gallimard, 2015), 147.

32 Cohen, *Bernard Berenson*, 125. Cohen makes reference to the short story 'Altamura' published in the *Golden Urn*, in which Berenson imagines a town where they could live aesthetically. See Robert Colby, 'Places Eternal and Serene: The Vision of Altamura and Isabella Stewart Gardner's Fenway Court', in Connors and Waldman, *Bernard Berenson. Formation and Heritage* (Florence: Villa I Tatti, 2014), 69–100.

33 This decision was the result of a meeting with Giovanni Morelli, discussed in Samuels, *The Making of a Connoisseur*, 97–105.

34 Berenson was one of the first art connoisseurs to stress the importance of photographic reproductions for the study of painting. His article on Marcozzi's photographs of the old masters at the Poldi Pezzoli in Milan, his first ever publication on art, instigated a collaboration with *The Nation* in USA. Bernard Berenson, 'Marcozzi's Photographs', *The Nation* 50 (February 1890): 130.

35 Michael Field, *Works and Days*, f.43 (1895), Add. Ms.46783, The British Library, London. Berenson let Michael Field stay at Villa Kraus for a fortnight, while he was away on a trip to Paris 'to take some rich Americans to Pisa, Lucca, Siena & Perugia' (f.40). Michael Field described the room in detail, with a particular attention to the colour pattern: 'His little study is a delight – stretched brown sacking on the wall & a dado of greenish matting. The greenish curtains with peachy flowers shaded with gold – trumpery things in themselves, tone perfectly with the sack & tawny cheap carpet' (f.43). I would like to thank Marion Thain for pointing me to this document. For a discussion of the friendship between Costelloe, Berenson and Michael Field, see Martha Vicinius, '"Sister Souls": Bernard Berenson and Michael Field', *Nineteenth-Century Literature*, 60: 3 (2005), 326–54, and Anna Gruetzner Robins's essay in this volume.

36 The collaboration between Bernard and Mary Berenson has been the object of recent scholarship. See Carl Brandon Strehlke and Machtelt Brüggen Israëls, *The Bernard and Mary*

Berenson Collection of European Paintings at I Tatti (Milan and Florence: Villa I Tatti and Officina Libraria, 2015); Ilaria della Monica, 'Notes on Mary Berenson's Diary (1891–1893)', in *Women's Expertise and the Culture of Connoisseurship*, ed. Meaghan Clarke and Francesco Ventrella, special issue of *Visual Resources* 33: 1–2 (2017): 140–57. In this essay I am only dealing with the years before their marriage in 1900, therefore I will always refer to Mary as Costelloe.

37 Mary Berenson, 'Life of Bernard Berenson', Chapter V, ff.8–9. 22c.5, BMBP.

38 Barolsky is very explicit on this aspect and in tracing a long male modernist genealogy of thinking of abstraction as 'impersonality' that goes from Winckelmann to Fried, via Goethe, Pater and Berenson, Fry, Bell and Greenberg. Barolsky, 'Walter Pater and Bernard Berenson', 139–53.

39 Mary Berenson, 'Life of Bernard Berenson', Chapter V, f.33. 22c.5, BMBP.

40 Patricia Rubin has already noted that Berenson's copy of Pater's *The Renaissance* is annotated with corrections of attributions and locations, mainly in the chapters on Botticelli and Leonardo. Rubin, 'Bernard Berenson, Villa I Tatti', 208.

41 For a discussion of Berenson's adaptation of the Morellian method see David Alan Brown, *Berenson and the Connoisseurship of Italian Painting* (Washington DC: National Gallery of Art, 1979), 41–9.

42 Mary Berenson's Diary, Wednesday 22 March 1893, BMBP.

43 From a leaflet which I found in the BMBP we read that the lectures were held at a private address in 93, Onslow Square, South Kensington, on Tuesdays and Fridays at 11am. The fee for the 10-lecture series was £2 2s.

44 Laurel Brake, 'Vernon Lee and the Pater Circle', in *Vernon Lee; Decadence, Ethics, Aesthetics*, ed. Catherine Maxwell and Patricia Pulham (Basingstoke: Palgrave Macmillan, 2006), 40–57.

45 Julia Cartwright, *The Life and Art of Sandro Botticelli* (London: Duckworth & Co., 1904), 3. Vernon Lee occupies an interesting place in the bibliography on Botticelli. The first pages of Cartwright's monograph give us a snapshot of Botticelli's scholarship in 1904. On the one side we have Pater, Symonds and Lee. In the middle are two very different approaches: Crowe and Cavalcaselle's lists and the iconological interpretations of Warburg. Finally both Berenson and Horne feature as champions of the new criticism which, for Cartwright, also meant followers of the Morellian method. Berenson is the only scholar who is given a footnote, and the last word, so to speak, especially because Horne was delaying having his.

46 Mandy Gagel, '1897, A Discussion of Plagiarism: Letters Between Vernon Lee, Bernard Berenson, and Mary Costelloe', *Literary Imagination* 12: 2 (2010), 154–79. The reference to Berenson's address in Lungarno allows us to date this meeting before 1893, when Berenson moved into Villa Kraus.

47 For a discussion of the intellectual exchange between Berenson and Lee see also René Wellek, 'Vernon Lee, Bernard Berenson, and Aesthetics', in *Discriminations: Further Concepts of Criticism* (New Haven: Yale University Press, 1970); Jo Briggs, 'Plural Anomalies: Gender and Sexuality in Bio-Critical Readings of Vernon Lee', in *Vernon Lee; Decadence, Ethics, Aesthetics*.

48 As a student, Berenson published a positive review of Lee's *Baldwin*; Bernard Berenson, 'Vernon Lee. *Baldwin: Being Dialogues on Views and* Aspirations', *Harvard Monthly*, 2: 5 (July 1886): 207–9.

49 Mary Berenson, 'Portraits: Vernon Lee', in 'Mary Berenson, Unpublished Writings', 5–6. 22D.0, BMBP. I am very grateful to Ilaria della Monica for bringing this typescript to my attention.

50 Charles Ephrussi, '*Deux fresques du Musée du Louvre attribuées a Sandro Botticelli*', *Gazette des Beaux-Arts*, 25: 2 (1882), 483. Ephrussi writes: '*le Louvre complétait cette collection naissante par un choix suivi de morceaux assortis, il offrait bientôt un ensemble sans rival des plus nobles spécimens de la grande peinture décorative italienne*'. With the Botticelli acquisition, the Louvre became the second museum in the world to display fresco fragments, alongside the Brera in Milan, which owned frescoes by Raphael and Ghirlandaio; the National Gallery London already owned Pintoricchio and Signorelli, purchased at the Barker sale in 1874.

51 Vernon Lee, 'Botticelli at the Villa Lemmi' [1882], in *Juvenilia: Being a Second Series of Essays on Sundry Aesthetical Questions* (London: Roberts, 1887), 82.

52 Lee, 'Botticelli', 84.

53 Lee, 'Botticelli', 85–6.

54 Pater, *The Renaissance*, xxix.

55 Bernard Berenson, *The Central Italian Painters of the Renaissance* (London: G. P. Putnam's and Sons, 1897), 34–5.

56 Lee, 'Botticelli', 106.

57 Lee, 'Botticelli', 88.

58 For a discussion of the influence of experimental psychology on Vernon Lee see Francesco

Ventrella, *The Body of Art History: Writing, Embodiment and the Connoisseurial Imagination*. Unpublished PhD thesis (University of Leeds, 2012).

59 Bernard Berenson, *The Florentine Painters of the Renaissance* (London: G. P. Putnam's and Sons, 1896), 89, 87. These terms are excerpted from Berenson's discussion of Michelangelo's nudes. Alison Brown has identified the Nietzschean influence on Berenson's emphasis about the life-enhancing capacity of tactile values. Alison Brown, 'Bernard Berenson and "Tactile Values" in Florence', in *Formation and Heritage*, 109–10. It is illuminating for me to notice that Brown's essay was instigated by a personal memory in which she recalls not being able to see how Botticelli's Venus could represent Berenson's tactile values. In a sense, she is right because Berenson used Botticelli's line to find 'movement' rather than 'tactile values'.

60 Berenson, *The Florentine Painters*, 73–4.

61 Berenson, *The Florentine Painters*, 73. Original emphasis.

62 Berenson, *The Florentine Painters*, 75.

63 Pater, 'Botticelli', 34. Cf. Barolsky, 'Walter Pater and Bernard Berenson', 148–9.

64 B. Berenson to M. Costelloe, 9 December 1893. 114.10, BMBP. The book is Hermann Ulmann, *Sandro Botticelli* (Munich: Verlagsanstalt für Kunst und Wissenschaft, formerly F. Bruckmann, 1893). Berenson's copy, with minor annotations, can be found in the Biblioteca Berenson ND623.B7 U55 1893.

65 Bernd Roeck, *Florence 1900. The Quest for Arcadia* (New Haven: Yale University Press, 2009), 13, 68.

66 Max Seidel, ed., *Storia dell'arte e politica culturale intorno al 1900. La Fondazione dell'Istituto Germanico di Storia dell'Arte di Firenze* (Venice: Marsilio, 1999).

67 B. Berenson to M. Costelloe, [11 December] 1893. 114.10, BMBP.

68 Bernard Berenson, 'Botticelli' [*c*.1894?], in 'B.B. Unpublished Manuscripts'. 132.21, BMBP.

69 Costelloe spent considerable time with her two daughters, who lived with the grandparents near Fernhurst in Sussex. In another letter Berenson expresses his regret at not being able to go to London to see the old master exhibition at the New Gallery: 'If I had the money I certainly should run up to London to see the pictures and it would be such fun to travel back together'; B. Berenson to M. Costelloe, 13 December 1893. 114.10, BMBP.

70 B. Berenson to M. Costelloe, [19 December] 1893. 114.10, BMBP. The New Gallery listed the portrait of Smeralda Bandinelli as item 110 in the catalogue. *Exhibition of early Italian Art from 1300 to 1550, The New Gallery, Regent Street, 1893–4* (London, 1893), 21.

71 Indeed it was Mary who carefully developed the famous *Lists* which interlinked their photographic collection with bibliographical information on each master and regional school. See Ilaria della Monica, 'Notes on Mary Berenson's Diary (1891–93)', in *Visual Resources* 33: 1–2 (2017): 140–57.

72 'Amico di Sandro', in *The Study and Criticism* (1901), 60. Berenson had seen Ionides's collection for the first time in 1896: 'Ionides was invited to meet us last night[…] He had read my last and fully understood "tactile values". We are to see his collection presently'. B. Berenson to M. Costelloe, 22 July 1896. 114.16, BMBP.

73 C. M. Kauffmann, *Catalogue of Foreign Paintings I: Before 1800* (London: Victoria and Albert Museum, 1973), 37–9. See the essay in this volume by Nicola Costaras and Clare Richardson.

74 B. Berenson to M. Costelloe [26 January] 1894. 114.14, BMBP.

75 M.C. [Mary Costelloe], 'Review of Sandro Botticelli, by Hermann Ulmann', *The Studio*, 3: 17 (1894), pp. xxi–xxxiii. Jonathan Nelson has discovered another manuscript by Mary's hand entitled 'Botticelli and his critics' (22E.4), in which she tidies up and elaborates some of the ideas already explored in Berenson's 'Botticelli' manuscript. Jonathan K. Nelson, 'An Unpublished Essay by Mary Berenson, "Botticelli and His Critics" (1894–95)", *19: Interdisciplinary Studies in the Long Nineteenth Century* 28, special issue: *Nineteenth-Century Women Writers on the Old Masters*, ed. by Maria Alambritis, Susanna Avery-Quash and Hilary Fraser (2019, forthcoming). I refer to his introduction for another analysis of the collaboration between Mary and Bernard. As Tiffany Johnston has demonstrated, in these years Berenson and Costelloe often worked together by first talking about a work, and then writing either collaboratively or simultaneously on the same topic. Tiffany Johnston, *Mary Berenson and the Concept of Connoisseurship*. Unpublished PhD thesis (Indiana University, 2001).

76 'Z.' [Bernard Berenson], 'Hermann Ulmann, Sandro Botticelli', *Revue Critique d'Histoire et Littérature* (4 February, 1895), 88–95. Cf. letter from B. Berenson to Senda Berenson, 11 February, 1895. 23.20 BMBP. '[…] I am sending you a number of the *Revue Critique* – a very influential French journal – with an article of mine in it on Ulmann's Botticelli, signed Z. I do not expect you to read it. I send it to assure you that in Paris I am somebody.' I want to

thank Michael Gorman for sharing the transcription of this letter with me. Berenson published another review signed 'Z.', *'Kunsthistorisches Sammlungen des allerhoechsten Kaiserhauses. Fuehrer durch die Gemaelde-Galerie. Alte Meister. I. Italienische, spanische und franzoesiche Schulen. Wien*], 1894', *Revue Critique d'Histoire et Littérature*, 29: 6 (11 February, 1895): 117–19. In the offprint at I Tatti Berenson has added his signature by hand. See also Samuels, *The Making of a Connoisseur*, 221, for letter to Senda and Botticelli review.

77 B. Berenson to M. Costelloe [22 January 1894]. 114.12, MBMP. Interestingly, one month later, in a letter sent by Costelloe to her mother we read about meeting with Vernon Lee: 'she talked like an angel about Botticelli, putting flesh and blood to the abstract "law" I have discovered about Botticellli's development. I felt like giving up the attempt to say a word about him!' M. Costelloe to Hannah Whitall Smith, 14 February 1894. Lilly Library Copies, BMBP. I am grateful to Michel Gorman for sharing the transcription of this letter. That the 'law' must be identified with Berenson's 'formula' is not in doubt. However, Mary and Bernard may have come up with the law/formula through their collaboration.

78 B. Berenson, 'Botticelli'.

79 Bernard Berenson, 'Rudiments of Connoisseurship', in *The Study and Criticism of Italian Art*, second series (London: George Bell, 1902), 111–48. NB 'Amico' is in vol.I, 1901, 'Rudiments' in vol.II, 1902.

80 While I was working on this article, Michael Gorman discovered a manuscript version of this review written in Berenson's hand. Although the letters seem to suggest that the article was co-authored, the presence of this handwritten manuscript also suggests that Bernard asked Mary to sign a review written by him. I therefore refer to the text printed in *The Studio* as 'Costelloe's review' only for convenience, and not to indicate her authorship.

81 M.C. [Mary Costelloe], 'Review of Sandro Botticelli', 32.

82 Both passages quote directly from Berenson's unpublished notes on Botticelli.

83 In December Berenson was in Paris with Isabella Stewart Gardner, and had a chance to work on his review with Solomon Reinach. Cf. Mary Berenson's Diaries, entries for 18 and 19 December 1894. 20.8, BMBP.

84 'Z.' [Bernard Berenson], 'Hermann Ulmann', 92–3. *'L'identité de détails ne prouve rien quant à la paternité d'une œuvre: c'est l'identité de qualité seule qui peut établir une présomption à cet égard. Mais cette idée de la qualité est tout à fait étrangère à l'esprit de M. Ulmann. Comme la généralité des critiques allemands, il s'imagine qu'en accumulant des considérations quantitatives, on peut obtenir l'équivalent d'une preuve qualitative. En critique d'art, il n'est pas de pire erreur.'* [my translation]

85 For a discussion of the competition between Morelli and Bode see Jaynie Anderson, 'The Political Power of Connoisseurship in Nineteenth-Century Europe: Wilhelm von Bode versus Giovanni Morelli', *Jahrbuch der Berliner Museen* 38 (1996): 107–19.

86 Ulmann, *Sandro Botticelli*, 11.

87 Cf. Berenson's copy, Biblioteca Berenson, ND623.B7 U55 1893.

88 B. Berenson, 'Botticelli', BMBP. Scott's *The Antiquary* recurs in other instances as an example of old-fashioned scholarship. Cf. B. Berenson, 'The Critic and Art' (1892). 129.8, BMBP; and B. Berenson to M. Costelloe, n.d., December 1893: 'I read part of the Antiquary last night. Thus far it is not at all so good as Guy Mannering. But the Antiquary's methods were precisely those the author of the Botticelli book is still using. This man makes C[rowe] & C[avalcaselle] seem angels, refined, tremendously artistic, scrupulously precise in comparison'. 114.10, BMBP.

89 B. Berenson. 'Botticelli'. BMBP.

90 Berenson. 'Botticelli', BMBP. Berenson's emphasis on 'touch' is crucial here, and is also underlined by Mary Costelloe's organisation of the titles in the manuscript. This may represent an alternative reference to 'tactile values' which I cannot pursue here.

91 B. Berenson, 'Botticelli', BMBP. These sentences too were merged into Costelloe's review co-authored for *The Studio*.

92 Angela Leighton correctly speaks of Pater's reforming of style, *On Form: Poetry, Aestheticism, and the Legacy of a Word* (Oxford: Oxford University Press, 2007), 74–98.

93 Roberto Longhi to Bernard Berenson, 4 September 1912, in *Lettere e Scartafacci 1912–1957*, ed., Cesare Garboli and Cristina Montagnani (Milan: Adelphi, 1993), 83. My translation.

94 Leighton here is reading Pater's essay 'Prosper Mérimée' (1890); Leighton, *On Form*, p.183.

95 B. Berenson to M. Costelloe, 2 August, 1895. 114. 15, BMBP.

96 B. Berenson to M. Costelloe, 3 August 1895. 114.15, BMBP.

97 B. Berenson to M. Costelloe, 31 December, 1895. 114.16, BMBP. Berenson soon accepted the Botticelli's *Three Angels* as by Botticini. See Berenson,'*Amico di Sandro*', in *Study and Criticism* I,

50: 'the famous Verrocchiesque picture in the Florentine Academy, which, after having passed for centuries as Botticelli's is now being fast accepted as Botticini's'. See also Donata Levi's essay in this volume.

98 For an analysis of Berenson's ambiguous anti-Semitism in the period following the Dreyfus affair in France see Rachel Cohen, *Bernard Berenson*, 128–30.

99 Schapiro, 'Mr Berenson's Values', 209–26. On these passages also see Catherine Soussloff, 'Introducing Jewish Identity to Art History', in *Jewish Identity in Modern Art History*, ed. Catherine M. Soussloff (Berkeley and London: University of California Press, 1999), 10.

100 Soussloff, 'Introducing Jewish Identity', 3.

101 B. Berenson, 'Botticelli'. BMBP.

102 Pater, 'Botticelli', 39.

103 This passage could also indicate what Warburg must have taken from Pater. See Claudia Wedepohl's essay in this volume.

104 B. Berenson, 'The Critic and Art: Pre-Raphaelites', in 'Bernard Berenson Notebooks, 1892–1893'. 129.8, BMBP.

105 Bernard Berenson, 'The Critic and Art: Pre-Raphaelites'. BMBP.

106 Berenson, 'The Critic and Art: Pre-Raphaelites', BMBP. These sheets are different from Costelloe's unpublished manuscript 'Botticelli and His Critics', but elaborate very similar points in a more accomplished fashion. Jonathan Nelson has already examined the Pre-Raphaelites' influence on Berenson's 'Amico di Sandro' in a paper that he has kindly shared with me, and which will soon appear as Jonathan K. Nelson, 'Swinburne, Berenson, and the Origins of the "Amico di Sandro"', in Michael Kwakkelstein, Paula Nuttall, Geoffery Nuttall, eds. *Filippino Lippi: Beauty, Invention and Intelligence* (Florence: Istituto Universitario Olandese di Storia dell'Arte and Brill, 2018 forthcoming).

107 Elizabeth Prettejohn, 'Botticelli and the Pre-Raphaelites', in *Botticelli Reimagined*, ed. Mark Evans and Stefan Weppelmann, with A. Debenedetti, R. Rebmann, M. MacMahon and G. Montua (London: Victoria and Albert Museum, 2016), 79.

108 '*Die Dargestellte ähnelt sogar etwas der venus dort. Dante Gabriele Rossetti, aus dessen Besitz das Portrait stammt (früher in der Sammlung Pourtales), hielt beide für die gleiche Persönlichkeit. Soweit jedoch möchte ich nicht gehen. Wie viel Anregung mag der unserem Meister geistesverwandte Begründer der Preraffaelitenschule aus diesem Werke des alten Italieners geschöpft haben für seine Frauenköpfe!*' Ulmann, *Sandro Botticelli*, 56.

109 B. Berenson, 'Botticelli'. BMBP.

110 Although originally the idea of Lady Chamberlain, the 1930 Exhibition of Italian Art at the Royal Academy confirms the meeting between two ideologies: fascism and Italianità. See Francis Haskell, 'Botticelli, Fascism and Burlington House. The "Italian Exhibition" of 1930', *The Burlington Magazine 141*, No.1157 (1999): 462–72. For a general discussion of fascist uses of the Renaissance see Claudia Lazzaro and Roger Crum, ed., *Donatello among the Blackshirts: History and Modernity in the Visual Culture of Fascist Italy* (Ithaca [N.Y.]: Cornell University Press, 2005).

111 '*Ad uguale risultato si giunge osservando una serie di bellezze femminili immortalate dai nostri stessi artisti (fig. 1 e 1bis). Invano in una qualsiasi di queste figure si potrebbe identificare un tipo regionale, esse sono al di sopra di ogni tipo regionale, perché rappresentano l'immagine reale della razza italiana.*' Guido Landra, '*Concetti del razzismo italiano*', *La Difesa della razza* 1: 2 (1938): 10. For a commentary on the visual culture of scientific racism in Fascist Italy see Marianna Aguirre, '*La Difesa Della Razza* (1938–1943): Primitivism and Classicism in Fascist Italy', *Politics, Religion & Ideology*, 16:4 (2015): 370–90.

112 Michaud, *Les Invasions barbares*. Michaud's argument is also summarised in English in 'Barbarian Invasions and the Racialization of Art History', *October* 139 (2012): 59–76.

113 On this topic, see the classic Allan Sekula, 'The Body and the Archive', *October* 39 (1986): 3–64.

114 See Sander Gilman, *The Jew's Body* (London and New York: Routledge, 1992).

115 Donald Kuspit, 'Meyer Schapiro's Jewish Unconscious', in *Jewish Identity in Modern Art History*, 202. Kuspit elaborates on the ambiguity of this sentence.

116 Kuspit, 'Meyer Schapiro's Jewish Unconscious', 204.

117 Kuspit, *Jewish Unconscious*, 214.

118 B. Berenson, 'Botticelli'. BMBP.

119 Pater, 'Botticelli', 36.

7. A woman's touch: Michael Field, Botticelli and queer desire

Anna Gruetzner Robins

The poet and dramatist Michael Field, the joint pen name of Katherine Bradley (1846–1914) and her niece Edith Cooper (1862–1913) (fig.2.17), had a passion for Botticelli that matches that of the best of his late nineteenth-century admirers.[1] They made a pilgrimage to Florence to see his two most famous paintings, hunted down his work in British collections, wrote poems about three of his pictures, made extensive notes about paintings by Botticelli and spent hours in their 'little Botticelli room', poring over their collection of photographs of paintings by him. Their letters, the diary that they shared and the poetry that they wrote together

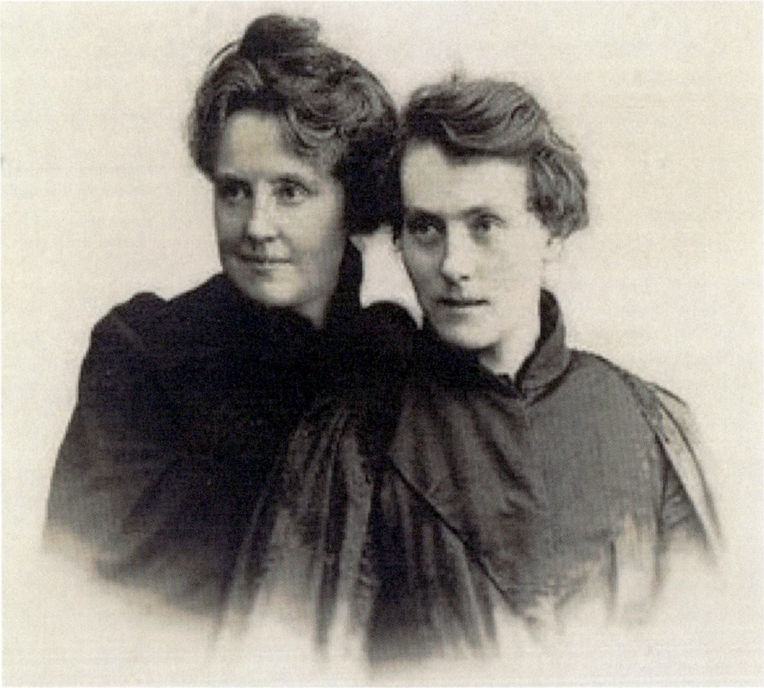

Fig.2.17 Michael Field (Katherine Bradley 1848–1914 and Edith Cooper 1862–1913), photograph, silver gelatin carte-de-visite (likely a copy of a platinotype), 1884-1889 by Bromhead, Clifton, Collection Mark Samuels Lasner, Special Collections, University of Delaware. © Wikimedia Commons.

reveal the complexities of the viewing experience of these two female beholders, whose writing celebrates their appreciation of the purely visual, 'the lines and colours of certain chosen paintings', and whose erotic engagement with the pagan figures in *The Birth of Venus, Primavera* (figs1.0 and 1.30), and *Mars and Venus* (fig.1.27) is unique. Michael Field looked, thought, talked together, and wrote in one seamless voice. Even in their diary, where the handwriting of each is easily identifiable, it is difficult to identify the observations of one from the other when reading their copious notes about pictures. They resisted the attempts of their peers to identify the contribution of each to what they regarded as a collaborative effort, explaining to the sexologist Havelock Ellis that 'we cross and interlace like a company of summer dancing flies; if one begins a character, his companion seizes and possesses it; if one conceives a scene or situation, the other corrects, completes, or murderously cuts away'.[2]

In summer 1890 Michael Field embarked on the first of many European tours taken together. They stopped first in Paris where they were introduced to Bernard Berenson, who, they noted, was 'qualifying to become an Art-historian'.[3] Within days they were meeting him in the Louvre for lessons in Morelli's critical approach. They left for Italy armed with a list of pictures given to them by Berenson that included *The Birth of Venus, Primavera* and other, less well-known pictures by Botticelli. As admirers of Walter Pater they knew his essay on the artist,[4] as well as the painting and the poetry of Dante Gabriel Rossetti, including his sonnet 'For Spring by Sandro Botticelli'.[5] As frequent visitors to the National Gallery in London they were already familiar with Botticelli's works, but meeting Berenson and going to Italy was a pivotal moment for them.[6]

Arriving in Florence on a whistle-stop trip around Italy, they soon made their way to *The Birth of Venus* in the Uffizi and *Primavera* in the Galleria dell'Accademia. The former was a key picture in Pater's influential essay; the latter was discovered and celebrated by the Pre-Raphaelite circle, and featured in Rossetti's sonnet. They were quickly back at the Uffizi where they spent part of the day in 'patient, continuous' looking at the *Birth of Venus* before making what they called 'a special study' of *Primavera* the following day. Their initial, highly visual, response to both pictures is recorded in a series of jottings that would find a voice in *Sight and Song*, a collection of 31 poems – each about a single picture that they had seen, including four about *The Birth of Venus, Primavera* (both in the Galleria degli Uffizi, Florence) and *Mars and Venus* (National Gallery, London).[7] The aim of the poems, they explained in the preface to the book, was to create an act of seeing 'as pure as the gazer can refine it of theory, fancies, or his mere subjective enjoyment'.[8]

Their efforts to record their attempt to see with an innocent eye is best illustrated in their diary which, as Marion Thain notes, functioned 'as both travel journal and notebook for the poems' – and also, I would add, a fascinating record of their observations about art.[9] Writing on the *Birth of Venus*, they recorded that Venus 'rises from a shell that floats on scallop-shaped wavelets, her back hair is bound in a sheaf, her locks about her face are bright and possessed by the wind', and 'this Venus, born out of her time, is shy at her own naked loveliness'.[10] Even Nature in its abundance was suffused with Venus's innocence:

> But what is this cool, cool sea, sprinkled with blown rose-leaves – & the shy recoiling girl-form that seeks to veil itself in its coiled wrappings of innocent hair?[...] The little green waves are indicated by their quaint foam-tips treated decoratively [...] There is strong covert in the great orange-trees & underneath them the sombrest of earthly shade, exquisitely contrasting with the lovely little innocent frilly pucker of the nipples under the shell.[11]

A finely tuned appreciation of the beauty of the natural world informs their writing on the painting:

> And I will greet the rosy garment of daisies broidery spring carries to wrap her. This attendant woman-form is clad in white sprinkled with blue cornflowers, her necklet of flowerless rose-leaves, her girdle of the rose in bloom.[...] The foot of Zephyrus moves the water shoreward. Roses fly like birds in the crisp air, which likewise makes the ends of Venus's hair flamboyant. To the right are lemon-trees – in the left hand foreground some rushes that tell of the coming to land of the Queen.[12]

These two aesthetes took equal pleasure in flowery hats, or the colour and pattern of a Brussels carpet ordered from Morris & Co – they noted the 'yellow mix on clouded cream [...] bordered or [*sic*] with blue in love with lavender seen through green stems with a fleck of rare pink for a bloom'.[13] The slippage between their writing on art and their writing on decoration reflects a similar heightened visual awareness and may explain perhaps why a fifteenth-century Italian painter from a very different cultural milieu could appeal to any number of English aesthetes, who placed such a premium on visual pleasure.

The Morris carpet was for their 'little Botticelli room', their carefully devised personal monument to an 'expressive, living Aestheticism'.[14] It was furnished with Morris wallpaper that would be increasingly covered with framed photographs of some of their favourite paintings, a 'dark mahogany' settle, cushioned and canopied in a 'lavender' colour (compare fig.2.18), commissioned from Herbert Horne – who 'insisted' they chose 'lavender velvet curtains' for the cream-coloured bookcase.[15] This old English type of furniture, refashioned by Horne in an aesthetic style, was quite literally the seat of their scholarly and creative endeavours. They were 'sitting in the settle together', they told Berenson, when preparing their comments on the proofs for his first book, *The Venetian Painters of the Renaissance,* 1894.[16] Since their first meeting in Paris, Berenson had, for a time, been a close friend and influential ally. They met up again

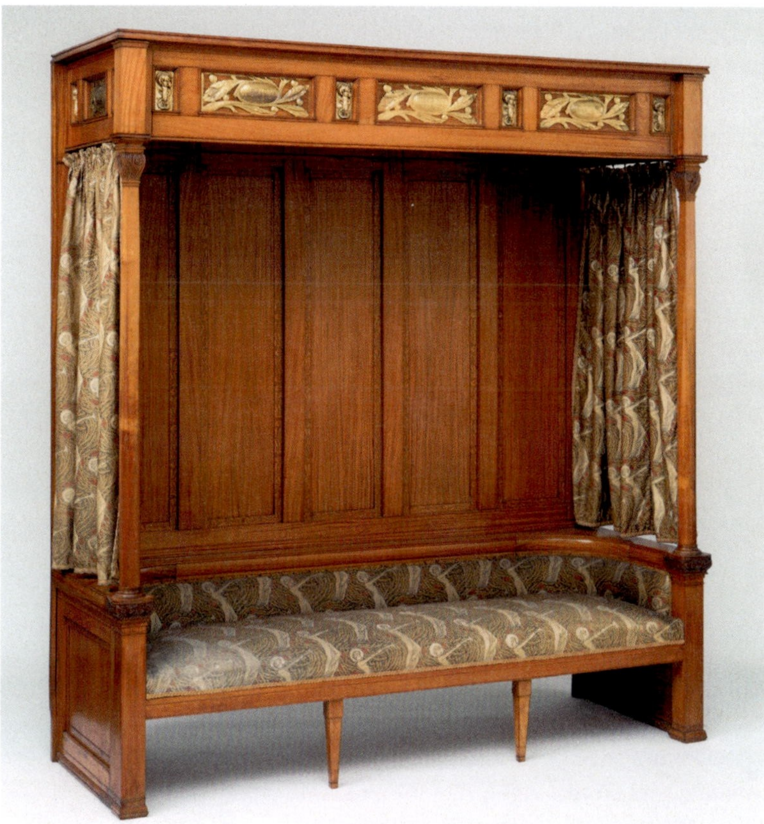

Fig.2.18 Settle designed by Arthur H. Mackmurdo and Herbert P. Horne (The Century Guild), made by E. Goodall & Co., 1886, satinwood, with panels of marquetry and brass; upholstery of printed cotton, Victoria and Albert Museum, London (W.16:1 to 4-1967). © Victoria and Albert Museum, London.

with him and his future wife Mary Costelloe in Paris and Italy, and paid to attend his self-arranged lectures in the National Gallery, London. Berenson advised what books on art they should read, supplied them with lists and sent them photographs of pictures; he also read a draft of *Sight and Song*. It was his suggestion to give 'the painter's names before all the pictures' in the titles of the poems, and they duly took his advice.[17]

On New Year's Day 1894 Michael Field met up with a group that included Berenson and Mary Costelloe at the New Gallery, London, to see the *Exhibition of Early Italian Art from 1300 to 1550*, which contained a significant number of Botticelli pictures. Soon after Berenson advised them to write a book on the artist. The book never came to fruition, but their notes about a range of Botticelli pictures suggest that they took the proposal seriously. They may even have been privy to Mary Costelloe's copious illustrated notes, starting in 1890, about pictures by, or attributed to, Botticelli in British collections. Any budding late nineteenth-century connoisseur would know that photographs of paintings were an essential tool for what Berenson described as 'a science reconstructing the unknown from the known'. I can imagine they spent time on their settle poring over their own collection, but the settle and the photographs had more than one purpose.

Before moving to Durdans (the house in Reigate where they lived with Edith's father and sister), Michael Field wrote a poem where they fantasised about sharing intimate moments together on a settee; it was to be a place for love-making.

> There's a lavender settee,
> Cushioned for my sweet and me;
> Ah, what secrets will there be
> For love-telling,
> When her head leans on my knee![18]

The planned-for settee took the form of Horne's settle, but it served the same purpose. The high mahogany seat, covered with lavender-coloured velvet, must have been imbricated with their many moments of close intimacy and erotic longing.[19]

Michael Field wanted to avoid a subjective point of view in *Sight and Song*, but this proved an impossible aim: ways of seeing are always subjective, and their particular way of seeing makes them a fascinating beholder. The two women had a strong emotional attachment and wrote endless declarations of their love for each other. They were a queer female couple, with a range of male nicknames for each other. They called each other 'boy' and 'he', as well as 'wife' and 'she', and thus played with gender identities that were slippery and unstable.

With no ready model of women who were desiring subjects of images of the female body, Michael Field reinvented and reimagined existing male conventions for exploring their queer desire.[20] Botticelli's female figures (and also those in other pictures) had a living presence for them, and were a trigger for the performative space where they acted out their erotic fantasies.

Katherine had studied at Cambridge where she read Classics at Newnham, and in 1879 both women enrolled to study the Classics at University College, Bristol. They undoubtedly knew examples in the writing of the ancient world, and also in eighteenth-century texts, in which a female marble statue becomes a living presence, to be admired, touched and coaxed into an erotic encounter by an amorous male admirer.[21] Katherine must have had these examples in mind as she gazed on three different occasions at three naked female statues – the Venus de Milo in Paris, the Medici Venus in Florence and the Capitoline Venus in Rome – during a European tour in summer 1880. She had also read Winckelmann on naked male sculpture,[22] and more than likely Pater's essay on him, but it took more than an ordinary imaginative leap for her to use these examples of male-female desire, and male-male desire for a sculpted body, as a touchstone when voicing her own desire for a sculpted female body. To illustrate this point, I refer to Katherine's letter written to Edith on 7 September 1880, in which she describes looking at the Capitoline Venus in the company of her two travelling companions, Miss Scott and Miss Blythe:

> The Venus of the Capitol is a perfect woman. Most happily her garments are beside her, not on her, and the lovely form from throat to foot is unmutilated and unshrouded, the dimpled back – the real beauty of the waist is only seen in the back – made me long again and again for the attendant Scott or Blythe to turn the statue for me; and all the circling beauty of the loins Kept me in lingering adoration[...][23]

Katherine also may have known the teachings of the Oxford don Benjamin Jowett, whose insistence that learning the stories in Greek myth was as important as learning the language opened the door to a model of male-male love in the ancient past that was influential for many of his students, including Oscar Wilde, as they explored their own male-male desire. But it still took a mental leap for Katherine to voice her desire for women. With the exception of the fragmentary writings of Sappho, which Michael

Field reformulated and extended in *Long Ago*, 1889, their first book of poetry, they had no other model of female-female desire to follow, which may explain why they adopted various private male identities during moments of intimacy.[24]

Pictures invite stories taken from our own biography. The male-male desire that runs through Pater's essays in *The Renaissance* has been well documented, but the disgust of the queer Pater on looking at *The Birth of Venus* has been overlooked. Pater imagined that the pagan goddess of love and beauty had a living presence, but the experience brought him little pleasure. An undercurrent of revulsion runs through his comments. He imagines Venus to be a worn-out sex worker, a woman of the streets, up before dawn, with 'sorrow in her face' at the thought of the whole long day of love yet to come.[25] This was no pagan Venus reconfigured by a fifteenth-century artist, but a shameful and shamed nineteenth-century prostitute. Pater thought he saw the 'shadow of death' tinting the grey flesh of Venus. Apparently he may have known the picture only from a chromolithograph issued by the Arundel Society. That apart, however, he was repeating a commonly held prejudice about Victorian female sex workers whose lives, it was believed, would be cut short by disease and death.

Katherine Bradley knew about sex workers. While living in Bristol in the early 1880s she came into contact with supporters of Josephine Butler's campaign to end the state inspection of prostitutes. She attended public lectures where Butler gave graphic descriptions, based on first-hand interviews, of an inhuman practice that required that female sex workers to undergo a painful examination for contagious disease. In September 1883 she travelled together with a group of women, including Josephine Butler, to attend the Third Triennial Congress of The British and Continental Federation for the Abolition of State Regulation of Vice, at The Hague. There Katherine gave a speech herself and listened to five days of speeches about prostitution.[26]

As we have seen, Michael Field believed that the figure of Venus in *The Birth of Venus* was an innocent young woman, 'a shy recoiling girl-form that seeks to veil itself in its coiled wrappings of innocent hair'; a figure who, 'not even by amorous bend of her head', gave any indication 'of that lusty sweeping male force on her left'.[27] Venus was not the Greek Venus, but 'how a Christian artist draws it: the soft guardian eyes of almost tearful shadow, the whole body timid, full of the instinct of fight[…] That the things of love are unspeakable, that the sorrow of it cannot be told – that shadowed face expresses to us'. Like Flora, who 'is contemplative, as woman of woman's beauty – the lips apart in wonder', they could gaze at this innocent Venus, and 'wonder & desire'.[28]

The premium they placed on Venus's virginity reflects the belief as described by the Social Purity Campaign that 'the possession of virginity is the sole source of female power, freedom and joy', and it is one that they upheld.[29] As they explain in the last two lines of their poem *Birth of Venus*: 'Virgin stranger, come to seek/ Covert of strong orange-boughs/ By the sea-wind scarcely moved-/ She is Love that hath not loved.'[30]

If anything, they took even greater visual pleasure in *Primavera*. While they had discussed the picture with Berenson when they first met in Paris, and would talk about the picture again with him in London at the end of the summer, seeing the picture in Florence was a revelation. These two passionate gardeners loved the scented, flowered and sensuous painted landscape as much as they admired the much copied aesthetic style of Flora's flowery gown.[31] And while Berenson would tell them that the three female figures whom they correctly believed to be the Three Graces were in fact the Three Fates (because they were 'too solemn and old' – a rather mean thing to say to the ageing Michael Field), they ignored his advice in the poem: 'They are the Graces in their virgin youth'.[32] The *Primavera* Venus, who is immersed in a flowery landscape of 'tulip, heartsease, strawberry-rose,/ Fringed pinks and dull grape-hyacinth', as the poem also tells us, was no innocent: 'Venus is sad among the wanton powers' and 'Her wide eyes have no allure,/ Dark and heavy with the pain'.[33]

In August 1890 Michael Field spent time together looking closely at a photograph of *The Birth of Venus*. While they undoubtedly took great pleasure in this act of contemplative looking, a letter from Katherine written to Mary Costelloe in December 1892 suggests that they shared a performative space with these painted images by Botticelli, which they imagined to be living beings. Berenson had sent them a 'huge' photograph of *Primavera*, which they immediately framed in 'brown paper' and hung in their 'little Botticelli room' (fig.2.19); it can be seen hanging above the cream bookcase in a photograph.[34] They explained that the picture was filling them with joy, especially the figure of Flora: 'I am fascinated by every little flake of her straight hair, every bit of design on her embroidered dress. And before her eyes & mouth I am dumb. She really is most terribly alive – herself, herself through every pore of her skin[…] I am laying down my pen to stare at her'.[35] Photographs such as this enabled them to imagine the living presence of Botticelli's women, and I would argue triggered their erotic desire and fantasy.

A fifteenth-century painted image of a female figure might seem like a poor substitute for the real thing, but Botticelli pictures unleashed deep erotic fantasies. No more so than with *Mars and Venus*, which

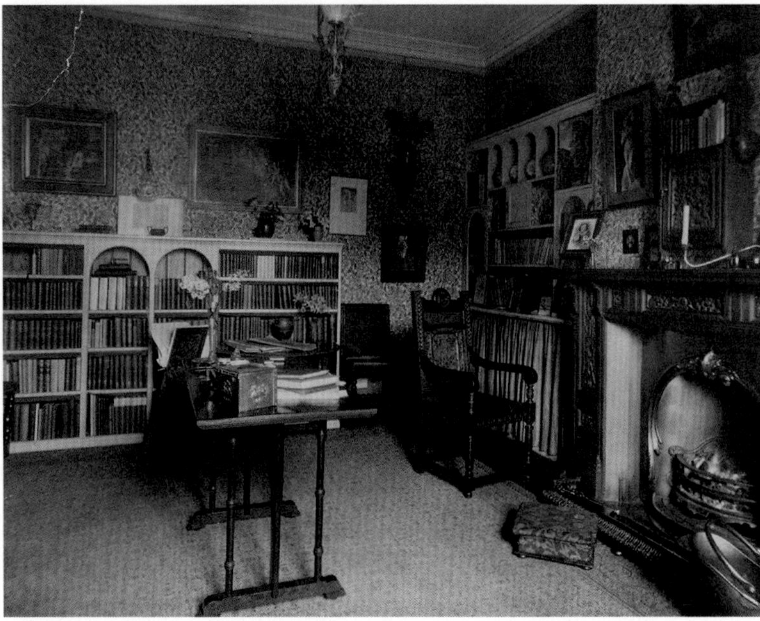

Fig.2.19 Photograph of the 'Botticelli room' at Durdans, Bodleian Library – Ms Eng Misc 304, 22 & 23. © The Bodleian Libraries, The University of Oxford (MS. Eng. Misc. c. 304, fol. 22r)

had entered the collection of the National Gallery, London in 1878. In July 1891 they 'sat long within sight of Botticelli's *Venus & Mars*', and recorded their response in their journal. John Addington Symonds's comment that 'the face and attitude of that unseductive Venus, wide awake and melancholy, opposite her snoring lover, seems to symbolise the indignities,/ which women may have to endure from insolent and sottish boys with only youth to recommend them', must have been a touchstone when they wrote:[36]

> Venus lies alert, her body lifted like a shoot after thunder-rain, triumphant for she has but received the storm: in him it is a spent fury & power that he has lost. He sleeps as if dead [...] This fulfilment of love is so like the fulfilment of life. How tragic are the two great figures male & female – he sleeping in illusion, she already above it, and watchful lest it cheat her ever again.[37]

The following month Michael Field was in Dresden where they saw Giorgione's *Venus*. The sleeping goddess was an example of 'perfect womanhood', they observed, while noting that her left hand 'lies near the thigh, the fingers bent inwards with unashamed simpleness – that profound universal of sex'.[38]

Their subsequent poem *The Sleeping Venus Giorgione* contains 'the only positive contemporary description about female masturbation':[39]

> Her hand the thigh's tense surface leaves, / Falling inward Not even sleep/ Dare invalidate the deep,/ Universal pleasure sex / Must unto itself annex-/ Even the stillest sleep; at peace/ More profound with rest's increase,/ She enjoys the good./ Of delicious womanhood.[40]

We might assume that they were writing from personal experience. Later the same day, after seeing the Giorgione *Venus*, Edith became sick with scarlet fever. While lying delirious in a Dresden hospital, she grew 'wild for pleasure' with Katherine, who was sleeping in her room. The presence of the nurse prohibited any intimacy, so instead she began to think about Botticelli's *Mars and Venus*, about which Michael Field had started a poem before leaving England. The memory triggered a highly erotic fantasy where she reimagined herself as Mars with Katherine as her Venus. She later described the moment in their diary:

> I am Mars, and, looking across at Sim's [Katherine's] little bed, I realise that she is a goddess, hidden in her hair – Venus. Yet I cannot reach her (I had been writing *Venus & Mars* (Nat. Gal.) just before I left home. I grow wilder for her or play check & madder against the ugly Mädchen. Sim comes to quiet me and assure me she is 'My Little Horse'.[41]

The precise nature of Edith's fantasy becomes clearer in the subsequent poem *Venus and Mars*, which describes Venus after she has masturbated Mars: She rears from off the ground/ as if her body grew/ Triumphant as a stem/ That hath received the rains/ and Mars '[…] supine who fell from her caress/ When love had had its sway'.[42] Its autobiographical origin, however, is suppressed in the poem and it is only through a close reading of the account in the diary that it becomes clear.

Following hospital practice, Edith's German nurse cropped her hair and gave her the name Henry. This change in her appearance and gender identity undoubtedly encouraged Edith to imagine herself as the young, androgynous figure of Mars. This gender slippage also speaks of a wider ambition to question conventional sexual norms, and is but one example of a 'rebellious femininity that worked with and against masculinity'.[43]

Patricia Rubin makes the point that the viewer's subjectivity is constructed by the nature of the gaze, whether the spectator is a man or a woman.[44] But even so Edith's erotic fantasy and cross-gender identification with the passive, naked, spent body of Mars is fairly extraordinary. No one else in the Victorian period except John Addington Symonds appears to have noticed the erotic nature of this viewing object, and even then the comments of Symonds, a queer man with a wife and children, were heavy with autobiography. Edith's fantasy took place at the beginning of what would become a growing obsession with Berenson, whose deliciously pretty boyish looks complemented those of the newly androgynous-looking Edith. By autumn 1891 Edith and Berenson were involved in a complicated, emotionally charged friendship, creating a 'queer triangle [of] two queer female poets and a young male aesthete'.

In a broader sense the androgynous adolescent male, able to 'absorb and reflect a variety of sexual desires and emotional needs', was a cultural paradigm of the 1890s – a well-known trope of homoerotic desire within the queer, homosocial sub-culture of bohemian aesthetic circles within which Michael Field moved.[45] Once again they funnelled their desire with the help of an existing male model. Edith's cropped hair made her look like an androgynous young man, and she – privately at least – took the name Henry; at the same time Botticelli's androgynous Mars was an image that enabled her to express her longing of sexual desire and fulfilment. Recognising and defining female sexual pleasure was a struggle when many still believed that it was improper for women to have sexual feelings; existing male models were the best on offer. Michael Field would have been better placed in the twenty-first century, with its ever increasingly fluid gender and sexual identities.

In 1899 Michael Field moved to the first house they owned together, the Paragone in Richmond, where their friends, the queer couple, Charles Ricketts and Charles Shannon, were their near neighbours. Since the previous year Ricketts had started a campaign to persuade them that Edward Burne-Jones was a far preferable artist to their beloved Botticelli. In spring 1900 Michael Field bowed to their influence and wrote in their diary:

> as for Botticelli he is a Vice. But one must constantly change one's Vices as a matter of hygiene & photographs of Botticelli have recently been unhung. Always change your vices – that is the golden Rule.[46]

This must have been a sad moment for Michael Field, for whom this fascinating artist had meant so much.

Notes

1 For a recent discussion of the Victorian taste for Botticelli see Elizabeth Prettejohn, *Modern Painters and Old Masters The Art of Imitation from the Pre-Raphaelites to the First World War* (New Haven and London: Yale University Press for The Paul Mellon centre for British Art, 2017), 147–66.

2 Katherine Bradley to Havelock Ellis, May 1886; cited in Mary Sturgeon, *Michael Field* (London: G. G. Harrap, 1922), 47.

3 See *Michael Field. The Poet Published and Manuscript Materials*, ed. Marion Thain and Ana Parejo Vadillo, (Peterborough, Ont.; Buffalo, NY: Broadview Press, 2009), 243. Their encounter with Berenson in the Louvre took place on 10 June 1890.

4 Walter Pater, 'Sandro Botticelli', in *The Renaissance: Studies in Art and Poetry*, ed. Donald L. Hill, (Berkeley, Los Angeles, London: University of California Press, 1980). The essay was first published in *The Fortnightly Review*, 1870, reprinted in *Studies in the Renaissance*, 1873, retitled in subsequent editions *The Renaissance*.

5 Dante Gabriel Rossetti, 'For Spring, by Sandro Botticelli in the Accademia of Florence', in *Dante Gabriel Rossetti: Collected Writings*, ed. Jan Marsh (London: Dent, 1999), 427.

6 1882 when Ruskin showed Katherine his copy of *Zipporah*, 1874, Ruskin Library, Lancaster University, a copy by Ruskin of part of the fresco of *The Temptation of Moses* in the Sistine Chapel,

7 Michael Field, 'The Birth of Venus, Sandro Botticelli, The Uffizi', 'Spring, Sandro Botticelli, The Accademia of Florence', 'The Figure of Venus in Spring, Sandro Botticelli, The Accademia of Florence' and 'Venus and Mars, Sandro Botticelli, The National Gallery', in *Sight and Song* (London: Elkin Matthews and John Lane at the sign of the Bodley Head in Vigo Street,1892).

8 Michael Field, 'Preface', in *Sight and Song*, v.

9 Marion Thain, '*Michael Field' Poetry, Aestheticism and the Fin de Siècle* (Cambridge: Cambridge University Press, 2007), 67.

10 Michael Field, *Notebook,* Book 3, vol.III (ff. iii+146). Jan. 1890–July 1891, which includes: f.27. Amy Katharine Mary Ryan, d. 1910 nee Coo[...], British Library, Add MS 46778; Accessed via the Michael Field Diary Archive, *Victorian Lives and Letters Consortium* (Center for Digital Humanities, University of South Carolina): http://tundra.csd.sc.edu/vllc/field. I am grateful to Leonie Sturge-Moore and Charmian O'Neil for their permission to cite from the Estate of Michael Field.

11 Michael Field, *Notebook*, Book 3, 136.

12 Michael Field, *Notebook*, Book 3, 137.

13 British Library, MS Add. 46779 f.26; cited in Ana Parejo Vadillo, 'Aestheticism and Decoration: At Home with Michael Field', *Cahiers Victoriens et* Édouardiens (September 2011): 19. I am indebted to this excellent article for my work on Michael Field.

14 Parejo Vadillo, 'Aestheticism', 19.

15 British Library, MS. Add. 46779 f.24 v.; cited in Parejo Vadillo, 'Aestheticism', 25.

16 Ms letter, Michael Field to Bernard Berenson, 24 April/ 182, Bernard and Mary Berenson Papers 1880–2002, Biblioteca Berenson, Villa I Tatti - The Harvard University Centre for Italian Renaissance Studies. Courtesy of the President and Fellows of Harvard College. A date of 1889 had been pencilled on the letter, but it must have been written in 1892 because Whistler's large retrospective exhibition, which took place in 1892, is mentioned in the letter. Horne's settle in the V&A collection (museum number W.16:1 to 4-1967) is a great example of the type of objects designed and produced by the Century Guild – a group of designers and craftsmen of which Horne was a founder member.

17 Ms Bernard Berenson to Michael Field, 28 February 1892, British Library. See also Ernest Samuels, *Bernard Berenson: the making of a connoisseur* (Cambridge, Mass. and London: Belknap Press, 1979).

18 Michael Field, 'An Invitation', in *Underneath the Bough: A book of verses* (London-New York: G. Bell, 1893), 81.

19 Rather confusingly the Fields describe the settle as a settee in their poem. Ana Parejo Vadillo ('Aestheticism', 25) assumes they ordered a settee from Horne, but both their diary and their letter to Berenson make it clear that it was a settle.

20 For a discussion of their role playing and queer identity see Virginia Blain, 'Michael Field, the "Two-headed Nightingale": lesbian text as palimpsest', *Women's History Review,* Vol. 6 (1996): 239–57.

21 For a discussion of these precedents see Caroline van Eck, *Art, Agency and Living Presence from the Animated Image to the Excessive Object* (Leiden: Leiden University Press, 2015).

22 See Katherine Bradley to Edith Cooper, September 1881; cited in Sharon Bickle, *The Fowl and the Pussycat. Love letters of Michael Field, 1876–1909* (Charlottesville and London: University of Virginia Press, 2008), 48, where she wrote 'Winckelmann Consoles me'.

23 Katherine Bradley to Edith Cooper, 7 September 1880; cited in Bickle, *The Fowl and the Pussycat*, 24.

24 Michael Field, *Long Ago* (London: 1889).

25 Pater in Hill, *The Renaissance*, 46.

26 Bickle, 99, n.1 reports that Katherine Bradley was among the representatives from Britain at this Congress that took place at The Hague in September 1883.

27 Michael Field, *Notebook*, Book 3, 111, 136.

28 Michael Field, *Notebook*, Book 3, 136–137.

29 Chris White, 'The Tiresian Poet: Michael Field', in *Victorian women poets: a critical reader*, ed. Angela Leighton (Oxford: Blackwell Publishers, 1996) 152; cited in Martha Vicinus, 'Faun Love: Michael Field and Bernard Berenson', *Women's History Review* 18 (November 2009): 753.

30 Michael Field, 'Botticelli's *Birth of Venus,*' in *Sight and Song*, 15.

31 For a full discussion of Michael's Field's diary entry on *Primavera* and the poem see Marion Thain, *"'Michael field": poetry, aestheticism and the fin de siècle* (Cambridge: Cambridge University Press, 2010), 66–79. I am also indebted to Hilary Fraser, 'A Visual Field: Michael Field and the Gaze', *Victorian Literature and Culture* 34 (2006): 553–71.

32 Michael Field, '*Spring,* Sandro Botticelli, The Academia of Florence' in *Sight and Song*, 24.

33 Michael Field, 'Botticelli's *Birth of Venus,* The Ufizi [*sic*]' in *Sight and Song*, 15.

34 Ms letter Michael Field to Mary Costelloe, 25 December 1892, Bernard and Mary Berenson Papers, Villa I Tatti, states that Berenson had written to say that he had sent the photograph of *Primavera* and that it had been framed.

35 Ms letter Michael Field to Bernard Berenson, 2 December 1892, pm, 242 Berenson Biblioteca, Villa I Tatti,The Harvard University Centre for Italian Renaissance Studies, courtesy of the President and Fellows of Harvard College.

36 John Addington Symonds, *Renaissance in Italy* 3 (London: Smith, Elder, 1877), 253.

37 Michael Field, *Notebook* 4; vol.IV, Jan.–Dec. 1891. British Library, Add MS 46779. Accessed via the Michael Field Diary Archive, Victorian Lives and Letters Consortium (Center for Digital Humanities, University of South Carolina): http://tundra.csd.sc.edu/vllc/field.

38 Michael Field, *Notebook*, Book 4.

39 Jill Ehnenn, 'Looking Strategically: Feminist and Queer Aesthetics in Michael Field's *Sight and Song*', *Victorian Poetry* (Spring 2005): 124. See also Rona Goffen, ed., *Titian's Venus of Urbino* (Cambridge and New York: Cambridge University Press, 1997).

40 Michael Field, 'The Sleeping Venus Giorgione The Dresden Gallery', in *Sight and Song*, 101–2.

41 Michael Field, *Notebook*, Book 4, vol.IV (ff.164). Jan.–Dec. 1891 includes: f.131, Amy Katharine Mary Ryan, d.1910 nee Cooper; wife[...], British Library, Add MS 46779; Accessed via the Michael Field Diary Archive, *Victorian Lives and Letters Consortium* (Center for Digital Humanities, University of South Carolina): http://tundra.csd.sc.edu/vllc/field. The entry was added towards the end of August after they returned to England.

42 Michael Field, 'Venus and Mars' in *Sight and Song*, 43–44.

43 Vicinus, 'Faun Love', 753.

44 Patricia Rubin, 'The Seductions of Antiquity', in *Manifestations of Venus: Art and Sexuality*, ed. Caroline Ascott and Katie Scott (Manchester: Manchester University Press, 2000), 24–38.

45 Vicinus, 'Faun Love', 754.

46 Michael Field, *Notebook,* Book 14, vol.XIV (ff. iii+ 189), 1900; British Library, Add MS 46789. Accessed via the Michael Field Diary Archive, Victorian Lives and Letters Consortium (Center for Digital Humanities, University of South Carolina): http://tundra.csd.sc.edu/vllc/field 120.

Part 3
Botticelli between art history and connoisseurship

Introduction

Caroline Elam

While part 2 focused on responses to Botticelli on the part of English artists and poets from the eighteenth to the early twentieth centuries, it also included an analysis of the tensions and ambiguities in the early writings on Botticelli of that celebrated 'scientific critic', Bernard Berenson. Francesco Ventrella's fascinating account of how Berenson's study of Botticelli was provoked by his distaste for the first monograph on the artist by Hermann Ulmann may be seen as a bridge to this third part, which turns to writings on Botticelli by art historians and connoisseurs.

Reviewing the historiography of the artist in 1930, Jacques Mesnil observed that writers on Botticelli always betray their nationality in their choice of approach and subject matter.[1] This is borne out by the works of the five authors treated in this part, whose English, Italian, German, Japanese and Franco/Flemish origins are evident both from their own methodologies and from their reactions to one another. That said, the study of Italian Renaissance art has since the nineteenth century been a strikingly cosmopolitan affair, in which personal contacts and collaborations have played important catalytic roles. However, the historiography of Botticelli in particular has a distinctively dialectical character, in which writers are inclined to lock horns with the perceived shortcomings of their predecessors.

The early decades of the period under discussion here were those of the Botticelli mania, launched in Britain by the Pre-Raphaelites and by the aestheticising critical writings of Swinburne, Pater and Ruskin. These are not pursued in detail in this volume, as they were well covered in the catalogue of *Botticelli Reimagined*. Another major figure who, for the same reason, is not individually treated in these essays is Herbert Horne, whose monograph of 1908 is generally acknowledged to be a milestone in the study of Botticelli. He and Aby Warburg turned their backs on the excesses of the aesthetic movement's response to the artist in order to pursue, in their very different ways, a historicising approach inspired by documentary discoveries and the critical and poetic language of Botticelli's own period. Both would have approved of the fact that all four contributions to this section are based on fresh new evidence derived from archival research.

The chapter on Botticelli in Crowe and Cavalcaselle's *New History of Italian Painting*, published in 1864–6, is an appropriate starting point. This is not just because it was the first serious consideration of Botticelli's life and work since Vasari, but also because, as shown here by Donata Levi, it provoked creatively antagonistic reactions, both from the critics Pater and Ruskin, and from the pioneers of 'scientific' connoisseurship Morelli and Berenson. It is ironic that, while making Vasari their starting point, Crowe and Cavalcaselle could not fully share the appreciation felt for Botticelli by the sixteenth-century biographer. Crowe's favourite critical terms for what he saw as Quattrocento weaknesses – 'want of selection', 'coarseness' and 'vulgarity' – seem to us now especially inappropriate in Botticelli's case. Levi shows that in his later, Italian edition of the book, Cavalcaselle appears completely oblivious of the Botticelli cult that had gripped the British since the 1860s; he is also silent in the face of Morelli's derogatory comments on his and Crowe's earlier text.

If Crowe and Cavalcaselle lacked interest in the peculiarities and mannerisms of what Berenson termed 'artistic personality', it was, Levi contends, because they were more concerned to identify a patchwork of formative influences on the artist, from Lippi, Pollaiuolo and Verrocchio. Nor did they accord special status to Botticelli's great mythological paintings. It is quite a shock to find the *Primavera* (fig.1.30) tersely summed up as 'a picture which is no longer fresh, but interesting as an illustration of the gradual growth of Botticelli's manner, and his characteristic treatment of half-heathen incidents in vogue at the time of Lorenzo de' Medici'.[2]

Such 'half-heathen incidents' and their parallels in the literature of Lorenzo's circle became the principal focus of Aby Warburg's epoch-making doctoral dissertation on *The Birth of Venus* (fig.1.0) and the *Primavera*. In her essay, based on new evidence in the Warburg archive, Claudia Wedepohl traces the fascinating false starts and methodological divagations that led to Warburg's eventual choice of subject, and left their half-concealed traces in his unwieldy but brilliant text. The consequences of Warburg's protean writings were to transform the study of meaning in art and institute a new kind of cultural history.

Warburg was reacting against the subjective vapourings of the aesthetic critics and the concentration on morphological detail of

Morellian connoisseurs such as Berenson. However, neither he nor Horne, in their search for a historically and culturally grounded Botticelli, could completely escape the influence of decades of Botticelli-mania.[3] Warburg included in his thesis (as did Horne in his book) the whole text of Rossetti's evocative poem searching for the meaning of the *Primavera*. Horne, who recognised himself to be a product of the late Victorian era, included Pater in the joint dedication of his 1908 monograph. He took his readers' familiarity with Pater's famous essay on Botticelli so much for granted that he did not bother to attribute the many quotations from it that he included in his own text.[4]

Yukio Yashiro's three-volume monograph on Botticelli, published in English by the Medici Society in 1925 (and never translated into Japanese), is something of a historiographical curiosity, in some ways the last gasp of subjective aestheticism. Probably the most influential aspect of the book in Europe was its superb array of specially commissioned detail photographs. As Jonathan Nelson observes, this aspect was to influence not only scholarly practice, most notably Roberto Longhi's studies of Piero della Francesca, but also more popular publications, such as Kenneth Clark's books of details from pictures in the London National Gallery. It is fascinating to learn that Yashiro's awareness of the importance of photographs had been stimulated both by Berenson's *fototeca* and by Sir Robert Witt's collection, which forms the nucleus of the Courtauld Institute's Witt Library. A photographic library became central to the Institute of Art Research that Yashiro founded in Tokyo.

Nelson points out very interestingly how Yashiro attempted to detach himself from preconceived notions of the East–West divide in art, which fed all too easily into political nationalism: 'Leaving geographical distinctions behind, Art is Universal'. It is in that spirit that he made comparisons between Botticelli's approach to the depiction of hands and flowers with those of Utamaro and Kyonaga. Reacting to Roger Fry's hostile review (which was essentially a defence of Herbert Horne), Yashiro resented Fry's faint praise of the 'poetic and mystic side' of his monograph – a Westerner's preconceived idea of what an 'Oriental' would write. But he himself had written to his champion Laurence Binyon in 1922 that he hoped to 'make clear what I, a man brought up in an artistic atmosphere utterly different from that of Europe, feel of Botticelli, that side of Botticelli which, as I think, was never or perhaps little appreciated by European connoisseurs'.[5]

It was the second, single-volume edition of Yashiro's book that elicited Jacques Mesnil's '*Connaissons-nous Botticelli?*', mentioned earlier. Mesnil paid tribute to the text's originality as an 'oriental poem' (Yashiro would not have liked this), but observed succinctly that the author preferred 'a transcendent to a contingent Botticelli', losing sight of the realities of Florentine life. Mesnil's own monograph, published eight years later, has been unjustly neglected in the anglophone literature, so that Michel Hochmann's reassessment of this sympathetic and tragic figure is especially welcome. His life-long relationship with Aby Warburg, who supported him both professionally and financially, is well evoked here on the basis of their exceptionally rich correspondence in the Warburg archive.

Hochmann shows that Mesnil was a pioneering figure in the social history of art, driven by a deep involvement with left-wing politics. Warburg described him in 1926 as '*un idéaliste pur sang*'.[6] His contextualised view of Botticelli was informed by the important archival discoveries he made during his early years in Florence from 1900 to 1906. Mesnil's approach was in some ways close to that of Horne, whose book he judged to be by far the best overall treatment of the master. But, as he wrote to Warburg, Mesnil detested England and its museums, describing the Victoria and Albert Museum as '*ce magasin de bric à brac*'.[7] He felt that Horne was part of a snobbish and elitist British environment, and had crucial limitations:

> He lacked direct contact with the Tuscan people ... and one senses in him the aristocratic type of English aestheticism, so distant from the populist and good-natured *allure* of the artists of the fifteenth century.[8]

Symptomatic of this, Mesnil felt, was the publication of Horne's monograph in a restricted number of copies and at a prohibitive price. Nonetheless, Horne would not have disagreed that Botticelli had to be studied as a creature of flesh and blood, an excellent artisan, involved in all aspects of design and craftsmanship. Recent and ongoing studies of Botticelli, for example those by Alessandro Cecchi, have given us both the painter for the elite and the master of the workshop who appealed to '*les gens pieux*'.[9]

In his brilliant discussion of the recovery of Botticelli in *Forms of Attention*, Frank Kermode noted that recognition of the artist's greatness 'depended in the first place on erroneous opinion', and that in the course of the nineteenth century one sees 'learning come belatedly to the maintenance of values established by ignorance'. However, Kermode also observed, historicism is not enough: the discovery of 'matters of fact' alone cannot 'maintain the life of a work of art from one generation to another'. For that, new interpretations and fresh approaches are needed.[10]

Notes

1 Jacques Mesnil, 'Connaissons-nous Botticelli?', *Gazette des Beaux-Arts*, ser.6, 4 (July 1930): 89–99.

2 J. A. Crowe and G. B. Cavalcaselle, *A History of Painting in Italy. Umbria, Florence and Siena from the Second to the Sixteenth Century*, ed. Langton Douglas assisted by G. De Nicola, vol.IV, *Florentine Masters of the Fifteenth Century* (London: John Murray, 1911), 254. (The wording is unchanged from the original 1864–6 edition.)

3 This point is well made in Jeremy Melius, *Art History and the Invention of Botticelli*, Ph.D. thesis, University of California, Berkeley, 2010, https://escholarship.org/uc/item/98rtqomq .

4 See Caroline Elam, 'Horne's Botticelli', in *Botticelli Reimagined*, 94–100.

5 Cited in Jonathan Nelson's introduction to *Yashiro and Berenson: art history between Japan and Italy*, yashiro.itatti.harvard.edu.

6 Aby Warburg to H. F. Kern, 6 January 1926, WIA GC [Warburg Institute Archive, General Correspondence].

7 Jacques Mesnil to Aby Warburg, 3 September 1903, WIA, GC.

8 Mesnil, 'Connaissons-nous Botticelli?'.

9 Alessandro Cecchi, *Sandro Botticelli* (Milan: Federico Motta Editore, 2005).

10 Frank Kermode, 'Botticelli recovered', in *Forms of Attention* (Chicago and London: University of Chicago Press, 1985), 1–32 and 'Preface', xiii–xv.

8. Crowe and Cavalcaselle on Botticelli: new results

Donata Levi

In a lecture on the 'Relation of Engraving to other Arts in Florence', given at Oxford in November 1872, Ruskin questions the very possibility of writing a history of painting in Italy:

> Such a title is an absurdity on the face of it. For, first, you can no more write the history of painting in Italy than you can write the history of the south wind in Italy. The sirocco does indeed produce certain effects at Genoa, and others at Rome; but what would be the value of a treatise upon the winds which, for the honour of any country, assumed that every city of it had a native sirocco? But, further, – imagine what success would attend the meteorologist who should set himself to give an account of the south wind, but to take no notice of the north! And, finally, suppose an attempt to give you an account of either wind, but none of the seas, or mountain passes, by which they were nourished, or directed.[1]

The target was Crowe and Cavalcaselle's *History of Painting in Italy*, a series of volumes published between 1864 and 1871[2] which, according to Ruskin, contained plenty of data of unequalled value, but was 'in fact only a dictionary of details relating to that history'. Ruskin was not alone in criticising Crowe and Cavalcaselle's works. Soon after the publication of these volumes a strong feeling arose against the historical-philological approach of the two scholars. Even more than from the connoisseurs (Giovanni Morelli and his friends and followers), the attack came from individuals, such as John Ruskin and Walter Pater who, thanks to their literary appeal, could address a larger audience.[3]

Again in 1875, in the third 'Morning in Florence', Ruskin criticised the 'rapturous' Crowe and the 'more cautious' Cavalcaselle for their scrupulous analysis of the state of conservation of Giotto's frescoes in the Bardi Chapel. To signal losses, interpolations and retouchings led to undermining the highly poetical and cultural meaning of the works. In Ruskin's view, actual authenticity differed from true authenticity, while a 'secure and wide knowledge of canvas, pigment, and tricks of touch' did not imply 'any knowledge whatever of the quality of the art itself'.[4] In 1877, in his essay on *Giorgione and his School,* Pater dismissed the 'new

Vasari' for having 'scrutinized thread by thread' the painter's reputation: 'all is not done when the real and the traditional elements in what concerns him [Giorgione] have been discriminated; for, in what is connected with a great name, much that is not real is often very stimulating'.[5]

As Paul Tucker has remarked, in advancing his critique Ruskin was rather thinking of a history of art as 'a form of mythography, in which the art of the past is "retold" as moral deposition'[6], while Pater inclined to interpret traditional imagery mythically in a sort of crystallisation of memory.[7] However, both of them were opposed to Crowe and Cavalcaselle's painstaking collection of data based both on archival sources and on visual evidence – and to their constant, though implicit, effort to point out the complex web of influences between painters, thus eroding the Vasarian scheme of the lives.

Within this framework the case of Botticelli is paradigmatic. The somewhat troublesome presence of Crowe and Cavalcaselle's chapter on the artist is evident both in Pater's essay on Botticelli (published in 1870) and in the passages of Ruskin's works dealing with the painter, such as *Ariadne Florentina* and *Fors Clavigera.*[8] Moreover, the mention in these texts of the *New History of Painting in Italy* is strictly connected with the *Lives*: for better or worse, Vasari and the so-called 'new Vasari' play an important and intertwined role in the new, mythological or evocative re-evaluations of Botticelli. For Ruskin, Vasari represents the apparent untruthfulness, but in reality, the deeper truth of the tradition (or myth), and for Pater Vasari's text is a sort of palimpsest or point of departure for further elaboration (for example on Botticelli and his illustrations of Dante, and on the famous painting by Francesco Botticini for Matteo Palmieri). For both writers Crowe and Cavalcaselle's new accounts of the painter, and of the history of painting in general, fail to penetrate into the real values of the artist's experience and so to make them either an emblem of a spiritual attitude or a source of a peculiar appreciation. Pater's opposition between 'general criticism' ('that sort of interpretation which adjusts the position of these men to general culture') and 'mere technical or antiquarian criticism' is transparent.[9]

Obviously, modern criticism has paid more attention to the innovative and much more evocative interpretations of Ruskin and Pater than to the apparently dry remarks of Crowe and Cavalcaselle. However, the latter constituted at the time the most detailed account of Botticelli ever published since Vasari. Before 1864 no analytic study of the painter existed, except for the comments and additions to Vasari's *Life* in the Le Monnier edition:[10] in this some paintings not mentioned by Vasari had been added to the artist's catalogue[11] and one of the editors, Carlo Pini, had corrected the erroneous attribution to Ghirlandaio of the Uffizi *Adoration* from the church of Santa Maria Novella.[12] Although (as Laurence Kanter has remarked) Crowe and Cavalcaselle 'found it difficult to justify even the relative importance assigned to Botticelli by Vasari' and clearly did not appreciate the artist's 'restless and disquieting poetry',[13] their account provided a narrative which included the results of new visual researches and provided the basis for successive art-historical studies.[14]

My aim here is first to go deeper into this account, searching for the sources used by the two scholars in their construction of Botticelli's biography and pointing out, in general, how they read Vasari in comparison with the approaches of Ruskin and Pater. Then I will follow the revisions of Botticelli's chapter, both in Crowe's reworking of it for an article which was published in the *Gazette des Beaux-Arts* in 1886[15] and in Cavalcaselle's Italian edition of the *History* (1894).[16] The comparison will allow me to outline the two art historians' reactions to the new evaluations of Botticelli's work in contemporary art criticism, during a time span which is of peculiar importance for the assessment of the artist.

As far as the construction of the chapter on Botticelli is concerned, one can refer to the huge archives left by Cavalcaselle and Crowe, respectively to the Biblioteca Nazionale Marciana in Venice[17] and to the National Art Library in London. The latter has been recently greatly increased with new correspondence (mainly from Crowe to his publishers) and more than 20 boxes containing sketches, engravings, photographs, drafts, transcripts from various sources, biographical notes, letters, newspaper cuttings, pamphlets, etc.[18] Given the way in which Crowe and Cavalcaselle worked together, the materials of the two archives complement one another. It is to be hoped that in future an integrated inventory will give easy access to documentation which, in addition to throwing new light on Crowe's and Cavalcaselle's activities as such, provides a comprehensive survey of the medieval and Renaissance art heritage in Europe between the 1850s and 1880s. Thanks to these working papers it is possible to trace the progressive accumulation of materials, and their elaboration with related doubts, hypotheses and approximations, which led to the composition of the chapter on Botticelli. Obviously I will limit myself to a few significant examples.

One case is provided by Cavalcaselle's notes on the *Saint Sebastian* in the Berlin Gemäldegalerie, taken during his European journey of 1852 (fig.3.1).[19] It may serve as an example of how their research proceeded. The painting had been attributed to Pollaiuolo, 'Schüler des Andrea del Castagno', according to Waagen's *Verzeichniss* of 1845,[20] and Cavalcaselle diligently writes down inventory number and attribution, adding '*grande intelligenza anatomica*' and singling out the details of the feet resting on the

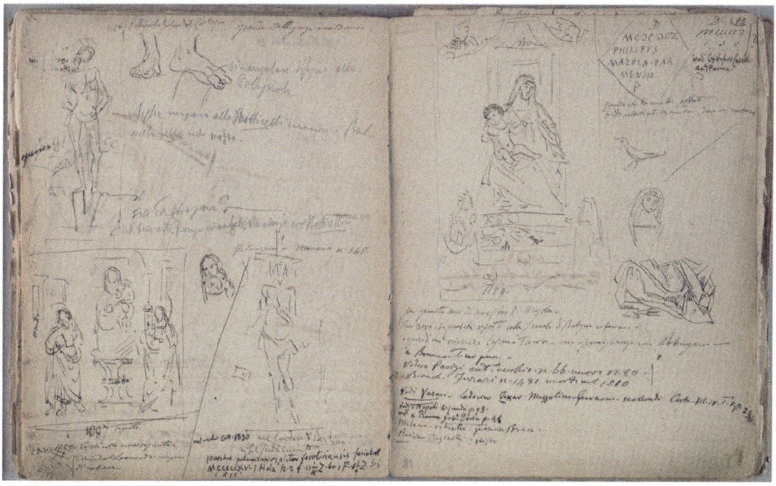

Fig.3.1 G. B. Cavalcaselle (1819–97), from S. Botticelli, *Saint Sebastian* (Berlin, Gemäldegalerie), Venice, Biblioteca Nazionale Marciana, cod.It. IV 2037 (=12278), notebook 15, c.80v. © Biblioteca Nazionale Marciana, Venice.

trunk. Later he added some remarks about the feet (*'sì angolare disegno alla Pollajuolo'*) and a first reference to Botticelli regarding the *'testa un poco alla Botticelli'*, a name which is a moment later denied: *'ma non è Botticelli – svelto, bello nella mossa'*. Cavalcaselle then hazards a guess: *'sia Castagno?'* Finally, possibly after having studied some paintings in the Accademia in Florence, either *Primavera* or the *Coronation of the Virgin*,[21] but in any case following his return to Italy in 1857, he writes down decidedly the name of Botticelli.

It is curious, however, that in the *New History* this painting is not integrated into the narration of Botticelli's early artistic life; it is mentioned only in the chapter on the Pollaiuolo, although with the right attribution and supported by a comparison with the *Fortitude*.[22] Though Crowe and Cavalcaselle adopted, at least in the *New History*, a biographical scheme, they seemed much more interested in tracing connections and links between artists than in reconstructing an artistic personality.

The next example is taken from a notebook regarding Rome, most probably written in 1859. At that time Cavalcaselle had already returned to Italy, after his long exile in Great Britain. John Murray, the well-known London publisher, together with Charles Eastlake and Henry Layard, had asked him to update Vasari's *Lives* and sent him to Italy to collect new materials. One port of call was Rome, where Cavalcaselle studied the frescoes in the Sistine Chapel. In this case he made no sketches, only notes: *'Pieno di forza et di animazione'* was his comment on the *Destruction of Korah, Dathan and Abiram*.[23] Rather more eloquent was the comment on the *Temptations of Christ*:

> Very fine the group of around the priest – recalling Filippino Lippi in the Uffizi[24] – seated and standing figures and I see here a proof that the painting in the little room in the Uffizi which had first been given to Ghirlandaio[25] is by Botticelli. Some point of contact with Signorelli – in the arrangement of the hair and the clothes and even the types[…] One of Sandro's fine [works] – there is movement and animation – the finest by Botticelli here.[26]

Just a fleeting, neutral note was devoted to the fresco representing *The Temptation of Moses* ('*dà da bere alla pecora*'; 'he is giving water to the sheep'), but not a single word on Zipporah, the figure who so greatly intrigued Ruskin and, through him, Proust.[27]

As shown by these notes, Cavalcaselle was mainly interested in defining affinities of style and in detecting resemblances among different works in order to produce trustworthy catalogues of painters. In the process, simple hypotheses could be confirmed while single intuitions might later be rejected. This is the case of a painting representing *Tobit and three Archangels*, now at the Uffizi and attributed to Francesco Botticini. In the *New History of Painting*, Crowe and Cavalcaselle mentioned the work in a footnote in the chapter devoted to the Pollaiuolo, as a picture from their workshop 'of a rude and dull colour'.[28] By contrast, sketching the painting presumably at the beginning of the 1860s, Cavalcaselle had been very careful to signal the affinities with Botticelli in the '*ombre verdette*' and '*ombre scure*' of the faces of two of the Archangels, which apparently led him to the provisional conclusion: '*ecco da dove viene Botticelli*' (fig.3.2).[29]

Through doubts, hypotheses and approximations, notebooks and single sheets show a systematic method of research that was carried on all over Italy and in many European museums and private collections. It involved every kind of painting, from celebrated works attested by Vasari down to workshop products: Botticelli 'filled the peninsula with productions originally feeble and now rendered more so by time and restoring', the two authors remarked.[30] The visual evidence was then matched with the literature on the artist in order to give shape to Botticelli's biography. Among the London papers, there is a short summary in Crowe's handwriting of the passages on the painter from Carl von Rumohr's *Italienische Forschungen* (1827). From this text he borrowed concepts such as 'vigour of expressing passions', 'effervescence of passions and unhesitating action', 'feeling for grace of position', the idea of the frequent repetition of types and themes, the

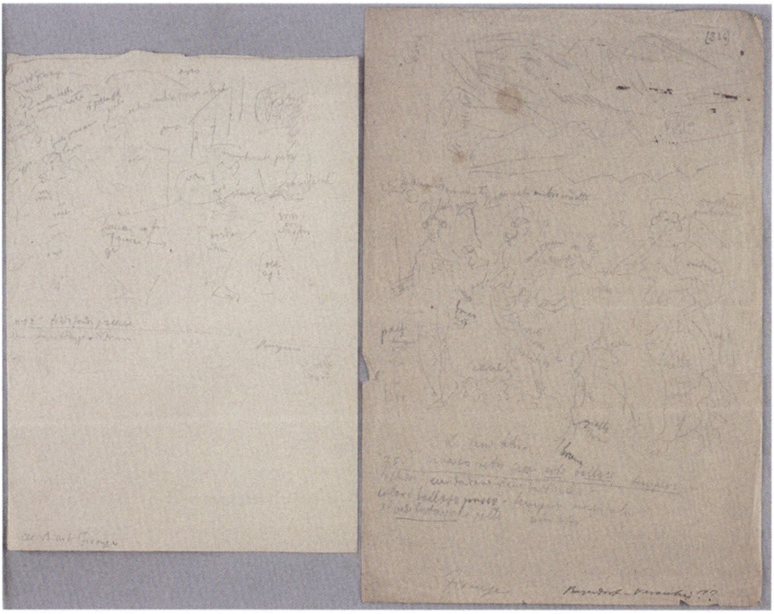

Fig.3.2 G. B. Cavalcaselle, from F. Botticini, *Tobit and three Archangels* (Florence, Uffizi), Venice, Biblioteca Nazionale Marciana, cod.It. IV 2030 (=12271), 16, c.334. © Biblioteca Nazionale Marciana, Venice.

'fine cut of the eyes', as well as the 'vulgarity of form in the cheeks, chin and jaw'. All were concepts that nurtured the image of 'vehemence' and 'activity' which characterises Botticelli's art, according to Crowe and Cavalcaselle.[31]

Along with this summary, there is a draft of the chapter on Botticelli, written by Crowe and commented on by Cavalcaselle;[32] it is one of the main examples of their close collaboration. This draft is heavily based on Vasari's *Life*, but at the same time shows a critical reading of that text and an attempt to translate it into a stylistic (or morphological or formalistic) discourse. For example, Crowe and Cavalcaselle commented on Vasari's observation that Botticelli had been apprenticed in a goldsmith's shop and noted (in a telling mixture of Italian and English languages) that there 'was in this age a great domesticity & quasi continua pratica between orefici et painters'. The comment is then exploited so as to create a more general framework to fit Botticelli's education:

> We have spoken of influence of sculpture & oreficeria, the latter even at a given time absorbing sculpture & we have the oreficeria drew painting along with it into its shop. The results of this in Pollaiuoli & Verrocchio and we have said all the painters up to Ghirlandaio issue

> from oraf. shops. In Pollaiuoli & Verrocchio painting was treated as a subordinate matter. We shall see that Botticelli in preference to sculpture and oreficeria spent his time chiefly in painting.[33]

This framework is then further enlarged to consider the 'exhaustion' on the part of Fra Filippo of the system (or 'technic', as Crowe writes) begun by Fra Angelico:

> It became necessary for following men to seek out fresh branches to the path. We have seen the efforts made towards improvements of method & chemistry of art in Baldovinetti & Pollaiuoli. Donato Uccello etc. striving in perspective of form, each of them with their failings. Having this framework before us the tendency of the time and of art at the time of Botticelli's birth, it is natural that he a man of talent as we shall find a man of an impetuous vehement character should so to say personify the entire condition of the art at his time.[34]

A critical and detailed reading is also given of Botticelli's apprenticeship with Filippo Lippi, whose influence is examined in Madonnas, such as the Madonna of the Magnificat at the Uffizi: 'Botticelli in part continued these subjects of Madonnas of Fra Filippo rendered in a new phase with a conjunction of the earth and the heavens. Maternity, affection in celestial scenes'.[35] Vasari is constantly on their desk, but his assumptions are made use of, scrutinised and also critically considered. For example, Crowe and Cavalcaselle discuss Vasari's praise of the cogitation and acute subtlety of the Ognissanti St. Augustine, but rather notice its:

> vehemence impetuosity force boldness frankness of execution, life in all parts which are remarkable showing the stamp of the man the vulgarity amongst other which is in all Botticelli's works and which has something of the Castagno and Pollaiuolo & from which Verrocchio was not free.

But at the same time they also add: 'Vasari who looked at art in the direction of form may have been right because as art and metier Botticelli is more skilled and at that time was superior'.[36]

The critical, balanced and sober reading of a historical text such as Vasari's is what mainly distinguishes Crowe and Cavalcaselle's method from the more ideological approaches of Ruskin and Pater. Crowe and Cavalcaselle were not accustomed to theorising. Their point of view is thus best expressed by a German art historian who can be considered as their spokesman. Max Jordan, who undertook the German translation and edition of their volumes,[37] explained their attitude towards Vasari in what may be described as a pre-review of the *New History of Painting in Italy*. This piece was published in 1864, some months before the publication – and possibly in order to induce the reluctant John Murray to print the first two volumes on painting in Central Italy without waiting for the third, which was to deal with North Italy and was indeed published in 1871. Jordan's article, significantly entitled *Vasari der Andere*, was published in '*Die Grenzboten*' – a periodical that embodied the political and literary tendencies of German liberalism.[38] Jordan explained that, though the *Lives* had a limited value in an absolute sense, they had an important relative value ('*unersetzlichem Belang*'): 'every piece of historical research may gain an excellent corrective and a certain guarantee of accuracy when it can take its starting point from a source you know from the outset you need to examine with a sceptical attitude'.[39]

Such a perspective, he added, was inherent in the significance of all historical sources, to the '*Literatur aller historischen Disciplinen*'. To stress a common approach to sources meant to assimilate art history to the other, more established, historical disciplines. Jordan considered Crowe and Cavalcaselle's history of painting to be an example of a non-instrumental, respectful, but sceptical approach to Vasari's *Lives*; he could therefore affirm the importance of a work which aimed to be a 'completion and fulfillment' ('*Vollendung und Erfüllung*') of Vasari, a Vasari 'inspected, newly worked, established and enriched with amazing literary apparatus' ('*gesichtet, neu durchgearbeitet, festgestellt und mit erstaunlichem literarischen Apparat bereichert*') on the basis of accurate examinations of the art objects themselves. While insisting on Crowe and Cavalcaselle's treatment of historical sources, Jordan pointed to the status of art history as a discipline: more than any other historical discipline, art history needed the 'police protection' ('*polizeilichen Schutzes*') of a definite and accepted methodology. He therefore hoped for a new status for the art historian as a historian, to be contrasted with either an amateurish or a merely scholarly approach. This claim was fulfilled by Crowe and Cavalcaselle's work:

> [...]certainly it deprives us of some cherished beloved illusions about alleged facts in the history of art and of the artists, but it enriches and deepens our knowledge, our intuition and our judgment to such an extent that all conventional complaints about 'disintegrating criticism' or 'sober intellectual tyranny', which similarly precise works tend to elicit, become childish chatter.[40]

Crowe and Cavalcaselle's *New History* was soon translated into German and edited by Max Jordan. Some additions were included which, however, left the structure of Botticelli's biography unchanged. The volume was published in 1870, the same year in which Walter Pater's article on Botticelli strove to distil from the artist's oeuvre 'the peculiar sensation' and 'the peculiar quality of pleasure, which his work has the property of exciting in us, and which we cannot get elsewhere'.[41]

What were the reactions of the two art historians to the new evaluations of Botticelli's work in contemporary art criticism? In 1886 Crowe contributed an article on Botticelli for the *Gazette des Beaux-Arts* and in 1894 Cavalcaselle published the volume containing the chapter on Botticelli in the Italian revised edition of *A New History of Painting*. Both men tried, in different ways, to supplement their rather meagre 1864 account with a richer narrative framework. Crowe in particular begins his article by delineating, on the basis of a recent Italian publication,[42] the contrast between Leonardo and Michelangelo: this was only a pretext for introducing Botticelli, who had been mentioned with equal deference by both artists.[43] Botticelli is now, according to Crowe, the painter who is capable of leading us into the 'atmosphere' of the Florentine court, in which the superb Lorenzo the Magnificent ambiguously protected both religious tradition and the free thinking of the Renaissance.

The main facts of Botticelli's activity and the main features of his style and technique are taken from the 1864 text in a slightly different order, but they are rendered in a more conversational, vivacious and light manner. Neither Ruskin nor Pater is ever mentioned. Only faint, indirect echoes of the new attitudes towards the painter can be detected and these remain on the surface or work at a general level, as a sort of inevitable patina of modernisation. A significant case may be cited, in relation to *The Birth of Venus* (fig.1.0). In 1864, in spite of new appreciations already expressed by critics (the brothers de Goncourt) as well as by artists (Gustave Moreau and Edgar Degas),[44] Crowe and Cavalcaselle had disposed of the picture in few sentences:

> Florence. Uffizi. First Corridor n.31. Allegory of the birth of Venus. The goddess issues from a shell which is driven to the shore by two flying allegories of the winds. Life size. The figures are a little out of balance. The picture originally belonged to the Medici and was painted for Cosimo's villa of Castello.[45]

After Pater's deeply inspiring interpretation of the painting, Crowe felt obliged to give it a more detailed consideration which, however, is based on academic criteria and a commonplace visual vocabulary. For example, he defines the *'formes'* of the goddess as *'sveltes et gracieuses, admirables dans le torse, les bras et les mains, trop grêles dans les chevilles et les pieds'* ('slender and graceful features, praiseworthy in the torso, arms and hands, too spindly in the ankles and feet') and criticises the promontories in the background for their lack of perspective. Pater's 'thin lines of foam' with their related image of the sea 'showing his teeth' become *'des méandres angulaires d'un parti pris tout à fait arbitraire'* ('angular twists of an arbitrary choice') by which *'le clapotement des vagues est bizarrement indiqué'* ('the lapping of the waves is oddly depicted').[46] Crowe's final remark on the similarity of types between Venus and the Madonnas and between *Primavera* and the angels of some Annunciation reminds us of Walter Pater's observation of the recurrence of the same figure types in Botticelli's paintings. However, it is totally devoid of the exemplary meaning it had for Pater as emblematic of Botticelli's peculiar character.

If Crowe was somewhat susceptible to the suggestions of the new trend, Cavalcaselle's rigorous and painstaking work to expand and refine Botticelli's catalogue is evidence of his essential indifference to the contemporary debate, and of his enduring effort to develop a 'positivistic' historical method in art history. Thirty years had elapsed since the publication of the *New History of Painting* and the figure of Botticelli had changed considerably in common opinion. In his *Introduction* to the 1908 monograph on Botticelli Herbert Horne referred to a peculiarly English cult of Botticelli, adding that around the 1880s Botticelli 'grew to be a catch-word among persons for whom early Italian art could never possess any real significance'.[47] Yet the taste for the Florentine artist does not seem to have affected the general interpretation of him offered in Cavalcaselle's Italian edition of the *New History*. The scheme remained essentially the same as in 1864, but the connoisseur systematically added a great number of paintings which he classified as works executed in the shop or under Botticelli's influence. He enriched the footnotes with references to recent publications, to historical sources other than Vasari, such as Albertini, and to archival documents (mainly from Gaetano Milanesi). Above all, he paid much attention to technical issues and to conservation, pointing out restorations and retouchings.

In the Italian milieu this apparently outdated approach appeared to Cavalcaselle to be instrumental for strengthening both the status of art history as a discipline and its role in the preservation of the national art heritage. Therefore, it is with a deep sense of loss that he mentioned the acquisition of the Villa Lemmi frescoes by the Louvre in 1882. They had been discovered in 1873 and Cavalcaselle had seen them before they were cut out of the wall by Stefano Bardini, restorer and art dealer, who later sold them to Pierre-Paul Both De Tauzia. Cavalcaselle regretted not only the export of the frescoes from Italy, but also the material deterioration caused by their detachment from the wall and the loss of their original setting.[48] He seems to echo both Ruskin, who in one of the lectures in *The Art of England* (1883) had denounced the damage caused by the transport and subsequent repainting of the figures,[49] and Vernon Lee, who had expressed her annoyance and disapproval concerning this removal of the frescoes from their original site.[50] However, it is unlikely that Cavalcaselle knew their writings. On the one hand, the accurate observation of the state of conservation of the paintings had been a constant feature of his studies since the beginning of his career. On the other, the rule of not removing works of art from their original site was among the guidelines he himself had contributed during his time at the Ministry of Public Education.

Cavalcaselle, especially in the last year of his life, appears to have been an isolated figure. He was unaffected even by the harsh attacks launched against him and Crowe by Giovanni Morelli. In the particular case of Botticelli, in the *Storia* Cavalcaselle seemed not to care about Morelli's criticism;[51] he generally confirmed his previous attributions, ignored Morelli's opinions and simply added to Botticelli's catalogue those few paintings that his rival had discovered. The Madonna Chigi had gone unnoticed in the *New History*, but, after Morelli's brief mention of it in his studies on the Borghese and Doria Pamphili collections,[52] Cavalcaselle described it at length in the *Storia* for the first time.[53] It is possible that psychological motives led Cavalcaselle to avoid sparring with so able a polemicist as Morelli. However, his behaviour was also in tune with a different approach to connoisseurship:[54] an approach which did not aim at apodictic opinions, cloaked by so-called 'scientific' evidence, but was based on hypotheses, constantly questioned and verified, and framed by an embryonic awareness that, as in the case of Vasari's text, sources (including visual ones) had to be scrutinised sceptically.

A final example may be useful to demonstrate the complexity of the factors that came together to delineate Botticelli's artistic personality, in the context of developments at play in the last years of the nineteenth century: the practice of connoisseurship, the reception of Vasari and the role of historical tradition, the new aestheticism, the intellectual dialogue among scholars. The painting in question is *The Assumption of the Virgin* painted for Matteo Palmieri, now in the National Gallery, London and attributed to Francesco Botticini.[55] Described at length by Vasari as a work by Botticelli, it had found no place in the *New History* because Crowe and Cavalcaselle had not yet seen the painting, then in the collection of the Duke of Hamilton.[56] A year after the publication of the *New History*, on his visit to Scotland in 1865, Cavalcaselle studied the picture and made a rough sketch of its composition (fig.3.3).[57] It was inserted in the German edition of 1870 as one of the *'lebensvollsten und hervorragendsten seiner Gemälde'* ('liveliest and most outstanding of his paintings'.[58]

In that same year the *Assumption*, together with the illustrations to Dante's *Divine Comedy* and *The Birth of Venus*, was to be the cornerstone on which Pater erected his image of Botticelli. In 1886 Crowe, too, hastened to insert a description of the painting, which had in the meantime been purchased by the National Gallery, in his article for the *Gazette*. However, also in 1886 Wilhelm Bode put forward his doubts about the authorship of the Palmieri painting and proposed to attribute it to the so-called 'Meister des Rossi Altars'.[59] In the Italian edition of the *New History* Cavalcaselle quoted Vasari's passage at length; he added a plain, objective description of the representation without comment or appraisal, but also did not mention Bode's new attribution.[60] In my opinion he did not know of

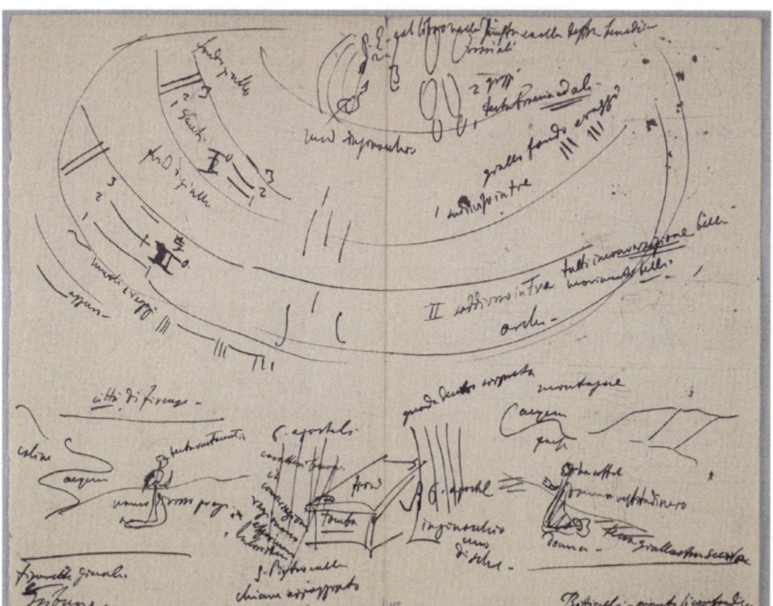

Fig.3.3 G. B. Cavalcaselle, from F. Botticini, *The Assumption of the Virgin* (London, National Gallery), Venice, Biblioteca Nazionale Marciana, cod.It. IV 2033 (=12274), XXII, cc.186v–187r. © Biblioteca Nazionale Marciana, Venice.

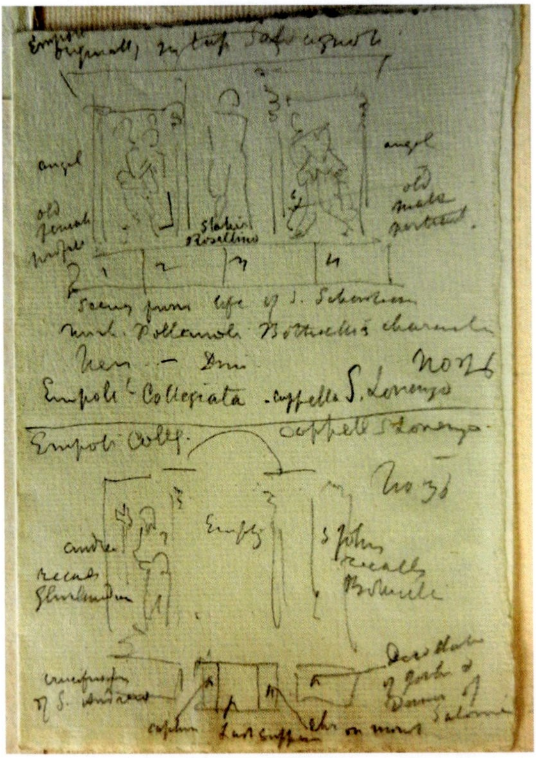

Fig.3.4 J. A. Crowe (1825–96), from F. Botticini, *Tabernacle of St Sebastian* (Empoli, Museo della Collegiata), London, National Art Library, 86.ZZ.33, box 1. © Victoria and Albert Museum, London.

Bode's article,[61] and he was perhaps too inclined towards Vasari (and – through Crowe – too intimidated by Pater's success) to exclude the painting from Botticelli's oeuvre; but it is also possible that he and Crowe were moving towards a different solution.

Their rough sketches and notes in the London and Venetian archives, presumably made during the 1880s, are evidence of the pair's never-ending interest in what in 1864 they had defined as that 'series of pictures of more or less merit whose character proclaims them to have issued from the hands of men subordinate to Filippino Lippi and Botticelli, who may have been of a wandering class of assistants assuming the style of their temporary masters without possessing talent sufficient to entitle them to an independent position as first rate artists'.[62] On that occasion Cavalcaselle and Crowe had listed the two tabernacles of St Sebastian and of the Sacrament and the Annunciation in the Museo della Collegiata of Empoli. After repeated visits and further studies on the spot in 1883

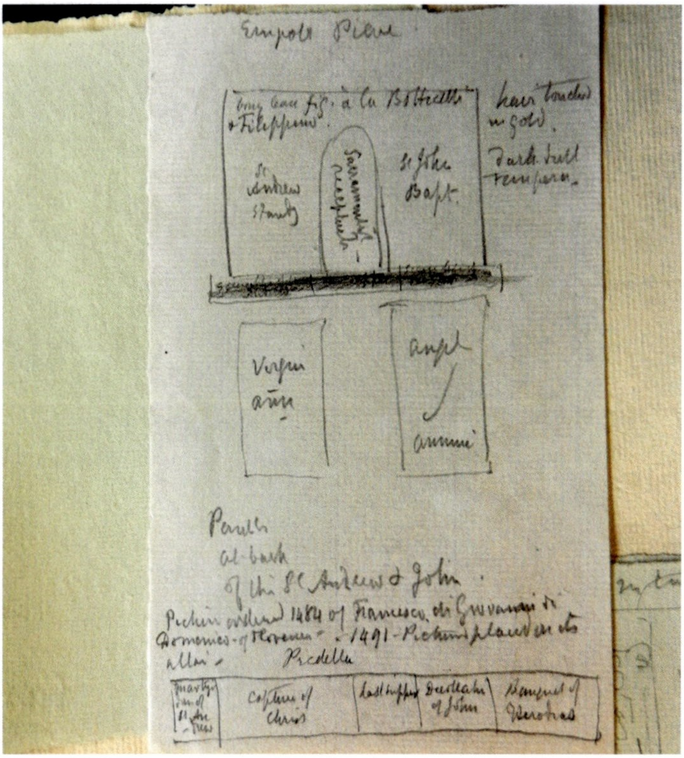

Fig.3.5 J. A. Crowe, from F. Botticini, *Tabernacle of the Sacrament* and *Annunciation* (Empoli, Museo della Collegiata), London, National Art Library, 86.ZZ.33, box 1. © Victoria and Albert Museum, London.

and 1886 (figs 3.4 and 3.5),[63] and thanks to the new archival documents published by Gaetano Milanesi,[64] they succeeded in giving a name to the author of these paintings: it was that of Francesco Botticini,[65] to whom the Palmieri *Assumption* was also attributed shortly afterwards by August Schmarsow.[66] Through the researches of a host of connoisseurs, one of the cornerstones of Pater's interpretation of Botticelli had thus been pulled down. But, as Pater himself had written, 'in what is connected with a great name, much that is not real is often very stimulating'. And in 1908 Herbert Horne was ready to admit that, in spite of the mistaken attribution of the Palmieri altarpiece, Pater's essay 'remains the subtlest and most suggestive appreciation of Botticelli, in a personal way, which has yet been written'.[67] To paraphrase Aby Warburg, the contrast between an 'unremitting feeling for documentary evidence' – to which one should also add visual evidence – and 'an element of scholarly imagination' or fantasy remains a methodological issue up until our own days.[68]

Notes

1 Published as separate issue in December 1873 and with the other 1872 Michaelmas term lectures under the title *Ariadne Florentina* in 1876; now Edward Tyas Cook and Alexander Wedderburn, ed., *The Works of John Ruskin* XXII (London: George Allen, 1906), 337–8. The subject of the course had been announced as 'Sandro Botticelli and the Florentine Schools of Engraving'.

2 Joseph Archer Crowe and Giovanni Battista Cavalcaselle, *A New History of Painting in Italy from the Second to the Sixteenth Century* (London: John Murray, 1864–6) and *A History of Painting in North Italy* (London: John Murray, 1871). For a general overview of Cavalcaselle and Crowe see Donata Levi, *Cavalcaselle. Il pioniere della conservazione dell'arte italiana* (Turin: Einaudi, 1988).

3 See especially Ivan Lermolieff [G. Morelli], *Die Werke italienischer Meister in den Galerien von München, Dresden und Berlin. Ein kritischer Versuch von Ivan Lermolieff. Aus dem Russischen übersetzt von Dr. Johannes Schwarze* (Leipzig: E. A. Seemann, 1880). On Morelli's circle see Jaynie Anderson, '*Dietro lo pseudonimo*', in Giovanni Morelli, *Della pittura italiana. Studii storico-critici. Le Gallerie Borghese e Doria Pamphilj in Roma*, ed. Jaynie Anderson (Milan: Adeplhi Edizioni, 1991), 493–578, *passim* and Donata Levi, '*Fortuna di Morelli: appunti sui rapporti tra storiografia artistica tedesca e inglese*', in *La figura e l'opera di Giovanni Morelli. Studi e ricerche* II (Bergamo: Biblioteca Civica Angelo Mai, 1987), 19–54. For Ruskin see notes 1 and 4.

4 Cook and Wedderburn, *The Works of John Ruskin* XXIII, 337–8 and 410. See Donata Levi, 'Esigenze di autenticità fra dichiarazioni di principio e pratica di intervento: Cavalcaselle ad Assisi', *Studi di Memofonte* 7 (2011): 1–13, especially 1–3.

5 Walter Pater, 'The School of Giorgione', *Fortnightly Review* 22 (October 1877): 526–38, then included in the third edition of *The Renaissance. Studies in Art and Poetry* (1880). Quoted from Walter Pater, *The Renaissance. Studies in Art and Poetry*, with an Introduction and Notes by Kenneth Clark (London and Glasgow: Collins, 1961), 139.

6 Paul Tucker, '"Reanimate Greek". Ruskin and Pater on Botticelli', in *Walter Pater. Transparencies of Desire*, ed. Laurel Brake, Lesley Higgins and Carolyn Williams (Greensboro: ELT Press, 2002), 119–32, quotation at 121.

7 Walter Pater, *The Renaissance*, 139: 'Giorgione thus becomes a sort of impersonation of Venice itself, its projected reflex or ideal, all that was intense or desirable in it crystallising about the memory of this wonderful young man'.

8 Tucker, '"Reanimate Greek"', 129–31.

9 Pater, *The Renaissance*, 77.

10 Giorgio Vasari, *Le Vite de' più eccellenti pittori, scultori e architetti*, (Florence: Felice Le Monnier, 1849), vol.V, 110–27.

11 Vasari, *Le Vite*, V, 123–7. However, some of these paintings were erroneously attributed to Botticelli, such as the series of the *Triumphs* by Jacopo del Sellaio (Fiesole, Museo Bandini).

12 Vasari, *Le Vite*, V, 116.

13 Laurence Kanter, 'Alessandro Filipepi, called Botticelli', in *Botticelli's Witness: Changing Style in a Changing Florence*, exh. cat., ed. Laurence Kanter, Hilliard T. Goldfarb, James Hankins (Boston: Isabella Stewart Gardner Museum, 1997), 21–7, quotation at 22.

14 Herbert Horne (*Alessandro Filipepi commonly called Botticelli Painter of Florence* [London: George Bell & Sons, 1908; repr. Florence: Spes, 1986–7], xx) admitted that 'although the chapter on Botticelli added much to our knowledge of the painter, it is not one of the more fortunate portions of the book'.

15 Joseph Archer Crowe, 'Sandro Botticelli', *Gazette des Beaux-Arts* XXXIV (1886): 177–87 and 466–75.

16 Joseph Archer Crowe and Giovanni Battista Cavalcaselle, *Storia della pittura in Italia dal secolo II al secolo XVI*, V: *Pittori fiorentini fin poco dopo la prima metà del secolo XV* (Florence: Successori Le Monnier, 1894), 203–310.

17 A selection of sketches was exhibited in Venice in 1973 (Lino Moretti, *G. B. Cavalcaselle. Disegni da antichi maestri*, with a preface of Rodolfo Pallucchini (Vicenza: Neri Pozza, 1973). See also Donata Levi, 'Per un progetto di pubblicazione della versione italiana della "History of Painting in North Italy", in Anna Chiara Tommasi, ed., *Giovanni Battista Cavalcaselle conoscitore e conservatore* (Venice: Marsilio, 1998), 11–21.

18 London, National Art Library, 86.ZZ.198 (Crowe family: papers and correspondence), 86.ZZ.19–29 (Manuscripts of *A New History of Painting in Italy* and of the *History of Painting in*

North Italy), 86.ZZ.30–3 and 40–1 (Notes on pictures in continental collections), 86.ZZ.42–3, 49 and II. RC.H.18–23 (Notes on Raphael and manuscript of *Raphael, his Life and Works*), 86.ZZ.44 and 47–8 (Manuscripts of *Titian, his Life and Times*), 86.ZZ.45–6 (Notes on the Italian schools of painting, chiefly medieval and upon the early Christian and medieval mosaics in Italy), 86.ZZ.50 (Notes on pictures in the National Gallery, South Kensington Museum, and provincial galleries), 86.ZZ.51–5 (Notes on Italian Painters), 86.ZZ.56 (Notes on Dutch and Flemish, and a few German and French Painters).

19 Venice, Biblioteca Nazionale Marciana, cod.It. IV 2037 (=12278), notebook 15, c.80v.

20 Gustav Friedrich Waagen, *Verzeichniss der Gemälde-sammlung des königlichen Museums zu Berlin* (Berlin: W. Moeser und Kühn, 1845), 361.

21 Both of them are now in the Uffizi Gallery, Florence.

22 Crowe and Cavalcaselle, *A New History*, 396.

23 Venice, Biblioteca Nazionale Marciana, cod.It. IV 2036 (=12277), notebook 13, c.61v.

24 Either the *Adoration of the Magi* (1496) or 'Pala degli Otto' (1486), most probably the former.

25 The reference is to the Uffizi *Adoration*.

26 Venice, Biblioteca Nazionale Marciana, cod.It. IV 2036 (=12277), notebook 13, c.62r.: '*Bellissimo il gruppo attorno il Sacerdote – ricorda Filippino Lippi agli Uffizi – figure sedute ed in piedi e qui vedo la prova che il quadro nello Stanzino degli Uffizi è di Botticelli che prima era dato a Ghirlandaio. Qualche punto di contato con Luca Signorelli – nelle acconciature di cappelli ed abiti ed anche tipi ... Uno dei belli di Sandro – vi è movimento ed animazione – la più bella qui di Botticelli*.'

27 Cynthia J. Gamble, 'Zipporah: a Ruskinian enigma appropriated by Marcel Proust', *Word & Image* 15.4 (Oct. –Dec. 1999): 381–94.

28 Crowe and Cavalcaselle, *A New History*, 397.

29 Venice, Biblioteca Nazionale Marciana, cod.It. IV 2030 (=12271), 16, c.334.

30 Crowe and Cavalcaselle, *A New History*, 423.

31 London, National Art Library, 86.ZZ.46, c.1593; C. F. von Rumohr, *Italienische Forschungen* II (Berlin und Stettin: Nicolai'schen Buchhandlung, 1827), 272–3.

32 London, National Art Library, 86.ZZ.46, cc.1569–99.

33 London, National Art Library, 86.ZZ.46, c.1569.

34 London, National Art Library, 86.ZZ.46, c.1570.

35 London, National Art Library, 86.ZZ.46, c.1572.

36 London, National Art Library, 86 ZZ 46, c.1571.

37 Joseph Archer Crowe, Giovanni Battista Cavalcaselle, *Geschichte der Italienischen Malerei.* Deutsche Original-Ausgabe besorgt von M. Jordan (Leipzig: S. Hirzel, 1869–76).

38 Max Jordan, '*Vasari der Andere*', *Die Grenzboten. Zeitschrift für Politik und Literatur* XXIII, 3 (1864): 481–95 and XXIII, 4 (1864): 18–32.

39 Jordan, '*Vasari der Andere*', 481 ('*Denn es giebt jeder historischen Forschung ein treffliches Correctiv und eine gewisse Gewähr der Richtigkeit, wenn sie ihren Ausgangspunkt von einer Quelle nehmen kann, zu welcher sie sich von vorn herein skeptisch verhalten zu müssen weiß*').

40 Jordan, '*Vasari der Andere*', 483–4 ('*freilich entzieht es uns manche mit Vorliebe gehegte Illusion über angeblichen Sachverhalt in der Geschichte der Kunst und der Künstler, aber es bereichert und verschärft unsre Kenntniß, unsre Anschauung und unser Urtheil in solchem Maße, daß alle herkömmlichen Lamentos von "zersetzender Kritik" oder "nüchterner Verstandestyrannei", wie sie derartigen exacten Arbeiten zu begegnen pflegen, zum kindischen Geschwätz werden*').

41 Pater, *The Renaissance*, 77.

42 Camillo Boito, *Leonardo e Michelangelo. Studio d'arte* (Milan, Naples and Pisa: Ulrico Hoepli, 1879).

43 Interestingly Pater too had introduced his essay on Botticelli with a reference to Leonardo's mention of the Florentine painter.

44 See the following contributions to *Botticelli Reimagined*, exh. cat. (London: V&A Publishing, 2016): Ruben Rebmann, 'Botticelli Enters the Museum: The Rediscovery of a Painter and the Invention of the Public Art Museum', 50–5, esp. 54, and Gabriel Montua, 'Botticelli's Path to Modernity: Continental Reception 1850–1930'. On the appreciation of Botticelli on the part of British artists, such as Dante Gabriel Rossetti and Edward Burne-Jones, see Susanna Avery-Quash, 'Botticelli and Victorian Art Collecting', 68–74, esp. 70, and Elizabeth Prettejohn, 'Botticelli and the Pre-Raphaelites', 76–81.

45 Crowe and Cavalcaselle, *A New History*, 423. In the draft quoted above (*c*.1581) they had even described one of the figures as 'out of balance'.

46 Crowe, 'Sandro Botticelli', 184–6.

47 Horne, *Alessandro Filipepi*, xix.

48 Cavalcaselle and Crowe, *Storia della pittura* V, 262: Lorenzo Orsini, *Per un catalogo critico degli affreschi staccati da e per Stefano Bardini* (unpublished MA thesis), University of Florence, 2017-18, 79-83.
49 Cook and Wedderburn, *The Works of John Ruskin* XXXIII, 313–14.
50 Vernon Lee, 'Botticelli at the Villa Lemmi', *The Cornhill Magazine* XLVI (July–Dec. 1882):159–73.
51 Ivan Lermolieff [Giovanni Morelli], *Kunstkritische Studien über Italienische Malerei. Die Galerien Borghese und Doria Panfili in Rom* (Leipzig: F. A. Brockhaus, 1890), 107–12.
52 Lermolieff, *Kunstkritische Studien*, 106.
53 Cavalcaselle and Crowe, *Storia della pittura* V, 285.
54 Donata Levi, review of '*I taccuini manoscritti di Giovanni Morelli* by Jaynie Anderson', *The Burlington Magazine* CXLIV, 1188 (March 2002): 170–1.
55 Jennifer Sliwka, *Visions of Paradise. Botticini's Palmieri Altarpiece* (London: National Gallery Company, 2015).
56 Crowe and Cavalcaselle, *A New History of Painting*, 429.
57 Venice, Biblioteca Nazionale Marciana, cod.It. IV 2033 (=12274), XXII, c.3.
58 Crowe and Cavalcaselle, *Geschichte der Italienischen Malerei*, 166.
59 Wilhelm Bode, '*Die Ausbeute aus den Magazinen der K. Gemäldegalerie zu Berlin*', *Jahrbuch der königlich preussischen Kunstsammlungen* VII (1886): 226–43, quotation at 233–4.
60 Cavalcaselle and Crowe, *Storia della pittura* V, 209–11.
61 Cavalcaselle still considers Lorenzo Dugolino de' Rossi as the author, not as the patron, of the Rossi Altarpiece in Berlin which had been examined in Bode's article (Cavalcaselle and Crowe, *Storia della pittura* VII, 130).
62 Crowe and Cavalcaselle, *A New History of Painting*, 452–3.
63 Venice, Biblioteca Nazionale Marciana, cod.It. IV 2032 (=12273), XXI and National Art Library, 86.ZZ.33, box 1.
64 Vasari, *Le Vite*, IV, 245–50; the documents were also published in *Il Buonarroti* , s. III, II. 10 (1887), 333 and in Gaetano Milanesi, *Nuovi documenti per la storia dell'arte toscana dal XII al XV secolo per servire d'aggiunta all'edizione del Vasari edita da Sansoni nel 1885* (Florence: G. Dotti, 1901).
65 Cavalcaselle and Crowe, *Storia della pittura* VII, 114–20.
66 August Schmarsow, *Italienische Malerschulen in der Londoner Nationalgalerie*, in *Festschrift zu Ehren des Kunsthistorischen Instituts in Florenz, dargebracht vom Kunsthistorischen Institut der Universität Leipzig* (Leipzig: Verlag von A. G. Liebeskind, 1897), 122–42, especially 125–6; the article had published in *Nationalzeitung*, Berlin, 19–26 August 1887 (see also Hermann Ulmann, *Sandro Botticelli* (Munich: Verlaganstalt für Kunst und Wissenschaft, *vormals* Friedrich Bruckmann, [1893]), 75–6.
67 Horne, *Alessandro Filipepi*, xix.
68 Caroline Elam, 'Herbert Horne's Botticelli', in *Botticelli Reimagined*, 94–100, esp. 100.

9. Why Botticelli? Aby Warburg's search for a new approach to Quattrocento Italian art

Claudia Wedepohl

Introduction

In 1944, expressing enthusiasm for the 'overwhelming achievements' of 'our father's generation' of art historians, Fritz Saxl chose to single out three expatriate 'Florentines': the English writer, architect, designer and art historian Herbert Horne (1864–1916), the German art and cultural historian Aby Warburg (1866–1929) and the Belgian journalist, physician and art historian Jacques Mesnil (1872–1940).[1] In the light of the Second World War Saxl's text – a lecture he delivered as director of the Warburg Institute (only about two weeks after its integration in the University of London) – was a plea for mutual understanding in the spirit of European identity. Three individuals with different nationalities, backgrounds and approaches to the subject were united by their scholarly interest in the Florentine Renaissance, particularly in a 'recovery of Botticelli'.[2] While living temporarily in Florence all three scholars knew and frequented one another.[3]

Because of their different approaches Horne, Warburg and Mesnil produced significantly different studies.[4] However, they pursued the same goal, namely a reaction against a formidable 'cult' of Botticelli. Their response to a normative aestheticism or infatuation with an artist's style – in Botticelli's case inspired on the one hand by Dante Gabriel Rossetti and the Pre-Raphaelites, on the other hand by the predominantly speculative writings of John Ruskin, Walter Pater and John Addington Symonds[5] – was based on solid archival research. Particularly time consuming, this new approach to Italian Renaissance painting (and to art in general) signified the manifestation of a critical art history.

In this respect their appreciation of one other's contribution was mutual. Warburg described Horne – a strong believer in the achievements of an attribution-oriented connoisseurship who named his own emphasis on documentary evidence 'scientific criticism' – as 'one of the few workers in the field who are inclined and able to appreciate the detail-work we have to do'. Such 'detailed work', later called the 'duty of reading old slips of paper', was in Warburg's view more important than 'opening large views, without anything real to point out'.[6] Exchanges between Warburg and Mesnil (who continued to unearth documents through meticulous research in the Florentine archives) demonstrate the same scholarly objection to any kind of subjective response to art.[7] As early as 1896 Warburg asked for Mesnil's help in identifying 'modern works in which Botticelli is either adored or dispraised' (*'angeschwärmt oder getadelt'*).[8]

Almost two decades before Horne's *Alessandro Filipepi Commonly Called Sandro Botticelli. Painter of Florence* appeared in 1908, and over 30 years before the publication of Mesnil's study, simply titled *Botticelli* (1938), Warburg had been the first to promote a new approach to the painter's most famous works.[9] In his doctoral dissertation on Botticelli's *The Birth of Venus* and *Primavera* (privately printed and published in 1893) he introduced a new methodology to reconstruct the milieu in which the two paintings were supposedly commissioned. At this stage, his strict objectivity was not yet underpinned by historical documents from Florentine archives, but by primary sources of a different kind, that is, contemporary literary works. Warburg thus applied a new method: a so-called philological reading of the artefact which adopted the textual exegesis practised by contemporary philologists.[10] Without access to the riches of the archives, the student Warburg thus believed that cross-cultural comparisons enabled him to reveal *symptoms* of a certain period mentality. His observations, namely a predilection for *all'antica* forms, sparked something bigger: the search for the solution of a 'problem' which was going to occupy him for the rest of his life. According to Saxl, it was 'the concern with images as the recurrent but variable expression of what is fundamental and unchanging in the human mind'.[11]

In a nutshell, Warburg claims in his 1891 doctoral dissertation that the poet Angelo Poliziano and the artist Sandro Botticelli relied on classical models, both texts and images, to find formulas for the expression of previously subdued emotions. In other words, by looking at Botticelli and his contemporaries, Warburg believed he had discovered distinctive signs of a post-medieval re-entry of emotions into art and literature. Its forms were animated accessories, initially remaining autonomous from the body of the wearer, later organically following the body's movement. Such apparently 'animated' peripheral objects – namely hair and draperies – were normally seen as purely decorative in aesthetic terms. Yet for Warburg the accessory as a phenomenon between aesthetics and psychology was only a starting point.[12] Although restricting himself to a few lines in the preface and to four highly abstract additional 'theses',[13] he tentatively drew a far more general conclusion that was based on theories of both perception and evolution. These theories were particularly crucial to him as they offered a scientific explanation for the reappearance of expressive formulas throughout the history of visual culture.

After the discovery of an assumed relation between motion and emotion, Warburg turned every subsequent enquiry into a case study. To put it in very simple terms, his theory considered both the genesis of a specific artefact in a specific historical milieu and, more generally, an artefact as such in the mind of any artist across time.[14] In the following pages I shall try to show how, even in his very first art-historical study, Warburg combined these two intrinsically distinct approaches. The former is guided by the idea that a particular artist selects and copies specific models, the latter by the notion that certain circumstances trigger a formally predetermined response to external forces – in effect, active choice versus passive subjection. For Warburg's work on Botticelli this means that he conflated what was at that time an entirely new iconological analysis of the artwork in its historical context with a nascent anthropologico-psychological theory.

Warburg's doctoral dissertation

Warburg handed in his doctoral dissertation to the University of Strasbourg on 8 December 1891. On 5 March 1892 he passed his exams, and two months later he was in contact with a publisher.[15] In the end his thesis was printed as a slim volume in December 1892, then published in the imprint in 1893 (fig.3.6). The print run is unknown, but a carefully compiled list of people to whom copies were sent documents Warburg's efforts to disseminate his new revisionist method (fig.3.7). Among the recipients were fellow students, former academic advisors and eminent scholars, such as Jacob Burckhardt and Adolfo Venturi.[16]

Didactically, Warburg's debut publication is far from exemplary. He presupposes his readers' familiarity with his objects of study and fails to frame a clear question or forge an argument that would lead his readers through his abundant materials. He seems to have assumed that his many textual examples and the visual evidence would speak for themselves.[17] Warburg explains his general aims only briefly in the preface. Firstly he sought to show how both contemporary art theory and poetics could be presumed to have influenced Botticelli; secondly to reveal how a non-specific 'antiquity' became a model for the expression of motion through 'animated accessories' ('*bewegtes Beiwerk*'); and, thirdly, to demonstrate how empathy was turned into a style-determining force.[18] The main body of the thesis, however, deals – at least explicitly – with only the first two of these aspects. Any conclusion regarding the third remains implicit.

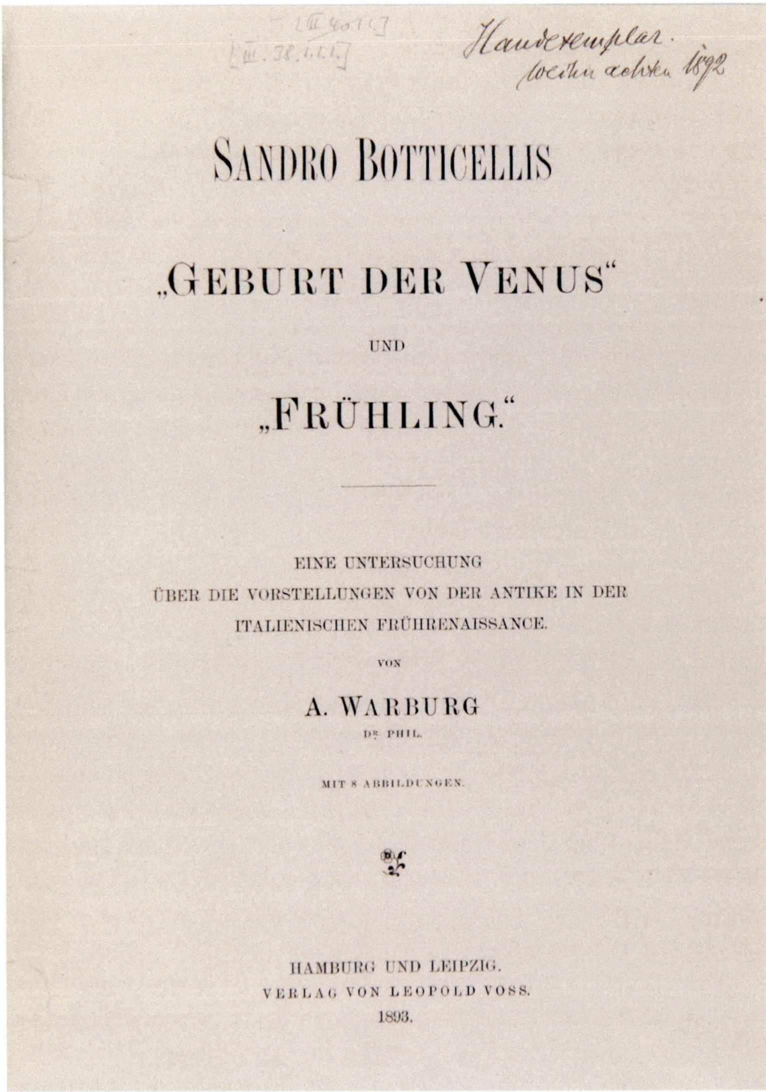

SANDRO BOTTICELLIS

„GEBURT DER VENUS“

UND

„FRÜHLING.“

EINE UNTERSUCHUNG
ÜBER DIE VORSTELLUNGEN VON DER ANTIKE IN DER
ITALIENISCHEN FRÜHRENAISSANCE.

VON

A. WARBURG

DR. PHIL.

MIT 8 ABBILDUNGEN.

HAMBURG UND LEIPZIG.
VERLAG VON LEOPOLD VOSS.
1893.

Fig.3.6 Title page of Aby Warburg's personal copy of his Sandro Botticelli's *'Geburt der Venus' und 'Frühling'. Eine Untersuchung über die Vorstellungen von der Antike in der italienischen Frührenaissance,* Hamburg und Leipzig, Leopold Voss 1893, Warburg Institute Archive, III.38.1.1.1. © The Warburg Institute.

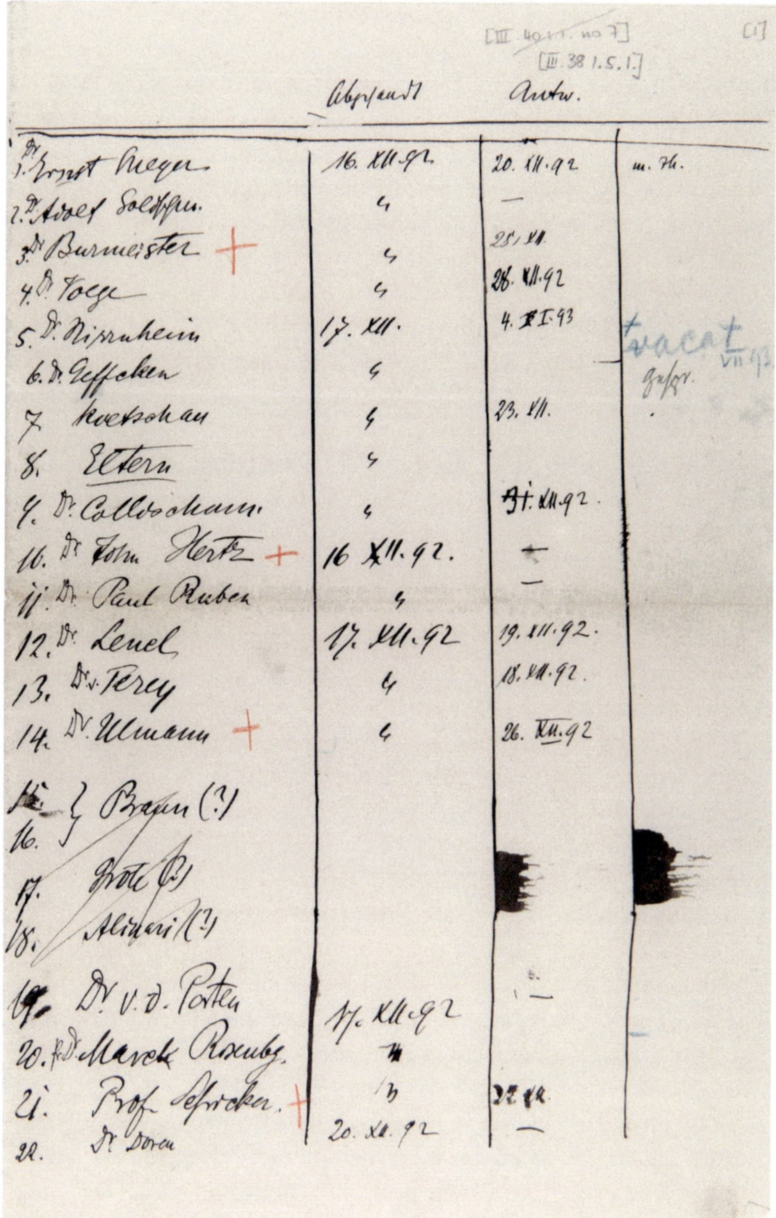

Fig.3.7 Aby Warburg (1866–1929), List of recipients of his Sandro Botticelli's *'Geburt der Venus' und 'Frühling'* (1893) and their responses, first of three folios, Warburg Institute Archive, III.38.1.5.1, fol.1. © The Warburg Institute.

Warburg begins by quoting the art historian Julius Meyer, director of the Berlin Gemäldegalerie.[19] In a footnote to his essay on the 'Florentine School of the Fifteenth Century' (with particular focus on the late Botticelli and Filippino Lippi) Meyer had related the iconography of *The Birth of Venus* (fig.1.0) to the second Homeric Hymn to Aphrodite. Stressing the presumed popularity of the text among Florentine humanists – a hypothesis based on the fact that it was printed as early as 1488 – Meyer concluded that Botticelli's iconography was inspired by this hymn.[20]

While Meyer went on to speculate about the learned Lorenzo de' Medici's role as Botticelli's intermediary, Warburg followed a different suggestion.[21] In 1888 Adolf Gaspary, a German scholar of romance philology, had been the first to observe analogies between Botticelli's *Venus* and Poliziano's verbal depiction of Venus Anadyomene floating on a shell. This reference was to an imaginary relief on the portal of Venus's palace in Poliziano's *Stanze per la Giostra*, the commemorative poem celebrating Giuliano de' Medici's joust in Piazza Santa Croce of 1475.[22] The *Stanze* famously recount the hero's platonic love for Simonetta Cattaneo Vespucci, the beautiful Genoese wife of the Florentine banker Marco Vespucci. Inspired, Gaspary believed, by the Roman poet Claudianus's *De nuptiis Honoriae at Mariae* (49–96), Poliziano's extensive 'painterly' digression on the 'Realm of Venus' competed with the newly revived art of painting.[23]

After Warburg had introduced these observations, he could forge his own central thesis that Botticelli's subjects were inspired by poems of Greek and Roman authors whose inventions were conveyed to him by Poliziano. But Warburg wanted not only to prove *if*, but also explain *why* painters such as Botticelli (and poets such as Poliziano) imitated classical models. He therefore went on to compare the classical originals with their post-classical copies. Through these comparisons, carefully documented in extensive tables (fig.3.8), he found that Poliziano had amplified the depiction of accessories in motion.[24] This observation provided the main clue for Warburg's subsequent interpretation.

To understand Poliziano's apparent emphasis on accessories, Warburg turned to Alberti's *De pictura* of 1435. Again two older scholars, the art historians Anton Springer and Robert Vischer, had already connected Alberti's now-famous passage, in which he instructs painters on the depiction of wind-blown hair and garments, with contemporary paintings.[25] While Springer linked Alberti's advice to Botticelli's wind gods,[26] Vischer, tellingly, made a connection between Alberti's words and supposedly typical mannerisms favoured by a whole group of painters who had been trained in Verrocchio's workshop.[27] According to Vischer, these 'garments and hair' were precisely 'the critical means of subjective

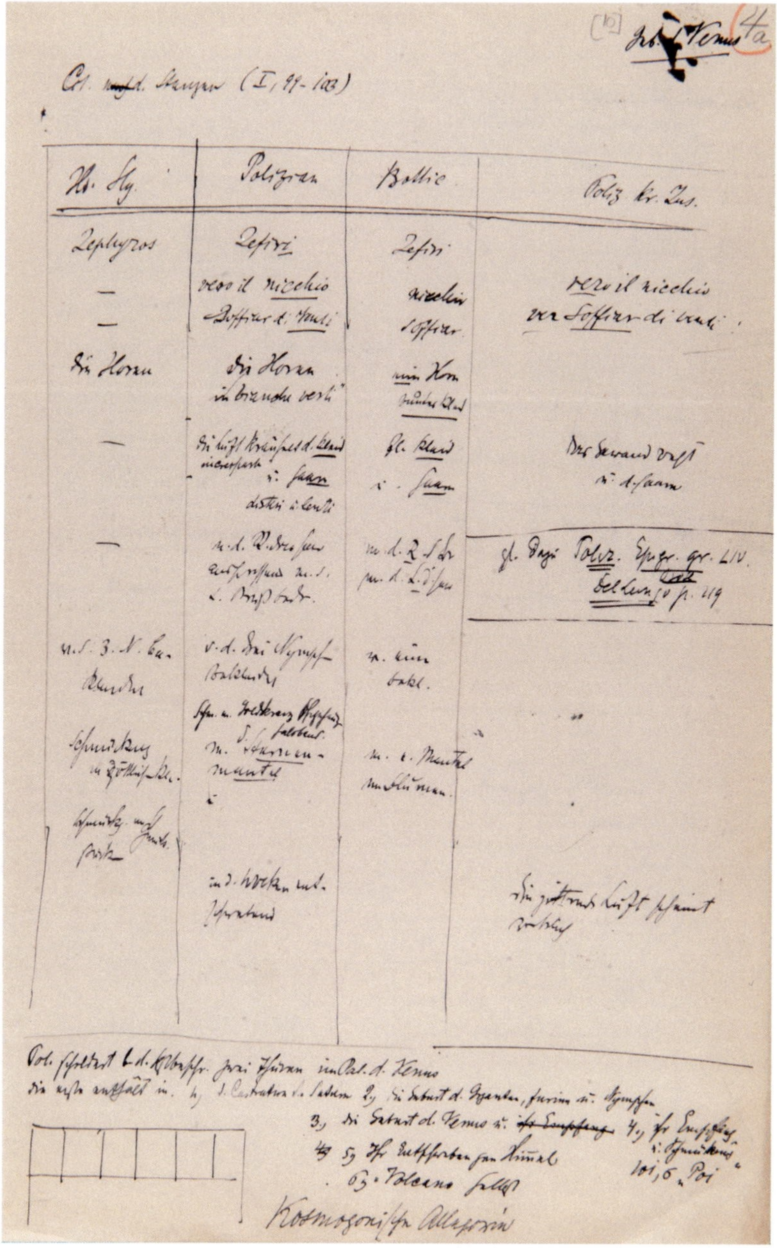

Fig.3.8 Aby Warburg, *Collation of the Homeric Hymn to Aphrodite, Poliziano's Stanze per la Giostra (I, 99–103) and Botticelli's Birth of Venus*, Warburg Institute Archive, III.39.4.2, fol. 7. © The Warburg Institute.

expression in painting', and subsequently 'the starting point[...] that prepares for Mannerism, right at the time when the desire to render nature as faithfully as possible was burgeoning'.[28]

For Warburg's attempt to offer a psychological explanation for the problem of the formation of style, Vischer's thesis was surely crucial. While Vischer was thinking of Signorelli, however, Warburg drew

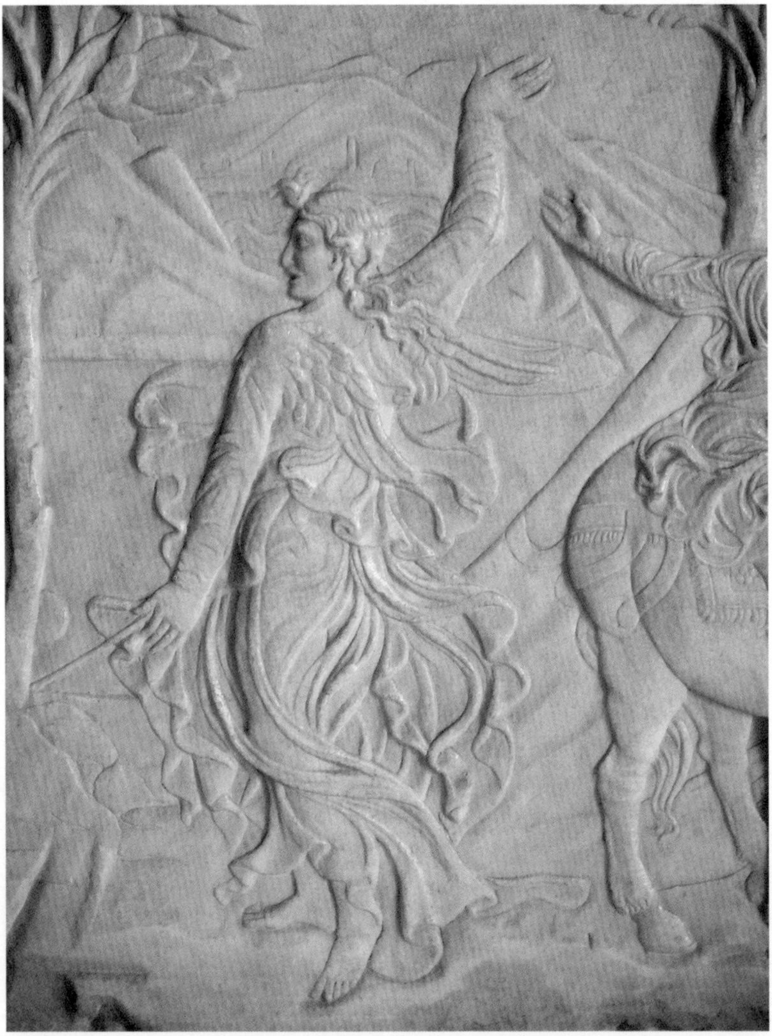

Fig.3.9 Agostino di Duccio (1418–81), *The Journey of St Sigismund*, detail of an angel appearing to the saint, *c.*1450, bas-relief (originally in the St Sigismund-Chapel, Tempio Malatestiano), Museo d'Arte Antica, Castello Sforzesco, Milan. © Photograph by the author.

attention to Agostino di Duccio, the Florentine sculptor whose principal works, dating from the 1450s, can be found in the *Tempio Malatestiano* in Rimini and in San Bernardino in Perugia (fig.3.9). Agostino was for Warburg the prototype of an artist who followed Alberti's advice excessively: '[He] filled the hair and the draperies of the figures[...] with such liveliness of movement that it devolved into Mannerism' ('*eine bis zum Manierismus gesteigerte Bewegtheit in Haar und Gewandung*').[29] The sculptor was thus a typical figure for whom form, as Warburg saw it, became detached from the emotions that initially had given rise to it.

Once Warburg had firmly established a link between Botticelli and Poliziano, he moved on to interpreting the *Primavera* (fig.1.30) which he believed was a companion piece to *The Birth of Venus*.[30] Warburg expounded once more on analogies with literary sources – particularly the Three Graces, for whose draperies Alberti, inspired by Seneca, had given another textbook example.[31] However, he also took into consideration contemporary artefacts, as well as the flesh-and-blood characters of Quattrocento festivals, as a source of inspiration for the prominent female figure with the flowery dress who is dispersing roses. He quotes Adolf Bayersdorfer from the Staatliche Gemäldesammlungen in Munich and Josef Bayer, who called this figure 'Flora'.[32] Warburg, however, believed that she was the goddess of spring, common in contemporary texts such as the *Hypnerotomachia Poliphili* (published about 25 years after Botticelli painted the *Primavera*) and here possibly modelled after a specific Roman sculpture of Flora or Pomona, formerly on display at Palazzo Pitti.[33] Warburg recognised the nymph 'Flora', instead, in the adjacent, much less colourful female figure with a rose twig growing from her mouth, precisely as Ovid had described her in his *Fasti*: 'As she spoke she breathed spring roses from her mouth'.[34] Warburg was convinced that Botticelli had presented the nymph precisely as she makes the transition from virgin to wife, when Chloris became Flora: 'In Ovid's *Fasti*, Flora tells how she was pursued, caught and overpowered by Zephyrus. As his bridal gift she has received the ability to turn whatever she touched into flowers.'[35] After quoting Ovid's passage in full, Warburg concluded:

> The description supplies the nucleus of the composition; and the necessary form in motion might have been regarded as Botticelli's spontaneous contribution, if he had not given more than one instance of his tendency to refer to established sources when depicting draperies in motion. The group turns out to be precisely based on Ovid's description of Daphne's flight from Apollo.[36]

That Poliziano, Botticelli's putative advisor, had adopted Ovid's depiction of Daphne's flight for his own description of the ravished Europa on the imaginary portal of Venus's palace, and had borrowed Ovid's words more than once, made Warburg conclude that Poliziano must have also influenced the composition of the *Primavera*. He also believed that this work and, subsequently *The Birth of Venus* in all likelihood related to his *Giostra*, namely his digression on the 'Realm of Venus'. Following Vasari's account of the paintings' common location on the one hand, and his identification of each central figure as Venus, on the other, Warburg identifies the two paintings as a pair, depicting two states of this mythical realm: Venus 'rising from the sea' and 'her appearance in her own realm', surrounded by her 'faithful helpers'.[37] To support the presumed link with Poliziano's *Stanze per la Giostra* he quotes, almost in passing, Jacob Burckhardt's observation that 'Italian festive pageantry, in its higher form, is a true transition from life into art' as an 'intuitive generalisation' whose validity could be proved through his very own analysis of the relationship between Poliziano's poetry and Botticelli's painting.[38]

Warburg's conclusion, based on a number of comparisons between classical poetry (namely Horace, Lucretius and Claudian) and that of Poliziano, finally allowed him to recognise – in both the Hora to Venus's left in *The Birth of Venus* and his goddess of spring in the *Primavera* – the idealised Simonetta Vespucci. She had died in April 1476, and her features had been portrayed by Botticelli in a painting mentioned by Vasari. Warburg's evidence is a detailed comparison with both the type and the proportions of two portraits of young women represented as nymphs and attributed to Botticelli, one now in the Gemäldegalerie in Berlin, the other in the Städelsches Kunstinstitut in Frankfurt.[39] The *Primavera* was thus for Warburg a 'pictorial allegory' that enshrined Simonetta's memory, putatively confirmed by the painting's date, based on Julius Meyer's analysis of style. Warburg believed that a veritable cult of Simonetta was the cause of Botticelli's *Primavera* – a conclusion he held to throughout his life.[40]

The genesis of Warburg's dissertation and its reception

Since Ernst Gombrich published his intellectual biography of Warburg in 1970, we have known that Warburg's first idea for a dissertation topic had been 'Filippino Lippi, art and progress in history' ('*Filippino Lippi, die Kunst und der Fortschritt in der Geschichte*').[41] Both topic and title date from December 1888, when Warburg spent the winter in Florence together with six fellow students; they were invited to attend a semester privately taught by the Breslau art historian August Schmarsow.[42] In 1927 Warburg recalled how this first idea came into being:

> Already [when I first came to Florence] Filippino Lippi's hyper-nervous mobility seemed to me like an inconceivable offence and almost a repulsive revolt against the law of beautiful composition that emerged from Italy's 'primitives', which precisely in its inner 'simplicity' represented the Italian traveller's ideal'.[43]

Again, in 1896, he reflected on the starting point of his lifelong interest in the afterlife of antiquity and described the original intriguing phenomenon as 'the baroque element in Early Renaissance art'.[44] Apparently a group discussion about Filippino's Pala Nerli of 1482 on 8 December 1888 in Santo Spirito sparked his initial interest in this artist.[45] Subsequently Warburg went on to draft a possible dissertation outline for Schwarsow's approval – the earliest document that demonstrates a specific attention to both *all'antica* costume and contemporary literature.[46]

We also know that while Warburg exchanged practical experience in Florence for his studies in Bonn, he continued an ambitious project to draft an objective theory of expression under the heading 'aesthetics'. In this he sought to define his own position between an empirical and 'materialistic' versus an 'idealist' approach to the problem. From the 'prolegomena' of Gottfried Semper's work on style[47] he recorded the statement that 'empirical aesthetics' ('*empirische Aesthetik*') would naturally have to follow speculative aesthetics.[48] To that effect, Warburg took lively inspiration from Darwin's *The Expression of Emotions in Men and Animals* (1872); on 26 November he recorded the much-quoted comment 'finally a book that helps me' ('*endlich ein Buch, das mir hilft*').[49] Most probably he turned to Darwin (after consulting Johann Caspar Lavater's essays on physiognomy)[50] in preparation for his first paper: a presentation on the 'types' in Masaccio's Carmine frescoes with a focus on facial expression. As a conclusion to his analysis of several frescoes, Warburg tried to demonstrate that there was an increase in physical movement over the time span of the execution of the cycle.[51]

From his diary we know, too, that Warburg visited all the Florentine galleries systematically, and acted as cicerone to his future wife, passionately discussing with her the relation between style, beauty and idealism.[52] This explains the loaded Hegelian term 'progress' ('*Fortschritt*') in his tentative dissertation title mentioned earlier. Shortly after his arrival in Florence Warburg had been studying a now little-known contribution to the controversy about historiography between empirical-materialist thinkers (led by the aspiring natural and technical sciences) and idealists (led by the humanities).[53] The text was Ernst Zitelmann's essay on 'Materialism in Historiography' – a response to Friedrich von Hellwald's purely materialistic interpretation of evolution in cultural history.[54] Informed by an idealistic-teleological approach, Zitelmann's response is essentially a plea for the application of Darwin's laws of nature – a putative empirical proof of Hegel's speculation about an *a priori* in history, and a goal ('*Zweck*') in its causality – to the interpretation of the evolution of culture.[55] Accordingly, for Warburg the transition from Tre- to Quattro- and to Cinquecento art demonstrated the existence of real progress towards naturalism with regard to the depiction of draperies. Florentine palaces, churches and collections offered manifold examples, and in his notes from Schwarsow's lectures we can see how he would mark every figure with garments in motion mentioned in them (fig.3.10).[56]

In May 1889, back at his home university in Bonn, Warburg presented his material to Carl Justi, his prospective advisor. Since Justi was not as sympathetic as he had expected, Warburg decided to change universities. After moving from Bonn to Strasbourg, where the eminent archaeologist Adolf Michaelis and the young art historian Hubert Janischek, editor of Alberti's treatises, taught, he continued to collect materials, and compile systematic tables and lists.[57] This kind of systematic approach is reflected

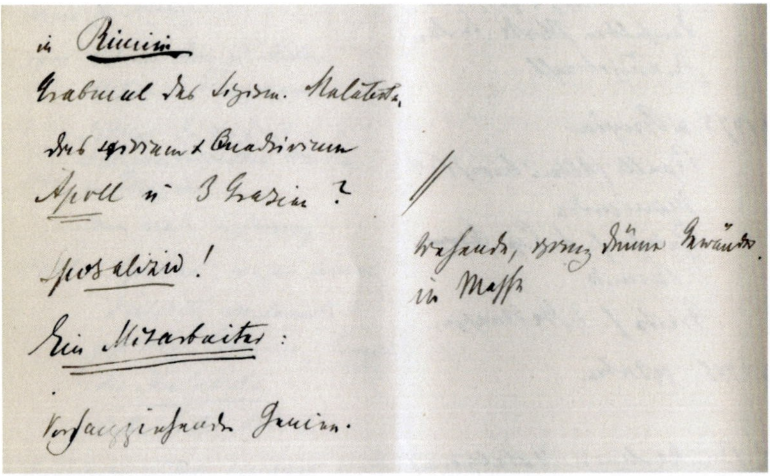

Fig.3.10 Aby Warburg, *Lecture Notes of August Schmarsow's 'Von Nicolo Pisano bis Michelangelo', Winter Semester 1888–89*, Kunsthistorisches Institut, Florence, Warburg Institute Archive, III.33.2.8, p.104: 'extremely sheer, fluttering garments en masse'. © The Warburg Institute.

in the structure of his dissertation. Successive drafts of the disposition of his thesis prove that he adhered initially to the idea of a systematic approach to the topic of fluttering draperies.[58]

The turning point came in April 1890. We find several diary entries referring to Warburg's reading of classical sources, underlined in red. Then, in a letter of 16 April 1890, Warburg told his mother proudly: 'I have now indeed explained the painting of which I spoke in Hamburg and I can finally eradicate this particular obstacle. So, what do you think?' Warburg later recalled:[59]

> A discovery (which, moreover, I made by virtue of how such images were translated in a German advertisement), namely, that the pursuit of Zephyr and Flora in Botticelli's *Spring* certainly must be a direct imitation of Ovid's *Fasti*, was thus decisive for me in choosing for my doctorate the theme of external, heightened movement beneath the sign of antiquity.[60]

Unfortunately we do not know which advertisement this was, but we do know that in April and May he wrote of having worked with Ovid,

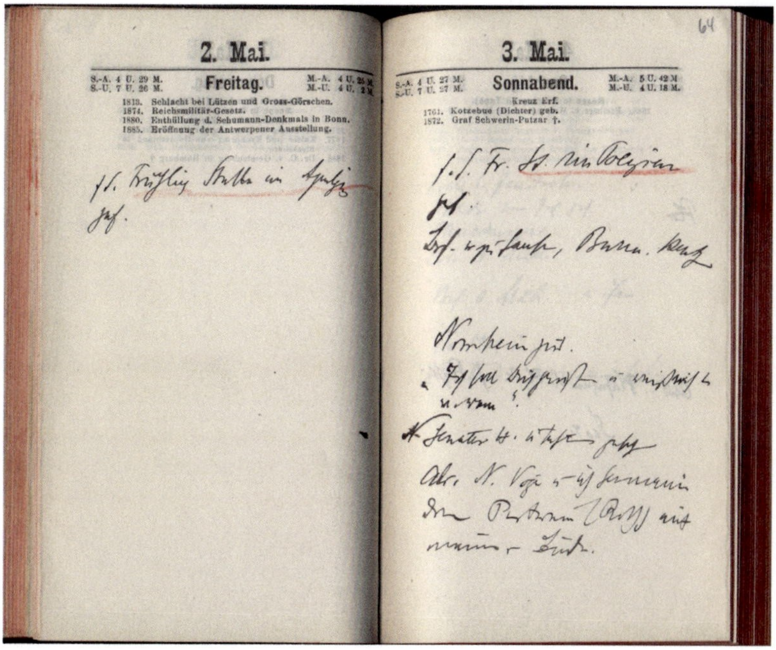

Fig.3.11 Aby Warburg, Diary entry of 3 May 1890: 'citation in Poliziano for the Spring found', WIA, III.9.6, p.64. © The Warburg Institute.

Horace and Apuleius, until he discovered a passage in Poliziano which he believed related to the *Primavera* (fig.3.11). This was the juncture that changed Warburg's plan. He was no longer going to produce a thesis about the fluttering draperies in Filippino's works – Botticelli's *Primavera* was now his topic. However, he had not yet abandoned the idea of making the development of style the main topic of his thesis. At the same time, he must have felt he was entering the territory of his fellow student, Hermann Ulmann, who was working on Botticelli's imitation of antique models and later produced the very first monograph on Botticelli. In July 1890 Ulmann replied to a letter, stressing that he had no hard feelings about Warburg's new topic, and adding that he had never come across any plausible classical source for the iconography of the *Primavera*.[61]

The question Warburg asked in his thesis triggered lively responses. With similar attention to detail, the classical philologist Richard Förster argued against the majority of Warburg's suggestions. Förster also vigorously denied the possibility that the painting's meaning could be determined by historical facts, and subsequently he discounted any connection with the death of Simonetta.[62] Warburg's friend and colleague Gustav Pauli also felt compelled to react. With a certain irony he remarked that the author narrowly missed his goal by drawing attention to garments instead of the naked bodies beneath, and that in fact he confused the means with the end.[63] Pauli in turn missed Warburg's arguably well-hidden point of departure: to investigate emerging mannerisms.

Style psychology and the afterlife of antiquity

Warburg's intrinsic goal is much more evident in his notes and drafts for the thesis than in the published text. Not only do they help us understand the somewhat disjointed discussion of Agostino di Duccio's sculpture, but they also clarify his epistemological interest in empathy. While in the final draft Warburg refers to Robert Vischer's theory of empathy, published in 1873, earlier versions include a reference to Heinrich Wölfflin's 'Renaissance and Baroque' of 1888,[64] and an explicit claim that his own study would help explain the phenomenon of mannerisms: 'The accumulation of stagy mannerisms,' he wrote confidently, 'is one of the psychological processes that accompanied every decline of art. This kind of touching mannerism is one of the most affective triggers of emotion in the viewer.'[65]

This claim, later to be abandoned, is the closest we get to Warburg's notion of the Pathos formula (*Pathosformel*) before the concept was properly born and the term coined in 1905.[66] His later remarks about Agostino di Duccio illustrate what I mean. Already in his thesis Warburg followed the archaeologist Franz Winter who treated Agostino as a typical epigone.[67] Later Warburg called Agostino an 'adept' ('*Adept*') who repeated 'Pathos formulas' mechanically, without an urgent inner desire' ('*ohne innere Not*') – that is, without 'breathing life into them' ('*beseelen*'). Products of this kind were for him 'disconnected dynamograms' ('*abgeschnürte Dynamogramme*')[68] and their repetition 'rhetoric' ('*Rhetorik*') or 'phraseology' ('*Phrasologie*').[69] That Hauser had found the same process in the works of neo-Attic sculptors was for Warburg a proof of psychological continuities, of synchronic truths.

Warburg's study of Botticelli's mythological paintings was triggered by a chance find. While in 1890 Warburg turned the discovery of a link between Ovid and Botticelli into an example to showcase psychological undercurrents in the formation of style – namely, the transition from naturalism to mannerism – he remained intrigued by the painter's personality. In a short article, entitled 'Sandro Botticelli' and published in 1898,[70] he tried to fathom the painter's 'temperament' through his biography and his works. The chief aim was to present Botticelli as a transitional character and thus the prototype of a transitional stylistic period. In his attempt to describe Botticelli's works as reflecting the painter's psyche, we observe the emergence of another fundamental idea: Warburg's concept of polarity. According to this the artefact is the manifestation of either its creator's or its patron's state of mind in a spectrum ranging between melancholy or inward-looking sentiment and more extroverted pathos. Warburg linked the former with Botticelli's religious subjects, angels, in particular, whereas the latter would characterise his secular paintings. On the other hand, Warburg's chance find of 1890 sparked his vivid interest in the afterlife of Ovid's works in post-classical art. For him Ovid was the most influential classical author to shape the expression of emotions.[71]

The reign of Venus

The Tenth International Art History Congress, held in October 1912 in Rome, is usually seen as the moment of breakthrough for Warburg's transdisciplinary approach. In his spectacular unravelling of the hitherto mysterious astrological calendar frescoes in Palazzo Schifanoia in Ferrara, he showcased his method of bringing together word and image.[72] Yet, in front of a broad audience, he felt also compelled to add something to his debut study – namely that, seen from the astrological perspective, Botticelli's 'Reign of Venus' was surely a celebration of the ruler over the month in which Simonetta Vespucci died.[73] He therefore utilised the attention of many to reinforce his old thesis.

Even if this assertion did not withstand the results of later investigations, we should recognise the immense potential of Warburg's debut study, developed at a time when art historiography was still dominated by writings on Botticelli soaked in aestheticism. After all, Warburg was the first to pay proverbial philological attention to detail. Gombrich called his deciphering of the allegorical meaning of Botticelli's *Primavera* a fruitful mistake, thereby laying the foundations for nothing less than what became known as iconology.[74] This is no surprise, since Gombrich considered Warburg's alleged attempt to replace aestheticism with a psychologised evolutionism a failure. His scepticism would leave room for a lengthy debate; yet I shall confine myself to noting that the history of art history seems to prove Warburg prophetic in granting images uncanny emotional power.

Notes

1 Fritz Saxl, 'Three "Florentines"': Herbert Horne, A. Warburg, Jacques Mesnil', in *Lectures* (London: The Warburg Institute, 1957), 331–44. Saxl delivered the lecture at the Courtauld Institute.

2 Jeremy N. Melius, *Art History and the Invention of Botticelli* (Ph.D thesis, Berkeley, University of California, 2010), 130–1; see also Michel Hochmann's essay in this volume.

3 Warburg and Horne met regularly and had a vivid exchange of letters in 1902–3. See Melius, *Art History*, 129–62; Caroline Elam, 'Herbert Horne's Botticelli', in *Botticelli Reimagined* (London: V&A Publishing, 2016), 94–100. Warburg became acquainted with Jacques Mesnil (whose birth name was Jean Jacques Dwelshauvers) in 1894; they remained close friends throughout their lives. See Saxl, 'Three Florentines', 342–4.

4 A. Warburg, *Sandro Botticellis 'Geburt der Venus' und 'Frühling'. Eine Untersuchung über die Vorstellungen von der Antike in der italienischen Frührenaissance* (Hamburg and Leipzig: Leopold Voss, 1893) and A. Warburg, ,'*Sandro Botticellis "Geburt der Venus" und "Frühling". Eine Untersuchung über die Vorstellungen von der Antike in der italienischen Frührenaissance*', in *Die Erneuerung der heidnischen Antike. Kulturwissenschaftliche Beiträge zur Geschichte der europäischen Renaissance* (Gesammelte Schriften I, II), Gertrud Bing, ed., in collaboration with Fritz Rougemont (Leipzig and Berlin: G. B. Teubner, 1932), 1–68, 307–28 (English trans. Aby Warburg, 'Sandro Botticelli's "Birth of Venus" and "Spring": An Examination of Concepts of Antiquity in the Italian Early Renaissance', in *The Renewal of Pagan Antiquity: Contributions to the Cultural History of the European Renaissance*, ed. Kurt W. Forster, trans. David Britt (Los Angeles: Getty Research Institute for the History of Art and the Humanities, 1999), 89–156, 405–31); Herbert P. Horne, *Alessandro Filipepi Commonly Called Sandro Botticelli: Painter of Florence* (London: G. Bell & Sons, 1908); Jacques Mesnil, *Botticelli* (Paris: Albin Michel, 1938).

5 Melius, *Art History*, 46–103, 129. Walter H. Pater, 'A Fragment on Sandro Botticelli', *Fortnightly Review* 3 (1870): 155–60; Walter H. Pater, *The Renaissance: Studies in Art and Poetry* (London: Macmillan 1893), 52–65. See Michael Levey, 'Botticelli and Nineteenth-Century England', *Journal of the Warburg and Courtauld Institutes* 23, no.3–4 (1960): 291–306, esp. 299–306; Frank Kermode, 'Botticelli Recovered', in *Forms of Attention: Botticelli and Hamlet* (Chicago and London: University of Chicago Press, 1985), 3–31; Adrian S. Hoch, 'The Art of Sandro Botticelli through the Eyes of Victorian Aesthetes', in *Victorian and Edwardian Responses to the Italian Renaissance*, Lene Østermark-Johansen and John Law, ed. (Aldershot: Ashgate, 2005), 55–85; Ulrich Rehm, 'The Critical Fortunes of "Vasari's Botticelli" in the Nineteenth Century', in *Botticelli Reimagined*, 48–9. Although Herbert Horne pays tribute to Walter Pater who induced the rediscovery of Botticelli, he also attributes the origin of 'that peculiarly English cult of Botticelli', the 'Aesthetic Movement', to his writings, see Horne, *Alessandro Filipepi*, XI–XIII, esp. XIII.

6 Horne, *Alessandro Filipepi*, XIV. Warburg was, no doubt, referring to Herbert Horne's meticulous reconstruction of Botticelli's life and work. See Warburg Institute Archive [WIA], General Correspondence [GC], Aby Warburg to Herbert Horne, 15 November 1902. See Elam, 'Horne's Botticelli', 96–100, esp. 100.

7 Mesnil was in Warburg's view undoubtedly a like-minded counterpart to whom he complained in 1897 that Ernst Steinmann's *Botticelli* (Bielefeld, 1897) was 'stilted and subjective' ('*ein durch und durch geziertes und unsachliches Buch*'). See WIA, GC, Aby Warburg to Jacques Dwelshauvers, 2 November 1897.

8 The context of this request was the preparation for Warburg's essay titled 'Sandro Botticelli', then published in *Das Museum* 3 (1898): 37–40. See WIA, GC, Aby Warburg to Jacques Dwelshauvers, 20 September 1986.

9 See n.82.

10 Warburg's so-called philological method owes much to his teacher at Bonn, the philologist Hermann Usener. Usener had stated that '[t]he philological descent into the detail ('*die philologische Vertiefung in das Detail*') leads to the vantage point from which new insights in the life and work of the nations can be gained' (trans. Davide Stimilli). See Hermann Usener, *Philologie und Geschichtswissenschaft* (Bonn: M. Cohen & Sohn, 1882), 27.

11 Saxl, 'Three Florentines', 341.

12 Spyros Papapetros, *On the Animation of the Inorganic. Art Architecture and the Extension of life* (Chicago and London: University of Chicago Press, 2012), 66. See Ernst Gombrich, *Aby Warburg. An Intellectual Biography* (London: Phaidon, 2nd ed., 1989), 47–52.

13 Warburg, 'Botticelli's Birth', 89, 144; Warburg, '*Botticellis Geburt*', 5, 58.

14 Warburg characterised his thesis as 'the attempt to use contemporary critical and classical literature to explain the genesis of artworks from their milieu' ('*den Versuch, die gleichzeitige kritische u. poetische Litteratur heranzuziehen und um so die Entstehung der Kunstwerke aus ihrem Milieu zu erklären*'). See WIA, GC, Aby Warburg's letter draft to Spemann (publisher), 31 May 1892.

15 Warburg, 'Botticelli's Birth', 405; Warburg, '*Botticellis Geburt*', 307; WIA, FC, Aby to Moritz Warburg, 5 March 1890.

16 WIA, III.40.1.1.1. About one-third of the recipients replied, notably Burckhardt and Venturi. As a sign of recognition the book was reviewed by a number of prominent German art historians.

17 Warburg's assistant and editor, Gertrud Bing, admitted that the dissertation 'may not exactly offer the easiest introduction to Warburg's writings' since 'the abundance of material does not seem to come under the same effortless conceptual control as in his later essays'. See Gertrud Bing, introduction to Warburg, *The Renewal*, 83 (English trans. of Gertrud Bing, introduction to A. Warburg, *Die Erneuerung*, XIV).

18 Warburg, 'Botticelli's Birth', 89; Warburg, '*Botticellis Geburt*', 5. See Gerhard Wolf, 'Warburg's Botticelli and Botticelli's Nymph', in *Botticelli Reimagined*, 102–4.

19 Warburg, 'Botticelli's Birth', 90; Warburg, '*Botticellis Geburt*', 6.

20 Julius Meyer, '*Zur Geschichte der florentinischen Malerei des XV Jahrhunderts. Sandro Botticelli in der zweiten Periode seiner Thätigkeit – Filippino Lippi, Raffaelino del Garbo, Piero di Cosimo*', *Jahrbuch der Königlich Preussichen Kunstsammlungen* 11, no.1 (1890): 3–35. See WIA, III.39.4.1.2, fols. 3–4.

21 Warburg, 'Botticelli's Birth', 90–1; Warburg, '*Botticellis Geburt*', 7.

22 Adolf Gaspary, *Geschichte der italienischen Literatur*, vol.2 (Strasbourg and Berlin: R. Oppenheim, 1885–8), 232–3.

23 Gaspary, *Geschichte*, 232.

24 Warburg, 'Botticelli's Birth', 91–5; Warburg, '*Botticellis Geburt*', 7–10.

25 Warburg, 'Botticelli's Birth', 95–7; Warburg, '*Botticellis Geburt*', 10–13. The observations of both Springer and Vischer were triggered by Hubert Janitschek's German edition of Alberti's treatise of 1877.

26 Anton Springer, 'Review of Hubert Janitschek, *Leon Battista Albertis Kleinere Kunsttheoretische Schriften (Vienna: W. Braümuller, 1877)*', in *Zeitschrift für bildende Kunst*, Carl von Lützow, ed., 14 (1879): 60–3, esp. 61.

27 Robert Vischer, *Luca Signorelli und die italienische Renaissance. Eine kunsthistorische Monographie* (Leipzig: Veit & Compagnon, 1879), 157.

28 Vischer, *Luca Signorelli*, 158: '*Gerade Gewand und Haar sind die kritischen Mittel des Subjectiven in der Malerei. Hier knüpft es, wie wir sehen, mitten im neu erstehenden Naturstreben an, um die Manier vorzubereiten*' (my translation). According to Papapetros, Vischer's statement was instrumental to the idea of the 'agency of the inorganic object'. See Papapetros, *On the Animation*, 45–6; 60–1.

29 Warburg, 'Botticelli's Birth', 96 (trans. modified); Warburg, '*Botticellis Geburt*', 12. See also Warburg's statement on page 141 of 'Botticelli's Birth': 'If the "influence of antiquity" then led to the unthinking repetition of superficially agitated motifs of motion, this was not the fault of "the antique" (which has subsequently inspired others, ever since Winckelmann, to describe it with equal conviction as the fountainhead of "tranquil grandeur"): the fault lay in the artists, and in their lack of mature artistic discretion.' See Papapetros, *On the Animation*, 55.

30 Warburg, 'Botticelli's Birth', 112; Warburg, '*Botticellis Geburt*', 26.

31 Warburg, 'Botticelli's Birth', 114–7; Warburg, '*Botticellis Geburt*', 27–8.

32 Warburg, 'Botticelli's Birth', 112; Warburg, '*Botticellis Geburt*', 26–7 with reference to Adolf Bayersdorfer Franz Reber, *Klassischer Bilderschatz* III (Munich: F. Bruckmann, 1891), VIII and Josef Bayer, *Aus Italien. Kultur- und Kunstgeschichtliche Bilder und Studien* (Leipzig: B. Schlickre, 1885), 269.

33 Warburg, 'Botticelli's Birth', 103–7, 126; Warburg, '*Botticellis Geburt*', 18–9, 38. Gerhard Wolf stresses Warburg's failure to recognise this figure as Chloris-Flora, represented in a 'pictorial metamorphosis' due to his determination to identify a historical person. See Wolf, 'Warburg's Botticelli', 103 and Elam, 'Horne's Botticelli', 96–100, esp. 100.

34 Warburg, 'Botticelli's Birth', 120; Warburg, '*Botticellis Geburt*', 32.

35 Warburg, 'Botticelli's Birth', 118; Warburg, '*Botticellis Geburt*', 32: '*In den Fasten des Ovid erzählt Flora, wie sie von Zephir ereilt und besiegt worden sei; als Hochzeitsgeschenk habe sie dann die Fähigkeit empfangen, was sie berühre, in Blumen zu verwandeln.*'

36 Warburg, 'Botticelli's Birth', 120; Warburg, *'Botticellis Geburt'*, 33: *'In dieser Schilderung ist die Komposition im Kern gegeben, und man würde das bewegte Beiwerk als eigene Zutat des Botticelli auffassen, wenn nicht seine Vorliebe, Beweglichkeiten der Tracht nach bewährten Mustern zu schildern, schon mehrfach zutage getreten wäre. In der Tat ergab sich, daß die Gruppe in genauer Anlehnung an Ovids Schilderung der Flucht der Daphne vor Apollo entstanden ist.'*

37 Warburg, 'Botticelli's Birth', 132–3; Warburg, *'Botticellis Geburt'*, 43–4.

38 Warburg, 'Botticelli's Birth', 125; Warburg, *'Botticellis Geburt'*, 37: *'Man erkennt hier, was Jacob Burckhardt, auch hier unfehlbar im Gesamturteil vorgreifend, gesagt hat: "Das italienische Festwesen ist in seiner höheren Form ein wahrer Übergang vom Leben in die Kunst".'*

39 Warburg, 'Botticelli's Birth' , 133–6; Warburg, *'Botticellis Geburt'*, 46–9.

40 Warburg, 'Botticelli's Birth', 139–40; Warburg, *'Botticellis Geburt'*, 49–52.

41 Gombrich, *Aby Warburg*, 45.

42 Hans W. Hubert, *Das Kunsthistorische Institut in Florenz: Von seiner Gründung bis zum hundertjährigen Jubiläum (1897–1997)* (Florence: Il Ventilabro, 1997), 14–15; Hans W. Hubert, 'August Schmarsow, Hermann Grimm und die Gründung des Kunsthistorischen Instituts in Florenz' in *Storia dell'arte e politica culturale intorno al 1900: la fondazione dell'Istituto germanico di storia dell'arte di Firenze*, Max Seidel, ed. (Venice: Marsilio, 1999), 339–58, esp. 340–7.

43 Aby Warburg, 'From the Arsenal to the Laboratory', trans. Christopher Johnson, annot. Claudia Wedepohl, *West 86th* 19, no.1 (2012): 106–24, esp. 114. Aby Warburg, *'Vom Arsenal zum Laboratorium'*, in *Werke in einem Band*, ed. Martin Treml, Sigrid Weigel and Perdita Ladwig (Berlin: Suhrkamp, 2010), 683–94, esp. 685: *'Deshalb erschien mir z.B. Filippinos übernervöse Beweglichkeit wie ein unbegreiflicher Verstoß und beinahe wie ein widerwärtiger Aufruhr gegen die Gesetze schönheitsvoller Zusammengefasstheit wie sie von den "Primitiven" Italiens ausging, die eben in ihrer innerlichen "Einfalt" das Ideal des Italienreisenden bildet.'* Objectivity was paramount for Warburg. In 1901 he sets his own method against a romanticising 'rediscovery' of the beholder's 'own primitive sensibility in the touching, unspoiled and simple Trecento painters'. See WIA, III.55.2, fol.12: *'Mit dem diskreten Lächeln innerer Überlegenheit wendet sich der moderne müde Kulturmensch auf seiner italienischen Erholungsreise von so viel banalem Realismus ab: ihn zieht Ruskins Machtgebot hinaus auf den Klosterhof, zu dem mittelmäßigen Giottesken Fresko, wo er in dem lieben, unverdorbenen, einfachen Trecentisten sein eigenes primitives Gemüt wieder zu finden hat.'*

44 Aby Warburg, *Fragmente zur Ausdruckskunde* (Gesammelte Schriften, Studienausgabe, IV), ed. Ulrich Pfisterer and Hans Christian Hönes (Berlin: De Gruyter, 2015), 16.

45 WIA, III.9.4, entry of 8 December 1888.

46 WIA, III.33.3.2. He probably discussed the draft with Schmarsow two weeks later. See WIA, III.9.4, entry of 24 December 1888.

47 Gottfried Semper, *Der Stil in den technischen oder tektonischen Künsten oder praktische Ästhetik. Ein Handbuch für Techniker, Künstler und Kunstfreunde* (1860) (Munich: F. Bruckmann, 2nd ed., 1878–9).

48 WIA, III.2.1. ZK 41, fols. 041/021155–8 contains sentences from the introduction of Semper's *Der Stil*, among them from page x: *'So erinnert die speculative Aesthetik in manchen Beziehungen an die Naturpsychologie. Wie diese die exacte Forschung, wird jene die empirische Aesthetik zur Nachfolgerin haben'*. See Spyros Papapetros, 'Aby Warburg as Reader of Gottfried Semper: Reflections on the cosmic character of ornament', in *Elective Affinities: Testing Word and Image Relationships*, ed. Catriona MacLeod, Véronique Plesch and Charlotte Schoell-Glass (Amsterdam and New York, NT: Radopi, 2009), 317–34: and esp. 317, 321–4.

49 WIA, III.9.4, entries of 26, 27, 29 and 30 November and 3 December 1888. See also Warburg, *Fragmente*, esp. 14, 30. Warburg never revealed how Darwin's book came to his attention.

50 WIA, III.9.4, entry of 16 November 1888.

51 WIA, III.33.2.6, fol.28.

52 Warburg, 'From the Arsenal', 114; Warburg, *'Vom Arsenal'* (as in n.43), 685.

53 See Johannes Heinssen, *'Der Indikator für die Probleme der Problemgeschichte: Kulturgeschichtliche Entdifferenzierung am Ende des 19. Jahrhunderts'*, in *Das Problem der Problemgeschichte. 1880–1932*, ed. Otto Gerhard Oexle (Göttingen: Wallstein, 2001), 39–84, esp. 50–63.

54 Ernst Zitelmann: *'Der Materialismus in der Geschichtsschreibung'*, *Preußisches Jahrbuch* 37 (1876): 177–96, 217–41; 38 (1876): 513–31, 650–63; Friedrich von Hellwald, *Culturgeschichte in ihrer natürlichen Entwicklung bis zur Gegenwart* (Augsburg: Lampart & Compagnon, 1875).

55 See Warburg's excerpt in ZK 41 [AE], envelope 30; WIA, III.9.4, entry of 29 December 1888; III.9.5, entry of 2 January 1890.

56 WIA, III.33.2.8.

57 WIA, III.39.2.2.1–7; III.39.3.

58 He was particularly excited to discover in Leonardo the reference to ancient sculpture as model for garments set in motion by the air. See WIA, III.9.5, entry of 11 July 1889.

59 WIA, FC, Aby to Charlotte Warburg, 16 April 1890: '*Jetzt habe ich das Bild von dem ich in Hamburg sprach wirklich erklärt und kann diese große Schwierigkeit beseitigen. – Na, und?*'

60 Warburg, 'From the Arsenal', 114; Warburg, '*Vom Arsenal*', 685.

61 WIA, GC, Hermann Ulmann to Aby Warburg, 14 July 1890.

62 Richard Förster, Review of *Sandro Botticellis* 'Geburt der Venus' *und* 'Frühling'. *Eine Untersuchung über die Vorstellungen von der Antike in der italienischen Frührenaissance* by Aby Warburg, *Zeitschrift für vergleichende Litteraturgeschichte* N.F. 6 (1893): 481–5.

63 Gustav Pauli, '*Antike Einflüße in der italienischen Frührenaissance*', Review of *Sandro Botticellis* 'Geburt der Venus' *und* 'Frühling'. *Eine Untersuchung über die Vorstellungen von der Antike in der italienischen Frührenaissance* by Aby Warburg, *Kunstchronik* 5, no.11 (1893–4): 174–7.

64 Robert Vischer, *Ueber das optische Formgefühl: Ein Beitrag zur Aesthetik* (Leipzig: Credner, 1873); Heinrich Wölfflin, *Renaissance und Barock. Eine Untersuchung über Wesen und Entstehung des Barockstils in Italien* (Munich: T. Ackermann, 1888).

65 WIA, III.39.4.1.2, fol.3: '*Man ersieht, wie die Bewegungsmotive, ursprünglich bewußt und besonnen vergleichend aus der Natur aufgenommen wurden, wie dann aber später die Künstler, angelockt von dem Wunsche, die als affectvoll empfundenen Motive sich nicht entgehen zu lassen, dieselben manieristisch häufen; sie verhält sich zu ihren Verkörperungen etwa wie die gedankenlose Analogie des mimischen Ausdrucks sich zur ursprünglich zweckmäßigen Handlung verhält. Es ist einer der psychologischen Vorgänge, wie sie den Verfall jeder Kunst begleiten. Mit diesem bewegten Manierismus entsteht jedoch auch für den Zuschauer eines der wirksamsten Reizmittel, die Empfindung.*'

66 A. Warburg '*Dürer und die italienische Antike*', in *Die Erneuerung*, 443–9, 623–5 (English translation, Aby Warburg, 'Dürer and Italian Antiquity', in *The Renewal*, 553–8, 729–31).

67 Franz Winter, *Ueber ein in Vorbild neu-attischer Reliefs* (Berlin: G. Reimer, 1890), 122–4. See Warburg, 'Botticelli's Birth', 97; Warburg, '*Botticellis Geburt*', 12.

68 WIA, III.2.1. 004/001235; III.102.1.4.1, fol.19.

69 WIA, III.61.6.1, fols. 29–30, 43. See Claudia Wedepohl, '*Von der* Pathosformel *zum* Gebärdensprachatlas. *Dürers* Tod des Orpheus *und Warburgs Arbeit an einer ausdruckstheoretisch begründeten Kulturgeschichte*', in *Die Entfesselte Antike. Aby Warburg und die Geburt der Pathosformel*, ed. Marcus Andrew Hurttig, in collaboration with Thomas Ketelsen (Cologne: Walther König, 2012), 33–50, esp. 40.

70 A. Warburg, 'Sandro Botticelli', *Das Museum* 3 (1898): 37–40 and Aby Warburg, 'Sandro Botticelli', in *Die Erneuerung*, 61–8, 329 (English translation, A. Warburg, 'Sandro Botticelli', in *The Renewal*, 157–64, 431.

71 See Aby Warburg, *Bilderreihen und Ausstellungen* (Gesammelte Schriften, Studienausgabe, II.2), ed. Uwe Fleckner and Isabella Woldt (Berlin: Akademie Verlag, 2012), 73–97.

72 A. Warburg, '*Italienische Kunst und internationale Astrologie im Palazzo Schifanoja zu Ferrara*', in *Die Erneuerung*, 459–81, 627–44 (English translation, Aby Warburg, 'Italian Art and International Astrology in Palazzo Schifanoia, Ferrara', in *The Renewal*, 563–91, 732–58.

73 Warburg, 'Italian Art', 585; Warburg, '*Italienische Kunst*', 478.

74 Gombrich, *Aby Warburg*, 56.

10. 'A Japanese Critic on Botticelli': fragmentation and universality in Yashiro's 1925 monograph

Jonathan K. Nelson

In a letter of 22 November 1922 to Laurence Binyon, Yukio Yashiro described his goals for a new book about Botticelli: 'I shall make clear what I, a man brought up in an artistic atmosphere utterly different from that of Europe, feel of Botticelli, that side of Botticelli which, as I think, was never, or perhaps very little, appreciated by European connoisseurs.'[1] Yashiro (1890–1975) was then a young Japanese art historian, recently arrived in Europe.[2] In London he sought out Binyon (1869–1943), an accomplished poet and specialist in Asian art at the British Museum;[3] he was also the author of a fine but now forgotten monograph on Botticelli.[4] Thanks to a letter of introduction from Binyon, stating that his 'Japanese friend [...] has come to Europe to study European art, but hasn't turned his back on his own', Yashiro met Bernard Berenson (1865–1959) in Florence and studied under his supervision at I Tatti.[5] Two remarkable aspects of the monograph that Yashiro published in 1925[6] – the fragmentation of Botticelli's works, thanks to the unprecedented use of detail photographs, and the interpretation of these details as expressing universal values – relate directly to the artistic atmosphere where the author was brought up.

What is uniquely Japanese about Yashiro's *Botticelli*? This question runs through all eight reviews of the first edition,[7] and four more of the revised and reduced monograph of 1929.[8] With the notable exception of Roger Fry, who published a highly critical and rather unfair article in *The Burlington Magazine*,[9] all the authors were extremely positive. Royal Cortissoz, a major figure in the American art world, opened his review by asking, 'How does an Oriental feel when he is confronted by one of our masters? [...] Does he recognize in it "the fundamental laws" [...] and do they, for him, make the West and the East seem essentially identical?'[10] Binyon himself, in an unsigned review for the *Times Literary Supplement*, 'A Japanese Critic on Botticelli', described the volume as 'an event of some importance. For the first time we have a full and complete study of an Italian master by the pen of a Japanese critic'.[11] An unsigned review in *The Spectator* even stated that the volume 'will remain the standard work upon his subject for decades'.[12]

Given the great interest today in historiography and transnational dialogues, one would expect scholars to take note of Yashiro's *Botticelli*. Instead, the monograph is cited in studies only when a diligent cataloguer wishes to cite all previous opinions on a given Botticelli painting.[13] The other exception is the very thin body of studies focusing on Yashiro himself.[14] In the online exhibition *Yashiro and Berenson: Art History between Japan and Italy*, available on the Villa I Tatti website since 2015, visitors can download the entire 1925 monograph, but there are only passing references to it in the letters between the two scholars, and in the related essays.[15] This paper will look first at one aspect of the *Botticelli* that Yashiro's contemporaries recognised as innovative, valuable and a reflection of the author's unique background: the beauty and abundance of the detail photographs. The second section addresses Yashiro's appeal to universal values, which acknowledges debates then raging in Japan.

All reviewers marvelled over the nearly 300 illustrations in the 1925 monograph, an unprecedented number for a study of any artist (figs 3.12–3.14). Yashiro's *Botticelli* appears to be the first publication to include detail photographs focused on only a hand, foot, drapery fold, flower or bird. On occasion earlier books included details limited to an individual, even to a face, but never the small fragments selected by Yashiro with such poetic sensibility. The plates in the Botticelli monograph, as noted by Binyon, 'endow us with fresh eyes for the beauty of dancing limbs, of clasping hands, of flowers in verdure, of some vistas of landscape seen in a radiant isolation'.[16]

In part Yashiro was inspired by the photographs he found in the collections of Berenson and Sir Robert Witt.[17] In these archives, unlike anything then available in Japan, Yashiro had found hundreds of detail images. As Yashiro wrote in his autobiography: 'During my stay in London, I saw that there was such a thing as an institute that ought to be called an "art library focused on photographs", where photographs of all kinds of art works were collected, divided and preserved. [...] I proposed to create such an institute in Japan'.[18] This, then, is the origin of the National Institute of Research that Yashiro helped to create in 1930 in Tokyo. Unknown to Western scholars, the methods used in the libraries of Berenson and Witt had a direct impact on how the Japanese study Japanese art in Japan.

Berenson used detail photographs primarily to establish the authorship of paintings, as he surely explained to his Japanese protégé. In *Botticelli* Yashiro discussed how Berenson, in his 'Rudiments of Connoisseurship' (1902), drew attention to the depiction of hands in order to determine the 'hand' of the artist. The Japanese author added, 'Hands treated as such do not interest me here'; instead, Yashiro was interested in how hands express deeper meanings.[19] In line with Berenson, Clarence Kennedy explained on the title page of his celebrated volume of photographs *Certain Portrait Sculptures of the Quattrocento* (1928) that the many details were 'taken expressly to facilitate the study of attributions and the critical analysis of style'.[20] Both scholars, of course, followed the methodology championed by Giovanni Morelli. As Yashiro himself explained in the first chapter of his *Botticelli*, Morelli 'studied the details of pictures very carefully, because in unnoticed corners [...] the artist reveals himself'.

Yashiro exhibited little interest in attributions, however, and his attention to details differs fundamentally from Morelli's. Yashiro's goals neatly correspond to those described by Bernard Berenson, in his 1899 article on the 'Amico di Sandro', where he expressed his desire to establish a 'distinct artistic personality'.[21] Similarly, a review published in 1894 by Mary Costelloe (Berenson's future wife) ends by stating: 'what other ultimate purpose art studies may have than definition of quality and reconstruction of artistic personality, we do not know'.[22] In his own monograph Yashiro used details to discover Botticelli's artistic personality. Decades later, in his autobiography, Yashiro wrote that small sections of the paintings revealed 'a mysterious slender beauty not found elsewhere [...]. Even when he is simply depicting wild flowers scattered in lush grass, one can sense in each flower's depths a concealed spirit.'[23]

This attention to details provided the foundation for the unique organisation of Yashiro's *Botticelli*. He devoted an entire chapter to the treatment of hands and feet, while other chapters focus on hair, draperies, flowers and landscape. We do not find this approach in any other book on Botticelli, or any other artist, before or since Yashiro. In his autobiography Yashiro explained that he wanted to demonstrate the 'idiosyncrasies' of Botticelli's art:

> I did this by selecting details from his representative works that went along with what I thought and by having taking numerous photographs taken of them. In some cases, I would specify a full-sized reproduction, and in other cases I would specify a clearly delineated crop.[24]

Yashiro could have followed the procedure used by most art historians, then and now: to print only a detail of an existing image. Instead he decided instead to commission new photography. The resulting images, Yashiro explained,

> surprised Giacomo, the son of the famous Florentine photographer Brogi, whom I asked to take these detail photographs according to my picky instructions. As he told me, 'Our studio regularly takes lots of detail photographs of various famous paintings for scholars from all over the world, but this is absolutely the first time we have had to photograph in such a sensuous, interesting way'.[25]

Brogi not only recognised the originality of the images; he also appreciated their economic value. He waived all charges for Yashiro in exchange for the rights to the works, which he sold as his own. One example is a postcard representing a detail of the grassy field in the *Primavera* (fig.3.12). This is one of several sent to Japan in 1928 by the philosopher

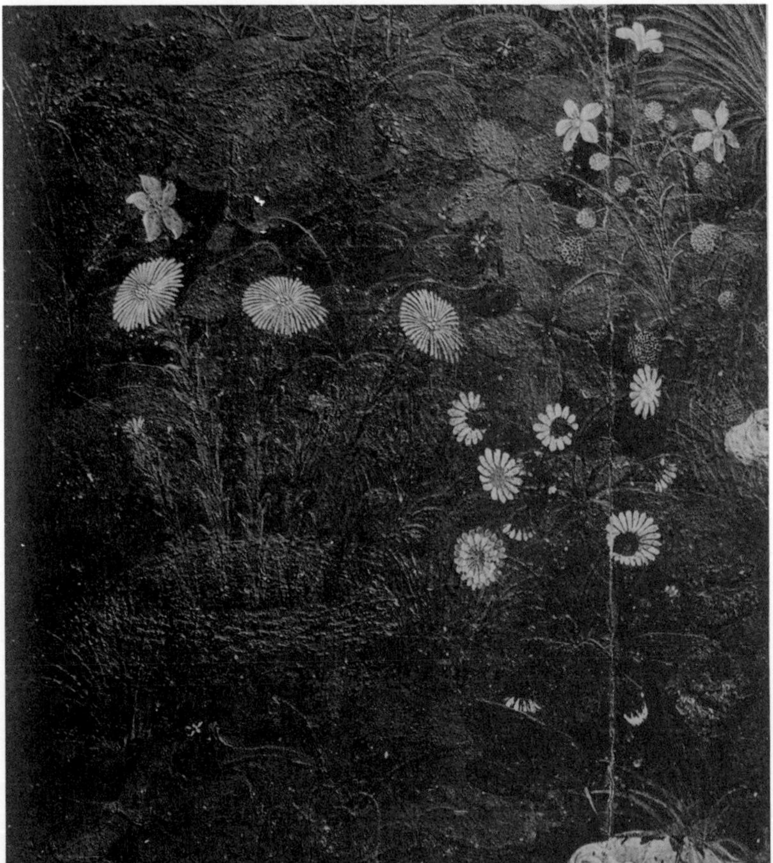

Fig.3.12 Yukio Yashiro (1890–1975), *Botticelli,* 1925, vol.II, 95: detail of *Primavera.* © Photograph by the author.

Watsuji Tetsurō with an accurate observation: 'I think that the picture cards must have been made as Yashiro proposed'.[26] These souvenirs indicate the impact of Yashiro's very personal vision of Botticelli on the memory of visitors to the Uffizi.

Three highly unusual aspects of Yashiro's approach in his 1925 Botticelli monograph – the decision to include more volumes dedicated to plates than to text, the use of custom-made images and the interest in details that reveal the personality of the artist – correspond closely to another work produced in Berenson's immediate circle, Arthur Kingsley Porter's *Romanesque Sculpture of the Pilgrimage Roads.*[27] In this series of 10 volumes, published in 1923, no less than nine are devoted to images; most of these were specially made by the author and his wife, Lucy Wallace Porter.[28] They were frequent guests at I Tatti when the young Japanese scholar worked there, and Yashiro must have learned about Porter's extraordinary project.[29] Indeed, Yashiro probably saw many of the detail photographs taken by the Porters in the early 1920s and given to Berenson. At I Tatti Yashiro developed his own idea for a Botticelli monograph that was not only richly illustrated, but also structured around highly detailed and original photographs. As Yashiro explained:

> precise, well-thought-out detail photography of famous paintings, although it has become commonplace nowadays, was in those days largely the first of its kind in the West. As such, not only did it generally receive a great amount of attention, but the detail photographs of Botticelli that came out especially well also received a great amount of praise from Mr. Berenson.[30]

Yashiro's contribution to Western photography has been entirely forgotten – in part because this observation appears in the autobiography of a little-known scholar, published only in Japanese. In the 1920s, however, Yashiro's monograph and his collaboration with Brogi had an immediate impact on the young Roberto Longhi. In 1927 Longhi collaborated with Brogi on a series of detail photographs, newly commissioned for an article on Rubens.[31] More importantly, in his 1927 monograph on Piero della Francesca Longhi included a large number of details.[32] Though none show only a hand, foot or drapery fold, several reproduce a lone tree, a building or a sliver of landscape. This innovative and effective use of detail photography, justly praised by modern scholars, most probably indicates Longhi's response to Yashiro's *Botticelli*, though neither scholar ever mentioned the other. In 1942, when Longhi published a new edition of his Piero monograph, he wrote in the preface that the reproductions from 1927 had the unwanted result of instigating an obsession with '"details", and with "details of details"'.[33] More recently, Massimo Ferretti aptly observed that 'a sequence of details, as one first finds in Longhi's *Piero della Francesca* (1927), presupposes a mental conception of space which is necessarily post-cubist'.[34] A Western observer could deconstruct a Renaissance painting only after the revolution led by Picasso and Braque. But a Japanese artist and scholar, brought up in an artistic atmosphere utterly different from that of Europe, conceived and realised a sequence of details of Botticelli's works several years before Longhi.

The young Kenneth Clark commented on the images in Yashiro's Botticelli monograph shortly after the volume appeared in 1925. On 14 February 1926, when writing to Mary Berenson about his forthcoming sojourn at I Tatti, Clark recommended that she acquire a new camera. In that way, he could take detail photographs of paintings, and 'we shall be able to Yashiro-ise anything we like'.[35] Clark published his views on this subject in *One Hundred Details from Pictures in the National Gallery* (1938). Detail photographs, he explained, 'had been taken for scientific purposes for many years before anyone thought of reproducing them for their own sakes, and I believe it was the Japanese critic, Yukio Yashiro, who first used them as aids to appreciation in his book on Botticelli'.[36] Here we see the most direct and important example of Yashiro's impact in the West. He inspired Clark, and subsequently countless others, to include a large number of details in their works and, indeed, to produce books of details.

Is there anything *Japanese* about the decision to include such details? The answer is yes, according to Binyon:

> Recently the Japanese, in reproducing their own masterpieces, have discovered the illuminating value of photographing many details on a large scale, as well as the complete picture. And Mr. Yashiro has applied this method with a lavishness that makes his two volumes of plates a series of enchantments and surprises.[37]

No one would know better about the origins of the Botticelli monograph than Binyon. In a letter sent to Mary Berenson, Yashiro recounts that at first

> I merely wanted to write articles on various phases of Botticelli's art, to which I had taken those detail-photographs as illustrations. The friends to whom I showed those photos became very much interested, & recommending a publisher, urged me to publish a book.[38]

One of these friends was Binyon; the other was his collaborator at the British Museum, Arthur Waley (1889–1966).[39] Binyon arranged for the volume to be published by the Medici Press, best known for its fine art prints. It was Binyon – a specialist in Asian art and inspired by Japanese publications with full-page details – who encouraged his Japanese friend to publish the Botticelli monograph in his highly unusual and influential format.

In earlier Japanese publications, details are usually limited to the central figure from a larger composition or a head, as in the splendid photographs by Ogawa Kazumasa.[40] These help us appreciate the striking originality of Yashiro's *Botticelli*, which included more focused details. Given that Yashiro was trained as a painter, his approach might reflect the use of *etehon*; these pattern books often included pages devoted to heads, flowers and animals.[41] Some of the details in the monograph reveal the same stylistic traits found in the Japanese woodblock prints that Yashiro compared to Botticelli. Though the author himself does not discuss the compositional qualities of the photographs or prints, both are characterised by a lack of perspective or shadow. More importantly, and more unusually in the West, the images are often highly cropped; in many cases, the main subject appears off centre (figs 3.13 and 3.14).

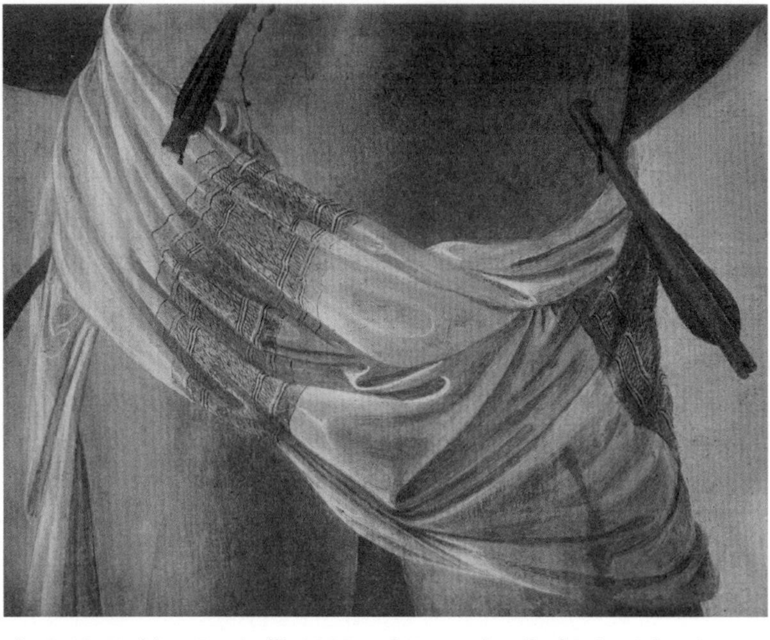

Fig.3.13 Yashiro, *Botticelli*, 1925, vol.II, 47: detail of *Saint Sebastian* (Berlin, Gemäldegalerie). © Photograph by the author.

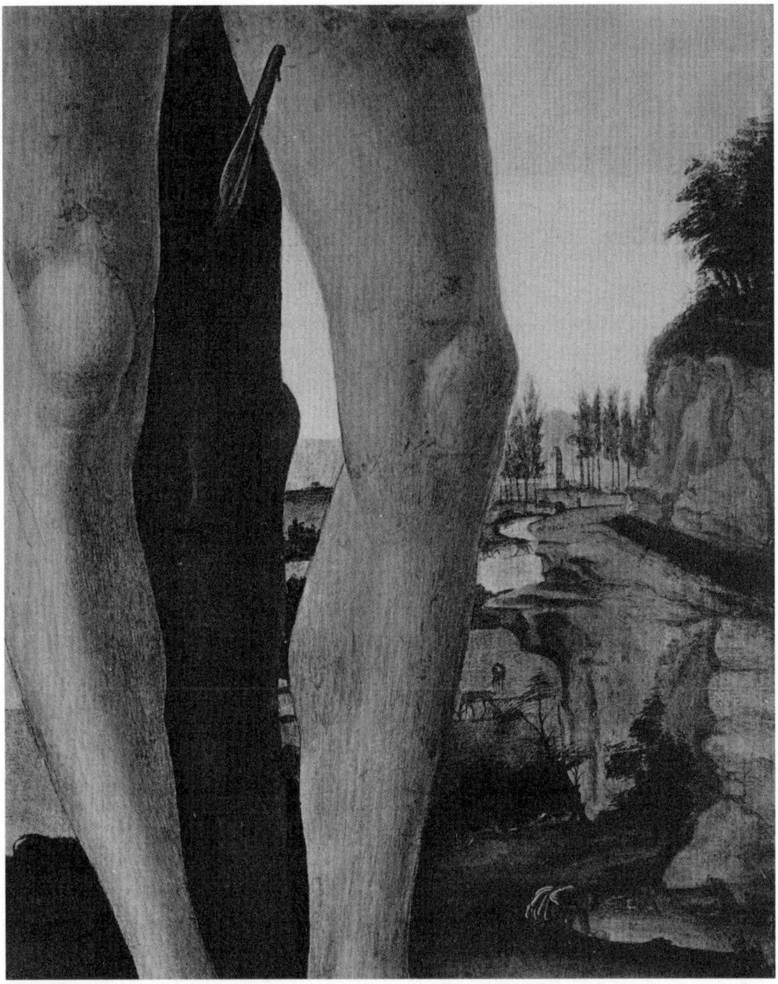

Fig.3.14 Yashiro, *Botticelli*, 1925, vol.II, 50: detail of *Saint Sebastian*. © Photograph by the author.

Yashiro's deep knowledge of Asian art certainly had an impact on his attention to details in Botticelli's paintings. For example, he writes that 'in Buddhism and other Oriental religions, all of which have strong tendencies to mysticism, hands play a large part in solemnities'.[42] Yashiro goes on to discuss these elements in both Eastern and Western art. Elsewhere he affirms that 'the only painter comparable to Botticelli for his sensuous appreciation of flowers is [...] that strange genius Utamaro'.[43] These parallels were praised even by Fry, for whom the most interesting parts of Botticelli monograph were those where Yashiro

> compares Botticelli's art, or rather his own impressions of that art, with that of his own country. It is, in the main, with regard to landscapes, flowers and shells in Botticelli's pictures that he finds at once affinities and differences which are illuminating.[44]

In his autobiography, Yashiro recounted that Berenson, upon hearing about his protégé's plans for a monograph, recommended 'a small book [...] since no one would think to learn about Botticelli from a Japanese'. Yashiro thought, 'I'll be damned', and vowed to 'publish in Europe a grand, full-blown work on Botticelli'.[45] He surely realised that this would be the first major monograph by a Japanese scholar to be written in English and dedicated to a Western artist. For this reason, I suggest, Yashiro decided to take on an ambitious project: to challenge the approach to world art he associated with Okakura Tenshin (1863–1913).[46] Okakura was one of the principal founders of the Tokyo School of Fine Arts, where Yashiro had taught Western art history before coming to Europe. In the realm of painting, Okakura attempted to develop a national painting style.[47] Yashiro, who never met Okakura, had studied with Kuroda Seiki, director of the Department of Western Art; like his teacher, Yashiro painted in a Western style. In his introduction to *Botticelli*, in reference to Okakura, Yashiro stated boldly

> He worked up all *The Ideals of the East* in sharp contrast to those of the West, and I know many young scholars in Japan who are following the same idea [...]. Generally speaking, Eastern writers hold very sharply contrasted views and consider that Western Art is the apotheosis of material welfare, and Oriental of the spiritual.[48]

Of course, Okakura and his followers recognised spiritual qualities in Western art. In his attack on the sharp opposition between East and West, Yashiro found a sympathetic ear in Binyon. His review of *Botticelli* states that 'Mr. Yashiro compels us to revise some of our presumptions. He is convinced that in the world of art the difference between East and West has been immensely exaggerated'.[49] Perhaps the English scholar also held a critical view of Okakura.

When Yashiro set himself in opposition to Okakura, he may have wanted to take on the mantle of the older scholar, who had died a dozen years earlier, as the most authoritative art historian from Japan in the West. Okakura's *The Ideals of the East* had first been published in 1903, and only in English, but Yashiro surely knew that it had been reprinted in London in 1920, and had possibly heard that some sections had recently been translated into Japanese. Today most Westerners know the author for *The Book of Tea* (1906), a poetic essay celebrating Taoist and Zen principles. Japan has developed a reputation as a peaceful nation and ally of the US and UK. At the beginning of the twentieth century, however, when many in the West feared the 'Yellow Peril', Okakura took a polemical stand, identifying the impact of European civilisation as 'the White Disaster'.[50]

After his death, some of his views were distorted and amplified by followers to provide an intellectual foundation for Japanese pan-Asianism.[51] During the cultural wars over Western values in Japan, which assumed dramatic importance during the 1920s, Yashiro wanted to distance himself from the views he ascribed to Okakura and his followers. In open contrast to Okakura's powerful image of a united Asia, Yashiro declared that 'East and West are antipodes in words: in reality, are there such fundamental differences? [...] Leaving geographical distinctions behind, Art is Universal'.[52]

We can see Yashiro's *Botticelli* as an effort to combat the cultural underpinnings of Japanese pan-Asianism. Botticelli was appropriate for this purpose because, more than any other Western artist, he revealed that spiritual quality which some scholars associated primarily with Asian art. For the same reason Yashiro pointedly disagreed with his former mentor in Florence. 'According to Mr. Berenson's way of thinking, in Botticelli's art one senses a spiritual element akin to the poetic or perhaps mystical properties of Eastern art.'[53] Yashiro did not follow Berenson and earlier writers, in associating this mystical property with Asian art. He also questioned the old notion that the East had an impact on the early Renaissance. For Yashiro, 'we must not exaggerate the influence of the Orient on Botticelli [...] of more importance [...] was the spontaneous confluence in his genius of the Oriental and Occidental ideals'.[54] Botticelli embodied 'the universality of art'.

Unfortunately for Yashiro, the search for universal laws had (and has) little interest for most art historians. Nevertheless, all can admire his perceptive analysis of then current developments in scholarship. Yashiro claimed that 'Historical research divides itself into two groups'. One of these was 'connoisseurship', represented by such authors as Berenson, and the other 'Art-History treated as illustrations to the history of civilization', as seen in the work of Aby Warburg and Herbert Horne.[55] One aspect of the latter approach that particularly galled Yashiro was the way in which Horne used a late fifteenth-century document that described Botticelli as having a 'virile' air.[56] Yashiro contested the importance of the 'period eye', and presented his own monograph as an attempt to reveal a dramatically different interpretation of the artist. Perhaps Yashiro's repeated attacks against the idea of a virile Botticelli relate to a *topos* in writings from the period: the contrast between the feminine Orient and masculine West. In his study of ceramics, for example, Henry Wallis explained that Italians 'created a masculine art wherein [...] delicate Oriental grace was skilfully and happily blended with Tuscan imaginative virility'.[57] In order to demonstrate the universality of art, Yashiro needed to show that Botticelli was neither virile in his style nor Asian in his sensibilities.

Yashiro explained in detail why he objected to the method championed by Warburg and Horne, who gave such importance to Renaissance texts in their analyses of Renaissance artists. He also distanced himself from Berenson and claims about 'scientific' connoisseurship. Instead, Yashiro explicitly placed himself in the tradition of Walter Pater in his search for Botticelli's artistic spirit.[58] As a student at Tokyo University, where he specialised in English literature, Yashiro studied the English aesthetic movement. Not only Pater but Algernon Charles Swinburne, Dante Gabriel Rossetti, Aubrey Beardsley and Oscar Wilde served as sources for his now-lost graduate thesis on 'Emotional Principles of Art'.[59] Yashiro used these principles in his *Botticelli* where, in the tradition of aestheticism, the author drew attention to his very personal reactions. Indeed, this was the very reason why Fry criticised Yashiro's monograph and celebrated that of Horne.

We see Yashiro's approach even more clearly in a book of essays, a slender volume that has not entered the Botticelli literature. Yashiro published *The Man Who Yearns for the Sun* in 1925, the same year as his monograph but in Japanese, and thus for readers who had not seen works by Botticelli in person.[60] One sentimental piece, entitled 'Sad eyes', focuses on a tondo from Botticelli's workshop.[61] Yashiro described not the work itself, but what he felt when he observed this painting. He would go see it in London whenever he was lonely. Yashiro recognised that everyone saw paintings differently, according to their personal experiences. This Madonna might remind some viewers of their mother, others of a beloved; for Yashiro, her sad eyes recalled those of a woman he had met on the ship he took to Europe. In this attention to the *reception* of Botticelli's work, and in the writing style of these essays, Yashiro reveals an awareness of his audience in Japan.

In the preface to his Botticelli monograph, he addressed himself quite explicitly to art lovers, again in the tradition of English aestheticism. 'My wish is to deliver Art from the guidance of specialists and return it to the simple desire of man. I loved Botticelli and studied him; that is all.' Yashiro did not write for scholars, and most specialists ignored him. Though his text had little impact on Renaissance scholarship, Yashiro's methodology informed his subsequent research on Asian art. His understanding of Botticelli, and his training in London and Florence, provided the foundation for the establishment of the Institute of Art Research in Tokyo.[62]

After his return to Japan, Yashiro continued his search for a way to analyse art outside of traditional Western paradigms. In an article for *The New York Times* from 1936, just five years after the Manchurian Incident, Yashiro asked if 'the art of sculpture must always be judged by the "classical" criterion', and wondered if 'there is not another kind of sculptural art which [...] tries to call forth and embody something of the spiritual'.[63] In his most ambitious study, the *Characteristics of Japanese Art* (1943), written in the midst of the Second World War, Yashiro identified the four essential qualities as impressionistic, decorative, symbolic and sentimental. This concept, as suggested by Shuji Takashina, developed out of ideas first presented in the Botticelli monograph, where Yashiro described Botticelli's landscapes as 'spiritual-decorative' and devoted an entire section to 'The Sentimental Botticelli'.[64] We are very far from the artist described by Horne as a 'Painter of Florence'.

Though Jacques Mesnil praised Yashiro's monograph as the most important since Horne's, he lamented that 'in this work we completely lose sight of the character of life in Florence'. He noted that Yashiro sought to present the artist 'in his pure essence, outside of space and time'.[65] This review hit the nail on the head. Yashiro presented Botticelli as an expression of 'the universality of art' in a monograph that reflects his familiarity with the woodblock prints, artist education, fine arts publications and religions of Japan. As a man brought up outside of the West, he focused on 'that side of Botticelli which [...] was never [...] appreciated by European connoisseurs' – mainly small details as a key to the artist's 'concealed spirit'. In this way Yashiro transformed Botticelli from a 'Painter of Florence' to a 'Universal artist'. Today, as nationalism is threatening both East and West, and overspecialisation threatens to limit the vision of scholars, we can draw inspiration from the spirit of internationalism, idealism and innovation that permeates Yashiro's *Botticelli*.

Notes

1 The unpublished letter is mentioned in John Trevor Hatcher, 'Anglo-Japanese Friendships: Yashiro Yukio, Laurence Binyon and Arthur Waley', *Bulletin of the Fukuoka University Research Institute* [*Fukuoka daigaku jinbun ronsô*] 23 (1992): 1011 [essay also in *Yashiro and Berenson. Art History between Japan and Italy*, ed. Jonathan K. Nelson, last modified, 25 June 2015, http://yashiro.itatti.harvard.edu/.] I thank the author for the transcription.

2 On Yashiro see Akira Takagishi, 'A Twentieth-Century Dream with a Twenty-First-Century Outlook: Yashiro Yukio, a Japanese Historian of Western Art, and His Conception of Institutions for the Study of East Asian Art', in *Asian Art in the Twenty-First Century*, ed. Vishakha N. Desai (Williamstown, Mass.: Sterling and Francine Clark Art Institute, 2007), 138–48 [essay also in Nelson, *Yashiro and Berenson*]; Shigemi Inaga, 'Yukio Yashiro (1890–1975) between the East and the West in Search of an Aesthetic Dialogue', in *Aesthetics and Cutures,* ed. Krystyna Wilkoszewska (Cracow: Universitas, 2012), 43–59.

3 On Binyon, see John Trevor Hatcher, *Laurence Binyon: Poet, Scholar of East and West* (Oxford: Oxford University Press, 1995). On Binyon and Yashiro see Hatcher, 'Yashiro, Binyon, and Waley' and Lino Pertile, 'I disegni di Botticelli per la "Commedia" da Bernard Berenson a Yukio Yashiro," in *Da Dante a Berenson: sette secoli tra parole e immagini. Omaggio a Lucia Battaglia Ricci*, ed. Chiara Balbarini and Anna Pegoretti (Ravenna: Longo, 2018), 243-67 [After submitting this essay, I found an important discussion of Yashiro's attention to details in his *Botticelli* as an early example of 'world art history'; see Mia M. Mochizuki. 'A Global Eye: The Perception of Place in a Pair of Tokugawa World Map Screens', *Japan Review* 29 (2016): 69–119.]

4 On Binyon's The Art of Botticelli. An Essay in Pictorial Criticism (London: Macmillan, 1913), see the brief discussions in Jeremy Norman Melius, 'Art History and the Invention of Botticelli', (PhD thesis, Berkeley, University of California, 2010), 163–6; and Frederick Morel and Marysa Demoor, 'Laurence Binyon and the Modernists: Ezra Pound, T. S. Eliot and F. T. Marinetti', *English Studies* 95.8 (2014): 912.

5 On Yashiro and Berenson see Carl Brandon Strehlke, 'Bernard Berenson and Asian Art', in *Bernard Berenson: Formation and Heritage*, ed. Joseph Connors and Louis A. Waldman (Florence: Villa I Tatti, 2014), 224–9 [essay also in Nelson, *Yashiro and Berenson*]; and Toshio Watanabe, '"No one would wish to learn about Botticelli from a Japanese": Yukio Yashiro, Bernard Berenson and the Historiography of Western Art in Japan', *Crossing Continents: Exile and Expatriate Histories of Art*, ed. Geraldine A. Johnson (forthcoming).

6 Yukio Yashiro, *Sandro Botticelli*, 3 vols (London: The Medici Society, 1925).

7 See J. B. 'Art Books', *The Manchester Guardian*. (2 December 1925): xiv; Edward Huttop, 'A Japanese Study of Botticelli', *The Observer* (3 January 1926): 5; and other reviews cited below.

8 Yukio Yashiro, *Sandro Botticelli and the Florentine Renaissance* (London: The Medici Society, 1929). See R. T. C. 'A Japanese Appreciation of Botticelli' [Review of Yashiro, *Botticelli,* 1929], *The Manchester Guardian* (9 January 1930): 5; the anonymous reviews in *New Statesman* 34.867 (1929): 306, *Apollo* 10.60 (1929): 366 and *The Connoisseur* 85 (1930): 187; and other reviews cited below.

9 Roger Fry, 'Sandro Botticelli', *The Burlington Magazine* 48.277 (1926): 196–200. In the preface to his *Botticelli* 1929 Yashiro gave an extended, point-by-point rebuttal to Fry's criticisms.

10 Royal Cortissoz, 'Sandro Botticelli Seen Through Oriental Eyes', *Scribner's Magazine* 79.2 (1926): 217. On the next page Cortissoz added, 'Yashiro published a work of really extraordinary significance ... he has made a study which shows at once that for a cultivated man of his origins, Western art has no barriers'.

11 [Laurence Binyon], 'A Japanese Critic on Botticelli', *Times Literary Supplement* 24.1243 (12 November 1925): 745.

12 *Spectator* 136 (1926): 331. The author added, 'It is doubly interesting, of course, to have the judgment of a Japanese expert upon Botticelli.'

13 Scholars also recognise Yashiro as the first to publish the *Trinity* (London, Courtauld Gallery [Inv.P.1947.LF.38]), but usually cite his article 'A Newly Discovered Botticelli', *The Burlington Magazine* 46 (1925): 156–67.

14 Yashiro's monograph provides the focus for the short essay by Toshio Watanabe, 'Botticelli, Yukio Yashiro and scholarship on Western art in Japan', in Mark Evans, Stefan Weppelmann et al. ed., *Botticelli Reimagined* (London: V&A Publishing, 2016), 110–13.

15 The exhibition was co-curated by Michiaki Koshikawa, Jonathan K. Nelson and Emiko Yamanashi. For the catalogue see Nelson, *Yashiro and Berenson*. I thank the Japanese co-curators for their invaluable assistance on this essay. The exhibition catalogue includes all the correspondence between the Berensons and Yashiro. For a Japanese translation, and new introduction, see the forthcoming publication edited by Emiko Yamanashi and Michiaki Koshikawa.

16 Binyon, 'A Japanese Critic', 745. In a similar vein see Eric MacLagan, *New Statesman* 26 (12 December 1925): ix. On the detail photographs he observes: 'Not a few among them are revelations of a beauty which has hitherto probably lain unnoticed by all but a handful of observers'.

17 Emiko Yamanashi, 'Yukio Yashiro and the Institute of Art Research: Realizing the Goal of Introducing Berenson's Methodology to Japan', in Nelson, *Yashiro and Berenson*.

18 Yukio Yashiro, *My Life in the Fine Arts* [*Watakushi no bijutsu henreki* (Tokyo 1972)], trans. Peter Bernard, in Nelson 2015, chap. 8.

19 Yashiro, *Botticelli*, 104.

20 Melissa Beck Lemke, 'A Connoisseur's Canvas: the Photographic Collection of Clarence Kennedy', in *Photo Archives and the Photographic Memory of Art History*, ed. Costanza Caraffa (Berlin and Munich: Dt. Kunstverl, 2011), 324.

21 On the late nineteenth-century interest in establishing an artistic personality, see Jeremy Melius, 'Connoisseurship, Painting, and Personhood', *Art History* 34.2 (2011): 288–309.

22 M[ary] C[ostelloe], [review of Hermann Ulmann, *Sandro Botticelli*], *The Studio* 3.17 (1894): xxxiii. Michael Gorman kindly informs me that the handwritten text of this review, which he discovered among the Berenson Papers at Villa I Tatti, is written in Bernard's hand, and that in a letter of 26 January (?) 1894, Bernard wrote to Mary, 'I will help you with a stunning review on *Botticelli*'. See also Francesco Ventrella's essay in this volume, and Jonathan K. Nelson, 'An Unpublished Essay by Mary Berenson, "Botticelli and His Critics" (1894–5)', in *19: Interdisciplinary Studies in the Long Nineteenth Century*, special issue, 'Nineteenth-Century Women Writers on the Old Masters', edited by Maria Alambritis, Susanna Avery-Quash and Hilary Fraser (2018, forthcoming).

23 Yashiro, *My Life*, in Nelson 2015, chap. 7.

24 Yashiro, *My Life*, in Nelson 2015, chap. 8, translation slightly revised.

25 Yashiro, *My Life*, in Nelson 2015, chap. 8.

26 Shigemi Inaga, 'Japanese Philosophers Go West: The Effect of Maritime Trips on Philosophy in Japan with Special Reference to the Case of Watsuji Tetsurō (1889–1960)', *Japan Review* 25 (2013): 134.

27 For this information I am most grateful to Kathryn Brush, who is completing a monograph on Porter. For now, see her 'Bernard Berenson and Arthur Kingsley Porter: Pilgrimage Roads to I Tatti', in *Bernard Berenson: Formation and Heritage*, ed. Joseph Connors and Louis A. Waldman (Florence: Villa I Tatti, 2014), 249–68.

28 Kathryn Brush, 'Medieval Art through the Camera Lens: The Photography of Arthur Kingsley Porter and Lucy Wallace Porter', *Visual Resources: An International Journal on Images and Their Uses*, vol.33: 3–4 (2017): 252–94, https://doi.org/10.1080/01973762.2017.1349623 .

29 However, the Porters are not mentioned in Yashiro's surviving correspondence with the Berensons.

30 Yashiro, *My Life*, in Nelson 2015, chap. 8.

31 For this information about Longhi I am grateful to Francesco Mariani, who is preparing a study on the use of detail photographs. For another Brogi collaboration with an art historian, in about 1935, see Alessandra Sarchi, '*Sulle tracce di Lányi e Malenotti: il fondo Brogi su Donatello nella Fototeca Zeri*', in *Photo Archives and the Photographic Memory of Art History*, ed. Costanza Caraffa (Berlin and Munich: Dt. Kunstverl, 2011), 227–39.

32 Roberto Longhi, *Piero della Francesca: con 184 riproduzioni in fototipia* (Rome: Valori Plastici, 1927).

33 Roberto Longhi, *Piero della Francesca* (Florence: Sansoni, 1956), vi (preface to 1942 edition), '*L'antico materiale illustrativo, che fu anch'esso esemplare a tante altre scelte e diede, involontariamente, fin troppo l'avvio alla smania, spesso sbadata, dei "particolari" e dei "particolari di particolari".*'

34 Massimo Ferretti, 'Fra traduzione e reduzione', in *Gli Alinari fotografi a Firenze 1852–1920*, ed. Wladimiro Settimelli and Filippo Zevi (Florence: Alinari, 1977), 135 (my translation).

35 Bernard Berenson and Kenneth Clark, *My dear BB ...: the letters of Bernard Berenson and Kenneth Clark, 1925–1959* (New Haven: Yale University Press, 2015), 10. A few lines earlier Clark explained that, 'With Sanderson half plate, a good Zeiss lens, pan chromatic plates & a little practice I should be able to take details of any picture in almost any almost any light. These details *could* be the actual size of the original.'

36 Kenneth Clark, *One Hundred Details from Pictures in the National Gallery* (London: National Gallery, 1938), 8. In his obituary he wrote that, 'Yashiro was the first man to make considerable use of photographic details from pictures. This has now become common form but at his time it was a revelation.' Kenneth Clark, 'Yukio Yashiro', *Times Literary Supplement* 3832 (22 August 1975), 946.
37 Binyon, 'A Japanese Critic', 745.
38 For the letter of 10 January 1924 see Nelson 2015.
39 On the friendship between the three scholars see Hatcher, 'Yashiro, Binyon and Waley'.
40 For his insight on early photography in Japan I am most grateful to Doshin Sato.
41 For this suggestion, I thank Yoshie Kojima. Yashiro would have also seen isolated hands and feet in Renaissance drawings, but he does not address these in his studies.
42 Yashiro, *Botticelli*, 106.
43 Yashiro, *Botticelli*, 82.
44 Fry, 'Botticelli', 197.
45 Yashiro, *My Life*, in Nelson 2015, chap. 8; on this passage also see Watanabe, 'Yashiro, Berenson'.
46 On Okakura and Yashiro see Watanabe, 'Yashiro, Berenson'; Inaga, 'Yukio Yashiro'.
47 See Victoria Weston, *Japanese Painting and National Identity: Okakura Tenshin and His Circle* (Ann Arbor: Center for Japanese Studies, The University of Michigan, 2004). I thank the author for helpful comments on an earlier draft of this paper.
48 Yashiro, *Botticelli*, 1925, xx. In the preceding line he wrote of Okakura, 'the Japanese can never be too grateful, if only for his initiative in preserving their national art at the time when it was in jeopardy'.
49 Binyon, 'A Japanese Critic', 745.
50 Kakuzō Okakura, *The Awakening of Japan* (New York: The Century Co., 1904), 107. The fifth chapter is entitled 'White Disaster'.
51 On this topic see Matsumoto Kenichi, 'Okakura Tenshin and the Ideal of Pan-Asianism', in Brij Tankha, ed., *Okakura Tenshin and Pan-Asianism: Shadows of the Past* (Folkestone: Global Oriental, 2009), 11–21.
52 Yashiro, *Botticelli*, 1925, xx.
53 Yashiro, *My Life*, in Nelson 2015, chap. 7.
54 Yashiro, *Botticelli*, 1925, 88.
55 Yashiro, *Botticelli*, 1925, xxii.
56 Jonathan K. Nelson, 'Botticelli's "Virile Air": Reconsidering the Milan Memo of 1493', in *Sandro Botticelli (1445–1510): artist and entrepreneur in Renaissance Florence*, ed. Gert Jan van der Sman and Irene Mariani (Florence: Centro Di, 2015), 167–82.
57 Henry Wallis, *The Oriental Influence on The Ceramic Art of the Italian Renaissance* (London: B. Quaritch, 1900), xiii.
58 On this tradition see Melius, 'Botticelli', 46–103, with further bibliography.
59 Watanabe, 'Yashiro, Berenson', based on Yashiro, *My Life*, chap. 2.
60 Yukio Yashiro, *Taiyo wo shitau mono* [*The Man who Yearns for the Sun*] (Tokyo: Kaizo-sha, 1925).
61 Yashiro, *Taiyo*, 41–6. For this summary I thank Shizuka Nishikawa, who informs me that Yashiro also mentions Botticelli in his chapters about 'Spring', 141–56, and 'Albiera and Giovanna', 90–102. For the tondo [London, National Gallery, inv.NG275], see *Botticelli Reimagined*, 268, n.11.8. Perhaps Yashiro knew that Mary Berenson had singled out this work for particular criticism, describing it as fit only for 'poetry of the depressed, nihilistic kind'; Mary Costelloe, 'The New and the Old Art Criticism', *The Nineteenth Century* 35. 207 (May 1894): 832.
62 Yamanashi, 'Yashiro and the Institute of Art Research'.
63 Yukio Yashiro, 'Artists of Japan Speak the Soul through Symbols', *The New York Times Magazine* (6 September 1936). In an autobiographical passage he added, 'No wonder Japanese artists travelling in Italy found their own artistic aspirations unexpectedly realized in the works of Masolino, Piero della Francesca and Botticelli'. Yashiro returned to the parallels between Western and Japanese art in 'The "Oriental" Character in Italian Tre- and Quattrocento Paintings', *East and West* 3.2 (1952): 81–7 [also available in Nelson, *Yashiro and Berenson*].
64 Shuji Takashina, 'Commentary', in Yukio Yashiro, *Sekai ni okeru Nihon Bijutsu no Ichi* [*Position of Japanese Art in the World*] (Tokyo: Kodansha Gakujutsu Bunko, 1988), 208. I thank Yuko Matsumoto for translating this passage.
65 Jacques Mesnil, 'Connaissons-nous Botticelli?', *Gazette des Beaux-Arts* 4 (1930): 96–7.

11. Jacques Mesnil's Botticelli

Michel Hochmann

Jean-Jacques Dwelshauvers (1872–1940), who published under the pseudonym of Jacques Mesnil, is a deeply moving personality (fig.3.15). His life was difficult. He studied medicine in Brussels and Italy, but chose to abandon this profession, because he wanted to dedicate himself to his political ideals and to art history.[1] He was initially an anarchist and an admirer of Élisée Reclus: after the First World War he became a communist. In 1924 Mesnil was excluded from the editorial board of *L'Humanité* and became close to Pierre Monate: he contributed to Monate's journal *La Révolution prolétarienne*, which criticised the new orientation of the communist party and of the Russian Revolution after Lenin's death.[2] As an art historian, Mesnil dedicated his life to Florence, where he lived almost constantly from 1900 to 1906, working in the archives and publishing various important documents. He became one of Aby Warburg's friends in 1895, because of their common interest in Botticelli, and remained in close relations with him until Warburg's death in 1929.[3]

Fritz Saxl paid homage to Mesnil, together with Warburg and Herbert Horne, in a lecture given at the Courtauld Institute in 1944; it remains the longest text dedicated to Mesnil as an art historian.[4] Saxl recalls his tragic death, when he was a refugee, 'in a monastery on a bed of straw soon after the Germans entered France in 1940'.[5] Saxl insisted that Mesnil was both a political writer and a scholar, with 'no split between the two sides of his nature'.[6] For him, 'the anarchist', the admirer of Rousseau, 'Tuscany [was] the land of the noble savage'. He saw 'Botticelli as a son of that vigorous race which he admired and loved in the family of Tuscan peasants with whom he had lived for years'.[7] Mesnil was acquainted with some of the major figures of his time – in addition to Warburg and Reclus, he also knew Romain Rolland – and the various aspects of his involvements in scholarship and in politics still need to be studied. In the present context I will naturally focus on his work regarding Botticelli, in particular the monograph on the painter, published in 1938 by Albin Michel.[8] As he recalled in the introduction, his book was the result of a lifelong involvement with the artist.[9] In a letter, he told Warburg he had already written a novel about Botticelli when he was 18 years old.[10] I will try to compare his achievements with other great studies of the painter at this period, in particular those of Horne and Warburg, and to understand

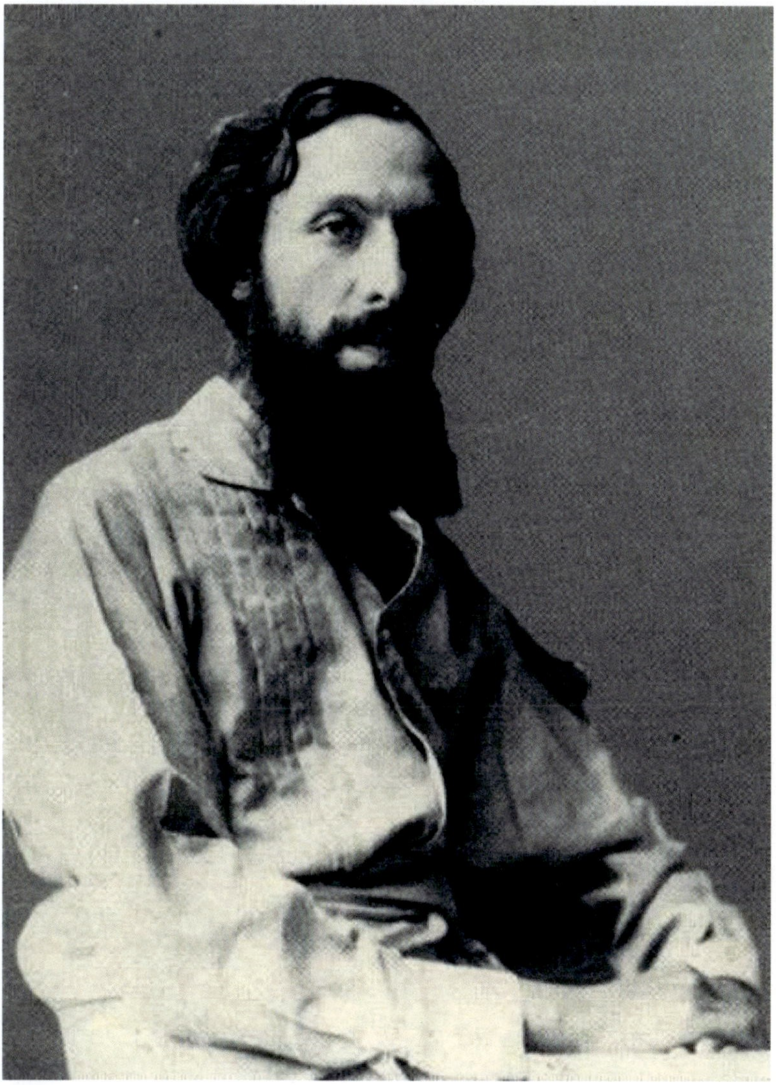

Fig.3.15 Jacques Mesnil (1872-1940), altered photograph (date unknown; 1905?). © Wikimedia Commons.

not only his points in common but also his differences with these other scholars, to whom he pays homage.

Mesnil tells us in the introduction that the book he finally published was not the one he had dreamt of during his youth (*'Ceci n'est pas le livre dont j'avais conçu l'idée première'*): he would have wished to embrace all Florentine life of the end of the fifteenth and the beginning of the sixteenth centuries, as seen through the 'âme émotive' (the emotional soul) of a great artist involved in its history. But his first project was delayed by other works, and the hardship that followed the First World War made it impossible.[11] In 1903 he had begun to publish his findings on Botticelli in two articles in the *Miscellanea d'arte*, the journal directed by Iginio Benvenuto Supino. The first one was dedicated to the *Virtues* of the Tribunale della Mercanzia, and established the date of Botticelli's *Fortezza* (1470); Mesnil also demonstrated that this painting had originally been commissioned from Piero del Pollaiuolo, and that Tommaso Soderini had insisted on calling upon Botticelli's services.[12] The second one, '*Quelques documents sur Botticelli*', confirmed Horne's findings regarding Botticelli's birthdate (1444 or 1445), by transcribing his father's declaration to the *catasto* of 1446; it also proved that Gaspare di Zanobi del Lama was the true patron of the *Adoration of the Magi* in the Uffizi (fig.1.8).[13]

These two articles would be very important in the monograph for the reconstruction of Botticelli's early years and of his relationship with the Medici family. Mesnil used his research regarding the *Fortezza* in another article published in *Rivista d'arte* in 1904; here he contradicted the idea that the painter had finished his education in the workshop of the Pollaiuolo brothers, underlining the profound differences between his work and theirs.[14] In the same journal he dedicated another article to '*Botticelli à Rome*', in which he harshly criticised Ernst Steinmann's work on the Sistine Chapel and his interpretation of its frescoes, proving that Botticelli was back in Florence in October 1482 and that the *Punishment of the Rebels* could not have been painted after December that year, as Steinmann had believed. He then commented on the painting known as the *Derelitta* (Galleria Pallavicini, Rome), confessing his doubts about the attribution of this work and suspecting it to be a fake.[15]

Mesnil developed very early a profound interest in the social history of art and in the painter's trade. He published, again in *Rivista d'arte*, various documents from the *Libri dell'Arte dei Medici e Speziali* regarding the guild regulations applied to painters, but his major text on the subject, on the education of painters in fifteenth-century Florence, appeared in the *Revue des idées* in 1910.[16] This pioneering work tried to establish the age of apprentices, the conditions of their contracts with their masters and the length of their apprenticeship. Mesnil's vision was idyllic, since he contrasted the unrestrained relationship between Renaissance masters and pupils, and the good humour of the *bottega*, to the conflicts and the rivalry of interests ('*rivalité aiguë d'intérêts*'), the reciprocal distrust between employers and workers in his own time.[17] Significantly Warburg, responding to this article, found Mesnil's vision too 'optimistic and bucolic': he thought that in the milieu of the merchants and clothiers of the fifteenth century all idealistic aspirations already tended to be defeated by materialism.[18] As an example of the happy life of the Renaissance painter, Mesnil quoted various *burle* described by the sources, which showed that artists treated life itself as a '*matière plastique*': their jokes showed the same sense of reality, the same visual accuracy that one finds in the works of art of that period.[19] Teaching was empirical, and did not consist in rules or laws, but in practical advice.

The same was the case for perspective, another of Mesnil's main fields of research. He was to dedicate several specific studies to this topic, in particular a lecture at the Warburg Library, which was published in the *Vorträge* of 1925–6. In this he summarised the main Renaissance sources on perspective and tried to reconstruct its use by Masaccio and his followers. In 1939 he published an article about Botticelli's linear perspective in the journal *L'Amour de l'art*, and many passages of his book on the painter were dedicated to this topic.[20] In his view, Renaissance artists did not follow systematic rules that could be applied mechanically without intelligence; good results could not be achieved without a natural talent for drawing.

In a review of Panofsky's famous work on the subject, he opposed Panofsky's ideas, asserting that perspective had nothing to do with symbols: it was instead an essentially artistic problem.[21] In his article in the *Revue des idées*, Mesnil stated that perspective had two functions. It provided an illusion of the third dimension, but (the most important aspect for artists of the period), by allowing a coherent composition, it gave paintings their 'unity as creations of the spirit'. Mesnil described in a very general way the studies from the human body, alive and dead, that could take place in the *botteghe*, and the difficulties there were in drawing from the nude at that period. He concluded with the problem of pictorial composition, emphasising once more that Renaissance artists followed no strict rules in this field, relying instead on their instinct and eye. The Florentine artist, in Mesnil's opinion, was no learned intellectual: he did not waste time in useless speculations; he assimilated forms and colours directly. Mesnil was highly stimulated by the character of the Florentine life, so variegated and colourful, '*animée et poignante*', 'lively and deeply moving'. It was these qualities that he wanted to reconstruct in the book he announced in this article, giving it the title *La Vie d'un Artiste florentin au XVe siècle*.[22]

Mesnil's relationship with Warburg was, as I have said, very close and lasting. He naturally paid homage to his friend in the introduction to his book on Botticelli, and also underlined what he thought their approach had in common: Warburg, like himself, was not content with purely aesthetic contemplation: he searched behind works of art for what they could reveal about the lives of those who commissioned or executed them.[23] In his youth, like Warburg, Mesnil had been opposed to the fashionable and snobbish taste for Botticelli among English aesthetes, Ruskin in particular.[24] He also disliked the Morellian approach, which Morelli himself, Bode and others presented as a new science: it seemed to him that these connoisseurs examined only the details, forgetting completely about the whole work and its soul.[25] But, as we shall see, he also had many reservations about Warburg's work. As Gombrich recalled, Warburg, for his part, thought that Mesnil did not quite understand the meaning of his research.[26]

In 1926, at Warburg's request, Mesnil wrote a remarkable review in the *Gazette des Beaux-Arts* about '*La bibliothèque Warburg et ses publications*'.[27] In this text, he summarised Warburg's ideas very effectively by saying that his friend had recognised in the works of art less an aesthetic expression than the symptom of a collective state of mind, the manifestation of the deep feelings and secret tendencies of those who commissioned them or admired them as well as those who created them. Although this summary was very illuminating, especially when one considers that it was among the first of its kind, Warburg was not entirely satisfied with it. In a letter to Mesnil, he singled out one of the sentences of this review, in which Mesnil had observed that Warburg wanted to understand 'what Antiquity really meant for the people of the Renaissance'.[28] Warburg asked him to publish one day an amendment in which he would add: 'A problem that later, in the course of years, was extended to understand the meaning of the survival of paganism for the whole European civilization'.[29]

Mesnil could not grasp the vision of fury and fear that paganism encompassed in Warburg's ideas. As we have seen, he thought of Renaissance Florence in an idyllic way. In one of his articles on the arts in communist Russia, he explicitly compared the Russian people with the Florentines, describing the Russians as 'a virgin people[…], a people whose profound life is not hidden by a uniform varnish of superficial notions and learned opinions'. They were instead, like the people of the end of the Middle Ages, whose soul he [himself] 'had tried to discover in the archive and in the monuments of Florence'.[30]

Like Horne, Mesnil was naturally impressed by Warburg's research on the *Primavera* and on *The Birth of Venus* (figs 1.30 and 1.0), which he already quoted in a letter to his friend in 1895, as we have seen. In his monograph he wrote that Lorenzo the Magnificent recognised in

Botticelli a sophisticated spirit, which made him the artist most qualified to translate into painting the literary fantasies and allegorical puzzles invented by the humanists who surrounded him. He mentioned that Botticelli had painted Giuliano de' Medici's banner for the *Giostra* in 1475, and that the artist had to translate into an image a riddle so clever that no one outside the narrow circle of the initiated courtiers understood it.[31] In 1905, replying to his questions on this topic, Warburg had written him a letter about the *Primavera*, stating once more that the work should be renamed the *Regno di Venere celeste* (and, in fact, Mesnil himself called the painting '*Royaume de Vénus*' in his book).[32]

Mesnil did not insist too much on the iconographic content of these famous works, however (in contrast to Horne, who dedicated a long passage to this question, completing Warburg's observations with his own). As he had said to Warburg, he thought that the important thing was to demonstrate, as Warburg had done, that someone had given Botticelli a programme based on elements derived from antique texts and contemporary poetry, such as Politian's works.[33] But, he insisted, what belonged to Botticelli himself was the conception and the execution of the painting, not its literary theme.[34] He thought that it was necessary to understand in a more precise way the exact nature and limits of the collaboration between the painter and the humanist who worked with him.

He also believed that scholars had given too much importance to the question of Simonetta Vespucci's presence in Botticelli's œuvre, instead of enquiring seriously about the painter's art. He blamed Bode and August Schmarsow but this was probably an indirect critique of Warburg too, since the latter had also tried to demonstrate the presence of Simonetta's portrait in the *Primavera*. Mesnil had already discussed the problem with Warburg in 1895, when he wrote to him enquiring about various paintings that were supposed to represent Simonetta, among them the famous example by Piero di Cosimo in Chantilly, and asking about her relationship with Giuliano de' Medici and with Botticelli.[35] However, Mesnil came to think, as Horne had already said in his monograph, that this was a sort of useless fanciful speculation: all the women in the *Primavera* simply reflected Botticelli's preferred feminine type. In a letter to him of 1905, Warburg was willing to admit that they were 'rather a syncretic evocation of various feminine souls, not only Simonetta's, but also Lucrezia Donati's and, perhaps, others'.[36]

Nor did Mesnil completely share Warburg's ideas about the vision of antiquity in Renaissance Florence in general and in Botticelli's work in particular. He quotes his friend on *The Birth of Venus* (fig.1.0), saying that, 'as Warburg has shown, the imitation of antiquity consisted above all ([...]) in the borrowing of different ways to suggest a movement, such as floating hair and draperies agitated by the wind', a statement he repeats several times.[37] Warburg's nymph appears in other passages of Mesnil's text: on the *Temptations of Christ* in the Sistine Chapel, he wrote that the influence of antiquity was visible in only one place: the group with a woman carrying a bundle of firewood and the child walking before her.

> The figure of a woman walking at a rapid pace, holding a burden with one hand on her head, and lifting her drapery with her other hand, to be more agile, was a motif that painters of the period introduced in their works to show their virtuosity.[38]

His view on that matter was very reductive, however: he seemed to consider as accessory and fairly meaningless a figure that had played a central role in Warburg's approach to Botticelli and to the Renaissance in general. Actually, Mesnil thought that Botticelli was indifferent to the spirit of antiquity all his life; he was not profoundly inspired by the Greco-Roman works he may have seen. He said that Botticelli's slender, undulating figures lacked the massive character and the monumentality of the antique: 'their arabesque, that sustains the whole composition, makes them look like the decorative creations of oriental art rather than the strictly balanced plastic of Greco-Roman art'.[39]

Mesnil's point of view largely ignored Warburg's famous theories about the presence of pathos in Greco-Roman art and its importance for the Renaissance. This must have been a conscious rejection (even if his own vision was much more commonplace), since Warburg had written him a remarkable letter in 1906 about his studies of how the style *all'antica* superseded the style *alla francese*, and about the problem of pathos.[40] Mesnil is even sometimes overtly polemical: when analysing one of the drawings for the *Divine Comedy*, he remarks that the Virtues there, although Dante describes them as nymphs in his canto 31:

> do not have any character *all'antica*, neither in their circular dances nor in their costumes, unless [and this is a direct attack on Warburg] one wants to find the influence of Greco-Roman art in the agitated draperies the Renaissance seems initially to have borrowed from the antique, but which had by now become a common property. The wild movements of these Virtues draw their inspiration more from popular dances than from representations of bacchanalian revels.[41]

Another direct quotation from Warburg in Mesnil's work is about the second series of engravings of the planets, which his friend had attributed to Botticelli.[42] As Mesnil himself recalls, Warburg had considered these engravings, probably dating to 1465, as symptoms of the critical transition period between autochthonous realism and *all'antica* stylisation, as in the woman in the Planet Venus engraving who jumps merrily, her hairstyle 'alla ninfa'.[43] But although he agreed that these figures are generically Botticellian, Mesnil saw no reason to believe that Botticelli himself provided the drawings.

One of the major strengths of Mesnil's monograph is his interest in the social life and historical framework surrounding Botticelli's work. In the monograph, he tried once more to reconstruct the personality of Gaspare di Zanobi del Lama, whom, as we have seen, he had discovered to be the patron of the Uffizi *Adoration of the Magi* once in Santa Maria Novella. He had found that this man was a broker, '*un métier de fripon*' (a scoundrel's trade) at that time.[44] By commissioning this painting, he wanted in a way to negotiate his salvation: this was typical of the Florentine of the time who acted as tradesman even with God.[45] But Gaspare's occupation might also explain how he had known the Medici, whom he had probably served, since they were bankers and no more honest than he was.

One might naturally compare Mesnil's observations regarding Gaspare's testament to Warburg's famous analysis of Francesco Sassetti's last will.[46] The problems were fairly similar, the relationship between business practices and faith, the Medici milieu, the insertion of portraits in a religious painting. But of course Warburg's approach was infinitely richer and more complex. Instead of reducing Sassetti to an 'absolute villain' (to quote Gombrich's analysis of his text), as Mesnil had done for Gaspare, trying to conciliate his mercantile spirit, his religion and his superstitious practices, Warburg wanted to show the delicate balance between Christian and pagan ideas, in a moment of transition between the Middle Ages and the Renaissance, in which men (I am quoting Gombrich again) 'still thought that they were able to harmonize the irreconcilable'.[47] Significantly, when reading his friend's article, Mesnil had admired it but found it far-fetched in its accumulation of hypotheses that were difficult to prove:

> *Le réaliste* [as Mesnil defined himself in opposition to Warburg] *aurait bien d'autres choses à dire*[...] *ça ne m'empêche pas d'avoir admiré les miracles d'équilibre réalisés pour échafauder les unes sur les autres des hypothèses de plus en plus hardies*[...] *Quel tour de force!*

on le regarde en retenant sa respiration, par admiration et aussi par crainte qu'un souffle trop vif ne fasse tout crouler.[48]

At the end of his book, Mesnil quoted another interesting document regarding a patron of Botticelli, first published by Horne in his monograph. This was the last will of Francesco del Pugliese, a Florentine merchant who had probably commissioned Botticelli's *Last Communion of Saint Jerome* (now in the Metropolitan Museum of Art, New York) and who was a fanatical supporter of Savorarola.[49] Del Pugliese mentioned several paintings in this testament, among them a head of Christ by a Flemish painter with two altar wings by Filippino Lippi (today in the Seminario Patriarcale in Venice) and a *Last Judgement* by Fra Angelico. Mesnil thought that this collection was a perfect example of the artistic tastes of pious Florentines of the time, and of the religious value they accorded to Flemish paintings. By placing Botticelli alongside Fra Angelico, this collection also showed that, at that period, like Fra Angelico, Botticelli was seen as a devout painter by all those for whom Christianity was above all a religion of piety and tenderness.

In the book, Mesnil summarised his research on the painter's trade, one of his major concerns. As we have seen, he probably intended to dedicate a much larger part of his monograph to this aspect, but some of his initial intentions remain in the book as published. He tried to sum up what he knew about Botticelli's *bottega*, using the *catasto* of 1480 to prove that the painter had three or four pupils with him at that time and giving some of their names. But he confessed that he had less information about his colleagues after that date, and especially between 1482 and 1498, when he was at the peak of his career. He uses the story recorded by Vasari of a joke Botticelli played on one of his pupils named Biagio. In it the artist sought to prove that the Florentine *bottega* had the characteristics of a shop where one could find not only paintings by the master, but also replicas and copies at a reduced price, painted by pupils or qualified craftsmen as well as other objects more or less related with the field of the art of painting.[50]

Mesnil studied with great care how cartoons were used by the pupils to replicate the *Madonnas* invented by the master.[51] In a note, he underlined the importance of Neri di Bicci's *Ricordanze* for the understanding of all these aspects. He had long ago tried to have this text published by the Kunsthistorisches Institut in Florence, but in vain.[52] Since Neri was one of the most mediocre artists of the period, no one really understood the importance of this document, even though Neri's *bottega* was similar to those of his more gifted contemporaries. Mesnil added that only in recent years, thanks to Giovanni Poggi, some parts of the manuscript had been transcribed, but its publication had been interrupted. In focusing on this document, Mesnil demonstrated once more his interest in the social aspects of art history: one may remember that his book was contemporary with Martin Wackernagel's pioneering study of such a topic, the famous *Lebensraum des Künstlers*, also published in 1938.

Mesnil's book ends naturally with the Savonarolian period. In an article published in the *Gazette des Beaux-Arts* a few years earlier, he had moderated Vasari's assertion that Botticelli was one of Savonarola's most enthusiastic supporters.[53] He observed that, although the painter certainly admired the friar, and although his brother Simone was a devout *piagnone*, Botticelli remained close to the Medici family – in particular to Lorenzo di Pierfrancesco, for whom he had drawn the famous illustrations of the *Divine Comedy*. Botticelli did not sign the petition addressed by Florentine citizens to the pope asking him to suspend the friar's excommunication.[54] But Mesnil acknowledged that some important works at the end of Botticelli's life proved that he was obviously shaken by Savonarola's prophecies. Botticelli came under the spell of his brother, whom Mesnil calls '*crédule*', and became the first among the painters who worked for '*les gens pieux*'.[55]

Mesnil studied the evolution in various aspects of Botticelli's religious imagery, for example the agitation in the poses of Christ and Saint John in the Virgin and Child subjects, as in the tondo then in the Lazzaroni collection in Rome, which Mesnil attributes to the *bottega* after Botticelli's invention. He also singled out other pious images produced by the *bottega* at that time, such as the suffering Christ then in the Lazzaroni collection in Paris. He insisted on the Flemish influence one could see in many paintings of the time, such as the *Agony in the Garden* painted for Isabella the Catholic, remarking that Botticelli was almost the only Italian painter present in Isabella's collection, which comprised mainly Flemish paintings and Flemish-inspired Spanish paintings. We should remember that Mesnil had also shared with Warburg his interest in the artistic exchanges between Flanders and Florence, and that in 1904 he had published an article on the relationship between Italian and Flemish painting during the Renaissance. Warburg's response was once more critical, noting that he was happy to see that the topic he had introduced was taking root, but that his view about the origin and achievements of Flemish art was different from Mesnil's.[56]

For Mesnil, Botticelli's last period showed how religious fanaticism had replaced the movement of liberation that had characterised the

Renaissance. His vision of the period was imbued with a sort of slightly naïve idealisation: for him, the Renaissance was the rediscovery of liberty and of the human body, which Christian faith despised. It was also the '*philosophie libre et purement humaine de la vie*', the free and purely human philosophy of life, representing concord between apparently hostile doctrines, between past and present. Again this was a theme that evoked some of Warburg's ideas, but reframed in an optimistic and rather commonplace formula.

Notes

1 In a letter to Warburg (Jacques Mesnil to Aby Warburg, 18 December 1895, WIA, GC [Warburg Institute Archive, General Correspondence]), he regretted that his studies in medicine prevented him from working on his art historical projects: *'Aussi ne puis-je consacrer la majeure partie de mon temps à étudier ce quinzième siècle florentin qui est pourtant mon milieu préféré; il faut que je me sacrifie en partie à la médecine "occupation professionnelle", nécessaire pour me faire une "position" dans ce monde (...)'.*

2 Marie-Noëlle Bonnet, 'Jacques Mesnil', in *Maitron-en-ligne* (accessed December 2016), https://rprenet.bnf.fr:443/http/maitron-en-ligne.univ-paris1.fr/spip.php?article153940 .

3 Letter from Mesnil to Warburg, 12 August 1895, WIA, GC: *'Une certaine similitude de goût doit nous rapprocher puisque nous aimons le même artiste et que ce sont en somme – la lecture de votre étude sur le "Printemps" & la "Naissance de Vénus" me l'a prouvé – les mêmes problèmes qui nous intéressent.'*

4 Fritz Saxl, 'Three "Florentines": Herbert Horne, Aby Warburg, Jacques Mesnil', in Fritz Saxl, *Lectures* (London: The Warburg Institute, 1957), vol. I, 331–44.

5 Saxl, *Lectures,* 342.

6 Saxl, *Lectures,* 342.

7 Saxl, *Lectures,* 343.

8 Jacques Mesnil, *Botticelli* (Paris: Albin Michel, 1938).

9 Mesnil, introduction to *Botticelli* [n. p.].

10 Mesnil to Warburg, 12 October 1896, WIA, GC. After severely criticising a passage about Botticelli in Zola's *Rome*, Mesnil adds: *'Moi-même dans un roman que j'ai écrit à 18–19 ans, alors que je n'avais vu que des photographies d'œuvres de Botticelli (roman que je me suis abstenu de publier bien qu'il ne soit pas plus mauvais que les trois quarts des élucubrations qui se vendent sous cette rubrique), j'ai rendu l'impression que fait à première vue Botticelli, d'une manière plus concentrée et plus vraie que celle-là'.*

11 Mesnil, introduction to *Botticelli*: *'Ceci n'est pas le livre dont j'avais conçu l'idée première à vingt ans devant les Botticelli de la National Gallery et dont le plan s'était amplifié au cours de mes années de jeunesse, passées presque entièrement en Italie'.*

12 Jacques Mesnil, 'Les figures de Vertus de la Mercanzia. Piero del Pollaiuolo et Botticelli', *Miscellanea d'arte,* anno 1, numero 3 (marzo 1903): 43–6.

13 Jacques Mesnil, 'Quelques documents sur Botticelli', *Miscellanea d'arte,* anno 1, numero 5–6 (May–June 1903): 87–98.

14 Jacques Mesnil, 'Botticelli, les Pollaiuoli et Verrocchio', *Rivista d'arte,* anno 3 (1905): n.2–3, 4–12 and 35–45. At the end of his life Mesnil would change his mind on that matter. In an article in *The Burlington Magazine* he wrote that Botticelli might have worked on the two *cassone* fronts now at the Musée Jacquemart-André in Paris that Mesnil attributed to the workshop of Antonio Pollaiuolo (Jacques Mesnil, 'On the artistic education of Botticelli', *The Burlington Magazine* 78 (1941): 118–23).

15 Jacques Mesnil, 'Botticelli à Rome', *Rivista d'arte,* anno 3 (1905): 112–23. Mesnil strongly disliked Steinmann's approach and his work on Botticelli. Cf. WIA, GC, Mesnil to Warburg, 6 July 1905: *'C'est un dur métier de prouver aux gens qu'ils disent des bêtises. C'est que Steinmann n'est pas un être, c'est un symbole: il pourrait s'appeler tout autrement au fait. Qui peut les compter? Steinmann, Ulmann, Guthmann et da capo ad infinitum. Et stultorum numerus est infinitus, soupirait l'Ecclésiaste.'*

16 Jacques Mesnil, 'L'éducation des peintres florentins au XVe siècle', *Revue des idées* 14 S., 8 (15 September 1910): 1–14.

17 Mesnil, 'L'éducation', 5: *'la méfiance réciproque qui existe à présent entre patrons et ouvriers'.*

18 WIA, GC, Warburg to Mesnil, 31 December 1910: *'Ihr Bild aus dem Leben der florentinischen Malerknaben habe ich mit sehr grossem Interesse gelesen. Sie sind aber doch etwas zu optimistich-bukolisch in der Beurteilung d. organischen Stellung d. Künstler im Milieu. Das Tuchhändlers – und Kaufmanns – Milieu hat sicher doch abplattend auf die idealistischen Versuche eingewirkt: d. Typ Pinturicchio ist in ganz Italien immer beliebter gewesen als Michelangelo – ehe er Mode ward.'*

19 Mesnil, 'L'éducation', 6.

20 Jacques Mesnil, 'Die Kunstlehre der Frührenaissance im Werke Masaccios', *Vorträge der Bibliothek Warburg* (1925–6), 122–46. Jacques Mesnil, 'La perspective linéaire chez Botticelli', *L'Amour de l'art,* XIXe année, no.9 (November 1938): 339–44.

21 Jacques Mesnil in *Gazette des Beaux-Arts* 6, Pér. 1 (1929): 319–20.

22 Mesnil, 'L'éducation', 14.

23 Mesnil, introduction to *Botticelli*: *'Puis mon souvenir va à l'ami défunt, au compagnon de ces belles années, à Aby Warburg, dont l'esprit pénétrant ne se contentait pas de la contemplation esthétique et cherchait derrière les œuvres ce qu'elles pouvaient lui révéler de la vie de ceux qui les commandaient et de ceux qui les exécutaient'*.

24 WIA, GC, Mesnil to Warburg, 12 October 1896: *'Je ne sais s'il [Botticelli] serait très flatté de voir qu'il remporte ses plus éclatants succès dans le monde des cocottes et des snobs et que ses créations ont été altérées jusqu'à en faire des images de mode! Tout ça, c'est la faute aux Anglais! Ces longs, filandreux, imprécis artistes anglais qui divaguent au milieu d'un peuple de marchands, parmi les brouillards ont eu le tort de se croire capables de saisir, et cela spontanément, l'âme des Florentins du 15e siècle. Ces Anglais, tous littérateurs avant d'être peintres, pleins de symbolismes extérieurs, pas plus coloristes que mes bottes, ces gens incapables pour la plupart de prendre pied dans la réalité sont allés accrocher leurs nébuleuses rêveries aux œuvres en somme si nettes, si claires, si directement réelles des Florentins. Tenez! ce que Ruskin m'embête, c'est indicible, et ce qu'il dit de Botticelli dans ses Mornings in Florence me semble d'une insupportable pose!'*.

25 WIA, GC, Mesnil to Warburg, 28 December 1895: *'La besogne que je vois s'accumuler devant moi me semble fastidieuse et vide, je suis presque convaincu qu'elle ne m'apprendra rien et je ne puis cependant l'éviter: je veux parler des questions de critique picturale, de cette nouvelle "science" qui fait la gloire des Morelli, des Bode et des Ulmann. Je vous avoue que j'éprouve à l'égard de ces livres une véritable antipathie. Je me demande vraiment à quoi peut aboutir ce travail de myopes qui promènent leur nez de tout près sur les tableaux, examinent les moindres détails, regardent dans tous les coins, et oublient invariablement de considérer l'ensemble et l'âme même de l'œuvre (...)'*.

26 Ernst Gombrich, *Aby Warburg. An Intellectual Biography* (London: The Warburg Institute, 1970), 307.

27 Jacques Mesnil, 'La bibliothèque Warburg et ses publications', *Gazette des Beaux-Arts* 5e période, vol.XIV, (1926): 237–41.

28 Mesnil, 'La bibliothèque Warburg', *'[ce] que représentait en réalité l'Antiquité pour les hommes de la Renaissance'*.

29 Quoted in Gombrich, *Aby Warburg*, 307.

30 Jacques Mesnil, 'L'art dans la Russie des Soviets', *Bulletin communiste*, no.8, troisième année (23 February 1922), accessed December 2016, https://www.marxists.org/francais/mesnil/works/1922/03/art.htm: *'(...) d'un peuple vierge, non gâté par la lecture des journaux (...) d'un peuple dont la vie profonde n'est point recouverte, dissimulée par un vernis uniforme de notions superficielles et d'opinions apprises. Bien souvent, en lisant des récits de la vie de ce peuple ou en entendant relater des événements de son histoire actuelle, ai-je pensé aux peuples de la fin du Moyen Age, dont je cherchais naguère à retrouver l'âme dans les archives et les monuments de Florence.'*

31 Mesnil, *Botticelli*, 45: *'Le rébus que le peintre eut à traduire en images était si ingénieux qu'à voir l'étendard personne n'en saisissait la signification.'*

32 WIA, GC, Warburg to Mesnil, 8 September; Mesnil, *Botticelli*, 51.

33 WIA, GC, Mesnil to Warburg, 6 July 1905: *'Mais que nous importe: il suffisait d'avoir montré qu'on avait fourni un programme à Botticelli & que dans les poésies contemporaines & dans les textes antiques on en trouvait les éléments: c'est ce que vous avez fait, & je trouve que tous les bavardages ultérieurs n'ont avancé en rien la question.'*

34 Mesnil, *Botticelli*, 50: *'Ce qui appartient à Botticelli, c'est la conception et l'exécution artistiques, non le thème littéraire.'*

35 Mesnil to Warburg, 12 August 1895, WIA, GC: *'A quel point en est la question de la Simonetta? Est-il décidé que le portrait qui se trouve au Pitti ne la représente pas? Je voyais dernièrement la reproduction du portrait authentique de la Simonetta qui se trouve maintenant à Chantilly: ce portrait est décidément fort déshabillé! Etait-il d'usage alors que les "honnestes" dames se fissent peindre dans des costumes aussi radicalement décolletés? A quelle catégorie de femmes appartenait en somme cette Simonetta Vespucci? Que fut-elle par rapport à Giuliano de' Medici – à Botticelli – au peintre qui l'a représentée dans cet agréable costume (est-ce P. di Cosimo ou Pollaiuolo?)? Le rôle de la femme à cette époque & ses rapports avec l'artiste – en tant qu'inspiratrice ou en tant que modèle – sont des questions qui m'intéressent fort.'*

36 Warburg to Mesnil, 8 September 1905, WIA, GC: *'Was die Identification der einzelnen Personen angeht, so bin ich dagegen bereit, im einzelnen Concessionen zu machen; denn es kann noch ein synkertistiches Rätselbild sein, auf dem verschiedene platonisirend verehrte Frauenseelen den Reigen der Seeligen tanzen: Lucrezia Donati und Simonetta und vielleicht noch eine andere Dame, deren Name uns aus vielleicht weitere archivialische Indiskretion bescheren wird.'*

37 Mesnil, *Botticelli*, 54: '*Comme l'a très bien montré Warburg, l'imitation de l'antique réside surtout (…) dans l'emprunt de moyens propres à suggérer le mouvement, telle la figuration des cheveux flottants et des draperies agitées par le vent.*'

38 Mesnil, *Botticelli*, 84: '*L'influence de l'antique est visible en un seul endroit: dans le groupe formé par la femme qui porte le fagot et par l'enfant qui la précède. Une figure de femme avançant d'un pas rapide, soutenant d'une main un fardeau posé sur sa tête, soulevant de l'autre son vêtement afin d'être plus alerte, était un "morceau" que les peintres de l'époque introduisaient volontiers dans leurs compositions pour faire apprécier leur virtuosité. Ils donnaient l'impression du mouvement en faisant flotter en arrière des draperies et quelques mèches de cheveux laissées libres à cet effet, un stratagème qui leur avait été inspiré, comme je l'ai dit, par l'étude des sculptures antiques.*'

39 Mesnil, *Botticelli*, 46: '*Leur arabesque, qui soutient l'ensemble de la composition, les apparente davantage aux créations décoratives de l'art oriental qu'à la plastique strictement équilibrée de l'art gréco-romain.*'

40 WIA, GC, Warburg to Mesnil, 2 October 1906.

41 Mesnil, *Botticelli*, 125: '*Les Vertus qualifiées de "nymphes" dans le XXXIe Chant du Purgatoire n'ont rien d'antique ni dans leur rondes, ni dans leurs costumes, à moins qu'on ne veuille retrouver l'influence de l'art gréco-romain dans les draperies agitées que la Renaissance semble lui avoir empruntées au début, mais qui étaient devenues, dès lors, bien commun. Les danses échevelées de ces "Vertus" s'inspirent d'ailleurs davantage des rondes populaires que des représentations des fêtes bachiques.*'

42 See attributed to Baccio Baldini, series of the 'Planets': Arthur Mayger Hind, *Early Italian Engraving, a critical catalogue* (London: British Museum, 1938–48), vol.III.1a (1845-8-25-474).

43 Mesnil, *Botticelli*, 136–7: '*Les traces d'influence septentrionale, très visibles dans la série des Planètes et dans celle des Sibylles tendent à disparaître dans la seconde version où les figures nouvelles sont d'un caractère "botticellien". Mais ce caractère est tout générique; nulle part on ne découvre l'inspiration directe du maître, on ne retrouve son dessin et nous n'avons pas d'éléments suffisants pour lui attribuer, comme le fait Warburg, le modèle des planches des Planètes à la manière large (…)*'. Mesnil is obviously referring to Warburg, '*Delle "imprese amorose" nelle più antiche incisioni fiorentine*' (1905), in Aby Warburg, *Gesammelte Schriften*, vol.I, *Die Erneuerung der heidnischen Antike. Kulturwissenschaftliche Beiträge zur Geschichte der europäischen Renaissance*, ed.G. Bing (Leipzig-Berlin: 1932), 77–88.

44 Mesnil, *Botticelli*, 47: '*Gaspard était courtier de banque: c'était un métier de fripon à cette époque*'.

45 Mesnil, *Botticelli*, 47: '*Tout ce beau monde croyait se concilier Dieu en faisant des cadeaux à l'Eglise (…).*'

46 Published in 1907: Aby Warburg, 'Francesco Sassettis Letzwillige', in *Gesammelte Schriften*, 127–58.

47 Gombrich, *Aby Warburg*, 172–6.

48 Mesnil to Warburg, 24 December 1907, WIA, GC.

49 Mesnil, *Botticelli*, 157–60.

50 Mesnil, *Botticelli*, 96–100. See also Alessandro Cecchi, *Botticelli* (Milan: Federico Motta Editore, 2005), 66–93.

51 Mesnil, *Botticelli*, 108.

52 Mesnil to Warburg, 1 January 1904, WIA, GC: '*A propos du père Brockhaus, je lui ai reparlé récemment de la publication du Libro di ricordi de Neri di Bicci. Il m'a dit qu'il n'y avait point de chance que l'Institut le fît. Je n'ai pas insisté, d'autant plus que je ne tiendrais nullement à devoir perdre mon temps à faire le commentaire, un commentaire "érudit" à la manière allemande, de cet interminable bouquin (…) Supino parle toujours de faire faire la publication du Neri di Bicci: mais il la prend plus à la légère: "Si farà copiare da uno che abbia tempo; poi si scriverà una bella prefazione e si manderà fuori". Mais là c'est une autre difficulté qui arrête: le gouvernement italien n'a pas de sous pour des publications de ce genre. Que voulez-vous? Il doit entretenir tant d'officiers pour défendre l'unité italienne (Boum! Boum!) & maintenir le prestige de Casa Savoia (en avant la musique!)*'. See Neri di Bicci, Le ricordanze (10 marzo 1453–24 aprile 1475), ed. Bruno Santi (Pisa: Marlin, 1976).

53 Jacques Mesnil, 'Connaissons-nous Botticelli?', *Gazette des Beaux-Arts*, ser.6, 4 (July 1930): 70–99.

54 Mesnil, *Botticelli*, 151–2.

55 Mesnil, *Botticelli*, 157.

56 Jacques Mesnil, 'Sur les rapports entre la peinture italienne et la peinture néerlandaise à la Renaissance', *L'art flamand et hollandais*, n. s., 1, 25, S, 4 (1904). For Warburg's reaction to this article cf. Warburg to Mesnil, 2 October 1906, WIA, GC.

Part 4
Botticelli now

Introduction

Stefan Weppelmann

Twentieth-century hermeneutics have discussed models that perpetuate themselves over a long period of time. I refer to the works of Aby Warburg, Wilhelm Worringer, Meyer Schapiro or Leo Steinberg, but I would particularly like to recall the influential study *The Shape of Time, Remarks on the History of Things* by George Kubler.[1] In view of current developments in the historiography of art I also want to mention Alexander Nagel's study *Medieval Modern, Art out of Time* in which the author projects the Middle Ages onto modernity and vice versa.[2]

Such new approaches promotes an alternative model which operates with the categories of either *prime object*, or series or mutation. The focus has thus shifted from the individual style and topographical context to questions of the function of an object, its iconological layering and common blueprints.

The results from this shift are narratives which spread like rhizomes, to use the apt expression of Deleuze and Guattari.[3] They do not evolve in a linear and thus apparently progressive manner, but instead diffuse, resembling a system of bamboo shoots. Yet this new approach to art – specifically to everything that can be called a visual formula (*Bildformular*) – is by no means a privilege of theorists of culture. In particular the artists themselves are often conscious of their own connection with the *prime object*, or rather *prime thoughts* when (re) producing today's world.

While chronology was an underlying principle for designing the exhibition *Botticelli Reimagined*, the universal availability of Sandro di Mariano's works shaped its concept. The above-mentioned tradition was both its curatorial leitmotiv and its methodological tenet. The three studies that conclude this volume of conference proceedings address that theoretical base. Georges Didi-Huberman refers to Aby Warburg's early notion of the Nymph or Maenad as a prototype. This figure plays, as we know, a major role in Botticelli's works. Yet Didi-Huberman extends his view beyond Warburg's observations when he discusses the syntax of both fluidity and eroticism, intrinsically associated with the nymph.

He demonstrates how one can find a series of poetical references to the interconnection between nymph-like behaviour and fluidity in Warburg's work, and shows how these references coincide with a proper revival of the *Ninfa ariosa* in nineteenth- and early twentieth-century art and literature. He then focuses on the psychomorphic role of air and water – in particular the sea – as fluid substances with sexual connotations, the *flux sexuel*. He thereby analyses the mutual exchange between word and image, extending his view into the sphere of twentieth- and twenty-first-century photography, film and video arts. He thus constructs a cross-media 'logic of fluidity' for which Botticelli's inventions gain the status of *prime objects*.

Didi-Huberman's observations create a fitting context for Riccardo Venturi's analysis of Salvador Dalí's Pavilion for the New York World Exhibition [World's Fair] in 1939. There, too, the erotically charged motive of the water nymph takes centre stage, again with reference to Botticelli's Venus. Through analysing the various stages of the design and development process of Dalí's surreal *Fun House*, Venturi shows how for the eroticisation of the body – namely the body of the emblematic figure of Venus – the artist creates a new meaning: the metamorphic interpenetration of both female forms and marine creatures. In this way Botticelli's Venus with the head of a fish appears as a vision in Dalí's imagination. Yet such kinds of hybrids are only *prima facie* original inventions. Bearing Didi-Huberman's essay in mind as a complement to Venturi's, it becomes clear that Dalí is perfectly in conformity with the tradition in which the male imagination associates the sea and its creatures, psychomorphologically, with the female body.

Dalí's reference to Botticelli is hardly surprising if we keep in mind that in the 1930s the surrealist painter made repeated references to Renaissance artists, including Raphael, Leonardo and Michelangelo. His further goal, according to Venturi, was the overcoming of a presumed distance between the Renaissance and modernity. Dalí presumably also wanted to identify surreal tendencies in Renaissance art – in other words to assign a much longer tradition to surrealist imagery, shaped by the subconscious, the grotesque and the absurd. The formulas Botticelli invented for *The Birth of Venus* and the *Primavera* are thus gaining the status of a dream vision which modernity begins to analyse. Above all, however, Venturi demonstrates convincingly, with the example of Botticelli, how images represent constructed realities. Hence while Dalí stressed the surreal notes of Botticell's inventions, the Italian government used the same images – thanks to their classical subjects and thus their implicit *italianità* – as political propaganda. Venturi thus points to the concurrence between Dalí's reception of Venus and the contemporary show *Italian Masters* at the Museum of Modern Art in New York, which featured the original *The Birth of Venus* (fig.1.0). This show had previously toured through the United States as a form of political propaganda.

After Venturi's discussion of this episode from the 1930s, Gabriel Montua analyses more recent sociocultural adaptations of Botticelli's works. He quotes several cases to highlight how in feminist debates about femininity and gender Botticelli's works, namely his *Venus* and the *Primavera*, are used as a kind of counterexample: they serve as ciphers for artistic and social conventions and for a typical male, Western system of power. Moreover, Montua's analysis of contemporary modes of reception of Botticelli's art even implies that his main pieces have become a kind of synonym for Western social norms and structures. Botticelli's masterpieces thus seem predestined for critical commentary on Western societies. Only the fact that the artist has apparently gained such status can explain the (at times curious) geopolitical statements by both Western and non-Western artists about these iconic images of the Renaissance.

All three essays lead to the conclusion that the reception of Botticelli in both the twentieth and the twenty-first centuries was based on two major yet alternative systems of reference. These systems allowed the painter to gain the unusual iconic status to which *Botticelli Reimagined* referred: firstly, the tradition of the ideal, erotically charged female figure with inherent, surreal, psychomorphic elements; secondly the politico-propagandistic constructions that use Botticelli's paintings – first and foremost the *Venus* and the *Primavera* (fig.1.30) – in a black and white manner to highlight geopolitical imbalances.

As an answer to anyone who looks for a dialectical connection between these two systems, the conclusion from all three essays is that the iconology described by Didi-Huberman and Venturi – that is, the typically Western, male sexualisation of the female and the fluid – contains a certain potential for a political utilisation of Botticelli. Botticelli's works do, quintessentially, contain Western, paternalistic constructions of the standard (the ideal form of female beauty, the role of the female as object and decoration, the sexualisation of femininity etc.). Some contemporary artistic expressions can thus be seen, as Montua demonstrates, as personal interpretations of the tensions inherent in these systems. They are thus still dependent on the 'shape of time' (George Kubler), namely the ramification of time-dependent permutations of the *prime object*.

Acknowledgements

The editors would like to express their gratitude to Claudia Wedepohl, who kindly translated this introduction.

Notes

1 George Kubler, *The Shape of Time, Remarks on the History of Things* (New Haven and London: Yale University Press, 1962).
2 Alexander Nagel, *Medieval Modern, Art out of Time* (London: Thames & Hudson, 2012).
3 Gilles Deleuze and Felix Guattari, *Mille Plateaux* (Paris: Éditions de Minuit, 1980).

12. *Ninfa fluida* (a post scriptum)

Georges Didi-Huberman

[...]

We come now to discuss *Ninfa* as a 'theoretical figure'. This signifies above all that the *images of fluidity* found in the works of Ovid or Lucretius, Botticelli or Ghirlandaio, Michelet or Victor Hugo, tell us something very fundamental about the *fluidity of images*. The play on words between *Einfühlung* (empathy) and *Einfüllung* (pouring in), which I noted in connection with Botticelli, characterising the empathy aroused by images and a certain sense of imaginary or symbolic (certainly *imaginative*) 'flow', was to find its development in a crucial concept. This concept, persistently reiterated by the author of *Mnemosyne*, was that of 'migrations' (*Wanderungen*) – the temporal as well as spatial movements through which every image finds its consistency, which, rightly speaking, is not stability, but rather fluidity, the play of 'sources' and 'influences', 'currents' and 'whirlpools'... At the end of his life, Warburg observed that 'there is law of energy governing the rotation of meaning (*es gibt ein energetisches Sinn-Drehungsgesetz*), even as there is a law governing the change in direction of the wind (*wie es ein Winddrehungsgesetz gibt*)'.[1]

The disappointment I felt 12 years ago on failing to identify a precise source for the French expression '*brise imaginaire*' (imaginary breeze) – used by Warburg in the German text of his thesis on Botticelli[2] – has now been alleviated by the discovery of several French texts which do use this phrase. All are to be found in his library. The first passage appears in an art-historical study by Paul Mantz, published in 1873 in the *Gazette des Beaux-Arts*. Describing a female portrait from the school of Rembrandt, he writes 'the flesh is a little white, the clothes are opulent and the draperies swell, blown out by an imaginary breeze...'.[3] One senses here a literary *topos* (without excluding other possible sources), particularly as other archaeological descriptions use the same formulation, somewhat in the manner of Wilhelm Jensen's novel *Gradiva*.

Here, for example, Gustave Mendel describes in 1912 a Greek relief sculpture in the museum of Constantinople:

> [...]the muse proceeds to the right, taking slow, deliberate steps. Her demeanour is noble and serene; the full weight of her body, which is vigorous without being heavy, is placed on her left foot, positioned flat on the floor. Her right leg is bent and trails slightly,

> her foot barely touching the floor with the tips of her toes, which extend over the plinth. With her left arm, she holds the lyre against her body, touching the strings both with the fingers of her left hand and with the plectrum she holds in her right. She is dressed in a light tunic which covers, without obscuring, her generous breast. The tunic floats at her feet, pleated with small, irregular, sinuous folds, while her mantle falls from her left shoulder over her back, covering her legs and rising up again, exposing the right side of her bust, towards her left shoulder; from this falls a fold, floating freely behind her as if lifted by an imaginary breeze[...]'.[4]

It is no surprise to find the expression 'imaginary breeze' invoked in the context of representations where references to antiquity predominate. However, it is much more surprising – and highly instructive theoretically – to find the same phrase in Villiers de l'Isle-Adam's *L'Ève future* (*Tomorrow's Eve*). Aby Warburg owned a copy of the 1891 edition of this work. In this great symbolist novel the *Ninfa futura*, an 'electro-magnetical' creature invented by the principal character Thomas Edison, is intended to embody the 'most surprising way in which to seek the ideal' in a woman. It is at the moment when this creature's kingdom is discovered – a veritable 'underground Eden', like the lair of an octopus or Josiane's palace in Victor Hugo's *L'homme qui rit* – that the 'caress of an imaginary breeze' causes veils, screens and petals to billow within this enchanted environment, described like a sexual organ seen from within.[5]

Such a possible reference by Aby Warburg to *L'Ève future* –after all, he quoted from another contemporary poet, Dante Gabriel Rossetti[6] – forewarns us, like many other indications, that it would be incorrect to see his interest in the 'survival of Antiquity' as pure nostalgia for the classical past. *Mnemosyne* speaks of desire as much as of memory; *Nachleben* is as much about modernity as it is about archaeology. Manet, for example, inspired Warburg to write an entire iconological study, while Arnold Böcklin, who made a painting entitled *Le Printemps* in 1862, also aroused his enthusiasm. Warburg admired Böcklin's energetic manner of representing in his paintings the '*vent rafraîchissant dans le vent et les vagues*', his naiads and nymphs sharing their watery frolics.[7] If we accept that the history of art as a literary genre cannot be disassociated from a certain *poetic history*, it will come as no surpise that Warburg's *Ninfa* brings together a whole universe of languages – not just of images – from Hölderlin's nymphs through to symbolist poetry and the 'erotic-fluidity' and 'tormented' production of the French Romantics.[8] Let us just revisit the first sketch of Hölderlin's *Hypérion*, when the nymph reappears, like Beatrice to Dante:

> A rustling in one of the side-walks startled me.
>
> Ah! Then, in this painful solitude with my heart all empty of joy, *she* appeared before me; woven as of light and fragrance, so gracious and delicate; above her smile, calm and full of unearthly calm, her great shinning eyes were enthroned in god-like majesty, and the golden crests of hair glinted about her face as the spring-breeze tossed them like little clouds in the first light of dawn.[...]
>
> Years passed; springs came and went; many a glorious picture, many a memorial of your beloved Italy, sprung from divine imagining, delighted me, but time has obliterated most of it: only *her* image remains to me and everything it entails. Still she stands before me as in the holy intoxicated moment I found her; I press her to my heart, the sweet phantom;[...]Everything hastened towards her. A part of her being seemed to communicate itself to everything[...].[9]

From this perspective, it is as true of the nineteenth century as of the fifteenth to say: these are *modern* periods *par excellence*, periods in which everything is reinventing itself thanks to certain techniques, around a certain notion of the human subject. At the same time, these are periods in which a tremendous passion was felt for everything *ancient*. There was never a time when Greek and Roman drapery were the topic of such intense study as they were following the writings of Léon Heuzey over a period of 50 years, from 1872 to 1922.[10] It is no coincidence that Maurice Emmanuel's work on Greek dance – studies with which Warburg's notion of *Ninfa* has specific associations[11] – addressed the *antiquity* of dithyrambic or bacchanalian gestures using a method that was pre-eminently *modern* – the chronophotography developed by Etienne-Jules Marey, the 'artist-scholar' who was so passionate about the forms of physical and physiological fluidity.[12] We thus begin to understand that with this 'fin de siècle Maenadism' the *immemorial* motifs that Warburg studied from the perspective of survival could be channelled through something resembling modern *cinematography*, as Philippe-Alain Michaud has seen.

Thus the ancient version of *Ninfa ariosa* found in Leon Battista Alberti or Antonio Cornazzano seems to reconfigure itself at the end of the nineteenth century, taking on the features of a *Ninfa auratica*. Loïe

Fuller would, of course, be the ultimate example of this. Celebrated by Mallarmé, she was already coming close to futurism, particularly in her 'avant-garde' use of light.[13] It is no surprise that Aby Warburg's interest in gestures and '*pathos formulae*' eventually culminated in an encounter with a certain style of contemporary dance, in which a real 'poetics of flow' developed around artists such as Isadora Duncan, Rudolf von Laban or Mary Wigman.[14] In the case of Isadora Duncan, we should remember that she wanted to dance Botticelli's *Primavera* (in terms of iconography) because (in terms of morphology) it had been the motion of the waves that first inspired her desire to dance:

> It was when I was contemplating the waves when I was very young that I first thought about dancing. I tried to follow the movements of the waves and to dance according to their rhythm. [...] When in Florence, we spent several weeks strolling ecstatically through museums, gardens and olive groves. It was at that point that Botticelli captured my youthful imagination. I would sit before *Primavera* for whole days; I loved it. A delightful ageing guard would give me a stool to sit on and observed my adoration with great emotion. I would stay there until I could actually see the flowers in the painting growing, the bare feet dancing, the bodies moving until a joyous angel came to visit me and then I thought: I will portray this image through dance[...]. Inspired by Botticelli's painting, I created a dance which sought to reproduce the gentle, marvellous movements he evoked, the tender undulations of the earth which was blanketed with flowers, the dance of the nymphs in a ring and the flight of the zephyrs, unfolding around the central figure, part Aphrodite, part Madonna, whose single meaningful gesture indicates the birth of springtime.

In his footnotes to the 'Preliminary remarks' prefacing his work on Botticelli, published by Gertrud Bing, Aby Warburg included some additional references and quotations, as a kind of epigraph. The first comes from Thomas Carlyle's *Sartor Resartus* and suggests precisely these ideas of fluidity, of the backwash of the waves, of ebb and flow ('many shall run to and from'). The second, taken from the philosopher Wilhelm Dilthey, evokes art as inherent in the 'spiritual balance sheet of human life' ('*der Kunst im geistigen Haushalt des Menschenlebens*'). The third comes from an article entitled *Zur Genesis eines ästhetischen Begriffs* ('On the genesis of an aesthetic concept'), which was published in 1894 by Theobald Ziegler and identified Novalis as the actual originator of empathy as an aesthetic concept.[15]

This helps us to get a better understanding of the *romantic* grounding of this *modern* aesthetic, at the point where *morphological* considerations (the objective forms of images with which we are presented) encounter *anthropological* questions (the subjective power of images deep within us). Before making the obligatory reference to Goethe, Wilhelm Dilthey also returned to the waves of the sea and to Leibniz's 'minute or dull perceptions';[16] headded that the 'difficult transformation of Leibniz's metaphysical aesthetics into a psychological aesthetics' was required.[17] This was a task to which the romantic – followed by the modern – revival of humanist theories of the imagination attempted to respond, and 'now for the first time *a real explanation of the most important psychical phenomena* became possible'.[18]

There can be no doubt that Aby Warburg wanted to adopt and extend Dilthey's proposition to understand 'how in a work of art image, form, feeling, thought and spirit are all connected from within'.[19] This demands a completely different idea of aesthetics from simple academic criteria of beauty, as is clearly – and almost violently – apparent in Schiller's letter to Goethe of 7 July 1797, cited by Dilthey as the epigraph to his 1892 article: 'Would that the demand for beauty finally be given up and once and for all replaced by the demand for truth!'[20] This was an agenda that Dilthey sought to follow, affirming that philosophical aesthetics should not be afraid of engaging with contemporary matters that are un-ideal and, so to speak, *immanent*, such as 'psychological depth', the materiality of the medium or even political questions, lying between 'naturalism' and 'socialism'.[21]

If indeed the notion of *Einfühlung* (empathy) seems so important in this regard, it is because, as Dilthey affirms,

> The way in which we become conscious of the external world – namely, as resistance to our will – explains the basic sense in which we spontaneously and inevitably attribute something inner to what is given to sense as outer. The essence of aesthetic apprehension and creation, i.e., the *relation of feeling and image*, meaning and appearance, inner and outer, is based on this.[22]

It is in this way that *images are immanent* to our existence within the world: *they flow* between our internal sensibilities and external forms. And this is how, in Dilthey's words, 'we learn to see through the eyes of the great painters. Through Shakespeare we learn to understand what happens on the stage of the world and through Goethe what comes to pass in the quiet depths of a human soul'.[23] It is from this starting point that an unwavering connection will be established, in which *survival* (the power of memory), *creation* (the power of desire) and the essential *fluidity* of images interact in motion.[24] We find this the connection not only in Warburg's writings, but also – with a remarkably similar vocabulary – throughout Bergson's philosophical dynamic.

Whether sculpted in marble, fixed beneath a painter's varnish or shown in motion through a cinema projector, images always *flow in and flow out again*. This living movement resembles the backwash of waves, bringing them both close to us (caressing, intimate) and distant (mysterious, retiring). This is their essential 'anadyomenic' quality, as found throughout *The Birth of Venus* (fig.1.0).[25] They whirl, they move, here and there, they pull away and return to us until the point at which they coil up into the 'octopus lair' of our unconscious psyches, out of our range of vision by being at our very core. That is what Aby Warburg chose to observe. That is why he found it essential to create an *historical anthropology of the imagination,* capable of penetrating the 'micro-history' of a single painting – even of a single detail. From this could be extracted a significant structural lesson, pertinent on the level of both the individual psyche and the whole sociohistorical fabric.

It will come as no surprise that his interest in the aesthetic and psychological notion of *empathy* caused Warburg, years later in 1893, to concern himself with Lucien Lévy-Bruhl's anthropological concept of *participation*. This phenomenon was first (and not coincidentally) observed by the ethnologist in connection with the 'survival of the dead', as envisaged by the so-called 'primitive mind',[26] but anthropologists soon recognised it early on in the heart of the modern and pre-modern West. In the *Carnets*, written at the end of his life, Lévy-Bruhl wanted to examine this notion of 'participation' further, although he insisted at the outset on the 'impossibility of clearly analysing participations' because, he stated, they originate from a very obscure realm of the human psyche.[27] This process, all the more powerful for being impossible to analyse, represented for Lévy-Bruhl an 'affective generalisation' (rather than a 'law'), what he would eventually call a fundamental 'mode of existence': 'For the primitive mentality *to be is to participate*'.[28]

For our purposes, it is intriguing to note that from the *illogical* nature of participation – which is 'resistant to contradiction' and made up of 'bi-presence', 'duality-unity' and entities which fall under the '*pars pro toto* principle'[29] – we can easily infer its *fantasmatic* or unconscious characteristics. From this starting point, it will be 'aesthetics which puts a first coherence in primitive man's mind', as summarised by Maurice Leenhardt in his preface to the *Carnets*.[30] And it is this aesthetic character – the constant employment of image and imitation, as for example causing our enemies to suffer by stabbing their effigies[31] – that gives these phenomena of participation their essentially *fluid* character.

> Accordingly, to feel participations between things and phenomena is to find oneself in the attitude familiar to the human mind when it feels itself in contact with the mythical world fluid reality, forces at one and the same transcendent and immanent. [...] and there is seen to appear, in place of the determinism of phenomena which seems to us the very framework of the ambient world, characteristic fluidity of the mythical world which is unaware of it.[32]

Even Claude Lévi-Strauss, in the section of his *Story of Lynx* entitled 'On the side of the wind', would remark on this essential character, which he in turn refers to as the 'fluidity of mythical forms'.[33]

One could find confirmation of such fluidity of images in Sandor Ferenczi's speculations on the paradigm of the sea (*Thalassa*) as a fundamental 'psychomorphism' in which the backwash of waves is understood as a principle of sexual flux (the impulse of life) and of a reflux or regression to the 'maternal womb' (the impulse of death).[34] It would also be fascinating to enter into Warburg's beloved labyrinths of comparative mythology: somewhere between the Aphrodite anadyomene of Hesiod or Botticelli and the African 'water gods', at the point where imagined equivalences between water and semen set in.[35] Equally intriguing would be Georges Dumézil's research into water deities as construed in the Indo-European world from Iran to Ireland, by way of Roman religion – which, for example, set up a polar opposition between female sea goddesses: the dangerous, boiling, swirling *Salaria* and the reassuringly calm *Venilia*.[36]

It would also be useful to return to Bachelard's analyses of the '*imaginary journey*' sparked by air and water, the two fluids *par excellence* (though remaining critical of some of his assertions). At the beginning of *L'Air et les Songes (Air and Dreams)*, Bachelard wrote that the imagination is essentially *open* and *elusive*. Within the human psyche, imagination is the very experience of *openness*.[37] Such openness and mobility will be necessary to grasp symbolic 'coherence' as well as 'unconscious dynamism'.[38] Certainly Bachelard would have found Warburg's '*brise imaginaire*' and 'accessories in motion' additional evidence for his claim that 'dynamic imagination' is [to be understood as] a *psychic amplifier* and at the same time as a dialectical process balanced *between the loss of shape and the regaining of shape*. 'Can the study of the *fleeting images* be a subject? Images of aerial imagination either evaporate or crystallize. We must seize them between the two poles of this constantly active ambivalence.'[39]

This is how Bachelard came to the crucial notion of the *material immanence of the imagination* as he describes it throughout *L'Eau et les rêves* (*Water and Dreams*).

> When I was meditating on the concept of the beauty of matter, I was immediately struck by the neglect of the *material cause* in aesthetic philosophy. In particular, it seemed to me that the individualizing power of matter had been underestimated. Why does everyone always associate the notion of the individual with form? Is there not an individuality in depth that makes matter a totality, even in its smallest divisions? Meditated upon from the perspective of its depth, matter is the very principle that can disassociate itself from forms. It is not the simple absence of formal activity. It remains itself despite all distortion and division. Moreover, matter may be given value in two ways: by deepening and by elevating. Deepening makes it seem unfathomable, like a mystery. Elevation makes it appear to be an inexhaustible force, like a miracle. In both cases, meditation on matter cultivates an *open imagination*.[40]

So it is with the idea that 'material imagination [is] an exhuberance of forms'[41] that Bachelard returned to romantic motifs of torment. Continuing in the same vein as Novalis and Michelet, he saw a whole ontology of adversity in the spectacle of the ocean, affirming that 'insofar as he is a source of energy, a being is, an *a priori* anger'.[42] The incarnation of 'aquatic melancholy' is what he refers to as the 'Ophelia complex', the nymph in whom desire and death are united.[43] For Bachelard this is an opportunity to re-examine a theme continuously reiterated and depicted in a vast poetic and iconographical tradition since antiquity – a perpetual *backwash of imagery*. In this nymphs and naiads appear as 'a mass of desires and images', where 'at the edge of the waters edge, everything is tresses' and 'the being rising out of the water is a reflection that materializes little by little; it is an *image* before it is a *being*, a desire before it is an image'.[44]

[...]

It was in relation to a dream described by Novalis in *Henri d'Ofterdingen* that Bachelard gave his fullest commentary on what he called 'water's feminine substance'. At this point in the poet's narrative there develops 'a profoundly materialized imagination, where water, in its volume and mass, not simply in the fairy-world of its reflections, appears like *dissolved maiden,* like the *liquid essence of maiden*'.[45] Such an imagination is haunted by the memory of Hesiod's Aphrodite anadyomene, by all the Oceanides and the sculpted *Auraï* (breezes) that adorn the mausolea of ancient Greece.

So that is the *Ninfa fluida:* always fleeting, always present. She comes and returns. She survives. Is it not a fluid being that lasts best, lasts longest? In the long confrontation between sea and promontory, it is surely the promontory that will crumble first, however enormous, phallic and intimidating it may be. The sea will 'endure', precisely because it is does not have a 'durable' form, because it does not impose itself *en bloc* and because it derives its strength from its ability to withdraw, in the incessant movement of the backwash, of ebb and flow. This is indeed *Ninfa fluida,* ancient and lost, but always present, enduring right up to the here and now. Our contemporary, then – but always, by her own desire, *in search of lost time*.

For we remember Odette, in Proust's novel.

> As she stood there beside him [Swann], brushing his cheek with the loosened tresses of her hair, bending one knee in what was almost a dancer's pose, so that she could lean without tiring herself over the picture[...] Swann was struck by her resemblance to the figure of Zipporah, Jethro's daughter, which is to be seen in one of the Sixtine frescoes.[46]

It was when she adopted an air of 'unrelieved sorrow' that Odette, who was a contemporary figure *par excellence*, evoked more than ever the 'faces of some of the women created by the painter of the *Primavera*'.[47] Equally, Odette was the contemporary of the celebrated dead beauty known as the *'Inconnue de la Seine'*[48] and of those modern Pythias – hysterical and psychic nymphs – who spat out their souls and conversed with ghosts.[49]

This is the era of Max Klinger's fascinating images in which we see excessive draperies, drowning lovers, antique centaurs along with modern-day girls, defecating in a meadow after a picnic, mermaids making love in the waves in a burlesque parody of ancient friezes, scenes representing the ravishing of women stranded on river banks, portraits of Nietzsche with fashionable nymphets dropping gloves while ice-skating.[50] This is the period of a 'return to antiquity' for the Viennese intellectual and artistic avant-garde.[51] While Warburg was pondering the fluid motions in Botticelli's paintings, Ferdinand de Saussure was discussing the two 'floating kingdoms' that constitute 'ideas' and 'sounds' – 'plastic' spaces, in the depths of which a linguistic act will operate its cuts and crossings.[52] (fig.4.1). It would soon be Wittgenstein's turn to adopt the same vocabulary in his concept of the 'flow of life' and the Heraclitan notion of *Alles fliesst* ('everything flows').[53]

This is also the period in which dreams and phantoms were being scrutinised for their *psychological truth*. Sigmund Freud's *Interpretation of Dreams*, for example, includes the unique 'illustration' of a typical dream, taken from the humorous Hungarian magazine *Fidibusz* and relayed to him by Sandor Ferenczi. Over the course of eight vignettes we are presented with a little boy and his young governess, first wearing city clothes, then semi-naked by his bed. Then comes the image of the child urinating; the flow of urine grows into a stream, then a river, then a canal, and then an expansive ocean[54] – another manifestation of the 'hypochondriac wave' (fig.4.2). At the end of the 1920s, going beyond the classic oppositions of 'outer content' and 'inner content', Ludwig Binswanger proposed a phenomenological approach to the *immanence of images*, both in dreams and fantasies. For example in a dream about falling, it is 'our whole existence (*Dasein*) [which] moves within the meaning matrix (*Bedeutungsrichtung*) of stumbling, sinking and falling'.[55]

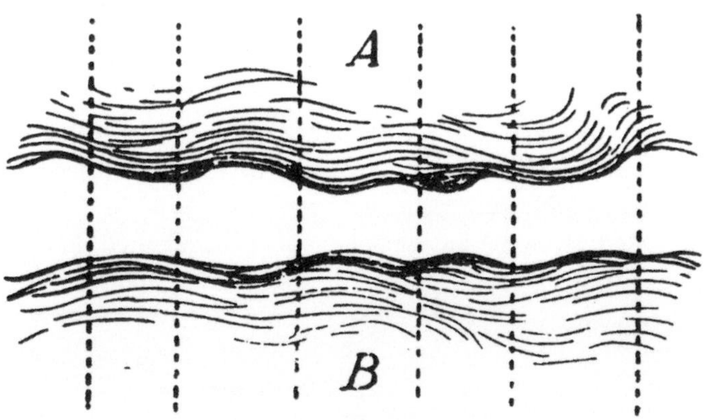

Fig.4.1 Ferdinand de Saussure (1857–1913), *Les 'royaumes flottants'*, 1906–11, in *Cours de linguistique générale* (1906–1911), ed. Charles Bally and Albert Sechehaye (1915), revised by Tullio de Mauro (Paris: Payot, 1972), pp.155–6.

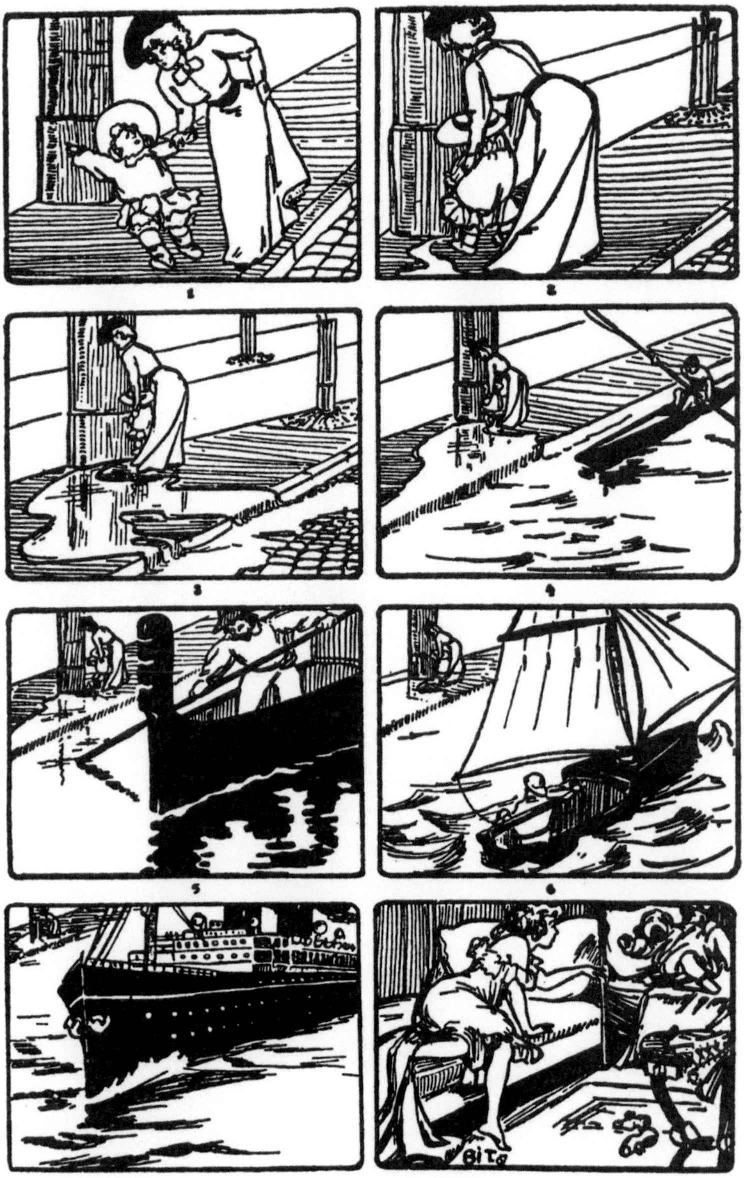

Fig.4.2 Illustration from Hungarian journal *Fidibusz*, 1900, repr. in Sigmund Freud, *The Interpretation of Dreams* (1899), trans. James Strachey (London: Allen & Unwin 1954), p.368.

This is the decisive moment in the history of theories of images, in which the notion of 'figurability' (*Darstellbarkeit*) was to achieve full recognition as a result of psychoanalysis, with its extraordinary heuristic value and its ability to function as a means of conversion between different levels of reality, perception and sensation. Thus the interplay becomes explicit between *nymphs* as gracious characters from classical antiquity and the French usage of *nymphes* to designate the labia minora of the female sexual organs – not to mention the metamorphic meaning in reference to butterflies.[56] There is a a similar interplay between the innocent grace of the *flower* (*'fleur'*) and the menstrual reference of *flow* (*'flueur'*). A beautiful drawing by Gustave Klimt, dating from 1916–17, depicts a young woman masturbating (fig.4.3).[57]

The realism of the pose goes along with an overall impression of disorder, as if the artist had decided to avoid representing the shapes precisely as he saw them. This disorder, in fact, arises from a notable decision about figurability: it is a likeness, not of the anatomical *aspect* of the body represented, but rather of the *process* observed by the artist in the intimacy of this presence – and still more of the *feeling* that is the predominant motif, or indeed mystery. The woman's drapery is therefore drawn as a disarray of lines returning feverishly to their starting point – evident in the way the material of her blouse is rumpled, but most of all in

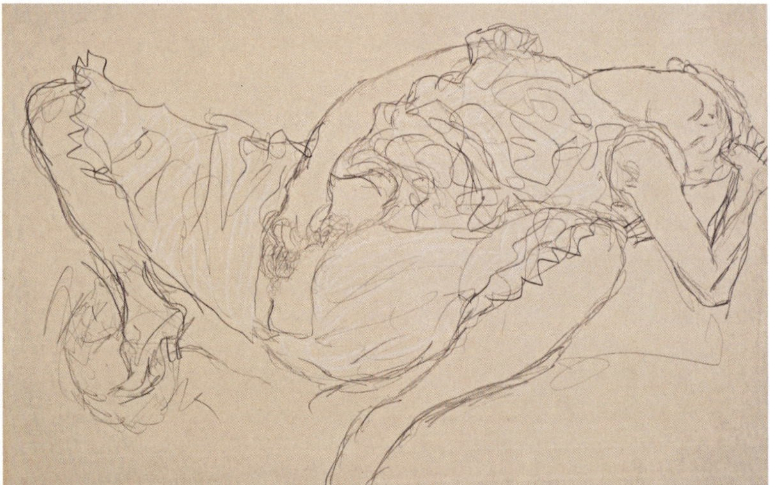

Fig.4.3 Gustav Klimt (1862–1918), *Reclining Female in Underwear with Spread Legs and Head Bent Backwards, Masturbating*, 1916/17, pencil, white chalk on Japanese paper, 37.4 × 57 cm, Leopold Museum, Vienna, Inv.1355. © Leopold Museum, Vienna.

the backwash of her pleasure itself. One might almost say that the artist himself drew his own finger over the sheet of paper, precisely at the point where the hand he has drawn was moving agitatedly, creating a central and blurred area on the sheet of paper – even more fluid than elsewhere. Here is the exact place where the viewer's glance questions female desire.

Going far beyond the depraved nymphs conjured up by Pierre Louÿs – one of them was called Chloris, although her friends were Connette, Laqueue, Vagine, Rosette and even Anus[58] – Georges Bataille took these themes to their landmark limits. In an article for *Verve* in 1937, the author of *Madame Edwarda* addressed the motif of female hair using alliterative wordplay, in which fluidity seemed to arise spontaneously from expressions such as 'fiery figures', 'fleeing figures' or 'fugitives'.

> On their heads are their flowing locks, as far removed from the fixed nature of worries as the most transparent jellyfish bathed in light, seen through the waves. Nothing appears closer yet nothing is further away than this hair as a body of light and water, so far away that the night sky, which is receding prodigiously, barely suffices to conceive of its strange presence. [...] If it were possible to *live* a hand or a foot, *to live* useless locks, it would seem that nothing would hold this life back at ground level, it would be nothing more than a lost flow of light in a dark space and it would no longer be anything more than the irremediable loss of self that a river represents.
>
> The most fleeting figures are therefore projected within the spirit and the figures flee the spirit: but is it certain that true unhappiness might not befall those who would not flee these figures just as they themselves flee it?[59]

Thus, from Aby Warburg to Georges Bataille, we understand that 'accessories of movement' – hair, draped clothing – will lose their classic status as 'decoration' or *parergon* and will be given new meaning in terms of intensification or even *excess.* In Bataille's *Le Mort* (*The Dead Man*), for example, the character of Marie will take her pleasure – not in the storm or in the wind, but, as it were, *from* the storm and *from* the wind.[60] Surrealist *ecstasy* fragments the body into pieces, from which drops or spurts of fluid are generated, like sperm. We find this in Salvador Dalí's texts for *Minotaure* in 1933,[61] or in Jean Arp's contribution to *Le Surréalisme au service de la révolution* that same year. In this illustrated poem the word 'root' is associated not only with the idea of 'air', but also with an undefined field of fluid shapes through which strange equivalences pass (fig. 4.4).

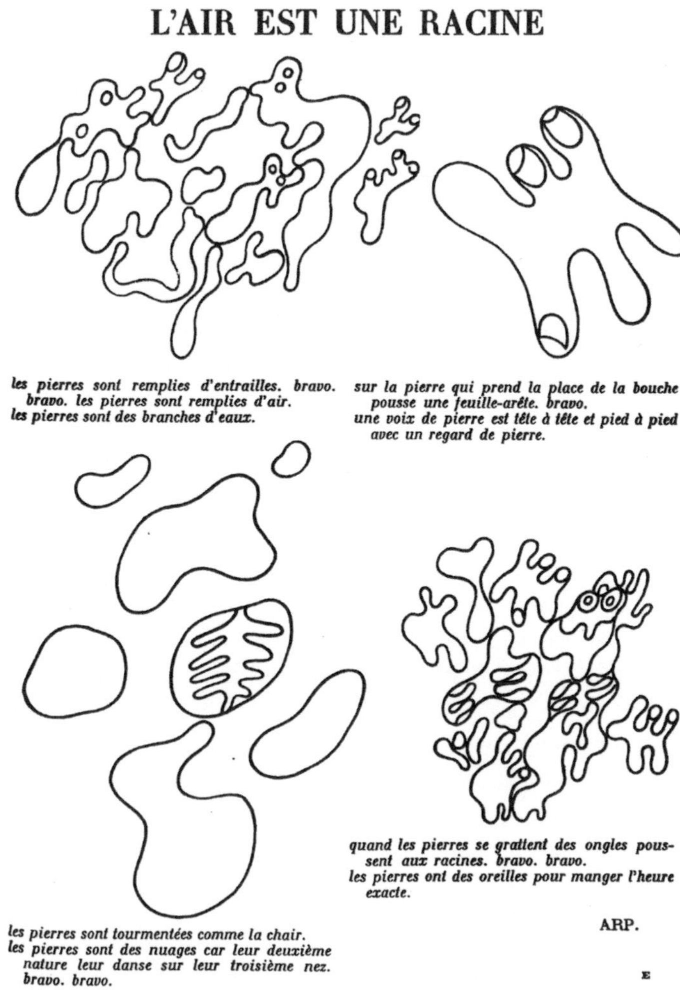

L'AIR EST UNE RACINE

les pierres sont remplies d'entrailles. bravo. bravo. les pierres sont remplies d'air.
les pierres sont des branches d'eaux.

sur la pierre qui prend la place de la bouche pousse une feuille-arête. bravo.
une voix de pierre est tête à tête et pied à pied avec un regard de pierre.

quand les pierres se grattent des ongles poussent aux racines. bravo. bravo.
les pierres ont des oreilles pour manger l'heure exacte.

les pierres sont tourmentées comme la chair.
les pierres sont des nuages car leur deuxième nature leur danse sur leur troisième nez. bravo. bravo.

ARP.

E

Fig.4.4 Jean Arp (1886–1966), *L'air est une racine*, 1933. Poems and drawings published in *Le Surréalisme au service de la révolution*, no.6 (1933): 33.

> THE AIR IS A ROOT
> stones are filled with innards, bravo
> bravo, stones are filled with air.
> stones are watery tributaries,
> stones are as tormented as flesh.[62]

And thus the nymph, having left her watery traces behind her – some emanating from her mouth as in photographs of 'psychic materialisations' (fig.4.5) – will herself become a character of sea spray and foam, as if to be reabsorbed into Hesiod's fantastical description of the birth of Aphrodite (fig. 4.6).

Going beyond the 'time-lapse effects' produced in the 'photodynamic' experiments of the Italian futurists,[63] the surrealists were to embark on an infinitely varied experimental realisation of a veritable *eroticism of fluids*. For example, in the admirable photographs of Rogi André (the male pseudonym of Rosza Klein, a Hungarian artist married to André

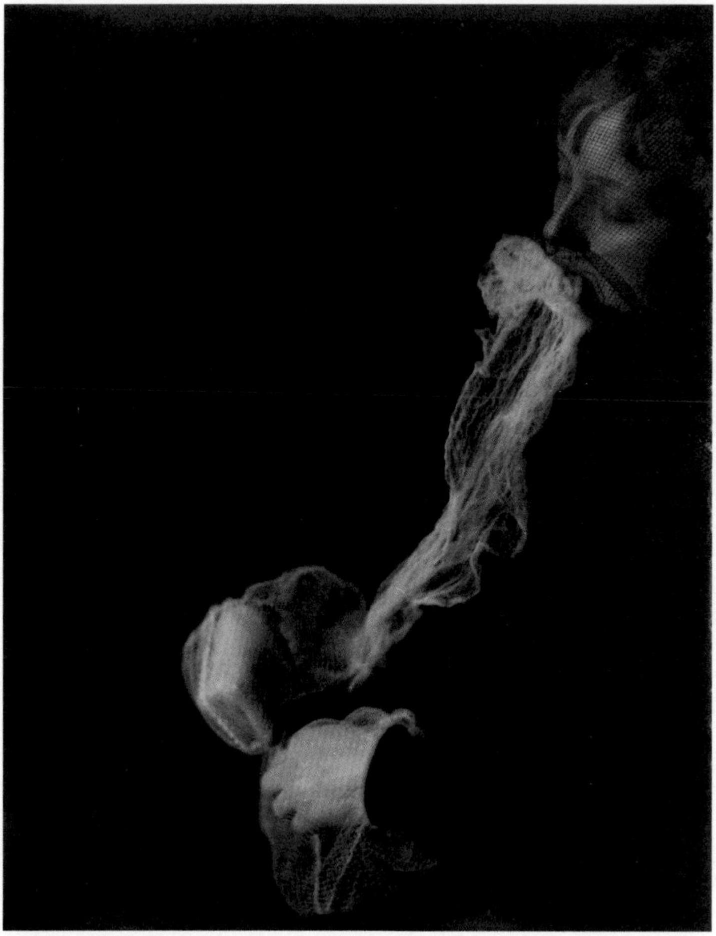

Fig.4.5 Albert von Schrenk-Notzing (1862–1929), *Le Medium Stanislawa P. avec un voile ectoplasmique*, 1913, photograph, Fribourg-en-Brisgau, Institut für Grenzgebiete der Psychologie und Psychohygiene. © Institut für Grenzgebiete der Psychologie & Psychohygiene e. V. (IGPP), Fribourg-en-Brisgau.

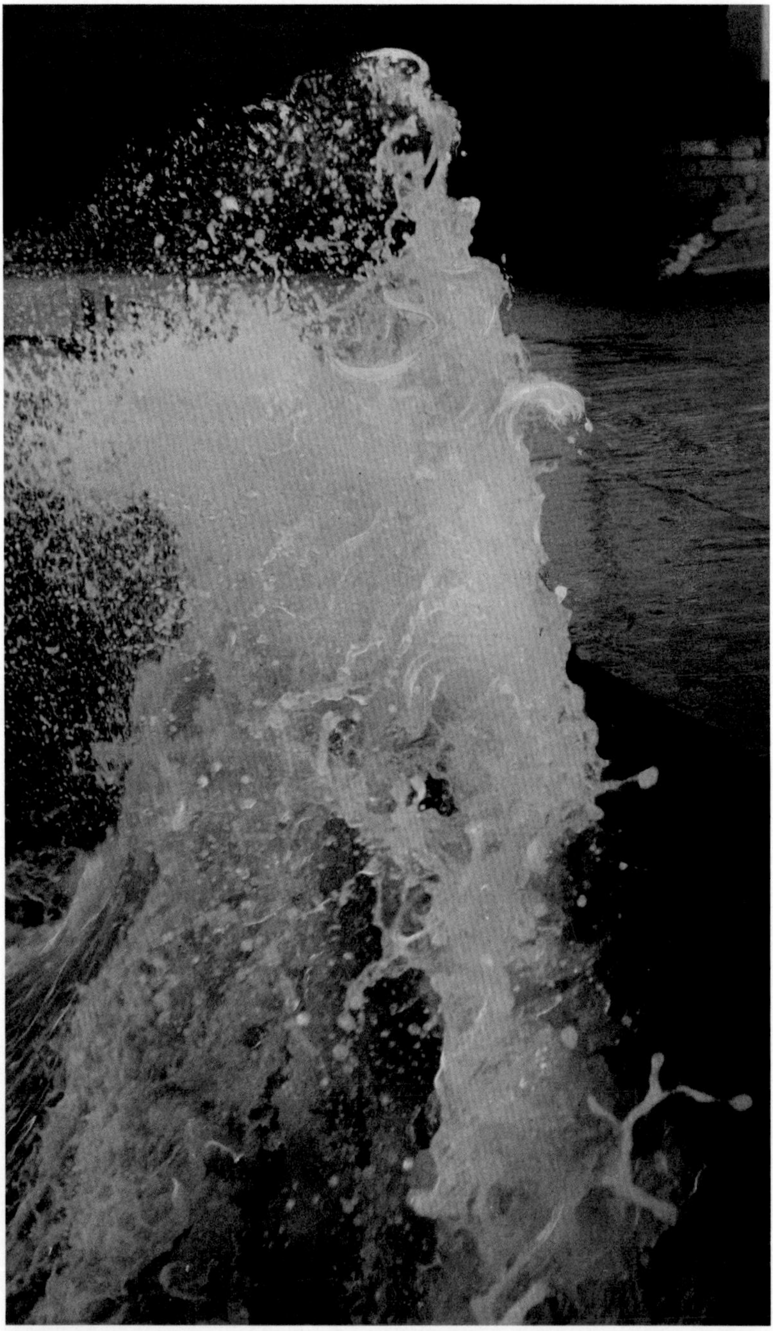

Fig.4.6 Pierre Jahan (1909–2003), *Jaillissement d'écume*, l'estacade, Le Havre, 1935. © Pierre Jahan/Roger-Viollet.

Kertész), a naked 'liquid woman' is depicted, swimming underwater in an aquarium (fig.4.7). The most famous image from this series, sometimes entitled *La Nymphe*, taken from Jacqueline Lamba, André Breton's 'muse' and companion, was published in *Minotaure* in 1935, and then in the edition of *L'Amour fou* in 1937.[64]

But no one travelled as far down this experimental route as Man Ray. From 1923, in *Le Retour à la raison*, Man Ray treated the roll of film as a single, directly imprinted photographic negative. The 'nymph' lying

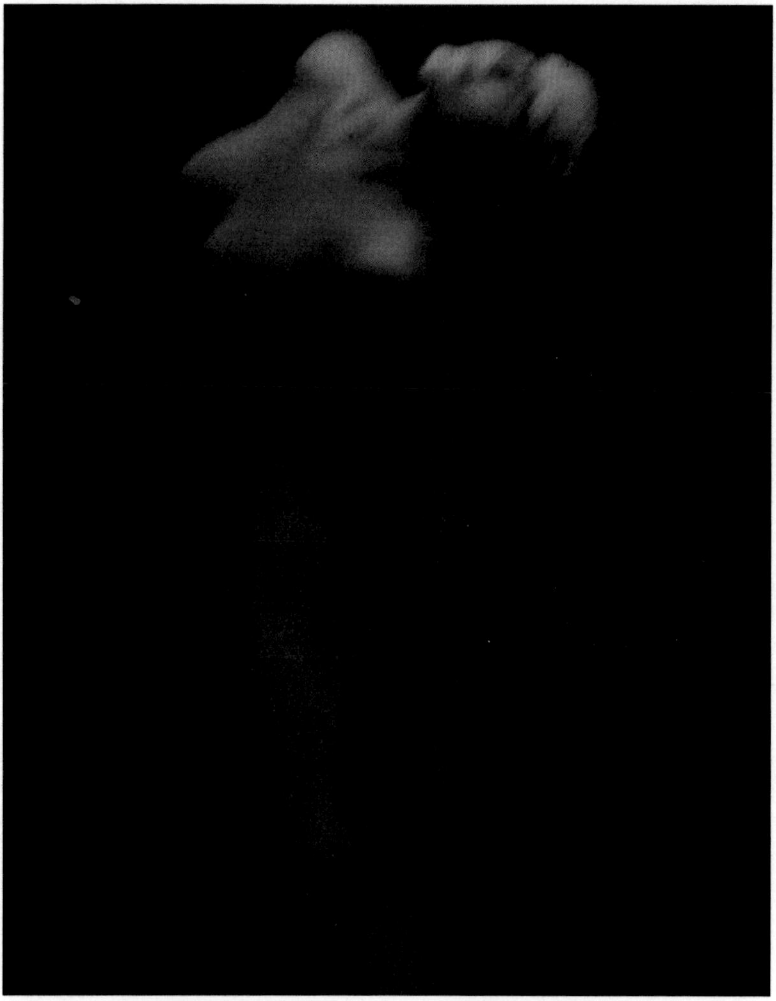

Fig.4.7 Rogi André (Rosza Klein) (1900–70), *Jacqueline Breton: la nymphe*, Recueil.EP-825-BOITE FOL. © Paris, Bibliothèque nationale de France (BnF). Photo © BnF, Dist. RMN-Grand Palais / image BnF.

on her back is only visible if one has the film in hand: she disappears as soon as the image is projected onto the screen (fig.4.8). As Patrick de Haas has commented in *Cinema intégral*:

> Whereas, in order to restore the semblance of continuous movement, cinema must be recorded discontinuously and projected discontinuously (with camera shutter and Maltese-cross projector mechanism), Man Ray makes continuous impressions which are then separated by the projector. Nothing more can be grasped by the eye.[65]

A radical way, in short, to create the 'dissolved young girl': she will have been pulverised within time itself, as in the sensory mechanism of the persistence of vision. Man Ray, we know, went on to make many other experiments of this type, particularly in *L'Étoile de mer*. Here the optic itself has become a *fluid medium* as if the nymph – Kiki de Montparnasse, in this instance – was being viewed through eyes filled with tears.[66]

This is what Pierre Kaufmann, in his great work on *L'Expérience émotionelle de l'espace* called the 'emotional spatialisation of desire': a process which generates all the dynamics of images, confronting us with the experience of a 'fluid world in which the fickle polarities can easily be reversed [as can] the content itself of what is being represented'.[67] To cite only one of many possible examples, when Jean Painlevé exaggerates the disproportion of a photograph of the male hippocampus, he produces an image that inescapably evokes a vulva with all the detail of its 'nymphes', i.e. the labia minora (fig.4.9).[68] This can also be observed in many cases of 'integral' or 'experimental cinema' which often evoke the effects of the *generalised fluidification* of the visible, moving world which these films show us.[69]

Before Eric Thouvenel mapped it out precisely,[70] Gilles Deleuze had expressed a philosophical view of the importance of the *fluid motif*

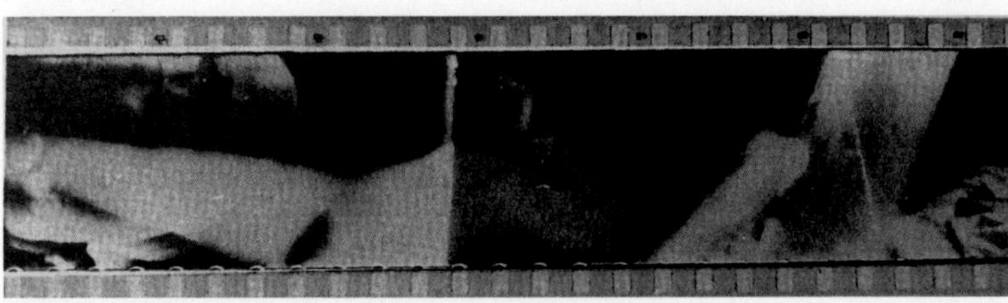

Fig.4.8 Man Ray (1890–1976), *Le Retour à la raison*, 1923. Segment of the film roll, Paris, Centre Georges Pompidou.

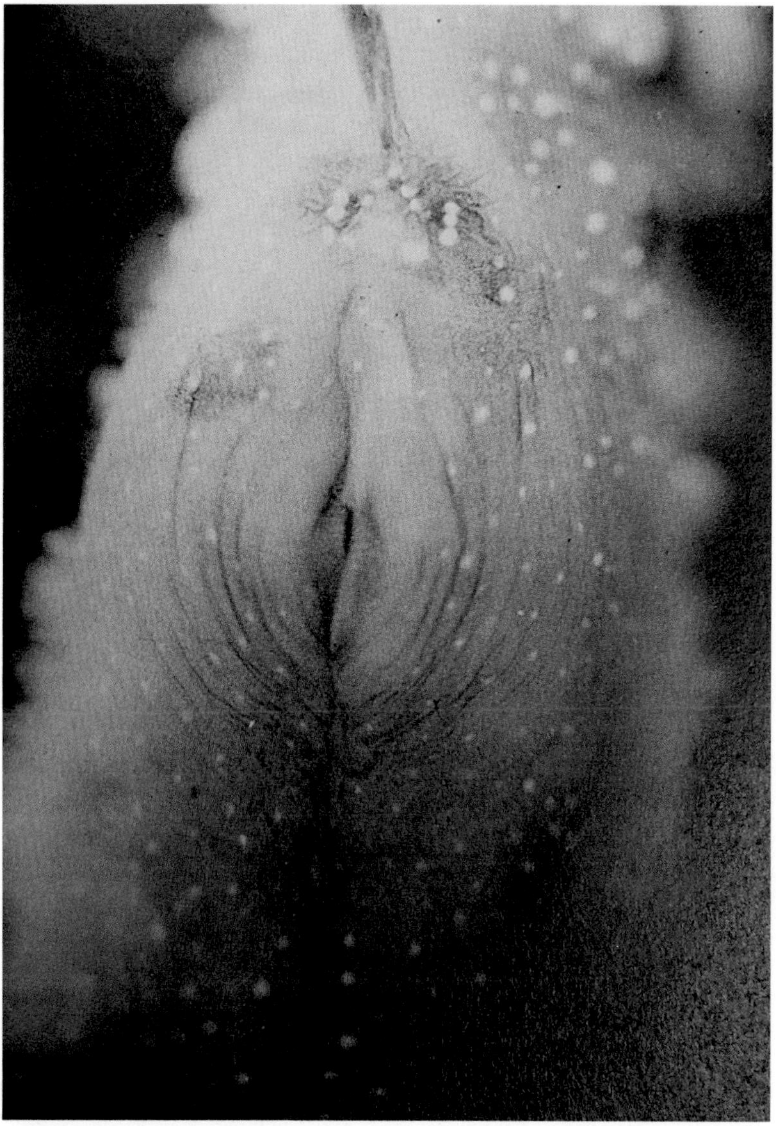

Fig.4.9 Jean Painlevé (1902–89), *Ouverture de la poche incubatrice du mâle hippocampe*, 1931. Silverprint. © Paris, Les documents cinématographiques.

in 1920s French cinema. Starting from his idea of cinematography as involving 'mobile sections', he observed that in Jean Epstein's work this created an original 'temporal perspective', inscribed in the image like an 'undulating' effect.[71] It is as if, at a certain time:

> the transition from a mechanism of solids to a mechanism of fluids[...] was going to find in the liquid image a new extension of movement in its entirety: better conditions in which to move from the concrete to the abstract, a greater possibility of communicating an irreversible lifespan to movements independently of their figurative character, a more certain ability to extract the movement of the object moved. [...] It was the French school that liberated the subject of water, giving it its own purpose and making it the form of things that lack organic solidity.[72]

Thus, in the work of Jean Renoir, Jean Vigo, Marcel L'Herbier, Jean Grémillon and Jean Epstein, Deleuze found that 'water is the medium *par excellence* from which we can extract the motion of the object moved and the mobility of movement itself'. This can be achieved through something that Deleuze would eventually call a 'liquid abstract', through which pure rhythms pass.[73]

What, then, is this 'liquid abstract' that Gilles Deleuze wanted to isolate in time itself, where it is also a question of isolating – abstracting, indeed purifying – this movement, starting from the moving subject? How is this possible in an image? Is it really possible to abstract 'pure movements' in the films in question? It is easily understood that they are 'aberrant', as demonstrated by David Lapoujade; this seems to be an essential element of their singularity.[74] But why do they need to be 'pure'? And why are they excluded from any form of 'organic consistency'?

No doubt Deleuze was seeking to liberate movement from its single figurative meaning, and that was why he proposed such a transition from the 'concrete' to the 'abstract'. But this is, in fact, a false polarity – or a false problem – as when a wave is photographed like the ghost of a body (fig.4.6) or when a simple, blurry opening conjures up a sexual organ in the montage itself and within the *Stimmung* (mood) that this image insinuates into our thoughts. How can we desire without our organs? And how, without our organs, would we feel desire taking hold of us? When we are looking at – and indeed even more when we imagine looking at – the intimate parts of a body or inside a body, does the opposition between the abstract and the concrete not fall away before the *emotional strangeness of the space* which comes into play at that moment? If there is a 'wave of hypochondria' in Victor Hugo's work – but also in that of Vigo or Epstein – is this not a question of *organic intensity* in the 'aberrant movements' and in the *de-figurative* space, rather than of an abstract or *a-figurative* grandeur?

In his 1931 film *La Natation par Jean Taris*, Jean Vigo in no way showed a 'pure environment' of fluidity or an environment of 'pure movements'. He rather portrayed the dialectic of a fluid environment, resculpted at every moment by the swimmer's organic and technical gestures – even down to his breathing – which transforms the watery space into a scene full of the splendour of the motions of the air and light escaping from his mouth.[75] In *L'Atalante* Vigo shows us in lyrical terms, just as Victor Hugo once did in *Les Travailleurs de la mer*, what it is to *sink into love* when love is unhappy. Here, the nymph becomes all too present and yet inaccessible. Inhabiting the depths of the water, she dances slowly down there like a ghost, while the man who still desires her is at the point of expiring (fig.4.10).[76]

Jean Epstein, for his part, never advocated nor filmed 'pure abstract movements', detached from the organ or material that produces them. When the movement of the waves goes into slow motion in that famous, magical moment in *Tempestaire*, a sort of anthropomorphism or animism (both words used by the director himself) is at its peak: the ocean becomes the organ of excess, *par excellence*. When the storm blows itself out, it is almost as if it had stopped breathing, or decided to suspend its murderous attack on the creatures that had set off on their marine

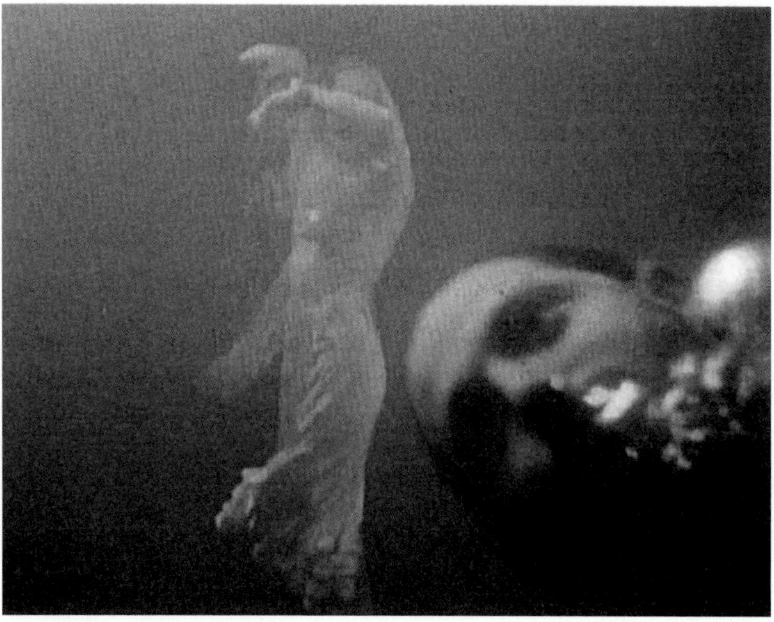

Fig.4.10 Jean Vigo (1905–34), *L'Atalante*, 1934; photographic still from the film.

adventure.[77] As early as 1928, Epstein had written that slow motion was a technique for making visible the idea of ebb and flow, the *intimate backwash of emotion* itself, whether it is the emotion – the motion, the internal movement – of a cloud, a wave or a face:

> I know nothing so completely moving as a slow-motion depiction of a face shaping itself into an expression. First the preparatory movement, a slow feverishness – we are unsure whether to compare it to a morbid incubation, to a progressive maturity, or, more crudely, to a pregnancy. Then, finally, all that effort overflows, releasing the stiffness of the muscles. Contagious movements animate the face. The eyelashes flutter and the chin trembles. And when the lips finally separate to let out a cry, we have been witness to a prolonged magnificent dawn.[78]

Both in his techniques and in his overarching themes, Epstein always conceived of cinema as an anthropomorphic drama consisting of 'moving spaces' and 'floating time';[79] it is driven by a 'fluid logic', created above all to 'penetrate into the self'.[80][...]The essential fluidity of cinema, its psychological effectiveness, was still a question of 'pathos formulae', empathetic processes and even survival. From that point onwards cinema did not need to choose to be 'concrete' or 'abstract', 'figurative' or 'non-organic', a 'thing in motion' or 'pure motion'. It generates all these states simultaneously and invents their very point of coalescence, in the place where *milieu and passion* are no longer opposites. Interestingly, in his famous article on 'cineplastics' of 1920, Élie Faure took issue with this opposition,[81] using the paradigm of a cloud of dust and a volcanic eruption to make us understand that this opposition cannot exist – as within cinema, as we so often see, the *milieu is the passion* and the *passion is the milieu.*[82]

One classic example of this coalescence is in Victor Sjöström's film *The Wind*. In his analysis of it Gilles Deleuze was anxious to maintain the distinction between the 'physical duel with the milieu' and the 'sentimental duel' that causes the heroine to struggle between the 'boorish cowboy who is in love with her' and the 'livestock merchant who wants to rape her'.[83] The whole film proceeds, right from the start, towards the ineluctable conclusion of *a rape by the milieu itself,* that is to say, by the wind. The significance of survival in this film becomes clear. Certainly, times have changed since Botticelli – the American desert lacks the charms of the Florentine springtime and Zephyr is no longer there to puff out his cheeks and launch the beautiful body of an antique god into flight.

But the terrible gusts of the desert wind, thrusting against the windows of the train and then against the young girl herself – surrendered to the elements as if to some cruel divinity – possess no less organic and ghostly power. This force is that of a *genitalis spiritus,* an atmospheric torment taking on the character of a terrifyingly violent sexual one.[84]

In this sense, we could take a fresh look at a number of famous films, starting with Roberto Rossellini's *Stromboli,* in which the excellent *mattanza* (tuna fishing) sequence engulfs the heroine in the cosmic and sperm-like aggression of the sea spray, whipped up by the slaughter.[85] Whether epic (as in John Ford's *The Hurricane*) or burlesque (as in Buster Keaton's *Steamboat Bill Junior*), the wind often appears as a separate character in itself – sometimes monochrome and evanescent, like Zephyr in Botticelli's *Primavera,* a god of desire in incessant pursuit of his nymphs. Just as it blows up faces out of proportion on the big screen (described so well by Jean Epstein), so cinema *blows up desire out of proportion* and takes it to fantastical levels of metaphor – as with Shohei Imamura's moving female fountain in *De l'eau tiède sous un pont rouge*, or in Hiroshi Teshigahara's troubled *Femme des Sables*.

Ninfa fluida is like the wind, which nonetheless threatens her: she can go anywhere, intrude, curl up or whirl here and there[...] Her very grace is the tenuous but tenacious sign of her survival. What an ignorant error it is to claim, as Alain Corbin did recently, that 'the girls who are the stuff of dreams vanished' after the nineteenth century![86] What pessimistic hyperbole it was for Peter Sloterdijk to draw a direct connection between 'being born of the foamy surf of the waves' (from Hesiod to Botticelli) and the gases used in the trenches of the First World War and in the death camps of the Second.[87] What reductivism to make a direct association between the 'life in liquid' and the 'life in fragments', as Zygmunt Bauman has done,[88] along with the idea of the 'young girl' as a pure product of commercial society.[89] Without even mentioning Warburg, should we not rather extend the 'domain of the nymph' in the terms that Elias Canetti might have used in *Crowds and Power* – to evoke the sea and the wind as paradigms that are always susceptible to new values?[90] Should we not simply say that *Ninfa* is indestructible in the sense in which Freud, following Spinoza, spoke of desire itself (a desire *Ninfa* embodies) as motion that is supremely indestructible?

Ninfa's youth is therefore ageless. For us she is so ancient only because she is able to navigate our contemporary era. She is so contemporary only because she never ceases to return from afar. She travels through the 'liquid intelligence' of photography referred to by Jeff Wall, and the 'poetry of fluids' of cinematic montage discussed by Térésa

Faucon.[91] She is everywhere in the 'figural unease' inherent in video images, from Nam June Paik to Bill Viola or Thierry Kuntzel.[92] We can recognise her just about everywhere, in the most diverse contemporary art forms.[93] Michael Diers has found her in the Dionysiac character invented by Pipilotti Rist; Luis Pérez-Oramas sees her once again in the dancing draperies of Brazilian *parangolé*, as interpreted by Hélio Oiticica, Lygia Clark or Willys de Castro.[94] Nor should we be surprised that the bouquet of flowers dragged along by the current in Jean Vigo's *L'Atalante* evokes some metamorphosis or immemorial ceremony, while at the same time pointing forward to the performances and films of Ana Mendieta – that contemporary *Ninfa* who wanted to dissolve her desire, and indeed her body, in the fluidity of the world (fig.4.11).[95]

Acknowledgements

This essay was originally published in French as the last section of Georges Didi-Huberman, *Ninfa fluida: essai sur le drapé-désir* (Paris: Gallimard, 2015), 125–67, 188–96. In agreement with the author, some passages have been omitted from the original text. These omissions are indicated in the text.

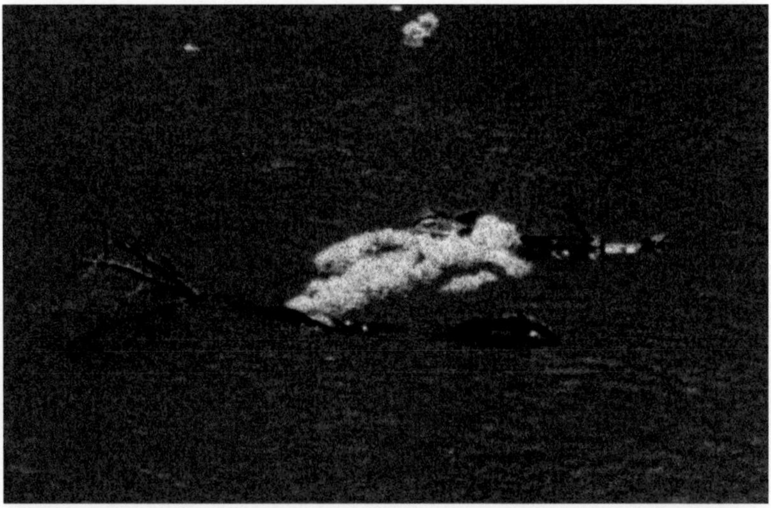

Fig.4.11 Ana Mendieta (1948–85), *Flower Person, Flower Body*, 1975, Super-8mm film transferred to high-definition media, colour, silent; running time: 6:20 minutes, edition of 6 + 3 Aps (GP1218). © The Estate of Ana Mendieta Collection, LLC. Courtesy Galerie Lelong & Co.

Notes

1 Aby Warburg, *Tagebuch der Kulturwissenschaftlichen Bibliothek Warburg mit Einträgen von Gertrud Bing und Fritz Saxl* (1926–8), ed. Karen Michels and Charlotte Schoell-Glass (Berlin: Akademie Verlag, 2001), 536 (25 September 1929); commented by Karl Sierek, *Images oiseaux, Aby Warburg et la théorie des médias* (2007), trans. Pierre Rusch (Paris: Klinksieck, 2009), 44–55.

2 Aby Warburg, *Sandro Botticellis 'Geburt der Venus' und 'Frühling'. Eine Untersuchung über die Vorstellungen von der Antike in der Italienischen Frührenaissance* (Hamburg and Leipzig: Leopold Voss, 1893), 20; repr. under the title *Die Erneuerung der heidnischen Antike: Kutlturwissenschaftliche Beiträge zur Geschichte der Europäischen Renaissance*, ed. Gertrude Bing and Fritz Rougemont (Leipzig: B. G. Teubner Verlag, 1932); trans. by David Britt, *The Renewal of Pagan Antiquity* (Los Angeles: Getty Research Institute for the History of Art and the Humanities, 1999), 107. [Note of the editors: the English translation does not keep the original French expression and reads 'imaginary breeze'.]

3 Paul Mantz, 'Galerie de M. G. Rothan', *Gazette des Beaux-Arts*, 2eme période, VII (1873): 283; repr. Paris: J. Claye, 1873, 11. I should like to thank Jean-Didier Wagneur for his help with this research.

4 Gustave Mendel, *Catalogue des sculptures grecques, romaines et byzantines* (Constantinople: Musées impériaux ottomans, 1912), 301.

5 Auguste de Villiers de L'Isle-Adam, *L'Ève future* (1886), ed. Alan Raitt (Paris: Gallimard, 1993), 166. The copy in the Warburg Library (Paris: Charpentier, 1891), 154, can be found under EBH pressmark trans. Robert Martin Adams, *Tomorrow's Eve* (Urbana: University of Illinois Press, 1982), 92.

6 Warburg, *The Renewal*, 112.

7 Aby Warburg, '"Le Déjeuner sur l'herbe" de Manet. La fonction préfiguratrice des divinités élémentaires païennes pour l'évolution du sentiment moderne de la nature' (1929), in *Miroirs de faille. À Rome avec Giordano Bruno et Édouard Manet, 1928–9*, ed. Maurizio Ghelardi, trans. Sacha Zilberfarb (Paris and Dijon: Atelier L'Écarquillé-Les Presses du réel, 2011), 125–36; see also Marie-Anne Lescourret, *Aby Warburg ou la tentation du regard. Une biographie* (Paris: Hazan, 2014), 150.

8 See Jean Rouch, *Orages et tempêtes dans la littérature* (Paris: Société d'Éditions géographiques, 1929); Simon Leys, *La Mer dans la littérature française (*Paris: Plon, 2003); Marie Blain-Pinel, *'La Mer, miroir d'infini'. La métaphore marine dans la poésie romantique* (Rennes: Presses universitaire de Rennes, 2003); Esperanza Guillén Marcos, *Naufragios. Imágenes románticas de la desperación* (Madrid: Ediciones Siruela, 2004). *'Cet immense rêve de l'océan'[...]Paysages de mer et autres sujets marins par Victor Hugo*, ed. Pierre Georgel (Paris : Maison Victor Hugo-Paris Musées, 2005); *Corps submergés, corps engloutis. Une histoire des noyés et de la noyade de L'Antiquité à nos jours*, ed. Frédéric Chavaud (Paris: Creaphis Éditions, 2007); *Muses et nymphes du XIXème siècle*, ed. Éric Francalanza (Bordeaux: Presses universitaires de Bordeaux, 2011).

9 Friedrich Hölderlin, *Hyperion, Thalia Fragment, 1794*, trans. Karl W. Maurer (Winnipeg: The Hölderlin Society, 1968), 15–17.

10 Léon Heuzey, *Recherches sur les figures de femmes voilées dans l'art grec* (Paris: Chamerot, 1873); Heuzey, *'Du principe de la draperie antique'*, in *Dictionnaire de l'Académie des beaux-arts* V (Paris: Firmin-Didot, 1896), 186–206; Heuzey, *'La chlamyde grecque étudiée sur le modèle vivant'*, in *Revue de l'art ancien et moderne* XXXIX, (1921): 12–31; Heuzey, *Le Péplos des femmes grecques étudié sur le modèle vivant* (Paris: Leroux, 1921); Heuzey, *Histoire du costume antique, d'après des études sur le modèle vivant* (Paris: Honoré Champion, 1922).

11 Maurice Emmanuel, *La Danse grecque antique d'après les monuments figurés* (Paris: Hachette, 1896; repr. Geneva: Slatkine Reprints, 1987). See Georges Didi-Huberman, *L'image survivante. Histoire de l'art et temps des fantômes selon Aby Warburg* (Paris: Editions de Minuit, 2002), 259–64.

12 Georges Didi-Huberman and Laurent Mannonni, *Mouvements de l'air. Étienne-Jules Marey, photographe des fluides*, exh. cat., Musée d'Orsay (Paris: Gallimard-RMN, 2004).

13 Philippe-Alain Michaud, *Aby Warburg et l'image en mouvement* (Paris: Macula, 1998, repr. 2012).

14 See Gerhard Neumann, Günter Schnitzler, Gabriele Brandstetter and Brygida Ochaim, *Loïe Fuller. Tanz, Licht-Spiel, Art Nouveau* (Fribourg: Rombach 1989); Giovanni Lista, *Loïe Fuller:*

danseuse de la Belle Époque (Paris: Stock-Éditions d'art Somogy, 1994); Lista, 'Loïe Fuller and her serpentine dance', in *Body stages: the metamorphosis of Loïe Fuller*, ed. Aurora Herrera Gomez (Milan: Skira, 2014), 29–41.

15 Warburg, *The Renewal*, 405. Warburg's own annotated copy including cut-out images (London, Warburg Institute Archive, III.40.1.1) refers too to the article by Ziegler regarding not only Novalis, but also Schiller and Schelling: Theobald Ziegler, '*Zur Genesis eines äesthetischen Begriffs*', *Zeitschrift für vergleichende Literaturgeschichte*, N.S. VII (1894): 113–20.

16 Wilhelm Dilthey, 'Three Epochs of Modern Aesthetics' (1892), in *Selected Works* V, *Poetry and Experience*, ed. Rudolf A. Makkreel and Frithjof Rodi (Princeton, NJ: Princeton University Press, 1985), 182–8.

17 Dilthey, 1892, 188.

18 Dilthey, 1892, 182–3.

19 Dilthey, 1892, 218.

20 Dilthey, 1892, 175.

21 Dilthey, 1892, 176–7.

22 Dilthey, 1892, 210.

23 Dilthey, 1892, 211.

24 Henri Bergson, '*L'Évolution créatrice*' (1907), in *Œuvres*, ed. André Robinet (Paris: PUF, 1959), *495–500; Creative evolution* (*L'Évolution créatrice*), trans. Arthur Mitchell (Mineola, NY: Dover Publications: 1998), 18.

25 See Georges Didi-Huberman, *La Peinture incarnée* (Paris: Les Éditions de Minuit, 1985), *130–2*. Didi-Huberman, '*La couleur d'écume, ou le paradoxe d'Apelle*' (1986), in *L'Image ouverte. Motifs de l'incarnation dans les arts visuels* (Paris: Gallimard, 2007), 67–95.

26 Lucien Lévy-Bruhl, *Les Fonctions mentales dans les sociétés inférieures* (Paris: Alcan, 1910), 68–110 and 352–78.

27 Lucien Lévy-Bruhl, *Carnets* (1938–9) (Paris: PUF, 1949, repr. 1998), 1; *The notebooks on primitive mentality*, trans. Peter Rivière (Oxford: Blackwell, 1975), 1.

28 Lévy-Bruhl, *The Notebooks* 1975, 18 (as well as 76–80).

29 Lévy-Bruhl, *The Notebooks* 1975, 4, 7–13, 83–6 and 191–4.

30 Lévy-Bruhl, *The Notebooks* 1975, xvi.

31 Lévy-Bruhl, *The Notebooks* 1975, 109–10.

32 Lévy-Bruhl, *The Notebooks* 1975, 119 and 134.

33 Claude Lévi-Strauss, *Histoire de lynx* (Paris: Plon, 1991), 251; *The story of Lynx*, trans. Catherine Tihanyi (Chicago: The University of Chicago Press, 1996), 187.

34 See Sandor Ferenczi, *Thalassa, a theory of genitality*, trans. Henry Alden Bunker (Albany, NY: The Psychoanalytic Quaterly, 1938), 73–107.

35 Cf. Karoly Kerényi in Carl Gustav Jung and Karoly Kerényi, *Essays on a Science of Mythology, The Myth of the Divine Child and the Divine Maiden* (1941), trans. R. F. C. Hull (Princeton, NJ: Princeton University Press, 1963, repr. 1969), 101–77; Geza Róheim,'Aphrodite, or the woman with a penis' (1945), in *The Panic of the Gods and Other Essays*, ed. Werner Muensterberger (New York: Harper & Row, 1972), 169–205; Marcel Griaule, *Dieu d'eau. Entretiens avec Ogotemmêli* (Paris: Fayard, 1991, repr. 1996); Georges Devereux, *Femme et mythe* (Paris: Flammarion, 1982, repr. 1988), 97–126 ('La naissance d'Aphrodite').

36 See Georges Dumézil, *Mythe et épopée,* III. *Histoires romaines* (Paris: Gallimard, 1973, repr. 1995), 1090–161, esp. 1149–55 ; Dumézil, *La Religion romaine archaïque* (Paris: Payot, 1974, repr. 1987), 393–4. On the Christian world see Pierre Saintyves, *En marge de la Légende dorée: songes, miracles et survivances. Essai sur la formation de quelques thèmes hagiographiques* (1930), (Paris: Nourry-Robert Laffont, 1987), 741–65.

37 Gaston Bachelard, *L'Air et les songes. Essai sur l'imagination du mouvement* (Paris: José Corti, 1943), 7; trans. Edith R. Farrell and C. Frederick Farrell, *Air and dreams: an essay on the imagination of movement*, (Dallas: Dallas Institute Publications, 1988), 1.

38 Bachelard, *Air*, 1988, 6–7.

39 Bachelard, *Air*, 1988, 12–13.

40 Gaston Bachelard, *L'Eau et les rêves. Essai sur l'imagination de la matière* (Paris: José Corti, 1942), 3–4; *Water and Dreams: an essay on the imagination of matter*, trans. Edith R. Farrell and C. Frederick Farrell (Dallas: Pegasus Foundation, 1983), 2.

41 Bachelard, *Water*, 1983, 10.

42 Bachelard, *Water*, 1983, 160.

43 Bachelard, *Water*, 1983, 80–92.

44 Bachelard, *Water*, 1983, 33–4 and 86.
45 Bachelard, *Water*, 1983, 126.
46 Marcel Proust, *À la recherche du temps perdu*, I. *Du côté de chez Swann* (1918–19), ed. Pierre Clarac and André Ferré (Paris: Gallimard, 1954), 222; *In search of lost time. 1 Swann's way*, trans. C. K. Scott Moncrieff and Terence Kilmartin (New York: Vintage, 2005), 267.
47 Proust, *Lost Time*, 2005, 337.
48 See Hélène Pinet, '*L'eau, la femme, la mort. Le mythe de L'Inconnue de la Seine*', in *Le dernier portrait*, exh. cat., Musée d'Orsay (Paris: RMN, 2002), 175–90 ; Bernard Tillier, *La Belle Noyée, Enquête sur le masque de l'Inconnue de la Seine* (Paris: Arkhê, 2011).
49 See Clément Chéroux and Andreas Fischer, ed., *Le Troisième Œil. La photographie et l'occulte* (Paris: Gallimard, 2004); Joseph Imorde, 'Schleier aus dem Nichts. Materialisationsphänomene und ihre Dokumente', in *Ikonologie des Zwischenraums. Der Schleier als Medium und Metapher*, Johannes Endres, Barbara Wittmann and Gearhard Wolf, ed. (Munich: Wilhelm Fink Verlag, 2005), 361–84.
50 Cf. Herwig Guratzsch, ed., *Max Klinger, Bestandskatalog der Bildwerke, Gemälde und Zeichnungen im Museum der bildende Künste Leipzig* (Leipzig: Seemann Verlag, 1995); Jo-Anne Birnie Danzker and Tilman Falk, ed. *Max Klinger: Zeichnungen, Zustandsdrucke, Zyklen* (Munich: Staatliche Graphische Sammlung-Prestel Verlag, 1996); Beatrice Buscaroli Fabbri ed., *Max Klinger*, exh. cat., Palazzo dei Diamanti (Ferrara: Ferrara Arte Editore, 1996).
51 See Jacques Le Rider, *Freud, de L'Acropole au Sinaï. Le retour à l'Antique des Modernes viennois* (Paris: PUF, 2002).
52 Ferdinand de Saussure, *Cours de linguistique générale* (1906–11), ed. Charles Bally and Albert Sechehaye (1915), revised by Tullio de Mauro (Paris: Payot, 1972), 155–6.
53 See Denis Perrin, *Le Flux et l'instant. Wittgenstein aux prises avec le mythe du présent* (Paris: Vrin, 2007).
54 Sigmund Freud, 'Urinary Symbolism' (1914), in *The Interpretation of Dreams*, trans. James Strachey (London: Allen & Unwin, 1954), 367–8.
55 Ludwig Binswanger, 'Dream & Existence', ed. Keith Hoeller, introduction by Michel Foucault, *Review of existential psychology & psychiatry* 19, no.1 (1984–5): 82.
56 See Georges Didi-Huberman, *Phalènes. Essais sur l'apparition* 2 (Paris: Éditions de Minuit, 2013), 9–78.
57 See Tobias G. Natter and Max Hollein, ed., *The Naked Truth, Klimt, Schiele, Kokoschka and Other Scandals*, exh. cat., Schirn Kunsthalle, Frankfurt and Leopold Museum, Vienna (Munich, Berlin, London, New York: Prestel, 2005), 181.
58 Pierre Louÿs, 'Connette et Chloris' (not dated), *Œuvre érotique*, ed. Jean-Paul Goujon (Paris: Robert Laffont, 2012), 432–66; see also Louÿs, *Le Crépuscule des Nymphes* (Paris: Briant-Robert, 1926).
59 Georges Bataille, 'Chevelures' (1937), in *Œuvres complètes* I (Paris: Gallimard, 1970), 495–6.
60 Bataille, *Le Mort* (about 1944), in *Œuvres complètes* IV (Paris: Gallimard, 1971), 44–5; *My Mother: Madame Edwarda, The Dead Man*, trans. Austryn Wainhouse (London: Penguin Books, 2012), 168–95.
61 Salvador Dalí, 'De la beauté terrifiante et comestible, de l'architecture Modern Style' suivi de 'Le phénomène de l'extase', *Minotaure* 3–4 (1933): 68–77.
62 Jean Arp, 'L'air est une racine', in *Le Surréalisme au service de la révolution* 6 (1933): 33.
63 See Giovanni Lista, *Cinema e fotografia futurista*, exh. cat., Museo di arte contemporanea di Trento e Rovereto (Milan: Skira, 2001); reviewed and augmented ed., *Cinéma et photographie futuristes*, trans. Lidwine Tamburini (Milan: Skira, 2008), 178–209.
64 André Breton, 'La nuit du tournesol', *Minotaure* 7 (1935): 48; Breton, *L'Amour fou* (Paris: Gallimard, 1937), 92; see Quentin Bajac and Clément Chéroux, ed., *La subversion des images. Surréalisme, photographie, film*, exh. cat., Centre Pompidou in collaboration with the Fundación Mapfre, Madrid and the Fotomuseum Winterthur (Paris: Éditions du Centre Pompidou, 2009), 368–9.
65 Patrick de Haas, *Cinéma intégral. De la peinture au cinéma dans les années vingt* (Paris: Transédition, 1985), 111.
66 See Jean-Michel Bouhours and Patrick de Haas, ed., *Man Ray, directeur du mauvais movies* (Paris: Éditions du Centre Pompidou, 1997), 58–83; Georges Didi-Huberman, 'L'espace danse. Étoile de mer Explosante-fixe' in *Les Cahiers du Musée national d'art moderne*, 94 (2005–6): 37–51.
67 Pierre Kaufmann, *L'Expérience émotionnelle de l'espace* (Paris: Vrin, 1967), 187–91 and 265.

68 For other examples see Ralph Rugoff, 'Fluid Mechanics', in *Science Is Fiction: the Films of Jean Painlevé*, A. M. Bellows and M. McDougall, ed. (Cambridge-London-San Francisco: The MIT Press-Brico Press, 2000), 48–57.

69 See Patrick de Haas, *Cinéma intégral*, 19–86; P. Adams Sitney, *Visionary film: the American avant-garde* (Oxford: Oxford University Press, 1979), 136–12. Adams Sitney, *Eyes Upside Down: Visionary Filmmakers and the Heritage of Emerson* (New York: Oxford University Press, 2008). I should like to thank P. Adams Sitney for bringing numerous 'fluid films' to my attention (in 2002 in Los Angeles) in the work of Ralph Steiner, Paul Sharits, Hollis Frampton, George Landow, Stan Brackhage, Su Friedrich, James Broughton, Jordan Belson and Michael Snow.

70 Eric Thouvenel, *Les Images de l'eau dans le cinéma français des années 20* (Rennes: Presses universitaires de Rennes, 2010).

71 Gilles Deleuze, *L'Image-mouvement, Cinéma 1* (Paris: Éditions de Minuit, 1983), 39.

72 Deleuze, 1983, 65.

73 Deleuze, 1983, 111–16.

74 See David Lapoujade, *Deleuze, les mouvements aberrants* (Paris: Éditions de Minuit, 2014).

75 Jean Vigo, *Œuvre de cinéma. Films, scénarios, projets de films, textes sur le cinéma (1929–34)*, Pierre Lherminier, ed. (Paris: La Cinémathèque française-Éditions Pierre Lherminier, 1985), 97–112. See also the film project 'La revanche des eaux', Vigo, *Oeuvre*, 1985, 411-12.

76 Vigo, *OEuvre*. 311.

77 See Philippe Dubois, 'La tempête et la matière temps, ou le sublime et le figural dans l'œuvre de Jean Epstein', in *Jean Epstein cinéaste, poète, philosophe*, ed. Jacques Aumont (Paris: Cinémathèque française, 1998), 267–323; Roger Odin, *De la fiction* (Brussels: De Boeck Université, 2000), 113–25. Vincent Guigeno, *Jean Epstein, cinéaste des îles. Ouessant, Sein, Hoëdic, Belle-Ile* (Paris: Jean-Michel Place, 2003).

78 Jean Epstein, *'L'âme au ralenti'* (1928). *Écrits sur le cinéma, 1921–1953,* I, ed. Pierre Leprohon (Paris: Éditions Seghers, 1974), 191; reprinted in *Écrits complets, III, 1928–1938*, ed. Nicole Brenez, Joël Daire and Cyril Neyrat (Paris: Independencia Éditions, 2014), 137.

79 Epstein, 'Le Cinéma du diable' (1947), in *Écrits sur le cinéma, 1921-1953*, I, 364–84.

80 Epstein, *'Le monde fluide de l'écran'* (1950), *Écrits sur le cinéma, 1921-1953*, II, ed. Pierre Leprohon (Paris, Éditions Seghers, 1975), 145–58 *; Epstein, 'Alcool et cinéma'* (1953), *Écrits sur le cinéma, 1921–1953* II , 210–15 and 229–34. It was in regard to Epstein that Edgar Morin spoke of the new 'realist universe of cinema' as a 'fluid universe'. Edgar Morin, *Le cinéma ou l'homme imaginaire. Essai d'anthropologie sociologique* (Paris: Éditions de Minuit, 1956), 71–2.

81 Élie Faure, 'De la cinéplastique' (1920), in *Cinéma* (Houilles: Éditions Manucius, 2010), 21.

82 Faure, 'De la cinéplastique', 31–3.

83 Deleuze, *L'image-mouvement,* 198–9.

84 See Fabienne Costa, 'La fiancée du vent', *Simulacres* 8 (2003): 75–81.

85 See Frank Fehrenbach, 'Mare nero. Meeresbilder bei Visconti, Rossellini, Antonioni und Fellini', in *Das Meer, Der Tausch und die Grenzen der Räpresentation* (Zürich: u.a., 2010), 163–90.

86 Alain Corbin, *Les Filles de rêve* (Paris: Fayard, 2014), 9.

87 Peter Sloterdijk, 'Foam: plural spherology', in *Bubbles: microspherology* 3, trans. Wieland Hoban (Los Angeles: Semiotext, 2011).

88 See Zygmunt Bauman, *Life in Fragments: Essays in Postmodern Morality* (Oxford: Blackwell, 1995, repr. 1998); Bauman, *Liquid Life* (Cambridge and Malden: Polity Press, 2005).

89 Tiqqun, *Premiers matériaux pour une théorie de la Jeune-Fille* (Paris: Mille et Une Nuits, 2001, repr. 2006).

90 Elias Canetti, *Crowds and Power* (1960), trans. Carol Stewart (Harmondsworth: Penguin, 1973), 75–90.

91 Jeff Wall, 'Photography and Liquid Intelligence' (1989), first published in French and English as 'Photographie et intelligence liquide', in *Une autre objectivité/Another objectivity*, ed. Jean-Francois Chevrier and James Lingwood, exh. cat. (Milan: Idea Books for Centre National des Arts Plastiques, Paris and Prato: Centro per l'Arte Contemporanea Luigi Pecci, 1989), now in *Jeff Wall: Selected essays and interviews*, ed. Peter Galassi (New York: Museum of Modern Art, 2007), 109–10; Térésa Faucon, *Théorie du montage, Énergie, forces et fluides* (Paris: Armand Colin, 2013).

92 See Sophie-Isabelle Dufour, *L'Image vidéo, d'Ovide à Bill Viola* (Paris: Archibooks-Sautereau Éditeur, 2008), 60–79.

93 See notably *Body as Membrane*, ed. Lene Burkard, Kirsten Justesen and Karsten Ohrt, exh. cat. (Odense, Denmark: Kunsthallen Brandts Klædefabrik, 1996); Karlheinz Lüdeking, *Grenzen des*

Sichtbaren (Munich: Wilhelm Fink Verlag, 2006), 195–212; Yvonne Volkart, *Fluide Subjekte. Anpassung und Widerspenstigkeit in der Medienkunst* (Bielefield: Transcript Verlag, 2006).

94 See Michael Diers, '*Die Gegenwart der Bilder. Zu Erinnerung der Antike bei Aby Warburg*' (2001) in *Fotografie Film Video. Beiträge zu einer kritischen Theorie des Bildes*, ed. Michael Diers (Hamburg: Philo & Philo Fine Arts, 2006), 299–332. Luis Pérez-Oramas, 'Parangolé-Botticelli: installation thinking and practical reason of the art history. Transitional form and carnival geometry', *ARS (São Paulo)* [online], 15, n.30, (2017): 233–54, ISSN 1678-5320. http://dx.doi.org/10.11606/issn.2178-0447.ars.2017.138471.

95 See Olga M. Viso, *Unseen Mendieta. The Unpublished Works of Ana Mendieta* (Munich, Berlin, London and New York: Prestel, 2008), 114–17; Anne Creissels, *Prêter son corps au mythe. Le féminin dans l'art contemporain* (Paris: Éditions du Félin, 2009), 55–70.

13. Into the abyss. On Salvador Dalí's *Dream of Venus*

Riccardo Venturi

The *Dream of Venus* (1939, fig. 4.12), the most uncanny environment the Catalan artist Salvador Dalí (1904–89) ever conceived, is one of the most accomplished examples of surrealist architecture.[1] Through looking at the role played by the art historical references Dalí makes to works such as Botticelli's *The Birth of Venus* (fig.1.0), this essay will address the artist's unresolved relationships with modernism.

The New York World's Fair & the *Dream of Venus* project

Realised for the 1939 New York World's Fair, the idea of the *Dream of Venus* started with the New York gallerist Julien Levy, the first to show surrealism in New York. Levy's idea was that a surrealist pavilion would make the French movement more popular in America. Ultimately, however, despite the huge public success of the Museum of Modern Art's *Fantastic Art, Dada, Surrealism* exhibition in 1936, Levy was persuaded not to use the word 'surrealism' for the pavilion. The name 'Laffland' (a neologism or a crasis/syneresis between 'laugh' and 'land') was initially suggested, as Levy saw the Fair as an opportunity to bring together French avant-garde art and American popular culture, surrealism and amusement, fine art and more commercial visual forms of attraction, glamour and spectacle.[2] He envisioned the pavilion as a prefabricated funhouse, far from a museum display: it was to be a sensual stimulation befitting the surrealist imaginary. A gallery of surrealist paintings was to have been coupled with a 'Dream Corridor', an 'Audible Staircase', rocking floors, pneumatic walls and so forth. The first sketch of the pavilion was outlined by the architect Ian Woodner (or Wooden Silverman) as a large eye shape 'whose iris would frame changing color projections'.[3] Inside this eye, reflecting its surrounding, a remarkable detail in the cornea would be visible: Botticelli's Venus shell. In this Venus would be replaced by two figures, one black, one white – perhaps a pagan Adam and Eve who, ejected from the Garden of Eden, sail away in a shell-shaped ship.

Levy's idea of a collective show with surrealist waxworks, a female automaton and a *cabinet de curiosités* referred back to the previous *Exposition Internationale du Surréalisme* held in Paris (17 January 1938). There Dalí had exhibited a mannequin, a lobster telephone and a *Rainy*

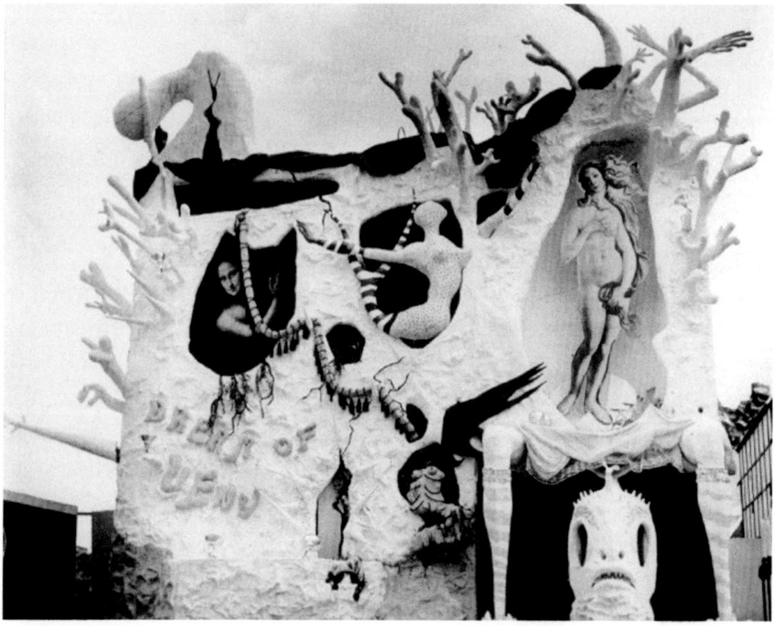

Fig.4.12 Facade of Salvador Dalí's *Dream of Venus* pavilion, 1939, The Dalí Museum in St. Petersburg, Fla. Dalí Museum/Fundacio Gala-Salvador Dalí via Agency Press.

Taxi. However, despite its originality and its visually shocking *mise-en-scène*, this project was dropped between the autumn of 1938 and early 1939 for lack of funds. The commission was assigned to a single artist, Salvador Dalí, as the star of the new artistic movement – the one who could 'condense the immaterial into being', as Levy wrote in his memoir.[4] As originally conceived, his surrealist house would have had to be built in an impossibly tight time frame, with just 'a day to sketch the interior and eight days to design the façade'.[5]

In the meantime, Dalí arrived in New York in February for his solo exhibition at Levy's gallery (21 March–15 April 1939). The display was anticipated by his collaboration with the Fifth Avenue department store Bonwit Teller, orchestrated by Levy, who had previously contacted Saks Fifth Avenue. After the *Fantastic Art, Dada, Surrealism* exhibition at the Museum of Modern Art, several surrealist artists had realised a series of windows for Bonwit Teller. (Artists such as James Rosenquist, Jasper Johns and Robert Rauschenberg were to collaborate on windows in the decades before the store was closed in 1979. It was demolished the following year to make way for the Trump Tower.)[6]

According to Levy's memoir, the window installation offered Dalí a chance to paint in three dimensions. But the commission ended badly. On 16 March, when Dalí realised that the store – in response to shoppers' complaints – had replaced his mannequins, he rushed through the store and, 'in an attempt to push the bathtub out the window and into the street', as Dalí reported in his *Secret Life*, both he and it crashed through the window and hit the pavement outside. As a result, he was almost 'decapitated by the Niagara of descending glass' and was arrested just two days before the opening of his show at the Levy Gallery.[7] Whether spontaneous or staged, this episode or publicity stunt received wide press coverage and provided the best *entrée en scène* that Dalí could have imagined. More than in his earlier 1934 exhibition at Levy's gallery, the artist's intentions were assertively affirmed in the explicit cover image for the 1939 show (fig. 4.13). It displayed the Fair's official icons – the Trylon and the Perisphere, which pointed toward the future, toward the 'World of Tomorrow' – destroyed by the arms of Helicline, the spiral ramp that partially encircled the Perisphere. Moreover, the Perisphere and the Trylon were put at the centre of the exhibition space; as reported at that time, 'the Perisphere is cracked in spots like an egg about to hatch and is surmounted by Beauty in the form of a cast of the Venus de Milo, while the Trylon is inscribed with such vaguely apposite names as Freud, Dalí, Caligula, and again, Dalí'.[8]

This violent animation of architectural elements was not only a clear sexual provocation, but also a critique of the educational goals promoted by the Fair, with its official discourse and rhetorical display of triumphant American capitalist power.[9] The radical innovation was clear. One only had to look at other pavilions, such as the bombastic and monumental Italian pavilion. Designed by the architect Michele Busiri Vici in a typical fascist Roman modern style, its classical female statue – a metaphor of Rome offset before a waterfall 60 m in height – utterly lacked the sensuality of Dalí's Venus.

When Dalí signed the contract on 10 April 1939, the pavilion was tentatively named 'Bottoms of the Sea' – in reference, according to Dalí, to 'the bottoms of man's minds, and everybody knew that there were no ends to *them*'.[10] Dissatisfied with this literal title, he and Levy started to think of more catchy names, including *Dalí's Dream Dive, Dalí's Visible Women, Dalí's Kala Pani* (a Hindu mythological reference to the ocean's murky waters), *Dalí's Fish, Flesh and Fowl, Dalí's Nude Aquarium, Dalínian Dearies; Dalí Trance Forms, Nude Drench, See! Sea! Si! Dalí!, No Nudes are Good Nudes, The Fair's Sex, Eros is Eros; 20M Legs Under the Sea, Swimmim' Women, Beauties of Disorder, Sea Nymphs and Maniacs, Sea Bottoms Up,*

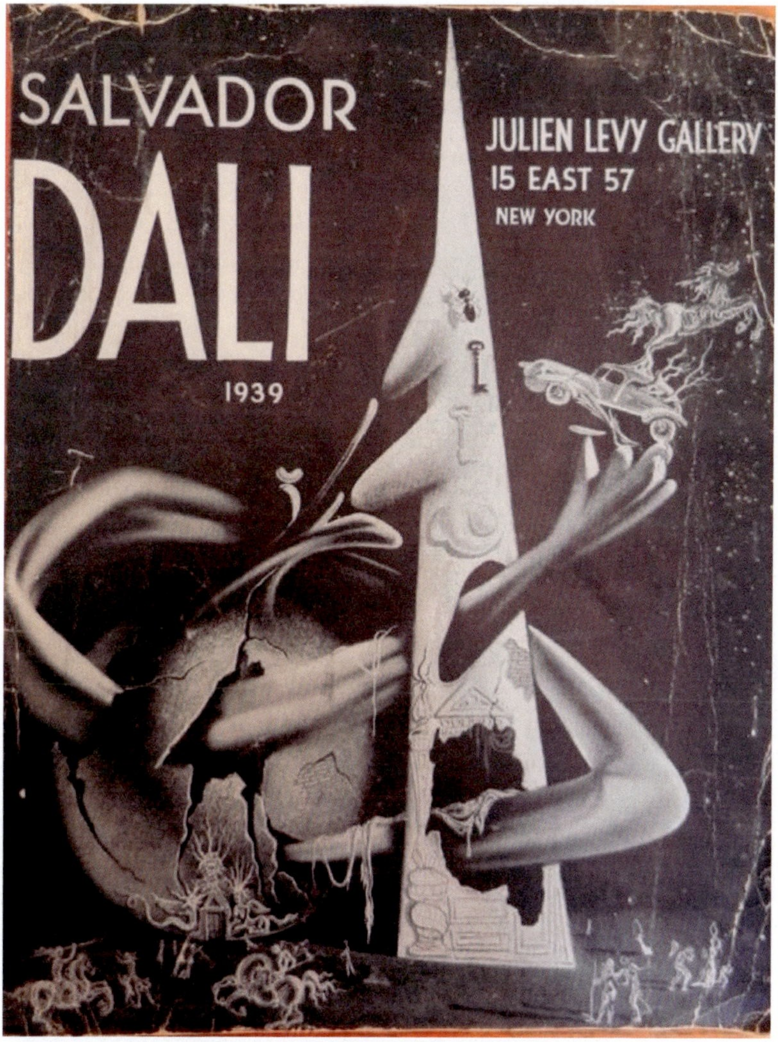

Fig.4.13 Salvador Dalí (1904–89), cover image of his solo show at Julien Levy Gallery, New York 1939. © Salvador Dalí, Fundació Gala-Salvador Dalí, DACS 2018.

Surrealism: Psychoanatomy, all the way through to *Dalí's Wet Dreams*.[11] On 9 May, the pavilion was christened 'Dalí's Dream of Venus'; it was to be renamed in the second season (the Fair closed on 27 October 1940) as '20,000 Legs Under the Sea'.

When the Fair officially opened on 30 April 1939, Dalí's pavilion was far from complete. While theirs was not the only unfinished pavilion, Dalí and Levy felt the urge to keep the media alerted, as they had with the Bonwit Teller display. A photograph by George Platt Lynes showed Dalí covering a female crotch with a lobster shell, evoking, in Fèlix Fanés's interpretation, the goddess born from the foam produced when the genitals of the castrated Uranus fell on the waves.[12] This photograph was coupled with another of the same model 'wearing [Dalí's wife] Gala's metal star necklace. Dalí drew over this print in ink, transforming a fairly banal shot into a fantastic mermaid with two fish-tailed feet. Fish tails also sprout from her shoulders and head, as does a unicorn horn'.[13] As in the invitation card for the pavilion (fig.4.14), where the lower part of the costume is more elaborate, the female body was transformed into an animal figure. Although the photographic documentation we have is not sufficiently detailed to be certain, these pictures may have been displayed on a platform next to the Pavilion entrance. And these manipulated prints that imbricate women and seafood, female genitalia and crustaceans, echo Dalí's manipulation of Leonardo's and Botticelli's female portraits.

Dalí's press agents, probably with his knowledge, issued a short press release headed with a question: *Is Dalí Insane?* It insisted on the artist's preoccupation with the materials of the subconscious, describing him as a 'tourist in the realm of insanity – collecting souvenirs and

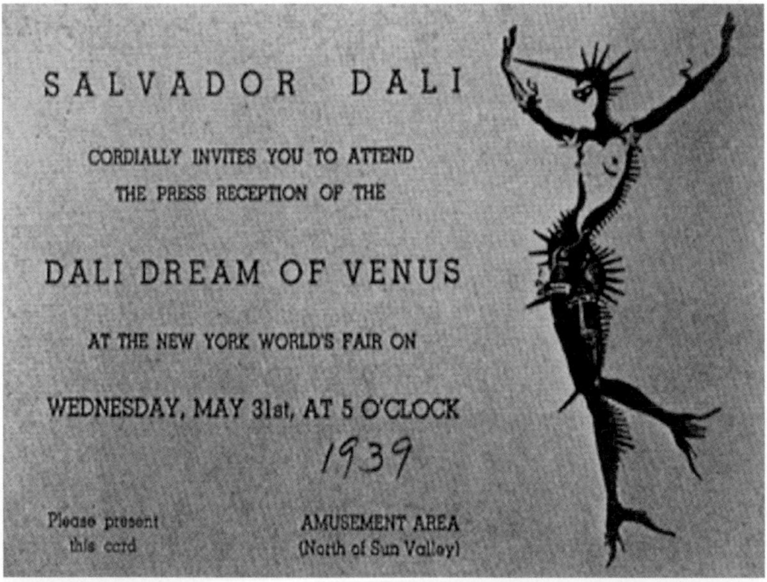

Fig.4.14 *Dream of Venus* invitation card, 1939, reproduced in Lewis Kachur, *Displaying the Marvelous. Marcel Duchamp, Salvador Dalí, and Surrealist Exhibition Installations*, Cambridge, Mass.: The MIT Press, 2001. © Salvador Dalí, Fundació Gala-Salvador Dalí, DACS 2018.

impressions' with 'his sensitivity and awareness of human dreams, and of the free-play of association within the mind of normal man'. The release also praised the artist's technique, declaring it to be 'comparable to that of the Flemish masters'.

Prior to the opening, a first sketch of the *House of Venus* was published in the June 1939 issue of *Vogue* (fig.4.15), announcing that 'the more erudite will recognize in the shape of the *cabaña*, and the deep-sea world inside, Dalí's symbolic conception of the maternal complex, the dark, safe dream of an atavistic watery world'.[14] Far from the final result, the version shown in *Vogue* stands in a Dalí-esque Venusberg – a vast and rarefied space with a chain of mountains on the horizon that resembles a theatrical backdrop, a connection also suggested by the plank floor. Yet this pink pavilion has a biomorphic and gelatinous quality that makes it almost a living creature, with a sexualised mermaid passing through the surface of the façade. Also of interest is the large platform, absent from the final version.

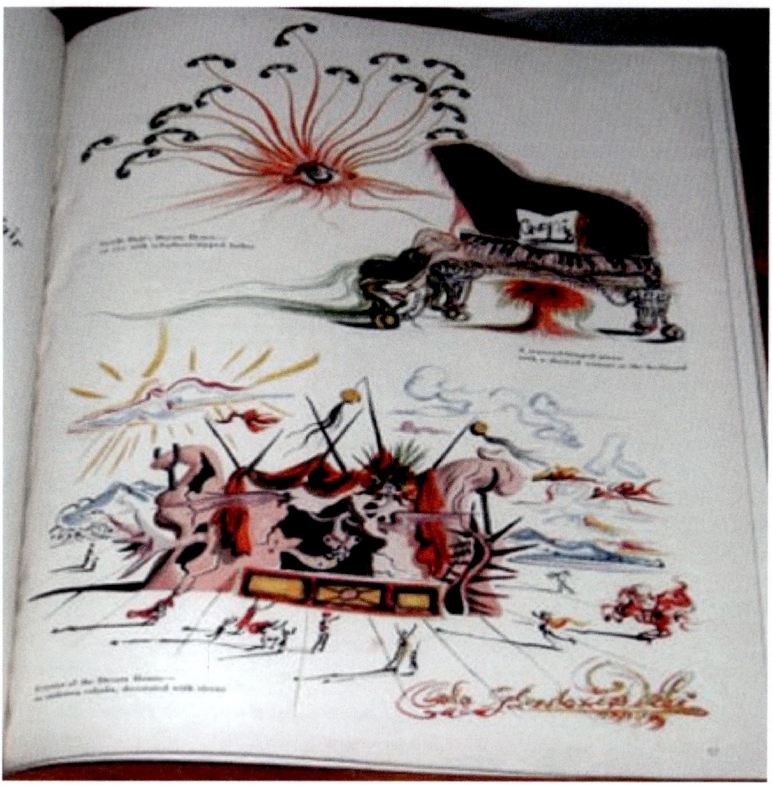

Fig.4.15 'Dalí's Surrealist Dream House at the World's Fair', in *Vogue*, June 1939. © Salvador Dalí, Fundació Gala-Salvador Dalí, DACS 2018.

In a later, more refined sketch (fig.4.16) – a collage made with pasted paper, closer to the pavilion's final version – the artist 'immodestly topped the building with the apotheosis of his own name, framed, in huge, three-dimensional letters'. He thus made it clear that it was as much the Dream of Dalí as the *Dream of Venus*.[15] 'I am not a Surrealist. I am Surrealism', he stated peremptorily.[16]

This was less the demise of subjectivity than Dalí's effort to reaffirm his role in the international art and public scene. As André Parinaud aptly pointed out when introducing Dalí's *Unspeakable Confessions*, 'Dalí never says the French *je* (I) without also meaning *jeux* (games), as his *I* implies all the tricks of the *eye*'.[17] This was particularly true at that moment in the United States, where he was acknowledged as the author of a doubtful portrait of Hitler (*Enigma of Hitler*) – one of the two paintings that remained unsold when it was shown at the Levy gallery in 1939 (the other being *The Endless Enigma*) – and known for his enthusiasm for Harpo Marx.

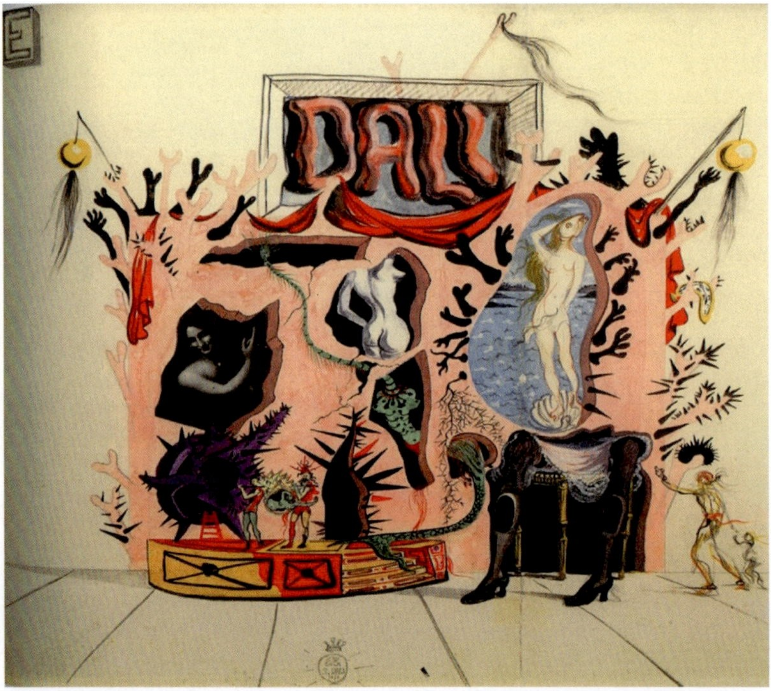

Fig.4.16 Salvador Dalí, sketch for *Dream of Venus*, 1939, tempera, charcoal, pencil and collage on illustration board, reproduced in Ingrid Schaffner, *Salvador Dalí's Dream of Venus. The Surrealist Funhouse from the 1939 World's Fair*, New York: Princeton Architectural Press, 2002. © Salvador Dalí, Fundació Gala-Salvador Dalí, DACS 2018.

Relative to the final version, this sketch is noteworthy for the Venus's elongated fish head. As in René Magritte's *The Collective Invention* (1934), it reverses the fish tail of the classic anatomy of the mermaid, removed from the water and lying lifeless on the foreshore. Dalí liked the idea of a fish head, specifically a shark's, as can be seen in Eric Schaal's startling 1939 photograph that shows both his eccentric public persona and his innate sense of self-promotion and advertising. When permission to put a fish head on Botticelli's Venus was denied, Dalí made a last artistic gesture, a *coup de théâtre*: though he could not attend the opening, he had hundreds of copies of a tract – 'Declaration of the Independence of the Imagination and the Rights of Man to his own Madness' – dropped over Manhattan (fig.4.17). In this text Dalí protested against 'the storm of obscurantism that is threatening' the United States, claiming that 'it is man's right to love women with ecstatic heads of fish'. Noteworthy in the image is the flaky skin of Venus's torso, as if Dalí had transferred the wavelets of the original painting directly onto the female body. If he had to give up the idea of putting a fish head on Botticelli's Venus and thus altering her human anatomy, he instead employed this motif for the ticket kiosk located between two open legs. The cashier was accessible through the fish's eyes, implying that viewers were penetrating into Venus's womb – or, as Dalí put it in the description he initially gave Levy, '*une chambre inter-uterine*' (an intrauterine room). He then added, in his typical cumbersome French, '*C'est très Hallucinang* [*sic*], – *tu verra* [*sic*]' (It's very hallucinating – you'll see).[18]

In the preliminary sketch, the female figure is surrounded by a Nordic marine landscape, a kind of archipelago where the undulating shape of black seagulls and white wavelets meld. The aquatic elements perfectly fit the aesthetic of the Fair, which used water as a spectacular element. As the producer Billy Rose advised Julien Levy and Ian Woodner: 'Anything writ in water will succeed, lagoons, fountains, aquacades, ice coolers, anything you please, but the public is disposed towards water'.[19] The fascination of the liquid element was key to the surrealist aesthetic and to Dalí's work. This had been revealed in his risky and marvellous performance at the International Surrealist Exhibition in London (1 July 1936), at which he delivered the lecture 'Authentic Paranoid Phantasies' wearing a suffocating deep-sea diving suit. The '*Dream of Venus*' was also influenced by the Parisian passageways that Louis Aragon described in aquatic terms (*Le Paysan de Paris*, 1926) – the shop windows like 'human aquariums' of 'primitive life', or, on a more anecdotal level, by André Breton's girlfriend Jacqueline Lamba dancing underwater at the Coliseum, an ex-swimming pool turned into a music hall.[20]

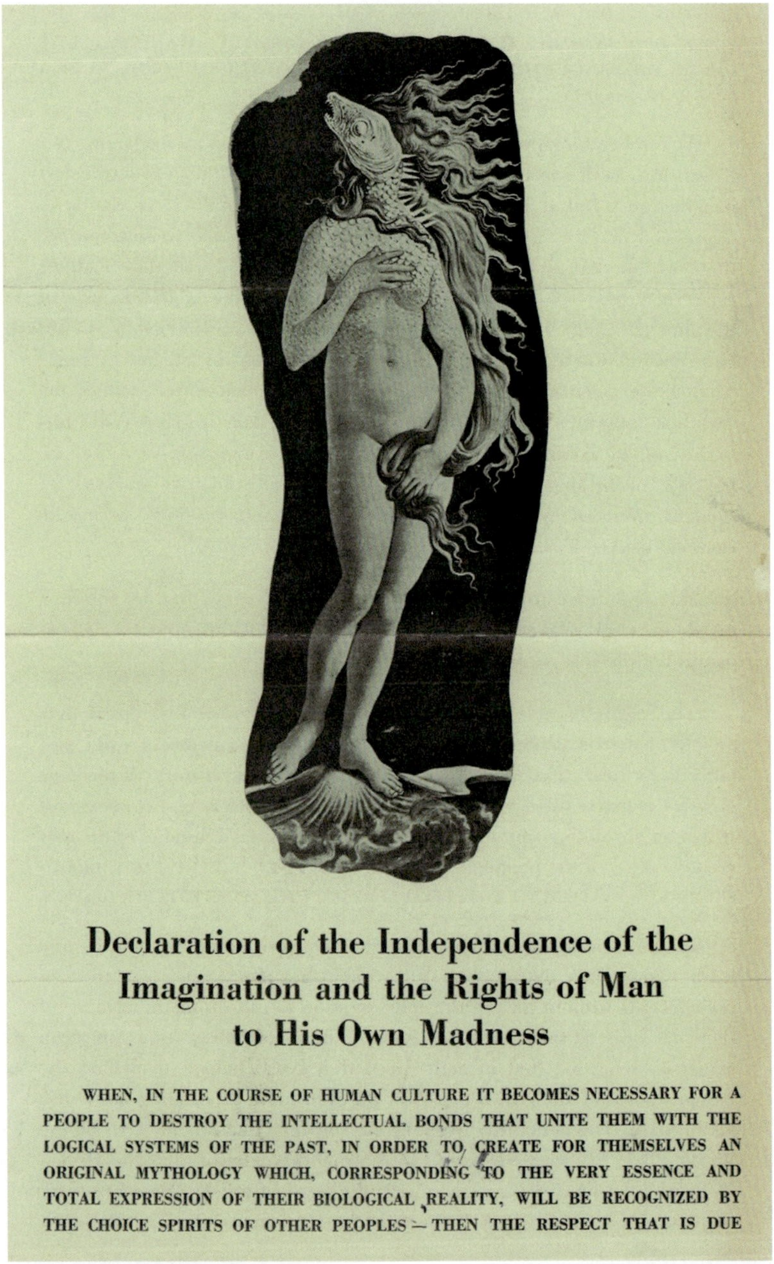

Declaration of the Independence of the Imagination and the Rights of Man to His Own Madness

WHEN, IN THE COURSE OF HUMAN CULTURE IT BECOMES NECESSARY FOR A PEOPLE TO DESTROY THE INTELLECTUAL BONDS THAT UNITE THEM WITH THE LOGICAL SYSTEMS OF THE PAST, IN ORDER TO CREATE FOR THEMSELVES AN ORIGINAL MYTHOLOGY WHICH, CORRESPONDING TO THE VERY ESSENCE AND TOTAL EXPRESSION OF THEIR BIOLOGICAL REALITY, WILL BE RECOGNIZED BY THE CHOICE SPIRITS OF OTHER PEOPLES — THEN THE RESPECT THAT IS DUE

Fig.4.17 Salvador Dalí, *Declaration of the Independence of the Imagination and the Rights of Man to His Own Madness*, 1939, ink on paper, 40.3 × 24.35 cm, National Art Library. © Salvador Dalí, Fundació Gala-Salvador Dalí, DACS 2018.

Despite all the efforts, the preview of the '*Dream of Venus*' scheduled for 31 May, one month after the Fair's opening, had to be postponed. Today, a telegram dated 30 May looks like a superb surrealist document: 'Salvador Dalí Dream of Venus press reception postponed for few days due to complexity of subconscious. You will be advised of opening date regretfully'. The pavilion finally opened on 15 June, although both Dalí and Gala had left New York the previous day to work on their next project.[21] Botticelli's Venus was to surface again in Dalí's mind and work, however. On his next trip to New York, on 2 September 1941, two months before the opening of the Miró-Dalí exhibition at Museum of Modern Art (MoMA) (18 November), he produced *Labyrinth* at the Metropolitan Opera House with the Ballets Russes of Monte Carlo, whose patron, the Marqués de Cuevas, was a friend. Dalí designed not only the sets and costumes, but also the two backdrops. One 'was based on Botticelli's *The Birth of Venus*. Dalí appropriated the latter's foam crested waves and translated the goddess to the sky, where her huge breasts and haunches doubled as clouds. The design was crude beyond description'.[22] Thus we can see that the dream of Venus was becoming more and more the dream of Dalí.

The *Dream of Venus* Pavilion

How to describe Dalí's surrealist environment, 'an assemblage of images, objects, paintings, and sculptures, all erotically animated by semi-nude female performers and housed in a small stucco building that looked like a tangled, bleached mass of beach debris'?[23] A puzzling and disorienting ambience far removed from institutional art spaces, an ambience in which artworks were radically transformed, activated, spectacularised. There was nothing similar at the World Fair, as shown, perhaps, by the fact that the house of Venus was hosted far away from the other art. Dalí's pavilion was in the Amusement Zone of the Fair – where, as *Time* magazine reported, there was 'more public nudity than any place outside of Bali', while the other art, including European and American masterpieces, was in the Communications Zone.[24] This distinctive placement underscored Dalí's extravagance and carnivalesque aspect.

Even before entering the freestanding building, visitors encountered Dalí's quirky world (fig.4.12): the exterior was, to use Rem Koolhaas's analysis of Manhattanism, 'a relentless assemblage of the Strange'.[25] On a rocky promontory, a whitish stucco far from the flesh-like pink of the previous sketch had blowpipe-shaped appendages sprouting from its facade: hands and elongated arms, or more organic forms resembling branches, cactus, corals or maybe weeds. A rampant accretion of tumescent protuberances, of non-structural excrescences reminiscent of Casa Milà by Antoni Gaudì or Pompeii as seen in a nightmare, grew around the vulnerable figure of Venus, protected only by an oval, architectural niche. It was as if Venus was in danger of being subjected to a metamorphosis like that of Daphne, if we follow Spyros Papapetros's reference to the female nymph who

> externalizes her presence in a series of *protrusions*. The nymph's petrified posture accumulates an excess of energy, which is externalized as an aerodynamic protuberance jutting out from the flatness of her wooden frame.[26]

More maliciously, the profusion of soft shapes was a blunt critique of modern architecture, particularly of Le Corbusier's international style. Dalí is known for his trenchant judgement of the French architect, whom he characterised as 'a pitiable creature working in reinforced concrete. Mankind will soon be landing on the moon, and just imagine: that buffoon claimed we'd be taking along sacks of reinforced concrete'.[27] Rem Koolhaas, however, saw Le Corbusier and Dalí (both of whom visited New York for the first time in the mid-1930s) as alike in that they made bold and individual attempts to 'reclaim' Manhattan – attempts that were seemingly antithetical, yet also complementary:

> Dalí abhors Modernism, Le Corbusier despises Surrealism. But Le Corbusier's persona and method of operation show many parallels with Dalí's PCM [Paranoiac-critical method].[28]

If some of Dalí's classical references were discreet, such as the copy of the Nike statue on the top of the fish head next to the torso of a nude woman, two were more flagrant. The first was St John the Baptist by Leonardo da Vinci, with a collage of the face of Mona Lisa. At the time of its exhibition, this hermaphrodite figure was taken to be Leonardo's original composition. More prominently, a 7.60m high reproduction of Botticelli's *The Birth of Venus* as a photomural or billboard was framed in a niche over the entrance.

This paradoxical display – over-exposed but protected within a niche – is reminiscent of the installation of the painting at the 1940 *Italian Masters* exhibition at the Museum of Modern Art in New York. There it was among 28 masterpieces including Titian's *Paolo III*, an early Michelangelo marble bas-relief, Raphael's *La Madonna della*

Seggiola, Andrea del Verrocchio's *David*, Gian Lorenzo Bernini's *Bust of Costanza Bonarelli* and Masaccio's *Crucifixion*. As expected, this was an incredibly popular exhibition, with a public attendance of 290,888 visitors and wide press coverage.[29] The museum's installation was striking in its theatricality. Botticelli's *Birth of Venus* was isolated, magnified by an empty room 80 metres square, spot lit and curtained off – it had a tremendous impact on viewers. All the theatricality boosted the painting's aura and heightened the feeling of privilege the public felt at seeing a Renaissance masterpiece. As one critic pointed out: '[T]his setting enabled the museum to orchestrate the viewer's encounter with the picture by re-enacting – in keeping with its subject – the origin myth of modernity'.[30]

While the *Italian Masters* run (26 January–7 April 1940) overlapped with that of the Fair (30 April 1939–31 October 1939; 11 May–27 October 1940), it is likely that Dalí had seen *The Birth of Venus* in previous shows which, much like the MoMA exhibition, promoted a dubious *italianità*. He might have seen the exhibition of Italian art at the Royal Academy's Burlington House in London in 1930 or, more likely, *L'Art Italien de Cimabue à Tiepolo* at the Petit Palais in Paris in 1935. The true object of these exhibitions – what Francis Haskell calls the 'Ephemeral Museum' – was less the exhibited objects themselves than 'the spectacle of cultural power, of high art in the service of politics' (Emily Braun). Both were intended to improve fascism's image internationally.[31] It did not go unnoticed that the 1940 MoMA show was promoted by the Italian government (the full title was *Italian Masters Lent by the Royal Italian Government*) and conceived on a highly ideological historical line that included the Roman empire, the Renaissance and – as Italy's final accomplishment – Mussolini's Third Rome. However Alfred Barr, the Director of MOMA, biased this ideological and political agenda: in an attempt to convince the Museum Trustees to host a show of Renaissance art in an institution consecrated to modern art, he cautiously hid it under his apolitical vision of the teleology of modernist art.

Returning to the facade of the *Dream of Venus*, it can be said that its indentations paralleled the maternal cavity of the internal space, its hidden nature. Dalí's pavilion was a grotto, an embryo that immersed the spectator in a world remote from the light of modernity. The uterine cavity between the women's legs led into a semi-obscure ambience where visitors' bodies moved in a submarine garden fantasy world. It was replete with real women, sleeping and dreaming; scantily dressed mermaids; and odd Dalínian elements scattered across the tiny space. These ranged from the soft, curved shapes (women-pianos, a divan in the shape of Greta Garbo's lips, a mummified cow, rubber telephones and typewriters), to the ceiling, covered by opened and closed umbrellas.

In the first two rooms, visitors encountered two glass tanks 11 metres long, one filled with paintings, the other with water. The latter was animated by 17 costumed 'Living Liquid Ladies'. These modern mermaids stayed, three or four at a time, in the tank for 20 minutes – displayed for, and fetishised by, the scrutiny of the masculine gaze. In another chamber a sumptuous couchette, 10m in length and covered in red satin, stood out, along with a dreaming Venus attended by two women. Here was the pulsing heart of the pavilion or, as the press release put it, 'the unexpurgated dream-substance of the goddess Venus'.[32] The same year Dalí showed himself lying on an elongated bed, with an umbrella (also present in his painting *The Enigma of Hitler*). Finally, the interior offered another example of art history according to Dalí. It referred not only to a Palladian proscenium in the backdrop, but also to Pompeii, the city overwhelmed and ruined by the eruption of Vesuvius.

Anachronisms: from Surrealism to Renaissance

The *Dream of Venus* is the result of free associations with mass culture, personal memory, psychoanalytic readings and, especially crucial in the context of the *Botticelli Reimagined* exhibition (5 March–3 July 2016, Victoria and Albert Museum), art-historical references. Dalí's interest in this went back to the outbreak of the Spanish Civil War in 1936, an event that had a profound impact on his life, ideas and art. Shocked by the traumatic events of the conflict and what he foresaw as the eventual catastrophe of Western civilisation, Dalí spent the summer of 1937–8 in Italy. There he enjoyed a moment of solitude – 'I wanted to be alone in Italy, overlooking the terraces of cypress and orange trees, the solemn temples of Paestum' – to cultivate the illusion of living in a distant past.[33] Italian Renaissance and Baroque art had never been so vivid: Raphael, Piero di Cosimo and Piero della Francesca, Andrea Palladio and Bramante, Leonardo and even Giorgio De Chirico, though Dalí's and De Chirico's anti-modernisms ultimately differ. As Michael Taylor put it:

> Dalí's reaction to the imminent destruction of centuries of European tradition and culture was to abandon his earlier interest in Surrealism in favour of the techniques and iconography of the old masters.

Instead of the 'Oedipal psychosexual dramas that had characterized his Surrealist paintings of the late 1920s and 1930s', the artist was now creating 'complex allegories of war and devastation'.[34]

Recollections of this Italian journey surfaced profusely in the 1939 Julien Levy Gallery's exhibition catalogue (*'Dalí, Dalí'*).[35] Here Dalí considers Leonardo as the 'authentic innovator of paranoiac painting', a reference to Leonardo's recommendation that his students look for inspiration in 'the indefinite shapes of the spots of dampness and the cracks on the wall' and try to find the precise moment at which the amorphous became a figurative scene. Later Dalí refers to Arcimboldo, Giovanni Battista Bracelli and, especially, to Piero di Cosimo's famous anecdote of finding 'enigmatic and atavistic compositions, fire and the horrible dragon of the oyster' in the 'viscous and mucous and bloody contours of tubercular spit'.[36] Dalí was thus historicising and legitimising his use of paranoiac phenomena and hypnagogic images by going back to the cave man, Aristophanes' *The Clouds* and Arcimboldo, Bracelli and Palladio.

Two years later, in the catalogue for his new exhibition at the Levy Gallery, *'Felice Jacinto'* (actually Dalí himself) makes a bolder claim:

> During these chaotic times of confusion, of rout and of growing demoralization [...] Dalí himself [...] finds the unique attitude towards his destiny: TO BECOME CLASSIC! As if he has said to himself: 'Now or never'. In 1941 – the 'year of Spiritual Sterility' – Dalí is striving for restoring the Renaissance tradition of 'Divina proportione'.[37]

This unattainable artistic programme is restated in 1942 in the conclusion of his autobiography *The Secret Life of Salvador Dalí*, with the triumphant *crescendo* of an avant-garde manifesto:

> Enough of disintegration; one must integrate, integrate, integrate. Instead of automatism, style; instead of nihilism, technique; instead of scepticism, faith; instead of promiscuity, rigor; instead of collectivism and uniformization – individualism, differentiation, and hierarchization; instead of experimentation, tradition. Instead of Reaction, or Revolution, RENAISSANCE!.[38]

Dalí's relationship with the Renaissance tradition of Raphael, Michelangelo and Leonardo da Vinci continued to evolve in the following decade under the aegis of his 'Nuclear Mysticism' (1952). More than just a deterrent to irrationality, classical sources were an imaginary repository that allowed Dalí to make scientific discoveries, especially those of modern physics, visible, according to David Lomas.[39] In *The Decadence of Modern Art* (1950) and *The Cuckolds of Antiquated Modern Art* (1956), Dalí famously attacks abstraction and modern art, in favour of 'the dazzling perfection of the masters of the Renaissance'.[40] In his *Diary of a Genius*, where he mentions Raphael, Vermeer, Velasquez and Piero della Francesca, Dalí quotes Georges Mathieu in the entry dated 1 September 1960, observing that he was 'in deeper communion with the cosmos' than any Western artist '[s]ince Dionysius the Areopagite'.[41]

As these passages make manifest, and as Fèlix Fanés remarked, 'Dalí never avoided the direct quoting of a work or a painter'.[42] And although the name and work of Sandro Botticelli rarely appears, in *Diary of a Genius* (1964), apropos of one of Botticelli's *Assumptions*, the artist evokes the vegetation, but not the female figures:

> The little crack is burning away. It feels like a mythological worm gnawing away at the corners of my mouth, which reminds me of one of the allegorical figures in Botticelli's *Primavera*, with its fascinating and obscure vegetation.[43]

A second reference will require a short detour before we move to our conclusion.

The spectral beauty of the Venus

Conscious of the gulf between his times and the Italian Renaissance, Dalí asked himself 'How to become anachronistic?' ('*Comment devenir anachronique*?'). The question was raised in a short text ('*Derniers modes d'excitation intellectuelle pour l'été*') published in the surrealist magazine *Documents* in June 1934. How should we consider this shift from surrealism to the Renaissance, from avant-garde to the old masters, from modernist to academic painting? Dalí's vehement and outrageous attempt to restore classical painting could be seen as a conservative move that hides his ideological, political (and even religious) views. Such an opinion is found in Nicolas Calas's malicious attack in the New York-based magazine *View* in 1941 – an internal critique, inasmuch as it came from a surrealist-oriented publication.[44]

More articulate was Clement Greenberg, whose influential 'Avant-garde and Kitsch' essay appeared in 1939, the same year as the New York Fair. From his modernist and formalist stance, the decisive question about surrealism was whether or not it provided painting with a 'new subject matter […] a new way of seeing as well as new things to be seen'. For Greenberg the answer was negative: the surrealist image was basically an aberration, an illustration of anecdotes, a disguised academic form of art, 'a new and interesting kind of pictorial literature' that, finally, 'requires no fundamental change in the conventions of paintings as established by the Renaissance'.[45] This is why the return to the Renaissance proclaimed by Dalí had few or indeed any relevant aesthetic consequences. According to Greenberg's reasoning, Dalí could easily switch from surrealism to Renaissance because the former was deprived of an artistic quality in relation to the latter, because it lacked specificity and originality. By the same token, Greenberg upholds abstract art as the most compelling art practice of his times, taking Western art history as an incontrovertible proof:

> Just as naturalism at the time of the Bellinis in Venice was the only tendency which promised a future to painting, in spite of the wonderful sideshows staged by Carpaccio and Crivelli, so abstract art today is the only stream that flows toward an ocean.[46]

In Greenberg's teleological thinking, the role played then by Carpaccio and Crivelli was now played by surrealism. In particular, surrealism is found guilty of entertaining too close an alliance with life and of having '*immediate* feelings about sex' that, in Greenberg's purist vision of cubism and abstract art, 'must first be transposed'.[47] Instead of making that transposition, Dalí promoted a puerile form of irreverence, 'no more revolutionary than fascism'. 'But of course Dalí,' pithily concludes the critic, 'is not to be taken seriously as anything other than a symptom. He is the Ossian of our day.'[48]

'Immediate feelings about sex': this decisive component of Dalí's aesthetics was more than a plain eroticisation of high modernism, just as his staunchly proclaimed return to the Renaissance – as technique, skill and craftsmanship, as a perfect and unparalleled model – was everything but classical. Julian Levy aptly described his role as part of 'the violent contribution to the menu of modern art Dalí offered with his imaginative snapshots of inter-cranial space, post-Euclidean composition, animalization of machinery, displacement of the orgasm, mobilization of the dream, intercourse of the eyes, the smashing of the mental molecule'.[49]

The pavilion for the New York Fair offers a privileged case in point. Although the facade and the interior were divided, the classical references to Leonardo and Botticelli and the real dancers found common ground in several ways. Photo documentation shows, for instance, beach chairs in front of Botticelli's Venus, with dancers in bathing suits catching the attention of passers-by through real strip-tease shows. Far from the celebration of rational order, a mechanical world built by human progress that the official discourse of the Fair promoted,[50] Dalí conceived an eclectic platform on which the Renaissance canon of beauty could meet what, at that time, was described as 'a reconstruction of very Freudian subconscious by means of what is known on Broadway as a *girl show*'.[51] If the *Dream of Venus* was a fun-show addressed to the male gaze, it was also an uncanny *mise-en-scène* of man's scopic desires.

The *Dream of Venus* was also, reciprocally, the unconfessable dreams of the patrons, and the mirrors in the installation echoed this effect of projection. Attending the 1939 fair as a young man, the modernist art historian and critic Robert Rosenblum describes Dalí's pavilion as 'the seductive invitation to surrealism's forbidden fruits' even if 'for reasons I can't dredge up, I never entered'.[52] Was what Rosenblum called 'the shock of modernity in art'[53] too strong for him? Did it provide an example of the difficult relations between modernism and surrealism, between modern art and the explicit erotic images of Dalí's mind and work?

A rare, intriguing photograph shows the reproduction of Botticelli's Venus lying horizontally on the ground, waiting to be installed in the niche over the fish-head entranceway. The image is surrounded by the 'liquid ladies' in their mermaid costumes (fig.4.18):

> This peripheral array of figures rehearses the theme of accessories-in-motion – the animated fabrics, which here are replaced by the living priestesses of the ancient goddess.[54]

Dalí copied the old masters for their erotic aspect. He never concealed the fact that this academic training aroused his sexual desires, that the copyist and the 'Great Masturbator' (to quote a Dalí text of the late 1920s) shared the same experience, as in Titian's *Worship of Venus* (1518–19) in the Prado, whose composition is probably at the base of Dalí's *The Lugubrious Game*. As Dalí confessed in the mid-1960s:

> I pause erotically at certain works, but I remain impassive. The thing that really draws me to a painting, especially to Ingres' nudes or any other nudes of the same period, is the erotic aspect. In my adolescence, copying these works served as an excuse for certain special practices. In the classics, the erotic and the feeling of death interest me more than so-called artistic perfection.[55]

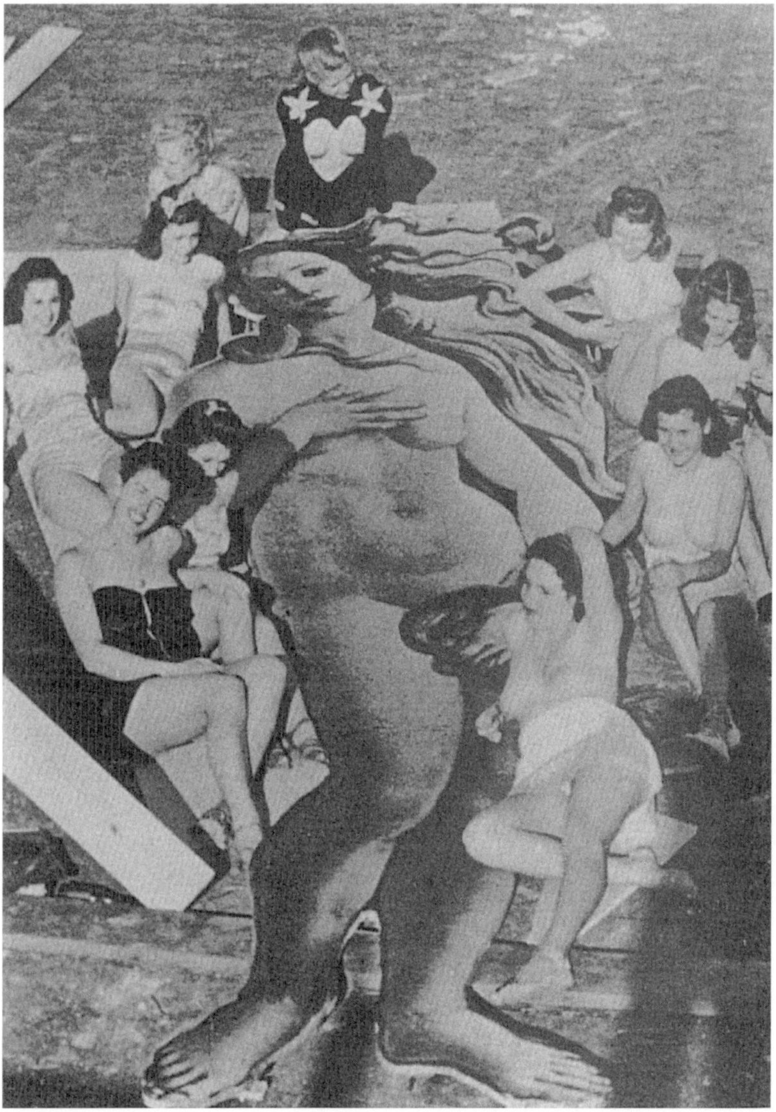

Fig.4.18 Photograph of female models for *The Dream of Venus* watertank show directed by Salvador Dalí, with a reproduction of Botticelli's *Venus*, 1939. Photographer unknown.

We should pause a moment to consider this 'feeling of death'. It surfaces in the *Dream of Venus* project in the *Declaration of the Independence of the Imagination and the Rights of the Man to His Own Madness* that was air-dropped during the pavilion's inauguration:

Man is entitled to the enigma and the simulacrums that are founded on these great vital constants: the sexual instinct, the consciousness of death, the physical melancholy caused by time-space.

But Dalí's interest in the translation of man's desires into plastic artefacts, of erotic desires into aesthetic forms, of morbid thoughts into a morphological vocabulary, date back to his collaboration with the surrealist magazine *Minotaure*. I am thinking in particular of three of Dalí's articles: 'Concerning the Terrifying and Edible Beauty of Art Nouveau Architecture' (December 1933), 'The New Colours of Spectral Sex-Appeal' (February 1934) and 'The Spectral Surrealism of the Pre-Raphaelite Eternal Feminine' (June 1936).

In the first article – in which Dalí called for renewing the bond between architecture and the unconscious, tectonics and human anatomy, the body and the built, the 'proximity between the human, the built, and the vegetal' – he sees architecture as having the power to materialise and solidify desires whose nature is to be fluid. Art Nouveau, with the soft flaccidity of its shapes, which Dalí compared to liquefied Camembert cheese, constitutes, in this sense, an astonishing case.[56] In the vein of the surrealist, the old-fashioned Art Nouveau was for Dalí a 'historical phantasmagoria', as Hal Foster puts it – hovering between the industrial and the outmoded, the modern and the démodé.[57] This is visible, for instance, in Dalí's female portraits such as the tree women he realised in the 1930s, as well as the novel *Hidden Faces* (1944), in which he fantasises about an 'architecture of passion' and buildings with 'stairs of pain, gates of desire, columns of anguish and capitals of jealousy'. Even more impressively, it appears in a double portrait of his wife Gala and her *doppelgänger* as a transparent cathedral structure (*My Wife Nude, Contemplating Her Own Flesh Becoming Stair, Three Vertebrae of a Column, Sky, and Architecture*, 1945). The work has been described by the critic Spyros Papapetros as 'an anti-modernist classicism made up of nothing *but* ornaments' in which 'the body disappears and is replaced by its accessories'.[58]

Dalí's interest in the death drive is more evident in the second text in his discussion of 'spectral sex-appeal'. The 'materialization of the idea of the phantom' is caused by the human libido that 'transforms metaphysical anxiety into concrete fat' – a kind of narcissistic tactility or, more plainly, into a conceptual and physical obesity. The spectre has the capacity of de-substantiating the phantom. Of course, these categories are not so different. Dalí tries to illuminate the distinction between them by asking 'How to distinguish a phantom from a spectre?' even as he mystified it. 'Freud, Chirico, Greta Garbo, La Gioconda [Mona Lisa]' fall on the side of the phantom; 'Picasso, Gala, Harpo Marx, Marcel Duchamp' on that of the spectre. Dalí is particularly interested in spectral representation or, more precisely, in the transition from sex appeal to the spectral – a transition on which the 'new sexual attraction of women' or 'the disarticulation and deformation of the female anatomy' depends.

Seeking a genealogy for this 'dismountable body', this *corps morcelé* (fragmented body), Dalí mentions Botticelli again in the third article. Here Dalí criticises Cézanne's apple as being a platonic idea without gravity – not the forerunner of cubist materiality, but the 'impetus toward the absolute idealism of formal lyricism'. It is not the Impressionists, but the Pre-Raphaelites, generally known for their immaterial silhouettes, who for Dalí are the real forerunners of surrealism, inasmuch they advocate languid, flesh and bones figures. The Pre-Raphaelites 'give us and make radiant for us women who are all at once the most desirable and the most frightening in existence'.[59]

Dalí's vocabulary leaves no doubts that he sees these figures through a surrealist lens: he speaks of terror, anxiety, repugnance like 'that of the soft belly of a butterfly seen between the luminescence of its wings'. If Cézanne's apples 'have volume without weight, a *virtual volume*', Pre-Raphaelite bodies, on the contrary, are made of 'turgescent, disturbing, and imperialist flesh'. They live in 'the blooming of this legendary necrophiliac spring of which Botticelli vaguely spoke'. The anachronistic association with the Renaissance is thus achieved. 'But Botticelli,' Dalí continues, 'was still too close to the live flesh of the myth to achieve this exhausted, magnificent, and prodigiously material glory of the whole psychological and lunar "legend" of the Occident'. Was this necrophiliac spring, this visceral spectral quality, what Dalí was attempting to perform in his *Dream of Venus* and in the presence of Venus on the facade?

The *Dream of Venus* – or should we say the Nightmare of Venus, as if dreamt by Hans Bellmer? – this Dalí-esque mysterious, sexualised deep-sea universe was a space or a grotto of negotiation and conflict between Renaissance, surrealism, and modernity. An outrageous displacement of classical sources, the *Dream of Venus* was also a visual embodiment of Dalí's ideas about the history of art and its role in contemporary art, beyond the then dominant narrative of modernism. As he told his gallerist Levy, the pavilion was an upside-down dream.[60] In transforming a venerated goddess into a sexy mermaid, insisting on its birth from the castrated genitals of Uranus, Dalí linked religion and sexuality, mysticism and erotic ecstasy, Beaux-arts and libido, metaphysics and entertainment.

But, like most dreams, Dalí's did not last very long. When the Fair closed, the pavilion was demolished (although some fragments were saved) and it survived mainly in a few pictures and reports of the time. Already by 11 August, during the opening times of the Fair, but presumably without Dalí's permission, the Venus billboard was removed from the facade, deprived of her shell and protecting niche, integrated within an anonymous seascape's squared painting, far from the marine landscape of a previous sketch, and stuck on the right side of the pavilion, next to the popcorn stand, practically invisible (fig.4.19). It was as if the sight of her, her spectral character, interfered with the attention and the desire of passers-by to enter the womb of Venus. Her former position was now filled by photo panels of two female figures displayed in a tree-like structure.[61] Like a Renaissance nymph, Venus had migrated. Dalí's *Dream of Venus* is ultimately a passionate achievement in the *Nachleben* of Botticelli's most iconic female figure.

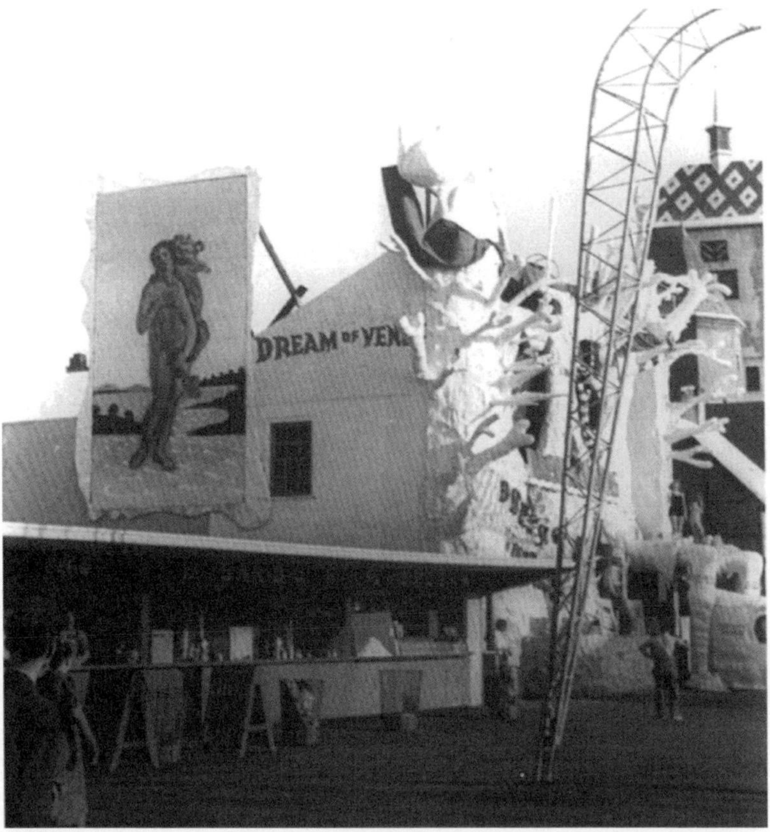

Fig.4.19 Carl Van Vechten (1880–1964), Dalí's *Dream of Venus*, side view of exterior, 11 August 1939, Museum of the City of New York, Print Archives.

Notes

1 Thomas Mical ed., *Surrealism and Architecture* (London-New York: Routledge, 2005).

2 Julien Levy, *Memoir of an Art Gallery* (New York: G. P. Putnam's Sons, 1977), 210; esp. 'Dream of Venus', 205–23. 'Those who understand surrealisme [*sic*] are probably fewer than those who feel competent to explain Einstein,' wrote Edward Alden Jewell in the *New York Times* in 1933, as quoted in Keith L. Eggener, '"An Amusing Lack of Logic": Surrealism and Popular Entertainment', *American Art*, vol.7, n.4 (Autumn 1993): 34.

3 Lewis Kachur, *Displaying the Marvelous. Marcel Duchamp, Salvador Dalí, and Surrealist Exhibition Installations* (Cambridge, Mass.: The MIT Press, 2001), 108, and see chap.3, 'Surrealism Goes to the Fair: Projects for an American Surrealist Display at the 1939 New York World's Fair', 104–63.

4 Levy, *Memoir*, 209.

5 Ingrid Schaffner, *Salvador Dalí's Dream of Venus. The Surrealist Funhouse from the 1939 World's Fair* (New York: Princeton Architectural Press, 2002), 72.

6 Designed in 1929, the entrance was a 'luxurious mix of limestone, bronze, platinum and hammered aluminium', 'with 12 stories of severe, almost unornamented limestone climbing to a ziggurat of setbacks'; at the top of the facade were two naked dancing women 'brandishing large scarves'. Quoted in Christopher Gray, 'The Store That Slipped Through the Cracks', *The New York Times*, 3 October 2014.

7 Salvador Dalí, *La vie secrète de Salvador Dalí: suis-je un génie?* (1942); *The Secret Life of Salvador Dalí*, trans. Haakon M. Chevalier (New York: Dial Press: 1942, third ed. London: Vision Press, 1968), 375.

8 Robert M. Coates, 'The Art Galleries: Dalí-Despiau-Art Young', in *The New Yorker*, 1 April 1939; in Schaffner, *Salvador Dalí's Dream*, 68.

9 It is interesting to remember that 'the steel structures of the Trylon and Perisphere in fact were later melted down to make bombs for WWII', http://www.italianmodernart.org/celebrating-modernity-dreaming-of-the-future-in-queens-the-new-york-worlds-fairs/ .

10 Dalí in Margaret Case Harriman, 'A Dream Walking', *The New Yorker*, 1 July 1939; Schaffner, *Salvador Dalí's Dream*, 74.

11 See Schaffner, *Salvador Dalí's Dream*, 82–4.

12 See Fèlix Fanés, 'Mannequins, Mermaids and the Bottoms of the Sea. Salvador Dalí and the New York World's Fair of 1939', in Montse Aguer, Félix Fanés, Sharon-Michi Kusunoki, ed., *Salvador Dalí. Dream of Venus* (North Miami: Museum of Contemporary Art, 2002), 93.

13 Kachur, *Displaying the Marvelous*, 115–16.

14 In Schaffner, *Salvador Dalí's Dream*, 102.

15 Kachur, *Displaying the Marvelous*, 111.

16 Salvador Dalí, *Comment on devient Dalí* (Paris : Editions Robert Laffont, 1973). *The Unspeakable Confessions of Salvador Dalí, as told to André Parinaud*, trans. Harold J. Salemson (New York: William Morrow and Company, Inc., 1976), 188.

17 In Dalí, *The Unspeakable Confessions*, 5.

18 Levy, *Memoir*, 205–6.

19 In Schaffner, *Salvador Dalí's Dream*, 50.

20 In Fanés et al., 'Mannequins, mermaids', 109, 113, n.63.

21 On 6 June according to Ian Gibson, *The Shameful Life of Salvador Dalí* (New York and London: W. W. Norton & Company, 1997), 446.

22 Gibson, *The Shameful Life*, 469.

23 Schaffner, *Salvador Dalí's Dream*, 30.

24 In Gibson, *The Shameful Life*, 447.

25 Rem Koolhaas, *Delirious New York* (New York: The Monacelli Press, 1978, repr. 1994), 275; see esp. '*Europeans: Biuer!* Dalí and Le Corbusier Conquer New York', 235–84. Koolhaas goes on to say that the Pavilion 'only demonstrates Manhattanism's wisdom in isolating the unspeakable behind the facade of the common. In trading his claim on the whole of Manhattan through words for the building of a specific fragment of actual Dalínian architecture, Dalí risks going from the sublime to the ridiculous'.

26 Spyros Papapetros, *On the Animation of the Inorganic. Art, Architecture, and the Extension of Life* (Chicago and London: University of Chicago Press, 2012), 285, see esp. chap.6, 'Daphne's Legacy. Architecture, Psychoanalysis, and Petrification', 263–314.

27 Alain Bosquet, *Entretiens avec Salvador Dalí* (Paris: Ed. Pierre Belfond, 1966); *Conversations with Dalí*, trans. Joachim Neugroschel (New York: E. P. Dutton & Co., 1969), 16.
28 Koolhaas, *Delirious New York*, 246.
29 See Alice Goldfarb Marquis, *Alfred H. Barr Jr. Missionary for the Modern* (Chicago-New York: Contemporary Books, 1989), 192–3.
30 Stefan Weppelmann, 'Branding Venus: Botticelli as Mirrored in American Art Since 1940', in Mark Evans and Stefan Weppelmann, ed., *Botticelli Reimagined* (London: V&A Publishing, 2016), 126. See Sandra Zalman, 'The Vernacular as Vanguard. Alfred Barr, Salvador Dalí, and the U.S. Reception of Surrealism in the 1930s', in *Journal of Surrealism and the Americas*, n.1 (2007): 44–67.
31 Francis Haskell, *The Ephemeral Museum. Old Master Paintings and the Rise of the Art Exhibition* (New Haven-London: Yale University Press, 2000), esp. chap.VII, 'Botticelli in the Service of Fascism', 105–27. Emily Braun, 'Leonardo's Smile', in Claudia Lazzaro and Roger J. Crum, ed., *Donatello among the Blackshirts. History and Modernity in the Visual Culture of Fascist Italy* (Ithaca and London: Cornell University Press, 2005), 181. See Sergio Cortesini, 'Italian Painters and Fascist Myths across the American Scene', *American Art* 25, n.1 (Spring 2011): 52–73; Raffaele Bedarida, 'Operation Renaissance: Italian Art at MoMA, 1940–1949', *Oxford Art Journal* 35, n.2, (2012): 147–69.
32 In Schaffner, *Salvador Dalí's Dream*, 102.
33 About Paestum, Dalí added that 'in order to satisfy my megalomaniac happiness and my thirst for solitude, I was lucky and glad enough not to like at all'. Salvador Dalí, *Diary of a genius*, Richard Howard, trans. (New York: Prentice Hall Press, 1965), 68–9.
34 Michael R. Taylor, 'The Dalí Renaissance', in Michael R. Taylor, ed., *The Dalí Renaissance. New Perspectives on His Life and Art after 1940. An International Symposium, Philadelphia Museum of Art* (New Haven & London: Yale University Press, 2008), 4–5.
35 In *The Collected Writings of Salvador Dalí*, ed. and trans. Haim Finkelstein (Cambridge: Cambridge University Press, 1998), 335–6.
36 Giorgio Vasari, 'Piero di Cosimo', in *Le vite de' più eccellenti pittori, scultori ed archittetori*, ed. Gaetano Milanesi, vol.4 (Florence: Sansoni, 1906), 131–44.
37 Felice Jacinto (Dalí), 'The Last Scandal of Salvador Dalí', Julien Levy Gallery, New York 1941, in *The Collected Writings*, 337–8.
38 *The Secret Life of Salvador Dalí*, 398.
39 Dalí 'discovered in Leonardo a fund of imagery that compensated for the relative paucity of such material offered by modern physics and that permitted him to give visual form to his sense of a world in a state of disaggregation'. David Lomas, '"Painting is dead – long live painting!" Notes on Dalí and Leonardo', in Michael R. Taylor, ed., *The Dalí Renaissance. New Perspectives on His Life and Art after 1940. An International Symposium, Philadelphia Museum of Art* (New Haven & London: Yale University Press, 2008), 171.
40 In Michael R. Taylor, 'The Dalí Renaissance', *The Dalí Renaissance*, 12.
41 Dalí, *Diary of a genius*, 197.
42 Fèlix Fanés, *Salvador Dalí. The Construction of the Image 1925–1930* (New Haven & London: Yale University Press, 2007), 142. In this work he quotes the example of the *Imperial Monument to the Child-Woman* (1929–34), in which Dalí 'cited Leonardo da Vinci, Jean-François Millet, Ernest Meissonnier, Arnold Böcklin, Modernist sculpture and architecture, himself and so on. The meaning of each of the quotations depended on the relations between them and with the work as a whole.'
43 Dalí, *Diary of a genius*, 25–6.
44 Nicolas Calas, 'Anti-Surrealist Dalí: I Say His Flies Are Ersatz', *View*, n.6 (June 1941): 1.
45 Clement Greenberg, 'Surrealist painting', in Clement Greenberg, *The Collected Essays and Criticism*, I, *Perceptions and Judgments, 1939–1944*, ed. John O' Brian (Chicago and London: The University of Chicago Press, 1986), 229.
46 Clement Greenberg, 'Review of the Whitney Annual and the Exhibition Romantic Painting in America', in Greenberg, *The Collected Essays*, 171–4.
47 Greenberg, 'Review of the Whitney Annual', 172.
48 Greenberg, 'Surrealist painting', 229.
49 Levy, *Memoir*, 71.
50 'Conceived as a victory of industrial progress and of capitalism, it unveiled a new era[…] one of technology converted into private consumer goods. […] All things considered, a world of home comforts, technological luxuries and new entertainment. In other words, a world of

commodities. The visitors, more than observers, were treated like future consumers (a way of doing things which had begun at the Chicago Exhibition in 1933).' Fanés, 'Mannequins, mermaids', 47.

51 'Freud + Minsky + Dalí', *The Art Digest* 13, n.18, (1 July 1939): 12, in Fanés, 'Mannequins, mermaids', 99. The confusion between the representation and the real woman, image and body is confirmed, on the contrary, by Dalí gallerist Julien Levy: 'When I was fourteen years old, I was conducted through the Uffizi Galleria in Florence by a plump, pretty woman named Hazel Guggenheim. For a length of time I would not pass beyond Botticelli's *Birth of Venus*, before which I stood stubbornly spellbound. "Come", said Hazel, taking my hand impatiently, "would you not rather have a real woman like me, for example, than that painted thing?" "No", I answered tactlessly and emphatically. "I would rather have that painted thing."' Levy, *Memoir*, 9. Dalí thought it was possible to get both at once.

52 In Ileen Sheppard and Marc H. Miller, ed., *Remembering the Future. The New York World's Fair From 1939 to 1964* (New York: Rizzoli, 1989), 14.

53 In Sheppard and Miller, *Remembering the Future*, 13.

54 Papapetros, *On the animation*, 287.

55 Bosquet, *Conversations*, 39.

56 Papapetros, *On the animation*, 281.

57 Hal Foster, *Compulsive Beauty* (Cambridge (Mass.): The MIT Press, 1993), esp. chap.6, 'Outmoded Space', 157–91.

58 Papapetros, *On the animation*, 280. 'Dalí's anus (markedly shadowed in both Gala's body and the "rear exit" of her temple) transform[s] into a skull – proof that the rectum, as Leo Bersani would say, has indeed the tendency to become a grave. This is the darker side of Gala's architecturally splendid and beautiful behind.' 281.

59 In Finkelstein, *The Collected Writings*, 311.

60 'This being upside-down is a familiar mechanism of Dream. But I will explain it for the public by two symbols, one inside the pavilion and the other on the façade.' In Levy, *Memoir*, 218.

61 'A contemporary cheesecake Venus replaced it over the entryway' according to Schaffner, *Salvador Dalí's Dream*, 157, n.79.

14. Giving an edge to the beautiful line: Botticelli referenced in the works of contemporary artists to address issues of gender and global politics

Gabriel Montua

The exhibition *Botticelli Reimagined* in Berlin and London, by assembling such a great number of works directly inspired by Botticelli, has made it all the more obvious that some of his figures have to be considered not only as icons, but also as quintessences of Western art. By this I mean that they are not only instantly recognisable to the viewer as familiar compositions, but that they can be taken to represent by themselves certain general qualities of Western art.

In this paper, I would like to propose that two qualities in particular can be attributed to Botticelli: his females, especially his nude Venus, stand for the iconic representation of women in paintings, while the ubiquity of some of his most famous figures makes his name synonymous with Renaissance art, with the High Art of Europe. Obviously, it is difficult to prove these assertions on an empirical basis, and such claims can also be made for most celebrated figures by other painters, some of them even more famous, such as Leonardo's *Mona Lisa*. The development of this paper will show, however, that Botticelli's inspirational quality is by no means limited to his two most famous paintings.

While the Pre-Raphaelites and their followers such as Evelyn de Morgan sought to imitate Botticelli's style and sensibility in the creation of genuinely new compositions, artists since the early twentieth century have drawn almost exclusively upon his motifs to create new works in which the whole or a part of a Botticelli painting is deliberately made visible as a reference to the original. It is important to keep the initial assertion of 'quintessentialness' in mind when examining two strings of questions that have guided contemporary artists to draw on motifs by Botticelli. If an artist wishes to express his or her concerns about imbalances in global politics, what kind of motif should be selected? A motif by Botticelli refers not only to Botticelli, but also to European culture at large. Thus this second layer of meaning raises the awareness of geography and facilitates the subsequent development of a geopolitical reading of the work, which is not the case when the source, lacking specific features, cannot be identified in the new work.

The same choice applies with even greater pertinence to artists wanting to express their concerns with gender relations. Botticelli is known not only as the author of *The Birth of Venus* (fig.1.0), one of the most beautiful female nudes in art history, but also as the painter of one of the most violent depiction of torture against women in classical painting in the second panel of his *Nastagio degli Onesti* series.[1]

Unlike this contribution, the aim of the exhibition *Botticelli Reimagined* was not to focus on particular themes of Botticelli's reception. Still, it presented a significant number of works related to gender issues by artists such as ORLAN, Valie Export, Ulrike Rosenbach or Joel-Peter Witkin. Also featured was a selection of works by non-Occidental artists such as Youssef Nabil, Yin Xin and Tomoko Nagao, which served to highlight the global dimension of Botticelli in contemporary art, even if political aspects were not at the forefront. In order to avoid repetition, these works will not be part of this essay.[2]

One first example of Botticelli's attraction for artists wishing to express imbalances in gender relations is an oil painting by Eglė Otto. In her 2012 work *Botticelli, Giotto, Grünewald, da Vinci, Dürer, Mantegna, Rossetti, Ensor, Parmigianino, Lippi, Raffael, van der Weyden, Ingres, Ernst* (fig.4.20), she fills the light blue background of her canvas with 14 circular forms. These are copies of halos illuminating the heads of saints in paintings of the artists she lists in the title of her work. Botticelli is first in line: the halo at the top left corner surrounds the infant Jesus in *The Virgin Adoring the Sleeping Christ Child* or *Wemyss Madonna* (*c.*1485, National Galleries of Scotland, Edinburgh). While pursuing her studies at HFBK art school in Hamburg during the 2000s, Otto noticed that the works presented in art history classes were almost exclusively by male artists. She started collecting the halos of male artists, which she copied, sometimes completing parts hidden by the heads, and assembled them on a pin wall like a collection of butterflies.[3] When transposing these halos to the canvas, the result resembles compositions by Hilma af Klint (for example, her 1907 work *The Childhood* from the series *The Ten Largest*). In this way, Otto transforms the work of male father figures of art history into an homage to the Swedish artist rediscovered in the 1980s as an early pioneer of abstract art.[4] This mother figure of abstraction thus plays the role of nemesis to the male-dominated art education that Otto (like so many others) received.

Another set of gender-related critiques is voiced in the work of photographer Matthias Herrmann, a former ballet dancer. In one work

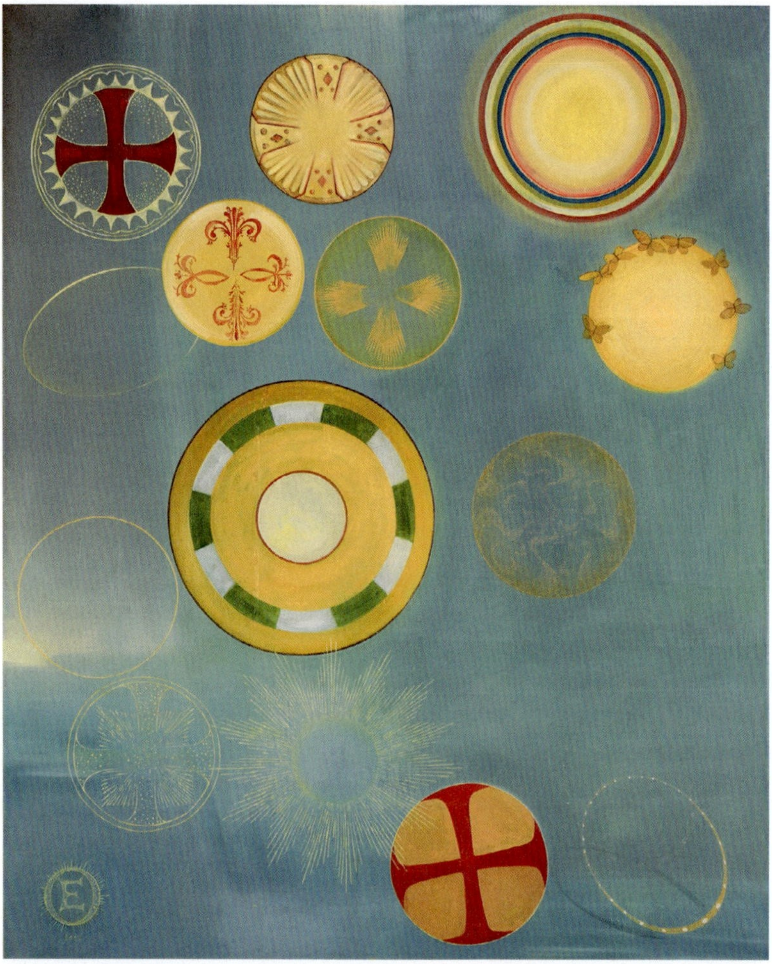

Fig.4.20 Eglė Otto (b. 1976), *Botticelli, Giotto, Grünewald, da Vinci, Dürer, Mantegna, Rossetti, Ensor, Parmigianino, Lippi, Raffael, van der Weyden, Ingres, Ernst*, 2012, oil on canvas, 130 × 107 cm. © Courtesy of the Artist.

from his artist's book *Paris Text Pieces*, a series of self-portraits in which some quotations convey additional meaning, one sees the artist with a blonde wig, donned in such a way as to reveal his real, short and dark hair, posing as *Venus pudica* (a possible shell at the bottom is not part of the photo). Next to his obviously male body a sign reads in French: '*Comment la Venus de Botticelli est devenue un top model anorexique*' (How Botticelli's Venus has become an anorexic top model).[5] On the one hand, this self-portrait can be aligned with other works in which the female characters of Botticelli undergo a sex change, such as Francis Picabia's

1930 oil painting *Salomé* (from the *Transparences* series). In this work Salomé's face has been modelled and feminised – through eye lashes, redder and fuller lips and a complete shaving of the beard – after the face of *Christ the Redeemer* (Accademia Carrara, Bergamo).[6] Joel-Peter Witkin's photographs featuring a transsexual Venus with breast and a penis featured in the exhibition,[7] while an even more sexually provocative version, *Botticelli's Venus, NYC* from 1982, depicts Venus holding 'her' erect penis in one hand. On the other hand, Herrmann's self-portrait draws attention to the well-known fact that Botticelli's *Venus* has been used abundantly in the fashion and beauty industry.[8] Both interpretations are a critique of contemporary society's use of Botticelli's *The Birth of Venus* to contribute to the formation of a normative female ideal of beauty. Such an ideal both denies beauty to queer forms of femininity and encourages women to undertake diets, cosmetic surgery and fitness training, fearing that their appearance might otherwise not conform to this canon of beauty and slenderness.

Sylvia Sleigh's 1974 oil painting *Maureen Conner and Paul Rosano* (fig.4.21) follows the composition of Botticelli's *Mars and Venus* (*c.*1485, National Gallery, London: fig.1.27). Leaving out the putti, she transposes the setting – appropriately for the hippie generation – into an idyllic garden; flowers in a multitude of species are reminiscent of the botanical profusion at the feet of the figures in the *Primavera* (fig.1.30). In Sleigh's painting, both protagonists are dressed in contemporary 1970s clothing, echoing the original garments. The two most gendered Olympian deities (Venus being the quintessence of femininity, Mars of masculinity) have just made love; Mars blissfully dozes off, while Venus contemplates him

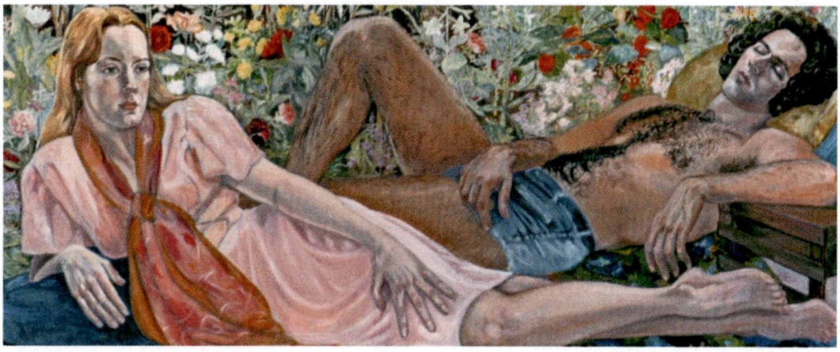

Fig.4.21 Sylvia Sleigh (1916–2010), *Venus and Mars: Maureen Conner and Paul Rosano*, 1974, oil on canvas, 69.2 × 173.7 cm, Milwaukee Art Museum, Gift of the Artist and Dr and Mrs James Stadler (M1990.137). © Courtesy of the Estate of Sylvia Sleigh and Andrew Hottle.

with a face not revealing her possible thoughts. In Sleigh's 1970s version Paul Rosano is also depicted in delightful slumber, while Maureen Conner looks out of the picture in a far less satisfied way. If we agree that intercourse has occurred here as well, this last detail seems to open up a reflection on male egoism in heterosexual encounters – a topic much discussed during the times of sexual liberation.

Moving on to gender concerns in the non-Western context, Turkish artist Gülsün Karamustafa produced three works featuring the Venus from Botticelli's *The Birth of Venus* during the 1980s.[9] The most notable of these is the 1985 assemblage, *Gold Venus with Mirror* (fig.4.22). It consists of a box covered with a glass panel to allow a view inside. The object thus creates a stage for something never seen before – the back side of Botticelli's *The Birth of Venus* – as an oblique look in the mirror covering the back wall confirms. Even if the auxiliary figures from Botticelli's original have been omitted, the shore setting is well recreated through crumbled aluminium foil and blue fabric, with the rain of roses hinted at by two large-scale artificial flowers. The most interesting part, however, is that the statuette is not the work of Karamustafa as a sculptor,

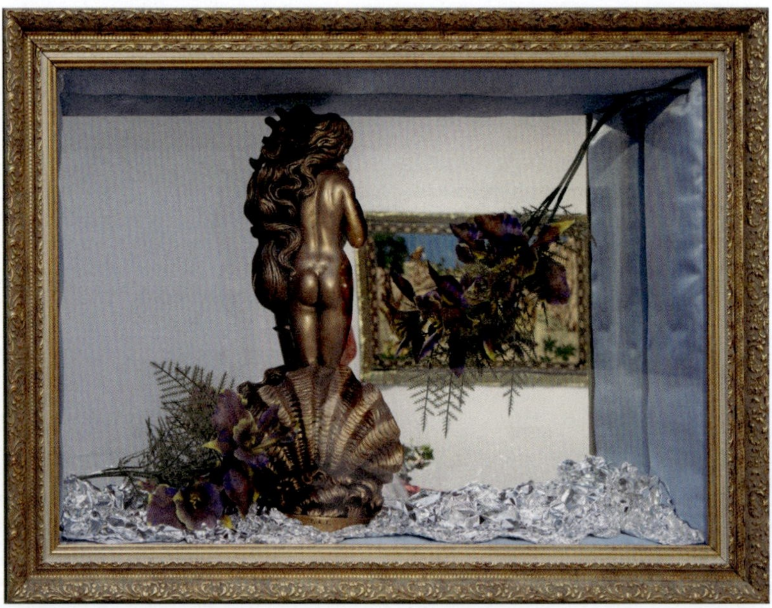

Fig.4.22 Gülsün Karamustafa (b. 1946), *Gold Venus with Mirror*, 1985, found object, wood, plastics, mirror, 65 × 88 cm, courtesy the Artist and Rampa Gallery, Istanbul. Photo © Thomas Bruns, Staatliche Museen zu Berlin, Nationalgalerie.

but the product of an anonymous industrial designer; it was bought by the artist in an Istanbul street bazaar selling cheap home decorations.

One aspect of this work plays with the notion of kitsch as a culture of interior decoration and explores its anarchic transgressions of origins and meanings. Karamustafa believes few potential purchasers would have been aware of the referenced original by Botticelli, or of the source of other statuettes for sale, such as the central figure in Botticelli's *Primavera* or the thirteen persons seated at a table from Leonardo's *Last Supper*, a subject devoid of its religious dimension for the predominantly Muslim buyers. The latter, if they take their religion seriously, should be averse to the female nudity in the *Venus*, though, according to the artist, this piece sold successfully.[10] Her work then presents the nude female halfway between a striptease dancer on stage and an item of natural history in a reconstructed habitat, not unlike a terrarium. Both readings present Venus as a forbidden fruit: to be seen through the glass, but not touched. The high value suggested by the display as a precious artefact (and the high cultural value commonly conceded to Botticelli's painting), combined with the cheap commercial value of the statuette, can be read as a metaphor for the status of women in Karamustafa's society. They may have value and prestige in notions of family honour, but few men value their choices for a self-determined life.

In yet another approach to the local condition of women, Iranian artist Farah Osūlī has created two gouaches in the style of Persian miniatures using the composition of Botticelli's *The Birth of Venus*. This symbiosis of miniatures, which are traditionally flat and two dimensional, with a painting by Botticelli works rather well, given the preference in his paintings for linear composition over depth, for which he is often criticised. Bernard Berenson linked this aspect of Botticelli's style to the Oriental tradition:

> The 'Birth of Venus' – take these lines alone with all their power of stimulating our imagination of movement, and what do we have? Pure values of movement abstracted, unconnected with any representation whatever. […] Well! Imagine an art made up entirely of these quintessences of movement-values, and you will have something that holds the same relation to representation that music holds to speech – and this art exists, and it is called linear decoration. In this art of arts Sandro Botticelli may have rivals in Japan and elsewhere in the East, but in Europe never.[11]

What is remarkable in Osūlī's *Birth of Venus* (2007) and *Botticelli and I* (2014, fig.4.23) is that the female nymph on the right side has been

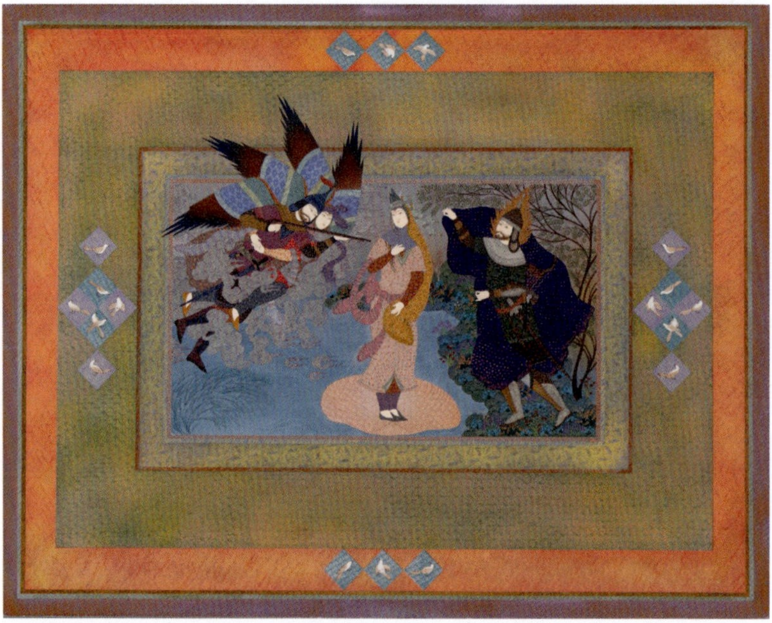

Fig.4.23 Faraḥ Osūlī (b. 1953), *Botticelli and I*, 2014, gouache on cardboard, 75 × 100 cm. © Courtesy of the Artist.

replaced by a man, holding up the cloth in which to clad Venus, arriving on a sea shell. However, this Venus is not naked, as Botticelli accurately rendered the account of her birth given by Hesiod in his *Theogony*, but already quite heavily clothed. The cloak which the man holds in readiness at the right is not meant to protect an undressed body from the cold, as in Botticelli's version, but to hide away an already clothed body. This is precisely the role of garments such as the *chador* or the *manteau* that women have been required to wear in public to cover their body shape in Iran since the Islamic Revolution.

In Osūlī's *The Birth of Venus*, the cloth the man holds is black and covered with stars. Interestingly, in Angelo Poliziano's *Stanze per la Giostra* – a poem composed between 1475 and 1478 – the veil the nymph holds is described as star-spangled, as a '*stellato vestimento*' (stanza CII). Botticelli did not follow this hint from Poliziano, but rather embellished the cloak with flowers, although he did adopt the sea shell proposed by Poliziano a few *stanze* earlier (XCIX), which was not mentioned by Hesiod. It appears that the man wants literally to cover and smother the woman in darkness, an interpretation reinforced in *Botticelli and I*. In the latter work the Zephyr-man on the left points an elaborately inlaid rifle at the female who, according to the title, might be the artist herself.

In *Botticelli and I*, the cloth is adorned with small swastikas, possibly a reference to the ancient religious symbol abundantly in use on the Indian subcontinent, culturally much closer to Persia in the heyday of Persian miniature paintings. But this symbol also has obvious reference to Nazi Germany and seems to reinforce the unyielding character of the ideology behind the dress codes imposed on women in present-day Iran.[12]

Shifting the focus from works expressing gender issues but remaining in the global dimension of artists' engagement with works by Botticelli, I would like to introduce David LaChapelle's adaptation of Botticelli's *Mars and Venus* in his photograph *The Rape of Africa* (2009). Even though it was included in the exhibition and received an entry in the catalogue, I believe the most important part for the perspective of this paper has not been presented adequately.[13] The more obvious message is suggested by the title: a hole in the back wall of the shack where the scene takes place is meant to evoke poor living conditions in Africa. The image offers a powerful view about excavators in an arid landscape busy removing natural resources from Africa, piled up in the lower right of the picture. The work is often undertaken in conjunction with heavy weapons, as indicated by the bazooka and machine gun held by the boys who take the place of Botticelli's putti, playing with the arms and armour of Mars.

The presence of supermodel Naomi Campbell as Venus gave the work another twist one year after its creation, as she had to appear in an international court as witness to a trial against former Liberian leader Charles Taylor. He had allegedly presented her with a so-called conflict diamond, the lack of traceability of its origins being linked to the financing of non-governmental armed groups. Campbell's testimony, the prosecutor hoped, would be another proof of the great stock of such diamonds held by Taylor, who was accused of dealing in them to finance rebels in neighbouring Sierra Leone.[14] But this detail should not make us overlook that the god of war is sleeping on gold and diamonds while others do the dirty work of obtaining and selling them – nor the fact that this god's skin is white, unlike that of Venus Naomi Campbell, who represents the title's raped Africa. The fact that Mars is incarnated by Caleb Lane, of far less celebrity than Campbell, could be a hint at the anonymity of those who profit, when compared to the flagrance of the suffering.

Another layer of interpretation can be deduced from the wallpaper of the shack, which is covered with cardboard boxes of washing powders and bleaches. Such items were abundantly advertised in the first decades of Western colonialism in Africa, with imagery linking the superiority of the colonisers to their higher standards of hygiene. In what were meant as attention-catching jests for Western consumers, some of these images implied that colonial subjects could move up the ladder of civilisation by using bleaches to reduce the darkness of their skin.[15] The racial discrimination implied by the use of bleaching agents is augmented by the blue contact lenses worn by Naomi Campbell and the boy on the far right. The rape of the continent made explcit in LaChapelle's title refers not only to the violent physical exploitation of its natural resources, but also to the technological methods of achieving this (excavators and fire weapons) and the psychological disposition (greed and consumerism, hinted at by the Warholian repetition of the detergent boxes). This destructive legacy of the colonisers has now been literally incorporated by the locals (Campbell's contact lenses) in what could be summarised as capitalism. The relative carelessness with which most people enjoy the ownership of diamonds or the sight of others wearing them is echoed in the luxurious and glossy C-Print, providing the material support for a message of such serious post-colonial implications.[16]

Another set of works places Botticelli's motives in a global perspective with political dimensions. In an oil painting called *Venus* (1975, Ludwig Forum für International Kunst, Aachen), the Icelandic artist Erró – known for his pop-art-style collages, including elements of Communist propaganda posters – has put Botticelli's Venus along with her shell and parts of the auxiliary characters in front of a Chinese *xuānchuánhuà* (propaganda illustration) showing Mao Zedong among workers and red banners. Once the clash of two distinct frames of references is acknowledged, further interpretations of this work appear rather limited and straightforward. Is Chinese propaganda art as beautiful as Botticelli's Venus? Is the Venus in itself propaganda and if so, for what? For Western hegemony in the visual arts?

A more complex message emanates from the minimal installation of the series *Triptychos Post Historicus*, by Yugoslav-born artist Braco Dimitrijević. Here a work of art from a museum's collection is grouped with both a personal, everyday object and a vegetable or a fruit. In 1996 Dimitrijević obtained permission from the Louvre to place an apple and a candle in front of Botticelli's *Portrait of a Young Man* (*c*.1470–5); he then personally lit the candle.[17] This series started in 1976, when it was one of the first ever systematic artistic interventions with museum collections. It questions the modes of tradition of heritage and history by engaging older works with present-day objects apparently devoid of value. What chain of circumstances is at play by which some objects are elevated to museum status while others are forgotten? Are the objects of a museum collection locked up in some kind of a-historicity, and how do they relate to the present? Is the cultural or financial capital they represent an objective quantity? In short, these questions are of an economic order, as they address the value of master paintings measured against other items or their utility.

These questions may seem less pressing today, since interventions into museum collections have become a regular artistic practice. However, it is worth noting that they were first articulated by an artist such as Dimitrijević, who grew up in a socialist society. The last work in this set is an almost literal copy of Botticelli's *Portrait of a Young Man with the Medal of Cosimo de' Medici* (*c.*1475, Uffizi, Florence: fig.1.7). However, the Iranian painter Aydin Aghdashlou has left out the face of the man, which he now presents framed by the medal in his hands (fig.4.24). The landscape, visible where the face should have been, seems at first to be a continuation of Botticelli's background, but is in fact the view seen through the window of Domenico Ghirlandaio's *Portrait of an Old Man and a Boy* (*c.*1490, Louvre, Paris). This detail further strengthens what Aghdashlou somewhat straightforwardly expresses with his entire 1970s

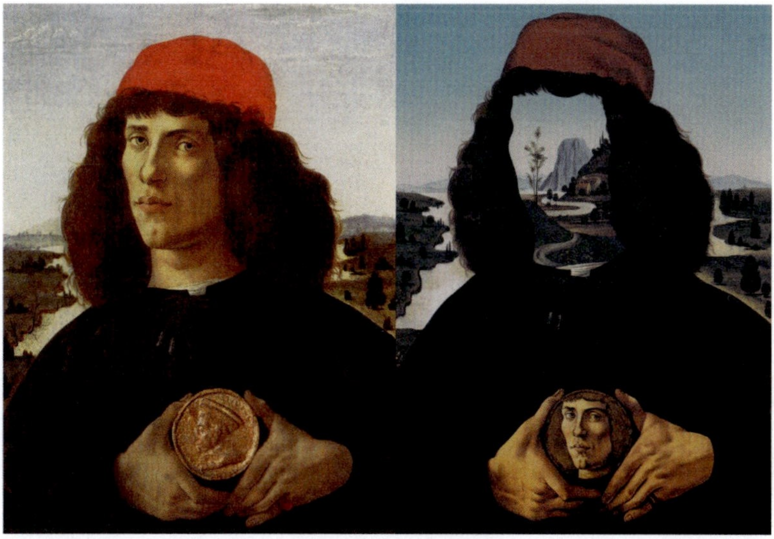

Fig.4.24 Left: Sandro Botticelli, *Portrait of a Man with a Medal of Cosimo the Elder*, *c.*1475, tempera and gilded stucco on wood, 57.5 × 44 cm, Galleria degli Uffizi, Florence; Right: Aydin Aghdashlou (b. 1940), *Portrait by Sandro Botticelli* (*Taṣvīrī az Sāndro Botteċellī*), 1975, gouache on paper, 71 × 50 cm, Tehran Museum of Contemporary Art, Tehran. © Courtesy of the Artist.

series *Memories of Annihilation*. This has many more Western sources literally disfigured, or Persian manuscripts shown burned or crumpled. The postmodern practice of mixing different sources, Aghdashlou seems to suggest, is another point in case of our era's unwillingness to value the artistic heritage as being of so much higher quality than our own productions. Aghdashlou thus reacts to the imposed Westernisation of his country during the reign of the two Pahlavi shahs (from 1925 to 1979), as well as to the physical dismantlement of Persian manuscript books into single leaves to obtain higher prices on the Western art market.[18]

A rather peculiar painting is the work of the Mexican architect and painter Juan O'Gorman, *Proyecto de Monumento al Nacimiento de Venus* (1976, fig.4.25). At least two Venuses and three shells form part of an elaborate and fantastic structure, reminiscent through the ponds from which it rises of the architectural elements of Hieronymus Bosch's *The Garden of Earthly Delights*. The main inspiration is credited to the *Palais Idéal* building in the French Drôme region, as indicated by a small portrait in homage to its creator, the postman Ferdinand Cheval. Another *cartellino* on the right hand side of the canvas explicitly states Mexico as the country where this monument was conceived. By mentioning this fact in writing, it seems that O'Gorman intends to challenge the geopolitical ownership of the *The Birth of Venus* – regarded, as I proposed in the introduction, as an exclusive possession of Europe (with some rights inherited by North America through cultural descent).

Last but not least, *Primavera* is an ensemble of works created in 2016 by Nigerian-born artist Sokari Douglas Camp. It consists of welded metal statues representing in different sizes all nine figures from the painting of the same name by Botticelli (fig.4.26).[19] The adult-size statue modelled after Flora has the face of a woman from Nigeria: brown eyes gaze out at the viewer over full red lips in a brown face. Like the light-skinned and blue-eyed woman in Botticelli's painting, Douglas Camp's statue carries flowers grouped as a bouquet in her hand and others strung like a garland around her dress, made of delicately welded and transparent leaves. They echo the pattern of the dress in Botticelli's painting, where the stems and leaves take up more space than the blossoms. However, a closer look at the petals, painted in bright colours, reveals metal items – toy cars – of equally gaudy colours, blending with the botanical decoration.

The painting's central protagonist has been constructed as another adult-size statue, a screen of branches radiating around her like a halo and crowned by the arrow-shooting putto. While the central figure and the putto have not been painted and present a uniform, silvery-metal appearance – save for the reds of the woman's veil and the putto's quiver

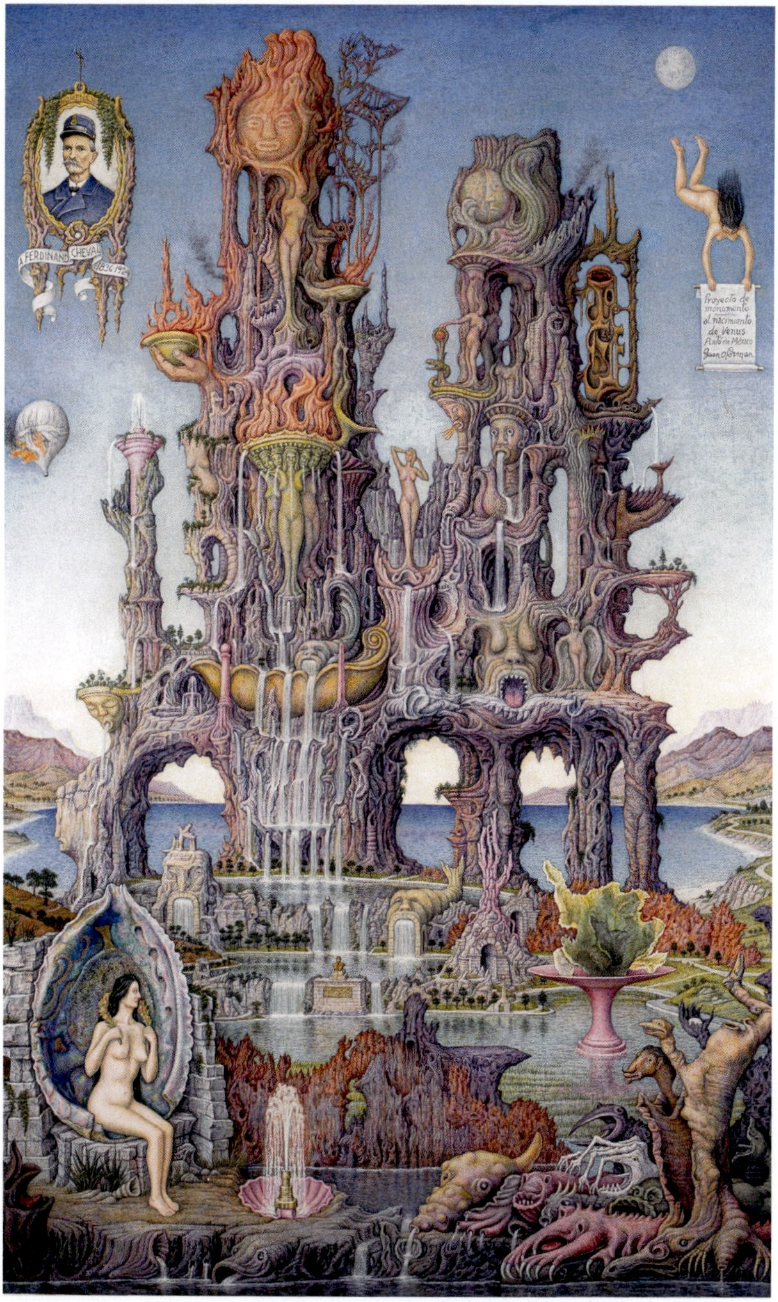

Fig.4.25 Juan O'Gorman (1905–82), *Proyecto de Monumento al Nacimiento de Venus*, 1976, tempera on wood, 122 × 82 cm, Pérez Simón Collection, México. © Pérez Simón Collection, México.

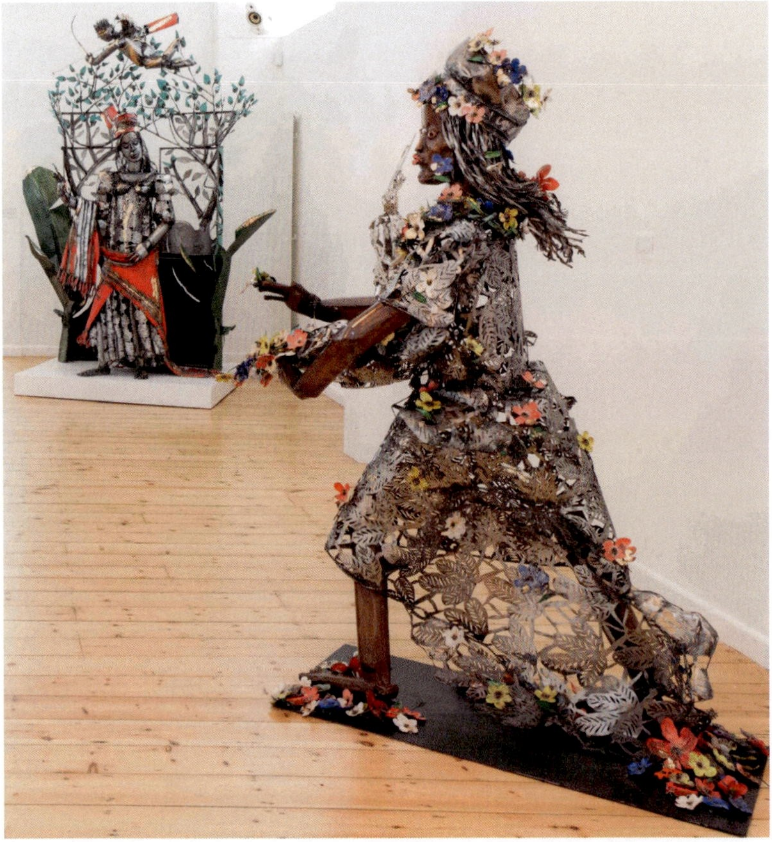

Fig.4.26 Sokari Douglas Camp (b. 1958), partial view of the work ensemble *Primavera* (presented at October Gallery between 7 April–14 May 2016), 2015–16, steel, gold and copper leaf, acrylic paint, various dimensions. © Courtesy of the Artist and October Gallery, London.

– the branches are coloured in two different greens: a more turquoise green for the small, almond-shaped leaves surrounding the head and a darker green at the bottom. This lower vegetation, covered by the other figures in Botticelli's painting, has been shaped by Douglas Camp in the form of large banana leaves. The metal she uses for the foliage is that of oil barrels, cut open to build the backdrop.

In summary, Douglas Camp not only transfers Botticelli's two-dimensional shapes to three-dimensional statues, as the maker of the Venus statue used by Gülsün Karamustafa had done, but Africanises them through two operations. One, more visible, is her rendering of Flora's face and the addition of banana leaves at the feet of Primavera.

The other lies in the references to oil, through the barrels used for the construction of parts of the Primavera group or the inclusion of toy cars, associated with her native Nigeria and its oil-rich Niger Delta region. This circumstance affects local life quite bitterly, in terms of pollution and especially politics. It is felt by many that most of the revenues from the oil extraction go to foreign companies and their corrupt local agents, while guerrillas conduct operations of sabotage, abduction and other violent interventions around oil-producing sites.[20] In Sokari Douglas Camp's ensemble *Primavera*, inspired by Botticelli, one finds similar concerns to those in David LaChapelle's *The Rape of Africa* – with the difference that in the former these are informed by the artist's close personal ties with the country, even after she took up residence in London.

In a brief conclusion, we should welcome the fact that Botticelli's originals do inspire contemporary works voicing serious concerns. They confirm that artists draw upon these sources in a reflective way and for a specific purpose, not simply because of their availability or the appealing quality of their designs. Touching on complex or edgy subjects represents an addition to the numerous possibilities of engagement with Botticelli. The new works are proofs of Aby Warburg's concept of *Nachleben* and facilitate the mediation of the originals with a contemporary public. Speaking both technically and metaphorically, an edge provides a further dimension. It is thus an enrichment to the beautiful and purely decorative line, criticised for its lack of depth by the likes of Bernard Berenson.

Notes

1 Georges Didi-Huberman, *Ouvrir Vénus: nudité, rêve, cruauté* (Paris: Gallimard, 1999). The brutality of the depiction is even more striking as the choice of subject, a side event taken from Boccaccio's *Decameron*, was a whim of Botticelli's patron in search of a wedding picture and thus lacked a great deal of the moral necessity conveyed by religious commissions depicting the martyrdom of female saints, especially that of St Agatha of Sicily.

2 Valie Export's *LIEBESPERLEN/Nonpareille* (1976) was only on shown in Berlin and had no entry in the catalogue. This large triptych consists of three black and white self-portraits of the artist on a white background, each re-enacting the pose of one of the Three Graces in Botticelli's *Primavera*. What looks effortless and graceful in Botticelli's painting is in fact quite a contorted pose to adopt. These works are in line with the artist's mid-1970s series *Body Configurations*, mentioned in the entry for her work *Expectation* (1976; cat. no.24).

3 Email from Eglé Otto to the author, 19 April 2016.

4 Emma Enderby, Melissa Blanchflower and Melissa Larner, ed., *Hilma af Klint: Painting the Unseen* (London: Serpentine Galleries and Koenig Books, 2016).

5 Matthias Herrmann, *Paris Text Pieces* (Toronto: Art Metropole, 1998).

6 See *Botticelli Reimagined*, exh. cat. (London: V&A Publishing, 2016), 284–5, cat. no.133.

7 See *Botticelli Reimagined*, exh. cat. (London: V&A Publishing, 2016), 160–1, cat. no.18.

8 To just quote two examples not mentioned in or around the exhibition: The cover page of the French fashion magazine *Le Jardin des Modes* (issue dated 18 June 1937) shows the photograph of a dressed model standing on a painted sea shell with the sea and waves visible, copied exactly from Botticelli's *The Birth of Venus* (thanks to Adelheid Rasche for providing me with a scan). The 1966 Italian science-fiction movie by Pietro Francisci, *2 + 5 Missione Hydra* (reissued as *Star Pilot* to the US and English-speaking markets) begins with a short sequence in which we see the shooting of an advertisement for a brand of bath salts (*sali da bagno*). In this the female main character stands in an elaborate and moving set design of waves modelled after Botticelli's *The Birth of Venus*, explicitly shown in the movie as a photograph in the hands of the directors supervising the production (thanks to Jean-Claude Lebensztejn for introducing me to the film).

9 For a more detailed account of Karamustafa's engagement with the Venus figure and the notion of kitsch, see Alice Bombardier and Gabriel Montua, 'À l'est de Chypre. La Vénus de Botticelli chez Āghdāshlū, Karamustafa et Osūlī. Etude de transferts artistiques Occident-Orient', *REMMM - Revue des mondes musulmans et de la Méditerranée, Arts visuels, Constexturaliser nos regards* 142 (2017): 33–52. For a reproduction of Karamustafa's other Venus works see Melanie Roumiguière and Övul Ö. Durmuşoğlu, ed., *Chronographia: Gülsün Karamustafa* (Vienna: Verlag für Moderne Kunst, 2016), 112 [*Panther Venus* (1985)], 116 [*Venus in Jar* (1988)].

10 Email by Gülsün Karamustafa to the author, 24 December 2016.

11 Bernard Berenson, *The Italian Painters of the Renaissance* (Oxford: Clarendon Press, 1930), 112.

12 For a more detailed analysis of these two works and their context with regards to the tradition of miniature painting and its present day use in Iran see Bombardier, Montua, '*A l'est de Chypre*'. The veiling of Venus in post-revolution Iran is addressed also in Marjane Satrapi's animated film *Persepolis* (2007), in which a teacher of art history introduces female students to a reproduction of Botticelli's *Birth of Venus*, with pretty much everything blacked out except for Venus's head and the shell on which she stands. When Iranian president Hassan Rouhani was given a tour of Rome's sites during a state visit on 26 January 2016, another *Venus pudica*, the Capitoline Venus, was covered, along with other statues, as a courtesy by the hosts. Stephanie Kirchgaessner, 'Rome spares Iranian president's blushes by covering nude statues', *The Guardian*, 26 January 2016, accessed 29 January 2017, https://www.theguardian.com/world/2016/jan/26/rome-spares-iranian-presidents-blushes-covering-nude-statues.

13 *Botticelli Reimagined*, 143–5, cat. no. 6.

14 Lizzy Davies, 'Naomi Campbell: I had nothing to gain by lying to Charles Taylor trial', *The Guardian*, 11 August 2010, accessed 29 January 2017, https://www.theguardian.com/world/2010/aug/11/naomi-campbell-denies-lying-over-diamonds. Thanks to Kumi Tanimura of the artist's studio for providing the name of the male model.

15 Anne McClintock, 'Soft-Soaping Empire: Commodity racism and imperial advertising', in Nicholas Mirzoeff, ed., *The Visual Culture Reader* (London and New York: Routledge, 1998), 314, analyses an advertisement poster for a British manufacturer with the slogan 'We are

going to use Chlorinol and be like de white nigger'. The advertisement depicts three coloured boys, one of whom has apparently already applied the bleach to his skin. The wording makes it quite clear that even a change of skin colour would not promote the colonised subject to equal rights with the white, an intermediate status being all they can hope for.

16 The link between the diamonds and the deadly methods of obtaining them is further highlighted by the reference to Damien Hirst's diamond-encrusted skull, *For the Love of God* (2007). A preparatory drawing by LaChapelle, shown in a video at the London venue of the exhibition, has the explicit mention: 'DIAMOND DH SKULL', the initials obviously referring to Damien Hirst.

17 For a reproduction of this work see Danilo Eccher, ed., *Braco Dimitrijević* (Milan: Silvana Editoriale, 2016), 243, or the artist's home page, accessed 29 January 2017: http://bracodimitrijevic.com/index.php?album=tryptichos&image=tryptichos_013.jpg.

18 For a more detailed account of the *Memories of Annihilation* series and the political circumstances in Iran see Bombardier and Montua, '*A l'est de Chypre*'.

19 *Primavera. Sokari Douglas Camp C.B.E.* (London: October Gallery, 2016).

20 Michael Watts, 'Petro-Insurgency or Criminal Syndicate? Conflict, Violence and Political Disorder in the Niger Delta', *Review of African political economy* 34, no.114 (2007): 637–60.

Index

Abegg-Stiftung, Riggisberg 79, 81
abstraction and abstract art 128, 280–1, 291
Adoration of the Magi 80, 95, 168, 220, 225
aesthetics and aestheticism 2, 121–4, 127–8, 150, 161–3, 183, 193, 198, 213, 240–3
altarpieces 7, 10, 17, 21
anti-Semitism 122, 133
architecture 284
art critics 4, 136
art dealers 101
art historians and art historiography 1–4, 120–1, 137–40, 149, 161–2, 168, 174–5, 183, 204–5, 212, 285, 291
Art Nouveau 284
Arte del Cambio 7
artistic personality 119, 121, 162, 169, 176, 205
Arundel Society 92
Asian art 210, 214
The Assumption of the Virgin: attrib. Botticini 176–7; Palmieri 176, 179

The Birth of Venus: painting 67–8, 73, 81, 92, 100, 149–50, 154–5, 174, 177, 184, 188, 191–2, 222–4, 234–5, 242, 266, 275–7, 291–5, 300; poem 155
'bourgeois' interpretations of art 3–5
Buddhism 210
Burlington House 277
busts 10, 26

The Calumny of Apelles 61
the Capitoline Venus 153
centaurs 58
Christianity 225–8
classical style 103, 184, 188, 195
colonialism 297
commissions for paintings 7–9
connoisseurship 2–4, 117–19, 124, 130–40, 152, 162–3, 176, 179, 203, 212, 214, 222
consumer culture 119
contemporary narratives on art 1–2, 5
cult of Botticelli 162–3, 175, 183
Cupid and Psyche 4, 9, 73–5, 78–85

death masks 24–6
The Decameron 61
Derelitta 220
The Divine Comedy 53, 94–104, 110, 177, 224, 227
Dream of Venus project 266–78, 282–6
dreams, study of 246–7

ekphrasis 61–2, 65, 67
empathy, concept and theory of 196, 241–2
eroticism and eroticisation 153–8, 234, 251, 281–4

fascism 27
'figurability' 248
films 254–60
Flanders and Flemish art 11, 16, 226–7
flogging 85
Florence 8–14, 19–20, 28, 53–4, 75, 82, 85, 95, 98, 103–4, 120–6, 129–30, 148–9, 164, 183–4, 193, 214, 218–22, 225–7
fluidity of images 237—60
Fortezza 220
Fortitude 7–8, 169
frescoes 85, 92, 95, 126, 166, 175–6, 197, 220

gender relations 3, 291, 294
genres 28
Greek dance 239
Greek myth 153

hands, portrayal of 163, 204–5, 210
heads, portrayal of 21, 26
hedonic criticism 132
hermeneutics 233
homoerotic desire 158
humanistic ideas 28

iconography and iconology 95–6, 198
'imaginary breeze' 5, 237–8
Inferno 96, 106
innamoramento pictures 66–7
Japan 4, 203–14
Judaism and Jewish identity 133, 139–40

kitsch 295

The Last Judgement (Signorelli) 104
The Last Supper (Leonardo) 295
lectio difficilior 57–8
Leda and the Swan 101

Madonna of the Pomegranate 125
mannerisms 196
marriage paintings 64, 68, 73
Mars and Venus 61–3, 149, 155–8, 293, 297
'masculine' art 213
masturbation 157, 248
materialism 194
medals 24
Medici Society 163
modernity and modernism 234, 238, 282, 285
Monarchia (Dante) 95
music 122–4, 128
The Mystic Nativity 92–3, 98–9, 110
mysticism 210
'mythologies' 4, 53, 61

nationalism 163, 214
naturalism 128, 194, 281
Nazarene artists 110
nymphs 192, 224, 233–4, 238–9, 244, 248–53, 257, 276, 296

old masters 2, 121, 282
'Ophelia complex' 244

paganism 222, 225
pan-Asianism 212
panels 7–8, 12–13, 21, 26–8, 73–6, 79
participation 242
pathos formula 196–7, 240
photography, use of 92, 155, 163, 203–9, 282
plagiarism 124
poetry 2–4, 59, 94, 136, 168, 188, 192
polarity, concept of 197
political propaganda 234–5
Pompeii 278
popular culture 117
pre-Raphaelite movement 3–4, 8–30, 136–7, 149, 161, 183, 285, 290
Primavera 4, 7, 9, 55–6, 64–7, 73–4, 80–5, 92–3, 100, 120, 122, 136, 149, 155, 162–3, 175, 184, 191–2, 195–8, 206, 222–3, 234–5, 240, 245, 293, 295
prime objects 233–5
'primitive' artists and paintings 94, 98, 103

The Punishment of the Rebels 220
The Punishment of the Sodomites 104–6

Quattrocento festivals 191

racial discourse 139

Saint Sebastian 168–9
St Lawrence Basilica, Rome 104
sculpture 95, 196, 237–8
The Seven Planets and Seven Heavenly Spheres 83
sexual feelings 157–8
sexualisation 235
Sistine Chapel 10, 80, 92, 101, 169, 220, 224
social history of art 164, 220, 227
Stanze per la Giostra (poem) 296
surrealism 3, 234, 250–1, 266, 269, 272–5, 278–82, 295

The Temptation of Moses 170
The Temptations of Christ 170, 224
the Three Graces, the 55, 66, 71, 76, 80–1, 85, 155, 191

universal laws 212
universal values 204
universality of the arts 214

Venice 21, 168
Venus (Erró) 298
Venus (Giorgione) 156–7
Venus: figure of 154–6, 234; reign of 197–8; seen as forbidden fruit 295
virginity 155
Vision of a Knight 110

wedding rituals 82
women, status of 2–3, 5, 295–6
Worship of Venus (Titian) 282